Growing and Managing an Entrepreneurial Business

Growing and Managing an Entrepreneurial Business

Kathleen R. Allen

University of Southern California
Marshall School of Business

UNIV. OF ST. FRANCIS
JOLIET, ILLINOIS

Houghton Mifflin Company   Boston New York

To Jon, Yvonne, Marianne, Jennifer, and Bryan. Thanks for your inspiration and support, and for always being there for me. You are the future of entrepreneurship, and that future looks very bright.

Sponsoring Editor: *Kathleen L. Hunter*
Senior Associate Editor: *Susan M. Kahn*
Senior Project Editor: *Fred H. Burns*
Senior Designer: *Henry Rachlin*
Senior Production/Design Coordinator: *Sarah Ambrose*
Senior Manufacturing Coordinator: *Sally Culler*
Marketing Associate: *January N. Gill*

Cover design and image: *Minko T. Dimov, MinkoImages*

Photo Credits: All part and chapter opening images Copyright © 98 PhotoDisc, Inc. *Young Entrepreneurs—Minicase* photos: Chapter 1, Courtesy of Young Entrepreneurs Network; Chapter 2, Photo by Krasner-Trebitz/Courtesy of Bulldog Entertainment; Chapter 3, Courtesy of Galbanum; Chapter 4, Courtesy of Toy Tips, Inc.; Chapter 5, Courtesy of Card Creations; Chapter 6, Courtesy of Kiyonna Klothing; Chapter 7, Courtesy of Perfect Curve; Chapter 8, Courtesy of Bravissmo; Chapter 9, Courtesy of Jolie Co.; Chapter 10, Chris Hartlove; Chapter 11, Alan Levenson; Chapter 12, Courtesy of Fitscape; Chapter 13, Courtesy of Screenshop Software; Chapter 14, Courtesy of Colorblock Corp.; Chapter 15, Photo by Krasner-Trebitz/Courtesy of East Side Sports; Chapter 16, Kelly Peterson; Chapter 17, Courtesy of Your Search Has Ended; Chapter 18, Andy Freeberg; Chapter 19, Courtesy of Kings River Expeditions.

All cases are reprinted with permission of their authors. All *Young Entrepreneurs—Minicase* features appear by permission of the subjects.

Printed in the U.S.A.

Library of Congress Catalog Card Number: 98-71973

ISBN: 0-395-90670-9

1 2 3 4 5 6 7 8 9 – DC – 02 01 00 99 98

Brief Contents

6 58.4
A 427

98

Wm. Dew

6-29-01

Contents

Note: Chapters contain a **Preview**, **Terms to Know**, a **Young Entre-preneurs—Minicase**, **Entrepreneurship in Action** boxed inserts, **Technology Tip** boxed inserts, **The Real World of Entrepreneur-ship** boxed inserts, **Cases Relevant to This Chapter, Issues for Review and Discussion, Experiencing Entrepreneurship, Re-sources,** and **Internet Resources**.

Part V   **Process Management in Entrepreneurial Companies**   **363**

Chapter 13

Part VII   Building a Business with Character   527

Preface

Business owners today are faced with a bewildering array of management theories and practices that range from reengineering to visualization. Should a company use an open-book policy, or empower its employees in self-directed teams? And what about quality circles, management by walking around, and just-in-time? With so many theories, proposals, and practices bombarding beleaguered business owners, it is no wonder that they often resort to throwing imaginary darts blindly at a board, choosing one practice and attempting to implement it—usually with less than satisfying results.

For those people in middle management in large, existing companies, implementing a new practice means radical change from traditional methods, a daunting task at best. But applying these newer management practices to entrepreneurial companies in the start-up and growth phases is a very doable accomplishment. In fact, it makes perfect sense. How much easier it is to begin building a company using state-of-the-art management practices than to re-engineer an existing company.

A Truly Contemporary Approach

This book breaks away from traditional small business management texts to introduce the reader—the up-and-coming entrepreneur—to the latest perspectives on organizational management. My students have corroborated the fact that by the time they take an entrepreneurship course, most of their previous management texts have typically taken one of two approaches: the management of mid-market and larger companies, or the management of small businesses. Their subject matter is typically organized in a functional manner without considering the company as a system of interdependent activities. Furthermore, they do not normally give in-depth treatment to the issue of how to build a company that will grow and endure. A company today that is not continually improving, innovating, and seeking ways to grow and give value to its customers will ultimately stagnate and die. The entrepreneurship books we use to teach our students should strongly reflect these values.

The paradigm that is threaded throughout this book emerged from the convergence of information technology, globalization, and a dynamic marketplace. It recognizes that the marketplace has dramatically changed, making many of the traditional business approaches and strategies obsolete or ineffective. It proposes that to compete and grow in this challenging environment, companies must do more than just give lip service to putting the customer at the center of the business and integrating total quality. Entrepreneurial businesses should integrate these values into every aspect throughout their organization. The principles espoused in this book are the result of the international research of many experts; they are proven philosophies that add value to the company and the customer. The concepts presented here of vision, agile webs, core values, virtual organizations, continuous improvement, core competencies, relationship marketing, and mass customization—to name just a few—are rarely found in other management texts; yet, they are very much a part of business practices today.

The key issues in this book revolve around the customer, the product/service, the process, the organization, and leadership, and are considered as interdependent components of an integrated organization. The topics discussed have value for small business owners and entrepreneurs alike who need to be proactive and flexible to meet the demands of rapidly changing customer needs in a global marketplace. I firmly believe that we must prepare our students to deal successfully with the changes occurring in business and organizational management today. That can happen only if we are willing to discard old thought in favor of new approaches that more accurately reflect this dynamic new environment and are proven to build successful and enduring companies.

Content and Organization

The book opens with Part I: Entrepreneurial Management for the Twenty-first Century, which in three chapters gives an overview of the nature of entrepreneurship, the entrepreneurial mindset, and the environment in which entrepreneurship occurs. This includes the industry and the legal environment.

Part II: The Nature of Start-up Companies focuses on the birthing process, considering life cycles, how businesses get started, and how resources are pulled together in the form of a team and a virtual organization.

Part III: The Nature of Rapidly Growing Companies looks at the preparations required to grow a company, from developing an effective management team and infrastructure to building a strong employee base and creating a strategy for growth.

Part IV: Marketing for Growth focuses on a customer-centered strategy for growing and marketing the company. In addition to addressing traditional topics such as the marketing plan and the "four P's," it also discusses virtual products, mass customization, relationship marketing, global marketing, technology issues related to marketing, and strategies for building customer relationships for life.

Part V: Process Management in Entrepreneurial Companies is a unique part of the book that is typically not found in other texts. In this part processes related to the development and manufacture of products and services are considered. The book looks at product development for entrepreneurs and how to achieve mass customization. In a chapter that focuses on product companies, it discusses manufacturing technology, purchasing, quality measurement, and distribution. Another chapter deals with process issues in retail/wholesale and service businesses such as trade area definition, facility decisions, and other business processes.

Part VI: Managing Finances for Growth addresses all the issues related to financial statement creation and analysis, managing cash flow, and accounts receivable and payable management. The last chapter in this part deals with strategies for financing for growth including the venture capital market, private placement, the initial public offering, and strategic alliances. It also treats the subject of harvesting the wealth of the business and succession planning.

The final part, Part VII: Building a Business with Character, discusses the critical issues of ethics and social responsibility. An Epilogue pulls everything together to describe the customer-centered entrepreneurial business.

Special Features of the Text

Growing and Managing an Entrepreneurial Business includes several pedagogical features of value to instructors and students.

▶ *Chapter Previews* outline key topics at the beginning of each of the nineteen chapters.

▶ *Terms to Know,* highlighted in boldface in the chapters and listed at the start of each chapter, give readers the key terms they will need to understand relevant to the topic.

▶ A *Young Entrepreneurs in Action Minicase* at the start of each chapter deals with the real-life stories and experiences of young entrepreneurs with growing businesses. Each reflects the content of the chapter with which it is associated. These minicases also provide a jumping-off point for discussion of the subject at hand.

▶ *Entrepreneurship in Action* boxed inserts feature extended real-life examples that show the application of key concepts discussed in each chapter.

▶ *The Real World of Entrepreneurship* boxed inserts provide concrete suggestions and strategies that entrepreneurs can apply immediately in their businesses.

▶ *Technology Tip* boxed inserts recognize the importance and pervasiveness of technology in today's business environment. These inserts suggest practical ways in which the entrepreneurial business can employ technology to be more productive and competitive.

▶ *Photographs* with extensive content-based captions supplement the text with real-world examples of entrepreneurs and how they meet the challenges of running a business.

▶ *Issues for Review and Discussion* are discussion-provoking questions about key points in the chapter. These can be used to stimulate interaction during class sessions or to help students review the material.

▶ *Experiencing Entrepreneurship* activities at the end of each chapter give students a chance to experience entrepreneurship first hand by getting them out in the marketplace to find information and interact with entrepreneurs.

- *Resources* provide a bibliography of additional books that students may consult to explore more deeply into a specific topic presented in the chapter.

- *Internet Resources* are listed at the end of each chapter to provide another critical source of information on chapter topics.

- *Case Studies* at the end of the book provide longer examples of real businesses dealing with the issues presented in the book. Each chapter lists cases relevant to the topics in that chapter.

- A *sample business plan* at the end of the book serves as a helpful model for students who are building their own business plan.

The Teaching/Learning Package

In addition to the pedagogical aids in the text itself, supplemental materials are provided for instructors and students.

- An *Instructor's Resource Manual* features suggestions for planning the course, learning objectives, lecture outlines, instructor's notes for the case studies, suggested answers to end-of-chapter questions, and supplementary lecture material that goes beyond what is presented in the text.

- A *Test Bank* contains over 80 questions per chapter, including true/false, multiple-choice, and essay questions that assess basic understanding as well as application of the concepts. A computerized version of the Test Bank is also available.

- *Electronic Slides* (prepared in Microsoft PowerPoint) provide aid for classroom presentation. For each chapter they include text as well as selected figures from the book.

- *Color Transparencies* featuring figures and tables from the text are also provided to help aid classroom presentation.

- *Videos* that explore various aspects of entrepreneurship provide additional real-world examples. An accompanying guide provides tips for using the videos in the classroom.

- *An Interactive Web Site* that will be expanded and updated as we receive feedback from our customers includes materials for both students and instructors. The student area of the site contains updates of resources and text materials, links to other useful sites on the web, video mini-cases, and examples of feasibility studies and business plans that can be used as models. The instructor's area contains the downloadable PowerPoint slides, updates, suggested answers to the materials on the student site, and additional teaching tips and information to enhance the learning experience. We look forward to receiving your feedback so that this web site will evolve into a truly useful tool. Visit the site by clicking on *Business* at Houghton Mifflin's College Division Home at *http://www.hmco.com/college.*

Acknowledgements

Over the course of several drafts of manuscript, I had the assistance of many fine reviewers. I am indebted to those people who teach the entrepreneurship course and were willing to share their ideas and provide constructive feedback:

John F. S. Bunch
Benedictine College

Melissa Cardon
Columbia University

Tony Enerva
Lakeland Community College

Craig Galbraith
University of North Carolina, Wilmington

Frederick D. Greene
Manhattan College

Steven H. Hanks
Utah State University

Sandra Honig-Haftel
Wichita State University

Frank Hoy
University of Texas at El Paso

Norris F. Krueger, Jr.
Troy State University, Malmstrom AFB

Thomas W. Lloyd
Westmoreland County Community College

Benjamin M. Oviatt
Georgia State University

Courtney Price
Entrepreneurial Education Foundation

Nick Sarantakes
Austin Community College

No author has ever worked with a finer publishing staff than the one I have at Houghton Mifflin. My gratitude for a very pleasant and rewarding experience to Susan Kahn, Senior Associate Editor; Fred Burns, Senior Project Editor; Sarah Ambrose, Senior Production/Design Coordinator; Henry Rachlin, Senior Designer; Tezeta Tulloch, Editorial Assistant; and Marcy Kagan, photo researcher and art editor.

A book of this size cannot be completed alone. In addition to the tireless work of the staff at Houghton Mifflin, I appreciate the excellent case studies contributed by my USC colleagues Tom O'Malia and Bill Crookston (Zotos-Stein and Zanart Entertainment), USC graduate Jim Mimlitsch (SB Networks), and research colleague Sandra Honig-Haftel (Marcus Food and Buckhead Beef). My thanks to the entrepreneurs who allowed me to spend time in their companies and write case studies from those experiences: David McDonald of Pelco, Inc. and Brenda French of French Rags and to all the young entrepreneurs featured in the minicases who inspired me with their courage, energy, and creativity.

I would like to thank my friends Steve Mariotti of the National Foundation for Teaching Entrepreneurship (NFTE) and Jennifer Kushell of the Young Entrepreneurs Network for helping me find so many exciting young entrepreneurs who were willing to be highlighted in the book. I want to give special thanks to my former student, project partner, and friend Jon Weisner who, in the midst of building his own exciting career, found the time to create the lecture presentation slides for the book, to answer all my technology questions, and to make sure I stayed humble.

My family keeps me going and striving to be better. Thank you, Rob, Jaime, and Greg. And as always, thanks to my husband, John, who makes my world go 'round.

Kathleen R. Allen

Entrepreneurial Management for the Twenty-first Century

*Only those who will risk going
too far can possibly find out
how far one can go.*
T. S. Eliot

Entrepreneurship and Small-Business Management

Preview

Understanding this chapter will give you the ability to

▶ **Discuss the three principles for a new marketplace.**

▶ **Describe the nature of entrepreneurs and the role of small business in the economy.**

▶ **Explain the difference between an entrepreneurial company and a small business.**

▶ **Decide whether you are suited to being an entrepreneur.**

Terms to Know

Young Entrepreneurs—Minicase

Jennifer Kushell
Young Entrepreneurs Network—Boston, MA

"**Y**ou're too young." "Wait until you graduate." "What do you know about running a business?" "Why don't you get a *real* job?"[1] Instead of frightening a very young Jennifer Kushell, these well-intentioned pieces of advice made her even more determined not to go the traditional route of working for someone else. Instead, she would learn about running a business by doing it.

Despite criticisms by the press about the lazy, misguided Generation X—the "twentysomething" generation—Kushell didn't see anyone around her who qualified as a "slacker." When she began looking around for young entrepreneurs, she found them everywhere, from a 23-year-old importer of fish from Fiji to a 21-year-old manufacturer of women's snowboarding apparel. These examples made Kushell more certain than ever that she needed to become a business owner.

[1]Jennifer Kushell, *No Experience Necessary* (New York: Random House, 1997), p. xiii.

In 1993, two friends who had formerly worked with the Association of Collegiate Entrepreneurs (ACE) approached her about starting a directory for young entrepreneurs to fill the gap left when ACE dissolved earlier that year. It seemed like as good a place to start as any, so the International Directory of Young Entrepreneurs (IDYE) was born. Its purpose was to provide resources for young entrepreneurs around the world. Over the course of a year, the three partners grew the membership and introduced a proprietary, contact-management software program designed by one of the partners. For an annual membership fee, members received quarterly updates of the directory on disk.

By the end of the first year, however, Kushell's two partners were no longer able to commit the time and resources needed to run IDYE. The partnership was dissolved, and Kushell became the sole owner in December 1994. She moved the operation from a bedroom in her parents' house in Los Angeles to a hallway in her apartment in Boston, where she had relocated to attend Boston University.

Without sufficient resources, Kushell needed to find creative ways to staff her new operation. So whenever one of her classes required a project, she found a way to bring in classmates to serve as interns. Since the business was labor intensive—collecting and verifying information for IDYE members—she often had as many as 10 interns working for her. She now had two full-time jobs—the business and school—but it was soon obvious which one took priority.

In the beginning, Kushell spent considerable time networking: going to charitable fund raisers, business forums, Venture-preneurs Network breakfast meetings, and any activity that would give her the opportunity to meet the movers and shakers of the business world. By the end of a year, she had hundreds of business contacts and was attending more business events than university events. But all this

came with a price. She lost friends who didn't understand her passion for business; she was stressed out from constantly being on the move and not taking care of herself; and sometimes she felt overwhelmed by being totally on her own at age 20 in a big city 3,000 miles from home. But Kushell never gave up.

When IDYE reached 300 members, it stopped growing. Kushell knew she had to find a new route to grow the company. In January 1996, she conducted a survey of her members to find out how many used the Internet. The results were astounding: more than 80 percent of the membership had Internet access, and the rest considered it a high priority. All believed it was important to put the directory online. This was a critical point in the life of the company, because putting the database online would allow members to update their own information and would almost eliminate mailing costs. Moreover, a web site would make it much easier to reach out to a global community of young entrepreneurs. The decision was made: Kushell hired a web site development firm to develop and host the site.

After graduation from Boston University in May 1996, Kushell moved her company to an office suite downtown. She also formed The Young Entrepreneurs Network (The Network) as an umbrella organization to include IDYE and a new consulting division, and she hired her first official employee. Now the company was better structured for rapid growth, but it was also going through some tough times. Members didn't understand the value of the service and were beginning to leave The Network. To keep itself afloat while it built up membership, The Network stepped up its consulting business. Clients included Mobil, Subway, Ernst and Young, and other large corporations seeking to reach young entrepreneurs. The Network also began holding monthly networking nights at local bars and restaurants in downtown

Boston. It was an instant success, attracting an average of 75 people per night.

At about this time, Kushell realized that the web site had become stale, so she hired two companies to build a search engine and an online database, as well as design a new site. The new site was launched in March 1997.

To create value for its customers, The Network instituted a discount program to help members save money on products and services they use every day. It also restarted its *Visions* magazine and made it possible for members to "search for entrepreneurs like themselves from all over the world, 24 hours a day, online." The Young Entrepreneurs Network is still a work in progress. It faces many challenges in its effort to continually add value for its customers through new products and services, but the future looks bright.

Jennifer Kushell has become the "guru" of her generation, according to *U.S. News & World Report* and the many public and private organizations to which she has spoken about the special needs of young entrepreneurs. In her "spare" time, she teaches classes in entrepreneurship at the National Foundation for Teaching Entrepreneurship (NFTE). Kushell has done more than most to encourage young people to take charge of their lives. So it's only fitting that she be the first of 20 young entrepreneurs whom readers will meet throughout this book.

What are some of the reasons Jennifer Kushell chose to start her own business rather than go to work for someone else?

Imagine that you can go to work whenever you want. You decide what needs to be accomplished, when you'll do it, and from where. You can choose to stay home today or do work from your boat on the lake. You decide how much you'll be paid, when and how many vacations you'll take, and how many people will help you do your work. Now imagine that you must work seven days a week, 12 hours a day, for little or no money, never getting a vacation and always taking the problems of work home with you.

Sounds like two extremes, doesn't it? Well, those two scenarios and everything in between comprise the many facets of business ownership; and if you decide to become a business owner, you—and only you—will ultimately determine what your business lifestyle will be. As a business owner, you will decide

‣ What kind of business you want

‣ Whether to start a business or buy an existing one

‣ Who will work with you

‣ Where you will get funding

‣ How the company will be run

‣ What role you will play

‣ How much time you will devote to the business

These are just a few of the hundreds of decisions you'll make as a business owner. Jennifer Kushell (see the opening minicase) quickly found that the independence that comes from being your own boss carries a heavy price in the early stages of a new business. Everything depends on you. You are the last to get paid, the last to go home at the end of the day, and you virtually eat and sleep with your business. But in Kushell's mind, the positives of business ownership far outweigh the negatives. She is in charge of her life, and she is creating something that is all hers.

This chapter will give you an overview of what business ownership is like today, the nature of small business, and what you need to consider before deciding to become an entrepreneur.

Three Principles for the New Marketplace

The decisions you make as a business owner will affect not only your business but your personal life as well. Business ownership is still the number one road to creating wealth. But the journey to business and personal success is not the same journey it was even 10 years ago. The convergence of information technology, globalization, and a dynamic marketplace with savvy customers has entirely changed the way we do business. Business transactions have an immediacy that never existed previously. We now expect communications to occur instantaneously, whether in our hometown or across the globe. Product life cycles have shortened due to technology and consumers' insatiable appetite for customized and leading-edge products. These are just a few examples of today's challenging and often chaotic business environment. Three principles have emerged for this new marketplace.

The first principle is a renewed focus on the customer as the center of the business. The customer is, in effect, the glue that holds all the pieces of the company together: without the customer there is no business.

The second principle is the importance of superior quality, not just in products and services but throughout the company—quality in everything we do as a business, and the highest levels of quality for our customers. Quality comes about when a company creates an environment that encourages innovation in all areas of management and organization, and when employees understand what they contribute to the satisfaction of the customer.

The third principle is the need for integration of all aspects of the business, or, as Peter Senge calls it, **systems thinking**. In his landmark book *The Fifth Discipline,* Senge proposes that "systems thinking is a discipline for seeing the 'structures' that underlie complex situations."[1] The kind of complexity with which most companies are familiar is what he calls "detail" complexity: the myriad details of running a business on a daily basis. Most companies, however, are unprepared to deal with "dynamic" complexity, where cause and effect are not readily apparent, and the results of actions by the company can vary significantly from short term to long term and even within various parts of the organization. In other words, we are often taught that breaking complex problems into smaller parts makes them more manageable, but in doing so we confront the classic dilemma: we can't see the forest for the trees. We lose sight of the whole and how all the various parts interact to produce a complete picture.

Achieving higher quality, lower cost, and better customer satisfaction is an example of a dynamic problem requiring integration. Short-term solutions to achieve the long-term goal of lower costs might actually raise costs in some parts of the organization. For instance, one way to achieve better customer satisfaction is to produce products the customer wants at the highest quality and the lowest price. In the short term, costs may go up as the company implements systems to increase quality; but in the long run, warranty costs will actually go down more than enough to offset the cost of the increase in quality. Product design costs may actually go down as well, because the customer is involved in the process from the beginning, thus reducing the need for redesign. The long-term result will be lower production costs, as well as lower marketing costs, because the company has produced something for a ready and willing customer. But these positive results for the whole organization are not easily seen when first implemented.

Looking at the company as an integrated whole and seeing how each aspect of the business interacts with every other aspect has become increasingly important as companies move away from rigid departmental structures to more flexible organizations. Certainly it is not possible to achieve total quality and the highest levels of customer satisfaction and loyalty without a focus on integrating product/service, process, organization, leadership, and customer in new and innovative ways (see Figure 1.1).

The three principles for a new marketplace will be emphasized throughout this book because they are essential for business success as we head into the twenty-first century:

1. The customer as the center of the business

2. Superior quality and innovation throughout the business

3. Integration of all aspects of the business

Now let's look at the role small business plays in the economy and how the entrepreneurial mindset is permeating all types of organizations, both profit and nonprofit, large and small.

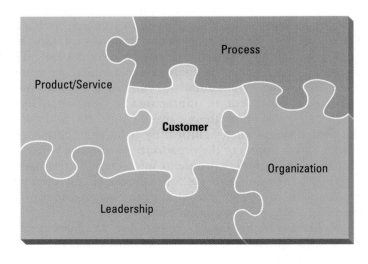

**Figure 1.1
An Integrated,
Customer-Focused,
Total-Quality
Company**

The Role of Small Business and Entrepreneurship in the Economy

Because the term *entrepreneur* is widely used to refer to anyone who starts a business, it is often difficult to understand why some ventures become the Home Depots and Microsofts of the world and others never go beyond providing a modest income for their owners. The reality is that the birth of a Home Depot or a Microsoft begins in the mind of the entrepreneur with world-class intentions to innovate, grow, and create value.[2]

Virtually every company starts out relatively small, but not every company stays small. Unfortunately, most of the research on entrepreneurship typically does not distinguish between those businesses that remain small and those that grow to become substantial companies. In fact, there is considerable disagreement about what constitutes a **small business**. The Small Business Administration (SBA) traditionally has defined a small business as one employing fewer than 500 employees. However, more than 90 percent of all businesses employ fewer than 500 workers, and most people find it difficult to think of a 400-person firm or even a 200-person firm as "small." In contrast, the Organization for Economic Cooperation and Development (OECD) and the U.S. Chamber of Commerce prefer to designate as a small business any firm employing fewer than 100 people. In the minds of many

 Entrepreneurship in Action

A World-Class Venture in the Recording Industry

You may not think of a rock group as a world-class business. But world-class entrepreneurship is almost a necessity to succeed in the intensely competitive recording industry.

For 30 years, until the death of lead singer Jerry Garcia in 1995, the Grateful Dead proved to be much more than a traveling '60s retro show. In fact, the Grateful Dead is recognized as being responsible for many innovations that are now widely accepted practices in the music industry.

1. In the 1970s, they pioneered the use of a floor pedal on the microphone on stage, allowing the singers to turn off their microphones with their feet when they weren't singing. This prevented unwanted sounds, such as talking between songs or during instrumentals, from being carried to the audience.

2. They were the first to set up their own mail-order system to sell tickets to hard-core fans. About 50 percent of their tickets were sold in this manner.

3. Their extensive merchandising operation involving promotional items has been emulated throughout the music industry.

4. Against tradition, they initiated the notion of touring even when they weren't bringing out a new album. They learned from their customers, the fans, that more important than the music was the event of being at the concert.

5. They pioneered the "cool opener" at stadium concerts, using such name performers as Bob Dylan, Traffic, and Sting, and turning the show into a mega-event. This practice is standard procedure today.

6. They innovated a telephone hotline that provided tour and recording information to their mailing list of more than 160,000 loyal fans.

Clearly, the Grateful Dead took the notion of "customer driven" to the max. They built an innovative, worldwide organization that lived for the customer. That is the essence of "world class."

In this book we make a distinction between small businesses and entrepreneurial companies. Sylvan Learning Systems, Inc. is an outstanding example of the latter. Douglas Becker and R. Christopher Hoehn-Saric acquired this company and, in just five years with their drive and vision, turned it into one of the fastest growing and most innovative educational companies in the United States. (Danuta Otfinowski)

business owners, however, even a firm with 100 employees does not seem small. Given the current trend toward downsizing, outsourcing, and virtual companies, the relevance of using the number of employees as a defining factor for *small business* has been called into question. How does one measure the size of a company by number of employees when the company **outsources** (uses contract workers rather than permanent employees) most of its primary functions such as manufacturing, distribution, and possibly marketing? However *small business* is defined, though, it appears to have a significant impact on the health of the economy.

Entrepreneurial Companies Versus Small Businesses

In this book, we make a clear distinction between small businesses and entrepreneurial ventures because they are generally two different types of businesses whose owners have different intentions. Small businesses typically start small and stay relatively small, providing a lifestyle, a job, and a modest level of income for their owners and having little impact in their industries. They are often referred to as "mom-and-pops," suggesting family-owned businesses, but many mom-and-pops have grown to become substantial firms with significant impact in their industries. Marriott Corporation (a hospitality company) and Davidson and Associates (an educational software company) are notable examples. Entrepreneurial ventures, on the other hand, have founders with different motives and goals. They are innovative and growth oriented. Their purpose is not to create a job or an occupation for their founders but to create value and wealth that the founders can harvest at some future date.

Job Generation in Small Business

The seminal work of David Birch in 1979 started a wave of further research supporting the notion that small companies generate a disproportionate share of new jobs in the economy.[3] This research argues that over the past 25 years, two-thirds of net new jobs in the private sector have come from small firms, which also accounted for about half of total private employment.[4] But measuring precisely the job creation effect of small business is difficult because of significant churning. **Churning** refers to the frequency with which businesses open, close, expand, and contract. Between 1988 and 1990, for example, more than 14.5 million jobs were created in small firms and more than 11.3 million were lost. In other words, to add one *net* job, nearly ten had to be created. According to researcher Zoltan Acs, the bottom line is " . . . no matter what industry sector you look at, small firms never create fewer jobs than their share of employment. And some of those small firms, like Nucor Steel, Microsoft, and Wal-Mart, grow rather quickly into large firms that create lots of jobs."[5]

Small-Business Failure

In recent years, Dun & Bradstreet (D&B) files have been the source of answers to many of the questions we have about small businesses. D&B tracks business failures and discontinuances over time. (**Failures** are firms that have gone out of business or have reorganized through Chapter 11 bankruptcy, resulting in losses to creditors. **Discontinuances** are firms that have ceased operations with no outstanding debts.) Looking at all firms that started business in 1985, D&B discovered that many more businesses were discontinued rather than failed. It also found, surprisingly, that 69.7 percent of those firms were still in business in 1994.[6] One reason for the discrepancy between its findings and those universally reported (that four out of five new firms fail) is D&B's definition of the firm. D&B does not include self-employed individuals or groups moving from venture to venture. Instead, it tracks businesses that are actively purchasing supplies, selling products and services, and in general doing things that put them in the spotlight. Along these lines, D&B also reported that those firms that survived were not necessarily the firms that had increased employment. In fact, the chance of surviving actually decreased as the size of the firm increased.[7] If a firm made it through the first two years of operation, its chance of succeeding increased with each passing year. This is generally because many of the failures were what are termed **casual businesses,** or businesses on paper, where either no significant effort was expended or it was determined that the concept was not feasible. An enormous number of these casual businesses are reported to the IRS on tax returns, nearly twice as many as are contained in the active records of Dun & Bradstreet. As a result, much of what we know about the economic contribution of small business is influenced by these casual businesses.

Gazelles

One subset of entrepreneurial companies has received a lot of attention recently. These companies, which researcher David Birch calls **gazelles,** have annual sales growth of at least 20 percent and comprise the fastest-growing segment of smaller companies. Although they represent only about 3 percent of all U.S. businesses, they created 5 million jobs between 1990 and 1994,[8] the largest number of jobs created by small business. They are, however, a paradox of sorts. Most of these fast-growing companies are in manufacturing, whereas the majority of net job growth generally is in services. Also, contrary to popular belief, they are not all high-tech companies. Birch claims that only 1 in 50 is a true high-tech company. The rest are found in relatively slow-growth industries such as paper products, rubber and plastic, electronics, and chemicals. Still, gazelles are responsible for 55 percent of all the derivative innovations in 362 industries and 95 percent of breakthrough innovations.

The State of Small Business

A look at the statistics on small business and the economy is encouraging. A strong economy certainly bodes well for small-business growth. If you compare the challenges business owners faced in the middle of a recession in 1991 with those they faced in the healthy economic times of 1996, you will find significant differences. In 1991, the top challenges were avoiding cash flow problems and keeping costs under control. In 1996, they were finding qualified employees and coping with increased insurance costs and taxes.[9]

A number of other sources of information give us a clearer picture of the nature of small business today. The following sections summarize the information on small-business health.

Number of Small Businesses

A look at all active, nonfarm businesses that pay unemployment insurance reveals that the total number of businesses has been growing at a rate of about 2 percent per year since 1992 and the number of new corporations has been growing at an annual rate of 2.8 percent. Moreover, the number of business failures declined by 26 percent between 1992 and 1996, while the average liability (loss to creditors) declined by almost 50 percent. Table 1.1 presents the state of small business between 1992 and 1996.

The number of home-based businesses skyrocketed from 12 million in 1991 to 16 million in 1996. In 1996, the top five start-at-home businesses were construction, cleaning services, retail stores, consulting, and design work.[10]

Job Creation

All the data indicate that small companies are growing and large ones are not. Industries creating the most jobs are personnel support services, eating and drinking establishments, and computer and data processing services. The home health care industry nearly doubled in size between 1991 and 1995. The biggest job losers were in aerospace and savings institutions.

Start-ups

More than 90 percent of the business population is composed of small businesses. Several studies have found that the overall prevalence of nascent entrepreneurs (those who are now or have been involved in a business of their own) is between 3.9 and 4.3 percent.[11] If we include those who are associated with a new business as part of their job, we find that about 6.8 million U.S. households have at least one person currently involved in a new start-up.[12] Men started twice as many businesses as women in 1996, and on a

Table 1.1   The State of Small Business, 1992–1996

Year	New Incorporations	Business Terminations	Total Number of Failures	Average Liability per Failure	Total Number of Businesses Year End
1992	737,000	819,000	97,069	$971,653	5,741,000
1993	776,000	801,000	86,133	$554,438	5,851,000
1994	807,000	803,000	71,520	$410,477	5,992,000
1995	812,000	869,000	71,128	$524,175	6,057,000
1996	820,000	823,000	71,811	$473,759	6,220,000

Sources: Office of Advocacy, U.S. Small Business Administration; Economic Analysis Department, Dun & Bradstreet.

per-100 people basis, most of those start-ups were in western states: Nevada, Idaho, Colorado, Texas, and Utah. Furthermore, most didn't use angel (private investor) or professional venture funds to fund their start-ups; rather, they used their own resources, including friends and family.[13]

Global Growth

Global expansion is no longer the province of large, multinational companies. Many factors have contributed to small-business's ability to join the party, among them GATT, which is working to protect intellectual property abroad, and NAFTA, which is providing trade opportunities free of tariffs among the United States, Canada, and Mexico.

The Internet provides a quick and less expensive way for entrepreneurs to establish a presence in the global arena. In 1995, 18,957 sites responded to a web survey; in 1997, an astounding 739,706 companies responded, proving that the Internet is definitely a new frontier.

Small business is experiencing positive economic times, and today, more than ever before, the incentives for entrepreneurship are many.

Incentives for Entrepreneurship

More than 35 million (one in three) U.S. households are involved in a new or small business. These are the preliminary findings of a national survey undertaken by the Entrepreneurship Research Consortium.* Why are so many people becoming business owners? Among the many reasons are these:

1. *Entrepreneurship is a way to take charge of your career.* Downsizing of large corporations in the 1980s and early 1990s pushed a lot of people into the ranks of the unemployed. The jobs they left no longer exist, and they face retraining before being able to reenter the work force. At that point, many people decide that it's time to take charge of their careers. One way to do that is to start their own businesses. When Peter Kim, kicker for the Tampa Bay Buccaneers, lost his job due to injury, he found himself sidelined early in his career. He returned to his Honolulu home and decided to become a restaurateur. Today his successful chain, Yummy Korean BBQ, has allowed him to further expand his interest in food services into other types of restaurants.[14]

    Immigrants often find that starting a business is the best way to get involved in their new culture and community. Many young people opt out of family businesses they could have easily entered in favor of making it "on their own." See the minicase on Bryan Rosencrantz that opens Chapter 12.

2. *Entrepreneurship is a way to build wealth.* Though it's clear that not all entrepreneurs will one day end up with the mega-businesses and fortunes

---

*The Entrepreneurship Research Consortium is an association of major universities across the country that are funding and undertaking ground-breaking research on nascent entrepreneurs. The consortium is based at Babson College, Massachusetts.

of the likes of Bill Gates of Microsoft or Republic Industries founder Wayne Huizenga, entrepreneurship does provide a way to create wealth that can't often be achieved by working for someone else. In their research spanning more than 20 years, Thomas Stanley and William Danko have discovered that the "prototypical" American millionaire is a 57-year-old male, married, with three children. Two-thirds of millionaires are self-employed. In fact, "self-employed people make up less than 20 percent of the workers in America but account for two-thirds of the millionaires."[15] Stanley and Danko define a *millionaire* as having a net worth of $1 million or more. Under this definition, only 3.5 percent of the U.S. population consists of millionaires.[16]

3. *Entrepreneurship is a way to take charge of your life.* The current generation of college students seems very concerned about quality of life issues. Of course, they want to make money, but—more important—they want to have time to spend with family, travel, and just have fun. And they want to give something back to the community. In short, they don't want to live the work-obsessed lives of their baby-boomer parents. So young people everywhere have embraced entrepreneurship as a way to achieve the quality of life they want. As a result, they are starting creative businesses that take advantage of flexible structures so they're not chained to the office. With laptops and modems, cell phones and pagers, they're doing business from anywhere and everywhere.

   World extreme snowboarding champion Steve Klassen wanted a lifestyle that would support his love of snowboarding and the outdoor life. So, after graduation from college, he saw an opportunity and opened a snowboard shop in Mammoth, California, hired snowboarders to staff it, and has built a successful venture and a lifestyle to match.

The incentives to become an entrepreneur are present in the economy, as is support for entrepreneurship.

Support for Entrepreneurship

In some ways it's more difficult to start a business today than it was 10 years ago. The marketplace is now global and changing rapidly, and the rules have changed. But in other ways it's easier, because entrepreneurship is supported and encouraged in so many ways.

1. *Formal and informal entrepreneurship education and training are available in some form in nearly every community.* From majoring in entrepreneurship at a large university to taking a class at a local Small Business Development Center (**SBDC**),* aspiring entrepreneurs and current business owners can prepare to increase their chances of success in

---

*Small Business Development Center: associated with the Small Business Administration, these centers provide counseling, training, and specialized services to prospective and existing small-business owners and entities.

starting and running a business. Go to any bookstore and you'll find hundreds of titles geared toward small business and entrepreneurship. Learning about entrepreneurship today is as easy as picking up a magazine at the grocery store.

2. *Entrepreneurship has developed the star quality of the entertainment and sports industries.* Some of the more famous entrepreneurs are being hounded by the press and deluged with fan mail. Entrepreneurship is accepted and respected; it has finally come of age. In fact, today it seems everyone wants to be known as an entrepreneur of sorts.

3. *Technology has made it possible for young, entrepreneurial businesses to compete on a level playing field with much larger companies.* Small businesses can set up shop right next door to AT&T on the Internet and look every bit as professional doing it. Point-and-click desktop publishing software has allowed small businesses to create professional-looking marketing materials without having to pay expensive designers. With interactive databases and contact-management software, they can keep better track of their customers, vendors, and other business contacts. The list goes on and on.

4. *The United States has a strong infrastructure to support entrepreneurship.* Professional advisers such as attorneys, accountants, and bankers now specialize in the needs of entrepreneurs and small businesses. Business suppliers structure deals that allow small businesses with limited resources to buy what they need.

5. *The global marketplace has opened up a wealth of opportunity for small business.* In a fast-paced environment, small companies shine because they can move just as fast, be as flexible, and meet the needs of global customers as well as—and often better than—their much bigger counterparts.

Opportunities abound for those who have the drive and passion to become entrepreneurs. Who are these new entrepreneurs? And what does it take to be one today? The next section provides some answers.

The Entrepreneurial Mindset

Much has been written about entrepreneurs, what makes them tick, and what makes them different from everyone else. In recent times an almost celebrity status has accrued to the likes of Microsoft co-founder Bill Gates, media giant Ted Turner, and retail innovator Anita Roddick of Body Shop International. This notoriety is evident in the proliferation of magazines, books, and television documentaries that examine every detail of the entrepreneur's business and personal life. Entrepreneurship has become the new breeding ground for legends, superstars, and heroes.

Over the years, academic researchers have focused on the characteristics, personalities, and behaviors of entrepreneurs in a vain attempt to categorize, define, and analyze them. It has been an impossible task, largely because entrepreneurs seem to defy categorization. They come in all shapes, sizes, and

Sometimes the passion to start your business overcomes all other goals, even a college education. Dineh Mohajer left college to make nail polish with Generation X slang names like "pimp" and "porno." Her $25 million a year business, Hard Candy, is on its way to becoming a significant force in the cosmetic industry. If Mohajer has her way, it will dominate. (Lara Jo Regan)

colors, with a diverse range of motivations and intentions. But they all have one fundamental characteristic: variously called "fire in the belly," "intense desire," or "the burning gut," it's essentially passion. Passion drives the entrepreneur to seek opportunity, take risk, and keep going forward when all around him or her are saying, "It'll never work."

The Psychology of the Entrepreneur

Several psychological characteristics of entrepreneurs have received considerable attention from researchers over the years. These characteristics certainly are not exclusive to entrepreneurs, but many entrepreneurs display them in varying degrees. For example, research has generally concluded that entrepreneurs are not high-risk takers; they are, in fact, moderate-risk takers.[17] They don't leave their future to chance; on the contrary, entrepreneurs tend to identify the risks inherent in their ventures and then look for ways to minimize those risks. At the same time, however, security is not something they consciously seek to achieve, since most entrepreneurs understand that opportunity lies in a changing environment. In that sense, they see change and the risks associated with it as a positive.

Entrepreneurs seem to have a tremendous drive to succeed. They enjoy problem solving and setting goals for themselves and their businesses. Consequently, they also have a strong desire to be their own bosses, to have total control of their lives and the work they do. This need for independence, however, often makes it difficult for entrepreneurs to delegate authority to others. In most businesses, the ability of an entrepreneur to give up the reins of the business to those who have the management skills needed to take it beyond the start-up and growth phases is a crisis point that must be recognized. Failure to do so has often led to the downfall of the company.

Parallel to the need for independence is the entrepreneur's typically high internal locus of control. **Locus of control** refers to the degree to which people believe events in their lives are within their control as opposed to being under the control of external forces. Many studies have found a strong internal locus of control among entrepreneurs.[18] This leads to more proactive behavior in comparison to the reactive behavior of people with an external locus.

Finally, because of the inherent nature of the entrepreneurial environment, entrepreneurs tend to have a higher tolerance for ambiguity and change. They seem to prefer environments that offer more challenge and opportunity.

It is important to note that these characteristics are based on average tendencies. For every entrepreneur who has one or more of them, you can find one who doesn't, yet is a successful entrepreneur. That is the inherent dilemma in trying to get a handle on who the entrepreneur really is.

The Behavior of the Entrepreneur

In his 1988 article "Who Is the Entrepreneur Is the Wrong Question," Bill Gartner broke new ground by suggesting that defining the traits or characteristics of the entrepreneur does not lead to an understanding of the concept of entrepreneurship.[19] At issue, he found, was the fact that many of the samples used in trait research over the years were not carefully defined in terms of what constitutes "entrepreneurship." Gartner argued that research needs to focus more on what the entrepreneur *does* rather than on who he or she *is*. The entrepreneur is only one component in the complex process of venture creation; therefore, many researchers have explored the behaviors of entrepreneurs in an effort to understand the nature of their contribution to the entrepreneurial process.

The entrepreneur's experience prior to starting the new venture has also been examined. Entrepreneurs tend to start businesses in industries with which they are familiar or in which they have some familiarity with the product, service, or market.[20] But experience in and of itself has not been shown definitively to increase the chances of success in starting and growing the business.

Of all the behaviors considered within the province of the entrepreneur, the theme of the entrepreneur as decision maker or problem solver has pervaded the research literature. Contributing much to the understanding of the relationship between decision making and environmental uncertainty, the seminal work of G. L. S. Shackle rejected mainstream economic theory and determinism for their failure to recognize the importance of time and uncertainty as a factor in entrepreneurial decision making.[21] In other words, what induces someone to be enterprising is essentially different from what induces someone to avoid uncertainty. Decision making under conditions of uncertainty is a way of life for most entrepreneurs.

Entrepreneurs as resource acquirers and creators of value are another behavior often found in the definition of *entrepreneur*.[22] And, of course, the opportunistic nature of entrepreneurs can't be denied. According to Stanley Kaish and Benjamin Gilad, "Opportunity, by definition, is unknown until discovered or created."[23] I. M. Kirzner calls this ability "entrepreneurial alertness."[24] In their study, Kaish and Gilad found that "entrepreneurs do seem to expose themselves to more information, and their alertness takes them to the less obvious places."[25]

The Entrepreneur for the Twenty-first Century

Because of the resources available today to entrepreneurs, we are also seeing a new kind of entrepreneur: the **professional entrepreneur**. As business writer Tom Richman puts it, "Professional entrepreneurs today don't just have great ideas; they have great education and know how to plan their execution and know which capital sources to approach."[26]

Inc. magazine's State of Small Business Edition for 1997 painted a portrait of the new entrepreneur for the twenty-first century that has replaced the lone gunslinger, shoot-from-the-hip image that pervaded for decades. Figure 1.2 depicts the new entrepreneur. This new entrepreneur is something entirely different from the traditionally male entrepreneur who lacked education, ran his business by the seat of his pants, took risks, and firmly believed that entrepreneurs are born, not made.

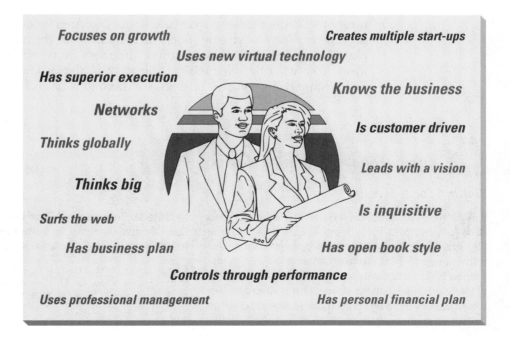

Focuses on growth　　　　**Creates multiple start-ups**
Uses new virtual technology
Has superior execution　　　　**Knows the business**
Networks
Thinks globally　　　　**Is customer driven**
Thinks big　　　　**Leads with a vision**
Surfs the web　　　　**Is inquisitive**
Has business plan　　　　**Has open book style**
Controls through performance
Uses professional management　　　　**Has personal financial plan**

**Figure 1.2
The Entrepreneur of the Twenty-first Century**

Today entrepreneurship is not just an art practiced solely by people who intuitively understand the nature of it. On the contrary, entrepreneurship is becoming more of a science, at least in the sense that potential entrepreneurs can learn and practice a great many of the skills and practices needed to succeed in an entrepreneurial venture. More people are studying the "art" and systematizing it so that everyone can understand what it takes to be an entrepreneur. "Professional entrepreneurs don't just do, they understand what they're doing."[27]

When we pull together what we know about entrepreneurs, we see someone who recognizes an opportunity and has the passion to put together the resources needed to develop that opportunity into a concept, test its feasibility, and turn that feasible concept into a business. We also see someone who knows how to create value, value that can be measured and converted to wealth. This ability to create value provides a variety of exit strategies that enable the entrepreneur to realize the wealth the business has created by selling a portion of his or her stock, selling the business outright, doing an IPO (initial public offering of stock), or merging with another company.

Making the Decision to Become an Entrepreneur

Before deciding to become an entrepreneur or a small-business owner, it's important to look at your personal values and goals because they will have an important impact on your decision. Successful entrepreneurs match their personal values, beliefs, and goals to business opportunities that are compatible and let them achieve both their business and personal goals. Remember Steve Klassen, who wanted to live and work outdoors doing his favorite sport, snowboarding? Would this entrepreneur have been happy starting a business in Los Angeles or Chicago? The reality is that Klassen actually had an opportunity to pursue a business venture in the Los Angeles area. It was an exciting concept for an extreme sports theme park. But the more he got into the planning and the search for capital, the more he found it was taking him away from what he loved most. Ultimately, he decided not to do the venture and is happily growing his business in Mammoth Lakes in new directions.

 Entrepreneurship in Action

Fishing for a Living

We often talk about the passion of the entrepreneur for what he or she is doing. Tracy Melton's passion for fishing lured him to skip his college graduation ceremony to attend a fishing tournament in Hawaii. It also pushed him to find a way to make a living from his love of the sport. His business concept? A mail-order company that sells big-game fishing tackle and accessories.

Melton International Tackle was started in 1993 in Los Alamitos, California, with start-up costs of $300,000. In 1996 sales were projected at $1.5 million.

Source: Janean Chun, Debra Phillips, Heather Page, Lynn Beresford, Holly Celeste Fisk, and Charlotte Mulhern, "Young Millionaires," *Entrepreneur*, November 1996, pp. 118–134.

Before you begin to search for opportunities, answer the following questions so that you'll be in a better position to judge whether or not a venture opportunity will be the right one for you:

1. What are your feelings about security?

2. Why do you want to own your own business?

3. How free are you to devote yourself to a new business?

4. What kind of lifestyle do you want to lead?

5. What kind of business environment suits you?

What Are Your Feelings About Security?

How important is a regular paycheck to you? Do you have enough money in reserve to cover your basic necessities until the business can afford to pay you? Some new ventures can take up to two years to show a profit or at least be in a cash position that allows you to pay yourself something. If you currently enjoy a regular paycheck and a certain lifestyle, you may have to make serious changes to allow the business to survive. And if you are undertaking entrepreneurship with responsibilities such as a spouse and children, you will need to have their support as well. What are their feelings about the lack of security you'll experience in the start-up phase of your business?

Why Do You Want to Own Your Own Business?

This is an important question. Most entrepreneurs would say they start businesses for reasons other than money: independence, freedom, creativity, power, fun. If you find yourself saying that you want to start a business just to make money, it's time to step back and look at yourself. There are easier, less risky, less time-consuming ways to make money than starting a business. You need to believe in and want to develop your business first and foremost. The value you create by doing the business well, by doing something you love, will be much greater because people always tend to do a better job at something they love. Be sure you understand your personal reasons for wanting to start a business. Realize that starting a business takes a huge commitment of time, money, energy, and devotion. Make sure that's what you want to do.

How Free Are You to Devote Yourself to a New Business?

Some types of ventures are more demanding than others in terms of time, level of stress, and even level of physical exhaustion. Some ventures take several years to develop and are far riskier than others. You need to seriously look at your ability to deal with these issues. Do you have what it takes in terms of time and endurance to make the business succeed at this stage in your life? At 22 you can afford to fail many times and recover to start another venture. Are you in a position to do that if you're much older or have many obligations? If you have many obligations in terms of family, mortgage, and so forth, how will you manage those while diverting needed resources to the new business? Do you have the support of your family in this effort?

What Kind of Lifestyle Do You Want to Lead?

The decision to start or purchase a business directly affects the kind of lifestyle you will lead, and where you want to live has an equal impact on the type of business you own. You can take one of two approaches: you can choose where you want to live first and then look around for a business opportunity that could be run from that location; or you can come up with a business idea and then find the best place to implement that business. The route you choose will depend on how important lifestyle is to you. For example, if the best place to locate your new manufacturing venture is near a port of entry for shipping, you will be somewhat limited in where you can live if you want to be involved in the day-to-day operations of the company. On the other hand, if living in a major city is not your style, you may choose to outsource the operations of your manufacturing venture to an existing company in the port of entry, thus freeing yourself to live in an outlying, smaller community some distance away and operate the company as a virtual company. If status and prestige are important to you, will your business allow you to do the things you need to do to achieve that status?

What Kind of Business Environment Suits You?

A lot of feelings and beliefs you didn't know you had will surface when you begin to think about what type of business you want to own. If you don't deal with these feelings honestly, you could end up with a business that makes you very unhappy and, as a consequence, probably doesn't do very well. You need to ask yourself about a number of issues, which include your feelings about

- The use of debt or having a business that is highly leveraged
- Unions and the use of union workers
- Employees and your ability to manage them
- Your religious beliefs and how they might affect the people you work with and the kind of business you choose
- Government regulation and paperwork (some industries are much more highly regulated than others)
- Dealing with people from other parts of the world or even other parts of the United States
- Getting involved in the community if your type of business requires that (and rare is the business that doesn't to some degree)
- Traveling, if your business requires that you be "on the road" a lot

Jim Koch tapped into the niche market of premium beers with his market leader, Samuel Adams beer. Koch believes that customers were ready to pay more to indulge in a really excellent American beer. He was right. Today sales exceed $214 million. (David Graham)

▶ Ownership, and your willingness to share ownership of the business with an investor or other person or persons (how do you feel about employing family members or giving them an ownership stake in the business?)

What You Need to Know to Succeed as a Small-Business Owner

It's important to understand that there is no one way to succeed as a small-business owner. There is no book of universally accepted rules you can follow. You need to be constantly aware that the way we do business today is substantially different from the way we did business several years ago. Therefore, much of traditional management thought has no place in today's marketplace. Whether you decide to become an entrepreneur or a small-business owner, you are still very much affected by the changes in the global marketplace. You still need to be competitive to survive and grow.

With this in mind, this book focuses on how to successfully grow and manage companies with an entrepreneurial viewpoint. The skills, tactics, strategies, and ideas presented are relevant to owners of all types of businesses who want to ensure that their businesses will ultimately survive in a highly competitive environment. Small-business owners today must think entrepreneurially just to stay in business. A good example of this is the independent booksellers that in recent years have seen the market they developed over 20 or more years suddenly devastated by the superstores—Barnes & Noble, Borders, Books-a-Million, and Crown. In Denver alone, four Barnes & Noble superstores surround independent booksellers, much as predatory animals stalk a kill. Nevertheless, some entrepreneurial independents have successfully competed by expanding their facilities and offering only those titles customers actually want. The point of view of the superstores reflects this focus on customer needs. They believe that if they succeed over the independents, it's because the independents obviously were not serving customers' needs.

This dilemma represents the key element in the success of any business going into the twenty-first century: giving customers exactly what they want. Today the customer *is* the business; it's as simple as that, and as complex. It is complex because to serve the customer completely, companies may have to change the way they do business. They must take advantage of new technology to gather and manage information about their products, services, vendors, and customers. They must focus more on integrating quality into every aspect of the business, providing one-to-one customer service, variable pricing, and a more flexible product mix. They must also develop their skills and resources while planning for the future in an unpredictable marketplace. To succeed as a business owner today, you must

▶ Be an expert on your market and your industry

▶ Know your customers well and get them involved in the business

▶ Integrate superior quality throughout your business

You now have some sense of what entrepreneurship is all about and what you should consider if you want to become an entrepreneur. In the next chapter, we will explore the entrepreneurial environment and how it affects your ability to become a successful entrepreneur.

Cases Relevant to This Chapter

French Rags
Zotos-Stein

Issues for Review and Discussion

1. What is an entrepreneur?
2. What is the difference between an entrepreneurial company and a small business?
3. Why are there more opportunities for entrepreneurship today than ever before?
4. What three questions do you need to ask yourself before you decide on a business to start or purchase?
5. What do you need to know to be successful as a small-business owner/ entrepreneur?

Experiencing Entrepreneurship

1. Interview an entrepreneur with a business less than five years old. How did this entrepreneur come up with the idea for the business? What other issues related to start-up did she or he face? What qualities made this person more likely to become an entrepreneur than the "average" person?

2. Interview a small-business owner and compare his or her mindset, goals, and business to those of the entrepreneur in question 1. How are they the same? How are they different? What conclusions can you draw?

Resources

Allen, Kathleen R. (1999). *Launching New Ventures,* 2nd ed. Boston: Houghton Mifflin.

Case, John (1992). *From the Ground Up.* New York: Simon & Schuster.

Drucker, Peter (1985). *Innovation and Entrepreneurship.* New York: Harper and Row.

Kushell, Jennifer (1997). *No Experience Necessary.* New York: Random House.

Naisbitt, John, and Patricia Aberdene (1990). *Megatrends 2000: Ten New Directions for the 1990s.* New York: Fawcett Columbine.

Peters, Tom (1987). *Thriving on Chaos.* New York: Harper and Row.

Senge, Peter (1990). *The Fifth Discipline: The Art and Practice of the Learning Organization.* New York: Currency/Doubleday.

Vesper, Karl H. (1993). *New Venture Mechanics.* Englewood Cliffs, NJ: Prentice-Hall.

Vesper, Karl H. (1994). *New Venture Experience.* Seattle: Vector Books.

Internet Resources

BizServe

http://bizserve.com/

Geared to small-business owners, this site gives information for new entrepreneurs and access to government and nonprofit resources.

Entrepreneurial Edge Online

http://www.edgeonline.com/

Resources for entrepreneurs and links to magazines, journals, and trade associations.

Small Business Administration

http://www.sbaonline.sba.gov

One-stop information source for business owners.

*The ability to learn faster than your competitors
may be the only sustainable competitive advantage.*
Arie P. de Gues
Royal Dutch/Shell, 1988

Entrepreneurship and the Dynamic Environment

Preview

Understanding this chapter will give you the ability to

▶ **Discuss the nature of the small-business environment and how technology has changed the nature of industries.**

▶ **Explain your industry's structure and how it plays a role in your competitive strategy.**

▶ **Identify significant trends in the business environment.**

▶ **Discuss the value of thoroughly knowing your business environment.**

Terms to Know

Young Entrepreneurs—Minicase

Jimmy Mac
BullDog Entertainment, Inc.

Jimmy Mac is the essence of entrepreneurial passion, and BullDog Entertainment is the expression of that passion. "BullDog is a way of life because it's the hungry dog that always wins." That kind of passion and persistence drove him to build a "mini Time Warner" in BullDog Entertainment.

This growing venture began in the heart of a boy from New Jersey who at 14 was a world champion cyclist and triathlete, getting product endorsements from major companies. In fact, Mac attracted so much attention from other athletes that he started

Pro-Elite, a sports marketing and management company, to represent other athletes for product endorsements. Eventually he also began receiving requests from European companies that wanted to increase their distribution in the United States. From October to March he would do his endorsement deals, then race for the rest of the year.

Bored with bicycle racing after several years, Mac decided to form his second company, UPJAM, in Philadelphia, where he also attended classes in entrepreneurship at the Wharton School of Business through NFTE (National Foundation for Teaching Entrepreneurship). There he met a disk jockey who introduced him to music. Subsequently, Mac opened a nightclub for kids and began managing regional acts. He also worked as a consultant to the USA Network for the program "Dance Party USA," whose executive producer ultimately became his mentor.

When his parents divorced, he felt he had to leave Philadelphia and head for New York. Having no place to stay, he was invited to live temporarily with a NFTE teacher who got him involved in teacher training for the program. Eventually, he found a studio apartment on 51st Street and began looking up old contacts so he could restart UPJAM. In the process, he realized his apartment was located in the same neighborhood that was home to all the major record labels. This was the first sign that coming to New York was the right move and that the environment he had chosen was conducive to what he wanted to do. The second sign was meeting his future business partner, Joel Sylvain, who at that time was working for an urban label called HUSH Productions. Sylvain introduced Mac to the vice president of HUSH, who got UPJAM involved in marketing for a couple of its acts on a consulting basis. This led to other contracts, and six months later HUSH hired Mac as an A&R person.

HUSH and UPJAM created a joint venture deal that called for financing UPJAM and sharing royalties and profits. The venture gave Mac an office on Central Park West and two years of valuable experience in a very complex and volatile industry.

At the end of the two years, Mac left HUSH and renamed his company BullDog Entertainment, Inc., in honor of UPJAM's logo, a bulldog, to reflect Mac's tenacity. With his partner, Sylvain, he used his money to bring the business home, and five months later had a deal with Elecktra Records that included a development deal for new acts like FTN Clique and a label, BullDog/Elecktra. The two partners then brought Diamond J on board to add the technical expertise they needed. In addition to recording, the company now does publishing, consulting, and marketing for such clients as Reebok, Fox Racing, Oakley, Izod, and Converse.

The music industry is extremely competitive; companies come and go with breathtaking rapidity. Mac's challenge is to find a way to meet the needs of the broad market while still offering something unique. BullDog's goal is to develop music with an R&B/alternative feel and build a company that has longevity. To accomplish this goal, Mac is forming strategic alliances with the best people in the industry under the umbrella of BullDog Entertainment. "We control everything in house, from contracts to administration—which is unique for an urban company." In 1997, they achieved about $1.5 million in revenues.

Mac believes in giving back to those who have helped him along the way, so he still devotes about 15 percent of his time each month to NFTE and lectures around the country on growing businesses for the year 2000. In 1997, he was nominated Rising Star of the Year for *Black Enterprise Magazine* and one of the Top 20 Young Tycoons of the year by the *New York Post*.

Jimmy Mac is a study in endurance, from his triathlon persistence to his business perseverance. According to Mac, "A natural element of entrepreneurship is bruises . . . 12–13 times is not a lot to try. You might not hit your success until the 81st try . . . but bruises go away."

How did Jimmy Mac's understanding of his industry enable him to make BullDog Entertainment stand out in a crowd?

The environment in which growing entrepreneurial companies operate and with which they interact has a profound impact on the success or failure of those companies. It also directly affects the strategies entrepreneurs develop to grow their businesses. Certainly Jimmy Mac (see the Young Entrepreneur minicase) believed that working in the recording industry for an established company gave him the contacts, understanding, and credibility he needed to grow his own company. In an industry such as the recording business, whom you know can mean the difference between success and failure. Failing to recognize this fact is like shutting the door to opportunity.

As depicted in Figure 2.1, the **environment** includes

1. The industry of which the business is a part
2. The market on which it focuses its efforts
3. The economy
4. All the various people and businesses with which it interacts: suppliers, distributors, retailers, customers, and so on.

One of the biggest mistakes aspiring entrepreneurs make is not taking the time to learn about and understand their industries so they know where the opportunities lie and how distribution channels work. Another mistake is failing to monitor economic trends that may signal opportunities or threats to the business in the future. Yet another error is failing to know their customers: who the customers are and what they want.

Businesses don't operate in a vacuum. They affect and are affected by everything that goes on around them. This chapter focuses on the industry environment; Chapter 10 deals with the customer.

The Nature of the Industry

Understanding the nature of the industry in which a business operates is critical to making effective choices about strategy. If, for example, the industry is very hostile to new companies and may even put up barriers to entry (such as tying up the best distributors with exclusive contracts so they won't work with anyone else) it will be important to formulate a strategy that permits entry. This may entail finding a **niche** in the market that no one else is serving so you're not competing directly with more established companies. This was the strategy employed by Gentech Corporation, a California-based manufacturer

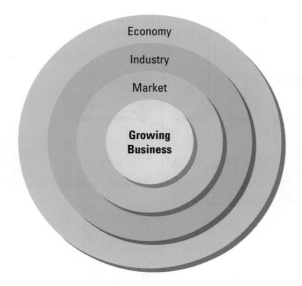

Economy

Industry

Market

**Growing
Business**

**Figure 2.1
The Environment for
a Growing Business**

of power source equipment. Its patented products and new technology spanned two very old, established, and very mechanical industries: the generator and compressor industries. Because it understood the nature of these industries, Gentech, with its combination air compressor/generator unit, was able to enter the market in a niche it created with its new technology.

The Importance of Technology in the Business Environment

Today technology has significantly changed the very nature of the environment in which growing businesses operate. It has changed the way industries look and act. New technology has made it possible for small, growing firms to acquire as much information as large firms—and as quickly. Using e-mail, the Internet, and interactive databases, to name just a few resources, small firms are becoming experts in very specialized areas that know no boundaries in terms of markets and industries. More and more, we are seeing the once unbroken boundaries between industries fading, making it difficult to even classify many new industries by standard measures. The prime example is taking place in the new **multimedia/information industry**. Five industries have come together to create a $1 trillion industry in a convergence unprecedented in this millennium. For the first time, five industries all use a common digital format that allows us to see on TV, view in the theater, read in print, and listen to and receive over airwaves information that is readily accessible to anyone. The multimedia/information industry presents a unique opportunity for anyone to study and learn from a new industry in the early stages when the environment is at its most volatile and the boundaries are ephemeral. Figures 2.2 and 2.3 depict how the world of information has changed over the past two decades. Figure 2.3 is not intended to be

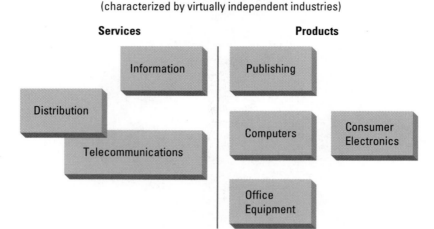

1970s: The Information Industry
(characterized by virtually independent industries)

Services   **Products**

Information   Publishing

Distribution

Computers   Consumer
Electronics

Telecommunications

Office
Equipment

What Was Available in the 1970s

Information Vendors
Consulting services, videotext, news services, photo services, advertising services

Distribution
Mail, courier services, Telex, e-mail mailgrams, cable networks, broadcast networks, FM subcarriers

Telecommunications
Telephone switching, telephones, PABXs, mobile phones and paging devices, international long distance, local telephone service

Publishing
Catalogs, film, TV, video, records, cassettes, newspapers, newsletters, magazines, journals, books

Computers
Mainframes, transaction processors, minicomputers, terminals, dedicated word processors, software

Consumer Electronics
Television, radios and receivers, tape decks, video game gear

Office Equipment
Point of sale hardware, printers, copiers, cash registers, typewriters, dictation equipment, microfilm, business forms, files

**Figure 2.2
1970s: The Information Industry (Characterized by Virtually Independent Industries)**

a comprehensive listing of all the latest technology. New technologies in the areas of telecommunications, networking, and data transfer are rapidly changing, and anything that is commonplace today will probably be out of date by next year.

Today even such tried-and-true categories as **high tech** and **low tech** have been called into question. For example, food processing companies have always been classified as low tech/low skills, but recently they have found global markets for their automated baking and packaging machinery, a more high-tech undertaking. Today a company identified as "high tech" may not

The Late 1990s and Beyond: The Information/Multimedia Industry

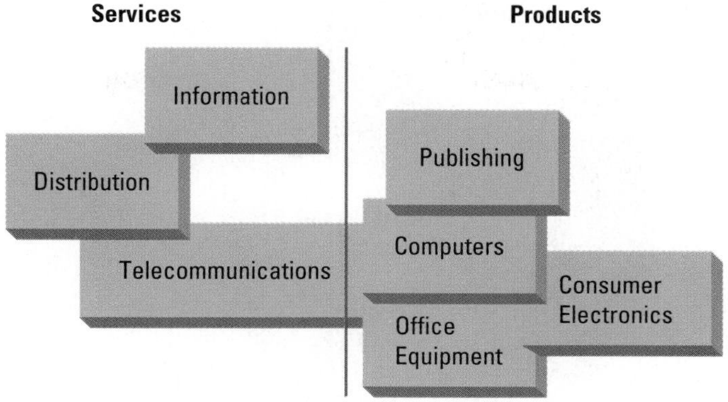

Services   Products

Information

Distribution

Publishing

Computers

Telecommunications

Consumer
Electronics

Office
Equipment

What's New

Information Vendors
Online databases and services, mail
order catalogs, shopping services

Distribution
EDI, Internet, cable modems,
ethernet, TCP/IP, networks, FTP,
ISPs, ATM

Telecommunications
Cellular phones, fax, caller ID,
e-mail, voice mail, alpha/numeric
pagers, 2-way paging, PCS

Publishing
Music CDs, DAT, DVD, software,
Internet publishing, network news

Computers
Modems, client-server computing,
packaged software, workstations,
personal computers, notebook
computers, CD-ROMs, laser
printers, color scanners, artificial
intelligence, audio, plug n' play

Consumer Electronics
Electronic PIMs, calculators, digital
watches, VCRs and videodiscs, spell
checkers, electronic references,
video games

Office Equipment
Business forms, fax machines,
desktop color copiers, credit card
verifiers

**Figure 2.3
The Late 1990s
and Beyond:
The Information/
Multimedia Industry**

necessarily produce high-tech products. A company may also be considered
high tech if it uses an advanced technology to produce its products and services—in other words, a technology process. Or it may be considered high
tech if it uses the latest technology to run the business: communicating with
customers, linking salespeople to the home office, or producing its own marketing materials through desktop publishing software. With the easy availability of the latest advances in technology to businesses of all sizes, we have
to broaden our definition of a technology-based company and a technology-
based industry.

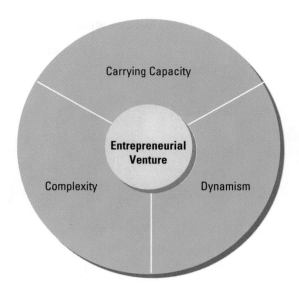

**Figure 2.4
Dimensions of the Industry Environment**

A Framework for Understanding the Small-Business Environment

The easiest way to look at the small-business environment is to start with the industry in which the business operates. Research has identified three dimensions of the environment: *carrying capacity*, *dynamism*, and *complexity*.[1] These three dimensions help to define the nature of the industry (see Figure 2.4).

Carrying Capacity

Carrying capacity is the extent to which the industry can support growth of new firms. In other words, does this industry provide a favorable environment for a new business to enter and become profitable? Entrepreneurs will naturally seek out an environment that allows the business to grow and obtain the resources it needs. Two signs indicate that an industry may be approaching its carrying capacity:

1. It is becoming increasingly difficult for new companies to enter the market.[2]

2. The rate of sales growth in the market has slowed.[3]

When this occurs, a new venture must enter with the plan to reshape the industry by creating demand for a product that didn't exist previously. This was Gentech's strategy. This is also precisely what is occurring in the multimedia industry, where consumers are generally unaware of new technology and its effect on, for example, the sophistication of the animation in a video game until a company such as Virgin Sound and Vision or Electronic Arts introduces it.

Dynamism

Dynamism, the second dimension of the environment, is the degree of certainty or uncertainty in the environment, as well as the stability or instability of the industry. Dynamic industries in volatile environments produce higher degrees of uncertainty; that is, things are changing so fast that we virtually don't know what might happen next. One example occurs in technology industries such as software and telecommunications. The speed at which technology changes and becomes obsolete creates high degrees of uncertainty and unpredictability in the environment of these industries. Uncertainty affects the structure of the business. As uncertainty increases, the amount of information increases and creates demand for more information to process decisions that will maintain a particular level of performance.[4] So the more uncertain the environment is, the more information the entrepreneur will need to make decisions and attempt to predict the future.

In contrast, relatively stable industries such as the mechanical tool industry have low information requirements and consequently move more slowly and are more predictable.

Complexity

Complexity, the third dimension, is the degree to which the number of inputs and outputs in the environment in which the business operates causes interdependence.[5] In other words, the greater the number of suppliers, customers, competitors, and government agencies the entrepreneur depends on, the more complex the industry. A global marketplace and changing technology have created more complex environments for most industries today. Growing businesses that operate in a network-type environment where outsourcing to other companies is the norm usually have to deal with more suppliers and customers. It has been argued that when a firm faces a more complex environment, it will perceive a higher degree of complexity and therefore require more information to make decisions.[6] For example, the greater the number of competitors in the firm's environment, the higher the information load and the more complex the environment, requiring the entrepreneur to obtain more information to make decisions.[7] Complexity can be measured by

▶ The degree of turbulence or volatility (how quickly things change)

▶ The degree of hostility among competitors

▶ The degree of heterogeneity among producers (how different they are)

▶ The degree of restrictiveness through the regulatory environment

▶ The degree of technical sophistication (see Figure 2.4)

Table 2.1   Characteristics of Highly Complex and Low-Complexity Environments

Highly Complex Environment: Software Industry	Low-Complexity Environment: Agriculture Industry
Very volatile	Stable and predictable
Hostile competitors	Collaborative competitors
Heterogeneous producers	Homogeneous producers
Restrictive—many controls	Unrestricted—few controls
High level of technical sophistication	Low level of technical sophistication

Table 2.1 compares a highly complex environment with one of low complexity for two industries.

Industry Structure and Competitive Strategy

As stated previously, it is vital that you, as the owner of a small, growing business, understand the nature of your industry so that you create strategies for your business that will give it the highest probability of success. The industry in which a firm operates is a significant portion of the total business environment and has an enormous effect on the competitive strategy of the firm.

The classic books written by Michael Porter set forth a framework for understanding the fundamental realities of the industry environment. Porter's **five forces model** analyzes the relationship between industry structure and strategic opportunities and threats, considering various strategic groups such as suppliers and buyers.[8] This model is used to demonstrate how a firm's strategy is influenced by opportunities and threats in the environment. According to Porter, five forces drive competition and affect the *long-run profitability* of a firm as well as other firms in the industry (Figure 2.5):

Technology Tip

Use the Internet to Understand Your Business Environment

An easy way to learn about the environment in which your business will operate is to get on the Internet and find other businesses in the same industry. Company web sites offer a wealth of information about a business's marketing strategy, customer base, philosophy of business, customer service strategy, and culture.

Also, try these sites for more information on your business environment:

Small & Home-based Business Resource
www.ro.com/small_business/homebased.old2

Statistics
http://www.lib.umich.edu/libhome/Documents.center/stecind.html

Small Business Administration
http://www.sbaonline.sba.gov/

Department of Commerce
http://www.doc.gov/bureaus/

**Figure 2.5
Forces Affecting the
Small Business**

▶ Barriers to entry in the industry

▶ Threat from substitute products

▶ Threat from buyers' bargaining power

▶ Threat from suppliers' bargaining power

▶ Rivalry among existing industry firms

Short-run profitability, in contrast, is affected by such things as economic forces, changes in demand, material shortages, and so forth. Let's look at these five forces within the business's competitive environment in more depth in the context of a small, growing business.

Barriers to Entry in the Industry

In some industries, barriers to entry are high and will discourage new entrants. These barriers may include the following.

Economies of Scale   Many industries have over time achieved **economies of scale** in marketing, production, and distribution; consequently, the established firms in that industry have attained production costs that have declined relative to the prices of their goods and services. It is therefore difficult for a new entrant to achieve these same economies. In terms of competitive strategy, this means that if your new business enters the industry on a large scale, it risks retaliation from those established firms. In contrast, if it enters on a small scale, it may be unable to compete because of high costs relative to rival firms. In this instance, a niche strategy whereby you create a market that you control may allow you entry. Domino's Pizza entered the saturated

When the big discounters set up entry barriers that are difficult to overcome, what should an up-start computer accessories company do? Alex Chen, AMT's founder, fought back by finding a unique channel of distribution—the Internet. There he can rival the likes of Fry's Electronics because he has virtually no overhead. (Tim Rue)

pizza market through a new channel of distribution—home delivery—that it controlled initially to give it a chance to compete and gain strength before competitors copied the strategy.

Brand Loyalty   Overcoming customers' loyalty to established products and services in the industry can require an extensive advertising campaign to create brand awareness. This can be a very costly strategy and a significant barrier to entry for new businesses.

Capital Requirements   Capital requirements are a daunting barrier in many industries. New entrants may incur enormous costs for plant, equipment, R&D, and marketing just to compete on a par with established firms. New businesses often have resorted to outsourcing expensive manufacturing to companies with excess capacity.

Switching Costs   It is difficult to get buyers to switch from one supplier to another. This is due to **switching costs,** the costs the buyer incurs in time and money to retrain staff and potentially learn a new technology or to build a new relationship with a supplier.

Access to Distribution Channels   It is often difficult to get distribution channel members to accept the new business's products or services without costly persuasion techniques. This is particularly true in the grocery industry, where shelf space is at a premium. A new venture may look to other types of outlets such as Trader Joe's to enter this difficult industry.

Proprietary Factors   Barriers to entry also include **proprietary technology,** products, and processes. When established firms hold patents on products and processes that the new business requires, they have the ability to keep that company out of the industry or make it very expensive to enter. Most favorable location is another form of proprietary barrier. Existing firms in the industry may own the most advantageous business sites, forcing the new business to locate in a less competitive site.

Government Regulations   By imposing strict licensing requirements and limiting access to raw materials through laws or high taxes, the government can effectively prevent a firm from entering the industry.

In most cases, the aforementioned barriers can be overcome by creatively exploring new avenues that may include a niche market, a new distribution channel, a new advertising technique, or a new process, to name a few.

Threat from Substitute Products

A company must compete not only with products and services in its own industry but with those that are logical **substitutes** in other industries as well. Generally, these substitute products and services accomplish the same basic function in a different way or at a different price. For example, a video arcade that is competing for consumers' entertainment dollars will also compete against movie theaters, bowling alleys, laser tag venues, and other establishments.

Threat from Buyers' Bargaining Power

Large buyers of products and services, such as Wal-Mart and Price/Costco, can force down prices in the industry through volume purchases. This is particularly true where an industry's products comprise a significant portion of the buyers' requirements. The largest buyers also pose a threat of **backward integration,** whereby they actually purchase their suppliers, thus better controlling costs and affecting price throughout the industry. A young, growing business that wants to deal with the discounters must be prepared to keep its costs low to meet the price demands of these major distributors. Marcel Ford, founder of Botanical Science, whose first product was a silk plant cleaner, used the major discounters as his distribution channel. One reason his company is successful today is that he kept his costs, both production and overhead, as low as possible so that he could take advantage of the volume sales these discounters produced.

Threat from Suppliers' Bargaining Power

In some industries, suppliers exert enormous power by threatening to raise prices or change the quality of the products they supply to manufacturers and distributors. If the number of these suppliers is small relative to the size of the industry, or the industry is not the primary customer of the suppliers, that power is magnified. A further threat from suppliers is **forward integration**—that is, that they will purchase the outlets for their goods and services, thus controlling the prices at which the products are ultimately sold and competing against others who must purchase their products at wholesale. An example is Intel Corporation, the principal supplier of computer processing chips to the PC industry. Intel is able not only to affect costs for PC makers but also to affect the product life cycle.

Rivalry Among Existing Industry Firms

In general, it can be said that a highly competitive industry will drive down profits and ultimately the rate of return on investment. To position themselves in a competitive market, companies will resort to price wars, advertising skirmishes, and enhanced service. These tactics are often seen in the airline, computer, and some food products industries, to name just a few. Once one firm decides to make such a strategic move in the industry, others will follow. To compete in this type of industry requires that the new entrant create a niche that has not been served by the established firms and enter without causing movement on the part of the major players. It also requires convincing the customer that the value you provide is worth your higher price.

How Do Small Businesses Compete?

Studying the industry via the five forces model is a valuable exercise that gives you a clearer picture of this aspect of the environment. However, examples abound of firms that have achieved a competitive advantage in industry environments that were less than inviting. For example, Wal-Mart has consistently earned a return on sales twice the average of its cutthroat, discount industry for the past 20 years. And entrepreneurial Nucor Steel saw its stock price soar through the 1980s and 1990s when other steel companies' stock remained flat or fallen.[9]

You need to ask yourself four important questions about your company:[10]

1. *Do you have the resources and capabilities necessary to take advantage of opportunities in the environment and neutralize threats?* The extent to which a company's resources and capabilities match the opportunities and threats in the environment can change over time. What may have originally been a strength for the company can suddenly become a weakness. Hunter Fan is a good example. Its market leader technology was created to cool large manufacturing plants; but with the invention of air conditioning, it lost its competitive advantage and was forced to change its strategy. When energy conservation became an issue in the 1970s,

Hunter saw an opportunity to exploit a new market—homeowners—and began creating fans with a decorative flair.

2. *How many competing firms already own the same valuable resources and competencies?* If several companies possess the same valuable resources or competencies, none are likely to have a competitive advantage. A resource or competency must be rare to offer an advantage in that sense. The advantage a common resource has is that it is a *requirement for survival* in the industry and therefore a *barrier to entry* to potential competition. Companies introducing rare resources or competencies will gain a significant temporary advantage over a period of time before others can acquire them.

3. *Do firms without a resource or capability face a cost disadvantage in obtaining it?* Competing firms often incur significant costs in acquiring the "rare" resources and competencies of companies that possess them. If this is the case, the firms that possess the resources and capabilities will be able to maintain a competitive advantage over a longer period of time. On the other hand, if a new competing business can find suitable substitutes for these resources, it may be able to achieve competitive parity over the long term.

4. *Is the firm organized to take full advantage of its resources and capabilities?* To exploit resources and capabilities, companies must have supporting resources, such as management control systems, a formal reporting structure, and compensation policies, and technology that will help them acquire and process information as well as or better than their competitors. As a new company begins to prepare for rapid growth, this infrastructure and these systems must be in place or strategies will quickly fall apart.

 Entrepreneurship in Action

Competing with the "Big Boys"

The lure of starting your own warehouse club is born out of the incredible successes of major discounters like Home Depot and Wal-Mart. For the young entrepreneur, it seems like an almost insurmountable task to compete in that market, but Brian Robinson had a dream and he decided to go for it.

After four years of working as a buyer for a discount store chain, Robinson believed he knew the industry well. He certainly had paid attention to customer complaints so that he also knew what his company would do that others weren't. With funding from his family, Robinson founded Advantage Store, smaller than the typical discount warehouse, yet offering significant savings to customers without making them buy in bulk. Advantage charges no membership fee and accepts credit cards and coupons. The strategy seems to be working; in 1996 he already had four stores on Long Island, New York, with plans for several more. The key to competing with the big boys was to find out what they weren't doing and to do it well.

Source: Janean Chun, Debra Phillips, Heather Page, Lynn Beresford, Holly Celeste Fisk, and Charlotte Mulhern, "Young Millionaires," *Entrepreneur,* November 1996, pp. 118–134.

To sustain a competitive advantage in the marketplace, a rapidly growing entrepreneurial company must consider not only the opportunities and threats presented by the environment but the strengths and weaknesses of its own resources and capabilities. A company with strong resources and competencies can successfully compete even in an environment that appears to have few opportunities and many threats. (See the Entrepreneurship in Action feature on page 37.)

Significant Trends in the Business Environment

Any study of the environment must include an examination of periodic fundamental shifts in the way business is done. These shifts often begin very quietly, receiving no attention until one day someone begins to notice a pattern and proclaims that what has always been done one way is changing. In the 1990s, three significant shifts occurred in the business environment that deserve attention because they affect the strategies business owners will develop to guide the growth of their firms into the next century: the resurgence of manufacturing, the technology revolution, and the change in the nature of jobs. In addition, a variety of other trends or minor changes over time that spell opportunity for the savvy entrepreneur should also be considered: cocooning, fitness and health, and the environment, to name a few.

The Resurgence of Manufacturing

Many believe that "not only the wealth but the independence and safety of a country appear to be materially connected with the prosperity of manufacturers."[11] The 1993 Congressional Research Service reported, "In 1987, the most recent year for which official data are available, a change in manufacturing output of $1 resulted in a total increase in output throughout the economy of $2.30." By comparison, the service sector, which is the largest sector, produced only $1.60 for every $1. In fact, manufacturing accounted for fully 31 percent of total economic activity if we include all the ancillary activities. Yet the reports continue that manufacturing in the United States is on the decline. Fortunately, there are many indications that the United States is actually making a manufacturing comeback. In their book *Making It in America: Proven Paths to Success from 50 Top Companies,* Jerry Jasinowski and Robert Hamrin outline several indicators of this resurgence in manufacturing (see Resources at the end of the chapter):

▶ In 1992, the United States became the number one exporter again.

▶ In the 1980s and early 1990s, manufacturing productivity grew an average of 3 percent annually, while the rest of the economy chugged along at less than 1 percent annually.

▶ Quality in products and services has improved.

▶ The United States is demonstrating leadership in industry. Between 1987 and 1992, the United States earned 50 percent of all profits in nine industries, Japan earned 2 percent, and Europe earned 0 percent.[12]

▶ Between 1985 and 1993, U.S. manufacturing exports grew 9 percent annually compared to 2.3 percent for Japan and 1.7 percent for Germany. In fact, during that period, manufacturing contributed 40 percent of the growth in the U.S. GNP.

Further, because world-class manufacturers have recognized the advantages of a global orientation, they have now seen their profitability increase and their growth take on unprecedented speed. A recent study that compared manufacturers' international orientation, strategic approach, and sales and profit performance from 1987 to 1991 found that companies whose strategy included internationalization of their marketing activities "grew faster in every industry and in all size categories than those without."[13]

The most recent Bureau of Labor Statistics data available at the time of this writing reported that the top five industries in terms of the growth rate of the fastest-growing companies were in some form of manufacturing.[14] Much of the credit for these indications can be given to the downsizing trend that forced U.S. companies to become competitive again and create hundreds of new niches for savvy entrepreneurs. In fact, downsizing actually paved the way for the creation of new jobs. In 13 percent of the downsized companies, a net increase in jobs occurred as companies actually expanded in those areas that had the greatest potential to create value.[15]

Inventions Are on the Rise

"Made in the USA" is also making a growing impact at the invention stage as well as U.S. patents increase their lead over foreign competitors. Traditionally, U.S. patents have comprised about 50 percent of all patents granted, but that is changing. Advances in such fields as biotechnology, telecommunications, food processing, and even household goods have made U.S. inventors

 Entrepreneurship in Action

From Magic to Technology

Imagine impaling your business partner in a sword chamber or burying her alive in a flaming illusion. There are partnerships no doubt where those thoughts have crossed many minds during trying times. For the Kramers, Bob and Judie, it was all part of the act. For years the Kramers toured as a nationally known magic act, performing at corporate functions and opening for big name celebrities. But when the corporate entertainment market shattered in the recession of the 1970s, they switched to a niche in the college market, which ended up being more lucrative.

When their agent of many years decided to leave the industry, it presented an opportunity to start their own entertainment agency. In 1984, Kramer Entertainment Agency was a serious business that developed live comedy and game shows as well as patented cyberspace adventures such as Omega, a machine that simulates roller-coaster rides. So successful were they that they were invited to provide entertainment for the Olympic games in Atlanta.

Keeping tabs on changes in the environment has proven to be an "ace in the hole" for this magical entrepreneurial team.

Source: Kate Convissor, "Getting the Show on the Road," *Nation's Business,* October 1996, p. 13.

the leaders in creativity and innovation once again. AT&T has won more than 25,000 patents, while IBM earns $500 million a year on the more than 800 patents it is issued every year—and that figure is up 67 percent in the past two years. This resurgence in interest in obtaining patents means more opportunities for U.S. companies to have an impact on the way we live. A prime example of the impact of inventions is the laser, the technology for which was patented in 1959 and is now used in everything from surgical procedures to supermarket scanners and compact disk players.

The Technology Revolution

To say that technology has changed forever the way we do business is clearly an understatement. The vast majority of new opportunities for entrepreneurs today, whether in products, services, or processes, can be traced in large part to technology. The availability of extraordinarily powerful technology has made information more readily accessible and in greater quantity than ever before. Today a company's competitive power—or an individual's, for that matter—comes from staying on top of new information and being able to access it, process it, and use it quickly and easily. The PC, fax, laser printer, LAN, and the Internet have changed completely the way business is conducted and the way information is processed. Not very long ago, larger companies touted information or data processing departments and/or records management departments. The ponderous systems with which these departments managed records and information were inconvenient at best, inefficient at worst. Paper shuffling from department to department and duplication of effort were an everyday occurrence. All that has changed with the arrival of individual computer-based workstations and network servers that allow users to create, store, retrieve, revise, disseminate, and dispose of information easily and quickly. With people in the organization networked across physical boundaries, states, and even countries, management of information in companies has truly arrived at the user level.

Technology and the Conduct of Business

Not only has technology empowered people at all levels of the organization, it has also changed our perceptions about how business should be conducted. We now expect business transactions to

- Have an immediacy they have never had before. Documents and responses of all types are expected instantly via fax, e-mail, or, at the very least, overnight mail.

- Have a higher standard of appearance. With powerful desktop publishing software and color laser printers readily available at declining prices, the expectation of higher-quality documents has increased.

- Have immediate access to company records: customer lists, inventory, production scheduling, and so forth.

- Have instant access to information worldwide via online databases.

▶ Be conducted from anywhere in the world via teleconferencing, cellular technology, faxes, and modems.

Technology and Small-Business Productivity

One of the most exciting aspects of the technology revolution is its impact on small-business productivity and competitiveness. Technology has given small entrepreneurial companies huge advantages over large companies in four primary areas: customizing products, service, flexibility, and productivity.[16]

Customizing Products   Smaller companies can use technology to augment their existing capabilities and produce customized products for customers in smaller quantities. Large manufacturers, in contrast, generally have been set up and equipped to handle mass production of commodity-type items.

Service   Large companies have tended to use technology to provide more efficiencies in activities such as stocking and production, but they have been less aggressive in using it to reach out to customers and serve their needs. In contrast, small companies are better able to track and communicate with their customers one to one, building databases of information about customer wants and needs that are more powerful than demographics alone.

Flexibility   Erik Brynjolfsson, an MIT professor, has found "a strong correlation between the growth in the 1980s in the U.S. manufacturing sector's information-technology investment and a decrease of 20% in the average number of employees in industrial companies."[17] Smaller companies can change direction more readily and respond more rapidly than cumbersome, employee-heavy large corporations. The film industry provides good examples of flexibility and virtuality. It regularly sees its best products turned out by small, innovative companies that concentrate on their core competencies and form strategic alliances with other small firms to capitalize on their strengths and create clout in the industry. That is how a tiny company like Pixar Animation Studios leveraged its 3D animation capability into the hit movie *Toy Story.*

Productivity   Because small companies operate with much less overhead and outsourcing for skills and technology outside their core competencies, and because they don't organize around a rigid, hierarchical structure, they can be far more productive. Their cost for technology is generally less because they often can purchase off-the-shelf products that are easily and inexpensively upgraded to the latest generation. In contrast, most large companies have heavy investments in mainframe technology that is very costly to change or update.

Technology Is a Matter of Survival

Technology has changed the way we do business and has created a wealth of new opportunities for entrepreneurs and business owners to take advantage of. It has also made possible the tremendous surge of entrepreneurship

In today's business world, each worker needs to think of him- or herself as a one-person business. Everyone must demonstrate the benefit they provide to their employers. Some workers have even started businesses to supply products and services to their former employers. (CATHY © 1997 Cathy Guisewite. Reprinted with permission of Universal Press Syndicate. All rights reserved.)

in this country as small, growing companies now compete alongside mega-corporations for the same markets. And, as Chapter 10 will discuss, technology has made possible a shift away from traditional mass marketing to one-to-one relationships with customers. In some industries technology is still a competitive advantage, whereas in others it is now a matter of survival. In either case, a business will not become world class without exploiting all of the opportunities technology presents.

Change in the Nature of Jobs

A quick glance through the headlines of any major newspaper reveals a drama that is sweeping the nation on a daily basis. Jobs are disappearing in record numbers in every industry and in every part of the country. But more than that, the very thing we call a "job" is disappearing as well. Traditionally, people who were laid off could ultimately find "their job" at another company or even at their previous company when things got better. That's not the case anymore, because those jobs that were lost no longer exist. The nature of "the job" as we know it has changed, largely because the very nature of business has changed. Building a successful company no longer automatically means creating jobs. In fact, today rapid growth may necessitate a "lean and mean" approach that involves outsourcing, strategic alliances, and flexibility.

To business owners, this means they must educate their current employees to these changes and show them how they fit into the new scenario. Employees must begin to understand that they are hired to contribute to the growth of the organization, not to do a job. So job descriptions are becoming very fluid, evolving and changing according to the needs of the business at any point in time. The new workers are being called **contingent workers**, that is, contingent on the goals of the business. They are essentially "businesses of one," and the length of their sojourn with the company will depend on their ability to provide a benefit to it.

Table 2.2   Industries That Offer Technical Opportunity for the Next Decade

The following challenges will provide opportunity for entrepreneurs in the next decade be-cause they represent important technological challenges that must be solved.

▶ Affordable home-based health care
▶ Personalized consumer products
▶ The convergence of technology in the home
▶ Protecting the environment and natural resources
▶ User-friendly interfaces for technology in the home
▶ Nutritional health
▶ Mobile energy—alternative fuels
▶ Micro-security
▶ Renewed infrastructure for cities
▶ Global business competition and the ability to control technology

Source: "Top 10 Challenges for 2007," *Engineering News,* June 23, 1997. Created by Battelle (http://www.manufacturing.net/magazine/dnl/).

Some Industries That Appear Strong for the Next Decade

Several industries appear poised for greatness, and entrepreneurs who have knowledge of, experience in, or an interest in these industries should look carefully for opportunities. In many cases, these industries are expensive to enter because of proprietary technology and huge research and development costs. But entrepreneurs can often find niches that are ancillary to the main-stream businesses in the industry or even support them in some way, and do quite well. These industries are just a sampling of those that present major opportunities for the savvy entrepreneur. See Table 2.2 for additional indus-tries where opportunity abounds.

The Women's Health Care Industry

The medical products industry is a $120 billion one, and the women's health segment is one of the fastest growing.[18] With prevention being at the core of many new product and service offerings, and because most diseases affecting women can be cured if caught early, there are many opportunities for entre-preneurs interested in health care issues.

The Telecommunications Industry

In a world where information means power, communication is critical, par-ticularly the speed of communication. "The Nineties will be remembered as the decade when everything got connected," says Roger McNamee of Inte-gral Capital Partners.[19] The phenomenal growth of the Internet and the insa-tiable appetite for speed have combined to create a constant demand for solutions to communications problems. The focus has shifted from simply creating new products to finding solutions that may include products, services, and people.

The Assisted-Living Industry

The fastest-growing segment of the U.S. population is elderly people, and with life expectancy increasing and the front end of the baby-boom generation just 15 years away from retirement, the market for assisted-living facilities is enormous. *Fortune* reports that the number of people who reach age 85 will increase by 44 percent by 2040.[20] Opportunities for creating new businesses in this environment are helped by the fact that only 2 percent of the total market is controlled by the 30 largest companies in the industry.

Continuing Trends

Several trends that emerged in the 1990s will remain strong for the next decade. Business owners who want to build competitive businesses need to be cognizant of these trends, taking the opportunities they present into consideration as they plan for growth.

An Emphasis on Social Responsibility

Today an increasing number of companies are doing much more than simply earning profits. They are also concerned about giving something back to their communities and demonstrating their interconnectedness with society as a whole. This community awareness may take the form of pollution controls, sponsoring community activities, recycling campaigns, and grants to community organizations. As an example, James Blackman, founder of the award-winning Civic Light Opera of South Bay Cities in Southern California, dedicates several nights of every production to give free admission to under-privileged and physically challenged children so they will have an opportunity to see and enjoy an aspect of culture previously unknown to them.

A Global Orientation

Technology has made access to other countries as easy as contacting the business in the next city. Fit-Net, a young company serving the fitness industry, decided to put its business on the Internet, thereby gaining global presence instantly without the cost of travel. Exporting products and services to other countries has become almost a necessity for a growing business to remain competitive. Today a company is just as likely to purchase some of its supplies overseas as it is to purchase them domestically. Many companies may even manufacture in another country. Studying the needs of customers in other countries is one way to open up new markets for an entrepreneurial business.

Fitness and Health

The business of keeping people healthy, physically fit, and youthful is a huge industry that began taking shape in the 1980s. The ubiquitous baby-boom generation, which has begun to reach age 50, provides the astute entrepreneur with an enormous customer base of people who want to stay "young" as long as possible.

Staying Home

Faith Popcorn, a noted market consultant to Fortune 500 companies, has observed a trend she calls *cocooning*. **Cocooning** is simply staying home, entertaining at home, or working from home as telecommuters, small-business owners, and entrepreneurs with virtual companies. In terms of opportunities for entrepreneurs, this means that people are purchasing more services such as delivery for food, groceries, dry cleaning, and so forth. Since they entertain themselves at home, they are purchasing in-home entertainment systems, renting more videos, and shopping from home via computers. With more and more people logging onto the Internet and using laptop computers, modems, and fax machines, business can be done from virtually anywhere, even from the comfort of one's bedroom. The cocooning effect opens up huge opportunities for new services, products, and channels of distribution to reach these people.

Women in Business

More and more women are starting businesses to find independence and to create organizations that reflect their particular collaborative management styles. In fact, women-owned businesses now employ more people than the Fortune 500 worldwide. With so many women in business, the economic result is that they now require the very services they used to supply for their families: housecleaning, child care, cooking, and so on. Consequently, some women are starting service businesses that help other women move into economic sectors previously dominated by men. Although the majority of women start businesses in the retail and service sectors, an increasing number are successfully venturing into traditionally male-dominated industries such as manufacturing and construction.

Business Owner: Know Your Business Environment!

It is the environment that has brought about the myriad changes businesses face today, from downsizing and global competitiveness, to the renaissance of manufacturing, to the change in the nature of jobs, and—perhaps the single most important change—that brought on by the technology revolution. Competing as a small, entrepreneurial company against giants would not be possible without technology. Technology is not a trend. It has become an

Catherine Muther, former senior marketing officer for Cisco Systems, is taking on a new challenge. Her business takes advantage of two of today's hot trends: She is underwriting a technology incubator for women-owned businesses in San Francisco. There she will provide low-cost office space as well as administrative and marketing support and mentoring from professionals. With her help, women will now find it easier than she once did to rise to the top. (Eric Millette)

integral part of business life and absolutely essential for a growing company that wants to compete effectively and sustain itself in a fast-paced market. Technology has brought about the new business paradigm. Without computers, databases, and networks, building one-to-one relationships with thousands of customers would not be possible. Giving customers what they want when they want it would not be possible.

Small is now beautiful, and fast and flexible are a way of life for most companies that want to grow and remain competitive in a global marketplace. Take a walk through the supermarket and notice all of the new microbrewery beers taking shelf space next to Bud and Coors. Flip through the pages of *PC Magazine* and be overwhelmed by the proliferation of computer hardware and peripherals suppliers, not to mention the hundreds of small software development companies that compete favorably against the giants. Take a stroll through any business district and calculate the number of small businesses that have developed to support the ancillary needs of large companies: payroll services, janitorial services, office supplies, and so forth. Small, growing, world-class companies are holding firm against the giants, and in some cases are outdistancing them in niches they have created, with global strategies and by taking full advantage of the new technology.

The environment in which a business operates should be thought of not as a challenge to overcome or a series of problems to be solved but as a fertile field of opportunities waiting to happen. Companies that understand their business environments well use this knowledge to gain a significant competitive advantage, even against much larger firms.

Cases Relevant to This Chapter

Pelco
French Rags
SB Networks
Marcus Food Co. and Buckhead Beef

Issues for Review and Discussion

1. Describe the nature of the environment for growing entrepreneurial companies today.
2. What is the role of technology in today's business environment?
3. What kinds of barriers to entry can an industry erect?
4. Discuss three significant trends in the business environment today.
5. Which continuing trends offer opportunities for entrepreneurs?

Experiencing Entrepreneurship

1. Choose an industry and apply Porter's five forces model to it. What conclusions about the nature of the industry can you draw based on the findings?
2. Interview two people in the industry you chose in question 1 to determine if your conclusions were correct.

Resources

Cornwall, J. R., and B. Perlman (1990). *Organizational Entrepreneurship*. Homewood, IL: Irwin.

M. Hanan (1987). *Fast Growth Strategies*. New York: McGraw-Hill.

Hannan, M. T., and J. H. Freeman (1989). *Organization Ecology*. Cambridge, MA: Harvard University Press.

Jasinowski, Jerry, and Robert Hamrin (1995). *Making It in America: Proven Paths to Success from 50 Top Companies*. New York: Simon & Schuster.

Porter, M. (1980). *Competitive Strategy: Techniques for Analyzing Industries and Competitors*. New York: The Free Press.

Porter, M. (1985). *Competitive Advantage*. New York: The Free Press.

Internet Resources
CNNfn
http://www.cnnfn.com/index.html
This site covers a broad range of topics. You can get headlines, in-depth reports, and other business information (i.e., Hoover's Online business profiles).

Department of Commerce
http://www.doc.gov
Provides links to many sites of interest to business owners.

IndustryLink
http://www.industrylink.com/
Offers links to sites of interest to people in a number of industries.

PR Newswire
http://www.prnewswire.com/
Good source of information about companies.

Securities and Exchange Commission
http://www.sec.gov/
Good source for researching specific industries.

SEC Edgar Database
http://www.sec.gov/edgarhp.htm
Contains documents that publicly traded companies must submit to the SEC.

Thomas Register
http://www.thomasregister.com:8000/
This is the online version of the Thomas Register of American Manufacturers. Contains information about products, services, and companies.

Wall Street Journal Interactive
http://www.wsj.com/
There is a charge for this site, but it may be worth it for the latest news from around the world. Also good information about the economy and specific companies and industries.

*Sometimes even
lawyers need lawyers.*
Billy Carter, 1980

Entrepreneurial Strategy and the Legal Environment

Preview

Understanding this chapter will give you the ability to

▶ **Choose the legal form of business that best suits your purposes with the help of an attorney.**

▶ **Understand the advantages and disadvantages of the various legal forms of organization.**

▶ **Discuss the effects of contract, agency, and trade laws on the strategies you develop for your business.**

▶ **Explain the competitive advantage of intellectual property rights: patents, trademarks, copyrights, and trade secrets.**

▶ **Discuss ways to protect yourself when you do business on the Internet.**

Terms to Know

Young Entrepreneurs—Minicase

Andrew R. Souter
Galbanum

Many entrepreneurs start businesses based on things they love to do, and Andrew Souter is no exception. Born in central Pennsylvania, Souter was a competitive swimmer at the national level as well as active in bodybuilding, martial arts, and team sports. In high school, however, the artistic, creative side of Souter emerged, and he resolved to teach himself music composition and performance via the piano. Coupled with his interest in science and technology, it was only natural for him to gravitate toward electronic music and computer technology.

When it came time to decide on a university to further his education, Souter chose the University of Southern California because, although born on the East Coast, he has always been "a true Californian at heart." Initially he thought he ought to study computer science and engineering, but his discovery of the Entrepreneur Program brought everything together for him, and he began to see his future as an artist/ entrepreneur. While at the university, he was also busy promoting multimedia events on both coasts, scoring short films and commercials, composing and recording material for future release, managing a web development venture, and refining his musical talent. "All of these experiences shared in preparing me for the formation of my current venture, Galbanum," he says. In fact, he devoted most of his senior year to researching and developing a feasibility study and business plan for the Software Division of Galbanum. In the summer of 1997, at age 22, he revised the short-term focus of Galbanum and, after market research revealed a demand for this type of service, he launched the Galbanum Production Division.

As a whole, Galbanum is dedicated to "developing, marketing, and distributing the premiere, next generation of digital media, art, entertainment, and creative tools, and putting these into the hands of professionals and nonprofessionals. Short-term projects include film, television, and multimedia scoring, album projects, audio installation artwork in museums and similar venues, and a software-based generative music production system that allows users to experience a new level of interactive music." Souter is also pursuing work with three-dimensional music and sound systems. Galbanum, which currently conducts the majority of its business in New York, produces all of its materials in-house, using a state-of-the-art digital facility with both new and emerging trends in digital audio systems. The nature of the business demands that Galbanum remain a bicoastal entity catering to both the New York and LA markets. This type of virtual operation is made possible by computer and communication technologies.

Galbanum's first project was providing the score to a television PSA created by JPL Video Production, a Harrisburg, Pennsylvania–based production company. That project won several awards and was broadcast approximately 1,500 times. In this industry, customers are found through a combination of "tenacious networking," quality product, and "undeniable serendipity." Souter also relies on an agent in New York who searches out and secures potential customers.

The company was funded through a combination of personal capital, private investment, and a line of credit through a commercial bank. Souter's in-depth understanding of the music industry allows him to use creative financing unique to the structure of that industry—recording advances—to prepay a percentage of his project costs.

One of the biggest challenges Galbanum faces is the ability to accurately project the future of technological evolution so that it can make sound, strategic decisions. Currently the music industry is struggling to reach agreement on a new technological standard, DVD audio. In the midst of the issues surrounding its acceptance, Souter is producing a product that "creates a compelling argument for consumers to adopt such a vision, both aesthetically and technologically."

Souter's family has always supported his dreams and efforts. From his father he learned that "we live in a time in which people must accept total responsibility for their own successes or failures. The days of laying your life in the hands of the giant corporations and mega-conglomerates are over." Souter strongly believes that today's business climate calls for autonomy, customization, personalization, and strong relationships with both customers and established strategic alliances.

Souter's biggest reason to start this business is probably the joy of the "journey." As he puts it, "Money, financial success, technological accomplishment, and material abundance may or may not accompany the entrepreneur, and in truth will most likely dance wildly in and out of focus throughout the entrepreneur's journey. This should not phase a person in the extreme, however, as it is not the possession of these things, but rather what is or is not done with them and the journey itself that truly determine happiness."

Which intellectual property rights will affect Galbanum in the development of its products, services, and markets?

Of all the environmental factors that influence a growing company in significant ways, none is more pervasive than the law. From the moment an idea for a business is conceived to the moment it is dissolved, the law plays a dramatic role in everything the company does and in every aspect of its organization. Today the impact of laws and regulations on emerging companies is rendered even more complex by the need to deal with international law and the specific laws of individual countries. Understanding these effects can mean the difference between a company that runs smoothly and one that is mired in lawsuits and compliance penalties. For example, Andrew Souter (see Young Entrepreneurs—Minicase) faced many legal issues in setting up his music company, Galbanum, and protecting his original works. Since he operates in a virtual and bicoastal environment, he must form strategic alliances that are the equivalent of legal partnerships, and he must make sure that the works he creates cannot be copied.

This chapter looks at the law from a strategic point of view: how the law affects the decisions entrepreneurs make about all aspects of their businesses, from forming the company to operations, intellectual property protection, and Internet law.

The Legal Form of the Company

All companies operate under one of four broad legal classifications: sole proprietorship, partnership, corporation, and limited liability company. Choosing the form that is most appropriate for a company at a particular point in time is a function of (1) the level of liability protection required, (2) the operating requirements, and (3) the effect on the company's tax strategy. It is possible to change forms during the life of the company, and each form has its own requirements. Some entrepreneurs choose to start their ventures as sole proprietors or partnerships because these are the easiest and least expensive forms to create. Later, as the venture takes off, they may switch to the preferred corporate form or limited liability company. Entrepreneurs with complex businesses, such as Galbanum, and more potential to incur liability generally start with these forms.

Sole Proprietorship

The **sole proprietorship** is certainly the most common and oldest legal form. More than 76 percent of all businesses in the United States are sole proprietorships. Reasons for its popularity are that it is flexible, is easy and inexpensive to start, and has few government regulations. To operate as a sole proprietor requires nothing more than a **DBA** (Certificate of Doing Business Under An Assumed Name) if the entrepreneur does not use his or her name as the name for the business. This certificate can be obtained by filing an application with the appropriate local government agency. The fictitious business name statement ensures that the company is the only one in the area (usually a county) using the name it has chosen and provides a public record of business ownership for liability purposes.

From a legal or tax perspective, the sole proprietorship does not exist apart from its owner; therefore, it pays no tax. Consequently, a salary or draw taken by the owner is not considered an expense of the business and cannot be deducted as such. The owner (the sole proprietor) *is* the business and is the only person responsible for its activities, profits, and liabilities. All profits of the company, including the owner's salary, are taxed at the owner's personal income tax rate whether or not they are ultimately put back into the business. In other words, sole proprietorships do not have retained earnings.

The Hobby Rule

Sole proprietorships fall under the **hobby rule** of the Internal Revenue Code. If a company makes no profit in three out of five years, it is in danger of being judged a hobby, with the result that losses suffered cannot be deducted from gross income to reduce taxable income. One test of the hobby rule is whether affairs of the business are conducted in a businesslike manner, for example, separate personal and business bank accounts, formal accounting records, and so forth. The hobby rule certainly points up the need for sole proprietors to keep their business and personal lives separate.

Disadvantages of Sole Proprietorships

Sole proprietorships have several advantages, as depicted in Figure 3.1. They are easy and inexpensive to create, give the owner complete authority, and tax income only once at the owner's personal rate. However, they also have several disadvantages that deserve serious consideration:

▶ The sole proprietor has unlimited liability for all claims against the business; that is, any debts incurred must be paid from the owner's assets,

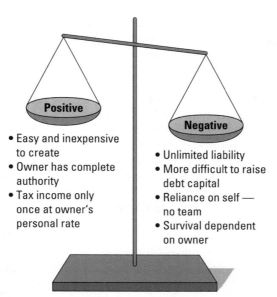

Figure 3.1
Sole Proprietorship

Positive
- Easy and inexpensive to create
- Owner has complete authority
- Tax income only once at owner's personal rate

Negative
- Unlimited liability
- More difficult to raise debt capital
- Reliance on self — no team
- Survival dependent on owner

which could include the owner's home, bank accounts, and any other personal assets. For this reason, sole proprietors should obtain general business liability insurance.

▶ It is more difficult to raise debt capital, because the owner's financial statement is usually the sole source to qualify.

▶ The sole proprietor often lacks a management team with diverse skills to help grow the company. To compensate, it would be important to put together an advisory team with these skills.

▶ The survival of the company depends on the owner. Succession agreements to the contrary, the business ends on the death or incapacitation of the owner.

Because of the serious disadvantages of this form of business ownership, it is not recommended for companies that intend to grow and deal in the global marketplace.

Partnership

Section 6 of the Uniform Partnership Act refers to a **partnership** as "an association of two or more persons to carry on as co-owners a business for profit." In this context, the term *persons* also includes companies and corporations, with the exception of charities and other nonprofit organizations, since they do not expect to earn a profit. A partnership is essentially a sole proprietorship involving more than one person in terms of its advantages and its treatment of income, expenses, and taxes. However, where liability is concerned, there is a significant difference. In a general partnership, each partner is held liable for the acts of another partner in the course of doing business for the partnership. This is called the **doctrine of ostensible authority** or *apparent authority*. For example, if a partner enters into a contract on behalf of the partnership, all the partners are bound by the terms of the contract. The ability of a single partner to bind the company and the rest of the partners to an agreement they may not like points to the need for choosing partners carefully and drawing up a partnership agreement. (Partnership agreements are discussed in the next section.) One exception to the doctrine of ostensible authority is that personal creditors of a partner—that is, for debt the partner has incurred in his or her personal life—can attach only personal assets of the partner who defaulted, including the partner's interest in the business.

Partners also have specific property rights. For example, each partner owns and has use of the property acquired by the partnership unless otherwise stated in the partnership agreement. In addition, each partner has the right to share in the profits and losses, each may participate in the management of the general partnership, and all elections, such as depreciation and accounting methods, are made at the partnership level and apply to all partners. The advantages and disadvantages of the partnership form of business are summarized in Figure 3.2.

Entrepreneurs sometimes form partnerships with co-founders during the development stages of a new product or in the early start-up stages of a new business. This is because it's easy, quick, and inexpensive to do. However, like the sole proprietorship, the partnership generally is not recommended as an appropriate legal form for a growing business, principally because it does

Positive
- Quick, easy, and inexpensive
- Advantages of a team — shared knowledge
- Shared financial strength
- Shared work load
- Taxed at personal level of individual partner

Negative
- No liability protection
- Control not with one person
- Fraught with personal conflict
- Shared equity

**Figure 3.2
Partnership**

not afford any liability protection. Nevertheless, since many companies form types of partnerships with other companies as they grow for the purpose of sharing resources, competencies, and risk, it's important to discuss some key issues related to partnerships.

How a Partnership Is Formed

A partnership can be formed with a simple oral agreement or can even be implied from the conduct and activities of the parties. In the latter case, the Uniform Partnership Act (UPA) says that the receipt by a person of a share of the profits of the business is *prima facie* evidence that he or she is a partner in the business. This is an important point, because if you receive a share of the profits of a business with which you're associated, you may also make yourself liable for its debts.

To this point, all references to partners have meant **general partners.** However, several other types of partners can be used in this form of business ownership, among them

▶ *Secret partners:* partners who are active but unknown to the public.

▶ *Silent partners:* usually inactive partners with a financial interest in the partnership.

▶ *Dormant partners:* silent partners not generally known publicly to be a partner.

▶ **Limited partners:** partners whose liability is limited to their capital investment in the partnership. These partners have no say in the management of the partnership. The penalty for actively participating is the loss of their limited liability status. The issue of private offerings as they relate to limited partnerships will be dealt with in a later chapter.

The Partnership Agreement

Though the law does not require it, it is critical that partnerships draw up a written partnership agreement based on the UPA. It should spell out in detail the business responsibilities, profit distribution, and transfer of interest should a partner die or leave the partnership. Many are the cases where a partnership failed to plan for these situations and found itself with a new, unwanted partner—namely, the spouse of the partner who died. Moreover, since partnerships are inherently fraught with problems arising from the different personalities and goals of the people involved, a written document executed at the beginning of the partnership will reduce eventual disagreements and provide for an orderly dissolution if irreconcilable differences arise.

A good partnership agreement, whether among individuals or companies, formal or informal, should address the following issues:

▶ The legal name of the partnership

▶ The nature of the business

▶ The duration of the partnership

◗ Contributions of the partners

◗ Sales, loans, and leases to the partnership

◗ Withdrawals and salaries

◗ Responsibility and authority of the partners

◗ Dissolution of the partnership

◗ Arbitration

In the absence of a partnership agreement, all partners are considered equal. At the end of the tax year, the partnership files a tax return and each individual partner files an information return, Form 1065.

Corporation

There are two types of corporations, C and sub-chapter S corporations. The specific differences of the S-corporation will be treated after a general discussion of corporations. The **C-corporation** is the only form that is a legal entity in and of itself. The U.S. Supreme Court defines the corporation as "an artificial being, invisible, intangible, and existing only in contemplation of the law." It is chartered or registered by a state and can survive the death or separation of its owners from the company. Therefore, a corporation can sue, be sued, acquire and sell real property, maintain perpetual succession, have a corporate seal, lend money, and make and alter its bylaws. The owners of the corporation are its stockholders, who typically invest capital in the corporation in exchange for shares of stock. Like limited partners, stockholders are liable only for the money they have invested in the corporation.

Although only about 17 percent of all businesses are corporations, they account for 87 percent of all sales, probably because they are the favored legal form for growing entrepreneurial companies. There are several types of C-corporations:

◗ A **domestic corporation** is organized under the laws of the state in which it incorporates.

◗ A **foreign corporation** is chartered in a state other than the one in which it will do business. A California corporation doing business in New York, for example, is considered a foreign corporation.

◗ A **public corporation** is one whose shares are traded on one of the stock exchanges. Growing companies often choose an initial public offering (IPO) as a way to secure the capital for further growth. IPOs are discussed in Chapter 9.

◗ A **closely held corporation** is one whose stock is held privately by a few individuals, often family members such as husband and wife.

How a Corporation Is Created

A corporation is created by filing a certificate of incorporation with the state in which the company will do business. It also requires the establishment of a board of directors that will make strategic policy decisions for the company and hire the officers who will run the business on a day-to-day basis. Another necessity to maintain the corporation's limited liability status is the formal documentation of board of directors' meetings. Many entrepreneurs with growing companies have failed to have the required board of directors' meetings and take minutes, which can cause them countless problems if they are ever questioned by a governmental agency. In addition, the state will also require articles of incorporation, which are generally standardized for each state.

Where to Incorporate

Where to incorporate is a decision that must be carefully made. For the most part, incorporating in the state in which the company intends to do the principal share of its business makes sense and is less costly in time and money in the long run, particularly if the company intends to conduct business on a national or international basis. In comparing states as sites for incorporation, the company should consider the following:

▶ Capitalization requirements, powers of directors, and flexibility of operations

▶ Incorporation fees and related taxes

▶ Cost of qualifying a foreign corporation in areas where the company will do business as compared with the cost of incorporating there

 The Real World of Entrepreneurship

Why Delaware?

Delaware has often been considered the ideal place to incorporate for a variety of reasons. Among them are the following:

▶ There is no corporate income tax for companies not doing business there, no tax on shares held by non-residents, and no inheritance tax on nonresident shareholders. In a state such as California, for example, a corporation will pay the minimum state income tax, which in 1997 was $800, whether or not it earned any taxable income that year.

▶ Corporate meetings may take place outside the state.

▶ The private property of shareholders is protected from liability for corporate debts.

▶ One incorporator is required.

▶ The corporation may be perpetual and can operate through voting trusts and shareholder voting agreements.

▶ Directors can make and alter bylaws even by unanimous written consent.

▶ No minimum capital requirements are imposed. Directors may determine what portion of the consideration received for shares will go to capital and what portion to surplus.

▶ The corporation can hold the securities of other corporations and property both in and outside the state. It can purchase its own stock and transfer or sell it.

▶ Dividends can be paid out of profits as well as out of surplus.

Whether or not to incorporate in Delaware should be weighed against such factors as the cost of operating as a foreign corporation in the state where the primary business is conducted and the cost and inconvenience of traveling to Delaware to settle legal matters that are typically filed in the state of incorporation.

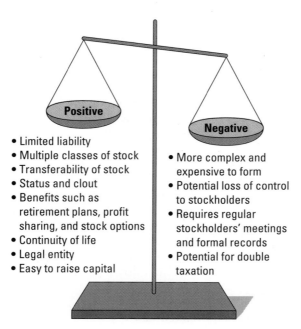

Positive
- Limited liability
- Multiple classes of stock
- Transferability of stock
- Status and clout
- Benefits such as retirement plans, profit sharing, and stock options
- Continuity of life
- Legal entity
- Easy to raise capital

Negative
- More complex and expensive to form
- Potential loss of control to stockholders
- Requires regular stockholders' meetings and formal records
- Potential for double taxation

Figure 3.3
Corporation

▶ Rules dealing with tender offers, if the stock will be widely held

▶ Annual fees and taxes

▶ State stamp taxes applicable to the original issue of the stock and any later transfers

See the Real World of Entrepreneurship box for more information on where to incorporate.

Advantages of Corporations

Corporations enjoy many advantages over sole proprietorships and partnerships (see Figure 3.3).

Limited Liability   The owners (shareholders) are liable for the debts and obligations of the corporation only to the limit of their investment. The only exception is payroll taxes withheld from employees' paychecks but not deposited for the Internal Revenue Service. This means that, with rare exceptions, the owners' personal assets cannot be seized as a result of something the corporation does.

Multiple Classes of Stock   The corporation can issue different classes of stock to meet the various needs of its investors. For example, it may issue nonvoting preferred stock to conservative investors, who will be first to recoup their investment in the event the corporation must liquidate its assets. It may issue common stock, which has voting rights, and common stockholders may share the profits remaining after the preferred holders are paid their dividends, assuming the corporation does not retain those profits to fund growth.

Status   Corporations often enjoy more status and deference than do other legal forms, largely because they are a legal entity that cannot be destroyed by the death of one or all of the principal shareholders. This is very advantageous to entrepreneurs dealing in a global market, as they are viewed as more serious contenders in the market. There is also the perception that corporations probably keep better records than other forms of ownership because they receive greater scrutiny from governmental agencies.

Benefits   Owners of corporations can benefit from retirement funds, Keogh and defined-contribution plans, profit-sharing plans, and stock option plans. These fringe benefits are deductible to the corporation as an expense and are not taxable to the employee.

Leasing of Personal Assets to the Corporation   Owners can hold certain assets, such as real estate, in their own names and lease the use of the assets to the corporation, thus giving them another income stream that is an expense to the corporation.

Disadvantages of Corporations

Like other legal forms, corporations suffer from disadvantages as well.

Complexity and Cost   The corporation is a more complex form that costs more to create. Although it is possible to incorporate without the aid of an attorney, it's not recommended.

Tax Issues   A more serious disadvantage derives from the fact that the corporation is a separate entity for tax purposes. As such, if it makes a profit, it must pay a tax whether or not the profit was distributed as dividends to shareholders. And unlike the partnership or sole proprietorship, stockholders do not receive the benefit of writing off losses to reduce taxable income (the S-corporation does enjoy this benefit). In a C-corporation, if those losses can't be applied in the year they were incurred, they must be saved to be applied against future profits. Accordingly, C-corporations pay taxes on the profits they earn and their owners (stockholders) pay taxes on the dividends they receive (already taxed as profit at the corporate level)—hence, the drawback of "double taxation."

Control   By creating a corporation and issuing stock, an owner gives up a measure of control and privacy to the stockholders and board of directors; consequently, unlike in the sole proprietorship or the partnership, corporate owners are accountable first to the stockholders and second to anyone else. For a young entrepreneurial company or closely held corporation, however, the reality is that the board of directors serves at the pleasure of the entrepreneur. Only if and when the company becomes a public corporation does the entrepreneur potentially lose some control. Nevertheless, in a private corporation, where several investors hold the stock, the entrepreneur will have to consider the input of those stakeholders (those who have a vested interest in the company).

S-Corporation

The **subchapter S-corporation**, or simply **S-corporation**, has become a popular legal form in recent years. Unlike the C-corporation, it is not a tax-paying entity. Instead, it is a financial vehicle that passes the profits and losses of the corporation to the stockholders, much as a partnership does, to be taxed at the individual partners' rate. It differs from the C-corporation in several ways:

▶ As in a partnership, owners are taxed on corporate earnings whether earnings are distributed as dividends or retained in the corporation.

▶ Unlike in a C-corporation, any losses the S-corporation incurs can be used as a deduction on the owner's personal income tax up to the amount invested in the corporation. If there is more than one shareholder, the loss is shared according to the percentage of ownership, as in a partnership.

▶ If the owner sells the assets of the business, a tax on the amount of appreciation on those assets is levied. With a C-corporation, in contrast, the gain is taxable to the corporation and the balance paid to the stockholder is also taxed.

If a C-corporation elects to become an S-corporation and then reverts back to a C-corporation at some later date, it will not be able to elect S-corporation status again for five years.

Businesses that don't have a need to retain earnings are suited to the S-corporation structure. However, some banks may not want to lend to S-corporations that distribute all their earnings, as this practice makes it more difficult for the company to grow. This negative aspect of the S-corporation is similar to the problem sole proprietors and partnerships face. Consequently, growing entrepreneurial companies with global intentions may prefer the C-corporation form. Furthermore, though most deductions and expenses are allowed, S-corporations cannot take advantage of deductions based on medical reimbursements or health insurance plans. Another consideration is that unless the business has regular positive cash flow, it could face a situation where it makes a profit, which is passed through to the owners to be taxed at their personal rates, but generates insufficient cash to pay those taxes. Also, S-corporations that operate in several states may experience problems with varying state regulations. If a company elects S-corporation status and later decides to do an IPO, it will need to convert to a C-corporation form first.

Companies that typically benefit from election of the S-corporation status include service businesses with low capital asset requirements, real estate investment firms during times when property values are increasing, and start-ups that are projecting a loss in the early years. Companies probably should not elect the S-corporation option if they want to retain earnings for expansion or diversification, or if they incur significant passive losses from investments such as real estate.

Limited Liability Company (LLC)

The most recent innovation in legal forms is the **limited liability company (LLC),** which is now available in at least 47 states. When formed correctly, an LLC often offers a better alternative to corporations, partnerships, and joint ventures because it combines the limited liability of a corporation with the pass-through tax advantages of a partnership or an S-corporation, in addition to the flexibility of a more informal structure. Many growing entrepreneurial companies are taking advantage of this form.

Most LLCs will be organized like S-corporations for tax purposes so that income tax benefits and liabilities will pass through to the members. In New York and California, however, the LLC will be subject to state franchise taxes or fees.

The Real World of Entrepreneurship

Guidelines for Forming an LLC

Following are some of the guidelines for creating a limited liability company. It is highly recommended that you consult an attorney specializing in corporate forms.

▶ The name chosen for the company has to contain any of the following words: *LLC, company, association, club, foundation, fund, institute, society, union, syndicate, limited,* or *trust.*

▶ The owners of an LLC are called *members,* and their interests are known as *interests.* These terms are essentially equivalent to *shareholders* and *stock.*

▶ An LLC will have two or more members and is formed by filing articles of organization, which resemble a partnership agreement. It should be formed in the state in which the company intends to do business.

▶ The management of the company can be undertaken by the members or by people elected by management.

▶ The members create an *operating agreement,* which is similar to a partnership agreement in that it spells out rights and obligations of the members. The LLC should keep a copy of the agreement and a list of the members. In most states, the operating agreement need not be made public.

▶ Managers, officers, and members are not personally liable for the company's debts or liabilities except as they have personally guaranteed those debts or liabilities.

▶ There is no limitation on the number of members or their status.

▶ The LLC must use a calendar year for tax purposes to coincide with the members' tax year. The cash method of accounting is available, although an LLC classified as a tax shelter must use the accrual method.

▶ The LLC may issue more than one class of stock.

▶ The LLC permits foreign ownership.

▶ An existing corporation can be converted to an LLC through a merger process. The merger documents are filed with the secretary of state, and the original corporation is listed as the nonsurviving entity.

▶ The LLC may be dissolved involuntarily by nonpayment of franchise or other taxes, by failure to maintain a registered agent and address within the state, or by order of the court. It may be dissolved voluntarily by vote of the members.

Table 3.1   The LLC Versus Other Corporate Forms

LLC Versus C-Corporation	LLC Versus S-Corporation
▶ No corporate tax	▶ More than 35 members allowed
▶ No double tax on liquidation	▶ Tax allocation not based on percentage of
▶ Pass-through taxation	ownership
▶ Debt in excess of basis may be put in LLC to avoid recognition of gain	▶ No restrictions on membership
	▶ Permits more than one class of stock
▶ Contribution of appreciated assets not subject to tax	▶ Step-up in basis at death of member

Only private companies can become LLCs, and they must be formed using very strict guidelines that may vary from state to state, so it is important to check state requirements for LLCs (see The Real World of Entrepreneurship).

LLCs are popular vehicles for companies with global investors, family-owned businesses, and professional service organizations. It is important, however, to check the special requirements of each state, as they do vary in some aspects. For a comparison of LLCs to other corporate forms of business, see Table 3.1.

The Nonprofit Corporation

Many entrepreneurs are finding opportunities that are well suited to a nonprofit corporate form. A **nonprofit corporation** is one established for charitable, public benefit (e.g., scientific, literary, and educational), religious benefit, or mutual benefit (e.g., trade associations, tennis clubs), all purposes recognized by federal and state laws. Like the C-corporation, the nonprofit (or not-for-profit) corporation is a legal entity and offers its shareholders and officers the benefit of limited liability.

There is a common misconception that a nonprofit entity cannot make a profit. This is untrue. As long as the company is not set up to benefit a single person and is organized for a nonprofit purpose as specified above, it can

 The Real World of Entrepreneurship

Qualifications for Nonprofit Corporations

To qualify to operate as a nonprofit corporation, a company must pass two distinct hurdles:

1. Meet the state requirements for designation as a nonprofit corporation.

2. Meet the federal and state requirements for exemption from paying taxes **(IRC 501(c)(3)** by forming a corporation that falls within the IRS's narrowly defined categories. Under this section, a nonprofit may not engage in substantial activity that is not for tax-exempt purposes.

make a profit on which it is not taxed if it has also met the IRS test for a tax-exempt status. The key requirement is that profits may not be distributed; that is, the nonprofit corporation cannot declare dividends. Income derived from for-profit activities, however, is subject to income tax.

The owners of a nonprofit corporation give up proprietary interest in the corporation and dedicate all its assets and resources to tax-exempt activities. If a nonprofit corporation is ever dissolved, its assets must be distributed to another tax-exempt organization.

One exception is mutual benefit corporations (trade associations, etc.), which can qualify for tax-exempt status under IRC§510(c)(6); however, contributions to mutual benefit corporations are not tax deductible. Also, these nonprofits do not qualify for nonprofit mailing rates and real and personal property tax exemptions. Unlike with other nonprofit types, when a mutual benefit corporation dissolves and all its liabilities are paid, it may distribute the remaining assets, gains, and profits to the members.

Advantages of Nonprofit Corporations

The advantages of a nonprofit corporation include the following:

▶ It is exempt from paying taxes.

▶ It has limited liability. However, directors or officers can be held liable when they have had to personally guarantee a loan or failed to withhold or deposit taxes for employees.

▶ It has perpetual existence; that is, like a corporation, it can exist in perpetuity.

▶ It is able to qualify for grants and receive corporate donations. Nonprofit companies often receive donations of equipment and supplies from companies that see a real benefit in helping the nonprofit.

▶ Employees can have benefits. Even the principals can be employees and eligible for tax-deductible employee fringe benefits.

The Real World of Entrepreneurship

The Culture of a Contract

Some U.S. companies believe Japanese companies don't honor their contracts. At the same time, Japanese companies often see U.S. businesspeople as aggressive and "out to take advantage" of them. The real issue is differing perceptions of the contract process between these two countries.

Japanese companies see the contract as the first step in building a relationship rather than the final result of a successful negotiation. The Japanese are more interested in finding good long-term partners than in signing long-term contracts. Consequently, their decision to sign a contract is made by the consensus of everyone with a vested interest. Furthermore, their contracts are much shorter than typical U.S. contracts, as they generally leave out clauses that deal with what to do if something goes wrong.

If a contract is signed, the Japanese partner will expect the U.S. partner to work out any disagreements that arise in a nonconfrontational manner—in other words, outside the courts.

SOURCE: David Andrews and Sherry Ridgley, "Negotiating with the Japanese," *Global Trade & Transportation*, September 1993.

Employment contracts are important in any business, but particularly in a family business. When David Shulman took charge of operating Grand Warehouse Corp., a corporation he formed with his grandfather, he soon learned that the only way to gain the authority he needed in the eyes of the family shareholders was to spell out his role in an employment contract. (Bill Bilsley)

Disadvantages of Nonprofit Corporations

Corporations have disadvantages as well. The usual red tape involved in organizing a corporation also occurs for a nonprofit. Recordkeeping and reporting can be a challenge, and the cost of incorporating is relatively high.

Contracts and Small-Business Strategy

Contract law plays a pervasive role in any business, from agreements with suppliers, lessors, and partners to contracts with independent contractors and employees. A well-written contract by an experienced attorney will be legally binding and will give a company legal remedies if the other party to the contract fails to comply with its terms. To be legally binding, a contract must have several elements:

- Capacity to contract
- Offer, acceptance, and mutuality
- Consideration
- A legal purpose
- Correct form

Capacity means that the parties to the contract must be legally able to enter into a fair contractual agreement. Those who cannot legally enter into a contract include intoxicated persons, persons who are not of sound mind and body, or minors. If someone in one of these categories does enter into an agreement, the contract may be contested and declared to be void, as never having existed.

Agreement consists of an offer or a promise to do something or refrain from doing something. For example, a lessor may offer to lease office space to a company, which constitutes an offer to do something. For the agreement to be valid, however, there must also be **consideration**, which in the current example is the company's promise to give up something in return, in this case a check for the deposit and the first month's lease payment. Furthermore, the contract must be for a legal purpose and in the correct form; that is, some contracts, such as real estate contracts, must be in writing to be legal. An illegal contract cannot be enforced.

Some companies regularly use oral contracts or "handshake" agreements; however, most courts will not enforce an oral agreement that extends beyond one year. It's a good idea for business owners to use an attorney for structuring contracts; however, if a particular type of contract is used often, the attorney may be able to create a template with blanks that can be used repeatedly.

Agency Law and Small-Business Strategy

Agency law can have a significant impact on a company's competitive strategy. Employees are the agents of the company, so the company is responsible for any damages or injury an employee causes while doing its work. Even a

The Real World of Entrepreneurship

Buy-Sell Agreements

Whenever a business has more than one owner, the issue of what to do if one of the owners decides to leave or dies arises. Inevitably, the **buy-sell agreement** is recommended because it is essentially a contract that states what will happen to an owner's share of the business. It's an important way to protect the owners from having to share ownership with someone they don't know or want in the business. Consider the following scenario. A company has three owners who have equal shares in the business. They have a buy-sell agreement that says the remaining two owners will buy out the third owner's shares at market value. This is typically done with insurance on the owners. Now suppose the owner, who subsequently dies, has a son who is working in the business. Because the buy-sell agreement did not address this situation specifically, the son will get cash from the insurance but have no ownership interest in his father's company.

This situation could have been avoided with an estate planning agreement. In the agreement, the shareholder purchases the life insurance and puts it in an irrevocable life insurance trust for the child. The insurance can be purchased using personal savings. If the subject owner lives three years beyond the transfer, the proceeds of the trust become free of estate taxes. When the owner dies, the trust pays for the stock with the proceeds from the insurance. The agreement will also provide that the child's stock carries no voting rights during the lives of the remaining owners.

SOURCE: "Buy-Sell Agreements: Does Yours Still Make Sense?" *Inc.,* September 1995, p. 106.

temporary worker or deliveryperson can be implied as an agent for the company. Domino's Pizza found that out when one of its drivers ran a red light and hit a woman in another car. The jury awarded the victim $750,000 in actual damages and $78 million in punitive damages.[1] As a result, Domino's no longer guarantees 30-minute delivery, which was a significant aspect of its competitive strategy.

Business owners should be familiar with several types of agency authority:

- ▶ **Express authority.** The company actually authorizes the agent to act for the company.

- ▶ **Incidental Authority.** The agent is given the authority to perform acts or carry out duties related to his or her job with the company.

- ▶ **Implied authority.** The agent has authority based on his or her job or previous responsibilities. For example, the buyer for a retail store has the implied authority to purchase from the established list of suppliers.

- ▶ **Emergency authority.** The agent has the authority to enter into contracts for the purpose of handling an emergency situation.

- ▶ **Apparent authority.** The conduct of the company toward the agent implies that the agent has the authority to act for the company.

- ▶ **Ostensible authority.** The company permits an agent to represent to a third party that he or she has the authority to act on behalf of the company.

In all of these cases, the actions and contracts of the agent bind the company. Therefore, it is important to clarify employees' and subcontractors' agency relationships with the company.

Trade Laws and Small-Business Strategy

In the United States, great value is placed on the free marketplace, and generally any attempts by government to interfere in the free market process are shunned. Nevertheless, since the 1800s, the government has imposed certain laws specifically designed to preserve competition and the free market. The

The Real World of Entrepreneurship

The Private Securities Litigation Reform Act

Until help arrived in 1995, many fast-growing companies found themselves targets for securities fraud lawsuits if they did not achieve financial projections. In the 1980s aggressive attorneys filed lawsuits aimed at junk bonds, but in the 1990s they moved in on small businesses, whose stock prices tend to be more volatile. In 1995, Congress passed the Private Securities Litigation Reform Act to protect companies from lawsuits filed by lawyers on behalf of investors. The law provides a safe harbor for companies that make optimistic statements about the potential growth of their businesses.

Sherman Antitrust Act of 1890, one of the first such laws, prohibited any restraint of free trade. Other regulations followed and are discussed in the following sections. Understanding the effect these laws and regulations will have on the company's competitive strategy will allow the entrepreneur to make more effective decisions and avoid the time and cost associated with lawsuits stemming from ill-informed decisions.

The Uniform Commercial Code

The **Uniform Commercial Code (UCC)** is a group of laws that affects everything from bank deposits and investment securities to sales. It is this latter category that affects business owners. Anytime a company enters into an agreement to sell a product, it creates a contract that is governed by the laws of contract. However, a merchant must also abide by the laws of the UCC, which can differ. To use a simple example, suppose a company has ordered some supplies from a manufacturer under a contract that contains the terms of place, delivery date, and quantity, but has failed to ask the price. The supplies arrive and the price is higher than expected. Under the regulations of the UCC, a price that is reasonable at the time of delivery is assigned based on the fact that both the purchasing company and the manufacturer are professionals that understand how the business operates.

Product Liability

The UCC also deals with product liability issues. Historically, the philosophy of the marketplace in the United States has been *caveat emptor* or "let the buyer beware." In contemporary times, however, the burden of that philosophy has shifted to "let the seller beware" as consumer groups and advocates such as Ralph Nader have forced businesses to take responsibility for the quality and safety of what they produce. Any company producing a product of any kind needs to consider product liability insurance to protect itself against potential litigation even when the company provides warranties. This is particularly true in the United States, where many customers will not think twice about suing companies for significant amounts of money if they believe a product has caused them harm. In the international arena, suits are far less common, but there is no guarantee that this situation will not change.

Implied Warranties

In instances where no warranty protects a buyer who is injured, **implied warranties** are present under the law of the Uniform Commercial Code. For example, an implied warrant of merchantability means the product does what the producer claims it will do. Beyond that, makers and sellers of goods that are inherently dangerous are held to strict liability, meaning they are liable under all circumstances. Whenever a company sells goods, it also sells a warrant of merchantability, an implied warranty that assures the customer that the product is of at least average quality and suitable for the purpose for which it was intended. This shift in the burden of responsibility has resulted in numerous lawsuits by consumers and higher premiums for product liability insurance. For example, it is estimated that about 25 percent of the cost of a football helmet pays for product liability insurance. Any company that intends to manufacture and sell a consumer product should be careful to include clear instructions on its use and warnings about the consequences of misuse. The liability can even extend to products served by fast-food restaurants, as McDonald's discovered when it was sued by a New Mexico woman in 1992 over burns from coffee she spilled on herself. Though she was awarded nearly $3 million in a federal court, a judge reduced the award, and the case was settled for under $600,000. In 1995, McDonald's was sued for $2 million by a Maryland man claiming he suffered first-, second-, and third-degree burns when coffee spilled on his lap.[2]

Consumer Credit Laws and Financial Strategy

Like consumer protection laws, the laws regulating consumer lending are pervasive in an effort to protect consumer rights. Understanding what is required of businesses dealing in consumer credit is essential to a successful financial strategy. The Equal Credit Opportunity Act (ECOA) provides for fair and equitable treatment of all borrowers without regard for marital status, source of income, race, gender, color, or national origin. It also requires prompt disclosure of the reasons for any denial of credit. The ECOA applies to all banks, credit unions, retailers, and business creditors. Before any credit granting can be completed, the Truth-in-Lending Act (Regulation Z) mandates detailed disclosures concerning the cost of credit, the method of billing on open-ended contracts, personal property leases, and credit card accounts as well as the number and amount of payments required, and the type of collateral given to secure the loan. Reg Z applies to anyone who regularly extends credit, imposes a finance charge, or permits an obligation to be repaid over more than four installments.

The Fair Credit Billing Act (FCBA) provides procedures for dispute resolution, and the Fair Credit Reporting Act (FCRA) mandates standards for reporting information on credit recipients to credit reporting agencies. If a company intends to grant credit to its customers, it must be aware of all the regulations that will affect its ability to do so. The bottom line is: merchant lender beware!

Truth in Advertising and Marketing Strategy

The Federal Trade Commission (FTC) is charged with protecting the rights of consumers against false or misleading advertising. It has come down hard on many a business for misleading customers about what a product can do, offering a reduced (sale) price on an item that was never advertised at a higher price, using list price as a comparison if the business has never sold the item at list, and using bait-and-switch techniques to lure customers into the store only to switch them to a higher-priced item.

Vivian Gibson knows how to protect her new product, Vib's Caribbean Heat, a hot seasoning sauce. She filed for trademark protection; she had her partners sign confidentiality agreements; and she secured product liability insurance to protect against liability if someone were to get sick from using her product. (Greg Kiger)

Consumer Protection Law and Customer Strategy

The greatest number of laws affecting trade come under the heading of consumer protection. They include

▶ Unscrupulous sellers

▶ Unreasonable credit items

▶ Unsafe products

▶ Mislabeling of products

One of the largest federal agencies monitoring product safety is the Food and Drug Administration (FDA), which is responsible for research, new-product testing, and inspection of the operations of food and drug manufacturers. If a new product is a drug, a food item, or anything that goes below the surface of the skin, it requires FDA approval before it can be marketed.

The Consumer Product Safety Commission was established in 1972 as the watchdog for consumer products that are considered hazardous. In addition, it is charged with setting standards for such things as toys for children under age 5. A company whose product falls into one of these categories will need to be aware of the standards and requirements for marketing and producing that product.

The Fair Packaging and Labeling Act was designed to provide consumers with information so that they could shop more wisely. The act mandates that manufacturers truthfully list all raw materials used in the production of the product on a clearly marked label in addition to the size and weight of the packaging. If the product is a food product, the label must display the percentages of nutrients—vitamins, carbohydrates, calories, and fat—contained in one normal-size serving. By becoming aware of the regulations affecting products manufactured for public consumption, a company can avoid both the possible recall of products and potential lawsuits.

Price Discrimination and Pricing Strategy

The Clayton Act of 1914 and the even stricter Robinson-Patman Act of 1936, enforced by the Federal Trade Commission, asserted that businesses cannot sell the same product to different customers at different prices without justification. In other words, they must demonstrate that the lower price was based on a quantity-sold discount, the quality of the product (seconds or slightly damaged), or a cost savings on the part of the seller (the manufacturer discounted the product to the retailer beyond the normal purchase price). Therefore, the company must be careful to be fair to all customers when setting prices.

Technology Tip

Going Online Can Mean Legal Problems

Every day hundreds of companies put up new web sites to provide information and advertise or sell products. But many of these companies are finding they haven't taken care of business when it comes to trademarks and copyrights and the insurance needed to defend them. Competition is fierce on the Internet, and companies are out there seeking to shut down rivals that have made mistakes on their sites. Usually it's a large company going after a small start-up, but the reverse may also be true.

Synet Inc., a small internet service provider based in Illinois, registered the name Internet Explorer in 1994. When the mamouth Microsoft Corporation came onto the market with its own Internet Explorer, Synet sued, claiming that the name is descriptive and too generic for a trademark. As of October 1997 Synet was in Chapter 11 bankruptcy, and 20 employees were out of work. Microsoft offered Synet $75,000 to end the litigation, but Synet refused, claiming that it wants the name "Internet Explorer."*

As a web site owner, be aware of the following:

▶ You're in the publishing business, and the same laws that apply to paper apply on the Internet.

▶ Never use someone's trademark or copyrighted material in any information, newsletter, or advertising materials without seeking permission or giving full credit to the source.

▶ Have your lawyer review any online materials.

▶ Check with your insurance agent to find out if you're covered for damages as well as the costs of a defense.

---

*Steve Young, CNN News. October 27, 1997.

SOURCE: Peter Weaver, "Covering the Bases for Your Web Site," *Nation's Business*, November 1996, p. 38R.

Intellectual Property Law

One competitive advantage many companies enjoy involves an area of the law called **intellectual property** rights, or *proprietary rights*. These are intangible ownership rights that include patents, trademarks, copyrights, and trade secrets. From a strategic standpoint, intellectual property gives the entrepreneur the opportunity to exploit a first mover and potential leader position in the market by introducing something that has not previously existed in its current form. It also enables the entrepreneur to license the intellectual property rights to someone to exploit, thereby expanding market presence much more rapidly. This has been the approach of many companies in the entertainment industry, such as Paramount Studios. Paramount owns the rights to Star Trek and its characters, which it has trademarked and licensed to a toy manufacturer, for example, to develop action figures.

It is important for an entrepreneur who develops an innovative product to investigate the potential to acquire intellectual property rights, that is, determine if there are legal ways to protect the product idea from competitor duplication until and after it goes to market. The issue of who owns an invention is a crucial one that could mean the difference between launching a successful product and a flop. The primary legal means to protect an original invention is through a patent.

Patents

Designed 200 years ago by Thomas Jefferson to protect the inventions of the independent inventor, the U.S. patent system has issued more than 5 million patents since 1790. Today, although most inventors work in the research departments of large corporations, the basic legal tenets of patent law still apply to the independent inventor.

 The Real World of Entrepreneurship

Still Seeking the "Better Mousetrap"

"**B**uild a better mousetrap, and the world will beat a path to your door." It has been claimed that Ralph Waldo Emerson in the 1800s uttered those prophetic words that entrepreneurs have heard over and over again. And many people have taken those words to heart, for the mousetrap is by far the most invented device in American history.

The Patent and Trademark Office (PTO) grants at least 40 patents for mousetraps every year. In fact, there are so many applicants that the device now has nine official categories that include such notables as "smit-ing," "choking or squeezing," "electrocuting and explosive." The original patent for a mousetrap was granted in 1903 (number 744,379), and this product is still manufactured by the Woodstream Corporation of Pennsylvania using the trade name Victor. Of the more than 4,400 patented mousetraps, fewer than two dozen have earned any money for their creators, proving that only the best have a path beaten to their door.

SOURCE: Jack Hope, "A Better Mousetrap," *American Heritage,* October 1996, pp. 90–97.

A **patent** is a grant to an inventor that gives him or her the exclusive right to an invention for a period of years, depending on the type of patent. It also prevents others from manufacturing and selling the invention during the period of the patent. At the end of this time, the patent is placed in the public domain. Two types of patents concern most inventors: utility and design patents. *Utility patents* are the more common type. They protect the functional aspect of machines or processes, as well as computer programs associated with hardware. Some examples are toys, film processing, protective coatings, tools, and cleaning implements. As of June 8, 1995, a utility patent is valid for a period of 20 years from the first effective filing date.* *Design patents*, by contrast, protect new, original ornamental designs for manufactured articles. The design must be nonfunctional and part of the tangible item for which it is designed. Some examples are a decoration, an item of apparel, or jewelry.[3]

Special Patents

The patent office watches for new technology that may not be covered under current patent categories. In 1980, for example, it created a new category of protection, life forms, which covers things such as microbes that break down crude oil, and human genes. Another special category of patents is the plant patent, which protects any sexually or asexually reproduced plant that is a new variety.

Computer programs present some special issues. They may be protected by a trade secret if the developer/owner merely licenses the program for distribution by someone else to a narrow market. If wide dissemination is the goal, a patent offers more protection and is available if the program contains at least one unique algorithm that is part of the machine or physical process. Copyrights are commonly used for programs that don't qualify for a patent. In addition, the name of the program can be trademarked and the instructions copyrighted.

Rules for Patents

Before deciding to file for a patent, it is important to first determine the patentability of the invention. There are four basic rules.

1. The invention must fit into one of the *five classes* established by Congress for utility patents:
   - Machine (fax, rocket, electronic circuits)
   - Process (chemical reactions, methods for producing products)
   - Articles of manufacture (furniture, diskettes)
   - Composition (gasoline, food additives)
   - A new use for one of the above

---

*Patents used to be good for 17 years from their issue date. The change came about as a result of GATT and NAFTA legislation.

Many inventions can be classified into more than one category. That does not present a problem, however, as the inventor does not have to choose into which category the invention fits.

2. It must have *utility*—in other words, be useful. This usually is not a problem unless the invention is something like an unsafe drug or something purely "whimsical." The PTO, nevertheless, has issued patents on some fairly unusual inventions, such as a male chastity device (number 587,994).

3. It must not contain *prior art.* Prior art is the state of knowledge that is publicly available or published prior to the date of the invention, which usually occurs sometime before the filing of the patent application. That is why it is important to document everything that is done in the creation of the invention. In addition, the invention must not become public or available for sale more than one year prior to filing the patent application. This is so that the invention is still novel at the time of application. Novelty consists of physical differences, new combinations of components, or new uses.

4. It must be *unobvious.* The invention must not be obvious to someone with ordinary skills in the field. In other words, the invention must contain "new and unexpected results." If the invention is rejected on the first pass as not being "unobvious," it probably means the patent examiner wants the inventor to demonstrate its unobviousness.

The Patent Process

The process for obtaining a patent is well defined; however, it is advisable to use the services of a patent attorney. The process consists of two steps.[4]

File a Disclosure Document   The inventor will normally file a disclosure statement that documents the date of conception of the invention. This statement is critical in the event that two inventors are working on the same idea at the same time. The one who files the disclosure document first has the right to file for a patent. The disclosure document is a detailed description of the invention and its uses, and may include photos; however, it is *not* a patent application. The inventor has a two-year grace period in which to file a standard patent application but must demonstrate diligence in completing the invention and filing the application. If the inventor publicly uses or sells the invention more than a year prior to filing the patent application, he or she will be prohibited from applying for a patent.

To file a disclosure statement, the investor sends

▶ A cover letter requesting that the PTO accept the disclosure statement

▶ A check for the required fee

▶ A copy of the disclosure statement

▶ A stamped, self-addressed, return envelope

It is important that the inventor not use the tactic of mailing a dated description of the invention to himself or herself by certified mail. It has no value to the patent office.

File the Patent Application   The patent application contains a complete description of the invention, what it does, and how it is uniquely different from anything currently existing (prior art). It also includes detailed drawings, explanations, and engineering specifications. The claims section of the application specifies the parts of the invention on which the inventor wants patents. The description of these claims must be specific enough to demonstrate the invention's uniqueness but broad enough to make it difficult for others to circumvent the patent, that is, by modifying it slightly and duplicating the product without violating the patent. The patent application should be filed within one year of offering the product for sale or using it commercially. It is infinitely preferable to file *before* making any public disclosures.

"Patent Applied For" Versus "Patent Pending"

Once the application is received, the patent office will conduct a search of its patent records. During this period the invention is said to be "patent applied for," which establishes the inventor's claim and dates relative to prior art. An invention can stay in the patent-applied-for stage up to two years. The primary advantage of this is that the public does not have access to the patent application and drawings, which might allow someone else the chance to design around the patent.

The patent office contacts the inventor and states that it either accepts the claims in the application or denies the application and gives the inventor a period of time to appeal and/or modify the claims. It is not uncommon for the PTO to reject the original claims in their entirety, usually because of prior art. If and when the patent office accepts the modified claims, the invention is in the "patent-pending" stage, that is, awaiting the issuance of the patent. The inventor may market and sell the product during this period, but should clearly label it "patent pending." Once the patent is *issued*, however, it becomes public record. If the patent examiner rejects the modified claims, on the other hand, the inventor has the right to appeal to a board of patent appeals within the patent office. If agreement is not reached at this point, the inventor may appeal to the U.S. Court of Appeals for the federal circuit. An inventor should realize that this process may take years.

Changes in Patent Law

Legislation to implement GATT and NAFTA has led to many changes in patent laws. One change is the term of the patent from 17 to 20 years from first application, as discussed earlier. Another is the recognition of provisional applications, which have been used for many years in other countries. The provisional patent is subject to minimal formal requirements and reduced filing fees. It is essentially the basis for filing a formal patent application later. This must be done within one year, after which the provisional application becomes abandoned in favor of the complete application. The

20-year clock starts with the filing of the complete application; so, effectively, patent protection is extended by one year if the provisional application is used. The provisional patent is an excellent tool for the small inventor who wants to be protected when talking to manufacturers and is not financially able to make a formal patent application.

Under the new laws, "offering for sale" and "importing" of products covered by U.S. patents have been added to the existing "making, using, or selling" definitions of what constitutes patent infringement.

Licensing Intellectual Property

An entrepreneur or a company does not have to own a patent to benefit from it. In some cases, it may be possible to license the right to use a patent from the inventor. For example, an inventor may grant a license to the company to manufacture and distribute the invention, while the inventor receives a royalty on sales. Alternatively, it may be possible for the company to purchase an assignment of a patent with the inventor, transferring ownership rights to the company. Inventors should be aware, however, that once the patent is issued, it is a powerful document that gives the holder the right to enforce the patent against infringers in a court of law. Under the law, the patent holder is entitled to a reasonable royalty from the infringer, and if the infringer refuses to pay, the patent holder can enjoin or close down the infringer's operation. If a company is planning to export products, it should file patent applications in the countries in which the product will be sold. This can be a costly process if the company is dealing with a number of countries. Furthermore, companies often have found that their patents are violated in countries that do not have patent laws as stringent as those in the United States.

The issue of licensing technology and intellectual property is discussed as a start-up and growth strategy in Chapter 4.

The Real World of Entrepreneurship

Who Decides Your Infringement Case?

For decades judges have determined whose patents have been enfringed on. Today, however, plaintiffs in a patent case are increasingly selecting juries to decide this matter under the assumption that they will be more likely to prevail with a jury and that a decision in their favor will be less likely to be overturned on appeal. A recent study by the American Bar Association Section of Intellectual Property Law, 1993–1994, looked at 79 decisions by the federal circuit that were appealed. It found that the jury was more favorable to the patentee in 59 percent of the cases. But when the appeal process was concluded, of the 47 decisions in favor of patentees,

only 27 were actually affirmed on appeal. In other words, 20 cases were reversed. In contrast, only three jury decisions in favor of the infringer were reversed.

When the patentee had a judge hear the case, the results changed significantly. On completion of the original verdict and the appeal, there was a 50-50 split between patentee and infringer on the favorableness of the decision.

The bottom line is: patentees will be more likely to prevail before a jury if they suspect that the infringer will not appeal. With a full appeal, the patentee's chances appear to be better before a judge.

Trademarks

A **trademark** is a symbol, word, or design that is used to identify a business or a product. For example, Apple Computer uses a picture of an apple with a bite out of it followed by the symbol ®, which means "registered trademark." A trademark has a longer life than a patent, with certain conditions. It must be renewed every 10 years. A business has the exclusive right to a trademark for as long as it is actively using it. However, if the trademarked term becomes part of the generic language, such as *aspirin* and *thermos*, it can no longer be trademarked. Furthermore, a trademark cannot be registered until it is actually in use. Before that time, the company should file an "intent to use" application with the PTO and use ^{TM} after the name until the trademark is registered or ^{SM} for service.

The Patent and Trademark Office also recognizes the registration of color where it can be shown that consumers recognize a particular product by its color. For example, pink has been registered for fiberglass and yellow and green for farm equipment. In some cases, shapes have been patentable, such as the classic Coke bottle, as well as sounds, such as the NBC chimes.

GATT has also affected trademark law with TRIPS (Trade in Counterfeit Goods), which sets the minimum standards of protection for intellectual property. Under TRIPS, the initial term of a registration and each renewal term are to be for no less than seven years. The trademark may be canceled only after an uninterrupted period of three years during which it is not used.

Trade Secrets

Trade secrets are those aspects of the business that need to be protected from disclosure by employees or others involved with the business. This form of protection generally is achieved through a written agreement. Aspects of the business that may be considered trade secrets are recipes or ingredients (e.g., Mrs. Fields Cookies), source codes for computer chips, customer discounts, manufacturer costs, and so forth. The only way to protect these items from disclosure is through an employment contract.

The Real World of Entrepreneurship

Trademarks on the Millennium

In an effort to capitalize on the turn of the century and the opportunities it means, thousands of entrepreneurs are seeking trademarks in every form on words such as "millennium" and "Year 2000." The U.S. Patent and Trademark Office has already awarded 117 trademarks including the word *millennium* (or, incorrectly, *millenium*) and more than 1,500 trademarks containing *2000*.

If fact, one entrepreneur in Maine, who has been using "Year 2000" on T-shirts for more than two years, received a cease-and-desist notice from Planet Marketing of New York City, which has trademarked the term and intends to bring out a variety of products under the trademark.

Source: "Thousands Drive for 2000 Profits," *Orange County Press Telegram,* November 3, 1997.

Copyrights

Copyrights protect original works of authors, composers, screenwriters, and computer programmers. Though not required by the PTO, it is recommended that to protect such a work, a notice of copyright be placed in a prominent location on the work using either the word *Copyright* or the symbol ©, the year of first publication, and the name of the copyright holder.

A copyright protects not the idea itself but only the form in which it appears. For example, a computer programmer can copyright the written program for a particular type of word processing software but cannot copyright the idea of word processing. This is why several companies can produce word processing software without violating a copyright. They are really protecting the unique programming code of their software. A copyright lasts for the life of the holder plus 50 years, after which it goes into the public domain.

Internet Law

One of the newest frontiers in the legal field is Internet law. With more and more companies conducting business over the Internet, lawyers are finding that the "the rules that govern conventional situations are sometimes difficult to apply in cyberspace."[5] In these situations, technology has created issues that have never been addressed in a court of law or by the legislature and thus

The Real World of Entrepreneurship

Protecting the New Media

One of the more interesting legal issues arising out of the new media formed by the intersection of books, records, film, and video is how to categorize it for legal purposes. Some titles are copyrighted as software and then licensed to the user, whereas others are classified as entertainment products and copyrighted like books or videos. The problem comes when the new medium contains music, film, written text, and programming code, and the purchaser wants to rent it. Under copyright law, software cannot be rented, but CD-ROM titles can if they are treated as a book or video. Distributors are interested in renting these titles because they believe, based on their experience with video games, that three out of five titles purchased will be rented first. Right now it depends on how the title is packaged. If packaged with a license agreement with the end-user, the end-user doesn't actually own the product but only has the right to use it on his or her computer. On the other hand, if the title is packaged as "finished goods," it is protected under the first-sale doctrine, which allows for copies for noncommercial purposes only.

It is always important for any developer of CD-ROM titles to obtain broad rights from all parties, including the creative and content contributors. The four publishing industries bring to the table four distinct ways of doing business, and it should never be assumed that one party understands what the others do. It is also important to seek out an attorney who has experience in various media. The attorney will make certain that the developer understands the rights and clearances needed to undertake and complete a project as well as the cost to obtain those rights.

The key point to remember about intellectual property rights is that they can't stop someone from infringing on the holder's rights. What they can do is provide the holder with offensive rights, that is, the right to sue in a court of law, a long and costly process. Consequently, intellectual property rights should never be the sole competitive advantage a company possesses.

put companies operating on the Internet on very slippery ground. This section examines two such issues: copyright infringement and contract issues.

Copyright Infringement

Downloading copyrighted materials is one of the most common activities on the Internet, and it will soon be possible to download and upload digital copies of music CDs and motion pictures. The relative anonymity of the Internet makes it that much easier for infringers to succeed in their efforts.[6] The current copyright law was discussed in an earlier section of this chapter. The question with regard to the Internet is whether a BBS (bulletin board system) operator can be held liable for violating copyright laws when users of the BBS download copyrighted materials.* The precedent-setting case discussed in the footnote (*Sega Enterprises Inc. v. MAPHIA*) holds BBS operators directly liable for reproducing video games without authorization. The law is still forming on this issue, but clearly BBS operators should be aware that the potential is great that they will be held liable if infringement is occurring on their system, with or without their knowledge.

Electronic Contracts

Many businesspeople are unaware that legal contracts under the UCC can be formed without paper and signatures or human interaction of any kind.[7] Such a situation would occur when a user purchased something from a company on the Internet. Those studying this area of the law believe that any symbol contained in the computer message that is put there to authenticate the message and indicate assent should satisfy the signature requirement.[8] Previously, letterheads and telegrams were accepted as signatures. For a symbol to satisfy the statute of frauds concerning computer messages, the contract should be sent using reasonably secure methods that ensure a forensic trail back to the signer.[9] It is recommended that businesses that deal in electronic commerce use the model agreement of the American Bar Association,

---

*The case that currently establishes precedent for holding BBS operators directly liable for unauthorized reproduction is *Sega Enterprises Inc. v. MAPHIA* 857 F. Supp. 679 (N.D. Cal. 1994). In this case, the MAPHIA BBS encouraged users to upload unauthorized copies of Sega video games, which MAPHIA would then charge other users to download, clearly aiding and abetting its users to infringe on the copyright. Another case, *Religious Technology Center v. Netcom Inc.,* 1995 U.S. Dist. LEXIS 18173 (N.D. Cal. 1995), found that there is no liability for direct infringement under certain circumstances, that is, when the BBS *automatically* stores materials for a brief time and then retransmits them. This is not considered to be making unauthorized copies. This situation occurs when a user uploads copyrighted material to the BBS, which happens to be connected to a usenet system, and the BBS transmits the materials to other usenet groups. However, yet another case, *Playboy v. Frena,* held a BBS liable for directly infringing on *Playboy*'s right to distribute photographs. Apparently, *Playboy* photographs were being uploaded and downloaded on the defendant's BBS without his knowledge. The court held, "It does not matter that Defendant Frena may have been unaware of the copyright infringement. Intent to infringe is not needed to find copyright infringement." Intent or knowledge is not an element of infringement, and thus even an innocent infringer is liable for infringement.

whose contract contains clauses that address these issues and requires computer messages to state their legal intent and whether the message is binding without formal acceptance (i.e., purchase orders).

Companies doing business on the Internet need to be mindful of the rapidly changing environment of Internet law. As more and more attorneys become familiar with the Internet, it will be easier for growing companies to obtain the advice they need.

Understanding the laws related to starting and growing a business is paramount to avoiding issues and mistakes that not only could be costly in terms of time and money but even result in business failure.

Cases Relevant to This Chapter

SB Networks
Zanart Entertainment

Issues for Review and Discussion

1. Compare and contrast the sole proprietorship, partnership, and corporate forms of organizational structure in terms of liability, life of the business, transfer of interest, and distribution of profits.
2. What is necessary for a contract to be legally binding?
3. Discuss how agency law can affect your business strategy.
4. What four requirements must an invention meet to be patentable?
5. In general, how are issues such as copyright infringement and contracts being handled in the Internet environment?

Experiencing Entrepreneurship

1. Find a business owner who deals with consumers and ask about the trade laws that affect the running of the business. Is the business owner fully aware of all laws that affect his or her business?
2. Conduct a random examination of business web sites to see how many businesses use copyrights or respect the trademark status of other companies.

Resources

Axtell, Roger E. (1996). *The Do's and Taboos of International Trade: A Small Business Primer.* New York: John Wiley & Sons.

Bangs, D. H. (1994). *The Start-up Guide,* 2nd ed. Dover, NH: Upstart Publishing.

Corporate Agents, Inc. (1995). *The Essential Limited Liability Company Handbook.* Grants Pass, OR: The Oasis Press.

Friedman, R. (1993). *The Complete Small Business Legal Guide.* Chicago: Dearborn Enterprises.

Jennings, Marianne Moody (1996). *Business: Its Legal, Ethical, and Global Environment (The Wadsworth Series in Business Law),* 4th ed. Cincinnati: Southwestern.

Kurz, Raymond A., Bart G. Newland, Steven Lieberman, and Celine Jimenez (1996). *Internet and the Law: Legal Fundamentals for the Internet User.* Government Institutes.

Nicholas, T. (1992). *The Complete Guide to Business Agreements.* Chicago: Dearborn Trade.

Nicholas, T. (1993). *The Complete Guide to "S" Corporations.* Chicago: Dearborn Publishing Group.

Whitmyer, Claude, and Salli Rasberry (1994). *Running a One-Person Business.* Berkeley, CA: Ten Speed Press.

Winston, Arthur (1996). *The Complete Guide to Credit and Collection.* Englewood Cliffs, NJ: Prentice-Hall.

Internet Resources

Advertising Law Internet Site
http://www.webcom.com/~lewrose/home.html
This site is maintained by a law firm and contains information about advertising law, choosing a name for your business, and business opportunities.

The Company Corporation
http://virtumall.com/CC/
How to incorporate quickly, cheaply, and online in any state.

Corporate Agents Inc.: The Business Incorporating Guide
http://www.corporate.com/cover_f.html
A site to help you incorporate.

Inventions and Patents
http://www.tucson.com/patents/
Good information for people who want to make money off their patents while protecting their interests.

MicroPatent
http://www.micropat.com/
This site charges to search for patent and trademark information.

Small Business Law Center
http://www.courttv.com/legalhelp/
This site is sponsored by CourtTV and has links to legal resources for entrepreneurs.

Trademark Law
http://www.law.cornell.edu/topics/trademark.html
Provides the text of U.S. trademark law (the Lanham Act) and recent U.S. Supreme Court decisions regarding trademarks.

The Nature of Start-up Companies

*The first rule of entrepreneurship
has to be that you do something you really love—
you can't make it otherwise.*
David Birch, economist, 1987

An Overview of the Journey

Preview

Understanding this chapter will give you the ability to

▶ **Discuss the life cycle stages of the average business and the focus of the entrepreneur at each stage.**

▶ **Contrast the nature of start-ups, rapidly growing companies, and mature companies.**

▶ **Discuss entry strategies for new businesses.**

▶ **List the pros and cons of starting versus buying a business.**

▶ **Identify financial resources available to start-up companies.**

▶ **Explain bootstrapping and how it can help the entrepreneur get a new business started with as few resources as possible.**

▶ **Describe the nature of angels and what they look for in start-up investments.**

▶ **List government sources of funding for new ventures.**

▶ **Distinguish between debt and equity financing.**

Terms to Know

Young Entrepreneurs—Minicase

Marianne Szymanski
Toy Tips® Inc.

As businesses grow and evolve, they sometimes become something quite different than what they started out to be. Today Toy Tips® is a national marketing and research firm that has made its founder, Marianne Szymanski, a sought-after media guest with regular spots on "Good Morning America," the Fox News Channel, CNN, "USA Today," "CNBC Power Lunch," and many others. But in 1991, Toy Tips® was the dream of a 23-year-old college graduate in marketing and psychology from Marquette University in Milwaukee.

Like many entrepreneurs, Szymanski was opportunistic and saw a problem that needed to be solved. Her experience in the toy industry revealed that there was no unbiased source of information on the best toys for kids at particular ages. In fact, Szymanski found that the magazines touting top 10 lists of toys were really paid by the toy manufacturers—hardly an unbiased source. Seeing an opportunity, she decided to make her yet-to-be company the source of that information.

Using her savings, Szymanski began the business as a 900 number, the National Toy Information Hotline, where people could call to receive the latest information on toy safety, product recalls, and tips on age-appropriate toys. Fortunately, the media picked up an appearance on a local talk show and the business took off faster than she expected. A letter to the Toy Manufacturers of America, the voice of the toy industry, resulted in information and hundreds of samples from toy companies. Working out of her home testing toys on the living room floor with neighbor children, Szymanski soon realized that she needed another location. She worked out a barter arrangement with a pediatrician, and ultimately was given the opportunity to work out of the child care center at Marquette University. By the end of 1991,

she was working with 50 manufacturers. By the end of 1992, the number had swelled to 140 and her revenues had doubled. To date she has tested more than 10,000 toys from more than 600 manufacturers.

Even though the business was growing, Szymanski couldn't afford to hire employees, so she asked the university to offer an internship program for students with her company. Engineering students tested the toys, journalism students helped her do fact checking and gather information for articles, public relations students helped her with her media tour, psychology and education majors participated in focus groups and testing, and marketing students developed questionnaires and researched the needs of parents. Media contacts gave Szymanski the publicity she needed to attract the attention of companies such as Toys 'R' Us, McDonald's, and Rayovac.

Her biggest challenge is to find the best way to structure the company so that she is free to do the consulting and media work she loves. This may entail splitting the company into two divisions and hiring someone to manage the day-to-day activities, such as the magazine and the research.

Today Szymanski combs the toy world to provide research allowing parents and companies to choose toys that are safe and fun. Her company has also taken on the adult world with the Toy Tips® Annual Executive Toy Test, a fund raiser to raise money for children's charities and a chance for executives to relive their childhood. Szymanski also publishes *Toy Tips® Magazine*, a semiannual publication with a distribution of 3 million copies. Toy Tips® Inc. now has two web sites, and Szymanski is publishing her first book, *Executive Toy Tips*, based on a five-year study of appropriate toys for the office.

In what ways was Szymanski able to bootstrap her way to entrepreneurial success?

Entrepreneurs have many choices about how they approach the start-up of their new ventures, and certainly no one approach is more successful than another. Some entrepreneurs, like Mo Siegel, founder of Celestial Seasonings herbal tea company, started from scratch because he wanted to live in Colorado and couldn't find an existing company that suited his needs. Other entrepreneurs choose to buy an existing company. Wayne Huizenga bought a fledgling young company and turned it into Blockbuster Entertainment Corporation. Marianne Szymanski (see Young Entrepreneurs—Mini-case) saw a need in the marketplace for a source that would give parents and grandparents the information they need to make wise choices about the toys they purchase. That moment of opportunity recognition resulted in the bootstrap start-up of the sole independent toy research company in the United States.

No matter how start-up is approached, once a business is started and a company is formed, it has much in common with other companies at various stages in their market lives. This chapter highlights the journey entrepreneurs make when they recognize opportunity and conceive the idea for a new business. It begins with an overview of the entire journey, looking at the various stages in the life of a business. This overview is important because, as the saying goes, if you don't know where you're going, you won't know when you get there. The chapter then turns to issues specifically related to start-up.

Business Life Cycles

Companies seem to have life cycles that parallel those of human beings. They begin at conception, go through the labor of start-up, are born, endure adolescence, become mature adults (though sometimes rather immature

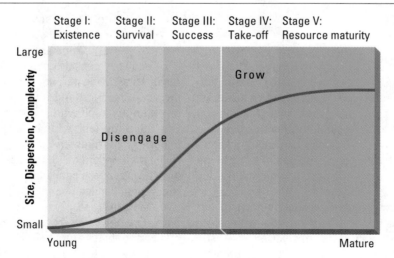

Figure 4.1
The Churchill-Lewis Growth Stages

Source: Neil C. Churchill and Virginia L. Lewis, "The Five Stages of Small Business Growth," in William A. Sahlman and Howard H. Stevenson, *The Entrepreneurial Venture* (Boston: Harvard Business School Publications, 1992). Reprinted by permission of *Harvard Business Review*. Copyright 1983, 1991 by President and Fellows of Harvard College, all rights reserved.

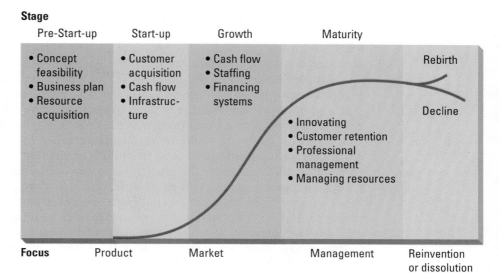

**Figure 4.2
The Life Cycle of the
Company**

adults), and ultimately die or are reborn in another form. For some companies the life cycle is brief, a rocket burst that lasts only a short time. For others life spans decades as is the case with the visionary companies discussed in Chapter 7.

At each stage of the life cycle, the needs and goals of the company differ. Terpstra and Olson reviewed the myriad theories and models of organizational life cycles and stages of development and concluded that in general, organizations tend to move sequentially through major stages of development, each with its own set of management issues.[1] For example, start-ups tend to be associated with marketing and financial problems, whereas strategic and management issues plague the growing company. [2]

Churchill and Lewis developed a simple model to describe the life cycle of small and growing businesses.[3] As Figure 4.1 depicts, the model contains five stages as well as measures of size, dispersion, and complexity.

As a company moves from young to mature, it typically grows larger in size, becomes less focused and more diverse, and attains a greater degree of complexity. As depicted, the model is static and doesn't reflect the changes going on in the organization as it moves through the cycles.

Figure 4.2 depicts the focus of the entrepreneur at each stage in the cycle. It includes an additional stage, the pre-start-up stage, which would precede the existence stage in the Churchill-Lewis model. This stage includes feasibility analysis (the testing of the new business concept) and the gathering of resources for start-up—in other words, all those activities that take place prior to actually going into business.

The pre-start-up stage takes place well before the business is actually operating. During this stage and the rest of start-up into early growth, the company tends to be very product focused. In other words, it tends to look inward to the concept that forms the basis of the business opportunity. This introverted period is the reason entrepreneurs are often accused of being "in love" with their products—the great idea. The products in this case may be manufactured products, services, or, more likely, a combination of both.

Start-up begins when the company is ready to do business in the marketplace. The product focus continues as the new venture tests its operations plan and puts an infrastructure in place to respond effectively to the demands of early growth. As the firm moves into the growth stage, if its operations are well honed, it begins to look outward to the marketplace and the potential customers with whom it will need to build lasting relationships. If the company successfully traverses the growth stage and establishes a loyal customer base, it becomes a mature company with relatively more predictable revenue flows. It now faces a new set of challenges, however: how to manage the resources it has accumulated over time and how to remain competitive. If at maturity the company becomes complacent and continues to operate the way it always has, it will ultimately decline. If, on the other hand, the company looks for ways to reinvent itself through new technology, new products, and new processes, it can experience a rebirth and go through another growth cycle. This is, of course, a very simplified rendition of a company's life cycle and reflects an average business.

In reality, the length of time from conception to maturity will vary with the industry, the type of business, and environmental factors present during the growth process, and it is by no means a sure path. Some companies fail before the growth stage; others can't gather sufficient resources or don't have the infrastructure in place to permit them to successfully pass through the

 Entrepreneurship in Action

Markets Change; Companies Must Too

Few companies can claim a successful life span of 63 years and then find themselves in Chapter 7 bankruptcy almost overnight. But that's precisely what happened to Dydee Diaper, a Boston-based diaper service founded in 1933. The company grew steadily on the strength of the baby boom and the fact that cloth diapers were the only option. Even when disposable diapers entered the market in the 1970s, the belief that disposables were not "natural" fueled continued growth for diaper services. In fact, from 1987 to Earth Day 1990, Dydee tripled its business to $5 million in sales.

But the next year saw a dramatic assault in the form of an advertising campaign by the manufacturers of disposable diapers to convert professionals of the baby-boom generation to the convenience of disposables. The result: Dydee's sales began dropping by 20 percent a year. In an attempt to save the company, Dydee added delivery, pickup, and recycling services, but the margins on disposables were too small, and by then most of its cloth customers had made the switch. Dydee found it could no longer cover its overhead and, in 1997, was forced to file bankruptcy.

This case points up the need for entrepreneurs to watch market trends carefully. Never assume that what has worked in the past will continue to work in the future. Customers' needs and preferences can change virtually overnight, and entrepreneurs must constantly stay just ahead of the market so they can be proactive rather than reactive.

SOURCE: Phaedra Hise, "Industry Bottoms Out, Disposes of Diaper Service," *Inc.,* June 1997, p. 32.

high-growth stage, and they fail at this point. Still others manage to survive the trials of start-up and growth to reach a mature stage, only to succumb to competitive pressures or dramatic changes in the market to which they are ill equipped to respond. Unlike human beings, however, a company can reach a mature stage and then—through the introduction of new technology, for example—be "reborn" and go through a new growth stage. Certainly technology has been the catalyst for many a rebirth and many a death as well when companies failed to recognize the substantial changes it has brought about. It is important, therefore, to understand the nature of companies at the five basic stages so that the growing company can adjust its strategies to effectively prepare itself for the next phase in its life cycle.

The Nature of Start-ups

Ambiguity is the ubiquitous companion of any new venture. Born into an uncertain environment, start-ups by nature must be flexible, able to change quickly in response to rapidly changing needs and requirements. Whereas in the past new businesses started with a narrow geographic focus, purchased equipment and technology to last for the long term, designed products and services before finding customers to purchase them, and built large, bureaucratic organizations, today the rules have changed. Today high-growth ventures have the distinct advantage of starting with flexible, dynamic organizations poised to respond to change and even create change as well.

The New-Venture Creation Process

Recall from Chapter 1 that the *entrepreneur* is only one component in the process of new-venture creation (see Figure 4.3). The behaviors and experience of the entrepreneur interact with all the other components of the new-venture process to create a company.

Every entrepreneur brings to a new venture a unique set of characteristics and behaviors that spring from the entrepreneur's cultural background, education, socioeconomic status, experience, and the family environment in which he or she was raised. All of these factors have given the entrepreneur a set of values that affect everything she or he does, from intentions to management style. And although we can say with some degree of confidence that all entrepreneurs have a special kind of passion that drives them to take a calculated risk to bring together resources to commercialize an opportunity, it is

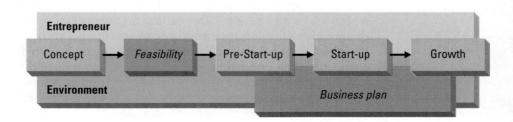

**Figure 4.3
The New-Venture
Process**

equally clear that other characteristics vary greatly among entrepreneurs. No two entrepreneurs are alike.

Another component, the **environment**, is the most comprehensive component in the venture creation process. It includes all those factors, apart from the entrepreneur's personal background, that affect the decision to start a business. Within specific industries and in specific geographic regions, environmental variables and the degree of their impact will differ. The bottom line is that the environment for start-ups is vastly different than it was less than a decade ago, so the strategies and tactics entrepreneurs use to start their businesses must change as well. The environment was discussed at length in Chapter 2.

The *new-venture* **concept**, the third component in the entrepreneurial process, is the development of the initial business idea, taking into consideration the entrepreneur's goals and the environment in which the business will operate. The business concept forms the basis for an analysis of feasibility to answer the question "Is there market acceptance for the concept?" A well-conceived concept that embodies a customer-centered focus and a goal of superior quality throughout lays the foundation for a world-class business.

Once feasibility has been established, the entrepreneur can begin to look at capital requirements to implement the concept and determine which resources will need to be gathered and whether they will be in the form of capital, labor, or equipment. Chapter 5 presents a complete discussion of the development of a business concept.

With feasibility established, the entrepreneur enters the **pre-start-up** stage, where all the activities related to developing a complete business plan, designing and building a prototype, and gathering the resources (equipment, labor, facility, capital, licenses and permits, intellectual property rights) prior to actually starting the business take place.

No real agreement exists on when the actual **start-up stage** begins. Some argue that a company is in "start-up" from the moment the idea for the business is conceived, whereas others see start-up as the early period in a company's life when it first begins to deal with its customers. This book will consider start-up that point where the new venture has gathered all the necessary resources and is ready to begin doing business with its customers.

An entrepreneur starts a business because the concept appears to be feasible. But testing the concept in the real world is what will actually determine if the business has viability, in other words, whether it has a life beyond the business plan. **Viability** is the point at which the company is generating internal cash flows sufficient to allow the business to survive on its own without cash infusions from outside sources such as the entrepreneur's own resources, investors, or a bank loan. Depending on the type of business and the capital requirements for getting into the business, the point of viability will change. If viability doesn't occur for two or more years due to substantial start-up costs, it will be important to consider ways to reduce those costs. One way may be through the use of a virtual corporation and subcontracting many of the more capital-intensive activities to a firm that has achieved greater efficiency in terms of cost. Chapter 6 discusses this option.

How Start-ups Will Look in the Twenty-first Century

Start-ups come from a learning curve that says bigger is not more efficient and the largest firms are not always the greatest source of innovation. The world-class start-ups of the twenty-first century will have several notable characteristics. They will

▶ Be smaller and more responsive

▶ Look for niche markets at a global level

▶ Innovate with teams and fast-paced product development

▶ Be oriented toward superior quality and customer service

▶ Have a flatter organizational structure

▶ Rely on outsourcing and use the virtual company form as their initial structure

▶ Create value by giving people (employees and customers) a major stake in the organization

Given that the start-up stage is characterized by ambiguity, uncertainty, volatility—even chaos—and usually a lack of sufficient resources, entrepreneurs typically have resorted to various techniques to keep the company moving forward. One of the most popular start-up forms to come out of the information revolution is the networked or virtual company. It is the antithesis of the vertically integrated, rigid, operational forms of the past that led to some of the huge, bureaucratic organizations that today are struggling to remain viable against an onslaught of scrappy entrepreneurial companies. The most successful start-up companies are those that can bring together a network of creative people and companies to supplement or supply the scarce resources the start-up needs. Some examples are Pixar Animation, the genius

The Real World of Entrepreneurship

Opportunities Sometimes Result from Breaking with Tradition

Entrepreneurs often are advised to find a unique product or service and an industry with no competition, or at least very little. Entrepreneur Norm Brodsky believes quite the opposite and suggests three criteria for selecting a new business:

1. Find a concept that has been around awhile, one that everyone understands, because educating the market is expensive.

2. Find an industry that isn't in touch with its customers, and get in touch to meet their needs.

3. Find a niche in the market that you can control.

SOURCE: Norm Brodsky, "The Three Criteria for a Successful New Business," *Inc.,* April 1, 1996, p. 21.

behind the movie *Toy Story,* and TLC, the company that produces three-dimensional foam maps for Rand McNally to help children learn geography.

Several recent forces have changed the nature of start-up strategies in such a way as to allow small companies to compete against much larger companies on a relatively level playing field. Among these forces are shortened product life cycles, the global marketplace, customers' expectations about quality and service, and the network economy.

Shortened Product Life Cycles   Brought about principally by faster product development and new distribution channels, shortened product life cycles have forced new companies to seek relationships with established companies to gain a competitive advantage. Most start-ups lack the capital resources to do fast-cycle product development or equip a manufacturing plant to produce their first product. However, start-ups usually have new, innovative products designed to serve a niche in the market. By forming a strategic alliance with an existing company in the industry, the start-up gets into the market more quickly, and both the start-up and the strategic alliance benefit.

The Real World of Entrepreneurship

Entertainment: The Virtual Industry

It is often stated that the information/technology revolution enabled the organization form that is now known as the "virtual corporation." But the essence of the virtual corporation, a network of strategic alliances, has been alive and well in the entertainment industry for almost 30 years. The primary reason Los Angeles (Hollywood) continues to be the undisputed center of the entertainment industry is the strength of its tightly woven network of small craft companies, which have produced outstanding levels of revenue even during recessions. Within this network, start-up companies offering an innovative product or service can quickly pull together a team of the best specialists in their fields to collaborate on large projects. When the project is complete, the company doesn't have to continue to carry employees it no longer needs; rather, it can seek out the most qualified people for the next project. In fact, only 19 entertainment companies in California employ 1,000 or more people; 95,000 workers in the industry are free lance or work in companies with fewer than 10 people.

One classic example is tiny Hammerhead Productions, a four-person start-up that was operating out of an apartment in Burbank, California in 1995 when it was approached by producer Alan Marshall to do the special effects for his upcoming movie, *Showgirls.* The company didn't even own a computer, so the entrepreneurs convinced Marshall to front the $75,000 they needed to lease some computer workstations. In 1995, they grossed $500,000 and were heading toward $1.5 million in the second year.

The reason these "cybergnats" have become a force in the special-effects industry is that they operate lean and mean in an industry that is growing at more than 25 percent per year with huge overhead. Major studios outsource to these small bootstrapping companies for small special-effects jobs such as those created by Illusion Arts for movies like *Courage Under Fire* and *A Walk in the Clouds.* The original models for the dinosaurs in the blockbuster *Jurassic Park* came from animatronics specialist Stan Winston. Moreover, these "cybergnats" generally are easier to work with in an industry where ego often gets in the way of good business decisions.

SOURCES: Joel Kotkin and David Friedman, "Why Every Business Will Be Like Show Business," *Inc.,* March 1995, p. 64; Joel Kotkin, "The Rise of the Micromoguls," *Inc. Technology,* 3 (1996), p. 65.

Furthermore, putting together a web of the best companies, each focusing on its core competencies, results in a competitive advantage in and of itself because it enables the entrepreneurial venture and its collaborators to create customized products and processes that are difficult to duplicate (see "Entertainment: The Virtual Industry" on page 90).

The Global Marketplace   A global marketplace puts more pressure on start-ups to think globally from the start. To successfully compete, the new venture must seek out raw materials, products, and customers beyond its domestic borders. It must also be prepared for competitors from anywhere in the world. The phenomenal growth of the Internet has given small companies a global presence they have never had before.

Customers' Mounting Expectations for Quality and Service   Customer expectations have compelled new companies to look to customization of products and services to differentiate themselves in the marketplace. To customize effectively, companies must know their customers well, on an individual basis. Therefore, one-to-one, relationship marketing becomes a crucial component of the competitive advantage of a new firm. Chapters 10 and 11 discuss relationship marketing.

The Network Economy   The new **network economy** can be seen in many industries today, most notably in the entertainment industry (see insert "Entertainment: The Virtual Industry"), but also in the Silicon Valley. In the 1980s, companies in the Silicon Valley faced a significant threat from well-financed Japanese and Korean firms that had succeeded in dominating the manufacture of microchips. The smaller U.S. firms knew that the future lay not in attempting to compete directly with Japan and Korea but in collaborating to develop unique, customized systems and components that were difficult to copy—a niche in the market. Collaboration of this type translates into the quicker development of more innovative products because the strategic team works like a well-oiled machine. In addition, the collaborative approach gives the smaller company great flexibility to respond to changes in customer preferences and market demand.

The Nature of Rapidly Growing Companies

Growth is not a natural extension of start-up; it doesn't often happen automatically, even when care has been taken in the creation of the company and the market. The choice to grow and how fast to grow is a conscious decision on the part of the entrepreneurial team. There are, however, some good reasons companies should make the conscious choice to grow:

▶ More businesses with fewer than 100 employees file bankruptcy.

▶ Survival rates double for companies that have grown.

▶ The most aggressive companies have an 80 percent survival rate.

▶ Companies need to have revenues greater than $500,000 annually to escape "small-business vulnerability."

▶ The probability of survival increases significantly after $1 million in annual sales. Only about 3 percent of all companies realize this level of sales.[4]

Growth is certainly an important component of any entrepreneurial strategy, but not all companies are destined to grow, even when growth has been the goal of the entrepreneur. Small retail stores and restaurants rarely achieve substantial size unless they become a chain or franchise operation. Other lifestyle-type businesses are intentionally kept small, as the purpose for their existence is to provide a job for the owner. This section focuses on the nature of companies with a potential for growth.

Stages of Growth

Sometime after start-up and the initial market launch of the product or service, entrepreneurial companies with good concepts and intentions to grow experience growth. This growth comes about in stages much like a miniversion of the life cycle of the business. The first stage of growth typically is that caused by an *innovative product or service* that allows the company to experience a period of time in which there is no direct competition to its offering. Companies that have started new industries, such as Federal Express (overnight delivery) and Digital Equipment (minicomputers), have given themselves an edge in this stage of the growth cycle. This early growth is usually controlled by the entrepreneur or founding team that assumes the responsibilities of sales, advertising, purchasing, personnel, and other functions of the business. At this point, others have little to say about decisions that are made. As growth increases, however, it soon becomes apparent that some of the core functions of the business must be *delegated* to others if the company is to grow effectively. This is a difficult time for entrepreneurs because generally they are very reluctant to relinquish control of any important aspect of the business. When they do, they are often unsure how to clearly assign duties and responsibilities, and give sufficient authority to others to carry them out. Eventually, if growth continues, those to whom responsibilities have been delegated will in turn need to delegate a portion of their responsibilities to others, creating yet another level of control. If left unchecked, the company ends up displaying the stereotypical bureaucratic hierarchy that may ultimately prevent it from remaining flexible and competitive.

An alternative to the traditional organizational growth pattern is *growth by participation* or *growth by empowerment and teamwork*. This strategy is discussed in depth in Chapter 9; for now, suffice it to say that a company that supports teamwork to accomplish its goals stands a better chance of reaching them.

Another problem is that growth often occurs too rapidly in the form of uncontrolled growth. Unlike the traditional growth pattern that moves through many stages, companies that experience immediate high growth shortly after or even during start-up barely have a chance to catch their breath before they face the need for an infrastructure that can respond to

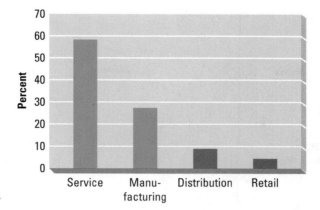

Figure 4.4
The 1997 *Inc. 500* by
Business Sector
Source: Inc. 500, 1997.

tremendous demand. This is because high-growth firms typically bypass the normal stages of growth, which can be very dangerous if the company is not prepared for it or doesn't respond quickly. Osborne Computer Corporation is one example of a company that experienced explosive growth and couldn't handle it. Compaq Computer, Inc., on the other hand, experienced equally explosive growth and survived to become one of the most successful computer companies in existence because it was prepared for growth.

The Fastest-Growing Private Companies

Every year *Inc.* celebrates the 500 fastest-growing private companies in the United States. Its report gives a snapshot of the nature of firms in the growth stage, specifically high-growth firms. The economic sectors represented by the 500 in the 1997 report are as shown in Figure 4.4. As expected, service dominated as the economic sector of choice, but manufacturing made a strong showing as well.

This group also displayed the changes in the environment for entrepreneurship that has shortened the start-up process. As Figure 4.5 depicts, more than half of all the 1997 Inc. 500 started in six months or less from conception of the idea.

Some unique characteristics emerged from this group that help us better understand the nature of growth companies:

▶ *They are optimistic and think big.* The co-founder of $5 million Computer Free America, Tony Cooper, reports that he had always wanted to be the largest employer in Clark County, Ohio.[5]

▶ *Computers are still the key to success.* The 1997 Inc. 500 list reported that 36 percent of the companies on the list were in some aspect of the computer industry. That is the highest percentage in the past decade.[6]

▶ *Entrepreneurship has become an extreme sport.* With more companies in the technology niche, the time from idea to start-up has decreased dramatically. Allyn Kramer, the founder of Dallas-based Kramer Lead Marketing

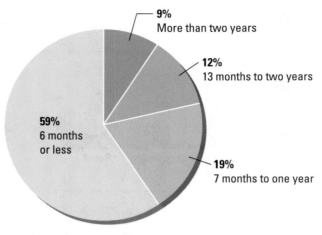

Length of Time from Idea to Start-Up*

9%
More than two years

12%
13 months to two years

59%
6 months
or less

19%
7 months to one year

Figure 4.5
Time to Start-up
Source: Inc. 500, 1997.

* Out of 412 respondents; numbers do not
add up to 100% because of rounding.

Group, started his business within six months because he understood the
industry and knew whom he needed to contact.[7]

▶ *The average number of employees per business has increased dramatically.*
In 1992, the average number of employees was 17; for the 1997 Inc. 500,
the average was 121.[8]

Fast-growth companies can be found in virtually every industry:

▶ The Home Depot, a chain of warehouse, do-it-yourself outlets, grew 7,000
percent in value in the 1980s.

▶ Liz Claiborne, an apparel company, grew 3,400 percent in value in the
1980s.

▶ Adobe Systems, a software company, grew 1,600 percent in the 1980s.

In general, fast-growth companies have experienced consistent 50 percent or greater annual growth over many years.[9] After an extended period
of fast growth, the company usually slows to a rate closer to 20 to 30 percent per year. Clearly, however, there are firms such as Cogentrix, a developer
and operator of cogeneration facilities, which grew by 141,681 percent in
five years in the late 1980s ($133,000 to more than $200 million in revenues), but that type of growth usually is not sustained over a long period of
time.[10] On the other end of the spectrum are industries such as steel, where
the modest 16 percent annual growth rate of a Worthington Industries is actually 5 to 10 times the industry average and is considered fast for that industry.[11] In general, fast-growth companies are found in the earlier stages of

the business life cycle—the period between 5 and 15 years into the life of the company.

Fast-growth companies are also responsible for the creation of considerable personal wealth and philanthropy. The Limited was started with $5,000 in borrowed money in 1963. Today its founder, Leslie Wexner, is worth more than $2 billion and is known for his philanthropy.[12]

The Risk of High Growth

The high-growth period is one of great risk for the company as it invests all of its resources into expanding the operations. This requires purchasing new equipment, increasing inventories, and hiring additional employees and perhaps management personnel. It is also the point at which the company begins to attract the attention of the competition, which previously may not have taken it very seriously. Because growth is expensive, it becomes increasingly difficult for the company to make large profits. Many an apparently successful company has found the downward fall from fast growth much steeper than the upward climb. This is true of companies such as ZZZZ Best, Chuck E. Cheese's PizzaTime Theater, Wedtech, and People Express Airlines, all of which are out of business. Nevertheless, on the whole, growth companies tend

 Entrepreneurship in Action

Fast-Growth Flowers?

The term *fast-growth company* usually brings to mind a high-tech company such as Genentech or Netscape Communications. It does not typically conjure up images of roses and daffodils. But no one can argue that New York–based 1-800-FLOWERS is a fast-growth company. Of course, Jim McCann didn't know that when he acquired the debt-ridden company in 1989 with sales at $6 million. By 1994, under his creative guidance, the company was generating $100 million in sales and in 1995 more than $200 million.

In 1976, McCann, then an administrator in a group home, got the urge to own his own business. A friend told him about a small flower shop for sale in Manhattan. The price was only $10,000, so he bought it, renamed it Flora Plenty, and brought someone in to manage it on a daily basis. Actually, the time was ripe for this type of business; the market was showing a strong interest in plants and flowers, so very quickly he opened 2 more stores, then 12 more over the next 10 years. He was blanketing New York City with flowers and enjoying growing profits: $200,000 in the second year and almost $500,000 in the third year. By this time

he had left his job. Things were going well when, in 1984, a company called 1-800-FLOWERS, a telemarketing company, opened in Dallas and asked him to fill their orders in New York. This opened up a new market for McCann. But by 1985, 1-800-FLOWERS was in trouble and turned to McCann, who by now was one of the top five florists in the country, to help it turn the company around. McCann didn't want to *work* for the company, however; he wanted to buy it and inject some fresh ideas.

It took two years of negotiation, but in 1987 McCann bought the company for $2 million, assuming $7 million in debt. Basically he bought the name and the telephone operation. He began the turnaround by moving the operation to New York and merging it with his retail operation, then set out to build back the customer relationships that had been lost by offering such things as same-day delivery and guaranteed freshness. In 1990 he began offering gift baskets, which ultimately became a $30 million profit center for the company. Jim McCann has always wanted to run a big company, and he fully intends to grow 1-800-FLOWERS to a billion-dollar company.

to be very durable. For example, when *Inc.* studied the 1985 class of the Inc. 500, it found that the failure rate is very low, only 57 companies out of 500. Furthermore, the aggregate annual sales of these companies swelled from $3.5 billion in 1984 to $29 billion in 1994. Microsoft was on the Inc. 500 list in 1985 with 75 employees and sales of $6.9 million in its base year of 1980. By 1985, however, it had reported sales of $97 million, and by 1994 it had exploded to 16,000 employees and $4.7 billion in sales. Though Microsoft is certainly the best performer from the class of 1985, it is not the only company that experienced meteoric growth during that period. But like Microsoft, the others tended to be in software publishing, computer distribution, and electronics manufacturing. There were notable exceptions, however, such as ABC Supply (a roofing and construction materials supplier), Amtran (a charter air service), and Drug Emporium (a drugstore chain).[13]

The Nature of Mature Companies

If the primary concerns during start-up center on gathering resources and the chief concern of companies in the growth stage is raising money and creating the infrastructure to grow, the focus of attention at the third stage, that of a mature company, is to consolidate and control the financial gains made during the growth phase. At the same time, the company doesn't want to lose the entrepreneurial spirit and flexibility it achieved during the first two stages. As, perhaps, a much larger company, the tug of war between the advantages of smallness and the need to professionally manage the company can threaten the company's very existence. It is at this stage that the company becomes something quite separate from the entrepreneur. Whereas in the early stages the entrepreneur or the founding team *was* the business, in the mature

The Real World of Entrepreneurship

Why Do Businesses Fail?

Michael Gerber, author of the successful *The E-Myth Revisited,* believes that small businesses, defined as 1 to 100 employees and $1 million to $5 million in revenues, fail because they haven't established the infrastructure necessary to grow. He has identified 10 reasons businesses fail:

▶ Lack of management systems

▶ Lack of vision and purpose by principals

▶ Lack of financial planning and review

▶ Overdependence on specific individuals in the business

▶ Poor market segmentation and strategy

▶ Failure to establish or communicate company goals

▶ Lack of knowledge about the market and the competition

▶ Inadequate capitalization or lack of funds

▶ Absence of a standardized quality program

▶ Owners concentrating on the technical rather than the strategic work at hand

Source: Michael Gerber, *The E-Myth Revisited* (New York: HarperBusiness, 1996).

stage, the company itself is at center stage. It now has the vision and culture, management talent, resources, and financial wherewithal to be a force in the economy if it manages to hold onto its entrepreneurial spirit.

Because mature companies are by nature more complex in terms of management structure, operations, customer relations, supplier relations, technology, and finances, they require systems, controls, and new strategies to manage these resources effectively. For example, whereas the micromanaging of cash flow consumes the entrepreneur in stages one and two, it becomes a less demanding issue in the third stage, where the loss of a customer or supplier will have a less dramatic impact on the company's financial position. In other words, the bootstrap strategies the entrepreneur used to keep the company alive in the early years become a waste of valuable management time in a mature company.

In new ventures, the entrepreneur, as the driving force, typically exhibits a more autocratic style of leadership, a need to be in control. Even where the venture is started by a team, as is the norm with growth ventures today, there is usually a lead entrepreneur on the team and the other team members generally share the philosophy and goals of the leader. The shift from an autocratic, lead entrepreneur to a professionally managed, participative mature company is not easy because the entrepreneur must learn to delegate authority and responsibility, something that generally is not part of his or her makeup. It is, however, crucial to becoming a successful, mature, entrepreneurial company that will live beyond the tenure of the original founding team.

To build a company that reaches maturity with a core ideology and an effective infrastructure in place that allows it to experience continued innovation and growth requires a different mindset than that of the pure entrepreneur who essentially wants to start a company, build it quickly, cash out, and use his or her accumulated wealth to do something else. Those who have the desire to create an enduring company generally have a drive for progress: continual improvement, a sense of purpose that goes beyond making money, and a desire to create something that will exist for decades beyond them. This is the key to maintaining the entrepreneurial spirit beyond start-up.

Starting a Business

Any journey begins at the beginning. For entrepreneurs that usually means with the idea for a new business that came from the recognition of an opportunity in the marketplace. (Opportunity recognition and the development of a new-business concept are discussed in Chapter 5.) Once you know what your product or service is and the kind of business you are creating, you must decide whether to start a new business or buy an existing business and turn it into an entrepreneurial venture that will satisfy your needs. In general, entrepreneurs start businesses from scratch when they can't find an existing business compatible with their product/service idea or goals. Starting a business is probably the most common route for entrepreneurs, but it's not the only one. Some entrepreneurs choose instead to buy an existing business.

Finding Resources for the Business

The Internet is an excellent source for beginning your search for resources for your business. Here are a few places to start. Remember: as you go to each site, look for hot links (icons or underlined words or addresses) that will take you to other sites related to what you're looking for.

For example, go to http://www.sbaonline.sba.gov/. From there click on *Your Local SBA Resources* to go to a United States map, where you can click on your home state. In your home state, you can find the city closest to you that maintains a local SBA office. So by typing in only one address, you can go to many other sites just by clicking your mouse button.

Here are some additional sites that will be useful in your search for resources for your business:

▶ http://www.moneyhunter.com

▶ http://www.themoneystore.com

▶ http://www.microsoft.com

Buying a Business

Buying a business has several advantages:

▶ It's less risky than starting from scratch, because facilities, employees, and customers are likely to be in place.

▶ It's an easier route to owning a business if the entrepreneur has limited business experience.

▶ The chances for success are increased, particularly if the business has a good reputation, because of established contacts in the industry and a customer base.

▶ The business may have established trade credit, which is crucial because relationships with suppliers and others take a long time to develop.

▶ The owner may be willing to stay on board for a time to help the entrepreneur learn the business.

However, existing businesses rarely come without problems. In the first place, the business may have been put up for sale because it was not successful. It may have developed a negative reputation, its inventory may be outdated, and its location may no longer be appropriate. On top of all this, chances are the owner will price the business at more than it's worth in the marketplace because he or she has put so much effort into it. To further compound the risk, an owner is not likely to confess the real reasons the business is being sold. These reasons may include the following:

▶ The company is being squeezed out of the market by larger companies.

▶ Key employees are leaving.

▶ The company faces the threat of a major legal action.

▶ Competitors' products are better.

▶ The owner has a better opportunity.

The owner is more likely to say the business is being sold because he or she wants to retire or is suffering from some illness. With this in mind, there are several questions to ask prior to purchasing a business:

▶ What is the potential for growth?

▶ Is the business profitable, with a strong cash flow?

▶ Does it have valuable assets?

▶ Is it free of legal problems?

▶ Does it have a good reputation?

▶ Are you capable of running the business?

▶ Is the location suitable?

▶ Is the business compatible with your goals?

Buying a business will take the same kind of research starting one does. You will need to

▶ Understand the industry and the market niche in which the business will operate

▶ Examine the records of the business

▶ Talk to employees, suppliers, and customers

▶ Examine equipment and facilities

▶ Examine all contracts

▶ Verify the value of the business based on industry statistics

There are several sources of information on business acquisitions. Probably the best source is talking to bankers, attorneys, and accountants who regularly work with businesses. The business opportunities section of newspapers such as *The Wall Street Journal* and trade publications are another source. It is also possible to investigate business liquidation auctions, but unless you're a turnaround specialist, taking on a business that has experienced severe problems may be riskier than starting from scratch.

Starting a New Business from Scratch

Creating a business has the principal advantage of allowing you to do everything exactly the way you want, in effect, starting with a clean slate. Often, however, the reality is that starting a new business is a matter of necessity. With limited funds, many entrepreneurs start out of their homes or garages because they do not have the financial ability to purchase an established business. Then, too, entrepreneurs frequently find it difficult to locate an ongoing business sufficiently compatible with what they are trying to do.

When the business you want to start doesn't exist, you need to start it from scratch. That's what Brenda Laurel did when she co-founded Purple Moon with Nancy Deyo. This unique software company targets the niche of girls 7 to 12 years old who aren't entertained by the current action software that caters to boys. (Andy Freeberg)

Starting a business, however, is generally more time consuming and potentially costlier than buying an existing business. That "clean slate" referred to earlier means the entrepreneur must purchase, rent, or borrow everything it takes to run the business. Furthermore, employees, suppliers, channels of distribution, and customers must all be identified and developed. In other words, start-up resources can be significant and not easy to come by.

Start-up Resources

The most commonly asked question of entrepreneurs is "where can I find money to start and build a business?" The answer is at once simple and complex. It is simple because at start-up there are few choices, and all those choices point back to the entrepreneur: his or her resources and whom she or he knows. The answer is complex from the standpoint that putting together sufficient resources to start a business requires enormous creativity and persistence, with the ultimate reward being a company that is able to reach critical mass and take advantage of significantly more choices for growth capital.

Bootstrappers are start-up entrepreneurs who have realized that to get what they need to start their businesses—location, equipment, money, and perhaps employees—they must possess a double dose of creative ingenuity and outright arrogance. Literally, bootstrapping is begging, borrowing, or leasing everything required to start the venture. It is the antithesis of the "big-money model" many espouse when they talk about entrepreneurial ventures.[14] More often than not, bootstrapping is a model for starting a business without money, or at least without any money beyond that provided by the entrepreneur's personal resources. Bootstrapping entrepreneurs generate money for the business any way they can. Papa John's International, the $164+ million pizza restaurant franchise, started with $1,600 in personal savings from its founder, John Schnatter, who founded the company in a broom closet in the back of a bar. In the beginning, he survived on profits from selling cheap beer. Later he sold the bar.[15] In the special-effects industry, tiny companies often lease rather than purchase their exceedingly expensive computer graphics workstations to keep start-up costs down.

Entrepreneur Resources

Most entrepreneurs start their ventures with their own resources. Bill Gates and Paul Allen started the software giant Microsoft in a cheap apartment in Albuquerque with virtually no overhead, a borrowed computer, and very little capital. Ross Perot, one of the great bootstrapping success stories, started EDS with $1,000. These entrepreneurs are the rule, not the exception; most new ventures are initially funded through the resources of the entrepreneur. There are many reasons for this:

1. New ventures by definition have no track record, so all the estimates of sales and profits are pure speculation and therefore very risky.

2. An enormous number of new ventures fail, so the risk for an outside investor is usually too high.

3. Many new ventures have no intellectual property rights or licenses that would give them a competitive advantage.

4. The founders often lack a significant track record of success.

5. Too many new ventures are "me too" versions of something that already exists. The owners have not identified or created a competitive advantage, so their chances of success are limited.

It's no wonder, then, that the only people willing to take the risk on a new venture are the entrepreneur and perhaps his or her friends and family. Entrepreneur resources include

- Savings
- Credit cards
- Friends and family
- Retirement funds from employment

▶ A part-time job

▶ Asset sales

▶ A second mortgage

Credit cards are an expensive choice for entrepreneurs, but when weighed against missing an opportunity to start a business, most entrepreneurs end up using them at start-up. At the extreme for this alternative were the three founders of Encore Productions, who predicted a boom in audiovisual shows for conventions and meetings. Every time the three founders received a credit card application in the mail, they sent it in. At one point, the three of them had accumulated 100 cards and $500,000 in credit. They used the cards like credit lines, paid them off quickly, and used them again. Started in 1988, Encore Productions today is a $16 million company.[16]

The Bootstrap Business Location

Many entrepreneurs stay close to home when they start their businesses, often literally *in* their homes. Businesses that don't require a storefront location can easily incubate in a spare room or the garage. This works well for "quiet businesses," but as Mark Ozkan—who started his $25 million computer mail-order business, Vektron International, in his home—found out, neighbors may not appreciate 18-wheelers coming down a residential street. Ozkan was cited by the city for violating an ordinance.

Some entrepreneurs have managed to negotiate free rent and lower lease rates in buildings where a tenant has gone bankrupt and the lessor is having difficulty releasing the space. Others have negotiated with larger companies to lease a portion of the larger company's space and take advantage of its reception area and conference room.

Hiring as Few Employees as Possible

Normally, the greatest single expense a business has is its payroll (including taxes and benefits). Subcontracting work to other firms, using temporary help, or hiring independent contractors can help to keep the number of employees and their consequent costs down. Marianne Szymanski founded Toy Tips Inc., a nationally recognized, independent product-testing and research firm in Milwaukee, using student interns from Marquette University and bartering for office space. The interns received university credit for working with her, and she didn't have to deal with payroll.

Leasing, Sharing, and Bartering Everything

At some point, virtually all new ventures need to acquire equipment, furnishings, and facilities. By leasing rather than purchasing major equipment and facilities, they don't tie up precious capital at a time when they badly need it to keep the new venture afloat. With a lease, there is usually no down payment and the payments are spread over time. A word of caution, however: new ventures should be careful about leasing new and rapidly changing technology for long periods of time, or they may find themselves with obsolete equipment but a continuing obligation.

When Marianne Szymanski (Young Entrepreneurs—Minicase) found that she needed a professional wardrobe for her media tour, she went to J.H. Collectibles and explained her situation. As a young businesswoman with a start-up company, she didn't have much money to spend, but she wanted J.H. Collectibles' clothes to wear on the tour. J.H. Collectibles liked her idea and gave her a wardrobe of clothes that she could promote on the tour while also promoting her business.

With more than $8 billion in goods and services exchanged in 1994, **bartering** is becoming a well-established tradition among entrepreneurs with new ventures.[17] More than 300,000 U.S. companies use some form of barter. In fact, large corporations going into global markets use it. In Russia, for example, Pepsico traded its surplus cola for vodka, which could be sold in the United States. Similarly, New Zealand traded dairy products for Russian coal. These barter arrangements are known as "one-to-one trades." In contrast, with barter exchange groups, a member can earn credits by providing products or services and then use those credits to "buy" products or services from another company when needed. Barter exchanges facilitate more complex barter agreements. The start-up fee for barter exchanges runs from $50 to $750 in addition to a fee of 10 to 15 percent of the value of each transaction.[18] At the end of the tax year, the exchange provides the participating company with a Form 1099 and also sends a copy to the IRS. Barter should always be considered a cash transaction.

Barter is a way for a growing company to conserve cash, reduce payables, collect on old receivables, and get rid of excess inventory. The only companies that are not appropriate for barter situations are those that have very specialized products and services that few people would need.

Any company considering joining a barter exchange should visit the trade exchange to talk to the people who will service the account and secure a list of clients and the various products and services they offer. It is important that the barter exchange's clientele have products and services that the company will use. The company should also do a background check on the exchange by contacting the National Association of Trade Exchanges, which is listed in the Resources section at the end of this chapter.

Other People's Money

Another key to bootstrapping success is getting customers to pay quickly and suppliers to allow more time for payment. Entrepreneurs must be willing to stay on top of receivables, which, if allowed to continue uncollected for too long, can put a young company in a dangerous position from a cash flow standpoint. Staying on top of receivables sometimes means walking an invoice through the channels of a major corporation in person or locating the person who can adjust the computer code that determines when a government agency pays its bills.

Suppliers are an important asset of any company and should be cultivated. Establishing a good relationship with major suppliers can result in favorable payment terms, since the supplier also has an interest in seeing the new venture succeed. Using several suppliers to establish credit is a tactic

Looking to American Indian tribes for start-up financing is becoming a growing trend because it offers substantial IRS savings. Ivan Makil, president of the Salt River Pima-Maricopa Indian community in Scottsdale, Arizona, looks for several characteristics when deciding whether to invest in a new business. The new business must be compatible with the tribe's vision and goals as well as be environmentally sensitive and profitable. The tribe has funded businesses such as Frozen Fusion, a retail store located inside Sky Harbor Airport in Phoenix. (Reed Rahn)

many entrepreneurial companies use when they can't get sufficient credit from one supplier. This approach has the additional benefit of identifying which supplier is the best source when the company is able to qualify for a larger credit line.

Bootstrapping Ethics

Whenever bootstrapping tactics are employed to allow a new venture to survive long enough to use other sources of financing, the issue of ethics arises. This is because when an entrepreneur bootstraps, by definition he or she is making the new venture appear much more successful than it is to gain some credibility in the market. In other words, many entrepreneurs walk a fine line between a desire to create credibility and deceit. Entrepreneurs must be careful, because credibility, if ill gotten, comes at a tremendous price to the business. Lying to survive will undoubtedly return to haunt the business at some future time.

Financing with Equity Sources

One way to raise capital for the new venture is to have people invest their money for an ownership share in the business. This ownership share is termed **equity,** and it means the investor puts his or her capital at risk; there is usually no guaranteed return and no protection against loss. Equity investors inherently differ from lenders; they are looking not for "repayment" but for an exit strategy with which they can cash out of the business with their investment having appreciated by a reasonable amount. Consequently, equity investors look first at growth in earnings and second at growth in assets. When they study the company's balance sheet, they look at inventory relative to sales. If it's growing, it may signal poor management practices. They also examine the current liabilities of the company and in particular look for loans to founders, which may be a sign that the company funds are being used to "bail out" the founder. The income statement tells them how profitable the company is in comparison to other companies in the same competitive market. It also indicates how capital intensive the company is. If the company has more than one product line, the investor will be interested to see if revenues are moving toward higher-margin products in the line. The most important statement to the investor will be the cash flow statement, because more businesses fail for lack of cash than for lack of profits.

Because of the inherent risks in start-up ventures, most entrepreneurs seek investment capital from people whom they know and who believe in them. Naturally, in the earliest stages of a new venture, the only people willing to risk their capital to fund a start-up are those who know the entrepreneur well. As the company gets off the ground and begins to show definite indications of market interest, others will be more willing to consider the risk. Family and friends present a unique dilemma from an investment standpoint, particularly if the company is using their money as well as outside investors'. They may feel they are entitled to more information and better treatment than outside investors. But it's important to treat all investors, whether friends, family, or others, the same in terms of offers and information provided.

In addition to personal resources already mentioned, entrepreneurs tap the equity in their brokerage accounts. Margin is, in effect, another source of credit, and when interest rates fall below those of the typical credit card, this source of funds becomes very attractive. With a margin loan, the security in the brokerage account is pledged as collateral for the money borrowed, similarly to pledging the equity in a home against a second mortgage. The collateralized security (buy or sell) can still be traded, but the owner cannot take possession of it until the loan is repaid.

The Nature of Angels

Private investors often are people the entrepreneur knows or has met through business acquaintances and networking opportunities. These **angels** are part of what is known as the informal risk capital market—the largest pool of risk

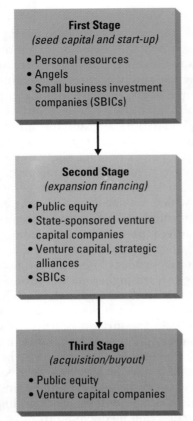

**Figure 4.6
Stages of Financing
for the New Venture**

Source: Kathleen Allen, *Launching New Ventures*, 2nd edition, Houghton Mifflin Company, © 1999.

capital in the United States, more than $50 billion. With all that power, it would seem they would be easy to find, but quite the contrary is true. Angels can't be found in a phone book. In fact, outside their own trusted circles of friends, they don't normally advertise their investment intentions. They come in all shapes and sizes, but they do have several characteristics in common:

▶ They typically are educated white men in their forties and fifties who have a net worth of more than $750,000 and have previously been entrepreneurs themselves.

▶ They normally invest between $10,000 and $500,000 in first-stage financing of start-ups or firms younger than five years.

▶ They tend to invest within a relatively short distance from home, as they like to be involved in the investment.

▶ They tend to prefer manufacturing, energy and resources, and service businesses. Retail ventures are less desirable because of their inordinately high rate of failure. They are also very active in financing high-technology firms.[19]

▶ They typically look to cash out of their investments within three to seven years. The risk/reward ratio they seek is a function of the age of the firm at the time of investment. If the venture is a start-up, they may want to earn as much as 10 times their original investment. If the venture has been up and running for a couple years, they may want up to five times their investment.

▶ They find their deals principally through referrals from business associates.

▶ They tend to make investment decisions more quickly than professional venture capitalists, and their requirements as to documentation, business plan, and due diligence may be lower.

The secret to finding these elusive angels is networking. Entrepreneurs need to get involved in the business community in such a way that they come into contact with sources of private capital or people who know these sources, such as lawyers, bankers, accountants, and other businesspeople. Developing these kinds of contacts takes time, so entrepreneurs shouldn't wait until they need the capital to begin looking for it.

Taking on an investor means giving up some ownership of the company. The process is normally completed through a private placement memorandum, which will be discussed in a later section. It is wise to include in the agreement a plan that allows the investor to exit the company should that issue arise. Including a buyout provision in the investment contract with a no-fault separation agreement will ensure that the entrepreneur doesn't have to wait for a criminal act such as fraud to end the relationship. Structuring the buyout to be paid out of earnings over time will avoid jeopardizing the financial health of the business. Above all, the entrepreneur should avoid using personal assets as collateral to protect an angel's investment.

The most common type of deal structure for private investors involves **convertible preferred stock,** which converts to common stock at an IPO if the entrepreneur decides to go that route. These securities include a "put" option that lets investors sell their stock back to the company at fair market value beginning at the end of the fifth year. Most puts have a three-year payout schedule so that the investor isn't totally cashed out until the end of the eighth year. This is good for a growing company that has limited cash resources.

Venture Capital

It has been estimated that fewer than 1 percent of all new ventures are funded with professional **venture capital,** a pool of managed funds. There are several reasons for this:

1. Start-up is the riskiest stage for a new company. Since there is always a steady supply of growing businesses that have a track record, the venture capitalist's money is probably better placed with those companies.

2. The bulk of venture capital today is supplied by institutional investors —pension funds, insurance companies, and so forth—and they tend to do larger deals than the typical start-up.

3. Venture capitalists normally want very high returns on their investments and a substantial stake in the company. Entrepreneurs, being control oriented, usually don't like to give up control of the company and tend to balk at the stringent requirements of the venture capitalist.

4. The goals of the venture capitalist often are at odds with the goals of many entrepreneurs. Venture capitalists have relatively short-term goals that revolve around getting a specific return on their investments in a specified period of time. Entrepreneurs, on the other hand, may have longer-term goals relative to building a company that endures.

Venture capital financing is discussed in more depth as a growth financing strategy in Chapter 18.

Financing with Debt

When entrepreneurs choose a debt instrument to finance a portion of the start-up costs, they are seeking a loan on which they will pay a market rate of interest. They will also be required to put up a personal or company asset as collateral, a guarantee they will repay the loan. The asset could be equipment, inventory, real estate, or the entrepreneur's house or car.

 Entrepreneurship in Action

Using Convertible Debt

When KnowledgePoint, a California software company, was founded in 1987, the entrepreneur, Michael Troy, calculated that it needed approximately $250,000 in start-up capital. Using its own resources, it was able to come up with the following:

$80,000 in salaries not paid for the first year
24,000 from Troy
20,000 from credit cards
50,000 home equity loan
―――――
$174,000

The company still needed another $80,000, which would come from friends, family, and business associates. Troy took an exit strategy approach to looking at the potential investment and chose convertible debentures as the investment vehicle. For investors it meant receiving an attractive rate of return (Troy decided on an interest rate of five points above prime with a cap at 15 percent) from day one and an opportunity to convert to equity at a prespecified future date. At the end of five years, the investors would receive their principal back, unless they had elected to convert the debt to common stock during the period.

When constructing a convertible debt deal, it is important to carefully spell out the conversion process in terms of when and how investors can convert to stock. Also, it often is more difficult to secure bank financing when using a convertible debenture offering, because for a time the company appears to have too much debt. That problem goes away if investors elect to convert the debt to equity during the prescribed term.

SOURCE: Jill Andresky Fraser, "Anatomy of a Financing: The Benefits of Convertible Debt," *Inc.,* February 1995, p. 115.

Commercial Banks

Banks are not a reliable source of either working capital or seed capital to fund a start-up venture. Since today banks are highly regulated, their loan portfolios are carefully scrutinized for risk, which they take great pains to avoid, and they are told in no uncertain terms not to make loans that have any significant degree of risk. However, with the availability of business credit cards, mutual funds, brokerage houses, leasing companies, and commercial finance and asset-based lending firms, even small companies have alternatives to commercial banks. In fact, the number of traditional banking customers declined several percentage points between 1989 and 1994 while the use of investment banks more than doubled during the same period.[20] The founder behind MicroVoice, an interactive-voice-response software company, uses a corporate checking account at Merrill Lynch that daily removes excess funds into an interest-bearing mutual fund so that it works for him day and night.[21] Using a brokerage firm is not a solution for every business, as these firms' minimum deposit and loan requirements are normally well beyond the level that a small business can achieve, and they generally don't give the same level of service on a personal basis unless the company's account is enormous.

Generally, banks make loans based on what is termed "the **five Cs**": character, capacity, capital, collateral, and conditions. In the case of the entrepreneur, the first two—character and capacity—become the leading consideration because the new business's performance is based purely on forecasts. Therefore, the bank probably will consider the entrepreneur's personal history carefully. It is important, however difficult, for the new venture to establish a lending relationship with a bank. This may mean starting with a very small amount of money and demonstrating the ability to repay in a timely fashion. Bankers will also look more favorably on ventures that have hard assets that are readily convertible to cash.[22]

It's important, once the company can do so, to use more than one bank to ensure that it receives the most competitive rates. A good bank will make suggestions, anticipate the company's needs, introduce the management team to people who can help the business, show the company how to save money, and generally treat the company with respect. In return, the entrepreneur should keep the banker apprised of important new developments with the business and avoid dealing with the banker only when the company needs money.

Commercial Finance Companies

As banks have tightened their lending requirements, commercial finance companies have stepped in to fill the gap. They are able to do this because they are less heavily regulated and they base their decisions on the quality of the assets of the business. Thus, they are often termed **asset-based lenders**. They do, however, charge more than banks by as much as 5 percent over prime. Therefore, the entrepreneur must weigh the costs and benefits of taking on such an expensive loan. Of course, if it means the difference between starting the business or not, or surviving in the short term, the cost may be justified.[23]

Government Sources of Funding

A variety of sources of both debt and equity financing are available through government agencies. A few of these sources follow.

Small Business Investment Company (SBIC)

Small Business Investment Companies (SBICs) are actually a type of venture capital firm licensed by the Small Business Administration under the Small Business Investment Act of 1958 to provide long-term loans and equity capital to small businesses. They get financing through the government to invest in small and growing businesses. Since their repayment terms with the government are generous, they are able to invest over longer periods of time. They can be found by contacting the SBA.

Venture Capital Institutes and Networks

Many areas of the country offer access to venture capital networks through institutes established on the campuses of major universities. The university acts as a conduit through which the entrepreneurs and investors are matched. It assumes no liability for or has no ownership interest in either the new venture or the investor's company. The entrepreneur typically pays a fee, in the $200 to $500 range, and submits a business plan to the institute. The plan is then matched to the needs of private investors listed in the database who subscribe to the service. If an investor is interested in the business concept, he or she will contact the entrepreneur. For example, the Oklahoma Investment Forum is a matchmaking program that was started by the Tulsa Chamber of Commerce to help small and mid-size companies find investment funding. The *Venture Capital Journal* is a monthly publication that chronicles these forums each year. In the case of the Oklahoma forum, more than $40 million has been invested in participating companies since 1991.[24]

In general, venture capital networks are a way for entrepreneurs to gain access to investors that they may not be able to find through other channels. Furthermore, the investors in the database are there voluntarily, so they are actually looking for potential investments.

Small Business Administration (SBA)

The small-business owner may also want to consider an SBA-guaranteed loan. The Small Business Administration was established in 1953 to provide aid, counsel, and protection to small businesses. Working with intermediaries, banks, and other lending institutions, the SBA has been able to provide loans and venture capital financing to small businesses that are unable to obtain such financing through traditional business channels. Between 1980 and 1991, the SBA guaranteed $31 billion in loans, principally for start-up and expansion. Small-business loans are those defined as less than $250,000. In 1993 alone, the SBA backed $6.4 billion in loans, a 40 percent increase since 1991.

The SBA guarantees to repay up to 90 percent of the loan to the commercial lender should the business default. A further incentive to banks is that SBA-funded ventures tend to be growth oriented and have a higher survival rate than other start-ups. In a study conducted by Price-Waterhouse, SBA-funded businesses and non-SBA-funded businesses were compared during the period between 1984 and 1989.[25] The results were astounding:

	SBA Funded	Non–SBA Funded
Employee growth	167%	0%
Revenue growth	300%	37%
Survival after 4 years	75%	<65%

Of course, since these loans are backed by the government, the documentation and paperwork are extensive, and interest rates usually are no different than with a conventional loan.

The Small Business Administration also has a micro loan program, which makes it easier for entrepreneurs with limited access to capital to borrow small amounts (up to $25,000). Instead of using banks as in its guarantee program, the SBA uses nonprofit community development corporations. The Answer Desk at the SBA (1-800-827-5722) can provide information on micro lenders in a particular area of the country.

State-Funded Venture Capital

Many states now provide a range of services to help new and growing ventures. From venture capital funds to tax incentives, states such as Massachusetts, New York, and Oregon are seeing the value of establishing business development programs. Texas, one of the most prolific states in terms of investment funds, has 44 state-based venture capital funds. They usually receive their funding from the state government, which enables them to seek larger investment amounts from private sources. States that do not have equity funding typically offer a loan program aimed at new ventures. For example, in Massachusetts, favorable debt financing is often exchanged for warrants to purchase stock in the new company. Pennsylvania was the first state to create a funding program aimed at minority-owned businesses.[26]

Small Business Innovative Research (SBIR)

The Small Business Innovation Development Act of 1982 requires that all federal agencies with research and development budgets in excess of $100 million give a portion of their budgets to technology-based small businesses in the form of grants to develop products in which the agencies are interested. Small businesses find out about these grants by checking the published solicitations by the agencies (Table 4.1) to see if they can provide what the agencies need.

These **Small Business Innovative Research (SBIR)** grants have three levels:

1. Phase I is the concept stage, providing up to $50,000 for initial feasibility.

2. Phase II provides up to an additional $500,000 for projects that have the most potential after completing Phase I.

3. Phase III brings in private sector funds to commercialize the new technology.

Table 4.1   SBIR Agencies

- ▶ Department of Defense
- ▶ Department of Energy
- ▶ Department of Transportation
- ▶ Department of Interior
- ▶ Department of Education
- ▶ National Aeronautics and Space Administration (NASA)
- ▶ Nuclear Regulatory Commission
- ▶ Environmental Protection Agency
- ▶ Health and Human Services
- ▶ National Science Foundation
- ▶ Department of Agriculture

To qualify for an SBIR grant, the company must employ fewer than 500 people, be independently owned, and be technology based.

There are as many roads to start-up as there are entrepreneurs who travel them. No one path works for everyone. What's important is that you learn about all the paths to becoming an entrepreneur and all the resources available so that you have the best chance to create a business that has value and that gives you satisfaction.

Cases Relevant to This Chapter

Zotos-Stein
Pelco
French Rags

Issues for Review and Discussion

1. How can entrepreneurs use bootstrapping to help them start their businesses?
2. Distinguish among the four stages in the life cycle of a company and the focus management takes at each point.
3. What particular challenges does a mature company face?
4. Discuss three ways companies can finance their start-up and growth with debt.
5. Identify three characteristics of angels.

Experiencing Entrepreneurship

1. Find a fast-growth company either in your community or in the news. Compare that company with the 1997 Inc. 500 characteristics described on pages 93–95. Which of those characteristics apply? How did you determine that this is a fast-growth company?

2. Find a start-up company in your community. Interview the entrepreneur about how he or she gathered the resources necessary to start the business.

Resources

Blechman, B., and J. C. Levinson (1991). *Guerrilla Financing.* Boston: Houghton Mifflin.

Blum, Laurie (1995). *Free Money for Small Business and Entrepreneurs.* New York: John Wiley & Sons.

Drucker, Peter F. (1985). *Management: Tasks, Responsibilities, Practices.* New York: Harper and Row.

Latus, J. (1992). *Cashing in on Free State Government Money.* San Diego: Lion Publishing.

Morita, Akio (1986). *Made in Japan.* New York: Dutton.

National Association of Trade Exchanges, 9790 Southwest Pembrook St., Portland, OR 97224.

O'Hara, P. D. (1989). *SBA Loans: A Step-by-Step Guide.* New York: John Wiley & Sons.

Schilit, W. Keith (1994). *Rising Stars and Fast Fades: Successes and Failures of Fast-Growth Companies.* New York: Lexington Books.

Timmons, Jeffry (1989). *The Entrepreneurial Mind.* Action, MA: Brickhouse Publishing.

Wilmeth, J. R., ed. *Directory of Operating Small Business Investment Companies.* Washington, DC: Small Business Administration, semiannual, June and December.

Internet Resources

American Institute of Small Business
http://www.aisbofmn.com
Educational materials to help people start their own businesses that can be ordered from the site.

NetMarquee
http://www.netmarquee.com/
Provides a broad range of information for entrepreneurs and family businesses.

Capital Quest
http://www.usbusiness.com/capquest/
This site is for entrepreneurs looking for investors, particularly angels or private investors. You can place an executive summary of your business plan online.

InterSoft Solutions FinanceHub
http://www.financehub.com/welcomef.html
Lots of information and links to sites about venture capital, other financing issues, legal issues, and more.

Small Business Administration
http://www.business.gov/
Information on starting, financing, and expanding your business, with links to other sites.

5

Prediction is very difficult,
especially about the future.
Neils Bohr, Nobel laureate in physics

Planning the Business

Preview

Understanding this chapter will give you the ability to

▶ **Test the feasibility of a new-business concept.**

▶ **Understand the role of a business plan.**

▶ **Identify potential readers of the business plan and their needs.**

▶ **Organize and structure a business plan to effectively present your business.**

Terms to Know

Young Entrepreneurs—Minicase

Alan Reed
Card Creations

Opportunity knocks in some very unusual places, but if you've got the entrepreneurial mindset, you're always ready when it happens. For Alan Reed, opportunity began as a shipboard romance. A young college student from Encino, California, Reed met a beautiful Italian college student, Dara DeResi, from New York, and a wonderful romance developed. But unlike most shipboard romances, this one didn't end when the boat docked. E-mail and phone calls spanned the more than 3,000 miles that separated them.

Then one day, Dara began sending pop-up greeting cards she had made herself. The sincerity and uniqueness of the cards spawned the beginnings of an idea for a business in Reed's mind. How could the cards be manufactured, distributed, and sold? And how could he possibly compete against huge, established companies in the industry? The solution seemed to lie in developing a card that was easy and fun to create by the purchaser— probably a child who liked to put things together and create personalized cards—and also a card that was more meaningful and from the heart than the typical off-the-shelf greeting card.

To survive on only $10,000, Reed had to convince his suppliers, artists, and designers of the benefits of a long-term relationship with Card Creations, that it would eventually become a multimillion-dollar greeting card corporation. To do this, he put together an advisory board of experts in the industry who believed in his dream and took advantage of all the contacts he had made during his senior year in The Entrepreneur Program at the University of Southern California.

Reed fell in love again, this time with his business concept for a company he planned to call Card Creations. With a determination born out of passion for his business concept, he capitalized the fledgling corporation in 1997 with $10,000 he had saved from gifts and odd jobs throughout junior and senior high school. He then asked Dara to design 10 greeting cards, which he took to several printers throughout Los Angeles to get bids on the cost of manufacturing the cards. He had put together a business plan that forced him to get out in the industry, and "pounding the streets" gave him many eye-opening experiences. Some manufacturers gave him quotes of $6.50 per card! Reed's market research told him to plan to retail each card for $3.50. It didn't take much education for Reed to realize that you can't run a successful business with those kinds of numbers. It was obvious that he needed to learn more about the printing business.

Fortunately, Reed's grandfather came to the rescue and introduced him to Ron Shwartz, a retiree with more than 30 years of experience in print estimation, production planning, and plant management. With Reed's enthusiasm and dedication and Shwartz's experience, 10,000 prototype greeting cards were produced and successfully test marketed in 20 stores throughout the greater Los Angeles area, including Hallmark and Card Factory.

Quickly realizing the complexity and expense of starting a manufacturing business, Reed chose to outsource all the work. This included the envelope, the greeting card, the die-cut sheet for the artwork, double-sided foam tape, artwork for the display bag, the bag itself, design and artwork for the greeting card, directions for use, the card rack, and the point-of-purchase display, among other components.

Today Reed has his cards in 25 stores and is negotiating with several major chain stores to carry his unique greetings across the country. He has found that he's really in the distribution business, spending much of his time training reps, meeting with manufacturers and buyers, and working on refining the product. The constant evolution of his business plan due to new information has led him to believe that he now needs to be in partnership with a major card company to give the cards the proper launch in the market. As Reed says, "I never had a love affair with my bed. For entrepreneurs to be successful, it's essential that they get out of bed every morning and work and hustle." Alan Reed is one of those young entrepreneurs who makes things happen.

How can the business plan be used as a living guide to the start and growth of a new business?

Business plans are a critical part of any start-up company, but their importance doesn't diminish when the business is up and running. At the start-up stage, a business plan is like a fast-moving storm, changing from minute to minute and never looking quite the same way twice. This is because a new venture is constantly seeking information that will help refine its goals, activities, and financial picture as it struggles to become an established company. Consequently, business plans for new companies are modified frequently until the right fit is achieved. Alan Reed (see Young Entrepreneurs—Minicase) finished his business plan and, within a very short time, found new information that changed some of his strategies. Had he relied solely on the information he had gathered for the business plan, he may have misjudged not only his production costs but his target market as well. From continuing research, Reed learned that card shops were not the best place to showcase his pop-up greeting cards. Rather, they would be more readily purchased in craft and toy outlets where children normally went to purchase creative items.

After start-up, the business plan becomes an integral part of the company's strategic planning process. It is a guide, a blueprint for the growth and development of the company. The business plan is often referred to as a *living* document because it changes to reflect changes in the environment in which the company operates. The plan contains the vision, purpose, core values, and strategies the company will use to grow, and serves as a benchmark against which to make decisions and measure its progress toward its goals. This chapter looks at how planning can increase your chances of having a successful business.

The Road to the Business Plan

In reality, most businesses probably start without formal business plans, at least in the beginning. A study of 2,994 new businesses by Arnold Cooper and colleagues found that 28 percent of entrepreneurs seized an opportunity because it existed without any formal planning, and another 13 percent did it because they had no better alternative.[1] But research has also provided some evidence that planning contributes to a successful start-up. For example, in a study of fresh-juice distribution companies, Donald Duchesnau and William Gartner found that the more successful firms actually spent considerably more time on planning than did the less successful firms.[2]

In today's complex and dynamic environment, planning for a new business and planning for the growth of an existing business are essential steps for most types of businesses. That planning process consists of four stages as depicted in Figure 5.1: opportunity recognition, concept development, feasibility analysis, and business plan.

Opportunity Recognition

Entrepreneurs recognize an opportunity in the marketplace when they become acutely aware of their environment and the problems, needs, and gaps

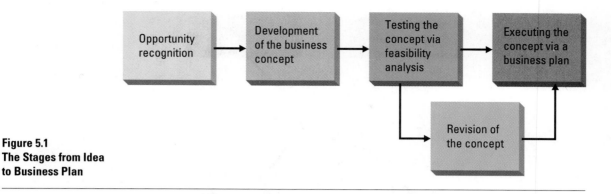

**Figure 5.1
The Stages from Idea
to Business Plan**

within it. They begin to see the world through an opportunistic lens; that is, they not only see problems, they see solutions and ways to create businesses that can provide those solutions. This is the idea generation stage, where creativity and an open, accepting mind take precedence over evaluation. In fact, at this stage, evaluation of ideas shouldn't enter the picture at all. Nothing should prevent the free flow of ideas. Doug Hall, master of creativity and inventor of the Eureka Stimulous Response™ Method, gives some unusual tips for freeing up your ability to generate ideas:[3]

1. *Look at paint chips.* Paint chips are an almost limitless source of stimulation, particularly if you go beyond the basic colors and get into such exotic hues as Glidden's chocolate kiss or smoked pearl. They stimulate images, moods, and emotions.

2. *Go to video rental stores.* Movies offer a wealth of images and ideas. Hall talks of the scene from *Rocky* where Rocky wakes up, heads into the kitchen, pulls a carton of eggs out of the refrigerator, cracks a half-dozen raw eggs into a glass, and chugs the liquid down. This image resulted in Hall's development of beverages in which his client's product is mixed with fruits and juices—easier to sell than raw eggs![4]

3. *Play with Play-Doh.* The smell of Play-Doh reminds most people of their childhood. Play with it. Mold it into sculptures. Build prototypes from it.

4. *Listen to music.* Music is a great idea generator. You will need to experiment to find the type of music that works for you. Dr. Yoshiro Naka Mats, the prolific Japanese inventor, prefers jazz or Beethoven's *Fifth Symphony.*

   In addition to these techniques, it's helpful to keep a notebook with you at all times. You never know when an idea or opportunity will strike you, and ideas usually come so quickly that if you don't write them down that instant, they will vanish. Other excellent sources of information are talking to people in many different industries, reading, and surfing the Internet.

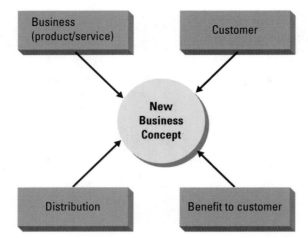

**Figure 5.2
The Business
Concept**

Once you have successfully put yourself in an opportunistic mode, you will find no lack of ideas for potential products or services. After several ideas have been generated, the question now becomes: which one to choose? So many ideas, so little time! Remember, this is not an evaluation stage—that is, whether the idea will or will not work. A good rule of thumb is to go with the idea you're most passionate about. The reason is that if you determine it's feasible and you attempt to start the business, it will take a tremendous amount of time, energy, and devotion to make it happen, so it's certainly better if you love what you're doing.

Once you have chosen an idea, you need to develop it into a business concept.

Developing a Business Concept

A **business concept** describes the four essential elements required to test whether or not a potential business idea is feasible. This is true for both a new business and a new growth strategy for an existing business. As the owner of a growing business, you may decide to add a new product line or develop a new service for the customer. The four elements of a good business concept will be used to test the feasibility of that new product or service. The four components of the business concept are the business (product or service), the customer, the benefit to the customer, and distribution, as depicted in Figure 5.2.

Suppose the idea for a new business involves providing West Coast location sites to film studios over the Internet. The concept for this new business can be defined more concretely by answering the following questions:

1. What is the product and/or service that is the basis for the business? In other words, what business are we in, and what is the product and/or service being offered? Using the example above: *We're in the information business, providing movie location sites on the West Coast.*

2. Who is the customer? That is, who will pay for the product or service (distributor, retailer, end-user, etc.)? *The customer in this case is the film production company.*

3. What is the benefit to the customer? What are we providing that the customer needs? *The business provides the customer with the ability to visually check sites, explore possibilities, and make decisions without having to travel or even leave the office.*

4. How will the benefit be delivered? *The benefit will be delivered via a web site that will provide still and full motion video of movie location sites and the ability to interact with the company.*

Once you have developed the business concept, you have something that can be tested, which is the next step in the planning process.

Testing the Concept

The business concept is tested through a process of analysis called the **feasibility study**. The feasibility study will answer the broad question: *Is there an acceptable market for the business concept?* In short, is it feasible, or "doable"? On a personal level, by doing a feasibility analysis, the entrepreneur is deciding whether or not to go forward with the business. Feasibility does not give all the information or answers needed to *start* the business, but

After three business failures, Mark Moore finally found the secret to a successful business concept—a focus on customer benefit, which in his case means filling a niche by providing specialized information services. Moore's company, TIS, started by supplying landlords with up-to-date eviction information about potential tenants. He later diversified into criminal background checks for employers. (Duane Hall)

it supports the level of confidence the entrepreneur needs to make a go/no go decision. It is the business plan that will ultimately deal with the issues related to creating a company to implement the business concept.

For all practical purposes, the feasibility analysis will answer the following three questions:

1. Are there customers and a market of sufficient size to make the concept feasible?

2. Do the capital requirements to start, based on estimates of sales and expenses, make sense?

3. Can an appropriate start-up or genesis team be put together to make it happen?

To answer these questions requires examining four broad areas of the business: product/service, industry, market/customer, and finance. Table 5.1 provides some in-depth questions that will help you do this.

Table 5.1   Feasibility Analysis

Area to Be Analyzed	Questions to Ask
Product/service	1. What are the features and benefits of the product or service?
	2. What product development tasks must be undertaken, and what is the timeline for completion?
	3. Is there potential for intellectual property rights?
	4. How are these products or services differentiated from others in the market?
Industry	5. What are the demographics, trends, and life cycle stage of the industry?
	6. Are there any barriers to entry? If so, what are they?
	7. What is the status of technology and R&D expenditures?
	8. What are typical profit margins in the industry?
	9. Have you talked to distributors, competitors, retailers, etc.?
Market/customer	10. What are the demographics of the target market?
	11. What is the customer profile? Who is the customer?
	12. Have you talked to customers?
	13. Who are your competitors, and how are you differentiated from them?
	14. Which distribution channel alternatives are available, and which customers will they serve?
Financing	15. What are your start-up capital requirements?
	16. What are your working capital requirements?
	17. What are your fixed-cost requirements?
	18. How long will it take to achieve a positive cash flow?
	19. What is the break-even point for the business?

Generally, the information available when the feasibility study is conducted is not as complete or detailed as it will be in the business plan, because entrepreneurs need to gather just enough information to make a go/no go decision. Nevertheless, a well-done feasibility study can prevent a company from throwing money at a new product or service for which there is no market, a market of insufficient size, or no efficient way to produce the product and make a profit. Of course, in a growing company, feasibility studies may not be necessary for every new product or service introduced. Typically, **derivative products** and services, incremental or small improvements on existing products and services, will not require a full-blown feasibility study, particularly if the customer has been giving feedback on the core product all along. However, a new family of products, **platform products**, will benefit from a more formalized approach, as they typically require substantial expenditures in product development and market research.*

Once you have determined that your business concept is feasible, it's time to turn the feasibility study into a business plan, which is a statement of your plan for the creation of a new company. Whether it's written for a start-up or a growing company, one critical purpose of the business plan is to persuade others, those third parties who may be potential investors, lenders, or key management personnel. This contrasts with the feasibility study, which normally is done for the entrepreneur or the founding team as a decision tool. Each of these groups interested in the business plan will be looking for different things, and it's important that the entrepreneur understand what those needs are.

Investors

Investors will focus heavily on the qualifications of the management team as well as on those factors that predict growth, usually found in the market analysis. They want to assure themselves that their investment will increase in value over the time they are involved with the company and that it's in good hands. Investors typically look for market-driven companies as opposed to product- or technology-driven companies because they are interested in such things as short payback periods for customers.[5] In other words, if customers recoup the initial investment in the product quickly, they are more likely to buy; therefore, the market holds more potential. Investors want to know that customers perceive a value in the user benefits through documented evidence of customer contact and research. They're interested in the amount of return expected relative to the amount of risk incurred. The farther along in the evolution a new product is, for example, the lower the risk and, consequently, the lower the expected rate of return on the investment. Investors will also look at the deal structure, that is, what their investment will buy them in terms of an equity interest and subsequent ownership

---

*A detailed discussion of feasibility analysis appears in Kathleen R. Allen, *Launching New Ventures,* 2nd ed. (Boston: Houghton Mifflin, 1999), which focuses on the tasks and questions to be answered prior to starting a business.

rights in the company. They will also want to know how they can liquidate their investment at some future date. Since most new ventures don't distribute dividends, investors often plan to harvest the benefit of their investment through an initial public offering of stock (IPO), a sale, or a buyout. These methods are discussed in Chapter 9.

Bankers

Bankers are interested primarily in the company's margins (the difference between sales and cost of goods sold) and cash flow projections because they are concerned about how their loans or credit lines to the business will be repaid. **Margins** indicate how much room there is for error between the cost to produce the product or deliver the service and the selling price. If the margins are tight and the business finds itself having to lower prices to compete, it may not be able to pay off its loans as consistently and quickly as the bank would like. Similarly, bankers look at cash flow projections to see if the business can pay all its expenses and still have sufficient money left over at the end of each month to grow the business. Clearly, bankers are also interested in the management team's qualifications and track record.

Bankers are discussed in Chapter 6 as a component of the professional expertise required of new companies.

Key Management

Potential key management will be interested in the business plan to get a complete picture of the business and the role they might play in its growth. Similarly, strategic partners, those companies with which the business will

 Entrepreneurship in Action

A Concept That's Going Places

Sometimes the best strategy is not to fight your competitors but to join with them to find a common enemy, a giant of a company that threatens all of your businesses. This was the strategy Alan Wolan and his wife, Natalia, chose to survive in the competitive niche of postcard advertising.

In 1994, when Wolan launched Five Fingers Inc. in New York City, he thought he had come up with an advertising vehicle that no one had yet exploited: postcards displaying the designs of their advertisers, from restaurants to retail stores to liquor companies. But as he studied the niche more closely, he discovered he had a small competitor in Los Angeles and one in Chicago. And all three had a common major competitor in Max Racks, a much larger company. So in 1995, the three companies met to form a network they called GoCard so they could sell national distribution to bigger accounts such as The Gap and Hanes. As time went on they added four more companies, and in 1996 they reported revenues of $6 million, which exceeded the $3 million reported by Max Racks. But, unfortunately, sometimes the loser can still get the last laugh. In January 1997, Max Racks claimed the domain name www.gocard.com and now routes Internet customers to its web site.

Source: Mike Hofman, "Dear Max: Drop Dead. Love, GoCard," *Inc.,* April 1997, p. 28.

have a working relationship, will want to review the company's growth plans and market strategy, as these sections of the business plan indicate how much business the strategic partners may get—in other words, what the value of the strategic alliance will be to them. They are also interested in the company's ability to pay them for the work they do. Key management issues are discussed in Chapters 6 and 7.

The Value of the Business Plan

Remember that doing a business plan is no guarantee of success. Companies have succeeded in spite of poorly written business plans and have failed even when the plan was carefully crafted. Some companies, such as Pizza Hut and Crate and Barrel, were successful in the beginning without business plans, although Pizza Hut wrote one later on before Pepsico acquired it. Today the business plan is a tool business owners use to enhance their chances of successful growth in a more complex global marketplace. As such, it is important that all the key management be involved in developing the business plan.

Some entrepreneurs choose to write several different versions of their plans, tailored to the needs of different interested parties. Others may decide to give only relevant sections of the plan to third parties. For example, it may not be prudent or necessary to give a deal structure section to a potential management employee or a detailed operations section to a banker.

In the first year, the company typically will reevaluate and update the plan several times to refine it and bring the activities of the company in closer alignment with the goals as stated in the business plan. If significant differences in estimates are observed, for example, the company will attempt to learn what may have caused the differences and adjust projections for the next period to account for any changes. In this way, the business plan always reflects what the company is actually doing and is always current when the company needs to approach an investor or a banker, or attract key personnel.

Technology Tip

A Cautionary Word on Business Planning Software

Sometimes technology can make a task seem easier than it really is. Such is the case with business planning software. Entrepreneurs who choose this route to complete their business plans often use a "fill-in-the-blank" approach that gives the plan a manufactured or artificial look. Unfortunately, savvy investors can spot these plans instantly.

The key danger in using business planning software occurs when the entrepreneur assumes the software creator really knows his or her needs and has taken them into consideration in designing the software. This is not always the case. Because each business is unique in at least some aspects, it's important that the entrepreneur be able to design the way the business plan is presented, including which information to present.

If you decide to use business planning software to format and lay out your business plan, be sure to choose one that gives you the flexibility to edit it to include information you need. A business plan is an expression of you, the entrepreneur. Don't let someone who doesn't know you or your business decide what should be in your business plan.

The Business Plan Structure

The first reason to undertake a business plan is to translate a feasible business concept into a company that can implement the concept. Recall that when the concept was being tested through feasibility, we were attempting to determine if (1) there were customers and a market of sufficient size to make the concept doable, (2) the capital requirements to start based on estimates of sales and expenses made sense, and (3) we could put together an appropriate team to make the concept happen. With the business plan, by contrast, the focus shifts to creating a company and issues such as process, marketing plan, and management enter the picture.

Table 5.2 presents a suggested outline of the business plan; however, any plan should reflect the personality and goals of the company, so there is no one format that works for every business. The following sections of the plan are those considered to be crucial to persuading the owners and others that the company has a healthy future. They are discussed in brief in this chapter and in more detail in later chapters where appropriate.

Executive Summary

A business plan should include a two-page executive summary that presents the most important points from all the sections of the plan. Potential readers of the business plan often read the executive summary first to see if they are interested in investing the time to read the entire plan. Consequently, it's vital

The Real World of Entrepreneurship

Business Plan Checklist

1. Did the executive summary grab the reader's attention and highlight the major points of the business plan?

2. Did the business product/service plan clearly describe the purpose of the business, the customer, the benefit to the customer, and the distribution channel?

3. Did the management team section persuade the reader that the team can successfully implement the business concept?

4. Did the market analysis support acceptance for the business concept in the marketplace?

5. Did the process plan prove that the product or service could be produced and distributed efficiently and effectively?

6. Did the management and organization section assure the reader that an effective infrastructure was in place to facilitate the goals and operations of the company?

7. Did the marketing plan successfully demonstrate how the company will effectively create customer awareness in the target market?

8. Did the financial plan convince the reader that the company has long-term growth potential and will provide a superior return on investment for the investor and sufficient cash flow to repay loans to potential lenders?

9. Did the growth plan convey a sense of direction for the company and demonstrate the potential to make money for investors?

Table 5.2   Business Plan Outline

EXECUTIVE SUMMARY (2-page summary in plan)

I. BUSINESS CONCEPT
   A. Business concept (product/service, customer, benefit, distribution)
   B. Purpose of the business
   C. Core values
   D. Description and uses, unique features/benefits
   E. The primary customer
   F. Spin-offs
   G. Environmental impact

II. MANAGEMENT TEAM
   A. *Qualifications of key management (founders)*
      1. Management team needs (gap analysis)

III. MARKET ANALYSIS
   A. *Industry Description*
      1. Industry size
      2. Industry status (growing, mature, in decline)
      3. Growth potential
      4. Geographic locations
      5. Trends and entry barriers
      6. Profit potential
      7. Sales patterns and gross margins
   B. *Target Market*
      1. Primary target markets
      2. Secondary markets
      3. Demographics of target markets
      4. Results of primary research on customer
         a. Customer profile
         b. Customer needs analysis
      5. Distribution channels—customer grid
      6. Entry strategy (initial market penetration)
   C. *Competitors—Competitive Grid*
      1. Direct and indirect
         a. Market share
         b. Description
         c. Strengths and weaknesses
      2. Emerging products/services
      3. Substitute products/services
   D. *Product/Service Differentiation and Competitive Advantage*
      1. Unique features
      2. Potential for innovation
      3. Proprietary protection
      4. Other competitive advantages
   E. *Pricing*
      1. Venture versus competitors
      2. Value chain

IV. PROCESS ANALYSIS
   A. *Technical Description of Products/Services*
      1. Uses, design, prototype
      2. Issues of obsolescence
   B. *Status of Development and Related Costs*
      1. Current status of development
      2. Tasks to be completed, time and cost to complete
      3. Potential difficulties, resolution
      4. Government approvals

Table 5.2   Business Plan Outline *(continued)*

    C. *Distribution Channels and Physical Distribution Plan*
    D. *Manufacturing or Operating Requirements and Associated Costs*
        1. Manufacturing cycle or service delivery process
        2. Materials requirements
        3. Inventory requirements (*also retail/wholesale business*)
        4. Production requirements (*also retail/wholesale or service*)
        5. Labor requirements (*all businesses*)
        6. Maintenance and quality control requirements (*all businesses*)
        7. Financial requirements (*all businesses*)
V. ORGANIZATION PLAN
    A. *Philosophy of Management and Company Culture*
    B. *Legal Structure of the Company*
    C. *Organizational Chart*
        1. Key management
        2. Duties and responsibilities
    D. *Compensation Programs and Incentives*
        1. Key management
    E. *Key Policies*
        1. Orders, billing, payment
    F. *Key Benefits*
VI. MARKETING PLAN
    A. *Purpose of Marketing Plan*
        1. Target market
        2. Unique market niche
        3. Business identity
    B. *Marketing Tools*
        1. Advertising and promotion
    C. *Media Plan*
        1. Uses and costs of specific marketing tools
    D. *Marketing Budget*
        1. Individual costs and total costs as a percentage of sales
VII. FINANCIAL PLAN
    A. *Summary of Key Points and Capital Requirements*
    B. *Needs Assessment* (Fixed costs, working capital, start-up costs)
    C. *Break-even Analysis and Payback Period*
    D. *Assumptions for Financial Statements*
    E. *Pro Forma Financial Statements*
        1. Cash flow (monthly yr1, qtr yr 2,3), income (monthly yr1, annual yrs 2,3), balance sheet (annual yrs 1–3), sources & uses (annual yrs 1–3)
    F. *Key ratios*
VIII. GROWTH PLAN
    A. *Strategy for Growth*
    B. *Resources for Growth*
    C. *Infrastructure Changes*
IX. APPENDIX
    A. CONTINGENCY PLAN
        1. *Potential deviations from the original plan and solutions*
    B. DEAL STRUCTURE (if relevant)
        1. *Debt and/or equity funding amounts*
        2. *Projected return on investment*
        3. *Harvest strategy*
    C. SUPPORTING DOCUMENTS
        1. *Resumes, contracts, maps, etc.*

that the executive summary grab the reader's attention in the first sentence with the key selling point or benefit of the business. This may mean, for example, introducing a problem and countering with the products and services the company will offer to alleviate that problem. Or the executive summary may open with a provocative statistic or statements that entice the reader to go further to learn more about the business concept. In any case, the first paragraph should contain a clear and concise statement of the business concept, answering the four questions listed on pages 118–119. In addition, the profitability of the company and potential for growth should be emphasized. Remember that the writers of the executive summary have only about 30 seconds to capture the attention of an investor, banker, or venture capitalist who probably sees many business plans each month.

Using the business plan checklist (page 124) as a guide, the remainder of the executive summary can be structured to present the most important points from every section of the business plan.

Business Concept

The first section, the business concept, gives the reader a clear understanding of the business: the purpose, mission, and product or service concept. The **purpose of the business** is a broad, enduring statement of why the company is in business. It speaks not to the specific products or services the company offers but to why the company is in business. For example, The Walt Disney Company is in business "to bring happiness to millions." Notice that the purpose represents the philosophy of the company and is stated in such a

 Entrepreneurship in Action

A Real Deal

Harry Davis and his partners learned a very important lesson. Not only is it important to write a business plan when you're seeking funding, but it's also important to continually update it. In 1992, when Harry Davis started his New York–based production company, Real-to-Reel Pictures Entertainment Inc., he raised $20,000 in a private placement stock offering to produce two short films. Then, in November of that year, he raised another $100,000 for a 30-minute television pilot called "Street Games," an interview-type sports show that features star athletes and their families. His five-year business plan effectively studied the target market, but his financial projections for production were far too low. He had to find a way to generate more revenue.

At that point, Davis decided to turn his company into a "nonlinear television and multimedia pre- and post-production house," meaning it would also do the work leading up to production and the editing and mixing required once the project was filmed. This new direction required significant changes in the business plan and even prompted a change in the company name to Reel Deal Inc. The business plan now had to reflect the restructuring of the company to do in-house filming, editing, graphics, and recording, which would also entail an additional $300,000 in capital for new equipment. With a current business plan in hand that described a business with greater growth potential, Davis was able to focus his efforts more clearly on increasing sales.

SOURCE: Carolyn M. Brown, " The Do's and Don't's of Writing a Winning Business Plan," *Black Enterprise,* April 1996.

way that no matter what happens in the business environment, the purpose will endure. The purpose also serves as a guiding principle for the company. All decisions regarding the operations, growth, customers, product development, and so forth are made based on their congruence with the company's purpose. As a result, The Walt Disney Company will not produce movies that are not family oriented and in line with its core principles. To produce more adult-oriented films, Disney formed another company, Touchstone Pictures.

Start-up company Gentech Corporation, has this overriding purpose: "to provide leading-edge, high-quality solutions to our customers."

The **mission statement** articulates a clear and compelling goal that focuses all the efforts of the company.[6] Unlike the purpose, it is something achievable. The mission is a way of translating the broad purpose of the organization into a defined goal. A goal must have an end point; therefore, the mission should clearly state by what date it will be achieved. For a complete discussion of purpose and mission, as well as the concept of company vision, see Chapter 7.

Recall that the business concept has four components: the business (what business the company is in), the customer, the benefit to the customer, and the distribution channel. A well-constructed business concept usually can be stated concisely in two to three sentences. For example:

> *Sunshine Learning Products* is in the business of helping children learn through computer technology. It will design and manufacture hardware and software for young children that will be sold through computer and toy retail outlets.[7]

What business the company is in is a broad statement of intent on the part of the company. As in the preceding example, it is broadly stated so as not to limit the company should the market for its products and services change over time. If Sunshine Learning Products had said it was in the business of providing computer keyboards for kids, it would have a problem someday when voice recognition makes keyboards obsolete. In contrast, saying that Sunshine Learning Products is in the business of helping children become computer literate—in short, it is in the education business—allows the company to think more expansively about how it can achieve its goals through a variety of products and services.

Sunshine Learning Products' direct customers are computer retail outlets. A company's **customer** is essentially the person or entity that pays the bill—in this case, the retail store—and the needs of that customer must be satisfied. But the end-user is also a customer, and the needs of the end-user—the child who uses the keyboards—are equally important. Ideally, the consumer's input has been part of the entire product design process and the marketing strategy as well so that the company can convince its customer—the retailer—that he or she will have sufficient demand for the product to make carrying it worthwhile.

The benefits to the customer include all those attributes of the product, service, and company that provide both the customer and the end-user with a way to satisfy their needs. The benefits are really the **central selling point** and the differentiating factor between the company's products or services and the competitor's. Those benefits are provided to the customer through a distribution channel; in the case of Sunshine Learning Products, it is manufacturer direct to retailer.

Creating a concept statement forces the company to focus on the most important aspects of its business. After reading a well-constructed concept statement, the reader should know exactly what the business is all about.

Product/Service Description

The product/service description presents a complete and detailed description of the products or services being offered, who the target customers are, the unique aspects, and the benefits to customers, as well as spin-off possibilities for additional innovation in products, service, or distribution. If the company is introducing a new product, one that needs to be designed and built, this section will summarize the product development process, leaving the more technical description for the process section of the plan. A more complete discussion of product development appears in Chapter 13. It is important to include tasks to be completed and time to completion. Zenas Block and Ian Macmillan suggest milestone planning.[8] This process includes 10 milestones or performance points at which the entrepreneur must make choices that will either enhance his or her chance of success or potentially result in failure:

1. Completion of concept and product testing

2. Completion of prototype

3. First financing

4. Completion of initial plant tests (**pilot** or **beta test**)

5. Market testing

6. Production start-up

7. **Bellwether sale** (first substantial sale)

8. First competitive action

9. First redesign or redirection

10. First significant price change

In addition, any perceived or actual environmental impact from the business and how the company intends to mitigate that impact should be noted.

Management Team

The management team section, the second section of the business plan, discusses the key members of the founding team (in the case of a new venture) or the principal management (in the case of a growing company), as well as the expertise they bring to the company. It also includes an analysis of any expertise that may be missing from the team and how the company intends to fill the gap, through either hiring employees, independent contractors, or consultants. The management team section is arguably the most important section of the business plan because, as it is often said, a great concept can fail because of a poor management team, but a great team can take a mediocre concept and make it a success.

If the growing company is seeking capital to feed the avaricious demands of growth—and few companies are not—investors, lenders, and other financial resources will likely look first to the people running the company. Just as the management team is the principal influence in the success of the company, it is also the chief reason companies fail.

Building a successful founding team is the subject of Chapter 6, while preparing the team for growth is discussed in Chapter 7.

Market Analysis

The market analysis is a critical section because it presents support for the contention that there is a market and a demand for the products and services the company is offering. It begins with a complete understanding of the nature of the industry in which the company is operating, including such factors as barriers to entry, stage of growth, competitors, market share, and potential for growth, as well as sales patterns and gross margin percentages. A good understanding of the industry will also facilitate zeroing in on the target market, the primary customer for the company's products and services. An in-depth analysis of the customer will include the size, location, buying habits, and needs of the customer base. An effective market analysis will also demonstrate that the company has talked to the customer and that there is market acceptance for the business concept. A complete customer profile based on interviews or focus groups will ensure that the company is on the right track.

In addition, a comprehensive analysis of both direct and indirect competitors and a description of emerging competitors and substitute products will demonstrate that the company has considered all possible competition. A **competitive grid** or table that compares competitors' products and services, benefits, distribution strategy, and marketing strategy with the entrepreneur's is essential to understanding what the new company faces by way of competition. It will also define those unique competitive advantages that the company enjoys. For more discussion on the industry and market as they affect the business, see Chapter 2.

Process Analysis

The process analysis section of the business plan presents a detailed description of the products and services, including engineering specifications in laypersons' terms and a description of the prototype. It will address the status of product development as well as additional steps that must be taken before having a product that is ready to sell to the public. It will also include the time and cost requirements for completing the development tasks. The business plan, however, is not the place to provide copious pages of technical specifications and details in an effort to describe how the product or process works. Most outside readers of the plan are more interested in the benefits than in the mechanics of the product or process. A second, more technical version of this section of the plan can be constructed for the management team; this is essentially an "in-house" version. In the version to be read by third parties, the benchmark question to be asked is: Does the reader need to know this piece of information to understand the product or service?

In addition, this section will contain a discussion of the distribution channels that will be used to move the product or service from the producer to the end-user. A major portion of this section is devoted to a description of how the business will operate, where it will get its raw materials, how they will be manufactured and/or assembled, and what type and quantity of labor are required to operate the business.

The outline of the business plan notes where businesses other than manufacturing have the same process information requirements manufacturing does. It is useful for nonmanufacturing businesses, such as retail and service businesses, to think in production terms, to see that every company produces something. Every company has a process and systems that need to be designed and prototyped. It is certainly not wise, for example, for a new restaurant to open the first day without having "walked through" the coordination of all the activities that will take place, from timing the preparation of the menus to ringing up the cash register. This is a process that can be laid out and monitored. For more on process analysis in product and service/retail businesses, see Chapters 14 and 15, respectively.

Organization Plan

The organization section of the business plan describes the company culture and management style (e.g., team-based, flat structure) that stems from the core values articulated in the business concept. It also discusses the legal structure and distribution of ownership in the company. In a growing company, a formal organizational chart is often used to depict key management personnel with their duties and responsibilities, compensation, and incentives packages. It may also depict outsourced capabilities and future personnel additions, as well as major policies regarding employees and benefits.

Chapters 7 and 8 present a more complete discussion of organization issues.

Marketing Plan

The **marketing plan** consists of the philosophy, strategies, and tactics the company will use to build its customer base. It begins with a statement of the purpose of the plan; in other words, what is the company attempting to accomplish? It follows with the plan for achieving that purpose and the benefits that will accrue to the customer as a result. Likewise, the plan will

Today branding is important in any business that wants to grow. Here Matthew Brown and Michael Grey are pictured among their DNA-like plastic linking toys called Zoobs. Brown and Grey have strengthened brand recognition for their new product by selling through specialty retailers like the Nature Co. and the Store of Knowledge instead of becoming lost on mass marketers' shelves. (Eric Millette)

identify the target market—the unique market niche the company intends to occupy—and the distribution channels it will use to reach the customer.

An important part of the marketing plan is establishing the company's identity, or how it will be perceived by the customer. The company's identity in the marketplace springs directly from the purpose it established for itself. For example, Starbucks Coffee places enormous importance on its employees. In an industry that regularly experiences high employee turnover and low wages, Starbucks views its employees as a competitive advantage and offers them a comprehensive compensation package, health care, and stock options to give them a vested interested in the company. This value is communicated to the customer in a very personal manner by the way Starbucks' employees treat their customers.

The marketing plan will also discuss the marketing tools (advertising, direct mail, trade shows, etc.) that will be used to create customer awareness and build customer relationships, the media plan with the schedule of uses and costs of each, and the total marketing budget as a percentage of sales.

Chapter 11 discusses the marketing plan in more detail.

Financial Plan

The financial plan presents the company's forecasts for the future of the business and the capital requirements for growth. Generally, these forecasts are in the form of **pro forma financial statements** broken out by month in the first year or two, and then annually for the next two to five years, in addition to a break-even analysis and other relevant ratios. The goal of this section is to demonstrate the financial health of the company and present the assumptions the company made in doing the forecasts. It's designed to reveal that all the claims about the product, sales, marketing strategy, and operational strategy can work financially to create a company that can survive and grow over the long term.

In a start-up venture, pro forma income and cash flow statements for three years are fairly standard. Balance sheets may also be included, but are more relevant to an existing business. Projections should be of two types: conservative and aggressive. That way the reader sees that the entrepreneur is not just expressing naive enthusiasm. An important part of a start-up financial plan is a **cash needs assessment**, which details how much capital in terms of fixed costs, working capital, and start-up funding is required to launch the business.

An existing business will have the advantage of a track record on which to base its projections. Therefore, it will present a full set of historical and current financial statements as well as pro forma statements for the future. A discussion of financial analysis with sample financial statements appears in Chapter 16.

Growth Plan

The growth plan presents the company strategy for growing beyond its current status and the methods by which it will obtain the resources it needs to successfully grow. The growth plan may call for an initial public offering, which may require some form of **mezzanine** (intermediate) **financing** in the short term to get the company through the IPO process. Or the company may be looking to franchise as a growth strategy and would need to look at the costs and payback period that strategy entails. These and other growth strategies are discussed fully in Chapter 9.

Appendix

The appendix is the place to put supporting documents and items that can be easily pulled out if they are not appropriate for a particular reader. Such is the case of the contingency plan and the deal structure. It's also a good idea to include résumés of key management members.

Contingency Plan

The **contingency plan** is simply a way to recognize that sometimes the "best-laid plans" don't work the way the company intended. It presents potential scenarios, usually dealing with situations such as unexpected high or low growth, or changing economic conditions, and then suggests a plan to minimize the impact on the company. This section is particularly helpful when a company is launching a new product, testing a new service, or going into a new market. Be careful, however, not to get too carried away building relatively rare pessimistic scenarios. Choose only those that have a good probability of occurring, and discuss how you will deal with them should they occur.

Deal Structure

The deal structure section usually is present in a business plan for a new venture or for a private or public offering for growth financing in a growing company. This section presents the offering to potential investors, including how much capital is required, in what form (equity, debt, or a combination), return on investment, and a plan for harvesting the investment at a later date. This section should be written from the investor's point of view and focus on the benefits to the investor of putting money into the company.

See Chapter 9 for a discussion of deal structure.

When Shift Media's Kim Heilman, Richard Grote, and Erin Jones wanted to expand their San Francisco-based web design and publishing firm, they tapped into a process called "kinesthetic systems modeling." Its developer, John Ward, helps entrepreneurs use modeling clay to turn one-dimensional business plans into three-dimensional tools. Modeling their business plan in clay unhooked the three from their technology and forced them to look at their business strategy. (Eric Caldwell)

Preparing the Business Plan

The general rule of thumb with regard to the length of business plans that others will read is that they should be less than 50 pages. There is no correlation between length and either quality or persuasiveness of a business plan. Clarity, conciseness, and directness will do a better job of selling the business than a plan that incorporates a lot of superfluous information. It's also important that the entrepreneur/team write the plan themselves rather than pay someone who doesn't have a vested interest in the vision to do it. The personality of the team, the enthusiasm for the concept, and the excitement about the potential for the new venture should be conveyed in the business plan, and outsiders will have a difficult time doing this. A good plan will take up to about six months of concentrated effort to compose. Once it's completed, however, updates will be easy to incorporate.

A business plan is not just for entrepreneurs starting new ventures. For the growing company, the business plan serves as a guide or benchmark against which the company can gauge its progress. It also establishes the purpose, values, and goals of the company that guide its decision making throughout its life. No entrepreneur ever plans to fail, but many fail to plan and find themselves reacting to external forces rather than moving their business forward proactively. A business plan helps an entrepreneur be proactive in a changing environment.

Cases Relevant to This Chapter

Zanart Entertainment

Issues for Review and Discussion

1. Why is doing a feasibility study important?
2. What is the role of the business plan and how does it differ from a feasibility study?
3. Who are the principal outside readers of the business plan, and what are they looking for?
4. What is the difference between the purpose and mission statements?
5. In your opinion, which is the most important section of the business plan, and why?

Experiencing Entrepreneurship

1. Interview an entrepreneur about his or her growing company with the goal of determining the purpose of the business, core values, and mission. Does this entrepreneur have a business plan? Why or why not?
2. Take an idea for a company you might like to build and write a statement of purpose, a set of core values, and a mission statement. What does this say about the kind of business culture you will build in your company?

Resources

Collins, James C., and Jerry I. Porras (1994). *Built to Last: Successful Habits of Visionary Companies.* New York: HarperBusiness.

Galbraith, J. R., Edward E. Lawler II, and Associates (1993). *Organizing for the Future: The New Logic for Managing Complex Organizations.* San Francisco: Jossey-Bass.

Shapiro, Eileen C. (1995). *Fad Surfing in the Boardroom.* Reading, MA: Addison-Wesley.

Tichy, Noel, and Stratford Sherman (1994). *Control Your Destiny or Someone Else Will.* New York: HarperBusiness.

Internet Resources

Business Opportunities Handbook: Online
http://www.ezines.com/
Features articles about running a small business. Also lists business opportunities.

National SBDC Research Network
http://www.smallbiz.suny.edu/
This site is administered by the State University of New York and is a good source of U.S. small-business development centers and links to many Internet resources.

6

*The path to greatness
is along with others.*
Baltasar Gracián, 1601–1658

Virtual Team Building

Preview

Understanding this chapter will give you the ability to

▶ **Discuss how to create a virtual company in a networked environment.**

▶ **Describe the benefits of using a team to start the business.**

▶ **Identify the most effective genesis team.**

▶ **Explain the role of independent contractors and the special rules relating to them.**

▶ **Know when to lease employees and use student interns.**

▶ **Describe how to create a successful strategic alliance.**

▶ **Identify and know how to choose the professional advisers you will need to start and operate the business.**

Terms to Know

Young Entrepreneurs—Minicase

Kim Camarella
KIYONNA™ Klothing

In January 1996, about to begin her final semester in The Entrepreneur Program at the University of Southern California, Kim Camarella was searching for a great concept on which to build her business plan. At the time, she was interning at a local computer software company. One day she and a co-worker, Donna Maldonado, were having a conversation, and Maldonado observed that there didn't seem to be any fashionable clothing for plus-size young women. In her entrepreneur courses, Camarella had learned the value of finding a need in the market that wasn't being met. Maybe Maldonado had just given her the opportunity she needed.

Camarella decided to do further research and gain some hands-on experience with a popular plus-size clothing designer. She conducted focus groups, did extensive research in the market, and discovered that indeed there was an untapped niche market of full-figured young women who wanted contemporary and stylish clothing. This realization marked the first step toward creating a company that would change industry perceptions of plus-size women's clothing.

Camarella, a petite woman herself, began discussions with Donna Maldonado and another acquaintance, Yvonne Buonauro, who had a degree from the Los Angeles Institute of Design and Merchandising. With a firm vision of what this company could become, the three young founders developed a business plan and decided to name the company after themselves—Kim, Yvonne, and Donna—KIYONNA Klothing. Kim would serve as president, Yvonne as VP of design, and Donna as VP of sales and marketing.

They immediately set to work to create a 30-piece line of clothing using the ideas generated in their focus groups and industry predictions about what would be fashionable in spring 1997. The next step was to find a pattern maker and a sample sewer to bring their ideas to life. In October 1996, the company debuted its first line of clothing for spring 1997 at the Big and Tall Women's Show in Las Vegas and got an overwhelming response. "Kiyonna Klothing walked away from the show with its first four customers," Kim said. As orders continued to come in, the company employed independent contractors to begin the first production run.

Although the partners had made personal investments to start the company, that money was quickly depleted. They managed to secure two short-term loans totaling $20,000 from Camarella's and Buonouro's fathers to cover production, marketing, and other operational costs. In January 1997, they hired an independent sales representative at the Los Angeles CaliforniaMart to promote the line, and in June 1997, they brought a Dallas representative on board.

As a growing, small company, they faced many challenges. Their volume had not yet reached the level of other apparel manufacturers, so it was difficult to find companies that would do the work for them. They also had quality control issues. Because they didn't have a quality control person to inspect the goods on site, they often received damaged or substandard goods. Another problem, typical of the fashion industry, was returns from retailers. A major department store, for example, would place a $1,500 order, pay in 30 days to get an 8 percent discount, and then return $500 worth of the clothing to KIYONNA while retaining the 8 percent on the full amount.

Yet another challenge was cash flow. As a small, unknown apparel company, KIYONNA lacked the clout to negotiate terms with vendors; yet its own customers, the retailers, demanded net 30 days. The three partners enrolled in the SBA's pre-qualification program for women business owners so that they would have more clout when they applied for a bank loan.

Having overcome all these challenges, by the summer of 1997, KIYONNA Klothing appeared in 17 boutiques around California and New York, as well as in the upscale Nordstrom department stores in southern California and Alaska. It has been featured in leading magazines such as *Big Beautiful Woman* and *Seventeen.* In one case, this free publicity resulted in more than 1,000 calls from plus-size women in less than one week.

Women love the stylish clothing; the challenge continues to be to find ways to convince retail buyers, who are typically reluctant to take a risk on a new line, to purchase it for their stores. KIYONNA is now considering mail order to reach the growing number of customers who don't have access to retail outlets that carry the line.

There are a lot of details in the apparel business. Camarella warns aspiring entrepreneurs to keep accurate records and "get automated from the start." KIYONNA uses Quickbooks® to manage its records and finances, and will eventually move to a program that will handle its growing requirements, but "you have to stay on top of it every day." Camarella says, "Listen to the customer, and listen to yourself." She believes strongly in her vision of a company that will give plus-size women the confidence that they look as stylish and attractive as smaller-size women. She knows the demand for KIYONNA Klothing is out there, and she's determined to find a way to reach every woman who wants it.

How did Camarella set up a virtual team to launch KIYONNA Klothing?

The 1990s have seen the rise of a popular new form of organization: the virtual organization or networked company, which allows a small company to look and act larger than it really is. The virtual organization is an opportunity-based form with the ability to create resources to develop and market complex products more rapidly and frequently than one company could do alone. The underlying philosophy behind the virtual organization is a focus on the firm's core competencies and forming alliances with other firms that can add their core competencies to the mix. The aggregation of many core competencies gives the virtual organization a critical mass that is unrealizable in any other organizational form. It makes it easier for a company to take earlier advantage of a window of opportunity by having in place a mechanism that coordinates all of the competencies needed to undertake the project.

Kim Camarella knew she couldn't get her new apparel company, KIYONNA Klothing, off the ground if she had to manufacture the clothes in-house (see the Young Entrepreneurs—Minicase). Since she lacked the needed money and expertise, she did the next best thing: she outsourced to an apparel manufacturer that already had what she needed as its core competency.

Virtual Organizations

In her book, *The Web of Inclusion,* Sally Helgesen describes the **virtual organization** as a living system in constant flux, much the way quantum science views the universe.[1] Goldman, Nagel, and Preiss refer to the same structure as an "agile web."[2] Figure 6.1 depicts the virtual organization in a web environment. Notice that the entrepreneurial company is in the middle, while its allied companies radiate out from it. For the most part, the customers are only aware of the lead company in an **agile web**. The agile web is really "an open-ended collection of pre-qualified partners that agree to form a pool of potential members of virtual organizations."[3] It has been compared to the Japanese *keiretsu,* with the exception that *keiretsus* have fixed memberships, whereas web members move in and out of the web as needed. The effect of a well-organized web of virtual organizations is to reduce time to market, reduce costs, decrease risk, and increase capability for all members of the web.

Goldman et al. suggest there are six strategic benefits to using the virtual organization concept:

1. The ability to share infrastructure, R&D, risk, and costs. This allows companies that otherwise would not be able to compete in the industry an opportunity to share and exploit their core competencies. For example, a new-product company that can't afford to set up a manufacturing plant can align itself with a compatible manufacturer to take care of its needs. Incubators such as the Ben Franklin economic development program in Bethlehem, Pennsylvania, and food courts that share common eating areas in shopping malls are other examples of this type of sharing.

2. The ability to link core competencies, as Hewlett-Packard did when it incorporated a built-in Motorola pager into its HP-100 palmtop computer.

3. The reduction of concept to cash time because new facilities don't have to be built and additional employees don't have to be hired and trained.

 Entrepreneurship in Action

Voodoo Lounge *a.k.a. The Virtual Corporation*

Sometimes a virtual company comes together for a purpose that has a definite time frame. When the goal is achieved, the company disbands or forms another virtual company that may look quite different. Such was the case of the Rolling Stones' 1994–95 *Voodoo Lounge* tour, which assembled 250 full-time employees to produce revenues of more than $300 million.

Michael Cohl, the chief operating officer, traveled the country with his office in tow: a crate of files, a laptop computer, and a fax machine. With this equipment networked to his people around the country, he could summon up the latest information on labor costs, travel schedules, and ticket sales.

Cohl contracted out the stage, lighting, sound, and many other provisions for the show to other companies.

In all, the production required 56 trucks and 200 stagehands and technicians to transport and install. In fact, since it took four days to build the set at each venue, they actually leapfrogged three stages around the country in various stages of construction.

With Joseph Rascoff, the operations officer in charge of production and the business end of the tour, Cohl dealt with issues such as merchandising of products and dealing with local government officials so that the stars of the show could focus on the creative aspect of the business.

SOURCE: Mark Landler, "It's Not Only Rock 'N' Roll," *Business Week*, October 10, 1994, p. 83.

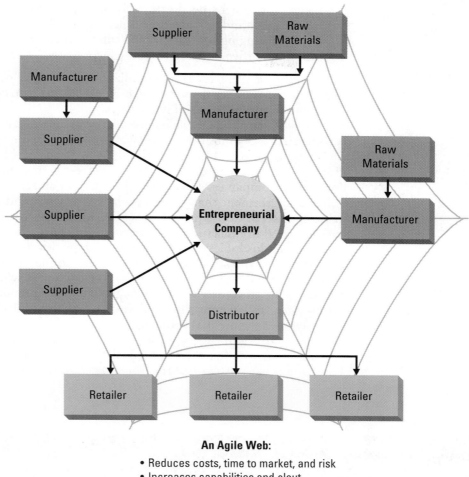

**Figure 6.1
The Agile Web**

An Agile Web:
- Reduces costs, time to market, and risk
- Increases capabilities and clout

4. The apparent increase in facilities and size that gives a small company the critical mass to compete against larger companies in the same market.

5. The ability to gain access to markets and loyal customers. This can be accomplished through franchising or **cobranding**, which means developing a product that uses another company's brand name as well. An example is Ben & Jerry's Homemade ice cream, which sells a flavor called Heath Bar Crunch. The OEM (original equipment manufacturer) concept, in which several smaller manufacturers put out products under a well-known name such as 3M, is yet another way to gain access to markets and customers.

6. The ability to migrate from selling products to selling solutions.[4] By cooperating with other companies, a firm is better able to sell a solution to

meet a customer's need rather than simply a product or service. In the construction industry, for example, a general contractor serves that purpose by bringing together all the subcontractors needed to provide a solution: an office building to house a company.

In addition, using a virtual organization strategy allows a small company to appear much larger than it is, thereby permitting it to compete against major corporations and expand its markets.

Many organizational mechanisms are available to companies that wish to become virtual organizations (see "Ways to Partner with Another Company"). These various forms of cooperation have existed for a long time. The web, discussed earlier, is actually one of the newest forms and provides a way to link virtual companies. To succeed, a virtual organization or an agile web requires an agreement that specifies who owns what and how profits will be made or shared. Consequently, it is also important that companies involved with a virtual organization or in an agile web have compatible management styles and philosophies about how their companies should be run.

Virtual organizations and agile webs are not necessary where companies have the core competencies they need to meet goals, where there is no clear benefit to the structure, where management styles among companies are incompatible, and where the legal framework is weak, thereby laying the groundwork for potential problems.

A virtual organization begins with the entrepreneur and the entrepreneurial team, whether the team consists of co-owners or outside advisers. This team is variously called the *founding team* or the **genesis team**.

 The Real World of Entrepreneurship

Ways to Partner with Another Company

▶ *Partnership.* This is a legal form that makes two or more companies partners in a new venture with all partners sharing losses and gains according to their contributions and the partnership agreement.

▶ *Joint venture.* This is a type of partnership that is less formal in nature. It is merely a contract between the participating companies to work on a particular project and share in the gains in some manner.

▶ *Strategic alliance.* This is an agreement to do business with a particular company or companies. It may be a formal arrangement, as in a partnership, or a less formal arrangement.

▶ *License agreement or royalty.* Under this scenario, the company licenses the right to produce its products to another company and receive a royalty based

on gross sales. Alternatively, the company licenses a character or name from a better-known company to increase brand recognition for its products.

▶ *New corporation.* The virtual organizations may form a new corporation to develop and market new products, with all companies involved holding stock in the corporation.

▶ *Outsourcing contract.* The company may have several contracts with suppliers and manufacturers to provide core competencies that it lacks.

▶ *Cooperative agreement.* This is similar to what has been done in agriculture for years, whereby farmers form co-ops to market their food products. Independent grocers have also done this.

Technology Tip

Networking the Virtual Company: The Electronic Keys to Success

The fundamental requirement of a virtual organization is the ability to exchange information rapidly and instantaneously. To accomplish this, growing companies should do the following:

▶ *Set up an e-mail system.* Besides reducing the amount of paper in the office, the response rate to memos and other information is much higher because of the ease of responding instantaneously. E-mail also facilitates cross-functional teaming and interaction with customers. To make it work, however, the company must be willing to forgo such things as paper memos and agree to communicate exclusively through e-mail.

▶ *Automate all activities that are time consuming, repetitive, and prone to error.* Automation in and of itself will not guarantee total accuracy, but if information is entered into the system only one time and

is automatically transferred to the appropriate files and documents (e.g., invoices, purchase orders) mistakes will be less likely.

▶ *Set up an electronic filing system accessible companywide.* This will allow the appropriate people to access files and documents from anywhere. The effect is to make travel time more productive.

▶ *Establish a system that allows everyone to easily monitor the performance of the company.* This may mean setting up security levels for each person and then assigning certain files or reports to that security level. In this way, all parties have access to that information that is important to their responsibilities. Because some people may not yet be comfortable maneuvering around the computer screen, programs to organize and analyze information need to be user friendly to encourage regular use.

Creating the Genesis Team

In their quest for independence, entrepreneurs often attempt a new venture as a soloist so they can retain sole ownership, make all the key decisions, and not have to share the profits. This is often a mistake. Although this autocratic approach to starting a business is still the most common one in small businesses and in the craft or artisan areas, in today's volatile, global market it is becoming increasingly difficult to succeed alone, particularly if the goal is to create a world-class company. With more new ventures operating in complex, dynamic environments and requiring more capital to start and grow, it is highly unlikely that any one person will have all the knowledge and resources to start a potentially great company as a soloist. It is also highly unlikely that any one start-up company will have all the competencies it needs to be competitive.[5] Therefore, at start-up and during initial growth, entrepreneurs tend to pull together a team, but often in a rather haphazard fashion and for reasons that frequently have nothing to do with what the team members can contribute to the organization. This, unfortunately, is also a mistake. Putting together a genesis or founding team is one of the most important tasks facing an entrepreneur with a new business concept, and should be undertaken with the greatest of care. This chapter will look at how to create a genesis team and then, taking it one step further, how to link your company to others in a virtual organization or network.

Collaboration is an essential ingredient in any world-class start-up. Studies of high-technology start-ups in particular have demonstrated that a team effort will provide a better chance for success than a solo effort.[6] There are several other important reasons for using a team effort:

▶ The intense effort required for start-up can be shared; thus, the load on any one person is lessened.

▶ Should any one member leave the team, the start-up is less likely to be abandoned.

▶ With a genesis team that includes expertise and experience in major functional areas (marketing, finance, and operations), the new venture can proceed farther on the growth path before it will need to hire additional personnel.

▶ A quality genesis team lends credibility to the new venture in the eyes of lenders, investors, and others.

▶ The ability to analyze information and make decisions is improved because the lead entrepreneur has the benefit of the varied expertise of his or her team members; in this way, ideas may be viewed from several perspectives.[7]

The founders of Compaq Computer Corporation, three former senior managers at Texas Instruments, used an integrated, interdisciplinary team approach to start-up that resulted in a phenomenal $111 million in sales in the first year. Their success was attributed to the "smart team" philosophy, which was that every member of the team should contribute to every facet of the venture. The engineer gave input to the market strategist, and the finance expert worked closely with the design engineer. In this way the company was able to cut its product development time in half, an important goal in an industry where new products are outdated almost before they are manufactured.

Starting as a team doesn't always mean you have to give up ownership. Your team members can also be people and companies to which you outsource certain functions or from which you receive needed advice.

What to Look for in a Team

When an entrepreneur decides to use a team effort to create the new venture, he or she generally looks for people who have complementary skills. In other words, if the entrepreneur happens to be an engineer, finding a market expert and someone who knows how to raise capital would be advantageous to the new venture. Clearly, since the start-up of a new venture is a multifunctional process, the entrepreneur and the venture will benefit greatly from a team comprising a variety of strengths and disciplines. Another advantage to forming a quality team is the fact that this genesis team has a vested interest in the new venture. Team members invest not only their time but usually their money as well. Thus, the burden of raising the resources necessary to start the venture is distributed among the team members, giving the lead entrepreneur access to the network of contacts of the other members in addition to his or her own. This vastly increases the information and resources available to the new venture and allows the venture to grow more rapidly.

A genesis team, no matter what the legal form of the organization, is for all intents and purposes a partnership with all the attendant benefits and problems. Chapter 3 discussed some of these problems. Anytime you decide to work with a partner, you must choose that partner for the right reasons. The fact that the partner is a friend may not be the right reason. Better reasons might be that the partner

▶ Shares your values and the vision for the company

▶ Has complementary skills to bring something needed to the mix

▶ Has integrity

All three of these qualities must be present if the partnership is to succeed.

It's important to divide responsibility in a way that makes each partner responsible and accountable for some aspect of the business. For example, where the team comprises two or three persons, ownership in the company probably is divided equally among the partners, especially if they originated the concept together. Nevertheless, it is important that one partner have the role of lead entrepreneur—CEO—and that duties and responsibilities be divided such that if a disagreement arises on a particular issue, one person can ultimately make the decision. For example, in a two-person partnership, one member might be the product development or creative end of the team and the other the business end. In a three-person team, duties may be split based on the three basic functions of the organization: finance, marketing, and operations. All partners should share the vision for the company, but individual partners will have responsibility for particular functions of the business.

A carefully chosen genesis team can carry the company through pre-start-up, through start-up, and usually well into the growth phase, at which time it often becomes necessary to bring in professional management if the original team doesn't have management expertise in mid-size companies (see Chapter 7).

Outsourcing for Expertise

Because growing companies usually don't have the resources to hire all the management staff they might need to run the company, and because many new companies start without the benefit of a multifunctional team effort, most entrepreneurs "bootstrap" in the early stages of growing a business. **Bootstrapping** is a term of art in business that literally means "beg, borrow, or rent everything." Bootstrapping represents collectively all of the creative techniques entrepreneurs employ in the start-up phase to gather resources. The general rules of thumb for bootstrapping include the following:

▶ Hire as few employees as possible (employees are usually the single largest expense of a business).

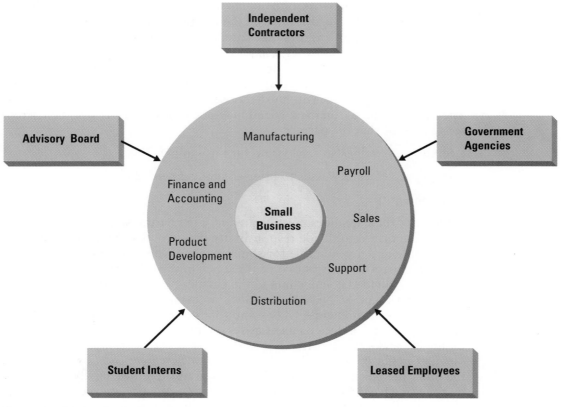

Figure 6.2   Outsourcing for Expertise

▶ Lease rather than buy so you don't tie up limited funds in equipment and facilities. With a lease, there is often no down payment and the cost is spread over time.

▶ Arrange longer terms with suppliers. The longer the term, the longer you have use of your limited funds.

▶ Where possible, get customers to pay in advance—if not fully, at least a substantial deposit. This was the strategy NordicTrack, the fitness equipment company, used when it started. Customers would pay the full amount up front and then wait for up to six months to receive the equipment. Up-front deposits or full payment are strategies many new manufacturers have used to jumpstart their companies, particularly where raw material costs are high.

These techniques make sense for a start-up, but how does a new venture survive with as few employees as possible and still grow? Three solutions are to use independent contractors (a process known as **outsourcing**), employee leasing, and student interns (see Figure 6.2). Strategic alliances, another source of expertise and help for a new venture, are discussed in a separate section.

Independent Contractors

Independent contractors own their own businesses and provide products and services to other companies under contract. They work under the control of the person who hires them *only* as to the result of the work they do and *not* as to the means by which that result is accomplished. When Marcel Ford of Botanical Science created his now successful silk plant cleaner, he hired an independent chemist and a packager to handle the design and manufacturing of the product.

There are several advantages to using independent contractors:

▶ They are usually specialists in their fields; in other words, they focus on their core competency.

▶ The cost of hiring an independent contractor is often less than that of hiring an employee because the entrepreneur doesn't supply benefits such as medical and retirement, unemployment insurance, income tax withholding, or social security tax. These benefits can amount to as much as 32 percent of the base salary or wage. Thus, an employee might cost the entrepreneur $52,800, including the above-mentioned benefits, whereas an independent contractor might cost only $40,000 to $45,000.

▶ The independent contractor pays his or her own withholding taxes, social security, Medicare, unemployment, and workers' compensation insurance.

▶ The benefit of using independent contractors not only accrues to the entrepreneur but to the independent contractor as well. Independent contractors can deduct 100 percent of their expenses related to self-employment on their income taxes.

Be Careful with Independent Contractors

An entrepreneur who does not follow the IRS rules regulating classification of workers as independent contractors can be held liable for all back taxes plus penalties and interest, which can result in a substantial sum. Therefore, entrepreneurs using independent contractors should always

▶ Consult an attorney

▶ Draw up a contract with each independent contractor that specifies that the contractor will not be treated as an employee for state and federal tax purposes

▶ Be careful not to indicate the time or manner in which the work will be performed

▶ Verify that the independent contractor carries his or her own workers' compensation insurance

▶ Verify that the independent contractor possesses the necessary licenses

There are, however, some protections for business owners who use independent contractors. Under the **safe harbor law** of the Revenue Act of 1978, companies cannot be held liable for employment taxes arising from an employment relationship if they

▶ Had a reasonable basis for treating the person as an independent contractor. A reasonable basis is normally a judicial precedent, such as an IRS audit or letter stating that this person is an independent contractor, or a long-standing industry precedent, as in the case of real estate salespeople.

▶ Has filed required returns with the federal government.

▶ Has not classified an employee with the same duties the independent contractor performs.

If the company does not pass these requirements, the IRS can choose to apply the more specific 20-point test for classifying workers as employees (see The Real World of Entrepreneurship on page 148). Even if all the IRS rules are followed, however, there is no guarantee that the IRS won't challenge the company's position. The 20-point test is not part of the tax code, so the IRS is not required to use it in making its assessments. Therefore, it's important to document the relationship with an independent contractor through a legal agreement that explicitly demonstrates that the independent contractor owns his or her own business.

 The Real World of Entrepreneurship

The Internal Revenue Service 20-Point Test for Independent Contractors

An individual is considered an employee if he or she

1. Must follow company instructions about where, when, and how to carry out the work
2. Is trained by the company
3. Provides services that are integrated into the business
4. Provides services that must be rendered personally
5. Cannot hire, supervise, and pay his or her own assistants
6. Has a continuing relationship with the company
7. Must follow set hours of work
8. Works full time for a company
9. Does the work on the company's premises
10. Must do the work in a sequence set by the company
11. Must submit regular reports to the company
12. Is paid regularly for time worked, by the hour, week, or month
13. Receives reimbursements for job-related expenses
14. Relies on the tools and materials of the company
15. Has no major investment in facilities and resources to perform the service
16. Cannot make a profit or suffer a loss through the provision of these services
17. Works for one company at a time
18. Does not offer his or her services to the general public on a regular basis
19. Can be fired at will by the company for reasons other than failure to produce specified results
20. May quit work at any time without incurring liability

Leasing Employees

Leasing employees is a growing trend among companies that are trying to better manage the most expensive item in their budgets. It is quite different from using temporary services in that employee management firms actually hire the company's staff and lease them back to the company. So the entrepreneur in effect hires the employees and then leases those same people back from the management company. The management company then handles payroll, files taxes, deals with insurance, and takes care of other human resource issues for a percentage of the total payroll. This saves the growing company time and money and usually provides the employees with broader benefits and less expensive health care premiums.

Several issues should be considered before signing a contract with an employee leasing company:

▶ The firm should be licensed, if that is required by the state in which it does business.

▶ Some firms are fully indemnified by large insurance companies to fund their benefits programs, whereas others are self-funded. The latter should maintain 15 percent of total premiums in reserve.

▶ It is important to check the banking track record of the firm to ensure that employees will receive their pay on time.

▶ Current and former clients should be contacted to determine how successfully the employee management firm conducted business and fulfilled the requirements of the contract.

▶ The management firm should have a broad range of insurance options.

▶ The leasing firm should supply the company with regular reports.

In contrast to leasing firms, temporary agencies send their own employees into the company on a temporary basis. Temporary agencies are another excellent source of personnel, particularly in instances where they are only needed for, say, a season or a specific event.

Student Interns

Any entrepreneur fortunate enough to live in a city with a college or university can take advantage of the many internship programs offered to give students real-life work experience in growing small businesses. Often interns are given course credit, so the company doesn't have to pay for them. In other cases, companies can offer paid internships to schools. Either way, the young company gets a temporary "employee" who is eager to work and learn and who could end up being a valued full-time employee later on.

Using interns at Marquette University in Milwaukee was the strategy Marianne Szymanski took to start Toy Tips International, an independent toy research company. See the Young Entrepreneurs—Minicase feature in Chapter 4 to read her story.

Strategic Alliances

One essential component of a virtual strategy is the **strategic alliance** or partnership with another company. It is distinguished from the independent contractor relationship in that it is a more formal and typically closer relationship. Moreover, *independent contractor* is a designation for tax purposes, whereas *strategic alliance* is not. Through strategic alliances, growing companies can structure deals with suppliers, manufacturers, or customers that will help reduce expenditures for marketing, raw materials, or R&D. Strategic partners are considered **stakeholders** in the company since they have an investment of time and money in its products or services. Moreover, in many cases their investment is irreversible; that is, if the new venture fails, liquidation of its assets will not make the stakeholder whole. This puts the stakeholder at significant risk and underscores the importance of minimizing

An effective strategic alliance should benefit both companies. Teaming a small company with a large one can do just that. Clotee McAfee (pictured) and her partner Ruby Eddie saw a perfect match with Macy's West. Their innovative school uniform company, Uniformity LLC, needed to get its products in front of school children and Macy's had a strong interest in entering the public school uniform market. The successful strategic alliance has plans to expand to an additional ten locations on the west coast. (Ulf Wallin)

stakeholder exposure and selecting partners who can bear the risk. Amar Bhide and Howard Stevenson suggest that the following characteristics should be present in strategic alliance partners:[8]

▶ *Diversification.* Those partners who have diverse investment interests generally are better able to bear the risk of investment in a new venture that is focused rather than diversified.

▶ *Experience in bearing this form of risk.* Partners such as 3M that are used to dealing with new ventures have a greater understanding of the nature of these small companies. Certainly such an association gives the new company more clout in the marketplace.

▶ *Excess capacity.* Firms that do not have to make additional investments in plant and equipment can provide their existing **excess capacity** to the start-up and thus benefit both partners.

The R&D Limited Partnership

One specific type of alliance is the **R&D limited partnership**, a vehicle whereby growing hi-tech ventures that carry significant risk due to the expense of research and development can share that risk with a more established company. The limited partnership (usually formed by private investors or venture capitalists) contracts with the new venture to provide the funding for the R&D to develop a market technology that will ultimately be profitable for both companies. Limited partners are able to deduct their investment in the R&D contract and enjoy the tax advantages of losses in the early years on their personal tax returns; they also share in any future profits. In this form of partnership, the new venture acts as a general partner to develop

 Entrepreneurship in Action

Paranoia Can Mean Lost Opportunities

A common mantra among small business owners is "the big guy is out to get me." Today that kind of paranoia can mean lost opportunities and higher costs.

Craftsman Customer Metal Fabricators Inc. is a 275-employee sheet metal–bending company located in Illinois. In the late 1980s its principal customer was Motorola, which had just decided to decrease its supplier base and make the suppliers it kept "partners." This meant Craftsman would have to share its trade secrets with the giant or suffer the loss of its best customer. The bottom line was *trust.* Could Craftsman trust Motorola with its secrets?

Fortunately, Craftsman decided to make the leap into a partnership with Motorola and discovered that the benefits far outweighed the potential negatives. With the expertise and strength of Motorola at its side, Craftsman began producing product in one to two days rather than the normal five days, and the company grew from $6 million to $30 million in 10 years. Because of the successful relationship with Motorola, Craftsman now seeks out other alliances that can help it save money and innovate for its customers.

Source: Jerry Useem, "Company Goes Crazy over Partnerships, Gets Committed," *Inc.*, June 1997.

the technology and then structures a license agreement with the R&D partner whereby the new venture can use the technology to develop other products. Often the limited partnership's interest becomes stock in a new corporation formed to commercialize the new technology. An alternative to this arrangement is an agreement to pay royalties to the partnership.

Strategic alliances are sometimes the only way to get the company out of R&D and into the marketplace with any credible level of strength. VORAD Safety Systems, a developer and manufacturer of on-board radar systems for vehicles, joined forces with Eaton Corporation, a $4 billion truck component manufacturer and distributor on the New York Stock Exchange that was interested in the technology but didn't have the in-house capability to develop it. In addition, M/A Com, a $341 million microwave manufacturer, and Allstate Insurance in Chicago joined the partnership, and a complex agreement resulted in a company that was worth $32 million, of which the founders retained a 35 percent interest. With this kind of strength and clout, VORAD was able to enter the market from a position of strength.[9]

Despite all the benefits of strategic alliances, entrepreneurs should never forget that they face the same negatives partnerships do. Companies have personalities, and sometimes those personalities clash. Therefore, it is important that communication be facilitated, clear duties and responsibilities be outlined, and procedures for disbanding the alliance be in place if that becomes necessary.

Professional Advisers

When a new venture is in the infancy stage, it generally doesn't have the resources to hire in-house professional advisers, such as an attorney or accoun-

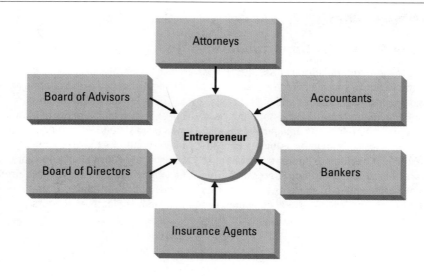

**Figure 6.3
Professional
Advisers**

Craig Johnson and his Venture Law Group (VLG) are redefining the relationship between law firms and start-up companies. They're doing it by acting like venture capitalists. VLG chooses its clients based on their potential for long-term success. Then they help form a professional advisory board to plan strategy for the company. This unique model has been very successful. (Bob Holmgren)

tant (see Figure 6.3). Instead, it must rely on building relationships with professionals on an as-needed basis. These professionals provide information and services that are not normally within the scope of expertise of most entrepreneurs, and they can play devil's advocate for the entrepreneur, pointing out potential flaws in the original business concept and the growth strategies. Growing companies that are putting all of their resources into growth often aren't able to hire in-house professional advice. This is not a problem, since continuing to use these advisers on an as-needed basis is probably a more effective allocation of resources. Because these professional advisers are essentially independent contractors, it is important to understand what they do and how to choose them.

Attorneys

The reputation of the legal profession has been under constant attack over the past decade, and lawyers have been the butt of many a joke for nearly as long as the profession has been in existence. It's no wonder, then, that many businesspeople attempt to avoid using lawyers until they get into trouble. This can be a costly error for a company, as a good attorney can often help a business avoid expensive litigation and protect its rights under the law. In fact, today stricter laws in the areas of antitrust, banking, the environment, and securities may affect a company's strategies and ability to do business as planned, even in the early stages of its life.

Attorneys are professionals who generally specialize in one area of the law, such as tax, real estate, business, or patents. Therefore, it's critical to select an attorney who specializes in the particular area of law you need. Attorneys can provide a wealth of support for a new and growing venture. Within their particular area of expertise, attorneys can

▶ Advise the entrepreneur in the selection of the correct legal organizational structure (sole proprietorship, partnership, or corporation)

▶ Advise and prepare documents for intellectual property rights acquisition

▶ Negotiate and prepare contracts for the entrepreneur, who may be buying, selling, contracting, or leasing

▶ Advise the entrepreneur on compliance with regulations related to financing and credit

▶ Keep the entrepreneur apprised of the latest tax reform legislation and help minimize the venture's tax burden

▶ Assist the entrepreneur in complying with federal, state, or local laws

▶ Represent the entrepreneur as an advocate in any legal actions

Choosing an Attorney

Choosing a good attorney is a time-consuming but vital task that should occur prior to start-up. Decisions made at the inception of the business may af-

 The Real World of Entrepreneurship

Understanding Legal Fees

▶ *Hourly fees:* Many attorneys bill in quarter-hour increments based on an hourly rate ranging from $150 to more than $500. That means that a five-minute phone call to an attorney who bills at $250 per hour in quarter-hour increments will cost the client about $60. It's important to question how various attorneys in the firm bill and also how time for paralegals and staff is billed.

▶ *Retainers:* Many companies put a firm "on **retainer**," meaning they typically pay a periodic fee (often monthly) to the firm for specified types of work such as reviewing contracts and phone calls.

▶ *Contingency fees:* **Contingency fees** are fees the law firm collects if it wins a case in litigation. In other words, the firm typically receives nothing until the case is resolved. Under this scenario, the entrepreneur should make sure he or she is in charge of the

case and determines whether the case settles or is appealed.

▶ *Stock:* In the case of young, growing firms that don't have the cash for attorney fees, law firms sometimes will accept stock. Obviously, to agree to this type of compensation, the law firm must believe the value of the entrepreneurial company will grow substantially. Giving up equity in the company probably should not be considered as the first choice.

▶ *Billable hours:* This is the method by which attorneys calculate the amount of work they do for a client. It may even include the time spent by a senior partner explaining the case to a junior partner or associate. The entrepreneur should request statements that detail the amount of time billed by each person in the firm on the client's work.

fect the venture for years to come; hence, good legal advice is critical. The following tips may facilitate the search:

1. Ask accountants, bankers, and other businesspeople for recommendations. This strategy is more likely to produce a good attorney who is also ethical in his or her professional or personal dealings.

2. Retain an experienced attorney who is competent to do what the company needs.

3. Look for an attorney who is willing to listen, has time to work with the management team, and will be flexible about fees while the business is in the start-up phase.

4. Check out the firm by phone first. You can learn a lot about the law firm by noting who answers the phone and with what tone of voice.

5. Confirm that the attorney carries malpractice insurance.[10]

The management team will also need to decide whether it wants to retain a large or a small law firm. Both have advantages and disadvantages. Large firms can often cover all the specific legal needs of a company—a one-stop shop of sorts—but are typically more expensive, and often a young company will find itself relegated to the youngest, most inexperienced attorneys. Large firms don't usually seek out small businesses as clients because the amount of legal business they may bring to the firm is not enough to cover the law firm's overhead; consequently, small, growing companies are often intimidated by the attorneys who represent them. Smaller law firms, in contrast, are less expensive but may have to refer clients to outside experts for specialties such as patent law. Nevertheless, they may be able to do the bulk of legal work required by the typical company in the early years.

To help keep legal fees in line, you should develop standardized documents based on the advice of your attorney that you can use in a variety of situations with minor modifications so that the attorney doesn't have to be involved each time. You should always go to meetings with your attorney prepared with all necessary documents in place and questions in writing. Above all, you need to practice preventive care by consulting an attorney *before* an issue becomes a real problem and realize that legal fees, like anything else, are negotiable.

Accountants

A lawyer is the company's advocate, but an accountant is bound by rules and ethics that do not permit advocacy. Therefore, where an attorney is bound to represent the company no matter what it does, the accountant, who is bound by the **Generally Accepted Accounting Principles (GAAP)**, cannot defend the company if it chooses to do something that violates the GAAP.

Accounting is a fairly complex form of communication that the entrepreneur needs to understand. In the beginning of the business, the accountant may set up the company's books and maintain them on a periodic basis. Or, as is often the case, the entrepreneur may hire a bookkeeper to do the day-to-day recording of transactions and go to the accountant only at tax time. The accountant will also set up control systems for operations as well as payroll. A growing business has to

◗ Verify and post bills

◗ Write checks

◗ Issue invoices

◗ Make collections

◗ Get suppliers to cooperate

◗ Balance the checkbook

◗ Prepare financial statements

◗ Establish inventory controls

◗ File yearly tax returns

◗ Prepare budgets

◗ Prepare stockholder reports

◗ Make payroll tax deposits

◗ Secure insurance benefits

◗ Keep employee records

The accountant can assist in all these areas. Once the new venture is beyond the start-up phase and growing consistently, it will need an annual audit to determine if the accounting and control procedures are adequate. In addition, the auditors may require a physical inventory. If everything is in order, they will issue a certified statement, which is important should the entrepreneur ever decide to take the company public on one of the stock exchanges. At that time, the investment banking firm handling the IPO will probably want three years of audited financial statements.

Finding an Accountant

Accountants are also a rich networking source in the entrepreneur's search for additional members of the genesis team. Much as attorneys do, accountants tend to specialize, so finding one who is used to working with young, growing businesses will be an advantage. It is highly likely that the accountant who takes the company through start-up and early growth may not be the same person who takes care of its needs when it reaches the next level of growth as a mid-size company. As the financial and recordkeeping needs of the business increase and become more complex, the entrepreneur may need to consider a larger firm with expertise in several areas.

When choosing an accountant, consider the following tips:

1. Choose an accountant who has experience dealing with small businesses.

2. Talk to other small-business owners and professionals for recommendations.

3. Ask a potential accountant if she or he will need to refer you to someone else for special issues such as taxation, audits, and so forth.

4. If you are in a complex business such as manufacturing, make sure your accountant has worked with manufacturers previously.

Bankers

Having a qualified banker on the company's professional advisory team is an issue not only when the company needs a line of credit for operating capital or to purchase equipment but from the moment the business account is opened. The company should think of a banker as a business partner who is capable of providing expertise in several areas. The banker should

▶ Be a source of information and networking

▶ Help the company make decisions regarding capital needs

▶ Assist the entrepreneur in preparing pro forma operations and cash flow analyses and evaluate projections the entrepreneur has made

▶ Assist the entrepreneur in all facets of procuring financing

 The Real World of Entrepreneurship

Why Bankers Reject Loan Requests

Entrepreneurs have problems with bankers because the two view the world in fundamentally different ways. Bankers tend to focus on the loss potential, whereas entrepreneurs focus on the profit potential. Other issues entrepreneurs face include the following:

Problem: Bankers don't know enough about the company.
Solution: The company should prepare a thorough business plan so the banker knows the entrepreneur understands the market and the customer.

Problem: Bankers don't understand exactly how much money the company needs and why.
Solution: The entrepreneur should request a specific dollar amount, show how it was arrived at, and how the money will be used.

Problem: Bankers don't see company numbers to support the request.
Solution: Bankers have to feel confident that the business will generate the funds to repay the loan. A start-up company will likely show a period of no profits and weak cash flow, so it's important to emphasize the company's successes and to state how the company expects to improve the situation.

Problem: Bankers don't see enough collateral.
Solution: Bankers typically don't value a company's assets dollar for dollar. Therefore, they often look outside the company to the entrepreneur's personal assets, which can strengthen the collateral status.

Problem: The business alone can't support the loan.
Solution: The entrepreneur may have to personally guarantee the loan to prove commitment to the business.

Choosing a Banker

Selecting a banker should be as careful a process as that for choosing an attorney or accountant. A list of criteria that defines the needs of the company with respect to the banking relationship will help narrow the search. Other business owners, as well as attorneys and accountants, are also excellent sources of relevant information on how well a particular bank works with companies in a specific industry.

When choosing a banker, it's beneficial to seek out an officer with a rank of assistant vice president or higher, as these officers are trained to work with new and growing businesses and have a sufficient level of authority to quickly make decisions that affect the new venture. The problem today is that banks, like other businesses, are consolidating and downsizing, so bank officers are frequently moved around. Therefore, it's useful to have more than one person of authority in the bank who knows the company.

When interviewing a prospective banker, be sure to ask the following:

1. Does the bank regularly work with small-business owners?

2. What are the costs related to the kinds of transactions your business will do with the bank? Fees vary, and too many small-business owners pay fees that are unwarranted for the value an account generates.

3. What kinds of services will the banker provide?

Working with a Banker

A good banker will want to see the company before extending a line of credit or a loan. The company should be prepared to show itself in the best possible light by introducing the banker to the management team and key employees. Any attempts to restrict access to certain parts of the business or to certain people will probably not be looked on favorably. It's also important to thoroughly know and understand the company's financials, including assets. Demonstrating products will give the banker a clearer understanding of the value of what the business is doing. It's always wise to anticipate any concerns the banker may have and discuss contingency plans in a positive way. Finally, the management team should demonstrate its awareness of safety and environmental issues and how the company is successfully dealing with them.

Insurance Agents

Many entrepreneurs overlook the value of a relationship with a competent insurance agent. A growing venture will require several types of insurance, including

▶ Property and casualty

▶ Medical

▶ Errors and omissions

▶ Life on key management

◗ Workers' compensation insurance

◗ Unemployment insurance

◗ Auto on company vehicles

◗ Liability (product and personal)

◗ Bonding

Major insurance firms can often handle all types of insurance vehicles, but many times the company will need to seek specialists for protection such as **bonding** (a common vehicle in the construction industry to protect against failure of a contractor to complete a project), product liability insurance, and errors and omissions (which protects the business against liability from unintentional mistakes in advertising). The company's insurance needs will change over its life, and a good insurance agent will help it determine the needed coverages at the appropriate times.

Boards of Directors

The decision to have a board of directors is influenced by the legal form of the business; consequently, if the new venture is a corporation, a board of directors is legally required. Furthermore, if the company at some point requires venture capital, the venture capital firm will probably demand a seat on the board. This is because directors are empowered. They can make decisions that affect the company, and they can hire and fire the CEO. Beyond this, boards of directors serve a valuable purpose because, if chosen properly, they provide expertise that will benefit the company, and in that capacity they act much like members of a board of advisers. They also assist in establishing corporate strategy and philosophy, as well as goals and objectives.

It's important to distinguish between boards of privately owned corporations and those of publicly owned corporations. In a privately owned corporation, the genesis team typically owns all or the majority of the stock, so

 Entrepreneurship in Action

"Key-Man" Insurance Is a Must

In many small companies, the fear of what will happen to the company should the founder die is a real concern. For PRP, the Massachusetts-based research and development company, the death of its founder, Francis Chao, in 1994 almost cost the company its life as well. At the time, PRP was in clinical trials on a new product: infusible platelet membranes used in the treatment of cancer patients undergoing chemotherapy.

Without a management successor in place, investors who were going to provide another round of capital became reluctant. The only thing that saved the company was the fact that it had a "key-man" policy for $2.5 million that saw it through the trials.

Whenever you have a situation where a single person is responsible for a key component of the business—R&D, securing capital—you need insurance and you should plan to purchase as much as the company can afford.

SOURCE: Jill Andresky Fraser, "Hindsight Advice on Key-Man Coverage," *Inc.*, March 1996, p. 97.

directors serve at the pleasure of the owners or entrepreneur who has effective control of the company. On the other hand, directors of publicly traded companies have legitimate power to control the activities of the company, and in many cases have been able to fire the lead entrepreneur if they felt he or she was preventing the company from achieving its goals.

Inside Versus Outside Boards

Boards can be composed of **inside** or **outside members,** or a combination of the two. An inside board member is either a founder, an employee, a family member, or a retired manager of the firm, whereas an outside member has no direct connection to the business. Which type of board member is better is a matter of opinion and circumstance, as research has provided no clear results on this issue. In fact, it reports that only 5 percent of closely held companies allow their boards to be dominated by outsiders, and about 80 percent of private companies tend to put outsiders on a board of advisers instead. In general, however, outside directors are beneficial for succession planning and capital raising because they often bring a fresh point of view to the strategic planning process and expertise the founders may not possess.

Insiders, by contrast, have the advantage of complete knowledge about the business; they are generally more available to meet and have demonstrated their effectiveness in the organization. They will usually have the necessary technical expertise as well. On the other hand, there are often political

Lindsay H. Frucci attributes much of the success of No Pudge! Foods, Inc. to the counseling she received from the SCORE (Service Corps of Retired Executives) Association. These volunteers (Jay Albert and Robert Fox) taught her everything she needed to know to grow her home-based business that produces fat-free brownies for revenues of more than $250,000 in 1997. (Richard Howard)

ramifications stemming from the fact that board members report to the CEO and for that reason may not always be objective and independent in their thought processes. Insiders may also lack the broad expertise necessary to effectively guide the growth of the business beyond its current state.

Whether or not the new venture requires a working board of directors must be carefully considered. Most working boards are used for their expertise, strategic planning, auditing the actions of the firm, and arbitrating differences. These activities are not as crucial in the start-up phase when the entrepreneurial team is gathering resources and raising capital. However, a board of directors can assist in those functions and network with key people who can help the new venture. Some investors will ask to be included on the board so they can monitor their investment in the company, whether that investment is money or time. This is common with large, private investors, bankers, and even accountants. To ensure that the company ends ups with the best people on the board, standards should be set in advance and strictly adhered to.

During the growth period of the company, the entrepreneurial team is normally burdened with operational details, the need to generate sales, and the problem of maintaining a positive cash flow. Dealing with a board of directors is not something they will want to do. But the board can offer the struggling team an objective point of view and the benefit of their considerable experience.

Choosing a Board

When choosing people to serve on the board of directors, the following issues should be considered. Does the person have

- The necessary technical skill related to the business?
- Significant, successful experience in the industry?
- Important contacts in the industry?
- Expertise in finance, capital acquisition, and possibly IPOs?
- A personality that is compatible with the rest of the board?
- Good problem-solving skills?
- Honesty and integrity?

When considering a board appointment, a time period should be specified; this is because if the entrepreneurial team is not careful, it may learn too late that a director it has appointed to the board considers the position an appointment for life, much like being appointed to the Supreme Court. To maintain the inflow of fresh ideas to the company, board members should serve on a rotating basis.

The board is headed by the chairperson, who in a new venture is typically the lead entrepreneur. The entrepreneur will also, most probably, be the president and chief executive officer (CEO). The additional positions of secretary and treasurer may be held by a single person, often another member of the founding team.

Boards normally meet an average of five times a year, depending on the type of business. How often the board meets will largely be a function of how active it is at any point in time. Directors typically spend about 9 to 10 days a year on duties related to the business and are usually paid a retainer plus a per-meeting fee; their expenses are also reimbursed. The compensation can take the form of cash, stock, or other perquisites. Additional expenses related to the development of a board of directors include meeting rooms, travel, and food.

Today, getting people to serve as directors is difficult. Because of the fiduciary responsibility they hold, in some cases they can be held personally liable for the actions of the firm, and the frequency with which boards are being sued is increasing. For this reason, potential directors may require that the business carry D&O (directors' and officers') liability insurance on them; however, the expense of this insurance is often prohibitive for a growing company. Some states—for example, Texas and Wisconsin—have passed statutes that protect directors of public and private companies from lawsuits.

Advisory Board

The use of **advisory boards** by entrepreneurs is a growing phenomenon in part because today's entrepreneurs often have educational backgrounds and corporate work experience that has taught them that boards are a valuable asset for a growing company. In contrast to the board of directors, the advisory board is an informal panel of experts and others interested in seeing the company succeed. They are generally unpaid and may meet once or twice a year to advise the entrepreneur; however, more and more boards of advisers are looking like boards of directors. They are even being paid for meetings, especially those where they are asked to contribute significant time and effort on the company's behalf. This has often resulted in the loss of liability protection, which is one principal reason boards of advisers have been chosen over outside boards of directors in the first place. Recent court rulings have led many to suggest that there is no difference, for liability purposes, between a board of directors and a board of advisers. In fact, in a state where protection exists for directors, it's a distinct disadvantage to be on an advisory board.

Advisory boards are often used when a board of directors is not required or in the start-up phase when the board of directors consists of the founders only. An advisory board can provide a new venture with the needed expertise and an objective viewpoint without the significant costs and loss of control associated with a board of directors. It is a good compromise when the company cannot afford to hire such advice on an in-house basis. The board's focus on strategic issues, for which most entrepreneurs don't seem to have time, can often save a company from potentially fatal mistakes. Its access to networks of potential sources of capital, technology, strategic partners, and favorable publicity are invaluable to a growing firm on a limited budget. Sport Tours International, a broker of American collegiate tours for foreign amateur basketball teams, gained significant advantages from its board of advisers. The board helped the struggling firm find its market focus, introduced

Sport Tours to World Wide Web marketing, professionalized the business, and found new clients.[11] Having the editor of *Basketball Weekly* on the advisory board also gave the company more clout.

Effective board members will have a broad spectrum of experience in business that gives them a perspective the entrepreneur lacks. Often entrepreneurs will also want a lawyer, an accountant, and other business professionals who can advise the company on particular issues.

Mistakes to Avoid When Putting Together a Team

Putting together the extended management team is a serious undertaking that, if unsuccessful, could have severe ramifications for the future of the company. Several common mistakes in forming the team should be avoided:

▶ Forming the team casually or by chance, that is, without careful consideration of the experience and qualifications each member brings to the team.

▶ Putting together a team whose members have different goals, which could impede the growth of the company.

▶ Using only insiders—that is, friends and family—on the board of directors instead of the people most qualified to advise the business.

▶ Using family members or friends as attorney and accountant for the business. Since these professional advisers must remain objective at all times to best represent and assist the entrepreneur, choosing relatives can cause unnecessary problems.

▶ Giving the founding team all stock in lieu of salary. The lead entrepreneur does not want significant shares of stock in the hands of people who may leave the company later. Furthermore, loose stock can land in the hands of the firm's competitors. Chapter 3 discussed the use of a buy-sell agreement to prevent this problem.

A well-chosen team can make the difference between a company that moves forward as a team for the good of all and one that is mired in conflicts

Technology Tip

Linking Your Team

When you operate a virtual company, communication is critical. While it's true that today you can do business from anywhere, to do it effectively you need to be linked with the people and companies you're working with.

All you need to stay in touch is a laptop with a modem and an e-mail service. Then wherever you go, you can plug into a phone jack and dial into the server at your business. There you can pick up any messages, send messages, and even access files you've created at the office, the company database, or files others have left for you.

If you're also on-line with your partner companies, you can get up-to-date information from them as well.

and disputes that drag the company down. Both the internal and external teams must be committed to the vision for the company.

The notion of the virtual company has definitely come into its own in this decade and will continue to be a solution for many start-up companies that want to compete successfully in a competitive global market. When employed as part of an agile web, it can give a young company the clout it needs to compete effectively against much larger rivals.

Cases Relevant to This Chapter

French Rags
SB Networks
Zotos-Stein

Issues for Review and Discussion

1. What are three key things entrepreneurs must not do when using independent contractors?
2. What three characteristics should be present in strategic alliance partners to minimize stakeholder exposure?
3. Describe the advantages and disadvantages of inside versus outside board members.
4. At what point in the growth of a company should the entrepreneur consider creating a board of directors or an advisory board?
5. Discuss three benefits to using the virtual organization concept. What are three mechanisms available to form a virtual company?

Experiencing Entrepreneurship

1. Interview a professional—lawyer, accountant, banker—about his or her experience with and ability to work with small, growing companies. What benefits can this professional provide you as an entrepreneur?
2. Identify a company that operates as a virtual organization. Create an agile web indicating the other companies with which it does business and the nature of their relationship (partnership, joint venture, etc.).

Resources

Covey, S. R. (1989). *The 7 Habits of Highly Effective People.* New York: Simon and Schuster Trade.

Ford, R. H. (1992). *Boards of Directors and the Privately Owned Firm.* New York: Quorum Books.

Goldman, Steven L., Roger N. Nagel, and Kenneth Preiss (1995). *Agile Competitors and Virtual Organizations.* New York: Van Nostrand Reinhold.

Helgesen, Sally (1995). *The Web of Inclusion.* New York: Currency/Doubleday.

Ward, J. (1991). *Creating Effective Boards for Private Enterprise.* San Francisco: Jossey-Bass.

Internet Resources

The Small Business Resource Center
http://www.webcom.com/seaquest/sbrc
Help with choosing, starting, and running a small business

Global Entrepreneurs Network
http://www.gen.com
Helps small businesses gain a presence on the web

The Nature of Rapidly Growing Companies

Growth is a by-product of the pursuit of excellence and not itself a worthy goal.
Robert Townsend
Former CEO, Avis, 1984

Preparing the Management Team and the Organization for Growth

Preview

Understanding this chapter will give you the ability to

▶ **Discuss the evolution of strategy and structure in a growing business.**

▶ **Explain the importance of a company vision and how it develops.**

▶ **Define your company's culture.**

▶ **Describe a learning organization and how it is achieved.**

▶ **Explain total quality management and how to successfully implement it in your company.**

▶ **Discuss open-book management and how it affects the way a business is structured.**

▶ **Define the components of an effective human resource policy.**

Terms to Know

Young Entrepreneurs—Minicase

Gregg Myles Levin
Perfect Curve

Sometimes the only way to solve a problem is to invent a solution yourself. Gregg Myles Levin had always struggled to create the "perfect curve" in the brim of his favorite baseball cap. While a student at Syracuse University in New York, he experimented incessantly using rubber bands to arrive at the "perfect curve."

Upon graduation in 1990, Levin took a job in New York as an account executive to begin what he thought was a career in marketing. Two years later, he moved back home to Boston to work for a direct marketing firm. It was then that he came up with an idea to solve the problem of achieving a perfect curve for his baseball cap. He developed a prototype of the device out of green PlayDoh and took it to an engineer to discuss how to design and build it. He also took pictures of fans at Fenway Park to convince potential investors of the need for what he planned to call PerfectCurve®.

Initially his family humored him. His father, an attorney, lamented, "This is why I spent $100,000 sending you to college?" To convince his father, Levin dragged him to several sporting goods stores touting the popularity of caps. His father was convinced. In 1994, Levin and his father founded PerfectCurve, Inc., and incorporated as a Delaware company. In addition to the initial investment of $5,000 from Levin and $12,000 from his father, along with countless hours of "sweat equity," Levin convinced landscape architect Roy S. MacDowell, Jr., to invest $200,000. This allowed Levin to leave his job and devote full-time effort to the fledgling venture. It also permitted the company to produce an initial production run of PerfectCurves for the Lids chain of baseball cap stores and about a dozen other stores throughout New England in time for the Christmas season. That first batch sold out in less than two weeks. This was a good sign of potential demand. According to MacDowell, 500 million caps/hats are sold in America every year. If PerfectCurve, Inc., could capture just 1 percent of that market, that figure would translate to 5 million PerfectCurves sold every year!

PerfectCurve can create a curved cap brim in minutes and actually provides three settings for three different looks: "Pro" is named for the slight curve preferred by professional ball players, "Varsity" is the setting for the most popular curve, and "Extreme" is an extremely tight curve popular with teenagers. What started as a basic solution to a simple problem has evolved into a company on its way to becoming the leader and innovator of what is now called the "cap/hat maintenance market." New products in the line include the Gzonta!™, a cap retention cord; The Perfect-Curve Cap Cleaner & Deodorizer™; The PerfectCurve Cap & Hat Water Repellant™; and the PerfectCurve Cap Rack System™, a cap display and storage system. PerfectCurve® is now available in more than 350 retail outlets and catalogs around the country.

Levin built the mold for the PerfectCurve and then hired a manufacturer with injection-molding technology to produce it. The finished product is then sent to a Boston area rehabilitation program site where people with disabilities assemble and package it. Levin then takes the finished packages to his office/warehouse, where they are stored and shipped. To date the company is shipping 10,000 units per month to retail locations. It also has a deal with Sony of Japan to distribute thousands of PerfectCurves throughout Japan. This was a real coup for the company, since it normally takes three to five years to break into the Japanese market. Levin and his father did it in seven months by building strong relationships with their customers and capitalizing on Japan's love for baseball. They have also shipped products to Israel, South Africa, and Australia.

Although Levin and his father have patents issued on the PerfectCurve, competitors are coming out with "knock-off" products. One competitor is literally copying everything PerfectCurve, Inc., does, but it doesn't have the distribution channels Levin does or the good customer relationships he has built. Levin is confident that the company will continue to grow and will double its revenues every year for at least the next two years. The possibilities seem endless, but both Levin and his father know they want to harvest the business at some time in the future.

Levin's father had always wanted to go into business with one of his children. Now that he is partnering with Levin, he dreams of giving up law altogether because he's having so much fun. It is not often easy for a kid to partner with a parent, because frequently neither is able to forget his or her traditional role and just become equal partners. What makes it even more awkward for Levin and his father is the fact that they have what Levin calls "a family business in reverse": Levin brought his dad into the business and is the principal decision maker. However, this arrangement has really enhanced their relationship and works very well. Still, Levin candidly advises that this may not be a good strategy for most young entrepreneurs. You need to have a strong relationship with your parent, bury your ego, be open to ideas, and have a good understanding of your role.

Levin's advice to aspiring entrepreneurs? "You're only as successful as the people you surround yourself with." Young entrepreneurs need to realize that there's a lot they don't know, and they can't do everything on their own. Gregg Levin has found a team that works, and he's very excited about the future of PerfectCurve, Inc. **http://www.perfectcurve.com**

How has Gregg Levin prepared his PerfectCurve team for growth?

The growth stage of the business life cycle is one of the most exciting periods of business ownership for entrepreneurs. It can also be one of the more frightening times if you haven't prepared for it, because without a plan securely in place, things can get out of control fairly quickly. Losing control during growth generally results from several factors, including

- ◗ Failing to have an appropriate infrastructure and systems in place
- ◗ Lacking the skills to manage growth
- ◗ Lack of sufficient working capital to support growth

Gregg Levin and his father (see the Young Entrepreneurs—Minicase) knew they wanted to keep their overhead costs to a minimum as the company grew so they could put all their limited resources into that growth. One way to do that was to outsource the manufacturing and packaging, which are labor-intensive tasks, to an established manufacturer and a rehabilitation center that was looking to provide useful jobs for its inhabitants. Levin knew the savings were not just in money but in time and expertise in hiring and managing employees, skills that he and his father lacked. By outsourcing the labor requirements, they were able to focus on what they did best: promotion and distribution.

Traditionally, management of organizations has been considered a three-step process consisting of (1) deciding what needs to be done (planning), (2) assigning jobs to appropriate people (organizing), and (3) evaluating the performance of those people and the results of their work (controlling). Today it's difficult to define management so rigidly because the business environment has changed. Environmental change means that if businesses are to be effective in the new environment, management structures must change as well. The conventional organizational chart with its multiple layers of management and rigid departmental boundaries is still alive and well in very large organizations, but it does not appear to meet the flexibility needs of growing

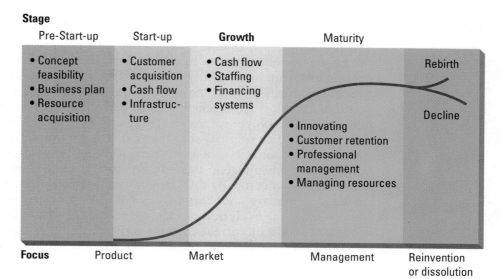

Stage

**Figure 7.1
The Growth Stage of
the Life Cycle**

entrepreneurial companies. It's not the hierarchical structure itself that is at fault but the new environment into which it has been thrust. The functional focus of hierarchies with rigid chains of command and authority does not respond as well to dynamic, chaotic environments as flatter structures do. In entrepreneurial companies, for example, people generally perform a variety of tasks in a team atmosphere where duties can overlap and functions are interdependent. At start-up, the founding management team may even perform all the tasks of the business; but as the business grows, it becomes necessary to bring in people with the expertise and experience needed to lead the company through this often turbulent period. Growth can quite naturally lead to hierarchy and more organizational structure because the creation of a hierarchy is an evolutionary process. The challenge is to manage the process so as to create an organizational structure that is appropriate to the type of environment in which the growing business will operate.

Recall the life cycle model first presented in Chapter 4 and reproduced in Figure 7.1. Notice that while cash flow certainly remains an issue in the growth stage, the entrepreneur's focus has begun to include staffing and systems issues that were not thought about during the bootstrap, start-up phase. Now the challenge becomes how to balance limited resources against the need to take on more staff and perhaps larger facilities and more equipment. Gregg Levin has increased his office/warehouse space three times in two years due to the demands of growth.

This chapter focuses on preparing the founding management team for growth and the potential addition of employees, and what that means in terms of coordination, delegation of authority, and the implementation of systems to manage greater demands on everyone's time and resources.

The Management Revolution for the Twenty-first Century

Today many of the rules generally associated with good management strategy have been bent, if not totally broken, in an effort to create an organization that can successfully compete and navigate in a dynamic, global environment while remaining entrepreneurial. Top-down, chain-of-command, rigid hierarchical approaches have been modified or even replaced by walking around, employee empowerment, participation, and open-book management styles. The result is that many of the traditional views of company strategy have moved from an external focus—"How can the firm achieve a competitive advantage in the marketplace?"—to an internal focus—"How can we build a company that satisfies the needs of the customers and provides a supportive and learning environment for our employees?" A brief overview of the evolution of management theory provides a natural segue to a discussion of current thought on such topics as company vision and culture, total quality management (TQM), the learning organization, and open-book management. These topics lay the foundation for a transition mechanism that allows entrepreneurs to move into professional management of their companies and develop a human resource policy for the growing company.

The Evolution of Strategy and Structure in a Growing Business

The competitive strategy focus that has long received so much attention was due principally to the work of Michael Porter,[1] although it actually had its origins in the work of A. P. Chandler, J. Bain, and I. Ansoff.[2] Chandler referred to strategy as "the statement of the firm's goals and its policies and practices for achieving those goals." The issue of management practice itself did not arise until later, when researchers began to look at the stakeholders of an organization and to view employees as one among several constituencies, which also included founders, stockholders, and others with a vested interest in the company.[3] U.S. management practices prior to the 1980s did not hold employees in high esteem as stakeholders. It was not until the globalization of the marketplace in the 1980s, when firms began studying Japanese management philosophy, that U.S. firms began to rethink the role of employees in the company's strategy. Japanese firms, even those operating in the United States, regularly ranked their employees higher as stakeholders; in fact, Japanese companies attained superior performance through the careful nurturing of what they considered their greatest asset: their human resources.[4] Therefore, much of current management practice is based on the original Japanese model.

Organizational Structure

Organization theory also produced many models of organizational structure designed to match a particular business strategy, beginning with the very early bureaucratic and hierarchical models. During the 1960s and 1970s, the work of P. R. Lawrence, J. W. Lorsch, and others taught us that environmental differentiation affects organizational structure.[5] In other words, the way a business is structured depends on the environment in which it operates. This theory was followed by the matrix model, which supported dual reporting relationships, and the contingency model, which said that the organizational structure is a function of critical elements in the firm's environment and customers. In the early 1980s, the concept of the strategic business unit (SBU) became popular and was shaped by the merger and acquisition fever of that period. Still, the basic concept of the hierarchy pervaded all these models, whether the company was organized based on function or on geographic location.

Beginning in the mid-1980s, however, total quality management (TQM) began to make inroads in the thinking of many business leaders as they sought ways to improve performance beyond mere strategy and structure. The goal of TQM was to respond more efficiently and effectively to the needs of the customer through the use of continuous improvement and just-in-time delivery. The important element in this new approach was that it was the first to move away from hierarchical modes of organization to a flatter, more decentralized structure. This required empowering employees at all levels to make decisions, as well as to self-inspect at every point of the process to ensure a quality outcome. The result was employees who worked in self-directed teams and were now significantly more important as stakeholders in the company. The timing of the entry of TQM is certainly critical, as it coincides with the emergence of the information/technology revolution, which made decentralization possible by linking all organizational functions via a local area network. Most recently, organizational structure and strategy have taken yet another leap to virtual organizations and agile webs, which create a very loose organizational structure that is flexible and easily changed as needed. Chapter 6 discussed these two types of structure more fully.

All of these changes have radically influenced the way leaders of organizations lead and managers manage. Today more than ever before, human resource management has become a driving force in the organization's development as business owners are realizing that employee development and business development are not mutually exclusive concepts but must occur simultaneously if the company is to achieve its goals.

A Great Company Begins with a Vision

Perhaps the most important function of an entrepreneur/leader is to be the catalyst for a clear and shared **vision** that the company will pursue.[6] It's possible for a company to be profitable without a vision, but research indicates that vision seems to be essential to an enduring company. It's the glue that binds everyone in the company to a common purpose. Vision is what makes a company independent of any individual person—in other words, enduring. It also provides a context within which decisions are made.

Contrary to some beliefs, vision is *not* an esoteric pronouncement by a charismatic leader or the ability to see the future. Rather, it's what makes the difference between a company that achieves superior long-term performance and one that is simply successful. But it's even more than this. Companies with vision have etched themselves into society's very foundations and changed the way we all carry out our lives. 3M's scotch tape and Post-it® Notes, GE's light bulbs and appliances, and Motorola's cellular phones and paging systems are but a few examples of enduring companies with a vision that translated into products that changed our lives. The answer to what makes these companies special, why they are a cut above their competition, and why they have survived lies in the vision that endures through decades of change in management, through economic ups and downs, and through changing technology and customer requirements.

Built to Last

In their ground-breaking book *Built to Last: Successful Habits of Visionary Companies,* James Collins and Jerry Porras present the results of six years of research on what they called "visionary companies."[7] The companies they chose to study were selected according to the following criteria:

- Premier institution in its industry

- Widely admired by knowledgeable businesspeople

- Made an indelible imprint on the world in which we live

- Had multiple generations of chief executives

- Went through multiple product (or service) life cycles

- Founded before 1950[8]

On the surface, this sounds like a big-business study rather than one that is relevant to entrepreneurs. But the lessons for entrepreneurs are clear: entrepreneurs who wish to create companies that endure well beyond their tenure as business owners and through significant changes in markets have much to learn about what it takes to do that.

Table 7.1 presents the companies that were chosen for the Collins-Porras study. These companies have been in their industries for decades and have "served as role models . . . for the practice of management around the world."[9] They have also significantly outperformed their competition in terms of return on investment. If on January 1, 1926, you had placed a $1 investment in each of (1) a general stock market fund, (2) the comparison companies (number 2s), and (3) the visionary companies (number 1s) and checked the growth on December 31, 1990, the results would have been astonishing. The return on investment of a visionary company was more than six-and-a-half times that of the comparison companies and 15 times more than the stock market!

What distinguishes these companies is the important lesson for entrepreneurs to learn about vision. Entrepreneurs tend to focus all their efforts and

Table 7.1   Companies in the Collins-Porras Study

Visionary Company	Comparison Company
3M	Norton
American Express	Wells Fargo
Boeing	McDonnell Douglas
Citicorp	Chase Manhattan
Ford	GM
General Electric	Westinghouse
Hewlett-Packard	Texas Instruments
IBM	Burroughs
Johnson & Johnson	Bristol-Myers Squibb
Marriott	Howard Johnson
Merck	Pfizer
Motorola	Zenith
Nordstrom	Melville
Philip Morris	RJR Nabisco
Procter & Gamble	Colgate
Sony	Kenwood
Wal-Mart	Ames
Disney	Columbia

energies on "the great idea," often to the exclusion of the notion of building a company. It's no wonder, then, that they can't answer the fundamental questions "What business are we in, and why?"

"The great idea" was one myth Collins and Porras buried as a result of their research. They found that very few of the visionary companies started with a great idea; in fact, most did not find entrepreneurial success early on at all.[10] This was astounding, but the research uncovered other characteristics relevant to entrepreneurs:

1. Visionary companies by and large did not have charismatic leaders at their origins. Rather, they had entrepreneurs who wanted to build a great and enduring company.

2. The driving force in these companies is not shareholder wealth or profit maximization but, first and foremost, adherence to their purpose and core values, the company's unique ideology.

3. Visionary companies zealously preserve their core values while striving for state-of-the-art products and processes.

4. These companies have not been afraid to take great risks when warranted. They often eschew strategic planning to go with their "gut."

5. Visionary companies are so firm in their beliefs and culture that only people who believe in their vision completely will be able to work for them.

6. Far and away, most CEOs of visionary companies came up through the ranks of the organization.

7. The primary competitor to a visionary company is itself. The visionary company is in a constant state of improvement.

8. They resist trade-offs that force them to compromise on quality in any area of the business. For example, instead of choosing between quality and low cost, they find a way to achieve both.

The Components of Vision

The Collins-Porras vision framework proposes that vision is composed of the company's core values, purpose, and mission.[11]

Core Values

Core values are the fundamental beliefs the business holds about what is important in business and in life in general—in other words, a "philosophy of life." (See Table 7.2 for the core values of three highly successful companies.) Core values derive from the personal values of the entrepreneur. They can't be "set" or created, but are actually a reflection of what already exists. The core values of any company are "a set of basic precepts that plant a fixed stake in the ground: 'This is who we are; this is what we stand for, this is what we're

Table 7.2   Core Values of Very Successful Companies

American Express	▶ Heroic customer service
	▶ Worldwide reliability of services
	▶ Encouragement of individual initiative
Merck	▶ We are in the business of preserving and improving human life All of our actions must be measured by our success in achieving this goal
	▶ Honesty and integrity
	▶ Corporate social responsibility
	▶ Unequivocal excellence in all aspects of the company
	▶ Profit, but profit from work that benefits humanity
Nordstrom	▶ Service to the customer above all else
	▶ Hard work and productivity
	▶ Continuous improvement, never being satisfied
	▶ Excellence in reputation, being part of something special

Source: James C. Collins and Jerry I. Porras, *Built to Last: Successful Habits of Visionary Companies* (New York: HarperBusiness, 1994).

all about.'"[12] Core values are so fundamental to the existence of the company that they rarely change over time. Johnson & Johnson, for example, established the following principle in 1943, which is still in force today:

> We believe that our first responsibility is to the doctors, nurses, hospitals, mothers, and all others who use our products. Our products must always be of the highest quality. We must constantly strive to reduce the cost of these products. Our orders must be promptly and accurately filled. Our dealers must make a fair profit.[13]

The visionary companies listed in Table 7.1 all had a set of core values that endured well beyond the tenure of the founding entrepreneur. In reality, these companies have become known by their core values.[14] It is also noteworthy that the core values of the top companies are about ideals, not profits; in fact, that is one of the principal characteristics differentiating the top companies from the number 2s. Sony Corporation, for example, has a simple but firm ideology:

> Sony is a pioneer and never intends to follow others. Through progress, Sony wants to serve the whole world. It shall be always a seeker of the unknown. . . . Sony has a principle of respecting and encouraging one's ability . . . and always tries to bring out the best in a person. This is the vital force of Sony.[15]

True, Sony started out with crude heating pads, sweetened bean-paste soup, and a failed rice cooker to stay alive while it moved toward the ideal of being a pioneer. But because Sony focused on its vision and core values, it was able to ultimately produce innovative products for which there was no demonstrable demand: the first magnetic tape recorder in Japan (1950), the first all-transistor radio (1955), the first pocket-size radio (1957), the first consumer videotape recorder (1964), and the Sony Walkman (1979). Kenwood, the comparison company in the study, had no set of core values, visions, or ideals.

It could be argued that entrepreneurs are too occupied managing cash flow and meeting customer demands to concern themselves with anything as esoteric as visions and core values. Yet Sony's ideals were set down in the earliest stages of its development, certainly long before it was ever profitable, and guided its evolution as a company. This is not to say that providing a quality product or service is not equally important in the early stages of a company, but in today's competitive environment, the company vision is critical to long-term success.

When deciding on the core values for the company, it's important to limit the number to no more than five or six so that they truly are core values that will endure over time. One test to use in deciding whether a core value will stand the test of time is to ask if the company will give the value up in the face of being penalized for holding that value. If the answer is yes, it's not a core value.

Purpose

Purpose is the fundamental reason for the existence of the business, and it emerges directly from the core values and beliefs. A purpose is analogous to trying to reach the end of a rainbow. You're always making your way toward it, but you never actually reach it.

Advanced Decision Systems' purpose, for example, is

To enhance decision-making power

It will never reach the day when it has completely enhanced people's decision-making power, but it will always have a purpose toward which it strives.

Mission

Mission is a statement of a clear and compelling but broad goal that serves to focus effort. In contrast to purpose, a mission is always achievable, and once it's achieved, the purpose is used to define a new mission. The mission is a way of translating the broad purpose of the organization into a defined goal. A goal must have an end point; therefore, the mission should clearly state by which date it will be achieved. It's also important that the mission be exciting, something people can grab hold of and feel and have an intense desire to accomplish.

In 1977, Sam Walton, founder of Wal-Mart Stores, Inc., set the following mission:

To become a $1 billion company by 1980

In practical terms, this meant doubling company size in three years. In reality, Wal-Mart achieved $1.2 billion.

Company Culture

In addition to changes in management philosophy, business strategy, and organizational structure, distinct changes in company **culture** have occurred. Researchers actually disagree as to exactly what culture is. Some believe it is the reflection of the core values of the company, which stem from the firm's history.[16] Others believe culture is changeable, that it really reflects the behaviors and attitudes of those in the company at the time.[17] In their 1982 book *Corporate Cultures: The Rites and Rituals of Corporate Life*, Terrence Deal and Allan Kennedy coined the term *corporate culture* to describe the organization's tendency to develop its own characteristic way of doing things.[18] In very simplistic terms, organizational culture is the personality of the company, that intangible set of values that determines how and why the people in the organization respond to their business environment as they do.[19] A description of the company culture may be spelled out in the company handbook, but the real culture is found in the attitudes and actions of the organization's people as they interact on a daily basis.

It is often said that entrepreneurial companies—start-ups in particular—have a distinct culture, one much different from that of large, established corporations. This is misleading, because not all start-ups are alike. If the

When was the last time you went for ice cream and were entertained at the same time? Well, you would have been if you went to Amy's Ice Cream in Austin, Texas where the employees have as much fun as the customers. The company's corporate culture based on having fun proves you don't always have to take business seriously. (Danny Turner)

founders came from the big corporate environment or from a traditional business school education, they are very likely to think in terms of elaborate organization charts and multiple levels of management that look much like those of GE or Xerox. Often it is the founders who don't have these experiences and basically organize to make the business happen, who end up with the maverick, "just do it" culture generally associated with start-ups.

Defining a Company's Culture

Some of the questions that lead to a definition of a company's culture are the following:

1. Do the organization's people work in teams or individually?

2. How does the organization deal with change?

3. How does the company deal with failure?

4. How are decisions made? Who makes the critical decisions?

5. How is work prioritized?

6. How is information shared within and outside the organization?

7. Does the company take a long-term or short-term focus on decision making?

**Figure 7.2
Defining Culture**

8. How does the company ensure employee competence?

9. Does the company encourage diversity?

10. How are employees treated, and what is their role in the company's vision?

Figure 7.2 depicts two distinctly different cultures based on these questions. Which one has the better chance to succeed in a rapidly changing environment? Undoubtedly, culture A is more flexible and better able to make changes. It will also be more likely to have employees who buy into the vision and are loyal to the company.

The Importance of Culture

Culture is an important attribute of a company for two reasons. First, culture has a significant impact on company performance.[20] A culture shared by everyone in the organization produces a sense of purpose and a drive to achieve goals, which results in a more successful business. Second, cultures are amenable to change with the times. Though the company's core values may endure unchanging over time, the culture reflects changes in the business environment and keeps the company moving forward. Although vision is the driving force for the company, culture is the reflection of how that vision is implemented on a daily basis.

CCTV manufacturer Pelco's corporate culture is about being fanatically customer driven. Talk to anyone in the company and within one minute you'll hear the word *customer*. Everyone in the company, from the president to the assembly worker who packages the product, knows what she or he contributes to the satisfaction of the customer. This culture is so ingrained that it will live on beyond the tenure of the founding team. (See the case study on Pelco, Inc.)

Moving from Entrepreneurship to Professional Management

Earlier in the chapter, we referred to a lack of resources, skills, and systems as significant inhibitors of growth in small companies. While all of these factors are vital, there is no doubt that the success of any growth strategy is predicated almost totally on the entrepreneur's ability to make the transition from being a bootstrapping entrepreneur to being a professional manager.[21] This is no easy feat because the skills required to start the venture are quite distinct from those needed to manage it through growth. The bootstrapping techniques and controlling, "just do it" attitude of most entrepreneurs that gave a new business the boldness it needed to break into the market can actually cause the business to stall or spiral out of control in a rapid growth phase. Hofer and Charen's research has resulted in a transition process that entrepreneurs should implement to ensure the successful growth and survival of their businesses:

1. First and foremost, the entrepreneur must recognize that change in his or her behavior needs to take place and that he or she must be willing to make those changes.

2. Formal decision systems must be put into place and more people given control over some aspect of the decision process.

3. The operational tasks that mean success or failure for the business must be institutionalized so they are not dependent on a single person.

4. Specialists in the company must be able to become functional managers, while functional managers must become general managers.

5. The company strategy with regard to growth must be reevaluated.

6. Systems and procedures must match the new strategies.

7. If not already in place, the company will need a professional board of directors.

Again, the key ingredient to success in this transition is the entrepreneur's ability to shift from an opportunistic, resource-gatherer mode to a resource management and more structured mode. For some entrepreneurs this is an impossible task, and they choose instead to put a professional manager in the operational role and step aside to concentrate on issues at a more strategic level.

Stevenson and Gumpert have identified five areas where entrepreneurs and professional managers differ in their thinking processes: strategic orientation, commitment to seize opportunities, commitment of resources, control of resources, and management structure.[22] Table 7.3 summarizes these differences.

Table 7.3   The Entrepreneurial View Versus the Management View

Entrepreneurial View	Management View
Motivated by opportunity; resource acquisition	Motivated by resources; resource management
Risk management	Risk avoidance
Revolutionary; breakthrough actions	Evolutionary; derivative actions
Unpredictable environment with limited resources	More predictable environment with committed resources
Rented, leased, borrowed resources	Owned or employed resources
Flat organizational structure; team approach; empowered employees	Hierarchical organizational structure; chain of command

Source: Howard H. Stevenson and David E. Gumpert, "The Heart of Entrepreneurship," *Harvard Business Review,* March/April 1985, p. 85.

Building the Learning Organization

Educators talk about the value of and necessity for lifelong learning. In other words, learning doesn't stop when formal education is complete. This principle is true for businesses as well. Growing companies need to put themselves in a learning mode so they are constantly prepared for changes in the environment.

In his best-selling book *The Fifth Discipline,* Peter Senge says,

> The organization that will truly excel in the future will be the organization that discovers how to tap people's commitment and capacity to learn at *all* levels in an organization.[23]

The **learning organization** is also a necessary foundation for the implementation of total quality management, which we will discuss in the next section. The learning organization is not about gathering new information, although that is certainly important. Rather, it is about the organization constantly renewing itself at both the organizational and individual levels, and it involves a systems approach that takes into account the interactions and consequences of everything the company does. Senge suggests there are five disciplines the company and the individuals within it must master to achieve a learning organization: personal mastery, mental models, a shared vision, team learning, and systems thinking. We will briefly look at each of these disciplines, which are essential to implementing total quality management.

First Discipline: Personal Mastery

At an individual level, **personal mastery** is a commitment by management and employees to lifelong learning and a superior level of performance. To accomplish this, management and employees need to identify what is really important to them as individuals. Senge has called the distance between what an individual wants and where he or she is at any moment in time **creative tension**.[24]

Creative Tension

Where I am   →→→→→→→→→→   **Where I want to be**

It's the job of management, particularly the entrepreneur/leader, to create a safe environment where employees can hold their own visions and become what they want to become, which will give everyone a sense of purpose. It is also the job of the entrepreneur/leader to facilitate employees' ability to do their best by offering training, incentive systems, and support.

Second Discipline: Mental Models

Every person in the organization brings to the company his or her unique **mental models** of how things should be and how things should work. These mental models or pictures are based on the individuals' own personal experiences and background. Yet because mental models and the behaviors they induce are not always congruent with theories of how things should work, people often behave at odds with theory.[25] In other words, we behave based on the reality we perceive whether or not that reality exists in fact. Thus, mental models are one of the primary reasons conflicts occur in companies. Each person sees a situation or an issue from his or her own perspective. Companies need to find ways to get beyond these content differences and focus on how everyone in the organization can communicate better. Regular meetings in a safe environment where communication can occur without threat to one's self-esteem or company position is one way to make this happen.

Third Discipline: Shared Vision

As discussed previously, vision is a strongly held belief, a set of principles and common purpose about what the company is and where it should go. It's a force that, if shared, drives everyone with a focus and an energy that an individual alone cannot achieve. But to accomplish this, the vision must be a commitment on the part of everyone, not an edict dictated by the entrepreneur with which everyone must comply. In fact, the most powerful **shared visions** often come from the ranks of employees early in the development of the company when everyone is working together for the survival of the start-up.

Data General's product development team was charged with developing an innovative new computer in a moment of great crisis for the company. During the process, it learned that the development of critical software was far behind schedule. The three engineers involved in the product development spent an entire night working on the problem and succeeded in completing two to three months of work in one night. This type of effort reflects commitment to vision rather than compliance.[26]

Fourth Discipline: Team Learning

Organizations learn not at the individual level but at the team level. When teams are able to suspend personal assumptions and develop a collegial atmosphere, they eventually become one, in alignment on their purpose and goals. Teams in alignment continuously improve their practice of the discipline of learning, and as a consequence they develop significant power as stakeholders in the company. That power comes from perfecting the discipline of learning so that they are always on the cutting edge in every function or task they perform. In companies that use a team-based philosophy, it is also important to reward based on team effort rather than individual effort, for the latter will prevent the team from ever achieving true coherency.

Fifth Discipline: Systems Thinking

According to Senge, "**Systems thinking** is a discipline for seeing the 'structures' that underlie complex situations."[27] It's about seeing the organization as a whole, looking for the effects of actions throughout the organization. When cross-functional teams are in place, systems thinking can occur. Every employee must be made aware of what she or he contributes to the organization as a whole. Employees must be able to see how their actions and the results they achieve affect the rest of the company. In an integrated company, no one operates in a vacuum.

Senge's learning organization is by no means a quick fix. Rather, it is a long, steady process that never really ends. It consists of establishing from day one a process of continual improvement in all aspects of the company and in every individual within it.

Total Quality Management

In the simplest terms, **total quality management** (TQM) is the application of the highest levels of quality in every aspect of the business. In the 1980s, TQM was a popular buzzword, the latest management fad. Many companies leaped to adopt its principles, and those same firms failed to achieve anything beyond mediocre results. Arthur D. Little Enterprises' 1992 survey of 500 U.S. firms found that two-thirds claimed their quality efforts had not had a "significant impact" on their competitiveness. Similarly, a British study of 100 firms found that their quality programs had not produced "tangible results."[28]

On the other hand, some companies have achieved outstanding results with their quality programs. Federal Express, for example, successfully employed TQM to achieve its goal of "100 percent service performance on every package delivered." Not only did it concern itself with on-time delivery, but it also instituted a service quality indicator (SQI) to measure various types of delivery problems, such as damage to packages and incorrect delivery time. Six years after establishing the system, package volume had increased 82 percent and its SQI had decreased by 4 percent, meaning the defect rate per 1,000 deliveries had declined significantly. The company also decreased its cost per package by 20 percent.[29]

Undoubtedly, Ford Motor Company would not be here today without TQM, and Toyota would not have invaded the auto industry so dramatically in the 1970s had it not implemented TQM.

Two reasons have been proposed for the lack of results by many companies in attempting to successfully execute the TQM principles. First, to effect change in the organization, its structure and culture must be amenable to change, and this is no easy feat because most established companies are well entrenched in their structures and cultures. Second, most of the new change literature (reengineering) focuses on one segment of the company without necessarily considering the company as a whole.[30] This is the problem to which Senge referred: a lack of systems thinking. Making a change in one area of the organization has important ramifications for every other part of the system. Therefore, to be effective, TQM must be applied to the organization as a whole and to every component in the system. It is "not a technique, but a way of life."[31]

Fortunately, new ventures that decide to implement TQM from the beginning have the highest probability of success because they can develop systems and hire people at the outset who understand what they are trying to accomplish.

 Entrepreneurship in Action

Honda: A TQM Success Story and Model for Growing Businesses

Honda is one of the great TQM success stories, both in Japan and in America. Following are the principles on which the company is built. These principles can be applied equally well in a small, growing company. Note how Honda has integrated all the aspects of total quality management into every area of the company.

- Honda is organized by teams rather than by function.
- Each team member is multiskilled and is called an "associate."
- Every team has a leader, and leaders have a strong understanding of all the components of production.
- There is no gap between labor and management. Everyone works together.
- Honda measures results at key points in its production process rather than solely at the end.
- Feedback is immediate and objective.
- Training is a constant. Everyone is continually learning.
- Just-in-time delivery and inventory are used in all areas of the business.

- Quality is built into the process and product, not inspected in.
- Any worker can halt the production line if a quality issue arises.
- All the principles are based on customer needs, both internal and external.
- The employee involvement program rewards through bonuses, profit sharing, and total compensation approaches for positive performance.
- Everyone shares a commitment to total quality.

Some CEOs who have been skeptical as to whether the "Japanese approach" can work in U.S. companies because the cultures are so different can look to the successes of Honda and Toyota in the United States, where the plants have workers who are virtually all Americans successfully operating under the Japanese system of management.

SOURCE: Adapted from *The Five Pillars of TQM* by Bill Creech. New York: Truman Talley Books/Plume.

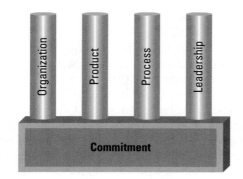

**Figure 7.3
Creech's Five Pillars
of TQM**

The Creech Model

Bill Creech, a four-star general who applied TQM to the Tactical Air Command in time to prepare the air force for the Gulf War and is probably the most successful practitioner of TQM since its inception, writes that the basics of TQM are supported by five pillars of the organization—product, process, organization, leadership, and commitment—as depicted in Figure 7.3.

The management system embodied in Creech's five pillars is designed to meet the requirements of a new, dynamic market environment. The five pillars are integrated in the following way:

▶ Commitment by everyone in the organization from the bottom up supports the other four pillars. If total commitment is not possible or is weak, the other four cannot stand.

▶ The product focuses the organization on purpose and achievement. Everyone in the organization produces a product or service, from the production people to the billing staff. Quality certainly begins with the product or service but is totally dependent on quality in the process as well.

▶ The process for producing the product or service is integrated with the actual product or service and dependent on the organization as a whole for its ultimate quality.

▶ The organization must allow for quality throughout by encouraging employee learning and empowerment through a decentralized structure that is flexible and supportive.

▶ The success of the organization depends directly on its leadership: the entrepreneur. The entrepreneur (leader) serves as a model of spirit, energy, and vision for the company and sees to it that the company remains on the path it set. The entrepreneur must be obsessed with creating a people-oriented company and, in that regard, must be willing to listen to its employees and adopt suggestions wherever possible.

**Figure 7.4
The Five TQM Pillars
Plus the Customer**

Adding the Customer to the Model

We would add one more element to the TQM model: the customer. If commitment is the foundation on which TQM rests, the customer is the roof that unifies the pillars and keeps them from collapsing. Without the customer there is no company, no business to conduct, and no organization to manage. Figure 7.4 depicts this new model.

Input by the customer into product/service and process clearly affects the way the company is organized to meet the needs of the customer. Likewise, leadership makes it possible for everyone in the organization to know the customer and to deal with the customer at some level. The commitment of everyone to this goal of achieving customer satisfaction in all areas of the business is what will ensure the ultimate success of the company.

A Seven-Step Process for Achieving TQM

In her book *Fad Surfing in the Boardroom*, Eileen Shapiro asserts that the process of TQM itself must be subjected to continuous improvement. She cautions companies not to focus solely on the process to the exclusion of outcomes. This was the problem at Florida Power and Light, the first U.S. company to win the Japanese Deming Prize for quality. The company found it was putting too much energy into process and procedures rather than simply relying on the fundamental principles of TQM. Its experience led to the development of a seven-step process improvement strategy using the following questions:[32]

1. What is the problem?
2. Where are we now?
3. What are the root causes?
4. What is needed to improve?
5. What happened from our actions?
6. How do we maintain the improvement?
7. What needs to be addressed next?

With this simple approach applied uniformly across the entire organization, total quality can be achieved and continually maintained.

To accomplish TQM, everyone must be committed. It cannot be left to a committee or a few chosen ones in a quality "power play." TQM principles and practices must be the province of everyone in the organization. Furthermore, quality must be achieved while at the same time allowing the company to achieve its profit goals. Making money is not an option for a company; it's a necessity to survive and provide customer satisfaction. Fortunately, small-business owners starting new businesses are probably in the best position to

CompuWorks, a Pittsfield, Massachusetts computer systems integrator, created a learning organization by letting employees get involved in every aspect of the business. Employees plan how to achieve their department goals and how to measure their progress. They record their achievements on huge charts they create and display where everyone can see them. (David Zadig)

put TQM strategies in place. They hire people who understand and share the vision and monitor the implementation of TQM as the company grows.

Open-Book Management

A natural outgrowth of employee empowerment and TQM is **open book management (OBM),** which gets everyone in the organization involved and thinking like an owner of the company. Proponents of this philosophy say the reason it works is that it gets people to think rather than just do. John Case believes there are three primary differences between an open-book company and a conventional company.[33] In an open-book company,

- All employees learn how to read and understand the company's financial statements. That way employees always know if the company is making money, how much it is making, and why.

- Employees learn that part of their responsibility is to keep the financial numbers moving in the right direction.

- Employees share directly in the profits of the company.

In some open-book companies, employees actually do all the purchasing and even have a voice in hiring decisions. In companies such as Cin-Made,

Entrepreneurship in Action

An Example of Open-Book Management

Recently, the press has touted a new style of management called *open-book management* in which employees are allowed access to the company's financials so that everyone knows what's going on. It sounds like a fine approach in theory, but how does it work in practice? John Strazzanti found out when he turned his company, Com-Corp Industries, a $13 million metal-stamping shop specializing in headlight parts for the auto industry, into an open-book company. The company is modeled, surprisingly, after the three branches of the federal government, with owner, managers, and employees all holding power. One of the things he does to maintain checks and balances on the system is to challenge the employees to find errors in the financial numbers, for which they can earn a 50-cent-an-hour raise. Strazzanti also provides his employees with workshops on issues that will help them make better choices in the marketplace, such as "how to manage a household budget" and "how the value of goods in the marketplace is determined."

Employees decide how compensation rates are determined by volunteering to serve on the Wage and Salary Committee. Their job is to collect as much information as possible on comparable businesses in the industry and what they are paying for everyone from the janitor to the president. In addition, a standardized performance appraisal form is used that divides the job functions into several measurable components. Employees are evaluated not only by their supervisors but also by their peers, and if they have a grievance, they take it to the Human Resources Assistance Committee.

Strazzanti also distributes a bonus pool of 17 percent of Com-Corp's pretax profits to employees and managers who have been with the company for a year or more. During hard times there's no profit sharing, but during high-profit years some of the line workers take home bonuses of more than $10,000.

SOURCE: Teri Lammers Prior, "If I Were President . . . ," *Inc.,* April 1995.

which makes metal and cardboard containers, profit sharing accounts for about 35 percent of employees' compensation.

To successfully implement open-book management requires that the company teach all employees the business skills they need to understand how the finances of the business work—such things as how the business makes a profit, what comprises its costs, and the sales patterns it has experienced over time. Management has to empower employees to make and be accountable for critical decisions that will allow them to improve the company's bottom line and share in the profits. Whether this comes about through a bonus incentive system or through stock ownership must be carefully weighed. Stack suggests that "equity is the basis for all long-term thinking. It is the best reason for staying the course . . . it's the best way to achieve lasting success."[34]

By itself, open-book management will not guarantee success; but as part of a systems approach to TQM, it goes a long way toward giving employees a vested interest in the company—in other words, a reason for making sure the company succeeds.

Developing a Human Resource Policy

As you can see, the human capital of a company is at the heart of what will make the company a success. It must be chosen wisely and nurtured as carefully as you do your customers. In the early stages of a developing small business, the focus is on hiring as few people as possible because labor costs are generally the biggest expense for any company. As the company begins to grow more rapidly, however, it feels pressured to increase its staff to support a growing demand for its products and/or services. It's at this point that the

 Entrepreneurship in Action

The Rise of the CEO Coach

What causes someone to leave a high-paying corporate job in an $800 million company to start a small business? For Kay Stepp, former president and COO of Portland General Electric Company in Portland, Oregon, the reason was she had "better things to do." Those "better things" included helping CEOs lead successful careers. In 1994, Stepp founded Executive Solutions, whose goal was to help CEOs create a learning environment and get rid of some of the behaviors that cause their organizations to become dysfunctional. She believes that the people side of business has been ignored for too long and that most management consultants focus on business problems rather than people problems. Her new business vowed to change that model.

For example, one of Stepp's clients found that in meetings where she was trying to get input so she could make a decision, she actually announced the decision ahead of getting input, so naturally she effectively cut off any meaningful discussion. Stepp pointed this out to her, and at future meetings, whenever that CEO started to control the conversation, Stepp would give her a look as a signal to back off. Stepp is constantly reminding CEOs that they always have choices they can make; they're always in control, whether or not they seem to be at the moment. For Stepp, leaving the presidency of a utility company was merely leaving a type of work, not leaving herself. Her new business is a reflection of herself and her priorities.

Source: Joshua Hyatt, "The Zero-Defect Coach," *Inc.*, June 1997, pp. 46–57.

company needs to put in place a policy for the management of its human resources so that they will become one of its most valuable assets and will more than justify their cost.

Traditionally, human resource planning has focused on management succession and development or on the staffing process, but today planning takes a much broader view, encompassing all the variables that work to improve organizational effectiveness.[35] For the first time, managing human resources has become a strategic issue that is integrated with all of the company's other functions and activities. If the primary mission of the company is to satisfy its customers, human resources in all areas of the company must be brought to bear on the task.

The integration of human resources (HR) with business strategy is evident in the research conducted over the past several years.[36] A study using a sample size of 2,961 respondents consisting of 223 of the Fortune Global 500, consultants, university faculty, and media in 12 countries defined what the researchers believe will be the state of human resource management in the year 2000:[37]

▶ HR will be responsive to a highly competitive and global marketplace and the resulting business structures.

▶ HR will be integrated with business strategic planning.

▶ HR will emphasize teamwork, quality, empowerment, and flexibility.

The Components of an Effective Human Resource Policy for Small Businesses

While other aspects of the company—product/service, process, and organization—must deal with rapid change, new technology, global competition, and the struggle for sustained competitive advantage, HR must not only deal with the same issues but be responsive to the staffing and human resource development needs of every component of the business. The development of an effective HR policy will be directly affected by the new principles of management and will incorporate the following:

▶ The organization will be built around processes using self-directed teams rather than departments, functions, or specific tasks.

▶ The organization will focus on its core competencies and do only those things that create value or add value.

▶ The customer will determine and have input into everything from product design to marketing to service.

▶ Rewards will be based on team effort rather than individual effort.

▶ Everyone in the organization will know the customer.

▶ Company information will be shared with employees so they can use it and have input into the direction the company is taking.

Technology Tip

Create a Virtual Team

Virtual teams are those that are called together electronically at a moment's notice. They may consist of people within your company or people on the outside such as customers, vendors, bankers, and so forth. What is unique about the virtual team is that the individuals don't have to be in the same room, the same building, the same town, or even the same country to meet and solve problems or address issues.

The important thing is to put in place a plan and procedures for when and how to call a particular team. All potential members should understand the system and know how to respond. For example, you may set up a system such as the following:

▶ For remote contact, use beepers, cellular phones, and voice mail.

▶ To disseminate information, use fax, e-mail, and application sharing over the network.

▶ For decision making, use e-mail, conference calls, and videoconferencing.

The choice of media is a function of need. For example, if you are calling together a team regarding a prototype for a new piece of equipment, you may choose videoconferencing so that all members can see the demonstration of the prototype.

Virtual teams are one way to increase your company's ability to respond to a fast-changing environment.

Source: William R. Pape, "Mastering Business in a Networked World," *Inc. Technology,* no. 2 (1997), p. 29.

Human issues are relevant to everything the company does and, in that regard, can determine whether or not a business effectively responds to change. Therefore, it is important to develop long-term strategies to deal with these issues. Of course, if the goal is truly integration of all business functions and activities, a separate human resource plan will not be necessary. It will simply be addressed in the context of all the other functions of the business in an effort to build effective processes for satisfying customer needs.

One of the core components of a human resource policy is employee empowerment through self-directed teams, the topic of the next section.

Employee Empowerment and Self-Directed Teams

The term **empowerment** has been used to describe formerly powerless individuals (employees) who now have control over the work they do.[38] In the organization literature, it consists of four dimensions:

1. *Choice:* a feeling of control over one's work.[39]

2. *Competence:* the individual's belief that he or she is capable of performing the task successfully.[40] Individuals who do not feel prepared to take on the responsibility of empowerment will typically fail if given that task.[41]

3. *Meaningfulness:* the belief that the task has value.[42] This means employees wish to have control over *nontrivial* tasks that have significance to the organization.

Patricia Louko, owner of an off-campus college bookstore in Lake Worth, Florida, has learned the value of cross-training her employees and empowering them to make important decisions. In 1995 when Louko became seriously ill, her employees were able to keep the business going because they knew how to perform every job. In fact, while the team was running the store sales actually increased, giving Louko the peace of mind she needed while she took time to recuperate. (Tom Salyer)

4. *Impact:* the belief that the work one does makes a difference or has an effect on company policy and performance.[43] Perceptions of impact on the organization by the individual result in increased intrinsic motivation.[44]

Of the four, choice has received by far the most attention in the literature, for it is believed that competence must precede empowerment and, though meaningfulness and impact are certainly important dimensions, they are most likely outcomes of empowerment rather than precursors or precipitators. The research has also proposed many surrogates for empowerment: leadership, participative decision making, job design, self-leadership, and so on. But true employee empowerment encompasses much more than participative decision making, which was favored as the ideal organizational form as early as the 1960s.[45] Employees do not merely give input into the process but actually have responsibility, authority, and accountability for the process. In other words, they don't just participate but *make the decisions, take responsibility for the consequences, and enjoy the rewards of success.*

Empowerment programs are popular not only in the research literature but in the popular press as well. In a 1994 survey by the CSC Index of 497 U.S. firms and 124 European firms, 84 percent of U.S. firms and 70 percent of European firms responding claimed to have employee empowerment programs in place.[46] But the success rate for these programs is yet to be determined. It is known, however, that the one factor that will keep an empowerment program from succeeding is a lack of knowledge by the empowered employees as to how to make decisions. Education and training must be an integral part of the mix if management is to feel comfortable that empowered employees are making decisions that are beneficial to the company.

Group Empowerment

Although the previous references have been to individuals, the same findings apply to empowered groups with the additional dynamic of a group leader. The findings from past research can be generalized to empowered employees and work teams today.[47] To successfully implement the empowerment process in groups, a growing company should do the following:

▶ It should provide an effort that is genuine and substantial, even if that means changing traditional job classifications and roles.

▶ It should transform the entire company to create and define interdependencies among all aspects of the organization. Only in situations of task interdependency do employees and work teams feel empowered.

▶ It should create small teams so that individual empowerment is not lost to group empowerment. Individuals should be encouraged to take control of their own personal growth.

▶ Because the company is asking individuals to participate in self-directed teams and take on more responsibility, it is likely that pay or incentives will have to be increased to offset this.

▶ It should continue to provide supportive leadership and learning opportunities for teams and individuals.

Entrepreneurs can receive assistance in their efforts to learn and implement managerial skills through suppliers, trade associations, chambers of commerce, the SBA, the Service Corp of Retired Executives, and consultants. Even professional advisers such as attorneys can help by recommending procedures to protect the company when hiring and firing.

The new approaches to human resource management are well suited to small businesses operating with scarce resources in dynamic environments. In fact, it is far easier to implement these approaches in a start-up company than in an existing company entrenched in traditional modes of organizational structure and strategy.

Cases Relevant to This Chapter

Zanart Entertainment
French Rags
Marcus Food Co. and Buckhead Beef

Issues for Review and Discussion

1. What are the components of vision, and how do they help the company become successful over the long term?
2. What is corporate culture, and which characteristics define a company's culture?
3. According to Peter Senge, what is a learning organization and how is it achieved?
4. What is meant by "empowered employees" and "self-directed teams"?
5. What should be considered before designing a human resource policy?

Experiencing Entrepreneurship

1. Visit an entrepreneurial company and talk to the entrepreneur, management, and employees. Write a one-page description about the culture of this organization. Refer to the questions on pages 179–180 as an example of the kinds of things you might ask.
2. Interview an entrepreneur to determine what his or her vision for the company is. Be sure to include a discussion of core values, purpose, and mission.

Resources

Case, John (1995). *Open-Book Management: The Coming Business Revolution.* New York: HarperBusiness.

Davis, S. (1984). *Managing Corporate Culture.* Cambridge, MA: Ballinger Publishing.

Kotter, J., and J. Heskett (1992). *Culture and Performance.* New York: The Free Press.

Porter, Michael (1980). *Competitive Strategy.* New York: The Free Press.

Senge, Peter (1990). *The Fifth Discipline: The Art and Practice of the Learning Organization.* New York: Currency/Doubleday.

Ulrich, D., and D. Kale (1990). *Organizational Capability: Competing from the Inside/Out.* New York: John Wiley & Sons.

Internet Resources

Advanced Consulting Group
http://advgroup.com
Free articles that help entrepreneurs with management concerns. Good links to other sites.

Training and Seminar Locators
http://www.tasl.com/
Provides information on staff training.

8

*Excellent firms don't believe in excellence—
only in constant improvement
and constant change.*
Tom Peters

Managing the Human Resources of the Entrepreneurial Company

Preview

Understanding this chapter will give you the ability to

▶ Do an effective job of recruiting and hiring personnel for your company.

▶ Explain the main components of a compensation strategy for employees.

▶ Develop a strategy for paying executives in the company.

▶ Discuss the key laws affecting companies with employees.

▶ Describe what an employee handbook should include.

Terms to Know

Job description, 200
Self-report
measures, 201
Equal Employment
Opportunity Commis-
sion (EEOC), 204
Temporary workers, 205

Gainsharing, 209
Flextime, 209
Individual retirement
account (IRA), 211
401(k) plan, 211
Simplified employee
pension plan (SEP), 212

Base salary, 213
Short-term
incentives, 213
Stock appreciation
grant, 213
Performance grant, 214

Benefits and
perquisites, 214
SERPs, 214
OSHA, 216
Workers'
compensation, 217

Young Entrepreneurs—Minicase

Jennifer Iannolo
Bravissimo!

Born in the Hudson River valley of New York, the last of seven children, Jennifer Iannolo was creating her first company while other little girls were playing with Barbie dolls. Working with a partner, she made and sold arts and crafts to schoolmates. The first important business lesson she learned? "Never sell on credit to 10-year-olds!"

She started her second two businesses while a student at New York University. The first, Nub Grafix, is a graphic design firm still being operated by her former partner. The second, The Quick Fix, a student-run store at NYU, was recognized as one of the top 10 U.S. student-run businesses in 1992.

In 1995, Iannolo packed up and moved to the Boston area to "face the challenge of starting a company in a new city." It was in Cambridge, Massachusetts, that Bravissimo! was born, with financing from credit cards and a small SBA loan from a commercial bank. Bravissimo! is a successful event-planning company with clients such as American Express and The Young Entrepreneurs Network. In addition to planning and coordinating corporate receptions and social events, Iannolo works with the country's most celebrated chefs coordinating culinary demonstrations for various projects throughout the United States and abroad. Her true passion lies in the culinary world, where she feels most at home because "foodies," as she calls them, are "the warmest, most gracious people I've ever worked with. I'm the last of seven children in an Italian family, so entertaining is an innate part of my character, and I want to be able to teach my generation how to do it with style, ease, and *lack of stress!*"

All of Bravissimo!'s clients have come from referrals, because as a premium service the company does no advertising or mass marketing. Most aspects of events, such as catering, music, and public relations, are subcontracted, while Iannolo performs the role of "traffic cop." This approach lets clients receive the best possible service from a single company. The challenge, then, is to grow the company without sacrificing the strong customer relationships she has built up.

As a firm believer in the benefits that come from giving back to her community, Iannolo devotes a large portion of her company's time to charitable

events related to the culinary field. She is vice chair for Boston's Taste of the Nation event, part of the national Share Our Strength program to raise money for the fight against hunger. "It's easy to devote your time to a cause when you simply incorporate it into your daily business activities," she says. The benefit to Iannolo is access to a vast network of business owners and corporate leaders who may ultimately do business with Bravissimo!

Jennifer Iannolo has this advice for aspiring entrepreneurs:

1. Never, ever give up no matter how many people tell you that you are a dreamer. Though there will be times when you can't afford a cup of coffee, be persistent and know that the struggle will make you strong enough to withstand adversity and the fear of risk. If you know you can survive on very little, it will give you the courage necessary to risk it all.

2. The only person who can make your dream come true is you.

3. Align yourself with other entrepreneurs, because they are the only people on earth who will understand you. This is a promise.

4. Learn from other people's mistakes. It will save you the pain of committing the error yourself.

5. Read *Atlas Shrugged* by Ayn Rand—it will help you better understand your value to this world.

6. Take a chance! What's the worst that could happen?

What does Jennifer Iannolo's experience teach you about the human resource component of your business?

Peple are arguably the most important asset of any company, but few entrepreneurs spend the time and effort needed to effectively hire and train this vital resource. One reason for this neglect is that during start-up, the founding team has typically filled all the functions of the organization and, assuming everything has gone well, the team has worked closely and well together. Hiring new people into the organization is much like bringing a stranger home to live with the family; he or she doesn't always fit into the culture that has developed through start-up and early growth, and it takes time to teach the newcomer how everything is done. Jennifer Iannolo (see Young Entrepreneurs—Minicase) knew her management style would make it difficult to bring someone in to work with her in the events-planning business. Iannolo knows how she wants things done and has a difficult time delegating to people who aren't experts in their field. But, with a growing business, she's not in a position to hire the finest people, so she chose the next best alternative: partnering with other small companies in the event-planning business so her clients could tap into the very best expertise in the industry. To ensure that these partners truly are the best, she checks references and track records, and relies on referrals from people in the industry whom she trusts.

In Chapter 7, we introduced the idea of a human resource policy and the importance of creating a vision and a culture for your company that employees will embrace. In this chapter, we'll look at how to find and keep good employees, as well as how to protect your company against unnecessary employee-related litigation.

Recruiting and Hiring

The time and effort spent recruiting and hiring employees, both the management and labor side, is time well spent because it will prevent many potential problems down the road. There appear to be two approaches to determining when it's appropriate to bring in new members to the management team. The first might be called the "when we have to" approach: you bring in new people when you're ready to delegate authority and the company needs some professional management and structure. This was the approach taken by Coldwater Creek, a $43 million catalog company founded in 1984. The point at which the founders, a husband and wife team, decided it was time to hire some help was when they and their employees were starting to work 80-hour weeks. Since the company was now six years old and had a good track record, they were in an excellent position to hire the best.[1] This strategy works well when the original team can manage effectively until the company generates enough revenues to justify additional employees.

The second approach is "start with a big management team": the company hires the best management it can based on its initial resources and continually adds to the team as profits grow. This allows the entrepreneur to focus on the aspect of the business that interests him or her most and delegate other functional responsibilities to the rest of the team. This approach was taken by PRT Corporation of America, a $14 million company that offers software planning, training, and development. PRT hired key management to handle all the major functions of the business but avoided building a traditional hierarchy by ensuring that no one reported to those managers, thus creating a flat organizational structure.[2]

Determining which approach is better for the company is generally a function of the type of company. For example, a software company that has spent two years in product development with a team of designers and programmers will probably find it critical to hire a professional management team to launch the product because the founding team's expertise is in product development, not business development. On the other hand, a service company may be able to develop its business to its fullest before adding management personnel to help it expand to other geographic locations. In either case, when to hire additional management will be determined by

- The founding team's ability to delegate
- The resources available for hiring
- The need to create more structure

Recruiting the Best Employees

Recruiting is the process by which a company locates individuals to fill employment positions. The recruiting function is perhaps the most critical and least attended-to facet of the employee hiring process; this is surprising, since it is the recruiting process that determines whether potential employees are in fact appropriate for particular positions. Small, growing businesses that lack experienced human resource management personnel tend to hire a person for a job rather than take an in-depth look at how well the individual will fit into the culture of the organization and whether or not she or he has the potential to grow with the company. If an advertisement for a position merely gives a broad job category such as "receptionist," the company will likely attract people who see the position as a job rather than a career. Though that attitude may be fine in a major corporation with substantial resources, it's not wise in an entrepreneurial company with limited resources and a need for employees who can do more than one task. So you may want someone who can not only assume the role of receptionist but also do some clerical or administrative work.

Hiring an HR consultant to help set up a recruiting and hiring process may be a wise investment that will save you money in the long run in terms of bad employment decisions. An alternative is to see if you can find an HR expert to serve on your advisory board. This is particularly important in businesses that are highly labor intensive and experience industrywide high turnover, such as the restaurant industry.

Employees can be found through a number of proven methods, including

- Advertising in the classifieds
- Recruiting at high schools, vocational schools, colleges, and universities
- Public employment offices
- Private employment agencies (headhunters)

When looking for good, loyal employees who take pride in their work, don't overlook workers with disabilities. David Morris and his father Saul are owners of Habitat International, Inc., a Georgia-based manufacturing company that produces indoor-outdoor carpeting. One day they were approached by a social service worker who presented an unusual idea. At her suggestion they hired a group of mentally challenged workers, who proved so good at their jobs that today 75 percent of Habitat's employees have some kind of disability. The Morrises attribute their current success to these workers. (Stephen Alvarez)

▶ Referrals from current employees and others in the industry

▶ Networking with local organizations

▶ Temporary help services

   Competition for good job candidates is great, so small-business owners must be prepared to sell the unique benefits of working for a small, growing firm. Some of these benefits include the ability to make decisions that directly affect the company, to move quickly into positions of responsibility, and to work in a more flexible work environment.

The Job Description

The best way to ensure a chance of interviewing the appropriate people for the position is to use a **job description**. A good job description will include the following:

▶ The educational and work experience required. This is an important initial screening device, but should be stated as "desired levels" rather than "required," because often the best person for the position does not have the exact educational or work experience stated in the job description, but is bright and capable of being trained quickly.

▶ The duties and responsibilities of the position in sufficient detail that the potential candidate understands what is expected, but not so detailed that it doesn't allow for some flexibility of tasks.

▶ The person to whom the candidate is responsible.

▶ The personal characteristics needed for the position, such as good communication skills, self-motivation, creativity, and so forth.

▶ A clause stating that the company can make some relatively minor changes in the job description without rewriting it.

In designing a job description, specifications, and an application for employment, it is important to recognize that the equal employment opportunity laws prohibit a company from discriminating based on age, sex, color, race, national origin, religion, and other factors during the recruiting and hiring process. For example, a job description cannot require a photograph of the applicant unless the position is one for which appearance is the primary attribute, as in modeling. This is to avoid discrimination based on race or physical size. The Real World of Entrepreneurship feature on page 204 presents some of the employment-related laws of which small-business owners should be aware.

Holding to the letter of the law is critical. In a time of increasing regulation and litigation, it is important that employers maintain excellent records during the hiring process as well as during employment, particularly since the burden of proof is on the employer to provide evidence that the company is innocent of discrimination.

The Selection Process

Once the criteria for the position and the candidate have been determined, it becomes necessary to find the most effective way to gather information on potential candidates and choose among them. There are two major sources of information: self-report and observation or empirical research, and these can be further subdivided into measures that tell the company something about the candidate's past experience, present character, and potential for advancement.[3] See Figure 8.1 for an overview of the recruitment and selection process.

Self-Report Sources

Two of the most common **self-report measures** to look at the past experience of the candidate are the résumé and the job application form. Both are good for screening applicants before the interview process; however, caution must be exercised because, particularly in the case of the résumé, applicants tend to embellish their achievements. Caution should also be exercised when using standardized job application forms, as they often contain questions that

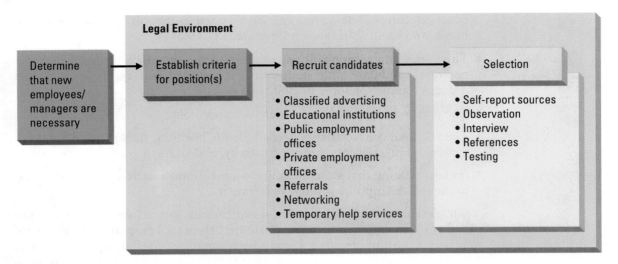

Figure 8.1
The Recruitment and Selection Process

could lead to accusations of discrimination. Here are some important clues to look for in a résumé:

▶ Did the applicant stay in previous positions for a reasonable length of time?

▶ Is the applicant's prior work experience relevant to the position being applied for?

▶ Does the overall appearance and quality of the résumé suggest a candidate who is serious about his or her career?

▶ Was the candidate successful in emphasizing skills, experience, and education needed in the position being applied for?

To learn more about the candidate's character and how he or she might fit into the culture of the organization, many companies give personality tests and integrity tests. These tests provide an insight into the candidate's values, interests, and needs. To learn about the candidate's potential for advancement, employers often use situational interviews. These are discussed in a later section.

Observation

Direct observation of the candidate is another way to gather valuable information. Employers can use observation to learn about a candidate's past experience by using references from previous supervisors or co-workers, performance appraisals, and drug tests,[4] and assess current abilities by observing work samples or the results of aptitude tests. Future potential is often measured through interviews that involve hypothetical or "what if" situations to which the candidate must respond.

Interviews

It is often said that the résumé is merely a tool to allow a candidate to get a foot in the door of the company. People are not normally hired based solely on the résumé but based on how well they present themselves in an interview situation. It's during interviews, however, that many employers cross the line, asking questions that are illegal to ask prior to the point of hire. (See The Real World of Entrepreneurship for some questions that should not be asked

The Real World of Entrepreneurship

Some Important Employment Laws to Be Aware of

The following laws were created to protect employees from discriminatory hiring practices. Entrepreneurs should be aware of these laws when they recruit and hire new employees.

Equal Pay Act of 1963—prohibits discrimination in the workplace based on sex. Women and men are to be paid the same wages for the same work.

Civil Rights Act of 1964—applies to companies with more than 15 employees; prohibits employers from refusing to hire, promote, train, or increase pay based on race, color, sex, or national origin.

Age Discrimination Act of 1967—designed to protect persons between ages 40 and 70 from discrimination in the workplace based on age.

Vocational Rehabilitation Act of 1973—designed to protect individuals with mental or physical disabilities from discrimination for jobs they are capable of doing. Section 503 of this act requires that employers with federal government contracts of $50,000 or more and 50 or more employees must actively recruit and hire individuals with disabilities.

Vietnam Era Veterans Readjustment Act of 1974—requires companies that have federal contracts in excess of $10,000 to make a concerted effort to employ and advance qualified disabled veterans and veterans of the Vietnam War.

Immigration Law of 1986—requires that all companies examine the documents of employees they hire to ensure they are not hiring illegal aliens. The documents must be listed on Immigration and Naturalization Service Form I-9 and kept for three years after the person is hired.

Americans with Disabilities Act of 1990—requires that businesses with 15 or more employees not discriminate against qualified persons with disabilities, conduct any kind of test to screen out such persons, inquire as to a disability, or deny a position to someone with a relationship with a person who has a disability. Moreover, employees must provide reasonable access to facilities, special equipment and training, and provide readers for blind individuals.

Civil Rights Act of 1991—applies to companies with 15 or more employees. It

▶ Allows women and employees with disabilities to collect monetary damages as minorities do in successful litigation

▶ Shifts the burden of proof to the employer to defend employment practices

▶ Requires employers to prove that allegedly discriminatory practices are job related and required for the operations of the business

▶ Caps punitive damages at $50,000 for companies with 100 or fewer employees and at $100,000 for companies with 101 to 200 employees.

and their acceptable alternatives.) Failing to exercise due care in the questions asked of candidates can result in a lawsuit for discrimination.

Another mistake many young (and some mature!) companies make in their hiring practices is failing to prepare for the interview process. Often this difficult but essential task is left to someone with little experience and an inability to convey the company's vision. Consequently, it's no surprise when the best people for the position are not identified or hired. Because today it is more difficult than ever to discharge someone from a position and costly to retrain someone new, a young, growing company would be wise to spend more effort investigating and learning about the people it hires. Following are some suggestions for achieving a successful interview:

- ▶ Choose a suitable place for the interview that puts the candidate at ease and permits a period of time without interruptions.

- ▶ If more than one person from the company is to participate in the interview process, all should be present at the start of the interview with plans in place as to how the interview will be conducted.

- ▶ A brief opening welcome and statement about the company by the interviewer gives the candidate a chance to get adjusted to the interview environment.

The Real World of Entrepreneurship

Interview Questions: What's Allowed and What's Not

In October, 1995 the **EEOC (Equal Employment Opportunity Commission)** released guidelines that allow for some prehiring discussion that previously had been disallowed. For example, if an applicant has an obvious disability (e.g., uses a wheelchair), it is permissible to talk about what accommodations might be necessary if the applicant were hired. Otherwise, the following questions may *not* be asked prior to the point of hire:

1. What is your age?

2. What church do you attend?

3. Do you have children or plan to get pregnant?

4. Have you ever been arrested?

5. How is your health?

6. You have beautiful skin; where are your ancestors from?

1. Only in the case of a young applicant can the employer ask if the person can prove he or she is of legal age after hiring. In other cases, age questions such as "when did you graduate from high school?" are not permitted.

2. No questions regarding the religion of the applicant or the applicant's family are allowed.

3. Questions regarding personal family plans or living arrangements are not permitted.

4. "Have you ever been convicted of a crime?" is permissible.

5. "Do you have any condition that would prevent you from doing your job?" is permissible.

6. Questions about ancestry, heritage, culture, etc. are not permitted.

▶ Open-ended questions provide more information than those that require short one- or two-word responses.

▶ Since experience, education, and basic skills are represented on the résumé, the interview should focus on clarifying any issues the résumé raised and getting at the character of the candidate. The goal is to answer the question "Can this person provide the company with the skills it needs and work well with others?"

▶ Sometimes the most innocent-appearing questions ("Do you like to travel?" "What do you like to do in your spare time?") really seek valuable information. In this case, will the person travel for the company? And does this person have demanding interests that will keep him or her from working long hours when needed?

▶ Questions such as "What is your definition of success?" or "What are your strengths and weaknesses?" tell the interviewer a lot about the character of the candidate and what is important to him or her.

▶ The interviewer should talk no more than 15 percent of the time and should take notes either during the interview or immediately after. The notes should refer to answers given by the candidate as well as feelings the interviewer had while listening and observing the nonverbal communication (body language) of the interviewee.

Checking References and Testing

Another area where young companies fall short in the hiring process is checking references. Often they assume that because a candidate listed someone as a reference, that person will necessarily give a good recommendation. That is not always the case! The fact is that well over half of fired employees who file a defamation claim recover damages. Wrongful-discharge claims can result in very costly verdicts. Consequently, many former employers will be

The Real World of Entrepreneurship

Using Temporary Employees

Today many small businesses are wary about hiring employees without a way to get out of the arrangement if it does not work out. Particularly in businesses where the need for employees varies seasonally, growing companies are looking for a way to have skilled employees when and where they need them but not have to carry them on the payroll when they're not needed.

One solution to this dilemma is to use **temporary workers** from an employment agency on an as-needed basis. Temporary help agencies have begun to special-

ize in providing specially trained workers for specific industries. This approach also works when a company wants to "try out" an employee before hiring him or her permanently. The National Association of Temporary and Staffing Services reports that 16 percent of former temporary workers took permanent jobs with the firms that hired them on a temporary basis.

SOURCE: "An Extended-Tryout Option," *Nation's Business,* June 1996, p. 26.

reluctant to give more than factual information, such as how long the candidate was on the job. To overcome this, you might consider hiring an independent firm to do background checks on potential employees, especially where the position is critical. In either case, it's important to check references.

Testing the applicant is another commonly used technique for screening. These tests may consist of psychological tests, performance tests, drug tests, and physical examinations. The benefit of doing these tests up front far outweighs their cost. Having to fire an employee and risk retaliatory litigation is far more costly, in both time and money. Remember that any test used to screen an applicant must be related to the job and must also come from a reliable source.

Compensation for Employees

It has always been the fate of growing entrepreneurial companies to have to do what large, established companies do but with better quality and far fewer resources. Despite limited resources, if they want to continue to grow, they need to hire the best people they can get and offer them a competitive wage and benefits package. The issue of compensation is central to the concerns of the employee in choosing to work for a particular company; likewise, for the employer, employee wages directly affect the cost of doing business. Before making micro decisions such as how much to pay for a particular position, it's important to gather some key information that will help you create an overall compensation strategy for the company. Some key questions to answer include the following:

1. *What are others in the industry paying for the same position?* To accurately assess this issue, you should compare total compensation costs per individual employee (including taxes and benefits) and per total number of employees, as well as the return on profit and sales for each dollar spent on labor.

2. *What is the supply and demand for employees in the industry, in particular those with the specific skills the company needs?*

3. *What responses or outcomes are being rewarded?* What is the employee expected to achieve for this compensation?

Be Careful About Personnel Files

The following are obvious benefits to a plaintiff's lawyer and should be carefully screened for by any company:

▶ A personnel file of a terminated employee filled with positive ratings

▶ Reasons given for termination that are purely subjective

▶ Personnel files filled with memos after the termination in an obvious effort to cover up a lack of documentation

▶ Evidence that money is being spent on training for younger employees only

▶ Different working terms and conditions for people performing the same job

It's standing room only at the Phelps Group when they hold their weekly staff meetings. That's because the first item on the meeting agenda at this Santa Monica, California marketing agency is to award a $100 bill to a randomly selected employee who can answer a question from the employee handbook. Then, sharing one-minute agenda items on such topics as technology, grammar, and office machines builds a sense of camaraderie that lasts all week. All this just goes to show that compensation and other efforts to motivate employees can take on unusual forms. (Voldi Tanner)

4. *What is the company's cost and profit structure?* How much is available for compensation packages?

5. *What is the typical turnover rate for employees in this industry?* (High turnover means higher costs for training.)

6. *What type of training can the company provide?* Can training be done on the job? Do we have to hire someone to do it?

7. *What is the potential for growth and promotion within the company's structure?* Are there opportunities for employees to move up and expand their skill base?

8. *What is the value of the pay level to employees?* What do employees perceive their pay should be for a particular position?

9. *To what types of rewards do employees in these positions respond?* Besides money, what other types of rewards do employees expect?

By answering these questions, the company is more likely to formulate a compensation policy that is realistic for the industry and the employees who work in it.

In general, pay comes in two types: cash and benefits. It has been reported that in the United States, 70 percent of pay comes in the form of cash, with the rest in deferred cash benefits such as health care, IRAs, and paid vacation.[5] Total labor costs will usually determine whether a company can afford to locate in a particular country or in a particular region of the United States. As productivity increases and more companies learn to work smart, however, labor costs as a percentage of total costs will decline.

Timing of pay and promotion is also part of the compensation strategy. Some companies prefer to bring employees in at a fairly low wage, but allow for significant growth over a period of time, whereas other companies hire people at an above-average rate but take much longer to promote and raise pay. The mix of compensation is also an important consideration. Many companies offer a base salary plus a portion of the compensation that is "at risk," that is, based on team or organization performance.

Compensation Should Match the Company Life Cycle

The work of L. R. Gomez-Mejia and D. B. Balkin provides some of the first evidence that choosing pay systems that match corporate strategies and objectives translates into better performance.[6] If companies go through a fairly predictable process of birth, growth, maturity, and decline, it makes sense that each of these stages calls for a different compensation strategy.[7] For example, pay based on outcome (performance) is very suitable for the growth period, when the upside potential is high, but a stable salary might better reflect a more mature company where gains are small. It has also been suggested that companies with unrelated products or a single product pose more risk than a company with a platform of related products.[8] Consequently, the

Technology Tip

Keeping Track of Employees

Be sure to set up an interactive database to keep track of your employees. A good database is user friendly; it may even contain a picture of the employee. In the data file you can keep records of performance evaluations, pay and promotions, things the employee has done above and beyond the job requirements, and notes on meetings with the employee.

These database files are important documents in case you ever have a dispute with an employee or if you're considering an employee for a promotion or new position. In addition, the address information is readily available for a mailing, and you can even set the database up to remind you about employees' birthdays.

Beyond providing information on individual employees, databases let you look at your company as a whole. For example, by selecting certain criteria—say, salary, gender, and age—you can quickly see if your company faces any potential charges of discrimination based on gender or age.

riskier scenario with the higher upside potential calls for outcome-based pay and a more decentralized approach to management.

Research has also found that money incentives are associated with the largest average increase in productivity.[9] Greater emphasis on short-term bonuses and long-term incentives based on base pay for middle- and upper-level management is correlated with higher profitability. Profit sharing has also been shown to be associated with higher productivity, but this should not be construed as a cause-and-effect relationship.[10] Similarly, employee stock ownership plans (ESOPs) appear to give positive results, but again no causal relationship has been established.[11]

Much attention has been paid to **gainsharing** and the positive results obtained from its use. This is generally attributed to the fact that employees can clearly see a relationship between what they do and what they receive.[12]

With a global economy now affecting virtually every business, it will be important for entrepreneurial companies to understand how compensation strategies in the United States may have to be modified to achieve the same results in another country. One example is the high need for risk avoidance in countries such as Japan, South Korea, and Taiwan, which may preclude the use of outcome-based pay that has been so successful in the United States.[13]

Noncash Benefits

Many growing entrepreneurial companies are unable to offer complex compensation packages that require a lot of cash outlay, but they can offer other benefits. One of those benefits is **flextime**, which allows, for example, two employees to share one job. This is a popular approach for employees who don't need to work full time and want more control over their time. One employee may work from 8:00 A.M. to 12:00 P.M., and another comes in from 12:00 P.M. to 4:00 P.M. Flextime also allows employees to take work home and communicate with the company via fax and modem. The benefits of flextime to the company are several. It tends to create a more positive work environment, one that meets the employee's individual needs. It increases employee productivity and empowerment, which also results in lower turnover. To successfully implement a flextime program, it is important to develop a detailed policy that spells out the company's expectations and reflects input from the employees. Entrepreneurs with small, growing companies and limited resources need to think creatively about how to provide noncash incentives until the business is in a position to add cash incentives to the mix. This may include such things as time off and intrinsic rewards that come from job satisfaction. See Table 8.1 for additional types of noncash benefits.

Intrinsic rewards are those things that come from the work itself, a cause to which everyone is committed—in this case, the success of the business. The problem is that once the business experiences success, entrepreneurs tend to forget that the people they hire need to feel that entrepreneurial spirit as well because extrinsic rewards lose their motivational effect fairly quickly. For example, if someone who believes in the company's vision is brought in to take the company through its high-growth period and is given a high salary but no

Table 8.1   Some Typical Employee Noncash Benefits

▶ Employee discounts	▶ Housing support
▶ Paid vacations and legal holidays	▶ Moving expenses
▶ Automobile or a specified allotment for an automobile	▶ Reduced-cost food service at work
▶ Travel expenses	▶ Recreation facilities or memberships
▶ Retention by employee of frequent-flyer mileage	▶ Education for employees and employees' children
	▶ Workshops and seminars for employee development

share of the results of his or her effort (the intrinsic rewards of ownership), that person will likely seek intrinsic rewards outside the company.

The 1996 *Inc.*/Gallup survey[14] of workers nationwide about the critical factors in their satisfaction and job performance found the following:

▶ Employees want the opportunity to do what they do best every day.

▶ They want to know that a supervisor or someone else at work cares about them as people.

▶ They want to know their opinions count.

▶ They want opportunities to learn and grow.

▶ They want to know that the company's mission sees their jobs as important.

▶ They want the materials and equipment to do the job right.

▶ They want to work in companies that are "family friendly."

It is clear from this survey that when employees are asked about what makes them happy on the job, the responses plainly focus on intrinsic values, the desire to be a significant contributor to the company's success.

Health Plans

The U.S. Chamber of Commerce reported that in 1994, the average benefit costs per employee for all industries was $14,678, down $129 from the previous year. Payment as a percentage of payroll declined to 40.7 percent. Still, the trend is for companies to offer health maintenance organizations and preferred provider organizations as a cost containment measure, as well as increasing deductibles that employees pay out of pocket.[15]

Some firms have chosen a self-funded health plan in an effort to reduce health care costs. In fact, the percentage of employers who self-funded health care benefits rose from 39 percent in 1985 to 57 percent in 1995.[16] Many believe the growth in self-funded plans would not have occurred without the federal regulations provided under ERISA. It allowed companies that operate in more than one state to design a system that is the same in each state.

Because of this, these plans generally cost less than insurance company plans. Furthermore, they are not subject to state laws requiring insurance carriers to include certain benefits in their plans, and doing their own paperwork allows them to save even more money. Companies can also limit their risk by purchasing stop-loss coverage insurance. They have a choice between aggregate coverage, which puts an overall cap on the number of claims a company might have to pay in a given year, and specific coverage, which pays claims that exceed a cap for each worker.

Before even considering self-funding, a company should investigate the following:

▶ Does the company have at least 50 employees?

▶ Is management comfortable with the volatility of a self-funded plan?

▶ Is the company fully committed to this approach?

▶ Does the company have a consultant or risk broker to help in making the decision, a stop-loss insurance carrier, and an outside firm to administer the benefits?

▶ Can the company carry both aggregate and specific stop-loss coverage?

▶ Does the company understand potential employee concerns about self-funding, and can it mitigate them?

Many small businesses are using their combined strength through trade associations to provide health coverage at a lower cost. This is an effective way to increase your clout when negotiating for health care premiums.

Pension Plan Options

In the United States, retirement income traditionally has been viewed as a three-part system consisting of social security, pension plans, and retirement savings. One of the many reasons this system has failed is that so many employees have no pension plans from their employers. Only a small percentage of small companies provide such plans because the options are limited and the administrative costs are high. Following are some examples of the options.

Individual Retirement Accounts (IRAs)   The Employee Retirement Income Security Act (ERISA) was established in 1974 to permit workers not covered by company pension plans to set aside tax-deferred income for retirement. In 1982, the Economic Recovery Tax Act (ERTA) extended that benefit to all workers. However, the 1986 Tax Reform Act limited the amount of money employees can contribute.

401(K) Plans   These are very beneficial to employees because they not only allow employees to contribute tax-free dollars to the plan but allow the *employer* to contribute as well. Small companies have avoided this benefit because of the high administrative costs, approximately $73 per employee;

however, since the tax benefits go to the employee, the employer can choose to pass this administrative cost on to the employee.

Simplified Employee Pension Plans (SEPs)   These plans benefit small-business owners with 25 or fewer employees who can't afford the more traditional plans. The small-business owner sets up the plan through a financial institution and makes tax-deductible contributions to the employee's annuity account. These contributions may amount to as much as 15 percent of the employee's compensation or $30,000, whichever is less. The employer can then deduct these contributions as expenses.

Compensation for Executives

In companies large and small, the issue of executive compensation is receiving a lot of attention from politicians—who see it as a way to use an "us against them" tactic to their political benefit—and the press, which seems to like to portray business as the enemy. But for growing entrepreneurial companies, deciding how to compensate the founding team and any hired management is a dilemma with no guidelines. An *Inc.* poll of its list of the 500 fastest-growing private companies found that the needs of the company were a significant factor in determining how much the CEO got paid, and that 39 percent of respondents believed their pay was below market average.[17] It also found that 71 percent of the CEOs used a pay-for-performance link, and 66 percent noted that bonuses made up a significant portion of their pay.

Executive compensation packages can consist of a varied combination of salary, stock, and bonus components. Consequently, the mix of these elements can have a critical impact on both the executive's accumulation of

 Entrepreneurship in Action

How One Growing Company Provided Benefits

Business Wire is a wire service company that was founded in 1961 by former *Stars and Stripes* correspondent Lorry Lokey. Here is a brief overview of how he built a benefits package for his employees:

▶ In 1966, Business Wire had three employees and began paying bonuses.

▶ In 1969, it created a pension trust and profit-sharing retirement plan for seven employees.

▶ In 1975, it added medical/dental/optical to supplement health insurance for 11 employees and $1.4 million in revenues.

▶ In 1986, it started a nursery staffed by working parents for 32 employees and $7.2 million in revenues.

▶ In 1992, it created a 401(k) plan with a guaranteed corporate match of at least 10 percent for 162 employees and $18.4 million in revenues.

▶ In 1994, it introduced a deferred-compensation annuity, subsidies for health club memberships and education costs for 200 employees, and $28 million in revenues.

The benefits package was designed to reward longevity and align individual interests with the company's goals.

SOURCE: Jill Andresky Fraser, "'Tis Better to Give and Receive," *Inc.,* February 1995, p. 84.

wealth and the company's profitability. Following are examples of some of these components.

Base Salary

Base salary is that part of the compensation package that is relatively "fixed"; that is, it does not vary with the performance of the company. Two trends are occurring with regard to base salaries. First, companies are starting to flatten their salary structures to permit broader ranges of base salary at every level to account for differences in performance. Second, the time between salary adjustments is increasing and the amount of change is decreasing relative to nonfixed or variable salary components. In start-up companies, the CEO/entrepreneur typically takes almost 80 percent of his or her total compensation in base salary. This is because the company can't afford the benefits and perquisites much larger companies offer.

Short-Term Incentives

Short-term incentives are given for a period of one year or less, usually on an annual basis, and are paid in cash, although they may include stock. Deciding who receives these incentives may depend on the company's reaching a target level of performance toward a goal, be based on a formula-driven share of a bonus pool based on financial results, or be determined purely at the discretion of the owners. This last approach is not uncommon in young entrepreneurial firms whose performance has not yet achieved any level of predictability.

Long-Term Incentives

Long-term incentives are based on performance for a period longer than a year and usually consist of stock appreciation grants, restricted stock or cash grants, and performance grants. Of these, the most common is stock options because they are an unbiased method of linking executive rewards and shareholder returns.[18]

Stock Appreciation Grants

Stock appreciation grants are based on future appreciation of the company's stock. They consist of *stock options,* the right to purchase shares of the company's stock at a fixed price for a specified period of time; *stock appreciation rights,* the right to receive direct payment for the option's appreciation during the term without actually exercising the option; and *stock purchases,* which permit the purchase of stock at a discount under either fair market value or full value, and sometimes with financial aid from the company.

Restricted Stock or Cash Grants

Restricted stock or cash grants are subject to restrictions on transfer outside the company and risk of forfeiture until the required employment tenure has been reached.

Performance Grants

Performance grants are grants or rights to receive stock, contingent cash amounts based on the company's long-term performance or a specified formula, or the right to receive dividend equivalents paid on a specified number of company shares.[19]

You should consult both an attorney and an accountant conversant in these types of incentives for advice on the best plan for your particular type of business and its stage in the life cycle.

Benefits and Perquisites

Typically **benefits** (health plan, IRA, etc.) **and perquisites** (car, club membership, etc.) amount to approximately one-third of the compensation package. In addition, many executives are seeking such things as "change-in-control severance agreements," often called "golden parachutes," and **SERPs,** special executive retirement plans whose pensions use a more generous formula than that used for other employees. These "perks" are generally prone to much scrutiny by people within the organization as well as by the government and are difficult to justify (see "The IRS and Executive Pay"). Again, seek expert counsel before implementing any of these highly scrutinized benefit plans.

The Legal Context of Human Resource Management

A significant portion of the already skyrocketing cost of employees is the result of legislation and regulation by the government. In addition to the cost of compliance, there is the confusion of multiple sources of regulation. Laws related to employment originate in the U.S. Supreme Court, Congress, the Immigration and Naturalization Service, the Department of Labor, and the National Labor Relations Board, in addition to state and local agencies and courts. Often both federal and state laws will apply to a given situation. The

---

 The Real World of Entrepreneurship

Don't Let Your Incentive Plan Fail

Often the best-laid incentive plans fail, not for lack of motivation and sincerity on the part of employers but for several very discernible reasons. Here are some tips to avoid incentive failure:

▸ Make sure employees understand the incentive system. Research points to the need to get employees involved in designing the plan. Usually this results in fewer but more meaningful incentives.[20]

▸ Focus on more than just cutting costs. Creating value may cost more initially, but the long-term payoff is much greater.

▸ Change incentive goals annually, but not without warning. This keeps the momentum going and helps to prevent people from attempting to outsmart the system.[21]

▸ Don't confuse employees with a lot of numbers. It's been suggested that three target incentives is the maximum an employee can focus on.[22]

remainder of this section presents some of the various laws that affect the management of workers in a company setting, including laws affecting compensation, safety, and liability.

Laws Affecting Compensation

The laws pertaining to the recruiting and hiring of employees were discussed in the first section of the chapter. This section addresses the laws that affect how the company pays its employees. Every company should be aware of the following laws:

▶ **Davis-Bacon Act of 1931.** Any contractor doing construction work in excess of $2,000 for the federal government must pay the prevailing wage as determined by the Department of Labor.

 The Real World of Entrepreneurship

The IRS and Executive Pay

It is not unheard of for companies today to receive a notice from the IRS under Section 162(a)(1) of the Internal Revenue Code claiming that an executive's salary is unreasonably high and demanding the company pay back taxes on the amount the IRS claims should have been declared as taxable profit. The IRS has no authority to dictate what a company can pay its employees, but it can state what it believes to be reasonable as a business expense. Generally the IRS targets smaller companies that can more easily manipulate income, often by using family members as employees. Recently, however, three small corporations decided to fight the IRS on this very issue and won. The judge in the case cited 12 criteria for reasonableness of executive pay in his January 1995 decisions:

1. Qualifications in terms of education and experience in the industry.

2. Nature and scope of work.

3. Size and complexity of the business.

4. Salaries versus net income, sales, and capital value. Often salaries are large relative to profit to make up for lean years in the early stages of the company.

5. Economic conditions. If the company is successful despite a weak economy, this is attributable to the leadership of the entrepreneur and can reasonably call for greater compensation.

6. Salaries versus payments to stockholders. If the company does not pay dividends, it sends up a red flag to the IRS that perhaps a portion of the tax deductible salary is really dividends.

7. Salary policy. The judge looked for a long-standing compensation policy.

8. Financial condition. The company needs to show that it grew substantially while the highly paid management team was leading it.

9. Comparable pay. The pay should be similar to that of other companies at the same level in the industry.

10. Previous years' pay. This refers to the fact that many entrepreneurs defer compensation in the early years to build the business.

11. Arm's-length dealings. Would an independent investor approve the pay?

12. Guaranteed debt. Have the executive/owners personally guaranteed company debts?

Some entrepreneurs have changed their companies' legal structure to an S-corporation to avoid problems with the IRS. In this form, all profits pass through to the owners and are taxed at the owners' personal income tax rates. Your tax attorney and accountant can advise you as to whether this is a good choice for your company.

Source: William Ringle, "Why the IRS Eyes Executive Pay," *Nation's Business,* October 1995.

▶ **National Labor Relations Act of 1935.** Employees have the right to bargain collectively for wages, benefits, and working conditions.

▶ **Walsh-Healy Act of 1936.** Any company with a federal contract in excess of $10,000 must pay the area prevailing wage as determined by the Department of Labor. Also, employees must receive time-and-a-half for all hours worked in excess of 40 per week.

▶ **Fair Labor Standards Act of 1938.** This law established the minimum wage and overtime pay as well as work rules for children under 18 years of age for companies engaged in interstate commerce.

▶ **Equal Pay Act of 1963.** All employers must pay men and women the same wage for the same work (i.e., skill, responsibility, and effort).

Laws Affecting Safety

No one would disagree that safety in the workplace is an important issue, and recently the trend has been toward more and more costly regulation. Two major areas of safety regulation are the rules under OSHA and workers' compensation.

OSHA

The issue of a safe and healthy work environment is the purview of the Occupational Safety and Health Act of 1970 (**OSHA**) and its administrative unit. OSHA requires that employers eliminate hazardous areas in the workplace and maintain health and safety records on all employees. OSHA inspectors regularly target companies in which certain hazards are inherent in the nature of the business, such as asbestos. They conduct rigorous inspections,

 The Real World of Entrepreneurship

Getting Advice About Paying Yourself

If you have based what your company pays you on cash flow and profitability, you're not alone. In an *Inc.* survey, 80 percent of the CEO respondents cited "company needs" as very important in their decisions about how much to pay themselves. But there are resources that can help entrepreneurs make this crucial decision:

▶ Published industry surveys by agencies and trade associations

▶ Executive search firms

▶ CEO roundtables—these are peer groups usually in companies of about the same size

▶ Trade magazines and the popular press

▶ Public company annual reports

▶ Industry consultants

▶ Compensation specialists

▶ Classified ads

▶ The American Compensation Association

Source: Edward O. Welles, "What CEOs Make," *Inc.*, September 1995, pp. 40–54.

Table 8.2   Staying on the Right Side of OSHA and Workers' Comp

▶ Develop a safety program with the input and commitment of everyone.

▶ Get employees back to work as soon as possible after an injury.

▶ Increase job satisfaction and commitment to the company. Happy employees translate into fewer claims.

▶ Pay premiums only on straight time (not overtime or vacation time).

▶ Check the rate categories for all employees carefully.

▶ Have the company pay the smaller claims itself.

▶ If the company has a higher-than-average safety record, ask for a discount in premium.

▶ Check insurance records carefully, especially for claims from people who don't currently work for the company or haven't for a long period of time.

▶ Shop around for the best rates, and don't be afraid to change agents midstream.

▶ Take care of injuries quickly.

▶ Help employees understand that high premiums mean lower profits, and less money in their pockets.

liberally dispensing fines and penalties where violations have occurred. Table 8.2 offers several tips to help a company avoid high premiums and the stress of OSHA audits.

Workers' Compensation

Workers' compensation is another significant safety-related expense, so much so that some companies have made location decisions based on the cost of workers' comp in a particular state. Workers' compensation insurance is a no-fault system under which workers receive guaranteed compensation for injury at work and employers are protected from unlimited liability by covering the cost of the premiums. The insurance has three components: the first covers medical bills and lost wages for the employee; the second covers the

 Entrepreneurship in Action

A Workers' Compensation Nightmare

Sometimes even when employees don't follow required safety procedures, they benefit from workers' comp. A shingler for a siding company on the East Coast fell from a scaffold due to his own carelessness as witnessed by several others. Because workers' comp is a no-fault insurance system, the man was eligible for wages and medical payments up to 160 months (13.3 years), and the employer would have to keep him on the payroll at two-thirds his pay, which was $28,000. The company protested, but each year, based on a doctor's statement, the company had to pay. Once, when the company advertised for a management position, the worker boldly applied. When the job was given instead to a person with executive experience, the former employee sued for discrimination against disabled employees.

Source: Robert A. Mamis, "Employees from Hell," *Inc.*, January 1995, p. 50.

owner should the spouse or children of a permanently disabled worker decide to sue; and the third is employment practices liability, which insures against lawsuits arising from claims for such things as sexual harassment and discrimination. The cost of worker accidents and false claims has threatened the life of many a business. On average a company spent $564 per employee on workers' compensation insurance in 1992, double the amount spent in 1985, according to the Small Business Administration. The dollar amount of claims has also risen, to an average of $23,000 per claim, double that in 1985. To further exacerbate the situation, premium rates, which are based on the type of business the company is in and its accident history, vary from state to state, resulting in some states having a competitive advantage over others in certain industries. Among the fastest-growing and most vexing claims are those for repetitive motion injury, such as carpal tunnel syndrome, and stress-related disabilities, although the most popular claim is for back injury (see "A Workers' Compensation Nightmare").

Laws Related to Liability

Another rapidly growing area of legislation and consequent cost to growing companies is liability for violating employee rights. Today a company may be held liable and be sued for damages for a long list of acts (see Table 8.3).[23] Not only are these suits expensive to defend, but if the company is found in violation, it potentially faces catastrophic damage awards. One Ohio jury awarded $7 million against a company for age discrimination (*Byrnes*, 1991).

Table 8.3   What a Company Can Be Held Liable For

- Race and sex discrimination (Civil Rights Act, 1993)
- Age discrimination (ADEA, 1993)
- Benefits discrimination (ERISA, 1993)
- Recordkeeping violations (Immigration Reform and Control Act, 1993)
- Improper use of a polygraph (Employee Polygraph Protection Act, 1993)
- Failure to provide adequate family and personal leave (Family and Medical Leave Act, 1993)
- Retaliatory conduct (*Lingle*, 1988; *Ostrofe*, 1984)
- Negligent hiring (*Malorney*, 1986; *Sheerin*, 1986; *Cramer*, 1985)
- Defamation (*Lewis*, 1986)
- Emotional distress (*English*, 1990; *Rojo*, 1989; *Johnson*, 1988; *Ford*, 1987; *Bodewig*, 1981)
- Invasion of privacy (*Saroka*, 1992)
- Unjust dismissal (*Gantt*, 1992; *Pierce*, 1980)
- Insufficient notice of layoff or closing (Worker Adjustment and Retraining Notification Act, 1992)

Family and Medical Leave Act

The Family and Medical Leave Act, which applies to companies with 50 or more employees, allows workers to take up to 12 weeks of unpaid leave each year to care for family members or deal with serious medical problems. Serious medical problems may be certified not only by physicians but also by chiropractors, podiatrists, midwives, clinical social workers, and many other caregivers. To qualify for this benefit, an employee must have worked for the employer for 12 months for at least 1,250 hours. Payment of health insurance premiums continues during the leave. If an employer believes medical certification is suspect, it can ask for a second opinion.

Religious Bias

Companies that require a worker to be on the job on a religious holiday can be found to be in violation of Title VII of the Civil Rights Act of 1964, which prohibits discrimination based on religion. This was the case in Arkansas, where a computer operator who was a practicing Seventh-day Adventist was fired for not working on Saturdays, a holy day in his church. The employee sued the company and was awarded nearly $100,000, and he got his job back.[24] The regulations regarding this issue come under the purview of the Equal Employment Opportunity Commission (EEOC), which requires that

When Threase-Mae Jacobs took a job at Domino's Pizza in Denver, she caused quite a stir when she showed up in the traditional garb of her Islamic faith. At first, the manager wouldn't permit her to wear it. But Jacobs consulted a friend who worked at Pizza Hut and learned that her manager was actually breaking the law. As an employer you must accomodate a person's religious beliefs as long as they don't place undue hardship on the business. Jacobs and her employer eventually managed to work out a compromise satisfactory to both. (Jeff Lowe)

employers reasonably accommodate their workers' religious practices as long as doing so doesn't pose an undue hardship on the company. Unfortunately, there is no clear definition of "reasonable accommodation" and, because of the wide variety of religious practices, the issue of accommodation is handled on a case-by-case basis.

Sexual Harassment

The rulings regarding unwanted sexual advances and harassment on the job began to get very tough in the 1980s. The courts have expanded the definition of *sexual harassment*, and businesses are now developing policies in an effort to ward off embarrassing and expensive lawsuits.[25] The EEOC reports that sexual harassment complaints grew from 4,400 in 1986 to 5,600 in 1990. In its first ruling on the subject, the Supreme Court held that sexual harassment violates Title VII of the 1964 Civil Rights Act when the act is unwelcome and represents an abuse of power in the workplace. Generally, harassment can be divided into two categories: *quid pro quo,* where advancement on the job or a raise is conditional on certain sexual favors, and *hostile working environment* cases, where the employee is subjected to a sexually offensive environment against his or her will. Harassment includes, but is not limited to, verbal and nonverbal assaults of a sexual nature, and physical harassment. As a result, business owners should establish policies that educate and make clear to employees what conduct is not acceptable in the workplace. In doing so, entrepreneurs can solicit guidance from the EEOC.

Protecting the Company Against Lawsuits

Fighting a lawsuit by an angry employee is a costly expense for any company, but especially for a growing, small business with limited resources. The problem is that employees can sue without putting up any money because they

 Entrepreneurship in Action

Regulation Isn't Just for American Companies

Though U.S. companies face regulations unheard of in other parts of the world, there are actually some regulations they don't have to deal with that companies in other countries do. In the Netherlands, for example, all companies must register with the chamber of commerce and provide information on how much they are paying their employees, what new products they are investing in, sales figures, and so forth. So anyone can access this information. The reasoning for this regulation is the government's desire to help suppliers determine whether or not they should do business with a particular

company. But of course, a company's competition is also privy to this information.

Terminating employees is no easy feat either, as Wally de Jong, the owner of InterActive Holding, BV, a flue system manufacturing facility in Didam, the Netherlands, found out. As a result of an agreement among the government, the union, and the industry, de Jong is required to pay severance pay to employees over age 50 in the amount of up to two months' salary for every year the employee has worked at the company.

typically seek out attorneys who work on a contingency basis and may collect more than 50 percent of the award if they win. If they lose, there is no cost to the client. Consequently, it's a win-win situation for the employee. Also, unaware entrepreneurs, who are focusing on acquiring customers and meeting market demands often forget to carefully document issues related to employment and are shocked at how seriously a disgruntled employee can hurt their already struggling business. A little effort on the front end can prevent costly litigation on the back end. A company can do several things to at least minimize the chances of being sued:

1. *Be very careful about whom you hire.* All expectations should be spelled out *before* the person is hired and documented for future reference. Every effort should be made to accurately assess the person's character and trustworthiness, and references should be carefully checked.

2. *Keep a file on each employee.* The file should contain documentation of all events of importance in terms of promotion, raises, training, performance evaluations, and potential for termination, written in a style that is factual and suitable as evidence in a court of law. It is also wise to have more than one person contribute to this file.

3. *Always put in writing any communications with an employee regarding performance.* The dates on which any violations of expectations occurred and the specific nature of those violations should be stated very clearly. *Make sure to obtain* written *confirmation of receipt from the employee.*

4. *Before terminating any employee, seek counsel from an attorney.* An attorney experienced in labor law can check the company's documentation for potential problems or openings for the employee to sue.

When You Have to Terminate an Employee

If it becomes necessary to terminate an employee, a company can take a number of steps to protect against a suit for wrongful termination:[26]

1. A neutral location rather than a manager's office should be used.

2. Two people should be present; one should be a neutral party who has no working relationship with the employee to be terminated.

3. The employee should receive a written termination notice documenting the events leading up to the termination, the rules or policies violated, and the procedures the employee must take following termination.

4. Management should state its case and answer questions. It is not wise to carry on a conversation with the employee.

5. No matter how the employee responds, management should always remain calm and in control.

6. Management should refrain from giving career advice, but can offer to help the person find a new job.

7. Management should never use the term *layoff* in a termination case. It suggests the person may be called back to work.

8. Management should accurately document the exit interview in writing and give a copy to the employee.

9. It is important to avoid giving a termination notice at the end of a workday, before a holiday, or after the employee has returned from a business trip.

Employee Handbooks

One of the best ways to communicate the vision, culture, and policies of the company is through an employee handbook. This handbook is both a legal document that protects both owners and employees and an enthusiastic rendition of the company culture. The handbook serves as documentation of everything from compensation and promotion to vacations and health care. It also lets employees know under what circumstances their employment can be terminated and what that process consists of.

The Problem with Employee Handbooks

In their exuberance to convey the corporate culture, employers often say things that can cause legal problems later. Sloppy language and broad statements of policy are often worse than no handbook at all. In the 1980s, a storm of wrongful termination suits put companies on notice about employee handbooks. In particular, the court in the landmark case *Toussaint v. Blue Cross and Blue Shield* (1980) ruled that an employer who reassured workers verbally and in the handbook that termination would come about only for "good cause" could not later dismiss them "at will." If a dispute arises, the company may find that the state court will bind it to the handbook as written, not intended; therefore, it's important to state all policies and procedures clearly without leaving room for ambiguity. Any vague provisions will likely go in favor of the employee, since the employer wrote the handbook.

Handbooks should avoid language that

▶ Suggests that employees can expect a long and enjoyable relationship with the company.

▶ Suggests that managers and supervisors can solve all employee problems.

▶ Establishes the specific rights of the employees.

▶ Tells employees exactly what is expected of them.

▶ States that certain absolute disciplinary steps will always be taken before termination. This allows no leeway for quick termination when necessary.

▶ Spells out violations for which people will be fired. It limits the company's ability to act on unforeseen problems.

The Company History

The story of how the company was founded should definitely be the first entry in the handbook because it sets the tone and gives the employees a sense of history, of belonging to something potentially great. The history should be related like a story; in other words, it should be personal, entertaining, and readable (it is not uncommon for this portion of the handbook to end up in some magazine!). Honesty about some of the troubles the company faced starting the business will make employees feel they are part of a *human* effort rather than a serendipitous occurrence.

The Company Philosophy

The company philosophy is essentially a statement of the identity of the company: what it is and what it stands for. If the history section describes the birth of the company's culture, the philosophy section ingrains that culture in the minds of the employees. After reading this section, employees should have a good sense of what the founders believe in, where the company is going, and how they fit into the picture. If the philosophy is that employees should be creative, assertive, productive, self-motivated problem solvers who aren't afraid to be wrong, they should know that up front. The reality is that most employees' experience with company cultures has been quite the opposite. The handbook should shake them up a bit and help them to clearly see that their experience with this company will be very different.

What Goes into the Handbook?

The best way to determine what to put into the handbook is to first consider what the employees want to know about the business; then the entrepreneur should look at the handbooks of other companies to see what he or she likes and dislikes. In general, the handbook should include the following information:

▶ *A section stating that the handbook is not a contract and is subject to changes.* This is important because business conditions may force work hours or vacation times to change and employees should be forewarned of this possibility. This section should also state that the employment relationship may be terminated at any time, for any reason, with or without cause or notice. The employee needs to sign a copy of this statement, acknowledging receipt of the handbook and agreement with its terms.

▶ *Employment policies* on such things as advancement opportunities, work hours, pay, performance reviews, vacations, sick leave, jury duty, and so forth.

▶ *Benefits* such as health, dental, insurance, disability, workers' compensation, and retirement. The law requires including mention of the Family and Medical Leave Act.

◗ *A policy on employee conduct,* including a written sexual harassment policy and dispute resolution procedure. It should be clearly stated that any situational examples included are merely examples of unacceptable conduct and not a comprehensive list.

◗ *An organizational chart* so employees know who is who and where they fit in the big picture.

◗ *Phone numbers* of key people.

◗ *Table of contents, question/answer sections, and an index.* The handbook should not be too cumbersome; 20 to 30 pages is plenty for a young company. It should be designed so that information is easily accessed.

A Word on International Human Resource Management

The global marketplace has increased the possibility that a growing company will ultimately have facilities and do significant business on a worldwide basis. This presents new dilemmas for companies whose only experience has been managing employees within the borders of the United States. It is widely believed that international human resource management (IHRM) is more difficult than domestic HRM because of macro environmental factors such as cultural, socioeconomic, institutional, and political elements, which differ in nearly every country.[27]

Research on IHRM is flourishing as more and more companies report their experiences in terms of (1) issues employees face when transferring overseas, (2) the IHRM function and activities, (3) the many factors that influence IHRM, and (4) IHRM in individual countries.[28] It is believed that firms intending to operate internationally need to understand and diagnose the contexts in which they will function so that they can integrate their domestic and international operations. When it comes to finding employees for overseas operations, companies seem to take three approaches:[29]

1. Find potential employees based on who is available or who volunteers.

2. Use local professionals knowledgeable about the market to locate the appropriate personnel.

3. Use transferees, that is, those from the domestic side of the company who have cross-cultural skills. Using locals for the bulk of personnel needs is usually a wise decision, particularly in marketing, as it is difficult for someone who has not lived in a culture for a long time to truly understand the nuances of communication in that culture. Unfortunately, recent research confirms that many firms do not pay attention to that advice.[30]

Some firms are making the effort to develop their employees for careers in the international arena by providing training and skills needed to function effectively in a particular cultural environment. However, attempts to transplant in whole or in part U.S.-type HRM programs such as employee empowerment and performance evaluation based on merit will often meet with failure because of tremendous cultural differences. Where the goals of the firm may remain intact on a global level, implementation of those goals will probably see variation country by country. Check the resources at the end of this chapter for more information on global HRM.

The issue of how to maintain some sense of company vision and goals when operating in diverse environments will be a challenge for a long time to come. Perhaps it will be in the global arena that human resource management, the management of the human assets of the company, will finally become a significant partner in the company's strategic planning.

Cases Relevant to This Chapter

Zanart Entertainment
Pelco

Issues for Review and Discussion

1. List three key items that should be part of any job description.
2. What are some questions that should never be asked of interviewees?
3. What are the various possible components of an executive compensation package? How does the IRS view executive pay?
4. Describe three noncash benefits used as employee incentives.
5. Discuss three of the many regulations affecting workers and employers in the workplace.

Experiencing Entrepreneurship

1. You are starting a restaurant business and need to create a compensation policy. List and gather the information you will need to do this. Then arrange to talk to a restaurant owner about his or her compensation policy to compare the results.
2. Find a company that is doing business internationally, and ask how its HRM policy has changed to accommodate the cultural differences in other countries.
3. Interview the CEO of a growing company about how she or he handles executive compensation. In particular, how did the founder(s) decide to pay himself or herself?

Resources

Briscoe, Dennis R. (1995). *International Human Resource Management.* Englewood Cliffs, NJ: Prentice-Hall.

Cardy, R. L., and G. H. Dobbins (1994). *Performance Appraisal: Alternative Perspectives.* Cincinnati: South-Western.

Ferris, Gerald R., Sherman D. Rosen, and Harold T. Barnum, eds. (1995). *Handbook of Human Resource Management.* Cambridge, MA: Blackwell Publishers.

Interview Questions: What You Can and Cannot Ask. New York: American Management Association.

Marquardt, Michael J., and Dean W. Engel (1992). *Global Human Resource Development*. Englewood Cliffs, NJ: Prentice-Hall.

Moran, Robert T., Philip R. Harris, and William G. Stripp (1993). *Developing the Global Organization: Strategies for Human Resource Professionals*. Houston, TX: Gulf Publishing.

Noe, R. A., J. R. Hollenbeck, B. Gerhart, and P. M. Wright (1994). *Human Resource Management: Gaining a Competitive Advantage*. Burr Ridge, IL: Austin Press/Irwin.

Shenkar, Oded (1995). *Global Perspectives of Human Resource Management*. Englewood Cliffs, NJ: Prentice-Hall.

Steingold, Fred S. (1994). *The Employer's Legal Handbook*. Berkeley, CA: Nolo Press.

The 1990 Americans with Disabilities Act and the Age Discrimination in Employment Act of 1967. U.S. EECO, Office of Communications and Legislative Affairs, 1801 L Street, N.W., Washington, DC 10507. Ask for "ADA Enforcement Guidance: Preemployment Disability-Related Questions and Medical Examinations," released October 1995; and "Job Advertising and Preemployment Inquiries Under the ADEA," released July 1989.

Weiss, Donald H. (1995). *Fair, Square & Legal: Safe Hiring, Managing & Firing Practices to Keep You and Your Company Out of Court*. Amacom. New York: American Management Association.

Internet Resources

Employee Relations Web Picks

http://www.webcom.com/~garnet/labor/

Focuses on New York State labor relations issues as well as a range of federal employment issues and U.S. Supreme Court decisions.

Institute of Management & Administration Business Pages

http://www.ioma.com/

Sample articles about topics such as employee benefits, compensation, and industry resources. Hundreds of links to other sites.

High profits stem largely from superior execution or forceful opportunism, not structural competitive barriers.
Amer Bhide
Harvard Business Review, 1986

Rapid-Growth Strategies for Entrepreneurial Companies

Preview

Understanding this chapter will give you the ability to

- **Explain the factors that permit or inhibit a company from growing.**
- **Describe the role of the customer in the growth strategy of a company.**
- **Identify strategies for growing within the current market**
- **Identify strategies for growing within the industry.**
- **Identify strategies for diversifying outside the industry and market.**
- **Discuss what a company needs to expand globally.**

Terms to Know

Stephanie Karp
Jolie & Co.

How many people can say at age 27 that they've been in business for 13 years? Small-business owner Stephanie Karp can definitely say that about her fashion accessories business, Jolie & Co., which she launched in Newton, Massachusetts, when she was just 14. Buying ready-made products from a wholesaler who was a friend of her family and making a few of the items herself, Karp found there was a willing market for her hair accessories. Just before entering high school, she attended Camp Pembroke on Cape Cod. Her wholesaler suggested that she sell hair accessories to her fellow campers, but Karp wasn't interested; she wanted to just have a good time. Nevertheless, her parents thought it might be nice if she made a few extra dollars while she was there and finally convinced her to do it. They gave her $200 to get started with a beginning inventory of accessories. Surprisingly, those sold out within a few days, and she had doubled her money. The sales experience at camp made Karp more excited about retail, and she realized she had a natural talent for it. So in the fall of her freshman year, Karp decided to sell the products at school to earn spending money.

It was at that point that she formalized her business with a name—Jolie—which means "beautiful" in French and is also the name of her French poodle. But it wasn't until Karp turned 16 and got her driver's license that the business began to grow beyond the students at her school. Her age was definitely a problem with suppliers, however. It was difficult to be taken seriously. "I got a lot of rejections, but it never bothered me; it made me want to knock on more doors," she claims. Her strategy was to offer accessories such as scrunchies, barrettes, purses, scarves, and vests at prices between $6 and $25. These are what she calls "impulse items" that women of all ages will buy just for fun. Her customers ranged in age from 3 to 100. In fact, she still has some customers today who were with her in the beginning.

After high school, Karp went to New York City to the Fashion Institute of Technology to study market-

ing and merchandising and learn more about the industry. She had a decision to make: whether to continue the business or quit until she had finished her studies. That's when Karp's mom stepped in and offered to continue the business while Karp was in New York. On weekends and whenever she had any time away from classes, Karp would walk the streets, talk to wholesalers, go to trade shows, and generally immerse herself in the 7th Avenue world of fashion. When Karp graduated in 1993, she was offered buying jobs by three New York–based companies. It was a difficult decision, one she considered carefully before turning down all three offers to return home and run the business. Karp had learned that working for someone else in the fashion industry meant long hours for very little money, too little to allow her to live in New York. Working for herself also meant long hours, but she would be doing something she loved and the money would be secondary. Upon her return to Boston, her mother took a back seat and began helping Karp service accounts and do trade shows.

The industry Jolie & Co. is in is a difficult one. Karp has constant concerns about finding new customers, maintaining inventory, shipping on time, customer service, and generally keeping up with fashion trends, which can change overnight. Today about 50 percent of her products are made exclusively for Jolie by contract manufacturers; the rest are imported. Whereas she used to have time to make a good portion of the accessories, the demands of the business have forced her to rely more and more on friends in New York. Karp enjoys the merchandising and sales part of the business. When her merchandise arrives, she checks it to make sure it's salable and not damaged. Then she personally delivers the goods to her customers. She admits to "spoiling" her customers, even those as far away as Florida, where she visits from time to time. But she's learning as she expands the business geographically that she can't do it all, that very shortly the time will come when she needs to hire some help.

Although Jolie & Co. is not close to competing with the major companies in the industry, Karp is enjoying success where others have faltered. One reason is her relationship with her customers; the other is that she permits small orders when her competitors demand minimum volumes. Revenues have grown consistently through word of mouth and weekend craft shows, and the company is profitable.

Jolie & Co.'s products now appear in more than 200 retail stores, including boutiques; hair and nail salons; and gift shops in hospitals, hotels, and schools. Most people cannot believe how young Karp is, because she runs her company with maturity born of experience.

Karp is now introducing a catalog of her accessories and believes the business is poised to take a big spurt of growth. Her mom has been by her side from the beginning, encouraging and helping. She won't take a salary, but Karp often treats her to special gifts such as a new suit or a trip to a spa. Like her daughter, Mrs. Karp believes money is secondary to independence and the pride of owning your own business. Stephanie Karp encourages other young entrepreneurs by telling them to "love what you do, or else you won't want to work every day. If you love what you do, it will show in your business."

What growth strategies do you see for Jolie & Co.?

Growth is not only a positive thing for a business, it's an absolute necessity if a company wishes to survive in the long term. Stephanie Karp certainly learned that as she looked for ways to expand her market and compete against much larger companies (see the Young Entrepreneurs—Minicase). Karp was smart enough to realize that a business can't stay the same over the long term in a fast-changing marketplace. So she's constantly looking for new ways to reach new customers and new products to sell to her loyal customer base.

Some trends in the current market give a good basis for looking at growth strategies:

- There is still a lot of opportunity in the computer hardware/software industry. Companies are emerging in segments of the market that are still relatively young, such as systems integration and wide area networks.

- Increasing government regulation has spawned an entire industry of businesses devoted to helping companies cope with regulations and the associated paperwork.

- With more and more companies focusing on their core competencies, temporary help firms and employee-leasing firms are a rapidly growing industry that is providing personnel needs to all types of companies.[1]

In this chapter, we'll look first at the role of the customer in the growth strategies of entrepreneurial ventures going into the new millennium, factors that affect the ability of a company to grow. Then we'll consider several broad strategies for growing the business, including those that (1) exploit opportunity in the current market, (2) involve growth within the industry as a whole, (3) exploit opportunities outside the current market or industry, and (4) take the business into the international arena (global strategies).

Factors That Affect a Company's Ability to Grow

Businesses don't automatically grow just because they exist. Many factors in the environment either inhibit or enhance the chances for growth. These factors also dictate the way growth may occur. Growth can be slow, be sustained over a long period of time, or explode in a very short period of time (hypergrowth). It can also vary between rapid growth and slower growth in the various stages of the company's life cycle. Therefore, it's important to be aware of those factors in the business environment that affect growth (see Figure 9.1).

The Entrepreneur's Intentions for Growth

The 1996 *Inc.* list of the fastest-growing private companies found that just 30 percent of the entrepreneurs had original intentions to grow rapidly or to make the Inc. 500, about 45 percent wanted to grow slowly, 22 percent wanted to grow enough to survive, and 3 percent expressed a desire to remain small.[2] Yet all of them ended up on the 1996 list of the fastest-growing companies. This can be partly explained by the fact that a very small company will naturally show a larger percentage of growth in the early years because it's starting from a small base, and entrepreneurs' intentions can change over

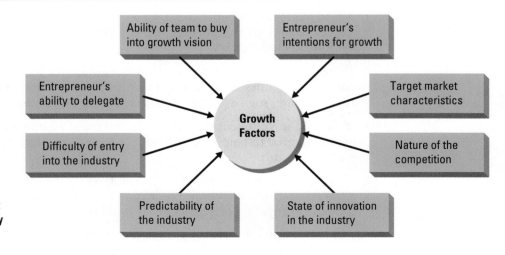

**Figure 9.1
Factors That Affect
a Company's Ability
to Grow**

time. Where an entrepreneur started with a business that was intended to be small, the market may have encouraged greater growth than expected.

Some entrepreneurs consciously or unconsciously choose not to grow their businesses. Perhaps they have read the many stories of entrepreneurs who failed during the growth period because they weren't prepared for it or lacked the skills they needed to manage the company during that time. To prevent a similar occurrence in their own businesses, these new entrepreneurs attempt in a variety of ways to slow the growth of the business to a manageable rate. Their fear of growth prevents them from understanding that growth is a natural by-product of a successful start-up period and that without growth they will miss the real excitement and challenge of owning a business. Instead they will slow the business to the point of stalling its growth, and ultimately the business will spiral into oblivion.

Some entrepreneurs also mistakenly assume that only high-tech companies experience rapid growth, so they are unprepared for it when it occurs. The reality is that businesses in a variety of industries experience high growth, including service companies, restaurants, product manufacturers, and clothing companies. Thus, while some industries, such as computers and telecommunications, operate in a seemingly natural environment for high growth, a similar level of growth can occur in other industries as a result of the entrepreneur's business strategy.

Several environmental factors also affect growth, including target market characteristics, the nature of the competition, the state of innovation in the industry, the predictability of the industry, difficulty of entry into the industry, the ability of the entrepreneur to delegate, and the ability of the team to buy into the company's vision.

Target Market Characteristics

The level of growth a company can achieve is somewhat limited by the sales and buying power of the customers within the niche it has chosen to enter. However, a strategy that includes expanding the niche on a global basis or finding other complementary niches to enter can increase the potential for growth.

The Nature of the Competition

The fact that the industry contains much larger companies that control a significant share of the market doesn't automatically preclude the entrepreneurial company from growth. Because it is smaller and carries far less overhead, the entrepreneurial company can be more flexible and change more rapidly with changing market demands. Today many large companies are outsourcing aspects of their business process to smaller companies in the industry for this very reason. Moreover, if the industry is stable and mature, the entrepreneurial company can create a niche and introduce new ways of doing business that will give it a solid chance to grow in the industry.

Sometimes the challenges a business faces can virtually stop its growth. Douglas Levin has had his share of challenges. First he paid too much for his fresh juice company, Fresh Samantha. Then he targeted the wrong market and his customers thought the price of the product was too high. Then a competitor sold a batch of apple juice tainted with E. Coli, which forced Levin to invest in pasteurization equipment. Still, persistence and a belief in his product paid off. Sales went from $2.8 million in 1996 to $7 million in 1997. (Seth Resnick)

The State of Innovation in the Industry

Being an innovative company, a company that is always looking for new ways to do things, in an industry that is known for innovation (e.g., computers, telecommunications, biotechnology) will not get the entrepreneurial company noticed. But being able to innovate more quickly and with higher quality than others in the industry will give the young company a competitive chance. On the other hand, if innovation is rare in the industry, introducing an innovation gives the growing company a chance to enter and establish the standards that everyone will have to follow to compete.

The Predictability of the Industry

Some industries are very volatile and, in some cases, appear to move at the whim of key industry players or major customers. These industries are fertile ground for opportunity and rapid growth. The toy industry is a good non-high-tech example. What is hot in December can become obsolete inventory in May. Toy companies come and go with the success and failure of their ability to read the market. Of the thousands of new products introduced at the toy fair in New York every February, only perhaps a dozen will find any success at all, and in only the rarest of cases (the Barbie doll is one) does a product achieve longevity as in other industries.

The Difficulty of Entry into the Industry

Many industry factors can make it difficult for a new business to enter the industry and gain a degree of market acceptance. Mature industry leaders may have established brand identity with customers. In some industries the costs of plant, equipment, and regulations are prohibitive for a new business. Moreover, if major companies own the rights to core technology the new business needs to compete, it may be effectively barred from entering if it cannot acquire a license on that technology. In instances where entry barriers are high, it will be important to consider if it's worth the effort to try to enter and grow in that industry. A compatible industry may be more inviting.

The Entrepreneur's Ability to Delegate to Professional Management

Countless entrepreneurial companies are hindered in their growth strategy by the very entrepreneurs who founded them. These entrepreneurs often don't realize they lack the management skills necessary to grow the company to the next stage. They excelled at bringing together diverse resources to create the company and see it to survival, but entrepreneurs and managers are two different breeds, and rarely does one person possess the distinct skills each role requires. If an entrepreneur doesn't recognize this inability to manage growth early on and delegate to someone who has the skills, the company will likely struggle and may even fail.

The Ability of the Team to Buy into the Growth Vision

By their very nature entrepreneurs have a vision for the growth of their companies, but that doesn't mean everyone else in the company understands or is ready to commit to this vision. Successful growth can only be achieved if everyone in the company is committed to seeing it happen. Vision starts with the entrepreneur, but it's implemented through everyone's efforts. Entrepreneurs who wish to grow their ventures must clearly communicate their growth vision to everyone, including customers, and be willing and ready to listen and accept feedback.

Customer-Centered Growth for a New Millennium

For now and into the twenty-first century, those companies that will see consistent high growth rates will be **customer centered** and experts at adding value for the customer. This means not just listening to the "voice of the customer" but, as Richard Whiteley and Diane Hessan, in their book *Customer-Centered Growth* call it, actually "hardwiring" the customer into the company.[3] The customer is the competitive advantage and, more than customer satisfaction, customer *enthusiasm* needs to be the overriding goal.

The entrepreneurs, who are the leaders of the organization, must be everywhere present, imbuing management, employees, and customers with the company vision and their enthusiasm. Bernie Moore and Arthur Blank, the founders of The Home Depot, wholeheartedly believe in this approach. In fact, they personally train store managers to ensure that their vision and enthusiasm for the company are passed on.

In their book, Whiteley and Hessan tell an inspiring story about a company called Fletcher Music, which grew entirely by focusing on the customer. Fletcher originally stocked most kinds of popular musical instruments in its stores, including the home organs for which they were known. It enjoyed success until well into the 1980s. Then the market changed; technology took over and changed the way instruments such as the organ were made. Unfortunately, traditional organs were Fletcher's most profitable product. At a point verging on bankruptcy, Fletcher made a bold move. It sold off all of its products with one exception—traditional home organs—while its competitor, Tune Town, continued to carry a full line of instruments. Everyone thought Fletcher was headed for disaster, but quite the opposite happened.

Fletcher had decided to look closely at its customers and found, to its astonishment, that the average age was 70. These older people were uncomfortable with the new technology and keyboards that were now designed for more agile fingers. What's more, Fletcher found the customer really wanted to be involved in something. So Fletcher created an organ designed for and by senior citizens, the Estey, and began offering "lifetime free lessons." Seniors began to pour into the store, and the Estey sold out quickly. Fletcher discovered that customers were using the music store as a meeting place, so it encouraged these activities. Today Fletcher considers itself to be not in the music business but in the "lifestyle enhancement business." It has succeeded enormously while its competitor has filed for bankruptcy.

The marketplace constantly entices companies such as Fletcher to pull away from their focus to take advantage of opportunities outside their core competencies. The end result is a shotgun approach to growth that ultimately fails. A better approach is to listen to your customers:

1. Identify the best customers.

2. Learn what they value.

3. Converge on that value and figure out ways to address it.

4. Develop an organization-wide obsession with a focus on what you and your customers believe you do best.[4]

Learning what customers value is best accomplished through a technique that Toyota developed to get at the source of a problem by asking "why" five times to a response. A modification of this technique can be used to learn what customers value by asking a series of five "whats," beginning with "What do you expect from us?" and following each response with "What does that mean?"[5] Finally, the company can ask itself "What resources do we have or need to develop to meet this customer need?" Table 9.1 presents an

Table 9.1   Using the Five "Whats"

Company	Customer
What do you expect from us?	Total quality
What do you mean by that?	Immediate response to problems
What does that mean?	A solution within 24 hours
What do you mean by "solution"?	A technical support person to fix the problem
What does that mean?	I need the tech person to come to the site

The need that must be met = The company must consider having field technical support for its products.

example of this technique. While focusing on the customer, entrepreneurial companies can consider four broad strategies for growth (Figure 9.2).

Growing Within the Current Market

One of the first broad strategies entrepreneurial companies consider is exploiting the current market fully; that is, they allow the company to expand its market share to the greatest extent possible by increasing the volume of sales to current customers and increasing the number of customers in the target market. Generally there are three methods for implementing a strategy of growing within the current market: market penetration, market development, and product development.

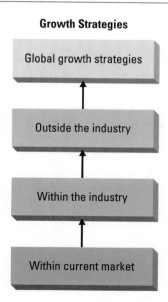

Growth Strategies

Global growth strategies

↑

Outside the industry

↑

Within the industry

↑

Within current market

**Figure 9.2
Growth Strategies**

Market Penetration

With **market penetration,** the company attempts to increase sales and gain more customers using more effective marketing strategies within the current target market. This is often the first growth strategy entrepreneurs use because it allows them to work in familiar territory while they get their infrastructure in place to grow more rapidly. So, for example, if you have designated Brookline, Massachusetts, as the start-up location, your initial target market might be the greater Boston area. You would focus your efforts on reaching and solidifying as many customers as possible in that area before moving out to other geographic areas or secondary markets.

Market Development

Market development consists of taking the product or service to a broader geographical area. One of the most popular ways to expand a market geographically is to *franchise,* because it's generally less costly than setting up a national distribution system and it allows the business to grow quickly in several geographical markets at once. Another approach is licensing. Both are discussed in the following sections.

Franchising

Franchising is the most common form of business venture opportunity and is one of the most popular ways to grow a company quickly without having to do all the work yourself. Franchising allows you to grow in several geographic areas at once and is less expensive than setting up a nationwide distribution system. It is estimated that franchises account for one-third of all retail sales. Franchising has several characteristics that distinguish it from other growth strategies:

▶ The business plan is licensed; that is, the franchisee purchases the right to implement the business plan.

The Real World of Entrepreneurship

Some Franchise Facts[6]

▶ Singer Sewing Machine started the first franchise in 1850.

▶ In 1992, franchising accounted for 40.9 percent of all retail sales in the United States.

▶ In the year 2000, franchise sales will exceed $1 trillion.

▶ Today 1 out of 12 businesses is a franchise. More than 600,000 franchised units exist, and more than 42,000 start up every year.[7]

▶ A new franchise outlet opens somewhere in the United States every eight minutes.[8]

▶ During the last 10 years, franchises added 2 million jobs to the economy.

▶ The business is identified by a common trademark used by all franchisees in addition to a common facility, service, and product design.

▶ The business receives initial training and ongoing assistance from the franchiser.

For these benefits, the franchisee pays a fee and a royalty on sales, typically 3 to 8 percent. Depending on the type of business, the franchisee usually receives for the fee:

▶ A product or service that has a proven market

▶ Trade names and/or trademarks

▶ A patented design, process, or formula

▶ An accounting and financial control system

▶ A marketing plan and national marketing support

▶ The benefit of volume purchasing and advertising

Franchises typically take one of three forms:

1. *Dealerships.* These allow manufacturers to distribute products without having to do the daily work of retailing. An example is an automobile dealership.

2. *Service franchises.* These provide customers with services such as tax preparation, temporary employees, payroll preparation, and real estate services. An example is Century 21 Real Estate Services.

3. *Product franchises.* These are the most popular; they offer a product, a brand name, and an operating model. An example is Chief Auto Parts.

 Entrepreneurship in Action

Great Harvest Bread Company: a Franchise with an Attitude

How would it feel to own a debt-free company, growing by more than 10 percent a year, with a gross income of $60 million and a quality of life that allows you to take off the summer to travel? Pete and Laura Wakeman know what this feels like because Great Harvest Bread Company of Dillon, Montana, has been their company for the past 20 years. With 119 domestic outlets in 34 states, Great Harvest's franchisees enjoy revenues of between $91,000 and $1.3 million each. And unlike most franchises, Great Harvest encourages its franchisees to be individualists. One of the only cardinal rules of the business is that everyone gets free bread.

Like Mrs. Fields Cookies, Great Harvest believes that great bread comes fresh from the oven, sliced only as it is used. It trains its new franchisees in this philosophy by requiring that during the first year a store can only produce six types of bread and one type of cookie. The bread has to be round and not sliced.

The Wakemans are very selective about who can buy one of their franchises. In 1996, only 14 of the 375 qualified applicants were accepted. This is far less than the industry average for franchises, but the Wakemans want to ensure that every franchisee has the right attitude.

SOURCE: Susan Gallagher, "Unusual Franchiser Prospering," *The Fresno Bee,* June 30, 1997.

Table 9.2   The Top Food Franchises in the United States

Franchise	Number of Domestic Units	Investment
McDonald's	10,655	$407,600–$646,350
Wendy's	4,334	$800,000–$1,000,000
Burger King	6,886	$300,000–$1,500,000
Dairy Queen	5,000	$506,600–$1,471,800
Sonic Drive-In	1,579	$495,000–$935,000
Checkers Drive-In Restaurant	491	$516,000–$940,000
Blimpie International	1,500	$95,000–$160,000
Fazoli's	243	$400,000–$1,000,000
KFC	5,112	$750,000–$1,000,000
Orange Julius of America	311	$130,000–$190,000
Pizza Hut	8,300	$263,000–$1,352,000
Schlotzsky's Sandwich Restaurants	564	$249,521–$309,767
Taco Bell	4,510	$200,000–$500,000
Baskin-Robbins	2,487	$55,000–$220,000

Source: "SUCCESS/Arthur Andersen Franchise Gold 100," *Success Magazine,* January/February 1997.

Not every business is suitable for using franchising as a growth strategy. In general, the business should have the following characteristics:

▶ A successful prototype store (preferably stores) with proven profitability and a good reputation so the franchisee will have the advantage of instant customer recognition

▶ Registered trademarks and a consistent image and appearance for all outlets

▶ The kind of business that can be systematized and easily replicated many times

▶ A product that can be sold in a variety of geographic regions

▶ Adequate funding, which may mean as much as $150,000 or more

▶ A well-documented prospectus that spells out the rights, responsibilities, and risks to the franchisee

▶ An operations manual that details every aspect of running the business

▶ A training and support system for franchisees both before they start the business and ongoing after start-up

▶ Site selection criteria and architectural design standards

▶ Financials that show that the company is profitable at the operating level (unit level)

Franchising is not without risks, however. It's virtually like creating a new business, because all processes and procedures must be carefully documented in a manual that will be used to train the franchisees. The franchiser must carefully scrutinize potential franchisees to ensure they are qualified financially and have the skills required to take on the responsibility of a franchise. Furthermore, the cost of preparing a business to franchise is considerable and includes legal, accounting, consulting, and training expenses.

The risk to franchisees who purchased the franchise as an entry into business ownership is also great. Franchisees will typically pay 2 percent to 10 percent of gross sales to the franchiser for monthly royalties and marketing fees, which translates into a tremendous challenge on the part of franchisees to control costs and get a return. But it may take up to three years to show a profit. Consequently, it's no surprise that one report, by Tim Bates of Wayne State University, found that only two-thirds of approximately 1,200 franchised units surveyed in 1987 survived under the same owner for four years.[9] Nearly 35 percent of franchises started between 1984 and 1987 went out of business by late 1991, compared to 28 percent for nonfranchised businesses. Another study, by Scott Shane of the Georgia Institute of Technology, corroborated the Bates study, concluding that of the 138 new franchise systems established in 1983, only 24.6 percent were still in business in 1993.[10] The reason behind the failures is that franchises are typically found in retail industries, primarily eating and drinking establishments, which have a pattern of high risk and low return.[11]

Entrepreneurship in Action

How Boston Chicken Became a National Phenomenon

George Naddaff, entrepreneur extraordinare, founded Boston Chicken, a restaurant chain, and took it public on November 8, 1993, to set a record for a single-day gain for an IPO.[12] With that success under his belt and years of experience with other franchises, Naddaff is constantly out there looking for the next Boston Chicken, a franchise concept with huge potential for growth. And he seems to have a proven strategy.

In doing the research on Boston Chicken, Naddaff studied all the stores carefully. He even stood in line and ordered food and, by doing so, learned that Boston Chicken customers are upscale, a step above those who buy at Kentucky Fried Chicken, so the mean price for a meal is higher, $5 to $6. Naddaff also looked hard at the entrepreneur and the management team. He wanted a person who would mortgage everything he or she had to make the business work. He also wanted real financials that showed the entrepreneur understood the costs of doing business. In short, he looked for passion and a concept that created value. Under his guidance, Boston Chicken grew to 1,100 stores in 38 states.

Naddaff sold Boston Chicken in 1992 to a group of former executives of Blockbuster Entertainment and attributes their troubles in 1997 to losing focus. At the time of the sale, it was a simple chicken store, but the new owners turned it into a market, Boston Market, and confused the customer with too many products, too many prices, and too many discounts.

In late 1997, Naddaff had just purchased Manhattan-based Ranch 1, a grilled-chicken sandwich shop, with intentions to grow it globally.

SOURCE: *Pittsburgh Post-Gazette,* November 7, 1997.

Bankruptcy of the parent company, the franchiser, should be another concern for potential franchisees, and it's not an uncommon phenomenon. In the past decade, dozens of franchises have experienced Chapter 11 bankruptcy, including 7-Eleven, Nutrisystem, American Speedy Printing, Church's Fried Chicken, and Days Inns. Most have emerged intact, but not without some harm to the franchisees. During the bankruptcy, the franchisees are left essentially in limbo, without support or information, and wondering if they will have a viable business when it's all over. The association of the franchisee with the bankrupt parent is also a negative, since customers assume that if the parent has financial problems, so does the child. Furthermore, most franchisees have invested their life's savings in their businesses. Under the arbitration clauses in most franchise agreements, franchisees don't have the option to go to court to recoup their losses. Even if the company comes out of Chapter 11, its image is tarnished. It will have to cut back somewhere, and savvy consumers will perceive this.

Licensing

Like franchising, **licensing** is a way to grow a company without investing large amounts of capital in plant, equipment, and employees. In very simple terms, a license agreement is a grant to someone else to use intellectual property and exploit it in the marketplace by manufacturing, distributing, or using it to create a new product. For example, suppose you have developed a new, patented process for taking rust off machinery. You could license that process to other companies to use on their equipment and receive a royalty. Conversely, imagine you have an idea for a new line of promotional products and you want to license a famous name and likeness to use on those products to make them more attractive to consumers. This would entail seeking a license agreement from the owner of the name and likeness to use it commercially, for example, seeking a license from Paramount Pictures Corporation to use the Star Trek characters on a line of products.

But licensing is much more than this, and entrepreneurs need to understand fully the value of intellectual property and how it can provide income in a variety of ways. For purposes of the discussion here, anything that can be patented, copyrighted, or trademarked, or is a trade secret, has the potential for licensing. If a company has intellectual property that someone else might pay to use or commercialize in some way, certain steps should be taken to ensure that both parties to the transaction win. Licensor and licensee depend on each other strongly for the success of the agreement, so the outcomes must be worthwhile on both ends of the deal. Following are some steps licensors should take to ensure a successful transaction.

Decide exactly what will be licensed. The license agreement can be for a product, the design for a product, a process for doing something, the ability to market and distribute, the ability to manufacture, or the ability to use the licensed product in the production of yet another product. It will also be important to decide if the licensee may only license the product as is or modify it in any way.

Understand and define the benefits the buyer (licensee) will receive from the transaction. Why should the licensee license from your company? What makes the product, process, or whatever unique and valuable? The licensee should clearly see that dealing with your company has many advantages and will be a much more profitable transaction than dealing with someone else.

Conduct thorough market research to make sure the potential customer base is sufficient to ensure a good profit from the effort. Of course, the licensee will have also done market research, particularly if she or he approaches the licensor with a proposal for a licensing agreement. But this situation is typical only with intellectual property that is well recognized in the marketplace, such as characters (e.g., Mickey Mouse, Batman). A company with new intellectual property (IP) that is unproven in the marketplace may need to seek out licensing agreements to get the property commercialized.

*Conduct **due diligence** on potential licensees.* It's important to make certain that any potential licensee has the resources needed to fulfill the terms and conditions of the license agreement, that the licensee can properly commercialize the intellectual property, and that he or she has a sound reputation in the market.

Determine the value of the license agreement. Several factors determine the value of a **license agreement,** including (1) the economic life of the intellectual property (that is, realistically, how long it will remain viable as a marketable product, process, etc.), (2) the potential that someone could design around the intellectual property and directly compete, (3) the potential for government legislation or regulation that could damage the marketability of the IP, and (4) any changes in market conditions that could render the IP without value.

Once the licensor determines the monetary value of the license based on these four factors, it becomes negotiable. Generally, the licensor wants some money up front to show good faith, and then a running royalty for the life of the license agreement. The amount of this royalty will vary by industry and by how much the licensee will have to invest in terms of plant, equipment, and marketing to commercialize the IP.

Create a license agreement. With the help of an attorney who specializes in licenses, a license agreement or contract will be drawn up that defines the terms and conditions of the agreement between the licensor and licensee. Following are some of the clauses that will typically be found in such license agreements:

1. A **grant clause** that specifies what is being delivered to the licensee and whether the license is exclusive (only the licensee has the right to this IP) or nonexclusive (others have a similar right).

2. A **performance clause** that specifies dates by which the licensee should have achieved certain agreed-on sales targets. This is important to avoid situations where the licensee ties up a technology through an exclusive agreement and then never commercializes it, leaving the inventor with nothing for his or her efforts.

3. A **secrecy clause** or *confidentiality clause* that spells out who may know the details of the intellectual property and for how long.

4. A **payment clause** that details the method by which payment will be made. If the license agreement deals with a foreign licensee, it will be important to designate the currency in which royalties will be paid. Normally, a U.S. licensor will definitely want to take payment in U.S. dollars, but a combination of dollars and the licensee's currency is also an option. Be aware that any foreign currency will fluctuate over the life of the license agreement, so royalty payments will vary as well. This could mean more or less income for the licensor and higher or lower payments for the licensee.

5. A **grantback** or *improvement* **clause** that permits the licensee to improve on the product and grant back to the licensor the right to any improvements. Likewise, there may be a **grantforward clause** that gives the licensee the right to use any improvements on the product made by the licensor.

6. A *definite term* for the license agreement.

7. A *sublicense clause* that specifies whether or not the licensee can sublicense the IP or assign the right to another party.

Being a licensee is also a way to grow your company without incurring the expense of always developing new products. From the licensee's point of view, here are a few things to remember:

▶ Search for a technology, product, logo, character, or other IP that you want to license.

▶ Prepare a business plan to present to the licensor showing what you propose to develop and market with the licensor's intellectual property. The plan should include such things as estimated sales, the target market, the plan for penetrating the market, and how you intend to finance the agreement, that is, what resources you have to carry out the agreement.

▶ Do due diligence on the licensor to ensure he or she is reputable, the IP is sound, and the licensor will be the kind of person you want to work with over the period of the license. Remember, this arrangement is much like a partnership, so it's important to choose a partner carefully.

▶ Try to negotiate favorable terms: conservative performance targets, lower royalties, little or no upfront capital, and so forth. Be aware, however, that if the intellectual property is well known or in great demand, there may be little room to negotiate, so you'll probably pay a premium for the agreement.

Again, licensing is an excellent way to move more quickly in the marketplace with less capital investment than other forms of growth require.

Product Development

As a customer-centered business, a third way to exploit the current market is to develop new products and services or offer new versions of existing products to current customers. As you will learn in Chapter 10, today more than ever it's important to take care of your current customers. More profit accrues from selling more products to existing customers than from trying to find new customers. This is because the cost of acquiring new customers is so high. Software companies use this strategy. They constantly update software with new versions that their customers must buy if they want to enjoy all the latest features.

Selling more products to existing customers is not as difficult as it sounds. Customer-centered companies get their best ideas for new products from their customers anyway. These new ideas usually come in two forms: **incremental changes** in existing products or totally new products, what are known as "breakthrough" products. Incremental products often come about serendipitously when engineers, sales personnel, and management spend time out in the marketplace with the customers learning more about their needs. Then these team members can come together on a weekly basis to discuss ideas that will help the company quickly zero in on those incremental products that are possible within the current operating structure and budget. The advantage of incremental products is that since they are based on existing products that the business already produces, they can usually be designed and manufactured fairly quickly.

New or **breakthrough products,** on the other hand, have a much longer product development cycle and are therefore more costly to undertake. Breakthrough products cannot be planned for; instead, they usually come about through brainstorming, exercises in creativity, and problem-solving sessions. In other words, if the entrepreneur creates a business environment that encourages creative, "off-the-wall" thinking, the chances are greater that it will eventually come up with breakthrough-type products. The breakthrough environment of necessity has no budget or time constraints and does not run on a schedule. It must be part of the company's culture on a daily basis. The most effective approach for product development is to use a combination of incremental and breakthrough products so that the speed and cost efficiency of the incremental products will keep cash flowing into the business to help fund the more costly breakthrough products. Over the long term, however, a significant breakthrough product can launch a company into hypergrowth. The impact of hypergrowth on marketing strategy is discussed in Chapter 12.

Growing Within the Industry

Traditionally, when entrepreneurs have wanted to grow their businesses within their industries, they have looked to vertical and horizontal integration strategies. But with the increasing success of outsourcing, strategic alliances, and virtual organizations, entrepreneurs with growing businesses are more often than not looking to a modular or network strategy. This section examines all three strategies.

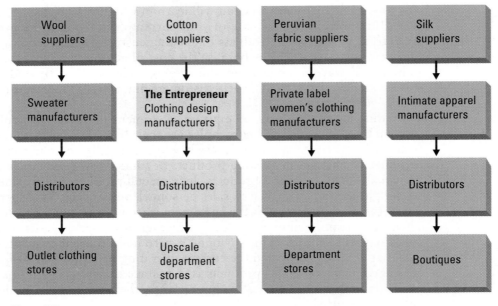

Figure 9.3
An Example of Vertical Integration

Vertical Integration Strategies

An entrepreneurial venture can grow by moving backward or forward within its distribution channel (Figure 9.3). This is called **vertical integration.** With a backward strategy, the company either gains control of some or all of its suppliers or becomes its own supplier by starting another business from scratch or acquiring an existing supplier that has a successful operation. This has been a common strategy for businesses that have instituted a just-in-time inventory control system. By acquiring the core supplier(s), the entrepreneur can streamline the production process, cut costs, and control inventory better. With a forward strategy, the company attempts to control the distribution of its products by either selling direct to the customer (i.e., acquiring a retail outlet) or acquiring the distributors of its products. This strategy will give the business more control over how its products are marketed and delivered to the customer.

Horizontal Integration Strategies

Another way to grow the business within the current industry is to buy up competitors or start a competing business (e.g., the same product under another label), an approach called **horizontal integration** (Figure 9.4). For example, a chain of sporting goods outlets could purchase a business that has complementary products, such as a batting cage business where customers

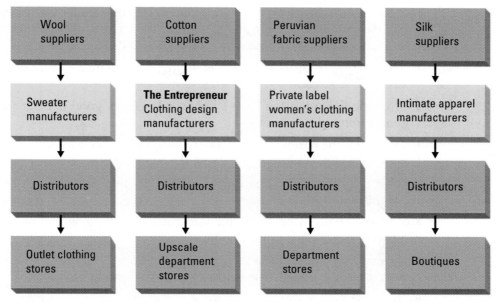

Figure 9.4
An Example of Horizontal Integration

can buy their bats, balls, helmets, and so forth from the retail store and use them at the batting cage. Another example of growing horizontally is to agree to manufacture a product under a different label. New York designer Mark Eisen manufactured a line of clothes for the Spiegel catalog under a different name in addition to his designer label line. This strategy has been used frequently in the major appliance and grocery industries as well. Whirlpool, for example, produced Sears' Kenmore washers and dryers for years. Likewise, major food producers put their brand name food items into packaging labeled with the name of a major grocery store.

Acquisitions

One of the more pervasive trends today is industry consolidation. Certainly we can easily see it in the computer/software industry, but it's also happening in banking, retail, and service industries. Savvy entrepreneurs are using consolidation to build empires and create a strong, defensible presence in the marketplace. But consolidation as a growth strategy is not new. In 1898, the automobile industry had more than 2,000 manufacturers that incorporated motors into their "buckboards."[13] Today the industry has just a handful of manufacturers that have consolidated to achieve synergies and savings and to build market power.

The **consolidation strategy** consists of entering a fragmented industry—perhaps with many smaller "mom-and-pop" type businesses—acquiring the best companies possible, and pulling them together under one umbrella to achieve economies of scale and synergies. It's what some analysts have referred to as a "Pac Man strategy," and it goes like this:[14]

▶ Acquire the strongest company in a particular region, usually in the $7 to $20 million range.

▶ Choose companies that have a long track record, good management, and good community relations.

▶ Make sure the partners fit into the philosophy and culture of the new company. It is important to get to know them personally.

▶ Use a combination of cash and restricted stock to provide an incentive to partners to build the business.

▶ Keep the original operators on board and charge them with looking for additional acquisitions in the region.

▶ Let each region become a separately incorporated business that centralizes common functions such as accounting, payroll, and purchasing.

▶ Use technology to integrate all the acquisitions.

Multitalented entrepreneur Wayne Huizenga used the consolidation strategy one garbage truck at a time to build billion-dollar Waste Management, Inc. He did it a second time with video stores to build another billion-dollar company, Blockbuster Entertainment Corporation. Now he's going for a third billion-dollar company with Auto Nation, which will consolidate and reposition the used-car industry.

Using an acquisition strategy requires the evaluation and valuation of the business being purchased. This will be discussed in Chapter 16. An attorney or a specialist in acquisitions can smooth the way financially and

---

 Entrepreneurship in Action

A Twist on the Pac Man Strategy

Most often, when entrepreneurs use the Pac Man strategy of consolidating a fragmented industry, they fold all the independents they acquire under one name. Jon Ledecky wanted to do something a little different: he wanted each of his acquisitions to retain its own name and identity within its community.

In a daring move, he approached 100 independent office suppliers with the idea of joining forces to create a monster company that would dominate the industry. Only 5 of the 100 would even listen to him. Undaunted, Ledecky went on a relentless search for a banker and finally found one in now-defunct Mabon Securities. With

the five companies that had agreed to come on board, he formed U.S. Office Products. Eventually a total of 67 of the original 100 companies he had approached signed up. The owners were bought out with 50 percent of the buyout in stock in U.S. Products. They were also given guarantees of employment for a minimum of two years.

In the first year of operations, Ledecky met his goal of $1 billion in sales. By 1996, he had 130 acquisitions and revenues of $3 billion.

SOURCE: "The Hidden Giant," *10th Annual Renegades,* ed. Michael Warshaw, *Success,* January/February 1997, p. 33.

Technology Tip

Gaining a Global Presence

If you want to gain an instant global presence, consider setting up a business site on the Internet. It will allow you to

▶ Reach millions of people and other businesses without having to leave your office, saving time and money

▶ Give other businesses and customers a place to go for the latest information on your business and its products and services

▶ Provide product pricing and availability information to vendors to whom you give access to classified areas of the site

▶ Give your customers a way to communicate with you and interact with the company in a variety of ways

procedurally for those entrepreneurs who have never acquired an existing business.

Modular, Agile Web, or Network Strategies

An excellent way for entrepreneurial companies to grow within the company's own industry is to focus on what the company does best and let others do the rest, that is, focus on the company's core competencies and outsource all other activities. This is known as a **modular** or **network strategy.** If the core activities of the business include designing and developing new products for the consumer market, other companies can make the parts, assemble the products, and market and deliver them. In essence, the company becomes the hub of the wheel with the best suppliers and distributors as the spokes. By doing this, the company can grow more rapidly, keep unit costs down, and turn out new products more quickly. In addition, the capital it saves by not having to invest in fixed assets can be directed to R&D and

The Real World of Entrepreneurship

Why Companies Outsource

1. To improve company focus and avoid wasting time on things it may not do well or isn't interested in

2. To gain access to world-class capabilities by forming alliances with much larger companies

3. To share risk

4. To free up noncapital resources such as people and equipment to focus on what the company does best

5. To make capital funds available by not putting limited resources into expensive equipment and facilities outside the core competency

6. To reduce operating costs

7. To look for cash infusion for a strategic partner

8. To take advantage of resources not available internally

9. To have access to a function that is difficult to manage in-house with the current resources and skills[17]

those activities that provide a competitive advantage. The electronics and apparel industries used this growth strategy long before it became trendy. Today many other industries are beginning to see the advantages to a modular approach. Even service businesses can benefit from outsourcing functions such as accounting, payroll, and data processing, which require costly labor.

Outsourcing noncore functions can often help a company get products to market faster and in greater quantities while at the same time spreading risk and delivering the capabilities of a much larger company without the expense. In fact, a Coopers & Lybrand survey of 400 fast-growing small companies found that two-thirds used outsourcing, and their revenues, sales prospects, and growth rates far exceeded those of companies that did not use outsourcing.[15] Outsourcing permits small, growing companies to have noncore functions completed more efficiently at a lower cost and a higher level of quality than they could achieve themselves. Innovative Medical Systems Inc., a New Hampshire–based manufacturer, outsources the manufacture of subassemblies, product design, computer networking, payroll administration, and direct mailing and advertising placement, and does only final assembly, quality assurance, strategic marketing, and customer service in-house.[16] Some companies have experienced explosive growth as a result of outsourcing. This was the case with Houston-based Paranet Inc., a provider of outsourced computer networking services. Founded in 1991, its resources

---

 Entrepreneurship in Action

Main Street Muffins

In 1987, Main Street Muffins of Akron, Ohio, was experiencing phenomenal success, and its founder, Steven L. Marks, was on top of the world at age 27. His breakfast and lunch café was very popular when in 1988 a restaurant owner called asking if he could bake Marks's muffins fresh in his restaurant rather than buy them. After much consideration, Marks decided to sell batter to the man, although he made the restaurateur come to the store every day at closing with a bucket and cash. The success of this new outlet for his muffins convinced Marks to begin his foray into the frozen-batter business to diversify his café concept. During that next year, Marks opened yet another bake shop/café and the frozen-batter business began to bring in about 30 percent of total revenues.

But rapid growth brought many problems, including high employee turnover, production mistakes, and negative cash flow. The company was focusing so much on increasing business that it lost sight of the customer, and systems and controls in the business were totally absent. The result: gross margins dropped from 50 percent to less than 40 percent. Main Street Muffins was on the verge of bankruptcy.

The solution seemed to be to focus on the part of the business that had the best chance for success, and that was the wholesale batter business. After much soul searching, Marks and his partner decided to sell the retail outlets with licensing agreements to maintain quality control and ensure an outlet for their frozen batter. This would free them from the tremendous load of day-to-day operations in a retail business to focus on their core business, making batter. The result was positive. Since 1990, their sales have grown an average of 100 percent a year, and they were named 1994 Small-Business Persons of the Year for the Cleveland district by the Small Business Administration.

SOURCE: Steven L. Marks, "Say When," *Inc.*, February 1995, p. 19.

grew to 66 million in 1996. In September, 1997 it was acquired by U.S. Sprint Corp. for $425 million.

Outsourcing to a provider of a single service means the company can obtain that service much more cheaply than it could do it itself. This is because the provider performs the same service for many companies and thus can buy in bulk and schedule equipment maintenance regularly. With outsourcing, fixed costs become variable and can be pared down when needed to meet changing demand. Funds that are not tied up in these functions can be put to use on core functions. It is reported that costs drop an average of 9 percent in outsourced functions.[18]

Like anything else, outsourcing has some negatives. If most functions are outsourced, it becomes difficult to develop a corporate culture that will bind workers together and make them loyal to the company. When "employees" are no longer employees of the company, some unique and pressing problems arise. Chapter 7 dealt with the issue of corporate culture.

The key to success with a network strategy is to have a good relationship with suppliers and distributors so that as the business begins to grow rapidly, they are willing to ramp up to meet demand.

Growing Outside the Industry

When entrepreneurs expand their businesses by investing in or acquiring products or businesses outside their core competencies and industry, they are employing a diversification growth strategy. Usually, but not always, this strategy is used when the entrepreneur has exhausted all growth strategies within the current market and industry and now wants to make use of excess capacity or spare resources, adapt to the needs of customers, or change the direction of the company because of impending changes in the market or economy. The last is exemplified by the collapse of the Houston oil economy in 1984. Many entrepreneurs who saw their oil ventures drying up found they had to diversify into new product lines or services to survive and grow.

One way to diversify is to use a **synergistic strategy,** whereby the company attempts to locate new products or businesses that are technologically complementary to its business. For example, a food processor may acquire a restaurant chain that can serve as a showcase for the food. Another way to diversify is to employ a strategy whereby the company acquires products or services that are *unrelated* to its core products or services. For example, a manufacturer of bicycle helmets may acquire an apparel manufacturer to make clothing bearing the company logo to sell to helmet customers. A final strategy for diversifying is called **conglomerate diversification** and involves acquiring businesses that are not related in any way to what the company currently does. The reason an entrepreneur might use this strategy is to gain control of a related function of doing business, for example, purchasing the building in which the business is housed and then leasing out excess space to other businesses to produce additional income and gain a depreciable asset.

Anthony Mark Hankins chose to move outside his industry to grow his $40 million clothing business. Using diversification strategy, he launched a line of home furnishings and intends to further expand into fragrances and men's clothing. The common thread among all these businesses is a finely-honed marketing strategy. (Jesse Hornbuckle)

Many entrepreneurs whose work causes them to travel extensively find it advantageous to acquire a travel agency to reduce costs and provide greater convenience.

A diversification strategy for growth is not something to be undertaken without careful consideration of all the factors and potential outcomes, particularly when it involves an acquisition. Though the entrepreneur can likely find consultants who are experts in mergers and acquisitions to help smooth the path financially and operationally, it is difficult to predict with any degree of certainty how the cultures of the two businesses will merge. Acquisitions and mergers cannot be successful based on financial and operational synergy alone. Organizational styles and individual personalities of key management all come into play when an acquisition or a merger takes place. As a result, the human side of the two businesses must be analyzed and a plan developed to merge two potentially distinct cultures into one that can work effectively.

Steve Snyder, founder of 21st Century Laboratories Inc. in Tempe, Arizona, was able to form a successful relationship with his Chinese distributor by making the effort to understand the culture of the country with which he was dealing. He learned that in the Asian culture you must build a relationship first before you do a business deal, and both take time. (Courtesy of 21st Century Laboratories, Tempe, AZ)

Global Strategies

With increasing competition and saturated markets in some industries, looking to global markets can add a new dimension to the entrepreneur's business. Many companies have found new applications for their products in other countries or complementary products that will help increase sales of their products domestically. Several events have made exporting U.S. products to other countries more attractive than ever before:

▶ Relatively low U.S. interest rates have made it easier for businesses to finance the exporting of their products.

▶ The North American Free Trade Agreement (NAFTA) eliminated trade barriers among the United States, Mexico, and Canada, which has made exporting to those countries more attractive.

▶ The decline of the U.S. dollar, though not good for U.S. travelers in other countries, certainly makes U.S. goods more affordable for other countries.

▶ The opening up and growth of untapped markets such as China and Vietnam means more potential customers for U.S. products.

▶ The establishment of the first four federal export assistance centers will give businesses considering exporting a new source of help. The four centers are located in Baltimore; Long Beach, California; Miami; and Chicago.

▶ The Uruguay Round of GATT (the General Agreement on Tariffs and Trade) reduces or eliminates tariffs among 117 countries. It also provides for improved patent and copyright protection, which has been a problem for businesses exporting protected products to other countries where proprietary rights may not be recognized or protected.

Although most companies should include a global strategy in any business planning, they will probably not be able to export successfully until the business is somewhat established and offers a high-quality product or service at a competitive price. Exporting is a long-term commitment that may not pay off for some time. During that period, you may have to adapt the product or service somewhat to meet the requirements of the importing country and develop good relationships with agents in that country. If you deal in consumer products, it's important to target countries that have disposable income and like U.S. products. If, on the other hand, you are dealing in basic or industrial products, you should look to developing countries that have needs for equipment and services for building infrastructure and systems. One example is Mexico, which is taking on the enormous task of building bridges and roads as it positions itself as a major player in the world market.

Finding the Best Global Market

Finding the best market for a product or service can be a daunting task, but some sources and tactics will help make the job easier. The *International Trade Statistics Yearbook of the United States,* which is available in any major library, is an excellent place to start. Using the SITC codes found in this reference book, you can find information on international demand for a product or service in specific countries. The SITC (the United Nation's Standard Industrial Trade Classification) system is a method of classifying commodities used in international trade. It is also important to be familiar with the **harmonized system (HS)** of classification, a 10-digit system that puts the United States "in harmony" with most of the world in terms of commodity tracking systems. If an international shipment exceeds $2,500, the company must know its HS number for documentation.

Demand for U.S. products is usually reflected in three areas:

1. The dollar value of worldwide imports of a specific type of product to a country.

2. The level of growth of these imports as determined by import demand records over time. Countries whose levels of import demand exceed worldwide averages for a product or service are good choices.

3. The share of total import demand to a country that U.S. products enjoy. This figure should exceed 5 percent. A lower figure could indicate that tariffs might be affecting growth.

4. Additional sources of information such as the district office or the Washington, DC, office of the International Trade Administration, and the Department of Commerce (DOC). The Commerce Department's database links all the DOC International Trade Administration offices and provides a wealth of valuable research information.

The successful launch of a program of global growth includes a marketing plan and budget directed toward that goal in the business plan. The company will also need someone on the team who has international management experience or export experience. Depending on the budget, a consultant who specializes in this area could be hired. It is also important to attend foreign trade shows to learn how business is conducted in the countries in which the company is interested in conducting business. You will also learn who the major players are and who the competition is.

Export Financing

To make a sale in the global market, the company must have the funds to purchase the raw materials or inventory to fill the order. Unfortunately, many entrepreneurs assume that if they have a large enough order, getting financing will be no problem. Nothing could be farther from the truth. Export lenders, like traditional lending sources, want to know the company has a sound business plan and has the resources to fill the orders. Entrepreneurs who desire to export can look for capital from several sources:

⬧ Bank financing

⬧ Internal cash flow from the business

The Real World of Entrepreneurship

Using IBEX for a Global Reach

The U.S. Chamber of Commerce, along with a consortium of businesses, has launched a system called the International Business Exchange or IBEX that allows small-business owners to sell products and services or buy supplies and components anywhere in the world. Using the proprietary computer software, a company can match up its offers to buy or sell with customers or vendors domestically and globally. It can even negotiate and complete the deal on the IBEX trading network.

IBEX works as follows. The company enters its offer to buy or sell on electronic forms. IBEX searches the system for potential matches and alerts the company via fax to log onto the computer and examine those matches. Then, using secure electronic mail, negotiations can take place as well as examination of company profiles. IBEX can also help locate freight forwarders.[19]

- Venture capital or private investor capital

- Prepayment, down payment, or progress payments from the foreign company making the order

A commercial bank will be more interested in lending money to a small exporter if the company has secured a guarantee of payment from a governmental agency such as the Import-Export Bank, which will limit the risk undertaken by the bank. Asking buyers to pay an up-front deposit large enough to cover the purchase of raw materials can also be a real asset for a young company with limited cash flow.

Letters of Credit

A **letter of credit** is a bank document that guarantees a customer's bank drafts up to a certain amount for a specific period of time. It is a firm agreement that must be met to the letter to remain valid. For example, if the export company cannot meet the ship date, the letter may lose its value. Many are the stories of international contracts that were invalidated by typos and other minor errors, or variances in weight and size. Consequently, exporters should not leave the details of the letter of credit to the customer, who can easily manipulate the sale to his or her benefit and to the detriment of the exporter. For example, the customer could specify that payment will occur when the goods are in the customer's warehouse rather than at the point from which the ship leaves the port. But what happens if the ship is wrecked and the goods are lost, or if the customs official will not release the goods without a bribe?

Following are some suggestions for constructing letters of credit:[20]

- Make sure the advising bank is the supplier's (exporter's) own bank.

- Make sure the company address on the letter of credit is exactly as it is on company stationery. Correcting an error here will result in a fee from the bank.

- Include an "at-sight" clause, which means that when the documents called for in the letter of credit are presented to the advising bank, the exporter will get paid within five days.

- Make sure the shipping date meets the company's production schedule.

- Ensure that the payment of the letter of credit can be made through a U.S. bank to avoid delays.

- Make sure the internal bank reference number is on all documents to avoid rejection.

- Include an expiration date for the letter of credit that is one month *after* the ship date to allow the exporter time to gather and present the documents to the advising bank.

◗ Ensure that the company has a "clean airway bill" or ocean bill of lading, meaning the wording is exactly as it is in the letter of credit, even down to spelling.

◗ Do not put the details of every item shipped in the letter of credit. Put them instead on the packing lists, invoices, and purchase orders to avoid the chance for discrepancies that would result in the rejection of the letter of credit.

◗ Do not allow for transshipments (taking goods from one aircraft or vessel and putting them on another), unless the customer allows it and takes responsibility for potential damage.

◗ Allow for partial shipments to speed up cash flow.

Foreign Agents, Distributors, and Trading Companies

Every country has a number of sales representatives, agents, and distributors who specialize in importing U.S. goods. It is possible to find one agent who can handle an entire country or region, but if a country has several economic centers, it may be more effective to have a different agent for each center. *Sales representatives* work on commission; they do not buy and hold products. Consequently, the exporting company is still left with the job of collection, which, when dealing with a foreign country, can be costly and time consuming. *Agents* provide a way to circumvent this problem. Agents purchase the company's product at a discount (generally very large) off list and then sell it and handle collections themselves. They solve the issue of cultural differences and the ensuing problems inherent in these transactions. Of course, with an agent the company loses control over what happens to the product once it leaves the company's control. The company has no say over what the agent actually charges customers in his or her own country. If the

Entrepreneurship in Action

How One Company Used Alliances to Go Global

Gerard Campain is the managing director of Paris-based Ingenico, one of the leading international vendors of smart card readers, devices that can read credit card–size cards that are embedded with a computer chip. They contain both information and money and have been used in Europe for about 20 years.

Campain's growth strategy is to find the most innovative entrepreneurs and companies in a country and sell them on a new-product idea such as the smart card reader, make it for them, and then go after other customers who can now see the product in use. He did this successfully with the Shanghai police, who use smart card readers to gather information on traffic violators and then transfer that information to the main computer at the end of the day. As a result of the success in Shanghai, readers will now be used in such places as Australian taxicabs and portable units for kiosk and newsstand owners.

SOURCE: David Carnoy, "Teaming Up," *Success,* April 1997, p. 20.

agent charges too much in an effort to make more money for himself or herself, the company may lose a customer. Companies that are just starting to export or are exporting to areas not large enough to warrant an agent should consider putting an ad in American trade journals that showcase U.S. products internationally. Companies producing technical products may be able to find a manufacturer in the international region they are targeting that will let them sell their products through its company, thus giving them instant recognition in the foreign country. They could also become a potential source of financing for the exporting company.

Another option is to use an **export trading company** (ETC) that specializes in certain countries or regions where it has established a network of sales representatives. ETCs may also specialize in certain types of products. What often happens is that a sales rep reports to the ETC that a particular country is interested in a certain product. The ETC then locates a manufacturer, buys the product, and then sells it in the foreign country. Trading companies are a particularly popular vehicle when dealing with Japan.

Choosing an Intermediary

Several things should be done prior to deciding on an intermediary to handle the exporting of products. Any company should

1. Check the intermediary's current listing of products to see if the company's products seem to fit in with the intermediary's expertise.

2. Understand with whom they will be competing (that is, does the intermediary also handle the company's competitors?).

3. Find out if the intermediary has enough representatives in the foreign country to adequately handle the market.

4. Look at the sales volume of the intermediary. It should show a relatively consistent level of growth.

5. Make sure the intermediary has sufficient warehouse space and an up-to-date communication systems.

6. Examine the intermediary's marketing plan.

7. If needed, make sure the intermediary can handle the servicing of its products.

Once an intermediary has been selected, an agreement detailing the terms and conditions of the relationship should be drafted. As it is very much like a partnership agreement, an attorney specializing in overseas contracts should be consulted. The most important thing to remember about the contract is that it must be based on performance so that the company does not tie itself up for many years with someone who is not moving enough products. A one- or two-year contract, with an option to renew if performance goals are met, should be drafted. This will probably not please the intermediary, as most will want a 5- to 10-year contract, but it's important to be firm; it is not in the company's best interests to do a longer contract until it knows the person is loyal and can perform.

Other issues the agreement should address include

▶ The company's ability to use another distributor; in other words, negotiate for a nonexclusive contract so that you will have some flexibility and control over the situation.

▶ The specific products the agent or distributor will represent. This is important because as the company grows, it may add or develop additional products and not want this agent to sell those products.

▶ The specific geographic territories for which the agent or distributor will be responsible.

▶ The specific duties and responsibilities of the agent or distributor.

▶ A statement of agreed-on sales quotas.

▶ A statement of the jurisdiction in which any dispute would be litigated. This will protect the company from having to go to a foreign country to handle a dispute.

To cut the costs of attorney-drawn contracts for every distribution agreement, the company can choose to use a software package, such as Caps User from Capsoft, that prompts the user through a series of questions about the agreement and then uses the responses to create the actual agreement.[21] Then the company will only have to pay its lawyers to review the agreement.

Choosing a Freight Forwarder

The freight forwarder's job is to handle all aspects of delivering the product to the customer. The method by which a company ships a product will have a significant impact on the product's cost or the price to the customer depending on how the deal is structured, so the choice of a freight forwarder

The Real World of Entrepreneurship

Using Trade Missions for Contacts

T**rade missions** offered by the government and private agencies provide small business (the overwhelming majority of trade mission participants) with an opportunity to make contacts in foreign countries and to establish a presence. Before being accepted for a trade mission, companies are asked to answer a few questions:

▶ Has the entrepreneur been to the particular country before?

▶ Is the company's product on the "best prospect" list?

▶ Does the entrepreneur have any exporting experience?

▶ Does the entrepreneur have a well-developed business plan?[22]

A trade mission is an intense round of interviews and discussions in a number of cities over a period of two to three weeks. Prior to going on the trade mission, the company will be asked to attend counseling sessions with trade specialists to match them with foreign agents, distributors, or partners.

Table 9.3   Additional Sources for Exporting

Directory of American Firms Operating in Foreign Countries
Europa World Year Book
European Directory of Marketing Information Sources
Exporters Encyclopedia
Guide to Canadian Manufacturers
International Marketing Handbook
Japan Trade Directory
Major Companies of the Far East
Moody's International Manual
Predicast's F&S International Index
Predicast's F&S Index Europe
U.S. Importers and Exporters Directory
United Nations Statistical Yearbook
Worldcasts

must be carefully considered. The ability to fill a shipping container to capacity is crucial to reducing costs. Freight forwarders prepare the shipping documents, which include a bill of lading (the contract between the shipper and the carrier) and an exporter declaration form detailing the contents of the shipment, and they can present shipping documents to the company's bank for collection. The company, however, is responsible for knowing if any items being shipped require special licenses or certificates, as in the case of hazardous materials or certain food substances.

Global Franchising

The first franchisers on the global scene were primarily the large food franchises such as McDonald's, Kentucky Fried Chicken, and Burger King. Today, however, even smaller franchisers are going global. In 1993, approximately 400 of the 3,500 U.S. franchises did business abroad.[23] Foreign governments generally welcome franchisers because they bring not only a product to the country but a way of doing business, which provides jobs for the citizens of the country. Those who have chosen to try their luck in developing countries or in the old Eastern bloc countries have consistently found that the cost of doing business there is much higher. In addition, they are likely to have to deal with unstable governments, volatile currencies, and a general lack of understanding of competitive market systems. Many international franchisers have discovered that having a local partner is one key to a successful global effort because it allows them to acquire an understanding of the business and consumer culture in the country. They also tend to look to establish master franchise agreements, which give the franchisee the rights to the entire country or region.

Some of the issues a company should consider before going global with a franchise concept are

▶ The suitability of the concept to the country's culture

▶ The potential for profit given royalties, development fees, franchiser duties, and costs

▶ Target market characteristics

▶ The current infrastructure

▶ Availability of supplies

▶ Currency and exchange rates

▶ Competition

▶ International relations and legal matters

▶ Real estate issues

▶ Labor

▶ Taxes

One challenge international franchisers face is to achieve the same level of productivity and service that they experience in the United States. In some countries, low productivity is simply a way of life, and changing old habits can require hours of training. One source of help for potential international franchisers is the International Franchise Association (IFA) located in Washington, DC. This organization has established a code of ethics and, through its Franchisee Advisory Council, provides dispute resolution for both franchisees and franchisers.

Failures occur when franchisers neglect to do market research. For example, a well-known hamburger chain failed in Malaysia because it overlooked the fact that two-thirds of the population does not eat meat. Similarly, a fast-food fish chain failed in Japan because its main product was made from a type of fish that the Japanese consider to be inferior. On the other hand, a party supply company looked at Puerto Rico seriously when it discovered that the country has 22 official holidays. Other obstacles faced by franchisers going global include the following:

▶ The concept is not easily adaptable to other languages or cultures.

▶ There are technical or legal barriers in the target country.

▶ The business is tied to an industry structure that does not exist anywhere else.

Overall, franchising still offers opportunities for growth and success, but that success is more likely to come to the founder franchiser from rapid growth in selling franchises and going public than it is to the person who purchases a franchise.

International Law Issues

Everyone has heard that laws vary from country to country, but until actually faced with a dangerous situation, few U.S. citizens believe they are not protected by the Constitution of the United States anywhere they go. Consider the case of an engineer who was hired by a Saudi Arabian hospital. While working, he discovered a problem that needed investigation and reported it. To his horror, he was accused of causing the problem and was tortured and beaten.[24] In another incident, a U.S. importer of goods from Taiwan flew to Taiwan to visit his supplier because he wasn't satisfied with the quality of the goods he was receiving. He was accused of fraud and put in prison. It took a year before he could leave the country, and he was forced to sell his stock in the company.[25] Although these cases do not represent the norm, they do point up the necessity to understand the culture and laws of

---

 Entrepreneurship in Action

One Company's Odyssey of Growth

Growth is not a phenomenon that occurs once in the life of a company but a continual process of starts, stops, reinventions, and fundamental changes. One example of such an odyssey is the story of TFN, The Future Now, Inc., a computer industry company doing about $800 million in sales. This is the path it took:

1. In 1986, the company was called Cincinnati Word Processing (CWP), and it sold one product, Wang Laboratories' word processing equipment. It had grown to $5 million in 10 years with gross margins of 25 percent. In that year its founder, Terry Theye, was no longer the owner but had stayed on as president.

2. Within two years, the buyer of CWP wanted out because he couldn't deal with the fast-paced computer industry. He helped Theye find an investment banker to structure a leveraged buyout of the company. The bank took an equity position and helped to find a lender to finance the balance. At this point, Theye had no equity but a lot of debt.

3. Meanwhile, by 1988, the personal computer had hit the marketplace. CWP's founder repositioned the company to carry PCs and changed the name to Future Now.

4. By 1989, TFN was a $20 million company that wanted to become a $100 million company just to survive in an industry that was consolidating and seeing declining margins.

5. Between 1989 and 1993, TFN acquired 11 other resellers and went to the public markets twice, with a $20 million IPO in 1991 and another $21 million in a secondary 18 months later. Theye now owned 2.5 percent of the company, and the company was doing $139 million in 1991. By 1993, it had exploded to $702 million in sales with a net profit of $9.3 million.

6. Theye took an innovative approach for that time, sending sales and service people into the field rather than waiting for customers to come into retail outlets.

7. Seeing the explosion of computer retailers in 1989, Theye decided to focus TFN's efforts on commercial accounts and cater to businesses rather than consumers. It shut down its retail outlets and reopened in upscale office parks.

8. By 1993, the company's margins on hardware had dropped from 22 to 8 percent and net profit had fallen to 1.3 percent. In March 1995, TFN agreed to merge with industry distribution giant Intelligent Electronics in a stock swap that gave TFN a source for its hardware and eliminated the need to carry inventory. TFN has effectively become a service company.

9. TFN is now shifting its work force to technical people and service rather than sales.

Source: *Inc.,* May 1995, p. 98.

the country in which the entrepreneur is doing business. A few suggestions will help the situation:

▶ Always get a receipt for anything bought in a foreign country, even if it's an inexpensive item purchased at a bazaar.

▶ Make sure all credit cards used in foreign countries are good, that is, not expired or over the limit, which could result in arrest.

▶ If detained or arrested, remain calm and request a phone call to an attorney familiar with international dispute resolution. According to the Vienna Treaty, officials of the country must inform the U.S. embassy in that country that they have detained a U.S. citizen.

▶ Always consult with an international attorney before leaving the United States to resolve an international dispute.

For additional information on marketing internationally, see Chapter 12.

Whichever growth strategy seems most appropriate to a particular type of business, it will only come about if the company is giving customers what they need when they need it. No other factor has more impact on growth than that.

Cases Relevant to This Chapter

Marcus Food Co. and Buckhead Beef
French Rags
Zanart Entertainment
SB Networks

Issues for Review and Discussion

1. What advantages do growth strategies within the current market have over industry and diversification strategies?
2. Why is it important to think about a global plan from the conception of the business?
3. What should you consider when using intermediaries for exporting?
4. What types of businesses are most suitable for franchising? Why?
5. How can acquisitions be used to grow the company more rapidly?

Experiencing Entrepreneurship

1. Visit or contact the U.S. trade office in your area (Department of Commerce) and investigate the programs available to help small businesses enter the global market.
2. Interview a franchise owner and build a profile of what it would take to purchase and successfully run that franchise.

Resources

Buying a Franchise and Business Opportunity. Entrepreneur business guide (1-800-421-2300).

IBEX (1-800-537-IBEX). Requires an IBM-compatible, Windows-capable personal computer with a modem. There is a one-time software and registration fee of $250. Users pay by function, not by minute. Average usage costs are $50 to $100 a month.

Trade Information Center (1-800-USA-TRADE, or 1-800-872-8723). Ask for an industry desk officer who is a specialist in your industry.

TradeNet. An Internet electronic mailing list for international importers and exporters. *TradeNet@cerfnet.com; TradeNet@ix.netcom.com; TACC5BA (Prodigy); TradeNetWS (America Online); 75144,3544 (CompuServe).*

Uniform Customs and Practices for Documentary Credits (UCP). *ICC Publication 500.*

U.S. Department of Commerce. "Flash Facts," a 24-hour free fax line for information on specific international regions: Eastern Europe (202-482-5745); Mexico (202-482-4464); Pacific Basin (202-482-3875); Africa, Near East, and South Asia (202-482-1064).

U.S. and Foreign Commercial Domestic Field Offices (1-800-USA-TRADE, or 1-800-872-8723).

Whiteley, Richard, and Diane Hessan (1996). *Customer-Centered Growth.* Reading, MA: Addison-Wesley.

Wolf, J. S. (1992). *Export Profits.* Chicago: Upstart Publishing.

Internet Resources

ExportNet
http://www.exporttoday.com
Tips for businesses that want to trade internationally. This is not a free service.

International Business Forum
http://www.ibf.com/
Geared toward entrepreneurs who want to get into the international marketplace. Contains lists of resources in various countries, opportunities, and associations.

The Internationalist
http://www.internationalist.com
An excellent source for information on a wide range of international issues.

International Trade Administration
http://www.ita.doc.gov
A division of the Department of Commerce. Offers help to companies that wish to export.

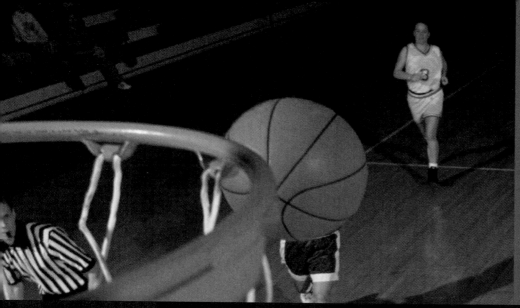

IV

Marketing for Growth

Customer-Centered Marketing

Preview

Understanding this chapter will give you the ability to

▶ **Discuss the newest aproaches to marketing for entrepreneurial companies and how they differ from traditional marketing strategies.**

▶ **Explain relationship marketing and its role in building a loyal customer base.**

▶ **Develop a strategy for building long-term customer relationships.**

▶ **Discuss the importance of virtual products and mass customization to the customer and your company.**

Terms to Know

Branding, 267
Paradigm, 267
Virtual products, 271
Mass customization, 271

Interactive
  database, 271
Flexible manufacturing
  systems, 271

Relationship
  marketing, 272
Transaction marketing,
  274

Positioning, 277

Young Entrepreneurs—Minicase

Mary Naylor
Capitol Concierge

Many companies are discovering the new marketing paradigm, one-to-one relationship marketing, the hard way. They reach a crisis point in the business where they learn they are spending the bulk of their time searching for new customers, the most costly aspect of marketing, instead of finding new ways to serve the customers they have. Capitol Concierge of Washington, DC is one company that has learned that lesson well. Founded in 1987, Capitol Concierge offers its "make a wish" services from concierge desks in 85 buildings in and around the District of Columbia. Mary Naylor, the founder, prides herself on being able to provide anything that's legal for her clients, from securing concert tickets to picking up dry cleaning.

Naylor was 24 years old and only two years out of college when she saw an opportunity to provide the kinds of services hotels offer to office buildings in large metropolitan areas. When she started her business, her initial focus was on getting more buildings because she figured that was the way to increase her bottom line. By 1992, however, as sales approached $3 million, Naylor began to look at her numbers more carefully. She had been charging property managers a flat fee per month to put a concierge in the building. From this money, she expected to cover her expenses and make a profit. She also planned to sell "a la carte" errand services to individuals for additional fees. Her analysis of the numbers made it clear that the first thing that would have to go would be the plan to make a profit from the monthly flat fee. Competition-induced predatory pricing soon reduced her margins to the point where she had no money for expansion, and sales of individual services lagged behind the building fees. It became obvious that she had to start focusing more on maximizing the business in the buildings she already had. This would require developing long-term relationships built on trust and performance.

By doing some research, Naylor found that many of her customers had no idea that she provided so many services beyond those she had done for them. This new-found knowledge led her to decide to (1) develop a system to interact with the customer and develop a relationship, (2) train her concierges so they would not only provide better service but also be better marketers for the company, and (3) rework her hiring practices to ensure that she hired only the best. Then she did some homework on her customers and the specific needs they had relative to their professions. Through one-

on-one executive roundtables, she developed more in-depth customer profiles, including where they enter the building, who their clients are, and how they like to receive information. Naylor used the advice of a consultant on personality testing to improve her hiring success rate. In fact, she became so good at hiring top-notch people that her corporate customers began hiring her concierges away.

By 1993, Capitol Concierge had reached $3.8 million in sales and had 70 employees. It also had a new mission: it would be a commissioned broker of products and services, collecting, on average, 15 percent of sales from its vendors and sharing profits with its concierges. This was good, but not good enough for Naylor, who had higher ambitions. Once she realized that her company needed the help of technology to track customer transactions, she really opened the door to growth. Using an interactive database and totally automating the system, she was able to increase individual sales to meet the building fees. The new system contains a streamlined order and invoice system, and the ability to generate a mock purchase order when the computer's tickler function says it's time to generate one. In this way, she can monitor whether the company is getting all the sales it should. The bottom line is that Naylor has learned the value of customer relationships in a business where maximizing existing customer satisfaction and value is more important than generating new customers. In 1996 she made the *Inc.* list of the 500 fastest-growing private companies.

SOURCES: Susan Greco, "The Road to One to One Marketing," *Inc. Magazine*, October 1995; Cara Hersh, "Office Cruise Directors," *Nation's Business*, November 1996, p. 16.

How did Mary Naylor use relationship marketing to differentiate and grow her business?

Customer-centered growth calls for customer-centered marketing strategies, and small, entrepreneurial companies are perhaps in the best position to implement these "one-to-one" approaches to building relationships with customers. Mary Naylor, founder of Capitol Concierge (see Young Entrepreneurs—Minicase), was shocked to find that her customers weren't even aware of some of the services her company offered. This new awareness sparked her plan to get to know her customers one to one and give them exactly what they wanted. This approach ultimately made her business unique and a success.

This chapter explores the new marketing principles and looks at marketing from a strategic point of view. It also considers the issue of building lifelong customer relationships, a critical strategy for small businesses.

During the 1990s, the ubiquitous marching, drum-beating Energizer bunny became a familiar fixture on commercial television. It has certainly been one of the best and longest-running series of commercials on TV, and Eveready eventually benefited from its success. But so did the company's major competitor, Duracell. Nowhere was this more apparent than in the 1990 Video Storyboard Tests Inc., which named the bunny ad the top commercial and congratulated Duracell! In fact, 40 percent of those who voted for the ad thought it was a Duracell ad, and Duracell's market share increased while Eveready's declined.

This is just one example of why traditional market-driven strategies to establish brand recognition and loyalty don't work well anymore. Mass advertising and promotion designed to identify customers, find ways to convince them to buy, create an image to entice them, and sell that image to them are not compatible with the current changes in customer behavior. Customers today are market savvy and demand choice, quality, and a high level of service. Conventional mass markets as we knew them don't exist much anymore. They have become fragmented into smaller interest groups, so mass marketing no longer translates automatically into brand loyalty. And because technology and innovation have made variety and customization more feasible, customers are demanding more individualized products. As a result, satisfying a customer today is like trying to hit a moving target.

Technology will continue to bring incremental improvements and breakthrough products, but the incremental value of those improvements will increasingly diminish as fewer people are willing to pay for them. Software purchase behavior is a good indicator of this trend. Once basic application needs are met—for example, word processing—users don't always upgrade to the latest version just to add bells and whistles they may never use. Moreover, the ability to purchase the latest software is a function of the ability of the customer's hardware to handle it. If going to the next version means an additional investment in hardware, the customer may not be willing to close the sale.

A similar situation occurs with commodity products, such as soft drinks, where customer loyalty is even harder to capture. The famous "cola wars" between Coca-Cola and Pepsico that came to a head in the mid-1970s saw market share go back and forth between them. Yet in spite of the enormous expenditures for advertising and promotion, it appears that neither side gained a clear competitive advantage. Both companies have similar resources and competencies, but they are not "rare"; that is, they have competitive parity. When Pepsico began its "Pepsi Challenge" campaign in the Dallas–Ft. Worth area with price discounts, coupons, celebrity endorsements, and so forth, its market share soared from 7 to 14 percent in six months. During that same period, however, Pepsi's selling price plummeted to one-half of its original. Pepsi doubled its market share and halved its price, a predictable result where competitive parity exists.[1] This example clearly shows that mass marketing may be a zero-sum game. The best deal for the customer usually results in little or no profit for the company.

Does this mean we are headed into an era of nameless generic products and services with no brand loyalty? Quite the contrary. In fact, **branding** and brand loyalty are more important than ever. Precisely because the cacophony from competing products is so loud, a company's brand and what it stands for must be distinctive. But branding, and the marketing strategies that produce it, is not the branding we have traditionally known, that is, the image or the icon for the product and business. Today branding must represent the qualities and philosophy of the company as much as the product. To achieve brand loyalty today, a company must be *market* driven, not *marketing* driven; the customer must be a key player on the team from the conception of the product or service through production, distribution, and service.

One entrepreneur who understands the value of a brand name is Martha Stewart. Stewart has created an empire based on making her name synonymous with fine living. In the 1980s, she saw a void in the market. Even though more and more women were in the workplace and led frantic lives that left little time for Stewartesque-type projects, they had dreams of leisure time for domestic crafts: home improvement, interior design, gardening, cooking, and entertaining. Stewart showed them how to do it, and her brand is now strong in all aspects of the media, from more than 18 books and a TV show to a very successful magazine and syndicated news column.

A Newer Approach to Marketing

The traditional marketing **paradigm** or set of principles has a transaction focus based on the "four Ps": product, price, place, and promotion. Firms operating under this paradigm typically attempt to achieve customer awareness through extensive mass marketing consisting primarily of advertising and promotion. There are two problems with this approach. First, many companies today are literally killing their brands with overpromotion and a focus on image rather than the company's credibility. Second, the four Ps don't take the customer into consideration. One of those Ps should stand for *people*. Today every component of the marketing mix has to create value for a customer who is jaded by advertising and myriad new products. Today's customers don't want to be told what to buy. They want to control what is produced so they get precisely what they want, when they want it. If a company is doing any of the following today, it will quickly find itself behind the times tomorrow in the twenty-first century. Here are some strategies to avoid:

1. *Marketing is a function or department in the business.* Marketing should not simply be a function; it should be a way of doing business. It is part of an integrated system that involves everyone in the company from the president to the bookkeeper and, certainly, the customer.

2. *The company identifies customers and then finds ways to convince them to buy the product or service it has created.* This approach is backward. The company needs to design the product or service to meet the needs of its customers as *they* have defined them. Products and services need to come out of solutions that the marketplace is looking for. The advantage to this approach is that it can be less costly in marketing terms because you're giving customers what they want.

3. *The company spends time and money creating an image to attract the customer.* Today's marketing is not about image; it's about character, the character of the company that stands behind the product. The cola wars were about image; they conveyed nothing about the quality, philosophy, or culture of the organization. Nothing in those ads would result in brand loyalty. In today's market, the philosophy of the company and the value and benefit to the customer are the attributes that need to come across to the customer. In a time of rapid change, a company's credibility is really the only constant.

4. *The company is concerned about selling things and making money.* Obviously those two events must occur for a business to succeed, but the means to the end has changed. Today entrepreneurial companies must be concerned about building relationships with customers for the life of the business, the by-product of which will be more sales and more profit.

Figure 10.1 depicts the marketing dilemma in the consumer market. Mass production and mass marketing go hand in hand, because shelf space drives the consumer market. To gain sufficient and competitively advantageous shelf space requires a critical mass of volume on the part of the company seeking it. To achieve that volume, mass marketing techniques are used. The resulting increase in volume then necessitates even more production, and a vicious cycle ensues. It is very difficult for a mass producer to break out of the cycle. To succeed, then, mass marketing depends on mass media and an audience of potential customers who agree to watch advertisements on TV, listen to them on radio, or read them in magazines and newspapers in exchange for programming, stories, and articles that entertain them. The problem is that customers have lived with commercials for years and have developed the fine art of tuning them out or using commercial time to visit the refrigerator. They skillfully glide over ads in newspapers and magazines to zero in on articles of interest. The bottom line is: the world has changed and customers have changed. These changes, which are a challenge for large

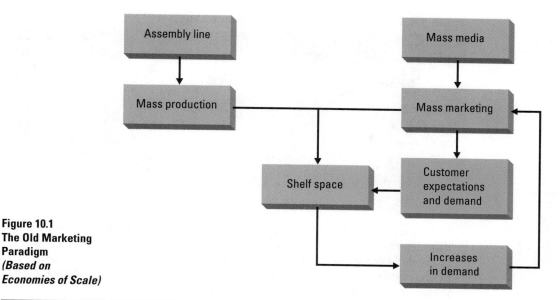

**Figure 10.1
The Old Marketing
Paradigm
(Based on
Economies of Scale)**

companies that rely on mass marketing, are the source of a distinct competitive advantage for small businesses. Entrepreneurial companies need to look to the customer for the answers to how best to market to them.

Key Factors in Marketing Today

Today we can say that at least three things are true about marketing:

▶ *Customers are an appreciable asset.* In fact, customers are the most important asset a business has, for without them there is no business. With the cost of acquiring a new customer rising rapidly—certainly it costs 5 to 10 times as much to acquire a new customer as it does to maintain an existing one—spending time cultivating this important asset is well worth the effort. Actually, the longer a company retains a customer, the more profitable that customer becomes in terms of additional purchases, referrals, and a savings in customer acquisition costs.[2] And these benefits don't even take into consideration the value the customer adds by giving his or her input to the company.

▶ *Quality is a competitive strategy.* The level of quality today's customers expect has increased substantially, so entrepreneurial companies need to go far beyond that level of quality. Like marketing itself, quality must infuse the entire organization, not just the product or service. It must be part of the character of the organization that is promoted to the customer.

▶ *Every industry is a service industry.* Today more than ever before, the boundaries between product and service industries are eroding. When GM

Table 10.1 The Changing Marketing Paradigm

The Traditional Marketing Strategy	The New Approach to Marketing for the Twenty-first Century
Marketing driven	Market driven
Producer capacity orientation	Customer demand orientation
Market share focus	Market creation focus
Mass production	Mass customization
Mass marketing techniques	One-to-one relationship marketing
Focus on seeking customers to increase sales volume	Focus on seeking and retaining customers as stakeholders

makes more money from lending its customers the money to buy its automobiles than it does from the sale of the automobiles themselves, it has effectively become a service business that happens to provide a product.[3] The primary service of most companies is solutions to customer problems, whether in the form of products or services.

Table 10.1 summarizes the changes in marketing strategy that have taken place in recent times.

It is not uncommon to see "The Customer is King" on the walls of companies nationwide, suggesting that they already have a deep-seated commitment to the customer. In reality, this isn't true. If anything, they have made a commitment to after-the-sale customer service, but are still putting target customers in their gunsights and attempting to pick them off with mass advertising. A start to be sure, but not good enough. The truth is that most companies don't have in place the policies and processes needed to effectively serve the customers' needs _before_ the sale.

It is extremely difficult to keep this "new" type of customer happy, which is why many companies mistakenly revert to strategies they are familiar with—strategies that, unfortunately, are out of date and out of touch with reality. New approaches always involve a period of uncertainty. Firms entrenched in the old ways find it easier to stick with what they know, even if it isn't working well, than to totally reinvent the organization to market under the new rules of the game. Learning a new set of rules is a painful process, but the end result is positive. The benefits to a relationship approach to the customer are many, and those who don't adapt may ultimately lose the game.

Virtual Products and Mass Customization

The power of the customer to "make or break" a company goes to the very conceptualization of the product or service and right through production and distribution; therefore, the importance of the process and procedures the company has put in place to work with the customer cannot be overstated. According to William Davidow and Michael Malone in _The Virtual Corporation,_ "The centerpiece of this business revolution is a new kind of product.

This product, though it has roots in the distant, artisan past, can only be built now thanks to the latest innovations in information processing, organizational dynamics, and manufacturing systems. Most important, it can be made available at any time, in any place, and in any variety."[4] It's called the **virtual product,** and it's a product whose output the customer controls.

We can already see evidence in the marketplace of virtual products and services that put the customer in control. Digital cameras give us instant pictures we can manipulate on computer screens; camcorders give us instant movies. For both these products, customers can create the images they want easily and quickly. ATMs provide instant access to cash, and the computer gives us instant access to information in whatever form we wish. The fact that these and many other "virtual" products already exist in no way makes the revolution less profound. These products and services are at the leading edge of a movement that will transform the way companies organize and operate.

Mass Customization

Virtual products go hand in hand with the concept of mass customization. **Mass customization** is providing a product or delivering a service designed to meet individual customers' needs in the most cost-effective way. Certainly this process requires continuous improvement and learning on the part of both the company and the customer, and the result is a bond between company and customer. Both have a vested interest in each other. In market terms, the customer will be less likely to shift loyalty to a competitor that does not understand the customer's specific needs. In fact, a company in a one-to-one relationship with its customers should be able to retain them for its life, assuming it continues to provide customized products and services that meet the customers' needs and assuming it stays at the forefront of technology.

Mass customization is a far different philosophy and process from mass production. Mass production is product focused and involves pushing inventory through the distribution channel to the customer, then selling the customer on the features through mass marketing techniques. Mass customization, by contrast, involves production systems in which the customer is involved in the design stage of the product or service and has input into everything from delivery to service. The end result is a relationship with a customer who now doesn't need to be "sold" on the product or service, and product differentiation becomes less important because products are adapted to the customer.

The possibility for mass customization to exist as a feasible market strategy is directly related to the development of **interactive database** technology, which lets the user look at and analyze information in a variety of ways, and information technology and **flexible manufacturing systems,** which let manufacturers shift to different products at will. These various tools make it possible to customize large volumes of goods or services for individual customers at a relatively low cost.[5] Again, the key is customization, not variety. Customers don't want more choices; they want *better* choices. Essentially, they want to design the product or service themselves. That way they know they will be satisfied. Andersen Corporation of Bayport, Minnesota, manufacturer of wood windows, found that its customers were literally overwhelmed by the variety of choices available to them as they designed their homes. To solve the problem, Andersen worked with its customers (contractors, architects, and end users) in designing a system called The Window of Knowledge. Using a multimedia workstation, the sales representative helps customers work through the thousands of design possibilities to generate manufacturing specifications and quotations for the windows they need. Hardin Industries, a manufacturer of upscale plumbing fixtures in Los Angeles, also uses multimedia technology to help customers design their own fixtures and send that information to the factory, where it's produced exactly to their specifications.

There is not one industry today where customization won't work to some degree. Automobile manufacturers such as Toyota will soon have the ability to let customers design their own cars (within some structural and regulatory limits) and have those cars delivered within 72 hours. Apparel manufacturer Levi Strauss is experimenting with the mass customization of jeans. Services are the easiest businesses to customize. Seminar providers like Boston's Management Roundtable, Inc. regularly customize their educational seminars to meet the unique needs of their customers. Even the music industry has gotten into the game. Long-time rock star Todd Rundgren, among others, has produced interactive music videos that let listeners remix a video to their own tastes.

Not only U.S. companies are jumping on the bandwagon for mass customization. National Industrial Bicycle Company in Japan (the Panasonic brand in the United States) is in the business of customized bicycles. It is able to make 18 million different types of bikes to order. The customer gets measured and picks all the components—color, handlebars, tires, and so on—and the custom bike is delivered in two weeks. The story goes that the company used to deliver the bike in three days (it is made in one night, and it takes a day-and-a-half for the paint to dry), but customers didn't believe they were receiving a custom bike, so the company stopped doing it.[6] That's truly a learning relationship with the customer!

With so many products chasing so little shelf space and customers who are no longer "sold" by advertising, mass customization is a new direction that entrepreneurial companies will use in conjunction with developing learning, one-to-one relationships with their customers.

Relationship Marketing

The essence of **relationship marketing** is building trust, satisfying customers, producing shared customer and company goals, communicating with customers, and making them part of the team. In their book *The One to One Future,* Don Peppers and Martha Rogers call this trend "share of customer."[7] Relationship marketing is about developing a learning environment where customer and company learn from each other with the goal of achieving a lifelong relationship that is beneficial and has value for both.

Next time you go on vacation, give your pet a vacation at a Ritz-quality hotel for dogs. Charles A. Cocotas wants to provide just that with his Best Friends Pet Resorts and Salons, headquartered in Norwalk, Connecticut. There he pampers pets with personalized services such as grooming, day care, and obedience training. To his customers, the dog owners, he provides the ability to use centralized registration to choose their dog's room and amenities as well as give them updates on their pet during the stay. Cocotas believes in building relationships with his customers so he tracks their demographics and preferences enabling him to provide "automatic" customized service to repeat customers. (Gale Zucker)

Developing relationships and creating value for the customer is a slow process that evolves over a long period of time. It definitely does not have the immediate impact of the "art of war" strategies that pepper the marketplace with advertising images and expensive promotions. Relationship marketing takes years to develop but is actually more compatible with global market strategies than the traditional mass marketing techniques of hype and personal selling, which in the global market are seen as untrustworthy. Relationship marketing is also not a new phenomenon. Other countries have been doing it for years. Maarten Voogd found that out when he started marketing the products of his company, Water Ventures, Inc. Voogd quickly learned that the American "hard sell" does not win sales in the Middle East or Southeast Asia, where he was marketing his resort equipment. In those countries, it is crucial to build relationships and a sense of trust over some time before people will risk their money on the company's products. Americans have a tough time being patient during the process and tend to want to push it along. Voogd recalls waiting months for a response to his faxed bid to a Middle Eastern company. Just when he had given up, a huge order from the company arrived. He had finally passed their test and could now look forward to many more orders.

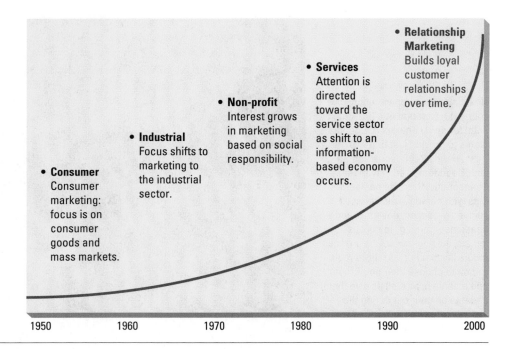

**Figure 10.2
The Evolution of
Relationship
Marketing**

Peppers and Rogers describe relationship marketing this way: "If mass marketing is wide, then niche marketing is narrow, and one-to-one marketing is not only narrow, but deep."[8] The importance of the customer to the business is embodied in the following text from the original 1943 Credo written by R.W. Johnson, Jr. of Johnson & Johnson, the company whose aim is to "alleviate pain and disease."[9]

> We believe that our first responsibility is to the doctors, nurses, hospitals, mothers, and all others who use our products. Our products must always be of the highest quality. We must constantly strive to reduce the cost of these products. Our orders must be promptly and accurately filled. Our dealers must make a fair profit.[10]

> Everyone in the company must think about the customer and how his or her needs can be met.

The Evolution of Relationship Marketing

Relationship marketing has evolved out of a series of different market focuses. Figure 10.2 displays this evolution. The first four marketing focuses (consumer, industrial, nonprofit, and services) can be aggregated and put under one title: *transaction marketing*. In **transaction marketing,** the focus is on the sale rather than on the customer. Comparing transaction marketing to relationship marketing produces the distinctions displayed in Table 10.2.

Table 10.2   Transaction Versus Relationship Marketing

Transaction Marketing	Relationship Marketing
Concerned with the single sale	Concerned with maintaining a long-term relationship
Focus on product/service features	Focus on benefits to customer
Customer service is an afterthought	Customer service is everything
Limited commitment to customer	Total customer commitment
Moderate customer contact	Continual customer contact
Quality is the province of production	Quality is everyone's business

It is clear from the comparison in Table 10.2 which approach is more customer centered. With customers becoming increasingly fickle, demanding exactly what they want when they want it, and with more products becoming commodities, the added value of a strong, long-term relationship with customers may not only be the best competitive advantage, it may also be the key to survival.

Figure 10.3 depicts the various marketing-related areas of the business in which the customer can become involved.

The Benefits of Relationship Marketing

Relationship or one-to-one marketing involves changing not only the company's philosophy but the very way it does business. Using interactive databases, companies can effectively focus on one customer at a time with the goal of supplying as many of their needs that are congruent with the company's capabilities as possible. One-to-one marketing is not just about collecting information from the customer, however. Merely asking customers

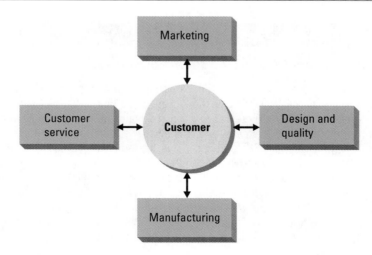

**Figure 10.3
Customer-Focused
Marketing**

where and how they bought the product, for example, doesn't answer the question "How do customers *want* to buy the product?" It only tells us the purchasing method the company made available to them. By asking the right questions and dialoguing with customers, Apple Computer, for example, learned that its Macintosh users prefer to purchase products by mail. Relationship marketing is about carrying on a dialogue with the customer over time. Moreover, if the focus is on one customer at a time, market share is no longer an issue or a relevant goal. The goal becomes to create lifelong customers who have a vested interest in the company, because the company sincerely wants to meet their needs.

The creation of customer relationships has a side benefit. When a problem occurs, the customer won't automatically shift loyalty to a competitor because he or she has spent time building this relationship with the company. Often that loyalty is actually strengthened after going through a problem-solving period together that results in a satisfying conclusion. This is because customers have typically had very negative experiences with companies when a problem arises. If the problem is not resolved satisfactorily, the customer never forgets. Today customers have a multitude of platforms from which to air their grievances, and one problem aired on national television can cause a public relations nightmare from which the company may never recover. A classic case in point is what happened to the Cunard cruise line when, in what could only be described as a moment of insanity on the part of management, it decided to launch its Christmas cruise of the renovated QE2 despite a shipful of builders who hadn't yet finished their work. Apparently Cunard believed its customers would overlook the mess!

Perhaps the most important benefit to the company of establishing lifelong customer relationships is that over time the full value of the customers is revealed. Customers no longer are viewed as a series of transactions but as bona fide, contributing members of the team that brings value to the bottom

The Real World of Entrepreneurship

How the CD-ROM Industry Discovered What Customers Want

The CD-ROM industry is a good example of the changes taking place in the marketing strategies of companies. CD-ROMs have specifically targeted audiences in education, entertainment, and business, and are very suited to relationship marketing. But until recently, relationship marketing was not used because competition was not significant, shelf space was available, and professional sales forces seemed to handle customer relations quite well. But the fall of 1994 saw the first real deluge of CD-ROM titles hit the market: 1,500 to 2,000 titles.[11] It was as if every CD-ROM developer had reached the same point on the learning curve at the same time. All of a sudden, margins, which are low to begin with, were squeezed by falling prices, and shelf space, the foundation of all their marketing strategies, became scarce. Today it is survival of the fittest for the CD-ROM producers. If the revenues on a title start falling, the retailer will quickly replace that title with another. Today the way to keep revenues up in this industry is to build lifelong relationships with customers that give customers a benefit equal to or exceeding the effort expended to establish the relationship.

line. The more the company learns from its customers, the better it becomes. And the better it becomes, the more difficult it will be for a competitor to adversely affect the business.

A Strategy for Building Customer Relationships

In a time of rapid change, when technology is constantly creating new markets, it is more important than ever to build long-lasting customer relationships. A strategy for building lifelong customer relationships should be based on the principles described in the following sections.

Forget Market Share Mentality

Worrying about market share is part of the old marketing paradigm. The goal of an entrepreneurial company should be to *own a market that it creates*. This means defining a niche market in which it can gain and sustain a leadership position. A company that owns a niche acts and is perceived differently by potential customers, suppliers, and competitors. It is in a position to set the standards for the market and encourage others to develop products and services compatible with theirs. This was the strategy of Fitscape, an Internet company that created a niche in the market by giving fitness professionals and fitness lovers a one-stop shop for information, resources, and products in the industry (*http://www.fitscape.com*). (See Young Entrepreneurs—Minicase in Chapter 12.)

Position the Company, Not Just the Product

Companies and their products and services are positioned in the market not only by the companies themselves but by distributors, sales reps, customers, and the industry environment in general. The most important **positioning** is

When you eat fish at a fine restaurant in Seattle, chances are it came from Mutual Fish, the 50-year old company started by Dick Yoshimura. By providing the highest quality and widest choice of fish as well as excellent service, Yoshimura has attracted a loyal customer base that now extends far beyond the Asian community. Today Yoshimura has taught the Seattle area to enjoy such unusual dishes as kasu cod and ocean (seaweed) salad alongside their traditional salmon and shellfish. (France Ruffenach)

not how the company sees its product but how others, particularly customers, see the product. Even two identical products can be perceived differently depending on the company name and strategies used to market them. This is why many customers will pay three times as much for the Nexus label on a shampoo bottle rather than purchase the less expensive store brand version with exactly the same ingredients. A key ingredient in brand loyalty, then, is the reputation and integrity of the company behind the product or service.

Build Credibility for the Company and Its Products

Credibility is built by investing in quality, service, and continued customer satisfaction. Concentrating on building referrals from satisfied customers, making customers aware of company successes and activities, and going after good customers who will consider themselves "stakeholders" in the business will all help to establish a desirable reputation and level of trust. Federal Express's guarantee of "absolutely, positively overnight" and L.L. Bean's "satisfaction guaranteed" have succeeded in developing trusting relationships between these companies and their customers.

Become a Mass Customizer Through Learning Relationships with Key Customers

Dialoguing with the customer is very easy today with interactive technologies such as electronic kiosks, online services, and database mail. From these dialogues will come the customers' preferences, and these preferences form the basis for customization. Basically, anything that can be digitized can also be customized. For manufacturers, mass customization means moving toward computer-aided manufacturing, flexible equipment, and virtual products that adapt in real time to customer needs. For example, Mattel will custom design Barbie dolls for customers such as Toys 'R' Us to reflect current trends or interests, such as "Barbie for President" during the 1992 presidential campaign and the "Ivana Trump" Barbie during Mrs. Trump's highly publicized divorce. Services are actually the easiest to mass customize. Maarten Voogd now understands the worldwide resort market and his customers so well that he can bid and supply a project that exactly meets the very unique requirements of the resort developer in any country. And he is doing it in a niche that he created. Building learning relationships with customers will help a company retain its most valuable customers and differentiate its products and services on a continual basis.

Focus on the Best Customers and Work to Keep Them

The twenty-first century will see the decline of the product manager and the rise of the customer manager. Instead of managing a portfolio of products, a world-class, entrepreneurial company will manage a portfolio of key customers for whom it will constantly seek new products and services based on their needs. This strategy will provide more opportunity for the company. Not only will the company have the first right to produce those new products for its customers, it can also act as a broker to find other products and services it may not be able to supply for customers, thereby providing yet another service that will encourage loyalty on the customers' part. With this in mind, entrepreneurial companies must develop smaller, key customer lists but keep them for life. They must treat their customers like shareholders so they won't be pulled away by strategic marketing tactics of image-driven companies.

Focus on the Intangible Aspects of the Product or Service

Intangibles are those things that are difficult to measure: quality, innovative technology, service, and reliability. Nevertheless, they are the key to differentiation in a market where products, services, and technology quickly become commodities in the eyes of the customer. The only way to differentiate commodity items is to add value through intangibles.

Why Current Customers Are the Best Customers

Growing entrepreneurial companies often get caught up in the constant search for the new customer. Without knowing how or why they feel compelled to do so, business owners make a sale and then set their sights on finding another sale with no thought for the customer they just acquired and no thought for how they will keep that customer. Most companies lose 25 percent of their customers annually.[12] If we assume it costs five times as much to acquire a new customer as to maintain an existing one, that translates into a lot of wasted expense for the company.

A number of research studies have underscored the significance of retaining customers:

▶ Fully 65 percent of the average company's business comes from current, satisfied customers.[13]

 Entrepreneurship in Action

How One Shoe Company Discovered the Value of the Customer

In 1989, Larry's Shoes, now a 10-store chain of men's shoes in Texas, was a discount shoe retailer focusing on volume sales. But Elliot Goodwin, the owner, was seeing his profit steadily decline no matter how much he sold, and he had to do something to stop it. The problem was that Goodwin's sights were focused on a five-year plan to achieve $50 million in sales with 15 stores. He was so busy with expansion-related activities that he lost sight of the marketplace, and in the interim the market changed.

For years the shoe industry had been dominated by small stores—independents—that knew their customers and what they liked down to the specific shoe style and color. The world of shoes today is something quite different. Dominated by department stores and discounters, it's a complex and difficult market. Goodwin's efforts to expand found him running the operation from 32,000 feet rather than from the floor with the customer.

In 1990, Goodwin commissioned a study of men's shoe-buying habits and discovered to his dismay that he didn't know his customer. In fact, his customer didn't know Larry's Shoes; two-thirds of potential customers had never even shopped at Larry's. They essentially thought it was a rack operation with no service. Furthermore, many men hate to shop for anything, let alone shoes. By 1994, Goodwin figured his regular customers represented 16 percent of the total potential customer base. His first strategy was to maximize the sales to his existing, regular customer base through direct mailings of catalogs and newsletters. He also gave his sales staff an incentive to bring a customer back within a year. They receive a 7 percent commission on the first sale, but if the customer returns within a year, the salesperson receives 10 percent on subsequent sales. Goodwin also supplies his salespeople with thank-you cards to send to every customer on every sale. And to give customers a reason to stop in, he has incorporated a coffee bar and a shoe museum. The results? In the first year of the "new" Larry's Shoes, sales jumped 24 percent, and he now has 10 stores.

Source: Jay Finegan, "In the Customer's Shoes," *Inc.,* May 1995, p. 45.

▶ A company that, each day for one year, loses one customer who generally spends $50 a week will suffer a sales decline of $1 million the next year.[14]

▶ About 91 percent of dissatisfied customers will never again buy from a company that gave them problems, and they will communicate this dissatisfaction to at least nine other people.[15]

Furthermore, 90 percent of dissatisfied customers won't let the company know why they are unhappy; they will just stop buying. It can't be any clearer: the best customer is the one the company already has, and the goal should be to find ways to satisfy that customer and solve his or her problems with new products and services.

The entrepreneurial company for the twenty-first century will live for its customers. Customers will decide what is produced, when and how it is produced, how much is produced, how much it will cost, and where it can be purchased and serviced. To paraphrase Ross Perot, the customers are the owners of the company. Keeping them happy is essential to the survival and success of the business. In a market-driven company, it is not just the sales personnel who deal with the customer. Everyone from the engineers to the plant workers to the office staff knows the customers. This means that those responsible for product development spend time with customers assessing needs; those who handle billing and invoicing spend time with customers to ensure that the service they provide is meeting its mark; and senior-line management spends at least a third of the time with customers so they don't lose touch with the company's greatest asset. In short, all actions the organization takes are first assessed based on their impact on the customer and second on their impact on the business.

In a world-class, entrepreneurial company, the customer is an integral part of the organization and is encouraged to participate in the company through letters, newsletters, visits to the company facilities, and attendance at special meetings. Customers are given numerous opportunities to express their feelings and give their suggestions, and are regularly sampled for their degree of satisfaction with the company and its products or services. When a world-class, entrepreneurial company makes promises to a customer, it keeps those promises no matter what the cost to the business to do so. The customer is always right.

The next chapter moves from the broader, more strategic view taken by this chapter to a more tactical view as we consider "guerrilla" marketing tactics to gain the attention of the customer and relationship marketing tactics to build a loyal customer base.

Cases Relevant to This Chapter

Pelco
French Rags
Zanart Entertainment

Issues for Review and Discussion

1. Compare the new marketing approach with the traditional, mass marketing principles.
2. What is mass customization, and how do virtual products fit into this scenario?
3. What is the essence of one-to-one relationship marketing?
4. Why is it less expensive to maintain current customers than it is to seek new ones?
5. Discuss three ways companies can build customer relationships.

Experiencing Entrepreneurship

1. Find a company that is customer centered, and interview employees and principals to determine what tactics they are using to build customer relationships.
2. Compare the company you found in question 1 with a company that uses more traditional marketing approaches. What conclusions can you draw?

Resources

Davidow, William H., and Michael S. Malone (1992). *The Virtual Corporation*. New York: Edward Burlingame Books/HarperBusiness.

McKenna, Regis (1991). *Relationship Marketing*. Reading, MA: Addison-Wesley.

Peppers, Don, and Martha Rogers (1993). *The One to One Future: Building Relationships One Customer at a Time.* New York: Currency/Doubleday.

Internet Resources
Guerrilla Marketing
http://www.gmarketing.com/tactics/weekly_02.html
Read weekly articles from marketing guru Jay Conrad Levinson.

American Marketing Association
http://www.ama.org
Resources on issues related to marketing.

Sell solution,
not just products.
Klaus M. Lesinger
Department Director
Ciba–Geigy, Ltd.
New York Times, 21 February 1988

11

Developing the Marketing Plan

Preview

Understanding this chapter will give you the ability to

▶ **Identify new company marketing issues**

▶ **Develop a marketing plan for a new business**

▶ **Describe the customer and the customer's needs**

▶ **Understand the product or service from the customer's point of view**

▶ **Develop an effective pricing strategy**

▶ **Build relationships and repeat sales through promotion**

▶ **Track customers**

▶ **Maintain customer relationships for life**

Terms to Know

Young Entrepreneurs—Minicase

Scott Samet and Douglas Chu
Taste of Nature and Tabacon
Cigar Company

Having multiple ventures while you're still a young entrepreneur is not an uncommon phenomenon today. Scott Samet and Douglas Chu were just two years out of the Wharton School in 1990 when they formed their first company, Taste of Nature, Inc., offering an alternative to the usual snacks found in movie theaters. Taste of Nature sells bulk healthy snacks and candy to more than 1,000 movie theaters nationwide, including AMC, General Cinema, Regal, Cineplex Odeon, and Sony.

It might seem unusual that these two financial analysts who had worked for two years at Bankers Trust would get into the food business. But they didn't see it as getting into the food business. Instead, they saw opportunity in a niche that wasn't being filled: the trend toward healthy foods in movie theaters. With $15,000 of their own money, they started the business in Santa Barbara, California, at the Metropolitan Theater chain. And the timing was perfect. While movie chains were testing Taste of Nature products, the press was covering reports that movie popcorn contains unusually high levels of saturated fat. The result was more and more theaters rushing to adopt Taste of Nature's healthy alternative.

In the meantime, Samet and Chu conducted additional research with moviegoers, who told them that packaging was important to attract their attention. So the two talked to Bill Hughes, vice president of theater concessions at Metropolitan Theaters, who helped them design Plexiglas bins in which to display their health snacks. Moviegoers and owners alike loved them because for $2.25, customers could scoop up whatever they wanted and put it in a bag. Samet and Chu had discovered not only a niche in the snack candy market but also a new and exciting way to deliver the product.

The challenge in this business comes from the fact that snack food companies are dependent on the success of the film industry in any given year. If the movies produced are successful, more people will go to the theater and buy their products. If not, they will be negatively affected. Currently Taste of Nature does close to $2 million in revenues, and its focus now is on bulk candy such as "pick and mix."

However, it recently introduced "chocolate-coated cookie dough," Taste of Nature's first packaged product, which will be sold both in theaters and as a bagged version in supermarkets.

But Taste of Nature was not the only venture for these two young entrepreneurs. Samet and Chu have always enjoyed cigars, and in 1994 they began to notice that cigars were becoming more popular. Recognizing that their first business was the successful result of identifying an unmet need in the market, they got the idea to start a mail-order club modeled after a popular beer-of-the-month club. With money earned from Taste of Nature, they started a club whose members would receive four cigars a month, along with a newsletter and the option to order more cigars at a discount. Their cigar supply at that time came mostly from factories in the Dominican Republic, although sometimes they had to buy from exclusive importers to get a specific type of cigar.

Things really took off for the monthly cigar club when they developed a 10-cigar sampler. Because cigars tend to be mainstream items, they personalized the sampler for specific department stores by designing a wooden box with the store's logo on it. Their "Premium Cigar Sampler," which is sold through the catalog divisions of Neiman Marcus, Saks Fifth Avenue, Bloomingdales, Brookstone, and others, was the number one drop-ship vendor for the Neiman Marcus catalog division in 1996. The monthly cigar club is devoted to serving the upscale cigar and cigar accessory mail-order niche. It sells a full line of cigar accessories and has more than 2,000 members.

Tabacon Cigar Company, the umbrella company, was launched after Samet and Chu developed five premium brands of cigars—Rosa Blanca, Del Valle, Don Jivan, Nivelacuso, and Tabacon—which have been well received in the marketplace and are sold through distributors, direct to stores, and through brokers. In fact, four of its five proprietary brands of cigars have been rated 95 or higher by *The Cigar Enthusiast*, an industry magazine. Tabacon provides its retail accounts—hotels, bars, clubs, and liquor stores—with attractive humidors in which to store and display the cigars. This has given them more exposure through better positioning on retailer shelves.

Much of Tabacon's revenue is generated using what Samet and Chu call the "Gillette method" of sales and marketing ("give them the razor and force them to buy the blades"). In other words, continuing sales are generated on the consumable aspect of the product, which is the cigar, while the humidor is provided essentially free of charge. International expansion to Asia with its new proprietary brands is the next goal.

The biggest challenge for Tabacon is that some brands of cigars have been around for hundreds of years and are recognized and held in high regard. As a new brand, it has the basic problem of brand name recognition. This is a whole different ballgame from Samet and Chu's first company, which essentially required no advertising. With Tabacon they must put their brand in front of the customer.

The partnership between Doug Chu and Scott Samet has worked well through two businesses because they are determined to be flexible in their thinking and to always communicate with each other. As a result, Tabacon Cigar Company is now one of the fastest-growing cigar companies in the United States. In 1997, its revenues exceeded $4 million.

What would a one-paragraph marketing plan look like for Tabacon Cigar Company?

As you have learned throughout this book, the customer is at the center of the business, a member of the team, and certainly the principal contributor to the bottom line. The customer's input should be evident from the concept development of the product or service through production, distribution, and after-sale service. For entrepreneurial companies, this customer focus begins at start-up and becomes an integral part of the culture, philosophy, and strategies of the company as it grows. Through one-to-one relationships with the customer, entrepreneurial companies can become learning organizations that believe in continual improvement. Scott Samet and Douglas Chu (see Young Entrepreneurs—Minicase) designed both Taste of Nature and Tabacon Cigar Company with input from the customer and end-user from the very beginning. As moviegoers and cigar smokers themselves, they knew their end-user intimately, and this made their businesses more attractive to their customers.

Marketing consists of everything you do to make your customer aware of your business and buy your products and services on a repeat basis. Marketing therefore includes the name of your business; the features and benefits of the product or service you sell; the process you use to manufacture or deliver products and services; the packaging; the location of the business; and the advertising, promotion, public relations, sales efforts, after-sale service, and follow-up needed to keep the customer.[1] Guerrilla marketing is a way for entrepreneurs with limited resources to reach their customers and build relationships as effectively or more effectively than large companies with significant resources. This chapter focuses on fundamental marketing strategies and guerrilla tactics that small, growing companies can use to create awareness of the company and build customer relationships.

New-Company Marketing Issues

A new company faces the dual challenge of marketing a new product or service *and* the company itself. A new, exciting product or service may attract initial customer attention, but customers also want to feel comfortable that a stable, healthy business backs up that product or service. Though company credibility is not always a prerequisite in the consumer products market (consumers will often buy from companies in Chapter 11 bankruptcy), it is certainly vital in the industrial or business-to-business products markets and in the service industry. So for new companies, marketing strategy takes place on two fronts: the product/service and the company.

The other problem new companies face (and often established companies as well) is that their founders have frequently learned about or gained experience in marketing from large companies, so they only know one side of marketing: the kind of mass marketing strategies used by giants such as Procter & Gamble, Kmart, and Intel. Small businesses, by contrast, have unique needs and face unique challenges, principally because of resource deficiencies; thus, they require different strategies. The fact that entrepreneurs look at marketing from a different point of view does not mean their strategies are "second class." Quite the contrary: some start-up marketing strategies, such as personalized customer service, have become so successful that large corporations are now adopting similar programs. World-class start-ups are recognizing that their ability to deal with the customer on a more personal level is a distinct competitive advantage and certainly a way to compete successfully against established firms.

For any company, an effective marketing strategy begins with a marketing plan. The following sections discuss how to put together an effective marketing plan.

The Marketing Plan

The **marketing plan** for an entrepreneurial company is a living guide to how the company plans to build customer relationships over its life to fulfill the mission statement in the business plan. It details the strategies and tactics that will create awareness on the part of the customer and build a loyal customer base over time. Marketing plans are written at many points in a business's life. Certainly the original business plan will contain a marketing plan for introducing the company and its products and services to the marketplace. Later the entrepreneur may develop a marketing plan to create market awareness for the company, introduce new products and services, and grow the business, perhaps in a new direction.

A few steps taken before the actual writing of the marketing plan will ensure that the plan is on target and is one the company can live with for a long time to come. One of the biggest problems with most marketing plans is that they are not followed long enough to achieve the desired results. Typically the business owner doesn't see immediate results from the marketing effort and decides it must not be working. So he or she automatically changes it and starts the cycle all over again. Changing the plan precipitously is precisely the wrong thing to do. It takes time to build customer relationships one customer at a time. It takes time for a particular marketing strategy to take hold and build confidence in the customer. From the first time a customer sees an ad to the point at which the customer actually buys the product may be weeks or even months. On average, the customer will see the ad 15 or 20 times before actually purchasing the product. The marketing plan, therefore, is an investment in the future of the business, and any investment takes time to mature.

To reap the benefits of a well-conceived marketing plan requires persistence and unwavering dedication until the plan has an opportunity to perform. Several steps should be taken *prior* to writing a marketing plan, and every member of the management team should participate in this effort.

1. **Make a list of the options.** To even begin to know which marketing options to consider, it is vital to talk to other business owners, customers, and suppliers. Reading books and articles on marketing strategies that successful companies have employed can also be a source of inspiration. This brainstorming process will produce a list of possibilities that may range from sponsoring a business conference to advertising in a national trade publication. The nature of the possibilities generated will reflect the needs of the company's particular customers. Determining which strategies are the most effective or even feasible can be left for later.

2. **Think like a customer.** The business must be imagined from the customer's point of view. What would entice a customer to enter your store, buy your product, and take advantage of your service? Richard Branson, founder of Virgin Airways, designed his planes and services based on how he felt as a passenger on an airplane. Scott Samet and Douglas Chu focused on what moviegoers wanted: the ability to design their own snacks. The most effective way to learn what customers want is to talk to them, observe them, and essentially become one of them.

3. **Study the competition.** Studying competing companies will give you a clear sense of what it takes to be successful and also what the company can do that is better than what the competition is doing. Which marketing strategies do they employ, and are they effective? How could your company improve on what the competition is doing? Consider becoming one of your competitor's customers.

4. **Analyze the options and rank them.** Marketing strategies that don't meet the needs of customers or are simply not feasible at this time (usually for budgetary reasons) should be eliminated. Then the top 10 choices can be rank ordered.

Figure 11.1
The Components of
the One-Paragraph
Marketing Plan

With these four steps completed, the marketing plan can be written. The primary market strategy for entrepreneurial companies that want to build a strong competitive advantage should be to build one-to-one customer relationships. Most large companies have not yet adopted the relationship marketing approach to its fullest extent. They are still too entrenched in the old mass marketing paradigm. Therefore, it is important that this customer-focused philosophy permeate the entire marketing plan. Figure 11.1 gives an overview of the components of the marketing plan.

The Marketing Plan in One Paragraph

Many experienced marketers suggest that the first step in creating the marketing plan is to condense all the ideas about the marketing strategy into a single paragraph that says it all. Impossible? Not at all. A single, well-written paragraph will force the company to focus carefully on the central selling point of the overall marketing strategy; that is what will grab customers' attention and entice them to buy. The paragraph should include the following elements:

▶ The purpose of the marketing plan
   What will the marketing plan accomplish?

▶ The benefits of the product or service
   How will the product or service help the customer or satisfy a need?

▶ The customer
   Who is the primary customer, and how will the company build a relationship with that customer?

▶ The company's convictions—its identity
   How will the customer define the company?

- The market niche
  Where does the company fit in the industry or market? How does it differentiate itself? How does it differentiate its customers?

- The marketing tactics to be used
  What specific marketing tools will be employed to create awareness and build relationships?

- The percentage of sales that the marketing budget will represent
  How much money will be allocated to the marketing plan?

Following is an example of a marketing plan in one paragraph:

The purpose of the marketing plan is to create awareness for ABC Corporation, which will sell innovative, portable power equipment at the highest quality and the lowest possible cost by positioning itself as the leader by providing reliable, dual power source products that reduce the number of pieces of equipment the user must own. The target market is the construction industry and, more specifically, those who use power tools in areas where no source of power is available. The niche ABC will enter is that of construction companies that own or lease power equipment. Initial marketing tactics will include direct sales to equipment rental outlets, advertisements in trade publications, and trade shows. ABC's customers will see the company as service oriented with a quick response to customer needs in both service and product design. Twelve percent of sales will be applied to the marketing strategy.

With the focus derived from the "one-paragraph marketing plan," the full plan can be undertaken. A complete marketing plan will cover issues related to the customer, the product or service, price, promotion, and distribution. (Distribution is addressed in Chapter 12.)

Understanding the Customer

Any good marketing plan begins with the identification of the target customer. The customer or *target market*, to use a traditional marketing term, is that segment of the marketplace that will most likely purchase the product or service—in other words, the primary market on which the company will focus its marketing efforts.

The target customer is not always the end-user of the product or service. Consider the simplified example in Figure 11.2. It depicts a manufacturer producing a product that is sold to a distributor, who in turn sells to the end-user—the consumer perhaps, or another business. The manufacturer's customer is the distributor who pays for the goods. The distributor's customer is the consumer or end-user. Even though the manufacturer is not selling directly to the end-user customer, it must know that customer well

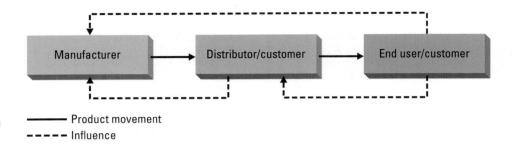

**Figure 11.2
Simple Distribution
Channel**

—————— Product movement

- - - - - - Influence

because that is the customer who is actually using the product and will ultimately determine its success or failure. The distributor, on the other hand, is also an important customer of the manufacturer because unless the manufacturer can convince the distributor of the value of the product, the manufacturer will not have an outlet to sell it other than to go direct, which would then put the manufacturer in the retail business. So both the intermediary (the distributor) and the end-user are customers of the manufacturer. Throughout this book, we will use the term *customer* without differentiating the two types, because the strategies and tactics discussed will generally apply to both, and it will be necessary for any company to establish lifelong, learning relationships with both.

Defining the Customer

Knowing as much as possible about the customer is critical to a successful marketing strategy. Recall that Mary Naylor of Capitol Concierge (see the Young Entrepreneurs—Minicase in Chapter 10) found that the more she knew about her customers—their habits, likes, and dislikes—the better she was able to meet their needs without expensive mass marketing techniques that may not have reached the specific customers she was targeting. How do we know who the customer for a product or service is? Who is purchasing it probably comes to mind. But how do we know who that *first* customer is? Learning that is a critical beginning for any company's one-to-one strategy, and it results from market research.

Traditionally companies have relied on demographic and psychographic studies done by such companies as Mediamark Research, Inc., and the Simmons Market Research Bureau. Demographics include such factors as age, income level, education, and race, whereas psychographics deal with attitudes and intentions, values, and lifestyles. These firms conduct random samples of the population to segment the consumer market in a way that will make it easier for companies to determine the size and characteristics of their markets. Market segmentation is a way to divide the target market into groups of customers with similar needs. Markets may be segmented in four basic ways: product or service, geography, psychographics, and demographics.

When Melba Wilson announced that Minton's Playhouse would re-open after decades of being closed, it was a sign that the best of Harlem was being revived. Wilson saw that the time was right to re-open the famous jazz club because Harlem is in the midst of a renaissance. With 35% of its residents having college or graduate level education and an average income of $33,000, Harlem provided Wilson with a promising customer base for her new venture. (Jim Lo Scalzo/US News & World Report)

In some cases, markets are segmented by the bundle of benefits the *product or service* provides the customer. Some customers may be looking for the highest quality and convenience and will pay for it, whereas others seek average quality and don't want to pay too much. Within this category, you may also segment based on how much of a product is purchased—that is, high-volume versus low-volume purchasers—and on how the product will be used.

Entrepreneurs often segment based on the *geographic area* where customers are located. This is because customers in different regions have different purchasing habits or desire different features and benefits. Segmentation by geographic area is also used to plan for more efficient distribution, warehousing, and servicing.

Segmenting by *psychographics* means looking at personality traits, motives, and lifestyles or values. Knowing a common personality trait in your target market, such as propensity to take risks, will give you a lot of clues that you can use to develop your marketing plan and in particular your media tactics.

Segmenting by *demographics* is another way to look at the target market. Market research firms can report down to the precise neighborhood what people typically buy, how much they spend, how much they earn, how they live, and what they say they do. Researchers use many demographic factors that affect buying behavior, including ethnicity, region, social class, age, and gender.[2]

Unfortunately, what people report they do on a survey form and what they actually do are not always congruent. Moreover, market research firms can't deliver information on why a particular customer chose a particular product or changed from one service to another. That information is not important to them, because the firms (their clients) that rely on this type of data are only after market size and market share, so statistical averages suffice; individual customers don't count. The goal of consumer product firms that use this research is to increase the *likelihood* that someone (anyone) will purchase from them, and statistical inference is all they need for this purpose. This type of "customer" information has worked well under the mass market approach. It will be of limited value, however, under a relationship marketing approach, in which knowing about individual customers is essential.

Entrepreneurial companies know that the first customer is found during the conceptual development of the product or service. In other words, customer acquisition begins *before* the company even has a product to sell or a service to offer. In this way, when the company is ready to launch the product or service, it will benefit from the collaboration of a pool of customers who, having a vested interest in the company because of their participation in the product development, are likely to "spread the word." Microsoft used this strategy in the development of the Windows platform. It created hundreds of **beta sites** (test sites) of potential users who tested the software during the development process and gave Microsoft "instant" feedback through e-mail. They also "spread the word" to potential buyers, who were ready to purchase when the product was launched.

How do we find out more about our target market? Through a process known as *market research*.

Conducting Market Research

In the beginning stages of market analysis, companies typically have a fairly loose description of the target market. This description is refined and may even change as discussions with potential customers take place during the field research. The key questions that need to be answered are

▶ Who is the customer?

▶ What do they typically buy, and how do they hear about it?

▶ How do they like to buy this type of product or service?

▶ How often do they buy?

▶ How can the company best meet the customer's needs?

Table 11.1   Steps in Market Research

1. Assess information needs. What do we want to know about the market?
2. Research secondary sources first. Secondary sources consist of information gathered by third-party sources such as trade journals and periodicals.
3. Measure the target market with primary field research. This means gathering the information yourself by talking to the customer.
4. Forecast demand for the product or service.

Most young companies lack the resources for professional marketing services. Doing your own market research has a distinct advantage. Who knows better than you do what is valuable in terms of information?

The research conducted on the target market will provide some of the most important data the company needs to decide if it is producing a product or service that customers want. To ensure that useful and correct conclusions will be drawn, the research methods must be sound. The four-step process listed in Table 11.1 will ensure that the information needed to make this crucial decision is gathered and used correctly.

Assessing Information Needs

Before you can begin to collect market data, you must determine exactly what you need to know about the market. Will the data demonstrate demand for the product or service? Will it describe the customer? Will it give a sense of trends in the market? Good researchers decide *first* what they are attempting to accomplish with the research so that they will gather the correct

Technology Tip

Be Your Own Publisher

Creating your own marketing materials has become easier than ever with software that literally guides you through the process. Invest in good publishing software, such as Microsoft Publisher 98, and you'll be able to create advertisements, brochures, flyers, business cards, and direct mail that looks as professional as any major company's materials.

If you have a very small business and your need for marketing materials is limited, you can also print your designs with a good-quality color printer that costs less than $500. For volume printing, your software will allow you to prepare the designs in a form that a professional printer can use and that you supply on disk.

You can even track the results of your advertising with spreadsheet software or a database.

Today it's easier than ever to take charge of every aspect of your business to ensure that you get the level of quality you want.

type of data for the analysis. Nothing is more discouraging to a researcher than collecting all the data only to find that a crucial piece of information is missing.

Research Secondary Sources First

Secondary data is information that someone else has already gathered and analyzed. It is important to study these data first because they may reveal reasons to either go ahead with or kill a particular product or service concept before primary research is begun. The library is a good place to start, because it contains a wealth of information on industries and specific markets from both government and private sources. The following sources provide secondary data on customers in various industries:

- *U.S. Bureau of the Census.* The 10-year U.S. population census, monthly *Current Population Survey*, and *Survey of Income and Program Participation.* Census data can be used to look at group demographic data within specific geographic regions and to estimate how many potential customers are within the geographic boundaries of the target market.

- *Community economic development departments.* Statistics on local population trends and other economic issues, as well as businesses locating in the community.

- *Chambers of commerce.* Information on the community in general as well as businesses.

- *Small Business Administration.* Broad-based information and services for small businesses.

- *Small Business Development Centers.* Branches of the Small Business Administration that contain a wealth of information and services for small businesses.

- *Trade associations.* Typically keep statistics on their members and their industries.

- *Trade journals.* What is happening in an industry: trends, problems, opportunities, and sources of information.

- *Government Printing Office.* The federal government provides free of charge pamphlets and documents on just about anything a business owner might want to know.

- *Trade shows.* Attending trade shows in your industry is an excellent way to learn who the competition is and to see what the latest trends in the industry and your specific market are.

- *Competitors.* Competitors can be a great source of information. Become their customers and study their strategies and how they deal with their customers. Who are their customers and why? What can you provide the customer that they are not providing?

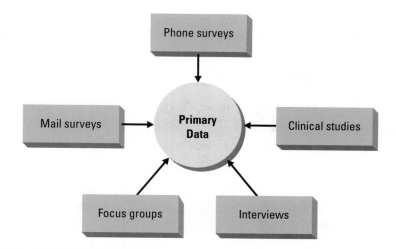

**Figure 11.3
Sources of Primary
Data**

▶ *The Internet.* Online databases with all kinds of information on the Internet, accessed via a web browser such as Netscape.* Some of those sites are listed at the end of the chapter.

Measuring the Market with Primary Data

For an entrepreneurial company, no data are more important than those the company itself collects through observation and talking to people. These are called **primary data.** There is no substitute for talking to customers, suppliers, distributors, lawyers, accountants, and anyone else who can provide information on the target market, because primary information will be more current than anything in print and will probably be more directly related to the business. Figure 11.3 summarizes the various methods for collecting primary data.

There are many ways to collect primary data on the target market, some more effective and less costly than others. Among them are mail surveys, phone surveys, interviews, focus groups, and clinical studies. Each has advantages and disadvantages, and a decision to use one or more of them is usually based on time and money. All have the common purpose of getting information on customer attitudes and preferences that can be used to make decisions about the four Ps of marketing: product, place, price, and promotion.

Mail Surveys   A mail survey entails designing a survey instrument, usually a questionnaire that will provide the desired information. Questionnaire design

---

* A cautionary note on Internet sites: the researcher should never assume that a site is a credible source of information just because it's on the Internet. Sources and authors should be carefully checked.

is not a simple matter of putting some questions on a piece of paper. There are, in fact, proven methods of constructing questionnaires to help ensure unbiased responses. It is beyond the scope of this book to present all the techniques for questionnaire construction; however, you should remember several key points:

1. Keep the questionnaire short with lots of white space so the respondent is not intimidated at the outset.

2. Be careful not to ask leading, biased questions.

3. Ask easy questions first, leading up to the more complex ones.

4. Ask demographic questions (age, sex, income) last, when the respondent's attention span has waned. These questions can be answered very quickly.

5. For questions that people generally hesitate to answer (age, income), group possible responses in ranges (e.g., 25 to 35 for age, $35,000 to $45,000 for income) so the respondent doesn't feel that he or she is giving away very private information.

6. Keep in mind that people generally increase their income classification one class and decrease their age one class.

7. Mail surveys are a relatively easy way to reach a lot of people in the target market and take less time than many other methods. However, mail surveys do have a few weaknesses.

   ▸ The response rate is generally very low, usually around 15 percent, which means about 85 percent of the people sampled did not respond. Consequently, the potential for nonresponse bias makes it difficult to trust the reliability of the results.

   ▸ Mail surveys do not have the benefit of nonverbal communication as an interview does. This is significant considering that at least 85 percent of all communication is nonverbal.

   ▸ There is no way to question or clarify a response.

   ▸ There is no control over the accuracy of the information given.

   ▸ Normally a second, follow-up mailing is necessary to achieve the desired response rate.

Phone Surveys   Like mail surveys, phone surveys use questionnaires to achieve consistency in the questions asked. Phone surveys have two advantages over mail surveys. First, they allow for explanation and clarification of questions and responses, and the response rate is higher. However, phone surveys take more time to administer and are more prone to surveyor bias; that is, there is more opportunity for the person conducting the survey to bias the results by the tone in his or her voice or the unscripted comments made. Second, phone surveys do not permit observation of nonverbal communication.

Furthermore, the frequency with which telemarketers contact consumers has made this method of inquiry less desirable as potential respondents are increasingly likely to refuse to participate in phone surveys.

Interviews   Although more costly and time consuming than mail or phone surveys, interviews have many advantages:

▶ They provide more opportunity for clarification and discussion.

▶ They enjoy the advantages of nonverbal communication. The interviewer is better able to discern the veracity of the interviewee's responses.

▶ The response rate is high.

▶ Interviews permit open-ended questions that can lead to more in-depth information.

▶ Interviews provide an opportunity to network and develop valuable contacts in the industry.

Where time and money permit, interviews are one of the best sources of valuable information from customers, suppliers, distributors, and anyone else who can help the company. A dialogue is an effective way to gather a lot of information that is not available from traditional surveys; it also allows observation of nonverbal communication.

It is possible to use a combination of surveys, phone calls, and interviews. For example, the company may start with phone surveys to obtain basic information and follow up with interviews with the most useful sources.

Focus Groups   One more efficient way to gain valuable information before investing substantial capital in production and marketing is to conduct a **focus group**. The company brings together a representative sample of potential customers for a presentation and discussion session. If the company is introducing a consumer product, it may choose to present the new product in concert with other products to test the unsolicited response to the product when presented with its competition. For example, if the product is a new type of nonalcoholic beverage, it might be served along with several competitors' beverages in glasses labeled with numbers. Feedback on taste, aftertaste, and so on can then be solicited.

Some products and services do not easily lend themselves to blind studies such as this, especially where there are no direct competitors. In those instances, the product can simply be presented to the focus group and their opinions and feedback solicited. It's important that the person leading the focus group have some knowledge of group dynamics and be able to keep the group on track. Often focus group sessions are videotaped so the management team can spend more time analyzing the nuances of what occurred. Thus, in many ways, focus groups can often prevent the company from making the costly error of offering a product or service for which little or no interest exists.

Clinical Studies   Clinical studies are one of the more expensive routes to gathering market data. Generally these studies are undertaken by professionals in controlled settings. Because most new, growing companies do not have the resources to conduct clinical studies, they are usually used by large, established firms introducing new products.

Choosing the Sample

All of these techniques to gather primary data require the selection of a representative sample from the target market. This step in measuring the market should be taken with great care, for it will determine the validity of the results. In general, a **random sample** of potential customers should be chosen, that is, one over which the company has as little control as possible over who will be selected to participate in the sample. Most companies, for reasons of cost and time, choose to use a **convenience sample**. This means that not everyone in the defined target market has a chance of being chosen to participate. Instead, for example, you may choose to select the sample from people who happen to be at a particular shopping mall on a particular day. Clearly, you will not reach all possible customers at that mall, but if you suspect the customer typically shops at malls, you have a good chance of achieving at least a representative sample from which you can derive fairly reliable results.

Even if a convenience sample is used, there are ways to ensure that participants are selected randomly. Using the mall example, the selection system may be to select and survey every fifth person who walks by. In this way, the person is not chosen based on his or her attractiveness (or lack of it) or any other reason, for that matter. Alternatively, using a random number generator on a computer, names can be selected from a telephone book. Whichever system is employed, the key point is that the selection of the sample must not be biased.

Sometimes entrepreneurs claim they took a sample of friends and relatives who loved the new-product idea. Friends and relatives may be able to provide some initial feedback, but they are *not* the best source of unbiased information. The market research a company does will result in a go/no go decision, so it is critical that it be done correctly. The credibility of the market research results will be directly affected by the quality of the sample selected.

Understanding the Product or Service

For marketing purposes, the product or service should be thought of as a bundle of benefits to the customer. These benefits include a wide variety of things: attractiveness, distinctive characteristics, quality, options, warranties, service contracts, delivery, and so forth. More important, perhaps, for the customer there are intangible benefits such as savings in time and money, or improved health. To feel comfortable about buying the product or service, the customer must know about and understand these benefits.

In a customer-focused marketing plan, it's assumed the customer has played a part in the design and development of the product or service. In other words, the product or service has been customized to meet the needs of the individual customer. For example, Motorola designs customized paging systems and can create more than 20 million types of pagers. The customer's specifications are sent via modem to the factory, and the entire production process is completed in just two hours. Part of the marketing strategy as it relates to the product or service, then, is to involve customers in the product development phase so that the ultimate product or service meets their exact needs. For more information about product development and mass customization, see Chapter 13.

It's also important to focus on the intangible aspects of the product or service. Intangibles are those things that are difficult to measure: quality, innovative technology, service, and reliability. They are the key to differentiation in a market where products, services, and technology quickly become commodities in the eyes of the customer.

Product/Service Positioning

Gathering primary and secondary resources will give you a good handle on how customers perceive the product or service. **Product/service positioning** is

One of the biggest problems facing small business owners is how to compete against the major chains and their low prices. Carmelo Mauro of Carmelo's Italian Restaurants in Houston, Texas decided that the best way to compete was not to compete on price. Instead he took a contrary approach and focused on quality and personal service. He used high cost ingredients, expanded his menu, and raised his prices. But he also greeted people at the door and made sure they had an elegant experience. His strategy has paid off with a successful business. (Courtesy of Carmelo's Italian Restaurants)

the way customers view the product or service in relation to competitors' offerings: is the product of higher quality, less expensive, more attractive, and so forth? In short, product positioning defines the product by its benefits to the customer. Consequently, products are typically repositioned several times during the product life cycle as customer tastes and preferences change.

Not only is the product or service positioned, but the company is as well. Savvy customers today are concerned more and more about the reputations of the companies they deal with. So, for example, if a company associates with distributors whose level of service is not up to its standards, that fact will ultimately reflect on the company. Realistically, a product's or company's position in the market will be a function of the customers' perception of where it should be. That is, the company may have designed its product to replace another, established product, whereas customers see it as a product they would like to have once they have already bought the competitor's existing product. Precious marketing dollars will be wasted if the company fails to respond to customers' perceptions. Using a one-to-one relationship marketing approach means you will have dialogued with the customer enough to know how she or he perceives the product or service.

A statement of the product's position relative to competitors' products should be written from the customer's point of view. For example,

> The customer will see EZ-Alert as a high-quality, state-of-the-art security device for parents who want to keep track of their children in public situations.

The positioning of a product or service should be tested in the market prior to doing a full product launch. Several methods can be used, which vary in the time and cost involved:

▶ *Peer review.* In a **peer review,** the entrepreneur or management team asks friends to give an opinion on the positioning statement for the product and on how the product will do in this position.

▶ *Distribution channel review.* In a **distribution channel review,** salespeople, distributors, and retailers are asked what they think of the position statement. Typically they have a good sense of where the company and its products fit in the industry.

▶ *Focus groups.* The company brings together a group of potential customers to get their feedback. These should be people who have not participated in the design and development of the product so that their opinions are unbiased.

▶ *Test marketing.* Test marketing involves producing a limited amount of product and selling it in a defined geographic region to determine if the product positioning is correct. The cost of this approach must be weighed against getting the product into the market as quickly as possible, particularly where there is a first-mover advantage to be gained. Time to market is becoming more important in light of rapidly changing technology and markets. Again, having the customer involved at every stage of product development shortens that time significantly and makes it more likely that the product will not experience problems after the launch. Chapter 13 discusses product development and prototyping.

The final positioning statement should be communicated to everyone in the company so that all will share a common philosophy and communicate a consistent message to the customer.

Branding

Building brand loyalty in a time of rapid change, when technology has created new media markets, is challenging at best. Today **branding** must represent the qualities and philosophy of the company as much as the product, but for many consumer product and service companies, building a brand name becomes a war of images. An ad featuring a young, slim, athletic-looking woman drinking a "light" beer seems to be an oxymoron, but subliminally it hits the mark. Drinking light beer is perceived as sexy, healthy, and youthful. Whether or not it's true is irrelevant; the image remains.

For companies that participate in the war of the images, the battle is everything. They will do anything to win. What's important is keeping the brand name in the public eye. Most times we don't even know which company is promoting the brand; often the name appears only briefly at the end of the ad. Such is the case with some Calvin Klein and Nike ads, for example. The strategy of these companies is not to sell product with these ads but to get people to pay attention to advertising once again. Today customers are so bombarded by advertising that they have almost become immune to its influences, so companies are taking drastic measures to regain their attention.

A countermovement, however, has begun to occur among entrepreneurial companies. A number of very successful companies, such as Ben and Jerry's Homemade, Smith and Hawkens, and Starbucks Coffee are resisting image positioning as the way to communicate their message. Instead of promoting brand names, they choose to communicate the philosophy of their company, which is at the core of all their products and by its very nature differentiates these companies from others in the market. They do not go head to head with their competitors in a war of images; they create their own niche in marketing strategy by seeking ways to increase pride and loyalty not only in their customers but in their employees as well. They break with tradition to make themselves stand out.

The differences in products that these new marketing strategists promote are real and measurable. These real distinctions not only separate them from the false reality of their competitors' images but also expose those images for what they are. Of course, developing a sound company philosophy or culture is not an overnight achievement. It takes time, and while the company is working at building that philosophy, the image builders will probably receive the bulk of the attention. Nevertheless, persistence will pay off when the company is able to deliver precisely what it said it would.

Brand name recognition, when achieved, must be protected from inferior products that might attempt to secure a competitive advantage by trading on a name or slogan that is associated with a successful brand. For example, McWilliams Wines, an Australian company, used the slogan "Big Mac" to promote a two-liter wine bottle. McDonald's, the famous American fast-food chain, took McWilliams to court, saying that its use of the Big Mac slogan would mislead the public into thinking a relationship existed. The court concluded that confusion might occur, but the slogan was not misleading because the term "Big Mac" is descriptive. Therefore, McWilliams had not infringed on McDonald's rights.[3]

In her book *Defending Your Brand Against Imitation,* Judith Zaichowsky suggests several things a company can do to protect a brand name:[4]

1. Use the trademark as an adjective in the name of the product, for example, *Sanka Brand Decaffeinated Coffee.*

2. Make sure the media use the trademark correctly. Check ads and articles written about the company, and report any errors for immediate correction.

3. Use a specific typographical treatment. For example,

EZ - A l e r t

4. Be careful in the selection of a brand name. Test it thoroughly and look to avoid names already in use or covered by copyrights, names too similar to existing trade names, and those already in use with unrelated products.

Packaging and Labeling

The packaging and labeling of products should reflect the philosophy of the company and the type of business. For consumer products, packaging actually becomes another form of advertising and promotion. Packaging has to grab the consumer's attention as it sits among many competing products on crowded shelves. When Jan Davidson, founder of Davidson and Associates, a leading educational software manufacturer, first studied the packaging of software back in 1979, she noted that most of it was in the form of plastic bags hanging on hooks in the store. Since she was an educator herself, she wanted her software to be more closely associated with books and education. So to differentiate her product at the retail level, she packaged it in binders that looked like colorful books on a shelf. That idea caught on, and today software is packaged in boxes that resemble books on a shelf. No one could have guessed in 1979 that today software would also be sold in bookstores. For another packaging example, see "Multimedia CD-ROM: The Packaging Dilemma."

Industrial products generally require packaging that is more utilitarian. The design doesn't need to attract attention because the packaging merely makes it more convenient to transport the product. Consequently, industrial packaging typically consists of brown boxes with bold, colored lettering to identify the contents and the manufacturer.

With products that are marketed globally, packaging may take on an even greater level of importance, not for shipping purposes but because in some countries—notably Japan—a premium is placed on the artistic design of the package, and customers are even willing to pay more for a beautiful box.

Just like the product, the packaging must be designed and tested for consumer response and distribution channel response. It should serve the functions for which it was designed. In general, packaging should

▶ Tell what the product is— this can range from product features to directions for use, ingredients, remedies for misuse, level of quality, and warranty information.

▶ Its key benefits to the customer—convenience, price, quality, features, and so on.

▶ The company philosophy—for example, "Our customers come first with us."

▶ In consumer products, be distinctive and attractive enough that customers can recognize the company's products from the package design alone without having to read anything.

▶ Use safe and recyclable materials wherever possible.

The Real World of Entrepreneurship

Multimedia CD-ROM: The Packaging Dilemma

Now that the distribution channels for CD-ROM titles have expanded to include not only software retailers but audio outlets, bookstores, and video stores, producers are challenged to create a packaging image that works well in all of these channels. Because the market is relatively young and small, multimedia titles don't enjoy the same type of advertising music CDs and videos do: full-page ads in magazines, movie trailers, and commercials. Therefore, the design on the box is the same one that appears in catalogs, only much smaller.

It's expected that the strict standards that now apply to packaging in the CD audio and video markets will soon extend to CD-ROM titles, creating a situation where packaging may need to vary depending on the outlet in which it's being sold. In any case, all media packaging must conform to industry standards so that it fits shipping cases and pallets, as well as store fixtures used to display the products. Producers of CD-ROM titles should design their packaging with the following in mind:

▶ The title and publisher should be in bold print on the front of the package.

▶ Primary colors or black should be used on packaging to attract attention.

▶ Subtitles must not confuse the customer.

▶ The packaging should have a consistent look so that the company and its image are readily identified on retail shelves.

▶ It has been estimated that a CD-ROM publisher has about 20 seconds of customers' time to grab their attention and encourage them to take the box off the shelf and read about the product. That's the importance of packaging today.

Package design is something that will require the services of a professional, which is not an inexpensive undertaking. However, many business owners can testify to the fact that good packaging sells product. Seckinger-Lee, an Atlanta gourmet cookie biscuit company, found it was losing sales because its customers, major retailers such as Saks and Neiman-Marcus, thought its packaging was too severe and its color scheme wasn't compatible with the gift item departments of their stores. Seckinger-Lee hired a design firm, spending $250,000 in the process, and was rewarded with a new look that gave it a 50 percent increase over the previous year at the fancy-food trade shows in Atlanta and New York. And, after 10 years of attempting to get its product into Macy's, it finally succeeded.[5]

Good design is rewarded by increased sales and also by the industry. Likewise, poor design receives its share of attention in the press as well. A classic example is L'eggs pantyhose. It received much criticism for its plastic egg used as the container for the hose. Nevertheless, the manufacturer refused to change the package by which it was recognized everywhere. By contrast, the original packaging of audio CDs (the plastic jewel box in a cardboard container twice the size of the CD) was changed due to consumer and distributor protest over excessive packaging.

The bottom line is that beautiful packaging cannot take the place of a quality product. It may grab the attention of the customer more quickly, but unless the customer finds satisfaction with the product inside, there will be no repeat sales—the most valuable part of a continuing customer relationship.

Understanding Pricing

Price is one of the most important features of a product. No matter how good the product or service is, no matter how attractive the packaging, it must be priced right to sell in sufficient quantities. The final arbiters of the price are customers, whose perception of quality determines the value of the product. But there are other determinants of price as well:

▶ *The demand for the product is strong relative to the supply.* Where demand is greater than supply, a higher price may be commanded.

The Real World of Entrepreneurship

Be Careful About What Is Labeled Recyclable

The Federal Trade Commission has issued guidelines for the use of environmental terms in advertising and product labeling. For example, a product can be labeled **recyclable** only if the entire product can be collected or separated from solid waste and used in the manufacture of other products. A product may be labeled **recycled content** if the recycled materials in the product came from a solid waste stream. Materials recycled from manufacturing and those from consumer waste must be distinguished by weight. To use the terms *degradable, biodegradable,* and *photodegradable,* there must be evidence that the product will completely break down and return to nature in a relatively short period of time. Otherwise, the label must qualify how degradable it really is.

▶ *The demand for the product is inelastic*; that is, people will buy no matter what the price because they need the product. This is typically true for commodities with no viable substitute, such as milk.

▶ *Intense competition* may force the price of the product down.

▶ *Additional features* may warrant a higher price.

▶ *New technology* may call for a higher price initially until the technology becomes more commonplace.

▶ *Product positioning* may be associated with a certain price level. For example, positioning a product among luxury items commands a higher price.

Pricing Policy

Before determining how to price the product or service, it's important that the company have a long-term pricing policy that takes into account both the level of sales the company wants to achieve and the profit margin it seeks. Companies often focus on price per unit of product produced, but total profit determines whether or not the company stays in business. Pricing presents problems when firms don't get enough information from customers, when they rely on comparing current orders with past orders, and when they have inadequate systems for calculating accurate costs. Therefore, having long-term goals in a pricing policy is critical to successful pricing, and customizing that pricing to reflect information from customers is essential. Long-term goals are typically statements of position in the market and give a marketing plan focus. Some examples of long-term pricing policies include

▶ Become the lowest-priced supplier in the industry

▶ Create the widest price range

▶ Maximize penetration of a market

▶ Create price leadership in the industry

▶ Position the company in a specific market segment

▶ Obtain a specific share of the market

Once the policy is in place, it's necessary to establish strategies to achieve the policy goals.

Strategies for Pricing

Pricing becomes a feature of the product when it's the central selling point. The product that is considered a commodity or the product that faces intense competition often will be pushed on the basis of lower price for the same quality. How a product is priced, however, is really a function of a company's

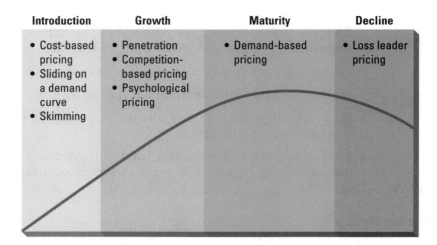

Figure 11.4
Pricing Strategies

Introduction	Growth	Maturity	Decline
• Cost-based pricing • Sliding on a demand curve • Skimming	• Penetration • Competition-based pricing • Psychological pricing	• Demand-based pricing	• Loss leader pricing

goals. Following are some possible goals and pricing strategies to achieve them:

▶ *Increase sales.* This may entail lowering prices to increase the volume sold.

▶ *Increase market share.* Lowering prices may increase volume, thus increasing market share.

▶ *Maximize cash flow.* Cash flow can be increased through a number of methods, including raising prices and reducing direct costs and overhead.

▶ *Maximize profit.* Similar to maximizing cash flow, this can be accomplished through several methods, including raising prices, lowering prices and increasing volume, or decreasing overhead.

▶ *Set up entry barriers to competition.* Lowering prices based on using efficient production methods, achieving economies of scale, and keeping overhead low often can set up entry barriers to companies that can't compete on that scale.

▶ *Define an image.* Setting a higher price based on higher perceived quality will help to enhance image.

▶ *Control demand.* A company that does not have the resources to meet demand can set prices higher to control demand.

Knowing what a pricing strategy is supposed to accomplish in advance of setting a price will ensure compatibility with the company's goals.

Companies use several pricing strategies at various stages of the business life cycle as well as the product life cycle (see Figure 11.4). Whichever strategy is chosen, it is important to understand what customers are willing to pay based on the perceived value of the product.

1. **Cost-based pricing.** This strategy adds together the cost of producing the product, the related costs of running the business, and a profit margin to arrive at a market price and is really the basis for all pricing decisions. In addition, a pricing strategy will need to consider the competition's prices and market demand. The channel of distribution through which the entrepreneur chooses to move the product will also affect the ultimate price to the customer, as each intermediary must be allowed to make a certain percentage of profit.

2. **Sliding on the demand curve.** With this strategy, the product is introduced at a high price; then, as technological improvements enable the company to reduce its costs, the price is reduced. In this way, the company can maintain a price advantage over competitors. This is a common strategy in the electronics market and is a variation of the skimming strategy.

3. **Skimming.** When the company has a product that no one else has or one that is significantly better than others in the market, it can enter the market at a high price until other companies begin to compete, forcing the price down. The initial higher price is used to recoup the development and promotional costs.

4. **Penetration.** Where a highly competitive market has similar products, the company needs to gain quick acceptance and broad-based distribution. To accomplish this, it needs to introduce the product at a much lower price with minimal profit. Once the product gains sufficient market share, the price is gradually raised to match the competitive market. This strategy is quite costly, as it entails extensive advertising and promotion for immediate product awareness. Low-priced goods are often introduced in this manner.

5. **Competition-based pricing.** As the company is growing and where the product has direct competition, the company can look at competitors' pricing strategies and price the product in line with theirs, higher if it is determined that the product has added value, or lower if competing on price.

 The Real World of Entrepreneurship

Warning Signs of Pricing Problems

If the company is regularly doing any of the following in its pricing strategies, it could face problems over time:

- Prices are always based on costs.
- Different people in the organization set prices with no agreement among them.
- Prices always follow the competition.
- New prices are generally a percentage increase over the previous year's prices.
- Prices to all customers are the same.
- Discounts are standardized.

Like any other aspect of a world-class company, pricing strategies are subject to change in response to fluctuations in the market and certainly feedback from customers. Failing to modify or revise a pricing strategy in response to these changes can cost the company valuable customers and significant profits.

6. **Psychological pricing.** Using an odd-even strategy can suggest a pricing position in the market: an odd number ($12.99) to suggest a bargain, an even number ($40.00) to suggest quality, or higher-than-average pricing to suggest exclusivity.

7. **Demand-based pricing.** This strategy is based on finding out what customers are willing to pay for the product, then pricing it accordingly. For new products for which there is no direct comparison, a combination of this approach and cost-based pricing often is used to arrive at a satisfactory price. In general, customers recognize several prices for any one product: the standard price, the price normally paid for the item; the sale price, the price paid for specials; and the relative price, the price of the item compared to a substitute product. For some products, customers may have to add to the normal cost of shipping, handling, or installation in their comparison with other, like products. With this strategy, price starts high and moves down gradually as demand is attracted at each price level.

8. **Loss leader pricing.** This is pricing below cost to attract customers to other products in your line because the original product no longer has value.

Building Relationships and Repeat Sales Through Promotion

The promotional plan establishes the identity and vision of the company that will be conveyed through all of its marketing efforts from advertising to public relations. Recall from Chapter 7 that vision is the fundamental belief in what the company aspires to be and is composed of the company's core values, mission, and purpose.[6] Identity and vision are quite different from image. An *image* is what the company wants the public to perceive it as being, whereas the company's character and vision define what it is in reality. A company that seeks to build lifelong customer relationships will stay away from image-creating techniques and focus instead on vision-conveying techniques. With this in mind, the promotional plan for growing the business is one the company will implement and use consistently for the long term. It's the plan in which the company invests to build a strong and loyal customer base.

The promotion function of the marketing strategy is the creative one, for this is where guerrilla advertising, publicity, sales promotion, and personal selling tactics—in short, the promotional mix—will be decided (see Figure 11.5). Not every company has the same promotional mix; it is a function of the type of business, the mission, the target market, and, of course, the budget. For entrepreneurs with new or growing ventures, the last item, the budget, dictates that they must be very creative in their promotional mix and strategy because normally their resources are very limited. Entrepreneurs have used several strategies to estimate how much money they will need to set aside in their budgets for promoting their businesses. These include

▶ *Using a percentage of sales.* If the companies in your industry typically spend about 5 percent of their sales on the promotion effort, that becomes a benchmark figure for your company.

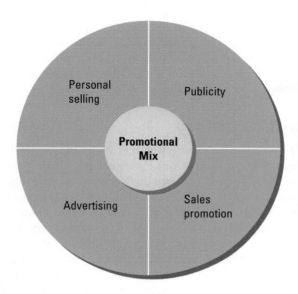

Figure 11.5
The Promotional Mix

▶ *Keeping up with the competitors.* You may decide to mimic the promotional mix of your competitors and spend what they spend.

▶ *Calculating what you will need to achieve your goals.* Some products and services require more promotion than others to create awareness. You will need to determine the most effective promotional tools available to you within the budget your company can afford and still take care of its other obligations.

Promotional creativity begins with a clear understanding of the customer, the economy, current trends, and even the daily news, because a creative idea for promotion can come from anywhere, including a current event. Today social responsibility is a big issue; hence the proliferation of ads, such as those of Mobil Oil, that depict a company that cares about people and natural resources. In fact, the ad may never mention the product it is trying to sell. Tying a marketing strategy to current trends such as social responsibility means the company must remain flexible and willing to change the strategy if the current trend changes. Customers are fickle, and no matter how sound or beneficial a trend may be, they will eventually tire of it, and a new strategy must be employed.

Promotion is also the way entrepreneurs convey their dedication to total quality and the highest levels of customer satisfaction. Recall the three themes in this book:

▶ A customer-centered business

▶ A dedication to superior quality throughout the business

▶ An integrated focus

A good promotional mix will incorporate the input of everyone in the organization to create an integrated plan. It should convey the dedication to superior quality in the types of promotion that are chosen and the way they are carried out. And all promotion should focus on the benefit to the customer of doing business with your company.

Advertising to Reach Customers

Companies advertise to create product awareness (product advertising) or company awareness (institutional advertising). It is impossible for a small-business owner to escape advertising because it is present everywhere, from the sign announcing your store or office to the salesperson or receptionist who greets the customer. Good advertising will attract the right customers and build a good company image. If done effectively, it will increase sales. But advertising cannot guarantee sales if the product or service doesn't have value for the customer or create continued sales if the company doesn't follow up with customers to ensure they are satisfied.

Whether you choose to use a guerrilla marketing approach to do the ads yourself or hire an ad agency, make sure all your ads do four things:

1. Target the correct audience

2. Present a positive picture

The Real World of Entrepreneurship

What About a Celebrity Endorsement?

Most growing entrepreneurial companies rarely consider celebrity endorsements because they bring to mind sports figures such as Michael Jordan and multimillion-dollar contracts that are beyond their budgets. But not all valuable celebrity endorsements are found in Hollywood or the sports world. Often a company can get a lot of press from a local celebrity or someone who is known for something. For example, Dee Pickett is a champion roper who promotes the products of tiny Callaway Ropes in Texas.[7]

There are several ways to begin the search for and acquisition of a celebrity endorsement:

1. Begin by contacting an ad agency or a public relations firm, which will add its fee to that of the celebrity. An alternative is to call a network, magazine, or newspaper to find out who a celebrity's agent is.

2. Choose a celebrity whose personality fits the product, and check out his or her reputation.

3. Find innovative ways to pay for the celebrity. For example, Dee Pickett is given all his rope supplies plus a fee paid in monthly installments.

4. Make certain that the endorser really uses the product; otherwise, the company is setting itself up for embarrassing and unwanted publicity. The Federal Trade Commission's testimonials guidebook states: "Endorsements must always reflect the honest opinions, findings, beliefs, or experiences of the endorser. . . . In particular, where the advertisement represents that the endorser uses the endorsed product, then the endorser must have been a bona fide user of it at the time the endorsement was given."

Check the end-of-chapter resources for additional information on celebrity endorsements.

3. Reflect the vision and culture of the company

4. Ask for the sale

There are three general choices of media for advertising: print media, broadcast media, and miscellaneous media. The choice of which to use will depend on the type of business you have and what is typically done in your industry. Where your customer usually looks to find out about products and services such as yours is where you need to put your advertising efforts. Look at the media comparison chart on pages 312–313 (Table 11.2) to get a feel for the options available to your business. Marketing on the Internet is a rapidly growing segment of advertising available to small businesses; this topic is discussed in Chapter 12.

This section has provided just a few of the hundreds of tips and techniques available to entrepreneurs who wish to advertise products or services in the most efficient and effective ways while the new venture is growing. The series of books on guerrilla marketing by Jay Conrad Levinson is highly recommended for its marketing suggestions geared specifically to young, growing companies.

 The Real World of Entrepreneurship

Tips for Getting Your Company Noticed

Here are five low-cost ways to win the attention of potential customers and put your company in the limelight:

1. *Create a special event that your company sponsors.* Silverado Furniture Company in Napa, California, stages a "Business After Hours" event to help raise money for the local chamber of commerce. The benefit to Silverado is that it gets to showcase its latest products to the more than 300 professionals who attend the event. This creates leads for its salespeople.

2. *Become an expert in your field.* Sandra Beckwith wanted to gain national recognition for her public relations firm in Rochester, New York. So she wrote a newsletter for women that took a "lighthearted" look at male behavior and called it *The Do(o)little Report.* She sent the first issue to 400 media outlets and got mentions in *USA Today* and *The Wall Street Journal,* among others.

3. *Give products away, especially to celebrities.* Recall entrepreneur Gregg Levin (Young Entrepreneurs—Minicase in Chapter 7), who sent cases of his PerfectCurve® device to professional baseball teams. He knew the media do many interviews with cameras in the locker room where baseball players park their caps on the PerfectCurve® to keep the bills curved.

4. *Offer free information.* It doesn't take much money to create and offer a free pamphlet giving tips to customers that will help them use your products and services better. Or go online with a free newsletter, as Azriela Jaffe did. In fact, she uses two newsletters to help her clients and gain attention for her business, *The Entrepreneurial Couples Success Letter* and *The Best Ideas in Business.* She also created a web site for her company, Anchored Dreams, at http://www.isquare.com/crlink.htm.

5. *Be the first to do it.* Metropolis Baker Café was the first coffeehouse in Twin Falls, Idaho, in 1992. Even though more than six coffeehouses now serve the tiny town of 32,000 residents, the Met continues to break new ground with such innovations as live entertainment, a fax mailing list, and an online cyber-café with links to other coffeehouses worldwide.

SOURCE: Julie Fanselow, "Budget PR," *Business 96,* October/November 1996, p. 48.

Table 11.2   Media Comparison Chart

Media	Advantages	Disadvantages	Hints
Print Media			
Newspapers	▸ Broad coverage in a selected geographic area ▸ Flexibility and speed in bringing to print and modifying ▸ Generates sales quickly ▸ Costs relatively little	▸ May reach more than target market ▸ Difficult to attract reader attention ▸ Short life	▸ Look for specialized newspapers for better targeting ▸ Include a coupon or 800 number ▸ Locate ad on right-hand page above the fold
Magazines	▸ Can target special interests ▸ More credible than newspapers	▸ Expensive to design, produce, and place	▸ Look for regional editions ▸ Use a media-buying service ▸ Use color effectively ▸ Check on "remnant space," leftover space that must be filled before magazine goes to print
Direct marketing (direct mail, mail order, coupons, telemarketing	▸ Lets you close the sale when the advertising takes place ▸ Coverage of wide geographic area ▸ Targets specific customers ▸ More sales with fewer dollars ▸ More information provided ▸ Highest response rate	▸ Not all products suitable. Need consumable products for repeat orders ▸ Response rate on new catalogs is very low, about 2%	▸ Create a personalized mailing list and database from responses ▸ Use several repeat mailings to increase the response rate ▸ Entice customers to open the envelope
Yellow pages	▸ Good in the early stages for awareness ▸ Good for retail/service	▸ Relatively expensive ▸ Targets only local market	▸ Create ad that stands out on the page
Signs	▸ Inexpensive ▸ Encourage impulse buying	▸ Outlive their usefulness fairly quickly	▸ Don't leave sale signs in windows too long; people will no longer see them
Broadcast Media			
Radio	▸ Good for local or regional advertising	▸ Can't be a one-shot ad, must do several	▸ Advertise on more than one station to saturate market ▸ Sponsor a national radio program ▸ Provide the station with finished recorded comercials ▸ Stick to 30-second ads with music
Television	▸ Second most popular form of advertising ▸ People can see and hear about product/service ▸ Can target at national, regional, or local level	▸ Very expensive for both production and on-air time ▸ Must be repeated frequently	▸ Time based on GRP (gross rating points). Range is $5–$500 per GRP. Use only if you can purchase 150 GRPs per month for three months. ▸ Seek help of media-buying service

Media	Advantages	Disadvantages	Hints
Cable TV shopping	▶ Good for new customer products ▶ Targets the consumer ▶ Good products sell out in minutes	▶ Not a long-term strategy ▶ Good only for products between $15 and $50 ▶ Product must be demonstrable	▶ Call network for vendor information kit ▶ Contact buyer for your product category ▶ Be prepared to fill an initial order of between 1,000 and 5,000 units
Infomercial	▶ Good for consumer items that can't be explained quickly	▶ Very expensive to produce ▶ Hit rate is about 10%	▶ Most profitable times are late nights, mornings, and Saturday and Sunday during the day ▶ Test time slots and markets to confirm effectiveness
Miscellaneous			
Affinity items (T-shirts, caps, mugs) Searchlights, Couponing, In-store demonstrations, Videotapes, Free seminars	▶ Good for grabbing consumer's attention ▶ Effective, yet inexpensive, way to showcase the company	▶ Value varies significantly with type of business and product or service	▶ Every company should make use of affinity items to create free publicity

Publicity and Public Relations

Publicity is essentially free advertising for a product or business through newspaper articles and radio and television stories and talk shows. **Public relations,** on the other hand, is the strategy for presenting the company and its philosophy to the public. Publicity is one of the best entrepreneurial marketing tools there is, because it gets attention and it's free.

The key to successful publicity is having a product or business that is newsworthy, in other words, unique in some aspect. For example, the product may be environmentally friendly, whereas the competitor's is not. Or the way the company was founded may be a newsworthy story. Companies such as Ben & Jerry's Homemade and Body Shop International have received millions of dollars' worth of free publicity because they have interesting stories and socially responsible messages. If the business or product is newsworthy, there are several ways to get some publicity. You can write to a reporter or editor to test an idea, then follow up with a phone call. You can also issue a press release answering the who, what, where, when, and why of the business and include a press kit containing the press release, bios, photos of the key people in the story, any necessary background information, and copies of any other articles written about the company. The key to success in receiving publicity is to make it as easy as possible for the reporter to write or tell the story. When an article is written about the business, the company should use reprints in future advertising and brochures to get even more value for the effort.

Whenever possible, the entrepreneur and the team should get to know people in the media on a first-name basis, perhaps even take them to lunch. This will give the company instant clout when it needs free publicity. The media are always looking for news and will appreciate the effort to give them something newsworthy.

Several publishing services also can be used to distribute information about the business. The *Contact Sheet*, a monthly publication, prints news releases written and paid for by companies. It is sent to more than 1,800 editors and reporters nationally who have free use of the material. Another publication is the *PR Newsletter*, a membership electronic service that also assists companies in writing messages targeted to a specific media audience.

Tracking Customers

For relationship marketing to work, the company needs individual information from transaction data. Instead of mass surveys, entrepreneurial companies need to run experiments.[8] For example, a mail-order company may be looking to find out if

1. The $19.95 price point is more effective in terms of number of sales than a $29.95 price point.

2. What the "look" of the mail order catalog should be: full color? a mix? a lot of information? a minimal amount?

3. Who responds best to a mailing: current customers? new customers? working women?

By testing several versions on various types of customers and measuring the results, the company can learn a lot about who its long-term customers will be. The secret to success is long-term tracking of individual customer preferences and buying habits so that future mailings can be better aligned to that customer's needs. American Express learned, after suffering substantial losses with its merchandise services division, that it had to shift to a "share of customer" approach, in other words, move away from selling products to managing customers and relationships.[9] To do this required shifting the product sales focus to rewarding salespeople for customer loyalty—repeat sales. Rather than concentrating on a portfolio of products, it began concentrating on a portfolio of customers for whom it could provide a variety of products and services.

In traditional marketing, customer feedback was commonly obtained through warranty registration, service plans, and company questionnaires. But to successfully implement relationship marketing requires a dialogue with the customer over time. It cannot be a one-shot deal today because customers basically see marketers as the adversary. Customers don't believe marketers have their best interests at heart—and they are probably right when it comes to traditional marketing. Furthermore, customers have endured this

Carole Ziter of Sweet Energy of Colchester, Vermont has learned the magic of relationship marketing. By carefully tracking the needs and desires of the customers for her mail-order dried fruit business, she can offer them things she knows they want. And she can even personalize messages to them. This strategy has paid off in a loyal customer list that is the biggest asset of her business. (Alan Jakubek)

type of marketing for so long that they are typically resistant and suspicious of a company's initial efforts to establish a "relationship." Consequently, Don Peppers and Martha Rogers recommend several approaches:[10]

◗ Don't try to sell something on every dialogue occasion. The next time the company calls, the customer will expect that and not respond favorably.

◗ Use a voice mail system for feedback. That way the customer can call anytime and voice his or her opinions and complaints.

◗ Consider a bulletin board service or web site where customers can go for free information and that offers incentives for the customer to give the company valuable information.

Establishing a Customer Information File (CIF)

Although the contents of a customer information file (CIF) will vary with the type of business, three broad areas of information are common to every business:[11]

1. *Recency:* When did the customer last make a purchase?

2. *Frequency:* How often does the customer purchase?

3. *Monetary value:* How much does the customer spend on average per purchase, and how much has she or he spent over the last six months or one year?

Of course, a company will want to collect a variety of other information that will help it segment and individualize its customers. Other information it might collect would include

- The customer's name, telephone, and address
- In the case of a business customer, who the principal decision maker is
- For consumer products and services, the composition of the household
- The date of first purchase and all subsequent purchases
- A projection for when the next purchase will take place
- Where the purchase was made and how
- Any purchases returned and why
- Method of payment and debt history
- Types of promotions and dates promotions were mailed to the customer
- Personal information gathered through dialoguing
- Complaints and resolution
- Perceptions of the company and its products/services
- Perceptions of competitors
- Assumptions the company makes about the customer from correlations in the database (e.g., pattern of purchasing gifts—will probably make a purchase for Mother's Day)

 Entrepreneurship in Action

From Products to Solutions: How One Company Gave Its Customers Added Value

Famous Fixtures is a small company in Wisconsin that supplies Wal-Mart with shelving. In an effort to monitor customer satisfaction, Famous Fixtures took its sales team (representatives from sales, engineering, production, and customer service) to Bentonville, Arkansas, home of the giant retailer, to meet with company executives.

During the course of the discussion, Wal-Mart executives related a problem they were having that had nothing to do with shelving. It seems they were having difficulty distributing a variety of manufacturers' store displays to the company's various locations and light-heartedly asked if Famous Fixtures could solve that problem! Famous Fixtures wasted no time and actually did solve it, proving the importance and value of focusing on getting more business out of the customers you already have. In fact, Famous Fixtures' salespeople don't take catalogs into the field anymore to show what the company carries. They figure they will supply the customer with whatever is needed from wherever they can get it.

Source: Laura M. Litvan, "Increasing Revenue with Repeat Sales," *Nation's Business,* January 1996, p. 36.

Collecting Information for Durable Goods

Durable goods—cars, appliances, major electronics—involve more time on the part of the customer and the salesperson, so there is more opportunity to gather valuable personal information on the customer's requirements during the sale and at point of sale. In addition, these products normally carry a warranty and/or service agreement, a club membership, or an application, all of which set up another opportunity to get input from the customer. The important point to remember is that multiple chances for contact with the customer will always produce better information because the customer is less suspicious of the company's motives and more likely to be agreeable to building a relationship with the company based on trust.

Collecting Information for Consumer Packaged Goods

Consumer goods is the more difficult arena in which to capture customer information because buying decisions are often made quickly and without a lot of careful thought or attention. Some techniques that have worked well for growing companies are the following:

- *Coupons.* Asking customers to put a name and address on a coupon they are redeeming for a purchase discount gives the company a way to contact the customer in the future with additional offers and also starts a file of the customer's preferences and buying habits. It's important that the company use a coupon clearinghouse that will validate the coupons and return them to the company to be entered into the CIF.

- *Affinity merchandise.* **Affinity merchandise** is items imprinted with the company's name, logo, and perhaps advertising, such as caps, T-shirts, pens, and so forth. It can reasonably be assumed that if the customer purchases or receives from the company as a reward an affinity item and uses it, the customer wants to be associated with that company; it is almost like an endorsement.

- *Contest applications.* These provide an opportunity to get more information from a willing customer who hopes such cooperation will increase his or her chances of winning the contest.

- *Store credit cards and membership clubs.* These provide an easy way to gather valuable customer information, again from a willing customer.

Royal Caribbean Cruise Lines keeps records of its customers and offers benefits to repeat cruisers in the form of affinity merchandise and a special reception hosted by the captain.

Collecting Information from Service Company Customers

Every company provides service to its customers, and some companies provide only services. In both cases, it's equally important to gather feedback

Table 11.3   12 Ways to Listen to the Customer

Focus groups of customers	Customer panels that meet regularly to provide input to the company
In-person interviews	Visits to customers (i.e., distributors, retailers)
Observing customers using product in natural setting	Customer tours of company facilities
Talking to customers at trade shows	Toll-free numbers to allow customers to give input
Telephone or mail surveys	Mystery shoppers who check on how customers are treated by company personnel
Customer exit interviews when you lose a customer	Customer service hotline where customers can get answers and problems solved quickly

from customers on how the service was rendered and whether or not the customer was satisfied. To most effectively gather information that will help the company determine exactly what its customers' needs are and where in the service process it can improve, it's important to identify the key points in the process where satisfaction of the customer is affected. These may be points of interaction with the customer or points where delays or problems could affect the quality of the outcome for the customer. Three such points are

▶ How the company handled a failure in the system

▶ How the company handled a customer's special request

▶ How employees responded under a variety of conditions

For additional suggestions on getting information from customers, see Table 11.3.

Identifying and Rewarding the Best Customers

It is totally unrealistic to think that a company will be able to build long-term relationships with all of its customers, especially if the number of those customers starts heading into the thousands and beyond. It is realistic, though, to search the company's customer base for the most valuable customers, those that warrant in-depth relationships. Who are those customers? Simply stated, they are the customers who account for the biggest percentage of the company's revenues. It is not uncommon for a company to find that as few as 24 percent of its customers account for 95 percent of its revenues. These are the customers the company needs to know well, and these are the customers it needs to keep happy. By the same token, the company should also identify the worst customers and get rid of them because they are wasting the company's time and money, and they will never be valuable customers. These are the customers who have a bad debt history with the company and buy so infrequently and in so little volume that it actually costs the company money to retain them.

After a company has been in business awhile, it becomes easier to identify the most valuable customers. One way is to calculate the lifetime customer value based on viewing the customer as a series of transactions over the life of the relationship.[12] A statistical method for doing this involves calculating the present value of future purchases using an appropriate discount rate and period of time for the relationship. Add to that the value of customer referrals, and subtract the cost of maintaining the relationship (advertising, promotions, letters, questionnaires, 800 numbers.) The result will be the customer's lifetime value. Another nonstatistical method is to simply dialogue with the customer and ask what his or her intentions are. The better the company knows the customer, the more valuable and reliable the information will be.

Companies can do a variety of things to provide special programs, incentives, and rewards for its best customers. The following sections discuss some of these approaches.

Frequency Programs

The airlines have used **frequency programs** with great success. Those who fly the most frequently with the airlines receive the most benefits in terms of free tickets, VIP service, and upgrades. Rewards increase with use; therefore, the customer has a vested interest in using that airline for all of his or her traveling.

Frequency programs have been used successfully with all types of businesses. Cosmetic companies, for example, have issued cards to customers that give them a free product after a certain number of product purchases. Similarly, small entertainment centers such as miniature golf facilities and water parks often offer discounts for season passes to customers who use the service the most.

Setting up a club or membership makes customers feel special, as though they have input into the company and receive special privileges for being a member, for example, informational newsletters, discounts, and other special programs. Young, upstart auto manufacturer Saturn invites its customers to pick up their new cars at the factory and meet the people who made them. Some companies offer next-day delivery free of charge to their best customers as well as access to a special, unlisted 800 number.[13]

Frequency programs derive their benefit from repeat purchases. The more a customer buys from a company (assuming satisfaction), the higher the probability they will buy repeatedly and the lower the cost to the company of each repeat purchase. In a one-to-one relationship approach, it's vital to single out the best customers for special treatment.

Just-in-Time Marketing

Keeping track of important dates for customers gives the company an opportunity to contact the customer on a special occasion such as a birthday, to remind the customer of his or her need to repurchase something, or to notify a customer of an impending sale of an item she or he typically buys. This approach is known as **just-in-time marketing**. Chris Zane of Zane's Cycles in

New Haven, Connecticut, became the most successful bicycle shop in the area by using one-to-one techniques. He availed himself of just-in-time marketing when he heard that another local shop was going out of business and the owner was leaving the area. He arranged with the phone company, for a small fee, to forward all calls going to the defunct business to his shop. In that way, the customers of the defunct business were directed to a new source for their cycling needs. He also bets on customer relationships by offering lifetime service on every bicycle he sells.[14]

Complaint Marketing

Recall the statement earlier that a dissatisfied customer will probably tell at least nine other people about the problem he or she faced with the company. And, of course, those nine people will tell their friends as well. It's easy to see how quickly one dissatisfied customer can destroy a company's reputation. Consequently, the company ought to think of complaints not as something to avoid dealing with but as opportunities for continual improvement. It should be easy for customers to make a complaint, and they should be able to carry on a dialogue with a human being who listens and attempts to understand. Nothing is more frustrating than to have to leave a complaint on a voice mail message. Pizza Hut provides an 800 number for customers. When a customer calls in to complain, he or she talks to a trained rep (Pizza Hut contracts this service out), who then communicates the nature of the complaint via computer to the manager of the appropriate store. That manager is then required to call the customer within 48 hours and resolve the issue.[15]

Some companies have used bulletin board services on the Internet to let customers communicate their complaints. Though effective, you should be prepared to handle more complaints by this method than by other methods. Companies using bulletin boards have found this system works almost *too* well, because customers communicating by computer feel freer to vent their frustrations more vociferously than when they are greeted with a soothing, caring voice on the other end of a phone line. And because anyone with access to the Internet can read these diatribes, a strong complaint can build momentum and create more problems than necessary.

One way to stem complaints at the source is to provide satisfaction surveys at every point of contact with the customer so the company can find any problems quickly and early before the customer becomes so angry that resolution and satisfaction will be nearly impossible. Following are several suggestions for effective complaint handling:[16]

▶ Recognize that the customer is a human being and treat him or her as such—never as a number, as someone without a name or feelings.

▶ Let the customer explain the complaint completely without interruption. In this way, the company is acknowledging that the complaint is important to it and worthy of attention.

▶ To find out what the customer really wants, ask the most important question: *What is one thing we can do to make this better?*

Table 11.4   The Cost of Losing Customers

Accounts lost	2,000	167 accounts every month
	x 1,200	Average revenue per account
	$2,400,000	Total lost revenue for the year
Profit lost	x .12	Profit margin
	$280,000	Total lost profit
Account closing costs	$20	Per account
	x 2,000	Number of closed accounts
	$40,000	Total costs to close accounts
Total costs	$280,000	Total profit lost
	+ 40,000	Closing costs
	$320,000	**Annual cost of losing customers**

▶ Diffuse the customer's anger by sincerely taking his or her side on the issue and then moving the customer from a problem focus to a solution focus. Get the customer to agree on a solution.

Contact the customer one week later to see if she or he is still satisfied with the solution, and express the company's desire for a continued relationship.

Maintaining Customer Relationships for Life

Customers stop buying from a company for a variety of reasons, including (1) dissatisfaction with aspects of the product or service, (2) ineffective complaint handling, or (3) a more competitive offer from another company, (4) changes in product, service, or personnel that the customer doesn't like. If a company that has an annual defection rate of 10 percent cuts that rate in half, the average lifetime of a customer relationship will double from 10 to 20 years and profits on that customer will increase from $300 to $525.[17] In her book *Serving Them Right*, Laura Liswood calculated the cost of losing customers.[18] Table 11.4 depicts a scenario based on her work where a company has lost 2,000 accounts in a year.

It should be clear from the table that losing customers is serious business for a company. Retaining customers, by contrast, can be very profitable for two reasons. First, over time the operating costs related to that customer decline in relation to increased purchasing on the customer's part. Second, in addition to base profit, the company earns profit from referrals, larger and more frequent purchases, reduced servicing costs, and price premiums.[19] Just as in production the goal is zero defects, in marketing the goal is *zero defections*.

Customer Satisfaction Programs

The success of any program to build lifelong customer relationships is totally dependent on the quality of communication between the customer and the company. The customer must feel that everyone from all levels of the organization is committed to customer satisfaction and quality. To achieve this, the company must establish companywide quality goals and policies, develop plans to achieve those goals, establish controls to evaluate progress, and provide incentives to management and employees to meet the goals. Inputs about the level of quality and service the company is providing will come from customer satisfaction surveys, management's perceptions of customer satisfaction, audits by mystery shoppers and customers, and observations during customer visits to the company.[20] Frequently observation is the only way to learn what the customer is really experiencing, because typically the customer will just suffer silently and not report the problem to the company. Certainly an excellent example is the problems consumers have with plastic bags in grocery stores; they are extraordinarily difficult to open. The frustration of customers dealing with these bags can be observed any time of day or night. Solutions such as Post-it® notes emerged from observing how people make notes to themselves.

Researchers at Texas A&M University developed five dimensions to describe a customer's experience with service quality.[21] They are summarized in the acronym *RATER* (see Figure 11.6):

Reliability—how dependably and accurately does the company provide what the customer wants?

Assurance—how knowledgeable and courteous are employees, and do they convey trust and confidence?

Tangibles—what is the appearance of physical facilities, equipment, and employees?

Empathy—how much individual attention is paid to customers?

Responsiveness—how willing is the company to help customers and provide prompt service?

Entrepreneurship in Action

How Giordano Listened to Customers[22]

Giordano is one of the fastest-growing retailers in the Pacific Rim, but in 1993 it experienced losses of more than $15 million in China. Its new chairperson, Peter Lau, determined to turn things around by focusing on customers. Here is what he did:

▶ He conducted customer surveys twice a year and used the data to improve all aspects of the company.

▶ In Hong Kong, he took a real chance running an ad in the newspaper that asked for complaints and offered a free T-shirt for doing so. He received 40,000 responses.

▶ Customers complained that sizes were too big for Chinese figures, so he added an extra-small to his T-shirt line.

▶ The conservative Chinese customers also thought the salespeople were too pushy, so he gave the employees lessons on how to deal with different customers.

The result of these and other changes is a company that today is doing more than $450 million with plans for 1,000 stores in China by the end of the decade.

SOURCE: Richard Whiteley and Diane Hessan, *Customer-Centered Growth* (Reading, MA: Addison-Wesley, 1996).

**Figure 11.6
Dimensions of Service Quality**

Service Quality

- Reliability
- Assurance
- Tangibles
- Empathy
- Responsiveness

Winning Back Lost Customers

Dealing with lost customers is a reality in today's volatile marketplace. Some companies (e.g., MCI) do it aggressively, and others merely retain the name of the customer in their files in case they want to contact the customer at some later date. Ending communication with the lost customer is a mistake, however. It is important, if possible, to get an exit interview with the customer, particularly if that customer has been a valuable one. During this brief discussion, the company will learn specifically why the customer is leaving and what it can do to improve its products or services so that this doesn't happen again. Often a positive exit interview leaves the door open for the customer to come back later.

The most important message you can send to your customers through your marketing efforts is that the customer is the most important part of the

The Real World of Entrepreneurship

How Do You Know When You're Really Customer Oriented?

To determine if your company is really customer oriented, marketing expert Don Peppers suggests that you need to ask yourself four questions:

1. *Do you treat different customers differently?* Do you give your best customers special treatment and spend more time and money on them than you do "low-value" customers? Do you treat them differently by customizing your products and services to meet their needs?

2. *Do you create a learning relationship with your customers?* Do you listen to your customers and let them teach you about their needs? For example, Dell Computers begins a learning relationship with its customers by asking what they need a computer to

do for them rather than how powerful a computer they need.

3. *Do you keep your customers?* Never let your customers get away. If they need something you can't supply, be sure you have a network of contacts to whom you can direct them. You want them to think of you as their primary source for whatever they need.

4. *Do you organize around customers?* Creating a learning environment will require organizing your company around the needs of the customer so that specific people are in charge of and responsible for specific customer relationships.

SOURCE: Alan M. Webber and Heath Row, "How You Can Help Them," *Fast Company,* November/December 1997, p. 128.

organization and you will do anything it takes to keep good customers satisfied. Though it's certainly true that a young, growing company needs to build a customer base by continually adding new customers, it will actually reap the greatest returns from investing in the customers it currently has.

The next chapter looks at the expansion of your marketing efforts into specialty markets, global markets, and the Internet.

Cases Relevant to This Chapter

Pelco
Zotos-Stein
French Rags

Issues for Review and Discussion

1. How do *identity* and *vision* differ from *image* in the promotional plan?
2. You have decided to start a business that provides payroll services to mid-market companies in the region. What type of promotional mix would be appropriate, and why? Which one-to-one marketing techniques would work in this situation?
3. Discuss the role of the marketing plan.
4. What is the importance of branding today?
5. Discuss three pricing strategies for growing companies.

Experiencing Entrepreneurship

1. Go into a business establishment and get served, such as dining in a restaurant or purchasing a product, and carefully observe how you are treated. Draw some conclusions as to whether or not this company is customer centered and how it could improve its service.
2. Interview a business owner about his or her marketing plan. Then write a one-paragraph marketing plan statement for that owner.

Resources

Bangs, D. H. (1995). *The Market Planning Guide,* 4th ed. Chicago: Upstart Publishing.

Electronic Retailing. Creative Age Publishing, 1-800-624-4196.

Federal Trade Commission, *Guides Concerning Use of Endorsements and Testimonials in Advertising* (16 CFR Part 255). 202-326-2222. Free.

Home Shopping Network, merchandising department. 813-572-8585.

Hoyer, Wayne D., and Deborah J. MacInnis (1997). *Consumer Behavior.* Boston: Houghton Mifflin.

LeBoeuf, Michael (1989). *How to Win Customers and Keep Them for Life.* Berkeley, CA: Berkeley Books.

Levinson, Jay Conrad (1993). *Guerrilla Marketing.* Boston: Houghton Mifflin.

National Infomercial Marketing Association (NIMA). 202-962-8342. Will refer to both ad agencies and direct marketers.

QVC, vendor relations department. 610-701-1000. Or fax name, company name, and address to 610-701-1356.

Response TV. Advanstart Communications. Provides details of pitching products on home shopping networks. 800-346-0085, ext. 477.

Reynolds, D. (1993). *Crackerjack Positioning: Niche Marketing Strategy for the Entrepreneur.* Tulsa, OK: Atwood Publishing.

Sewell, Carl (1992). *Customers for Life: How to Turn That One-Time Buyer into a Lifetime Customer.* New York: Pocket Books.

The Standard Directory of Advertising Agencies. National Register Publishing. Found in the reference section of the library.

Treacy, Michael, and Fred Wiersema (1995). *The Discipline of Market Leaders: Choose Your Customers, Narrow Your Focus, Dominate Your Market.* Reading, MA: Addison-Wesley.

Zaichowsky, Judith Lynne (1994). *Defending Your Brand Against Imitation.* Westport, CT: Quorum Books.

Internet Resources

AdvertisingAge
http://www.adage.com/
This is the online version of the magazine that focuses on the advertising industry.

American Demographics/Marketing Tools
http://www.marketingtools.com/
This site will help you learn how to target your marketing efforts.

American Marketing Association
http://www.ama.org/
Focuses on the services of this organization.

*Don't forget that it [your product or service]
is not differentiated until the customer
understands the difference.*
Tom Peters
Thriving on Chaos (Knopf, 1987)

Strategic Marketing for Global Growth

Preview

Understanding this chapter will give you the ability to

▶ **Discuss how changing demographics have affected marketing strategy.**

▶ **Explain the role technology plays in marketing strategy.**

▶ **Discuss issues related to global marketing.**

▶ **Discuss the role of distribution as a marketing strategy.**

Terms to Know

Young Entrepreneurs—Minicase

Bryan Rosencrantz
Fitscape

Not all young entrepreneurs who have family businesses in their backgrounds decide to go into the

business when they graduate from college. Even
though to outsiders it would seem like the easy thing
to do, for some people it just doesn't make sense—at
least not right away. Bryan Rosencrantz was raised in
a world of entrepreneurs. Originally from the Portland,

Oregon, area, Rosencrantz grew up around his father's successful real estate development company and his grandfather's steel business, the largest scrap exporter in the United States and the largest steel company in the western United States.

Rosencrantz remembers growing up in and around the family business as a positive experience that gave him a real-life education. "I learned that I didn't want anything handed to me. . . . [Going into the family business] I'd be making a lot of money and probably be happy, but I'm more into accomplishment right now."

Rosencrantz attended the University of Southern California as a business major with an emphasis in entrepreneurship. He was, however, never one to wait for things to happen in an orderly fashion. Before he entered the Entrepreneur Program in the fall of 1995, he had developed a concept for a new business; and before the first semester of a year-long program had ended, he was already in the throes of starting his new business. The business was Fit-Net™, a one-stop Internet shop for fitness enthusiasts where they could get the latest information, buy equipment, products, and services, and check out local gyms. At the time no one had tapped the fitness market on the Internet, and Rosencrantz was determined to get a foothold and brand name recognition before anyone else decided to enter the market. This meant moving quickly to line up key alliances with nationally known gyms, instructors, and big-name fitness gurus such as Lou Ferrigno, former star of "The Incredible Hulk" TV show.

Before the second semester was over in the spring of 1996, Rosencrantz had completed his business plan and had the business up and running on the Internet. It wasn't easy trying to finish college and start a business at the same time. Many times he had to choose between going to class and meeting with a potential client. He always chose the latter, because the business had become the most important thing to

him and his passion to make it a success overtook everything else in his life.

The business had many highs and just as many challenges. Rosencrantz found it relatively easy to form relationships with companies and people in the fitness industry, but not always easy to keep them happy. One challenge was to expand his services so that he could meet all their needs and lessen the chance they would go to someone else to provide the service they needed. Under the umbrella of a new company, Fitscape™, he began offering total Internet service provider (ISP) services, which included web page design for clients' own web sites. One of his major clients is World Gym®, which has many franchisees around the world and was founded by Joe Gold, the original founder of Gold's Gym®. Fitscape developed the web site for the franchisor and is now attracting franchisees to develop their own local sites that are located on the home site. Of course, becoming an ISP entailed significant investment in hardware to give Fitscape's system the capability to handle the demand. World Gym alone received more than 100,000 hits in its first three days of operation.

In 1997, Fitscape also began developing software for a company called Apex Fitness™, which licenses a complete program for health clubs that is essentially a diet and exercise prescription. Apex's products are found in more than 500 clubs around the world, so this arrangement broadened Fitscape's presence in the marketplace.

Rosencrantz admits he was luckier than most young entrepreneurs. He had a big financial safety net from his family, but he still didn't have unlimited funds to do anything he wanted. When he first started the business, the biggest challenge was graduating from the university so he could devote himself full time to the business. Fortunately, since much of the work he had in the USC Entrepreneur Program was related to the business plan for his company, he was able to finish successfully on time. Now "everything is a challenge—getting clients—it's easy to spend money, hard to make it; staffing is difficult and capital requirements are high in technology." Rosencrantz believes success comes in the details. "When you're a young entrepreneur, it's a continual learning process. You are defined by how you deal with your defeats. People get caught up in their successes. Don't let your ego get the best of you. Be open to the learning process."

Bryan Rosencrantz's background taught him to be successful, "but my business and my personal life have taught me the real meaning of success"; to him that is the key to life. "I think I've accomplished something . . . if everything fell apart tomorrow, I'd know I did something."
www.fitscape.com

How can Rosencrantz enhance the global possibilities for his online business?

To this point in our discussion of marketing for small businesses, we have focused on the role the customer plays in your marketing strategy and in the tactics you employ to implement that strategy. But other factors come into play as well. A company attempting to expand its market boundaries domestically and globally must be well grounded in the fundamental market trends that affect any marketing strategy to one degree or another. These trends can be classified into four broad categories: changing demographics, the impact of technology, global marketing, and distribution strategies.

Changing Demographics

Companies that have stayed too long in one market or one region of the country and have not stuck their heads above ground to see what's going on in the rest of the world are often blindsided by rapidly changing demographics in many significant arenas where they will ultimately do business. This section looks at three significant demographic shifts that futurist Barry Minkin, in his book *Future in Sight,* claims will affect the way we live and do business for decades to come.[1]

China

The first of the three demographic shifts is taking place on an international scale. By now many small-business owners have felt the impact of foreign markets because they already sell to these markets, import supplies, manufacture in other countries, or face foreign competitors. But small-business owners need to look into the future and prepare themselves for a market that will include the "sleeping giant": China. China has been called the fastest-growing economy in the world. It is projected that in the first half of the next century, China will become the number one economy, followed by the United States, Japan, and the European Union.[2] Today China is actively seeking foreign technology and equipment and is expected to become the world's largest importer of steel. Its $200-billion-a-year retail market is also expected to triple by the year 2000.

For new companies, this means a vastly expanding new marketplace for goods and services and the potential for an enormous competitor that all companies will need to watch and understand. The Chinese market will be revisited in more depth in a later section.

The Sunbelt Surge

Another trend taking place is the Sunbelt surge. The demographic center of the United States is shifting inexorably toward the Southwest, the so-called Sunbelt states, fueled by declining death rates and increasing birth rates among the steady stream of immigrants to the area. The Asian American population, as well as the minority American population, is growing at eight times the rate of the white population, with Hispanics growing at four times the rate and African Americans at a slightly lesser rate. This means that over the next decade, a major share of new households will be formed by Asians and Hispanics. It is projected that by the year 2050, the United States will comprise more than 180 million non-Anglos, almost half of the projected population. The greatest increase will be among Hispanics, who will surpass African Americans to become the largest minority group.[3] One interesting example of the increasing dominance of the Latin influence is the fact that in 1990 tacos surpassed pizza as the most popular ethnic food.

 Entrepreneurship in Action

Doing Business in China

The U.S. Chamber of Commerce has found more than 200 small U.S. companies successfully doing business in China. But it's definitely the Wild West, or at least as risky as a trip to Las Vegas. Chris Barclay and his wife left a teaching job in Florida to come to Guangzhou in 1994 with only a $150,000 loan and the idea to start a hardware exporting business. After making a couple of bad deals and discovering that Americans pay a lot more than locals to live, they found a few fellow expatriates and started offering English classes to Chinese government officials and businesspeople. They began to look for a joint venture partner for this business that they called The American Language & Technology Education Center. Finding a suitable partner in China is an expensive proposition, particularly in entertainment expenses.

A typical evening of drinks and karaoke ran about $300. Finally, the Barclays found a provincial educational institute with a good reputation. They also managed to avoid the political corruption reputed to be so prevalent in the area. Companies are constantly approached by government officials looking to extract a fee for a nonexistent service under the threat of closing the business down. The Barclays persevered and now have offices in Guangzhou, Beijing, and Chengdu and clients such as Nike, Reebok, and DHL. The important lesson learned was that, as with Las Vegas, you have to know before going to China how much you're willing to risk.

SOURCE: Evelyn Iritani, "On the Front Lines," *Los Angeles Times,* October 8, 1997.

Staffing an inner-city plant with minority, unionized workers has not traditionally been perceived as a recipe for success. But Quam-Nichols, a Chicago-based manufacturer of loudspeakers proved that isn't necessarily so. William G. Little, the president and CEO, sets high standards and hires the best from this local, multicultural pool of applicants. (T. Michael Keza/Nation's Business)

Much has been written about the changing U.S. population, and entrepreneurs would be well advised to learn about these changes so that they don't assume a stereotypical consumer who may no longer exist.

The Growth of Urban Centers

Infrastructure failures in many of the world's largest cities will slow economic development. Often, as cities merge with urban areas and more and more companies move to those urban areas, the city core is left with no economic resources to repair and upgrade its roads, buildings, and sanitation systems, and it must repair infrastructure to attract business back to the inner cities. In Asia, for example, thousands of people swarm to the major cities seeking the products and services of a more westernized culture, but find instead sky-high unemployment rates as companies move out to be closer to where people live and where costs are lower.

Cities all over the world will expand along major transportation routes. Jobs, however, will be found in urban areas where businesses will find it more economical to operate. For small business, this means opportunities abound in construction and redevelopment in major cities. Often government funds are available to support a company's effort. It also suggests making more careful decisions about where to locate a business if you want to be in the path of growth.

On the surface it may appear illogical that major cities are a hotbed for new entrepreneurial ventures, particularly since people seem to be moving out of the major cities in droves. The Regional Plan Association of New York found that between 1992 and 1996, more than 861,000 people moved out of the New York City area. Moreover, the cost of living and doing business in a major city is astronomical compared to the suburbs. Still, many find signs that the big city is returning to prominence and reinventing itself to cater to particular types of industries. For example, in 1995 both San Francisco and San Jose, California, created a total of 60,000 new jobs in high-end business services, communications, and high-tech manufacturing. Even more impressive, in 1995 Los Angeles saw job growth reach 70,000 to 90,000 new jobs.[4] The reason touted is that entrepreneurs who start businesses in major cities can take advantage of an international work force. Therefore, it's no surprise that industries such as textiles, design, movie production, fine arts, graphics, and trading services find a home in major cities. This is a significant trend of which business owners should be aware.

The Impact of Technology on Marketing Strategy for Growth

The second major trend, and arguably the most important one, is technology. A consistent theme throughout this book is the notion that technology has been at the root of most of the more dramatic changes we see occurring in business today. If we see the organization as an integrated system where changes in one part ripple throughout the system, causing major and minor shifts in every other part, it's logical to conclude that marketing strategy has not been left untouched. It was precisely the conception of economical, fast, and innovative computer technology, as well as networks and online services, that gave rise to mass customization of products and services and the ability to take relationship marketing to the extreme. Bryan Rosencrantz (see Young Entrepreneurs—Minicase) was able to customize a marketing strategy for his fitness customers online that exactly fit their particular needs.

Technology has also leveled the playing field for small, growing companies and allowed them to compete successfully with giants in the same markets. E-mail, teleconferencing, multimedia CD-ROM, and networked databases have all contributed to entrepreneurial companies' *chutzpah* in the marketplace. For a very modest investment in computer-related equipment, small companies can emulate the marketing tactics of much larger companies. They can even set up a home page on the World Wide Web right next door to Wal-Mart.

Finally, technology has affected the way we structure and manage our businesses. Electronic networks and the Internet have facilitated the decentralization of businesses and the ability to outsource activities to other companies.

Strategies and Tactics Employing Technology

From a strategic viewpoint, technology has influenced marketing in a number of significant ways:

▶ The emphasis has shifted from products to information and solutions.

▶ Products can be launched from marketing tactics based on identifying specific customer needs.

▶ Technology makes relationships with customers easier, which enhances product acceptance and minimizes costs due to redesign.

▶ Technology allows companies to target specific products and services to specific customers.

▶ Technology supports the integration of engineering and marketing to get the product to market in the least amount of time.

▶ Technology helps prevent midcourse corrections in product design that always result in higher costs and longer time to market.[5]

From a tactical viewpoint, the latest information technology can help a growing, entrepreneurial company market its products and services in a number of innovative ways:

▶ E-mail allows the company to communicate rapidly and easily with customers, strategic partners, suppliers, distributors, and others all over the world. This reduces the costs of travel and speeds up response time.

▶ Teleconferencing lets the company hold international sales meetings and meetings with strategic partners without getting on a plane.

▶ Networked databases provide small, growing companies with online access to research ad development information through such sources as the Small Business Innovation Research program.

▶ Modems and laptop computers let employees work from virtually anywhere in the world, increasing productivity and bringing the company closer to the customer.

▶ Voice mail lets small, growing companies receive messages even when they are not available "in the office" to answer the phone. It is also a good way to get customer feedback.

▶ Satellite systems, which a retail company can lease from a provider, permit the company to receive sales broadcasts from chain manufacturers that help move product. The company doesn't have to incur the cost of producing the broadcast itself.

▶ Laser/color printers let companies quickly produce signs, banners, cards, price tags, and so forth that look as good as preprinted ones from a professional.

▶ Some industries have CD-ROM services that companies can tie into to receive updated information on such things as equipment and supplies on a regular basis. It also makes it easier for a company to quickly locate customer items that it normally doesn't carry in stock.

▶ The World Wide Web as a marketing tool is putting smaller companies on an equal footing with larger ones. Though the effectiveness of web advertising is still up for debate, there is no doubt that the medium is growing rapidly.

▶ Online databases have put information at the hands of anyone who chooses to access them. Moving information is something small companies do very well.

The important thing to remember about technology is that it's a tool used to improve the way companies do business—nothing more, nothing less. It cannot replace personal contact with the customer, nor can it replace the entrepreneur's unique ability to take vast amounts of information and make sense out of it in terms of a marketing strategy for the company. It can, however, make it easier to integrate all the activities of the company, automate routine tasks, and generally free up more time to focus on the customer and quality.

When Technology Is the Company's Product: Tornadoes and Growth

Today a company's competitive strategy often centers on technology it has developed or licensed. Technology can be used to create a competitive advantage by creating barriers that keep rivals from successfully entering the market.[6] A company can do this by using a leader or a follower strategy. With a pioneering strategy, the company takes a leadership role in its industry by creating technologies that require radical product or process innovation.[7] The intent is to capture premium segments, achieve economies of scale, set industry standards, or control distribution channels.[8] This is a risky strategy

 Entrepreneurship in Action

How the Customer Benefits from the Company's Technology

Many companies are using information technology to give their customers more personalized service. Retailer Stephen Silverman, owner of a men's apparel chain in North and South Dakota, likes to make sure his customers leave with exactly what they want. He has created a massive database from information collected from customers over several visits to the store. Silverman can tell you how many suits the customer bought over the past year, how much he spent, what kinds of clothes he likes, and when he likes to shop. Armed with this information, Silverman's salespeople can meet the customer at the door and provide his exact needs when he needs them.

In the retail business, another advantage of an electronic database system is the ability to help people who come in to buy gifts for regular patrons of the store. These concerned shoppers can relax and have a cup of coffee while a salesperson puts together a gift that is sure to please its recipient based on information in the database. This is one-to-one relationship marketing at its best.

SOURCE: Stephen M. Silverman, "Retail Retold," *Inc. Technology,* Summer 1995.

because it requires substantial investment in R&D. Microsoft is an example of a company that has been successful in pioneering technology.

With a follower strategy, by contrast, a company essentially copies another's technology and makes incremental improvements to create value for the customer.[9] The key disadvantage to being the follower is that the pioneering firm sets the standards by which the follower must abide. Whichever route the entrepreneur chooses to follow, it's important that the company have a technology strategy to achieve superior performance. Research suggests that companies benefit from pursuing product technologies early in the product life cycle and focusing on process technologies later in the cycle.[10]

When technology is the product, it necessitates a different approach to marketing strategy than other types of products and services. This is because its adoption life cycle is quite different. When a company introduces new technology in the form of a product that will shatter the equilibrium of the status quo, a few early adopters will purchase it; most of the market, however, will wait to see how things "shake out." If the product achieves acceptance by the early adopters who "spread the word," chances are it will experience what Geoffrey Moore has called a "**'flash point'** when the entire marketplace shifts its allegiance from the old architecture to the new."[11] Pent-up demand results in a purchasing frenzy that takes the company into **hypergrowth**. Moore calls this being "inside the tornado." Though the tornado has touched down more often in Silicon Valley than anywhere else, other industries have not escaped its grip, notably aerospace, pharmaceuticals, and broadcasting. Moore describes a technology adoption life cycle that explains the existence of tornadoes (see Figure 12.1).

The Technology Adoption Life Cycle

The first stage marks the introduction of the product and initial enthusiasm and acceptance by early adopters, those who always want to own the latest technology the moment it's available. But between the early stage and mainstream acceptance lies what Moore calls **the chasm**, that period when the mainstream market is still not accepting of or comfortable with the product. If the company, through its marketing efforts, is able to cross the chasm, it establishes a niche in what is known as the **bowling alley**. In this stage of the cycle, the product is starting to gain acceptance from a variety of niche markets but has yet to achieve widespread, mainstream adoption. Actually, the goal for the company while in the bowling alley is to rack up enough niches to start a momentum going that will drive the product into the tornado. In each niche market, the company drives out the existing competition in its forward advance.

Moore suggests that to get out of the bowling alley, a company must go after competitors of the same or similar size (don't take on a giant) and focus efforts on the end-user customer rather than the technical community.[12] One of the trickiest points for a new technology company is to decide when to move. Moving too soon may result in systems that still have bugs, while moving too late may cost the company its window of opportunity and put it at a competitive disadvantage. When the company and its vendors decide it's time to move, it happens very quickly, unleashing a flood of demand that

Inside the Tornado, focuses on mapping the marketplace beyond the chasm. It focuses on three subsequent stages in the life-cycle model, illustrated here.
The Early Market, a time of great excitement, when customers are technology enthusiasts and visionaries who are looking to be first to jump on board with the new paradigm.
The Chasm, a time of great despair, when the early market's interest wanes but the mainstream market is still not comfortable with the immaturity of the solutions that are available.
The Bowling Alley, a period of niche-based adoption in advance of the general marketplace, driven by compelling customer needs and the willingness of vendors to craft niche-specific products.
The Tornado, a period of mass-market adoption, when the general marketplace switches over to the new infrastructure.
Main Street, a period of aftermarket development, when the base infrastructure has been deployed and the goal is to flesh out its potential.
End of Life, which can come all too soon in high tech because price/performance are driven to unheard-of levels, enabling new paradigms to come to market and supplant the leaders who themselves had only just arrived.

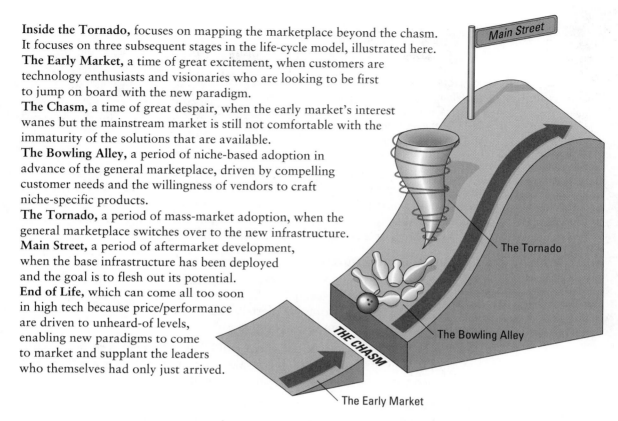

Figure 12.1
The Technology Adoption Life Cycle
Source: "The Technology Adoption Life Cycle," from *Inside the Tornado* by Geoffrey A. Moore. Copyright © 1995 by Geoffrey A. Moore Consulting, Inc. Reprinted by permission of HarperCollins Publishers, Inc.

cannot totally be met. This is often very disconcerting to marketing people, who are used to figuring out how to create demand. In the case of the tornado, they literally have to stand out of the way and just facilitate the shipping of product as quickly as possible. This is where focusing on the process becomes important. There is everything to be gained by becoming the best at producing and distributing the product as quickly as possible.

The Final Stage

Once the company has been through the tornado, it arrives at what Moore calls "Main Street," where it now has to dramatically shift gears and become end-user focused, something it has never done before. Moore says the defining characteristic of Main Street is that "growth no longer comes from selling to new customers." Instead, companies must develop **niche-specific extensions**—in other words, sell more product to the same customers.

Technology Tip

Thumbnails for Speed

If your web site requires a lot of graphics and/or photographs, try using "thumbnails" to speed up their
downloading. A thumbnail is a small version, about an
inch square, of the larger graphic or photo. Then make
it possible for the visitor to click on the small picture
and increase the size to see it in more detail.

Not all high-technology companies experience tornadoes; some lucky
ones simply benefit from the ride on the coattails of the market leader, as so
many small companies partnering with Microsoft have done. It's a wild ride
that will end up either an enormous success, as it did with Hewlett-Packard
and Microsoft, or a complete bust, as Word Star experienced.

Lessons from the Tornado

Moore believes that the two greatest tornadoes of the 1980s were the mid-
range computer war between DEC and Oracle, and the laser and inkjet
printer breakthrough from Hewlett-Packard. He says there are several
lessons to be learned from these companies:[13]

1. The competition must be attacked ruthlessly. The goal is to become the
   standard in the industry, so every sale a competitor loses is another brick
   in the mortar of the new company's foundation.

2. The distribution channel must be expanded as quickly as possible. This
   may come at the expense of the customer in the short term, but it is the
   only way to become the market leader, which is critical to achieving full
   acceptance and dominance.

3. Forget the customer while in the tornado, because this is a very unique
   environment. The product is hot and customers are lining up. The only
   thing they care about at the moment is getting the product as quickly as
   possible. After the company is out of the tornado, it can concern itself
   with building long-term loyalty on the part of its customers.

4. Focus on the process above all else. The most exciting, innovative product in the world will fizzle if the company that produces it can't ship it
   quickly and reliably. At the same time, the company has to stay on top
   of potential problems that could, as in the case of Intel and its Pentium
   chip problem, cost it millions of dollars.

5. Extend distribution channels to every type of outlet possible. This is important because the price of the product usually comes down very
   rapidly when it's in the tornado, and the company will need to expand
   its outlets to increase volume.

6. Drive to the next lower price point. The first vendor to hit the new price
   point gets first chance at a whole new class of customer that was waiting

for prices to come down. If the leader company fails to move to the new price point, it will lose customers to clones. Hewlett-Packard is one example of a company that has always moved to the next price point to successfully keep out competitors.

7. Have good partners in place before entering the tornado, and "institutionalize" them and the company as the standard bearers in the industry.

8. Bundle products with partners so that customers buy more than one product. Microsoft did this when it designed office product suites such as Microsoft Office97®; it's called **commoditizing** the product.

Not every company that experiences the tornado comes out positively. Usually, when a company attempts to control the tornado, its efforts fail. For example, 15 years ago Sony found itself in the tornado with its Betamax technology for VCRs. In an attempt to control the tornado, Sony refused to license its technology to other vendors, so it was unable to keep up with demand. Consequently, vendors went around Sony to VHS technology, which was more readily available—and the rest, as they say, is history.

In the early days of word processing software, Word Star had 50 percent of the market. In the midst of the tornado, it switched direction and, instead of coming out with an upgrade of its successful product, produced an entirely new product, thereby negating a possible impact of switching costs. Customers therefore had no reason to stay with Word Star and switched to WordPerfect.

Marketing strategy is affected not only by technology products but by technology-based distribution channels such as the Internet, the subject of the next section.

Marketing on the World Wide Web

The **World Wide Web,** an area of the Internet, is a virtual, global, open-ended array of interconnected information sources. It's a distribution system that any company, big or small, can join, and it's far and away the quickest and easiest way to market products and services globally to people who access the Internet. It's easiest to think of a web site (home page) as an electronic brochure that lets readers know everything that's important to know about the company or individual that owns the site.

The hype surrounding the WWW is only surpassed by the hype about its parent, the Internet. Every business owner has been encouraged by the media and by **Internet service providers** (those who sell access to the Internet) to set up a web site and make money marketing on the Internet. Only recently, however, have we been able to ascertain if anyone was actually making money doing this. On October 30, 1995, Commerce Net and Nielsen Media Research published the findings of landmark research on Internet usage.[14] They interviewed randomly by telephone more than 4,200 current and potential Internet users in the United States and Canada age 16 years and older who fell into one of three categories: Internet users, online service users, and nonusers. They also stratified the sample frame by geography to achieve a proportionate geographic distribution. All telephone numbers in the frame for each area had an equal probability of being selected. This study is more valid than previous ones in that earlier studies used Internet users, which introduced the bias of self-selection among those already using the Internet.

Some of their findings include the following:

- More than 24 million people used the Internet in a three-month period prior to the interview.

- Of these, 2.5 million made a purchase through the Internet.

- The U.S. and Canadian users spend as much time on the Internet as they do viewing videotapes.

- 11 percent of the population 16 years or older use the Internet, and 8 percent use the Web.

- Two-thirds of users are male and account for 77 percent of total online time.

- 53 percent of users are between ages 16 and 34.

- 66 percent have access through their work.

- 31 percent access the Internet at least once a day.

- Users stay online an average of 5 hours, 28 minutes a week.

- 25 percent of users have incomes in excess of $80,000.

- 64 percent have a college degree versus 28 percent for the total population.

 Entrepreneurship in Action

How About a Life Outdoors?

Imagine having 27,000 customers coming to your company's headquarters every day while you hike in the wilderness or schuss your way down a mountain. If you're the founder and owner of Cool Works, that's exactly what you do. Bill Berg thinks he has probably the best business in the world. Coolworks.com is the largest recruiting site on the Web for jobs in ski resorts, dude ranches, national parks, and other wilderness areas.

In April 1997, the site went from 60,000 hits to 106,000 hits on the home page alone. His full site got 800,000 hits for the month. Why? Because Bill Berg knows his customer. In 1995, Berg quit a good job to go back to school to get an MBA in environmental management, which is where he first saw the Web. Immediately he recognized that lots of companies are trying to hire college students for summer jobs, and where do college students spend their time? On the Web!

Berg collaborated with Great Outdoor Recreation Pages (GORP), an index of outdoor recreation information, and the linkage produced more revenues for both companies. He's had to add four people to his staff, but like a true technology junkie, his staff is miles away connected via modem. Sounds like it's time for an intranet!

SOURCE: Adapted from Ann Burgund, "Create a Website and Spend the Rest of Your Life in the Great Outdoors," Microsoft Office Website, 1998, http://www.microsoft.com/Office/office 97/documents/Cool/Wks

For a growing company, these findings spell opportunity. Certainly Bryan Rosencrantz (see Young Entrepreneurs—Minicase) saw the Internet as a niche market in the saturated fitness industry. But this opportunity has to be considered carefully because marketing on the WWW is still like surviving a gunfight at the OK Corral. It's the wild, wild West with no holds barred for the most part, and many businesses have failed because they didn't understand the nature of the market. Nevertheless, rules and traditions are slowly developing, so the uninitiated may often find their inappropriate Internet tactics "flamed" by users and providers alike. One small publishing company learned that lesson quickly when the owner attempted blatant selling on an online forum and was summarily dismissed from the forum. The key is to get the message across without sounding like an advertisement.

Online forums on the Internet (newsgroups) and message boards on commercial services such as CompuServe and America Online are essentially electronic postings by users that anyone can read. A **bulletin board service (BBS)** is basically a host computer with storage capacity, software, a modem, and a dedicated phone line. In cases where usage of the BBS is high, multiple modems and hard drives will be necessary. It is estimated that 67,000 BBSs are in operation.[15]

Getting Started

The easiest and cheapest way to establish a company beachhead on the Internet is to start with **forums** where users come to ask and answer questions, give advice, or just state their opinions on issues related to a particular forum. For example, AOL has a popular travel forum where the owners of Rail Pass Express of Columbus, Ohio, got their start. They began by posting information about train travel in Europe and secondarily mentioning that they happened to sell tickets. Signing with the name of the company was also an excellent, yet subtle way to market the company. These tactics were a way to establish their reputation with those interested in travel issues. After a year of participating in forums, they decided to buy an *online advertisement,*

 Entrepreneurship in Action

How One Company Started a Forum

In 1994, E. David Ellington, an entertainment lawyer, had an idea for an online forum on America Online. He saw great interest in African American culture, everything from R&B to jazz to the early days of the Negro Baseball League, and thought an online forum would bring all these people together.

AOL liked the concept and gave him $100,000 in seed money to create NetNoir. It was one of six forums

it funded out of 1,700 proposals. Ellington now runs the forum full time with a partner and claims a market value of $6.5 million.

SOURCE: Robert McGarvey, "Ready, Set, 'Net: From Restaurants to Retailers, Small Businesses Are Connecting with Customers Online," *AOL,* June 1996.

which cost $750 a month, and set up their own web site. This constant presence on the travel forum's message board took their online revenues from $60,000 in the first year to more than $300,000 in the second.

Using *e-mail* in tandem with the previous two approaches enhances the opportunity to establish a relationship with the potential customer. Notifying users of a forum where they may contact the company for a list of frequently asked questions (FAQs) on the topic of interest gets the customer to the company, where it can promote its products and services.

A third step in increasing involvement online is to actually *operate a forum* for an online service. This entails approaching a service provider with a proposal for content and operation, including the justification for interest on the part of users. Often the service provider will front the money to create the forum, which can run as high as $100,000 or more. Then the company will receive revenues from a percentage of online fees paid by the users of the service, from advertising, and from sales to users. Of course, setting up a forum does have some challenges, since hundreds of others are also considering doing the same thing. Competition is, in a word, intense (see "How One Company Started a Forum").

Setting Up a Web Site

Companies can bypass the commercial online providers and set up a web site on the WWW. The cost of doing this will start at well under $1,000 using software that can be purchased at any retail outlet. Or, if the company wants to save time, it can hire someone to design the site. The cost for this service can range up to $100,000 depending on the level of graphical sophistication of the site. Finding a designer is not a problem because everyone from high school students to professional firms is designing web sites. The problem, then, is to choose wisely. It certainly is important to look at other sites a designer has developed to judge the quality of the work. It's also wise to come prepared with a sketch of what the company wants to accomplish to make sure the developer can do it. Then it will be necessary to hire an Internet service provider (ISP) to put the site up online. Check Table 12.1 for a listing of some of the information you should collect from potential ISPs.

 The Real World of Entrepreneurship

Why Will People Come to Your Web Site?

A recent study by IntelliQuest Web Evaluation Services found that 56 percent of respondents revisit a web site because it's "very entertaining." This was closely followed by "it grabs the reader's attention" and "contained very useful content."

Like any marketing materials, a web site must get the user's attention, hook the user in to spend some time, and then provide valuable, thought-provoking, and visually appealing content.

Source: IntelliQuest Web Evaluation Services, 1996, appearing in *Inc. Technology* no. 2 (1997), p. 26.

Table 12.1   Checking Out an ISP

Here is a checklist of information you need to know when choosing an Internet service provider:

- Standard rates (for comparison)
- Length of time in business
- The modem rates the ISP supports
- Security measures and number of backups
- The availability of e-mail and electronic ordering blanks
- The reports the ISP provides: what they contain (visitor's domain names, number of hits) and how often they are provided.
- Who has the intellectual property rights to the web site? Does the designer want copyright rights to graphics and icons? (This is not uncommon.) Also, any artwork that is scanned in may involve another copyright.
- Who owns the programming code? If the company uses proprietary software from the provider, it may not be able to take that software with it if it leaves that provider.
- Who owns data? It is important for the company to protect any data about its site, for example, hit rates the ISP may use in its own promotions.

Getting Noticed

The biggest problem on the WWW is getting the company noticed. Vermont Teddy Bear Company tried an eight-page online preview of its catalog featuring teddy bears in bikinis. But because the web address was poorly marketed offline, few people saw the site and no one ordered. Yahoo, one of the principal directories on the Web, claims to receive 2,000 new web site submissions a day. The competition for the user's attention is fierce, so innovative thinking is definitely an asset. One approach is to link up with a noncompeting but compatible web site. For example, a travel agency could link with the web site for a resort. Then, when users land at the resort site, they will see a button that takes them directly to the travel agency. Similarly, the travel agency will have a button for the resort on its web site.

How Important Is the Name?

One important thing a business should do immediately is register the business name as an Internet **domain name**. This is usually done through the ISP. It is not uncommon to find the company's name has already been taken, often by Internet providers wanting to secure the company as a customer. This was the case when the founder of Princeton Review, a test preparation service, registered "review.com" and also "kaplan.com" for its competitor, Kaplan Educational Centers. Kaplan, however, fought the registration, claiming that trademark laws should apply to Internet domain names. An arbitration panel required Princeton to give up "kaplan.com."[16]

Some Tips for Marketing Online

The difference between marketing the company's message on TV and doing so online is that online is interactive, so the audience has to come to the company's site by choice—and that's the hard part. Following are some tips for producing a web site that will effectively market the company and its products and services:

- *Keep your site fresh.* Change the content often, and be sure to let the visitor know about new content by flagging it on the home page with a "new" sign. Make sure your site appeals to the audience you are trying to reach.

- *Design your site with search engines in mind.* Remember that search engines such as Yahoo use key words. Find the key words that will get people to your site.

- *Let readers know where they are at all times.* Documents online are non-linear, so wherever the visitor is on the web site, he or she must have a continuous picture of the whole site. This continuity can be accomplished through uniform graphics or icons with the company name prominently displayed.

- *Keep things short and concise.* People have short attention spans on the Web, much as TV channel surfers do. They should be able to get the main point quickly and move on.

- *Make it easy to find information.* Don't assume users will read every page.

- *Don't use memory-hogging graphics.* Animation and 3D graphics are exciting and fun, but the average user is working with a 28.8 baud modem and will have to wait much too long for the graphics to download. Use small graphics.

- *Use shorter sentences and paragraphs.* A lot of people don't like to read great amounts of material onscreen.

- *Let people interact with the company.* The site needs to have the ability to interact with the customer, and customers want to feel they can "talk" to the company. This may mean providing e-mail, an 800 number, or a bulletin board service. Some companies have found their customers enjoy games and contests as ways to interact.

- *Keep track of "hits."* **Hits** are the number of times the site is accessed during a specific period of time. Currently technology doesn't let the company know if the same person is accessing or new, potential customers.

- *Provide "hot links."* **Hot links** are highlighted text or buttons that take a user immediately to another page of information or to another site. However, be careful not to direct visitors away from the company's site before they have had a chance to see everything they need to see.

- *Offer something free.* Usually this takes the form of information, FAQs, or an invitation to join a forum.

▶ *Check out how the site functions from various platforms.* These would include various configurations of PCs, Macs, and workstations.

▶ *Ask the ISP if the company can pay for services with a percentage of on-line sales monthly.*

▶ *Use global graphics.* Although most people who use the Internet speak English because it's a global information service, it's important to use graphics that universally identify the company and its products and services.

▶ *For speed, keep graphics horizontal and use few colors.*

▶ *Make it easy to sort through lists.* A search routine, a categorical listing, or an alphabetical listing will help.

▶ *Use a hypertext link (hot link) to take users directly to the order form.*

▶ *Give people a reason to come back.*

Don't forget to market your web site offline as well in traditional media such as newspapers, magazines, business cards, stationery, and so forth. More and more people are looking for web site addresses in business advertisements.

Like China, the World Wide Web is a new frontier for marketers. Knowing what is out there and which companies have been successful marketing online will go a long way toward saving time and money for the growing entrepreneurial company.

Global Marketing

With 95 percent of the world's population and two-thirds of its purchasing power found outside the United States, it's no wonder so many businesses are planning to market their products and services in the international arena.[17] In a survey conducted by Deloitte Touche Tohmatsu International, 86 percent of the companies interviewed sold outside their own countries and 46 percent had foreign manufacturing operations. The U.S. Department of Commerce reports that 60 percent of the U.S. firms now successfully exporting are small businesses with fewer than 100 employees. There are many compelling reasons to consider the global market:[18]

1. You can achieve a broader marketing base, which will minimize any adverse economic conditions that may be affecting your home country.

2. You may be able to reduce the effects of seasonality by going into complementary countries.

3. You can more fully employ any excess capacity when dealing in the domestic market alone.

4. You may be able to increase your product's life.

5. You may be able to lower production costs by establishing foreign production facilities.

In any business market research is vital, but learning how "the system" works in other countries is equally important. Izabel Lam of Izabel Lam International was experiencing problems selling her unique cutlery and dinnerware in Europe until she learned that focusing on the distribution of her art is just as important as the creation of the art itself. To finally succeed, she had to set up her own distribution warehouse in Germany. (Dale May)

The decision to market goods and services globally can come at the start of the new venture or several years down the road after the company has established a strong domestic market. In the case of the new technology product in a tornado, it will definitely happen in the tornado. But for many other types of businesses, a "wait and see" attitude may be more appropriate. These businesses choose to perfect their products, processes, and services in domestic markets before they tackle the cultural, political, legal, and general differences in doing business in other parts of the world.

Still, the question for any growing company is not *"should we go global?"* but *"when should we go global?"* Entrepreneurial companies have many reasons to consider the global market even as early as during the development of their original business plan. First, technology today is not the sole province of the United States. Gone are the days when U.S. firms could ship their obsolete technology and products to other countries to extend their market life. Other countries now expect to receive the latest technology in the goods they purchase, and it may not always come with a "United States" label.

Second, the United States, though a huge market, represents less than half of the total global market. Other countries are becoming increasingly entrepreneurial. In Europe today, there are fewer family-owned, small businesses and more growth-oriented, entrepreneurial ventures.[19] In China, the number of town and village enterprises has increased from 1.4 million to 20.8 million.[20] In Eastern Europe—Hungary, Poland, the Czech Republic, Slovakia, Bulgaria, the former German Democratic Republic, and Romania—there has been an enormous privatization program to return businesses to individual ownership.[21] With privatization, entrepreneurs benefit from several types of opportunities. Individual owners can now make purchasing decisions, which means more sales opportunities for exporting entrepreneurs. Since privatization requires major restructuring, opportunities open up for new products and services to facilitate that restructuring. Finally, entrepreneurs are finding investment opportunities through joint ventures in other countries.[22]

Third, due to rapidly changing technology, product lives are increasingly shorter, and with R&D being so expensive, companies are forced to enter several major markets at once to gain the maximum advantage from the window of opportunity. Entrepreneurs who attend world trade shows know their strongest competition may come as easily from a country in the Pacific Rim as from the company next door. Entrepreneurs also know they may have to rely on other countries for supplies, parts, and even fabrication to keep costs down and remain competitive.

But global marketing is much more than simply taking the company's domestic marketing strategies abroad. Global marketing is about finding new markets and niches, developing buying and selling opportunities, marketing goods and services, and researching international markets. Traditional global marketing has consisted of

1. Developing a country risk profile that includes economic, cultural, and political data.

2. Conducting a company analysis to include product, price, promotion, distribution, and the firm's competitive advantage.

3. Making national marketing decisions about opportunities, analysis, and strategy.[23]

Countries are then ranked according to the risk they present to the company. More recently, however, nontraditional global marketing has added some new frames of reference to the original model:

▶ The **political frame**, which now includes reinventing nation-states and free trade regimes as contexts.

▶ The **technological frame**, which takes into account decision making under conditions of uncertainty; multimarkets across technologies, industries, and nation-states; and information technologies.

- ▶ The **cultural frame,** which includes such factors as demographics, youth and young adult culture as a driving force for change in markets, the freedom lifestyle factor, and the contingency perspective.

- ▶ The **marketing-management frame,** which looks at such elements as product diffusion, the learning curve, segmentation, positioning, and imagined differences.[24]

The Council of American Survey Research Organization (CASRO) recently conducted a survey of 313 executives at major U.S. corporations who carry on research or hire research firms in an effort to learn if they intended to conduct research overseas.[25] A surprising 61 percent said they will devote a larger percentage of their research budget to overseas research. These executives believe that because the global market is still so new, research has to take priority. Today researching global markets is critical to the decision about where to invest the company's resources. Understanding, for example, that the Japanese government promotes economic change and development through its public policy means less risk for U.S. companies than that faced by the more regulated countries of Latin America. As another example, the rate of change of technology outpaces any strategy the company could devise, so companies have to find better ways to speed up product development and the processing of information on a worldwide basis, and that means they must find the best resources, suppliers, processors, and distributors globally.

Douglas Lamont has suggested that the research should answer four basic questions about a particular country or a particular region of the world:

1. *Who uses the product?* How are these buyers similar to or different from U.S. buyers? How are U.S. products incorporated into the country's lifestyle?

2. *How do the people of that country define value?* Is value based on timeliness, quality, service, or price? How do products and services need to be changed to meet customer needs?

3. *What signals will indicate change in the market?* Does the country accept foreign ideas? Are there cross-cultural trends?

4. *How can the company increase market share?* Who are the local competitors? Are any of them foreign companies? How much disposable income do consumers have?[26]

The remainder of this section looks at four regions that represent four types of global markets. Although this chapter cannot possibly cover the issue of global marketing strategy in depth, a look at these four regions of the world will give you an appreciation of the importance of developing a global strategy that takes into account the distinct differences among countries.

Mexico

After years of taking an opposing stand, Mexico became part of GATT in 1987, signed on to NAFTA, and in 1995 was asked to become a member of the Organization for Economic Cooperation and Development (OECD), a group of the 24 richest countries in the world. This may seem odd for a country where only 1 percent of citizens are super rich, 7 percent are middle class, 12 percent are lower middle class, and 70 percent live in poverty.[27] But Mexico has been making a concerted effort to reinvent itself for the global marketplace. Since 1983, Mexico has followed a policy of privatization, selling off 80 percent of the companies it used to run.[28] This signaled that the government no longer wanted to shape business policy and set prices. Large manufacturing companies have seen productivity rise, but mid- to small-size companies have been unable to adopt new technology fast enough. This is because "each unit of foreign investment in Mexico pulled in 1.8 units of imports," so there is not enough free cash to improve productivity.[29]

The range of consumer tastes is affected by the cultural differences within the country and runs the gamut from very traditional to more North American. Southern Mexico is generally more traditional with its indigenous Mayan tribes that are more closely aligned with Central America. This area is experiencing a great deal of unrest. Central Mexico, by contrast, is considered ethnocentric—more closely tied to its traditions but with pent-up demand for contemporary goods and services in Mexico City—whereas northern Mexico is nonethnocentric, most probably because it shares a border with the United States and is more influenced by U.S. products and services.

Companies that have gone into Mexico have taken different routes to do so. For example, Ford made a wholly owned investment; Costco took on an equity joint venture with a Mexican firm; I Can't Believe It's Yogurt Ltd used a local franchising agreement with Mexican investors; and Coca-Cola bought 30 percent of Femsa, a beer and soft-drink bottling company. All of these approaches have helped companies diffuse their products throughout Mexico. There is, however, continued concern about the economic stability of the country in terms of the peso and such issues as deregulation and privatization.

It is also difficult to collection information on consumers in Mexico because the Mexican people are generally not willing to talk about themselves. In contrast to Americans, Mexicans understand from birth their status in society: rich, upper middle class, or poor. Whereas the United States has a huge middle class, Mexican society appears more like a triangle, with the bulk of society at the bottom. Refer to Table 12.2 for examples of some of the problems marketers face in learning about the Mexican customer.

Nevertheless, it is known that customers of many Mexican firms tend to prefer goods made in the United States rather than the same goods with a Mexican label. In Mexico, as in other countries, learning about the customer from a variety of sources will provide more accurate information for marketing purposes.

Europe

When studying Europe as a potential market, demographics become very important. There is no European national culture; in fact, huge cultural differences exist among the countries considered to be part of the European Union

Table 12.2   Why the Mexican Customer Is Difficult to Research

Here are some reasons marketing researchers have difficulty gaining good information from Mexican respondents. They point up the importance of understanding the culture before attempting to gather research data.

1. *Translations from English are imprecise.* Many English words do not translate directly into Spanish, particularly American concepts such as "shelf space" and "stocking fees."

2. *"Me versus us" mentality.* Whereas U.S. consumers may ask, "What's in it for me?", Mexican consumers will be more concerned with what's in it for their friends and family.

3. *Individualism versus collectivism.* Mexican respondents tend to make collective decisions based on the family rather than individual decisions.

4. *Too many polite responses.* Mexicans are more reticent to talk about personal issues than Americans are.

5. *Unfamiliarity with research methods.* Many Mexicans are not familiar with research questionnaires and methods, and therefore may not know how to answer.

Sources: Douglas Lamont, *Global Marketing* (Cambridge, MA: Blackwell Publishers, 1996); Charles S. Mayer, "Multinational Market Research," *European Research*, March 1978, pp. 77–83.

(see Table 12.3). Marketers often talk about the differences between the "potato" culture of northern Europe and the "spaghetti" culture of southern Europe, but that is a simplistic approach. It does suggest, however, that the importance of country history, language, and religion cannot be ignored when planning a marketing strategy.

Although the European Union (EU) is moving toward a common currency and a "borderless" community, it is still a conglomeration of independent states with a multinational commission in Brussels that makes decisions related to GATT issues and tariffs. It has been suggested that dividing the EU into six cross-cultural, cross-national clusters or markets is appropriate.[30] See Table 12.4 for a listing of these six markets.

Mintel, a London-based marketing research firm, conducted a formal study of 7,000 Euro-consumers in 8 of the 15 EU nations to determine how

Table 12.3   Who Is Considered *European?*

French	Germans	Italians	Dutch
Belgians	Luxembourgers	British	Irish
Danes	Greeks	Spanish	Portuguese
Swiss	Austrians	Norwegians	Swedish
Finnish	Icelanders	Poles	Czechs
Hungarians	Estonians	Latvians	Lituanians
Byelorussians	Ukrainians	Russians	Moldovans
Rumanians	Bulgarians	Georgians	Armenians
Azeris	Turks		

Table 12.4   Cross-cultural and Cross-national Clusters

Cluster	Population (Million)
United Kingdom of Great Britain and Northern Ireland, and the Republic of Ireland	60.4
Belgium, Luxembourg, and France	54.5
Portugal and Spain	56.4
Southern Germany, Austria, northern Italy, and Corsica	71.5
Southern Italy, Sicily, Sardinia, and Greece	31.3
Flemish-speaking Belgium, the Netherlands, northern Germany, Denmark, Norway, Sweden, Finland, and Iceland	57.6

cultural differences might affect market strategy and came up with some interesting results:

▶ The French are more likely than the average European to sample a new product if a celebrity endorses it.

▶ Fifty-one percent of Italians versus 31 percent of Spaniards were influenced to buy through advertising.

▶ The French are more likely (22 percent) to eat outside the home than are the Italians (6 percent).[31]

These are just a few examples of the enormous diversity in the European community. This diversity presents a huge challenge for marketers who have resorted to using four cultural-free typologies to seek out cultural information that will help them market across Europe: uncertainty avoidance, individualism, power distance, and masculinity.[32] Note that this framework can also be used to analyze customers and culture in any country.

▶ *Uncertainty avoidance.* How do individuals in particular countries handle uncertainty, and how does their tolerance of ambiguity affect their buying habits?

▶ *Individualism.* How willing are European youth to break away from their country's traditions to try new things—to become *European* rather than *British*, for example?

▶ *Power distance.* How do individuals of various countries feel about and deal with hierarchies, power, and the distribution of wealth? For example, wealth and power are fairly evenly distributed in Denmark, but France displays enormous inequities.

▶ *Masculinity.* Some countries—for example, Austria and Italy—tend to be more masculine in nature. Consequently marketers, knowing this, use ads displaying assertive behavior, an achievement orientation, and a focus on material possessions. By contrast, the Netherlands and Denmark are perceived as feminine countries, so ads there focus on concern for the environment, caring, and championing the underdog.[33]

The conclusion to be drawn is that where cultural differences are small, sharing products across borders works well, as in the case of the United States and the United Kingdom. On the other hand, where cultural differences are vast, as in the case of France and Germany, products of one country may not do well in the other. Consequently, it is important to look for cross-cultural clusters rather than national segments. Still, Euro-consumers have little loyalty to the EU when compared to the loyalty they show to their home countries.

One thing that has made researching the European Union easier is the existence of ESOMAR, the equivalent of the American Marketing Association in Europe. It tracks demographics on 65,000 households so that marketers have a sense of the quality of life and standard of living in each country. ESOMAR's research has found that although significant cultural differences exist across countries, there is a general preference for individualism, trend-setting products, and high-tech products.[34] Many marketers have resorted to using age to segment the Euro-consumer, for example, children, youth, teenagers, young adults, middle-aged people, retired people, and those in their sunset years.

It is true today more than ever that both European and U.S. lifestyles are present in the EU. Marketers are challenged with the dual effort of attracting Euro-customers with traditional national themes and young European professionals with more pan-European themes.

Japan

Japan is special in its ability to maintain its unique culture in the face of an onslaught of U.S. products. The government encourages collectivism and, from all appearances, Japan is moving at glacial speed toward individualism. But other trends are surfacing. More women are working, producing more family income and more consumption, and more young people are waiting to marry and are forming smaller families. Still, Japan has unique cultural traits that are distinct even from those of other Southeast Asian countries. It is, in effect, a closed society that cannot be looked at by segmentation. It must be considered as an integrated whole. Though even Japanese youth are not readily accepting of U.S. and European goods, young working adults probably have the most in common with their counterparts in the United States. Still, the risk for businesses in Japan is equivalent to that in the United States or Europe and is less than in Mexico or China. Like Mexico and unlike China, Japan takes a long-term view of marketing.

Japan appears to have some structural problems. For example, "the average consumer product in Japan goes through 5.2 hands before reaching the consumer."[35] Moreover, conducting business in Japan is expensive, complex, and time consuming. Japanese firms, whether a small business or Toshiba, take a long-term view of marketing relationships.

One method marketers have used to understand the Japanese culture and mindset is through the *manga* or Japanese comic books. In Japan, one-third of all magazines sold are comic books.[36] And they are not read only by children; a variety of *manga* are targeted toward young women, male executives, and other groups. One reason the *manga* are so popular is the Japanese propensity toward visual communication.

Those companies that have found success marketing in Japan have learned to provide advertising and products that make use of five fundamental beliefs: humor, fantasy, harmony, *nihonjin*, and collective material success. In Japan, mocking, nonthreatening humor is very popular. For example, rapper MC Hammer appeared in a commercial that showed Coke (the market leader) turning people into nerds; consequently, Pepsi's sales shot up 19 percent in 1991.[37] The Japanese love fantasy, which is why the Tokyo Disneyland has been so successful. Though it may seem ironic that a totally American phenomenon such as Disneyland is accepted in the heart of Japan, it is not surprising when you consider that when they step inside the gates of Disneyland, they feel they are stepping into a dream world where they can play out their fantasies of becoming a cowboy, an astronaut, or even Mickey Mouse.[38]

Harmony is important to the Japanese (the use of odd numbers of objects in design, for example), as is *nihonjin*, that which is uniquely Japanese. So strong is the desire to promote and retain the Japanese culture that many U.S. companies operating in Japan have found themselves becoming more Japanese. For example, Kentucky Fried Chicken (KFC), one of the most popular franchises in Japan, has started serving *yaki-musubi* (grilled rice balls) alongside its chicken, as well as *yakitori* (chicken on skewers). McDonald's stopped serving ketchup with its fries because the Japanese found it too messy; instead, it serves seasoned salts. And because of the Japanese love for harmony and beauty, KFC has to think more about how to package its product so that it's more appealing to Japanese tastes.

Marketers have learned many other things about Japanese tastes and preferences:

▶ The youth market (18 to 21) is looking for products that show assertiveness, green chic (environmental), and value; casual apparel; and products that are easy to use.[39]

▶ Consumers want products that save time.

▶ Tokyo consumers like products that are trendy.

▶ Consumers want products with an established reputation.

▶ They can't afford private homes, so they tend to spend a lot on luxuries such as vacations and jewelry.

▶ They want the highest quality.

▶ They display strong gender differences.

In Japan, perhaps more than in any other country, understanding their traditions, religion, and love for things Japanese is important to marketing success.

China

China's communist government maintains political control over every aspect of business, although recently it has allowed some deregulation and privatization and has encouraged investment by the United States and Japan. The economy is volatile, and poverty among peasants and factory workers is an enormous problem. This, coupled with a short-term planning horizon, ranks China higher as a business risk than Mexico. Culturally, the population may be divided among devoted communists, young executives, and overseas Chinese (those who have chosen to live and work in other countries but maintain their Chinese traditions). All of these groups prefer overseas Chinese products.[40] Consequently, marketing efforts by U.S. companies have focused on young executives and overseas Chinese. Material success appears to be important, but as in Japan, it is a collective rather than individual success. Chinese youth will try new Western products that their overseas Chinese counterparts also use.

It has been found that foreign products that get into the market first, ahead of Chinese equivalents, usually do well and ultimately become household names.[41] Some examples are Coke, Johnson waxes, and Singer sewing machines.[42] Still, China does not yet have the same market segments the rest of the global economy does. It is experiencing labor unrest, price inflation, and a volatile economy. Access to information is difficult because it is generally guarded by the government. Add to all this the Chinese desire to avoid uncertainty, which makes them tend to shop for Chinese goods, and you have a difficult marketing situation.

Nevertheless, several marketing methods have been identified as promising in the Chinese market:

▶ Direct selling has been an effective strategy. Avon began advertising its products well ahead of actually selling them in China.[43] Then, upon entering China, its strategy was to direct-sell to women at the factories so that it didn't have to deal with the Chinese distribution system. Avon did, however, partner with Guangzhou Cosmetics Factory, a prosperous team that has made Avon a $60 million business in China.[44]

▶ Partnering with local companies has been another successful strategy. For example, Procter & Gamble sells its own shampoos as well as a local brand, Jiejua, through Hutchinson China Trade Company, and the Guangzhou government's Construction Import & Export Corporation.[45]

▶ Discovering a luxury niche market is also a good strategy. In China, Coke is considered a luxury item, and Coca-Cola sends its trucks into every corner of China to encourage sales. As a result, Coke's sales are 10 times higher in China than in the rest of Asia.[46]

China is a new frontier in terms of marketing strategy. Learning about the successes and failures of the pioneering companies in China will help a young, entrepreneurial company build a sound strategy for penetrating the market.

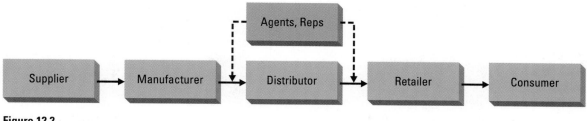

Figure 12.2
Indirect Consumer Channel

Whenever you look at building a marketing strategy across cultures or within a specific culture, it's important not to begin your research with a preconceived notion or stereotype of that culture. The global marketplace is affecting all nations. Every culture is evolving, and what has traditionally been true in the past may not be true tomorrow. It's therefore vital that your research be current and ongoing. And it's essential that those involved in creating your global marketing strategy have firsthand knowledge of the culture.

Distribution as a Marketing Strategy

Today distribution offers as many opportunities for growth, innovation, and competitive advantage as any of the other marketing functions. In fact, many successful companies, such as PriceCostco, a wholesaler to the public, and Ferguson Enterprises, a distributor of plumbing and heating equipment, have built their businesses on effective distribution of products. In marketing terms, the distribution decision involves finding the most effective way to get products to customers. But that's only part of the story. Where the company lies in the distribution channel determines what kind of business it is in and who its primary customer is.

Consider the consumer distribution channel in Figure 12.2. The manufacturer is the producer of the product and also the customer of the supplier that supplies the raw materials or parts to produce the product. The manufacturer's primary customer is the distributor, which buys product and sells it to its primary customer, the retailer. The retailer, in turn, has the consumer as the primary customer. This is known as an **indirect channel of distribution** in that there are intermediaries between the producer (the manufacturer) and the consumer. Notice that independent reps and agents may also enter the channel in addition to the other members or to replace the distributor. Their role will be discussed shortly. In a **direct channel,** the manufacturer cuts out the intermediaries and sells direct to the consumer.

In an **industrial channel** of distribution, businesses sell to other businesses. For example, a manufacturer may be targeting another manufacturer for the sale of its products. As Figure 12.3 shows, the options for industrial

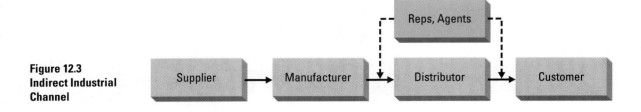

**Figure 12.3
Indirect Industrial
Channel**

markets are similar to those in the consumer market, with the exception that the ultimate customer or end-user is another business.

The manufacturer can choose to sell direct to the industrial user using no intermediaries or can use distributors or manufacturer's reps, who market to end-users. Another alternative is to work with agents, who act as a sales force for the manufacturer and either go through a distributor or directly to the industrial user.

Depicting the distribution channel graphically has great value. Apart from the obvious benefit of showing the various options available to get the product or service to the customer, graphing the channel will help you to

▶ Judge the time from manufacture to purchase by the end-user customer.

▶ Determine the ultimate retail price (or wholesale price in the case of industrial channels) based on the markups required by the intermediaries.

▶ Figure the marketing responsibilities and costs. Manufacturers may help distributors and retailers with promotion, but the heaviest responsibility and cost fall on the channel member that deals with the ultimate customer: the end-user.

The graph of the distribution channel can also become a **value chain** depicting the markups along the channel, as in Figure 12.4. At each stage, the channel member adds value to the product by performing a service that increases the chances the product will reach its intended customer. For example, the manufacturer charges the distributor a price that covers the costs of

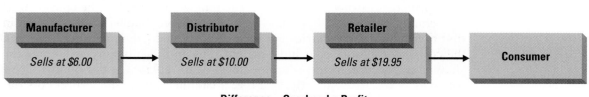

**Figure 12.4
Value Chain**

producing the product plus an amount for overhead and profit. The distributor, in turn, adds an amount to cover the cost of the goods purchased and his or her overhead and profit. Likewise the retailer does the same and charges the final price to the customer/end-user. The amount of markup at each point is a function of the industry and the demand for the product. A wholesaler, for example, will generally have an established markup or gross profit margin for a particular product line. Price is critical to the wholesalers because most retailers purchase based on price. Wholesalers offer discounts and terms based on quantity ordered.

On the surface it appears the final retail price could be substantially lower, perhaps even priced at the rate the distributor sold to the retailer in the example in Figure 12.4. However, that reasoning is flawed. The distributor performed a valuable service. He or she made it possible for the manufacturer to focus on producing the product and not incur the cost of warehouses, a larger marketing department, a sales force, and a more complex shipping department. All these activities now become a cost to the manufacturer of doing business with retailers and must be factored into the decision to choose a direct distribution channel.

Wholesalers/Distributors

Wholesalers or distributors (the terms are interchangeable in common usage) buy products in bulk from manufacturers and then seek retail outlets to reach the consumer or other businesses in an industrial channel. The wholesaler removes from the manufacturer the responsibility of finding suitable retail outlets for the products. A distributor can mean the difference between success and failure for a business. When a company entrusts its most valuable assets—its customers—to the distributor, it becomes conspicuously clear that selecting a good distributor is a crucial part of the marketing plan. Good distributors not only will contribute to increased sales but will help with product planning for the future. The specifics of what a distributor may do depend on the distributor. Some of the tasks performed by them include

- Warehousing of products
- Advertising and promotion
- Packaging and displays
- Training of retail sales personnel
- Transportation to retailers
- Service backup
- Restocking of retailers' shelves

The key to finding a good distributor is knowing to whom to talk. Some sources of information on distributors are customers, suppliers, lawyers, business consultants, and bankers (they will have knowledge of a distributor's payment record). Business owners should look for a distributor who provides good service, prices competitively to retail outlets, and is trustworthy. When that distributor is chosen, the company should execute a written contract with the distributor and monitor performance on a regular basis by sampling retail customers to determine if they are satisfied with the product and the service they are receiving from the distributor.

Logistics Firms

It takes a long time before a young, growing company can justify having its own distribution center. Consequently, many growing companies are outsourcing their packaging, warehousing, inventory control, and trucking requirements to third-party **logistics firms**. In distribution terminology, logistics is the timely movement of goods from the producer to the consumer. In addition to providing other services, logistics firms can negotiate the best deals and the most efficient carriers, potentially saving the growing venture thousands of dollars.

Agents/Manufacturer's Reps

Often manufacturers/producers will retain agents, brokers, or manufacturer's reps to find suitable outlets for their products. **Agents** will arrange agreements with wholesalers and retailers for the manufacturer. Agents usually do not buy or hold an inventory of goods from the manufacturer; instead, they bring together manufacturers and distributors or retailers to establish the most efficient distribution channel. The manufacturer or producer shares the cost with other manufacturers represented by the agent and pays a commission only on what the agent sells.

Manufacturer's representatives are essentially independent salespeople paid on commission who handle the manufacturer's business in specific territories. Unlike agents, who bring buyers and sellers together for individual transactions, manufacturer's reps work with a specific manufacturer on a continuing basis, receiving a commission per product sold. Reps may also provide warehousing in a territory and handle the shipping of the product to the retailer.

Specialty Markets and Distribution

Many entrepreneurs have taken advantage of specialty markets and distribution strategies. These include selling to industrial customers, selling commodities, and selling to superstores. We begin this section with trade shows and exhibits, which are excellent venues for reaching people in specialty markets as well as global markets.

Trade Shows and Exhibits

For some entrepreneurs, trade shows, fairs, and exhibits are a primary way to expose their products to a large audience and to reach specialized audiences that might otherwise be difficult to find. Trade shows and the like are also a good way to find out who the competitors are and what marketing techniques they are using. It's the place to meet and negotiate with sales reps and get names for a mailing list. But the primary reason to display products at a trade show is to eventually make the industry aware of your company and its products and, ultimately, to sell more product. To accomplish this effectively, a company should do the following:

1. Rent booth space. Then hire a display designer to design and produce a quality display booth that will attract a lot of attention. Visiting several trade shows prior to doing your own will give you some ideas as to what works and what doesn't. You may also be able to work out a deal with another company that has compatible products to share a booth and combine resources.

2. Hire someone personable to distribute an information sheet to as many people as possible and invite them to stop by the booth. The expensive brochures should be saved to hand out to potential customers at the booth. It is also important to ask for business cards for follow-up with people who took the brochure. To avoid wasting money handing out expensive color brochures to people who will merely leave them in their hotel rooms, one company took a high-tech approach. It brought two laptops, one with database software and the other with fax software and a modem. Potential customers typed their names and addresses into the database, then went to the second computer, where they selected from the onscreen display the information they would like to receive. That information was immediately faxed to the potential customer's place of business. Anyone who is willing to do this is probably a good lead.

3. Have enough knowledgeable, personable people in the booth so that potential customers don't have to wait to talk to someone. That way breaks can be staggered so that the booth is always staffed.

4. Consider renting a hospitality suite in the hotel where the trade show is located to entertain key people in the industry.

The Real World of Entrepreneurship

Trade Show Savvy

To learn about trade shows and conventions where a company can display its products, check the library for the *Trade Show and Convention Guide,* which can also be ordered from Budd Publications, P.O. Box 7, New York, NY 10004.

5. Offer something free at the booth: a sample or a contest.

6. Follow up with letters to anyone whose business card was collected and phone calls to all serious prospects.

Resources in a start-up company are normally limited, yet it's often possible to partner with a compatible company to share the expenses of a trade show booth.

Marketing to Industrial Customers

When the target market the company is trying to reach is other businesses, the marketing strategy differs somewhat in terms of advertising and promotion. Consumer products and services require a lot of high-profile advertising and promotion to entice customers away from the myriad other choices they have. With industrial products and services, the focus is on letting the targeted businesses know that the product or service is available and what it can do for them. In general, industrial products and services do not use broadcast media or the most popular print media. Instead, they rely heavily on direct mail, personal selling, trade shows, and articles and advertisements in trade journals.

Since most industrial product manufacturers distribute their products through wholesalers, it becomes the wholesalers' job to market to and locate retail outlets. If you are dealing with industrial customers, you need to investigate how products are promoted in that industry. That will give you a good idea of where your customers typically look when they are trying to find a product or service. Talking to customers about the marketing strategies in the industry and how effective or ineffective they are is an important way to see if you can innovate a new marketing strategy that will better serve the customers' needs.

Selling to the Superstores

For many consumer product companies, a substantial portion of their revenues come from a few customers known as "superstores": discount outlets such as Target, Kmart, and Wal-Mart, **category killers** such as Home Depot and Toys 'R' Us, or warehouse clubs such as PriceCostco. These giant outlets have enabled small manufacturers and others to market on a national and international level, whereas without them, the companies may have been forced to take a more conservative regional approach. It is estimated that mass merchandisers account for 40 percent of all U.S. retail sales.[47] Despite the fact that they comprise less than 3 percent of all retail outlets, the very top discount chains—those with 50 or more stores—account for 11 percent to 13 percent of all retail sales. It's no wonder, then, that attracting and keeping these valuable customers is important to the financial well-being of small manufacturers. It affects product development, brand visibility, factory efficiency, and the company's ability to retain quality sales reps, not to mention the ability to pay back lines of credit and maintain a positive cash flow.

If your marketing strategy includes marketing to the mega-retailers, it's important to do it carefully and correctly. Find the right person to approach and present the company's case; usually this is a buyer. It will probably take several phone calls before the buyer calls back. It may also take the help of a good sales rep who is used to doing this kind of thing. The company should also consider the trade show route to attract the attention of buyers from the major chains it may be having trouble reaching.

As in everything else entrepreneurs do, the pitch is crucial. The company must show it understands who the consumer is, who the competition is, and how the company's product will sell. You should never approach a large chain unprepared to deliver when that first order comes. Usually, if the chain likes the product, it will place an initial order to test it in a few of its stores before rolling it out nationally. It's important to remember that these chains, if they do take the product to all their stores, order tremendous quantities, and you must have the infrastructure in place to handle the volume.

The marketing job is not over when you get an order from Wal-Mart. Southern California entrepreneur Marcel Ford's company, Botanical Science, sold his silk plant cleaner to PriceCostco. It did well initially, and then sales slowed. Ford learned that if he periodically did demonstrations of the product in the store, he increased sales substantially. So he hired some people part time to do the demonstrations and has successfully maintained his presence with the retailer on a national basis.

Selling a Commodity

Many companies face a time when high quality and service have become the standard in the industry and the only differentiating factor among companies' products is price. The company finds it is seeing sales increase but profits decline along with margins; so essentially, the owners are working harder and making less money. The phenomenon is known as *commoditization*, and it is something that can happen almost overnight. Here are some signs that portend this problem:

1. Customers begin treating the company as just a bid, and face-to-face contact decreases. This is typical in the construction industry where a low bid often wins over quality because the product, a building, is perceived as a commodity.

2. **Bundling,** which the company used to enhance its products and sell more to the same customers, is being pulled apart by customers who are focusing on price and doing more of the service part of the bundle in-house.

3. The company's salespeople constantly have to deal with customer complaints about price. Suddenly the product has lost its inherent value.[48]

Where it has been determined that the product is becoming a commodity, it is vital to understand that the value the product once had has now shifted to the value of the relationship among the company, its sales reps, and the customer. The company must now look for that unique value that only it can deliver. Unfortunately, many companies become reactive rather than proactive. They add more services to the product, thereby decreasing margins even more, or they downsize the business, which is a move backward in a growing company. Instead, they need to take the focus off price and put it on what the customer perceives as added value. They need to begin rebuilding customer relationships from the customer's point of view.

Cases Relevant to This Chapter

Pelco

SB Networks

Marcus Food Co. and Buckhead Beef

Issues for Review and Discussion

1. How does the promotion strategy for consumer-oriented businesses differ from that of industrial businesses?
2. What impact is technology having on an entrepreneurial venture's marketing strategy in general? Give three specific examples of this impact.
3. What are the steps in setting up a web site for global marketing?
4. Discuss the importance of national culture to the diffusion of products into Mexico, China, Japan, and Europe.
5. If the product or service your company provides is becoming or already is a commodity, what steps should you take to remain competitive?

Experiencing Entrepreneurship

1. Interview a businessperson from Mexico, China, Japan, or Europe and verify the cultural and business conduct issues presented in the chapter.
2. Log onto the Internet, find a commercial site, and evaluate it based on the criteria discussed on pages 342–343.

Resources

Balachandran, M., ed. (1993). *Encyclopedia of Business Information Sources: Europe.* Gale Research.

BBS Magazine. For callers and system operators. (1-800-822-0437)

Boardwatch Magazine. Monthly coverage of the Internet. (1-800-933-6038)

Bryant, Alan D. *Creating Successful Bulletin Board Systems.* Reading, MA: Addison-Wesley. Includes Bread Board bulletin board software to run a BBS.

De Mente, Boye Lafayette (1993). *How to Do Business with the Japanese: A Complete Guide to Japanese Customs and Business Practices.* NTC Publishing Group.

Engholm, Christopher (1994). *Doing Business in Asia's Booming "China Triangle" (The Prentice-Hall Emerging World Market Series).* Englewood Cliffs, NJ: Prentice-Hall.

Entrepreneur Magazine. Business Guide 1390, Electronic Bulletin Board Service. (1-800-421-2300)

Howard, Thomas J. (1995). *Global Expansion in the Information Age: Big Planet, Small World.* New York: Van Nostrand Reinhold.

Howells, Jeremy, and Michelle Wood (1993). *The Globalisation of Production and Technology.* Belhaven Press.

The Interactive Services Association (301-495-4955).

Johnson, Michael, and Robert T. Moran (1993). *Robert T. Moran's Cultural Guide to Doing Business in Europe.* Butterworth-Heinemann.

Kenna, Peggy, and Sondra Lacy (1994). *Business China: A Practical Guide to Understanding Chinese Business Culture.* NTC Publishing Group.

Kenna, Peggy, and Sondra Lacy (1994). *Business Japan: A Practical Guide to Understanding Japanese Business Culture.* NTC Publishing Group.

Lamont, Douglas (1996). *Global Marketing.* Cambridge, MA: Blackwell Publishers.

Moore, Geoffrey (1995). *Crossing the Chasm: Marketing and Selling High Tech Products to Mainstream Customers.* New York: HarperCollins.

Moore, Geoffrey (1995). *Inside the Tornado: Marketing Strategies from Silicon Valley's Cutting Edge.* New York: HarperCollins.

Newman, Gray, and Anna Szterenfeld (1992). *Business International's Guide to Doing Business in Mexico.* New York: McGraw-Hill.

Nothdurft, William E. (1992). *Going Global: How Europe Helps Small Firms Export.* Washington, DC: Brookings Institute.

Winsor, Anita (1994). *The Complete Guide to Doing Business in Mexico.* New York: AMACOM Book Division.

Internet Resources

Business Information Sources on the Internet
http://www.dis.strath.ac.uk/business/
Provides a great number of links to other sites in England and Europe.

The Business Times
http://www.asia1.com.sg/biztimes/
Provides business-related information from the Far East, including Taiwan.

The Economist
http://www.economist.com/
An excellent international business journal.

EXPOguide
http://www.expoguide.com/
A large list of trade shows and conferences.

Global Trade Center
http://www.tradezone.com/
A source of many business links and listings of international business opportunities.

Process Management in Entrepreneurial Companies

V

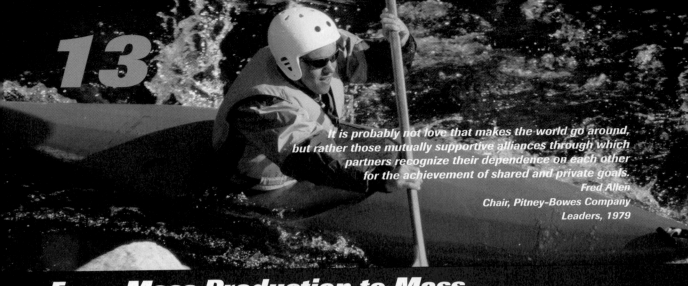

> It is probably not love that makes the world go around,
> but rather those mutually supportive alliances through which
> partners recognize their dependence on each other
> for the achievement of shared and private goals.
>
> *Fred Allen*
> *Chair, Pitney-Bowes Company*
> *Leaders, 1979*

From Mass Production to Mass Customization: Product Development in Entrepreneurial Companies

Preview

Understanding this chapter will give you the ability to

▶ **Explain the move from mass production to mass customization.**

▶ **Discuss the nature of product development for entrepreneurial companies today.**

▶ **Describe the product development cycle.**

▶ **Discuss the unique issues of product development in small companies.**

▶ **Explain ways to design right the first time.**

▶ **Discuss the value of designing for manufacturability.**

▶ **Explain how to achieve mass customization.**

Terms to Know

Mass customization, 366
Breakthrough
  products, 371
Platform products, 371
Demand factors, 372
Structural factors, 372
Time to market, 373
Fast-cycle product
  development, 373
Aggregate project
  planning, 377
Derivatives, 378
Partnered
  projects, 378
Licensing, 378
Electronic data
  interchange (EDI), 383
Quality function develop-
  ment (QFD), 384
Design for manufactura-
  bility (DFM), 387
Design rules, 387
Design for
  producibility, 387

Young Entrepreneurs—Minicase

David H. Meadows
ScreenShop Software

One common entry strategy that entrepreneurs undertake is the niche strategy, in which they find an area of the market that is not being served and fill it. Even the smallest niche can potentially be a winner for a young entrepreneur. David Meadows found that out when he created a niche that crossed over both the software and corporate gift markets. ScreenShop, based in New York City, develops computer screensavers for promotional, incentive, and training purposes. Its ScreenShop™ software raises traditional screensavers to a new level by merging entertainment, information, and technology into a customized package that lets companies reach their targets—whether customers or employees—in a unique and exciting way, right on their desktops. The screensavers incorporate text, photos, sounds, animation, and often time-released messages.

David Meadows didn't start out in the computer software industry. In fact, he took a variety of roads to his current business. Raised in Akron, Ohio, Meadows finished high school six months early and took off for his first year of college, first at the University of Colorado at Boulder and then Saint Petersburg Junior College in Clearwater, Florida. Finally, he returned to his home state to attend Ohio University, where he graduated in 1991 with a bachelor of science degree in communication and a bachelor of business administration. Over the next year, he traveled around the United States and worked in his family's business in Florida. In August 1992, Meadows moved to New York City to become the full-time national campus development director for the Association of Collegiate Entrepreneurs (ACE), an international organization created to support and inspire entrepreneurship among college students. In August 1993, however, the entrepreneurial bug bit him. He left ACE to start his own company to market a product called Worldbits!® Country-A-Day Calendars, which was to become the number three seller on Rand McNally's retail best-seller list.

A European trip was the genesis for Worldbits. Meadows recalls that at one point a European said to him, "You Americans are so '#*@$'; you know nothing about the rest of the world!" This brash statement, though not directed at Meadows personally, inspired him to create a product that would help promote international awareness. With personal savings, loans, and credit cards, Meadows bootstrapped Worldbits into existence. The product was a printed daily calendar that explored counties of the world with facts and information as well as maps. He managed to sell the product as a customized promotional gift to AT&T for its clients, but soon found it was too costly to produce and customize. Although the product was successful and sold out on retail shelves of small bookstores, in the Rand McNally outlet, and at the United Nations, Meadows took a loss on the company and closed it in December 1995.

From this experience, Meadows learned that screensavers essentially could act in the same way as a daily calendar and be produced at a fraction of the cost. The Worldbits concept evolved into a screensaver, and a new company was born. On November 29, 1995, Meadows applied for a trademark on the name "SmartScreen" for his new software company. Six months later, however, he discovered that Pointcast, a "push" screensaver technology company, had applied for the same trademarked name on November 19, 1995. Meadows therefore was forced to change the name of the company to ScreenShop.

ScreenShop Software was profitable from the start. "The software industry has a certain magic to it," says Meadows. To help finance its growth, Screen-Shop requires deposits up front for customized work. There are many industry competitors because the entry barriers are low and the technology is not highly advanced. The trick to survival, according to Meadows, is to find a niche market. ScreenShop found its niche in the personalized corporate screensaver market. In July 1997, ScreenShop Software introduced its newest product, IncentiveScreen™, which was inspired by research indicating that a screensaver is used 38 percent of the time a computer is on and that having a goal enhances employee performance. Suppose Xerox has 6,000 employees competing for a trip to Hawaii. ScreenShop will customize a screensaver with photos of Hawaii, along with motivational quotes and other information. The screensaver is then distributed to all employees to promote the program and motivate them with a visual reminder on a daily basis.

Meadows provides another example. "Imagine the concept of going into a Mercedes dealership and having your picture taken with a digital camera, and then you're handed a normal floppy disk. Once you get home, you place the disk in your computer and install the new Mercedes screensaver. You then see all of the Mercedes cars drive across the screen with your picture in the driver's seat."

The biggest challenge facing ScreenShop is growth capital. "I have wanted to maintain a wholly owned company financed through growth, and therefore, it's a slower process," Meadows says. Meadows is learning that growth from internal cash flow requires patience, which is not always easy in the volatile software industry. Being first in the market with a new niche product requires large amounts of capital, but it's an exciting place to be because, as Meadows claims, "First to the market usually wins, but now the race is on."

Meadows advises aspiring entrepreneurs to "Seek advice from seasoned entrepreneurs and never, ever, ever give up. . . . I [didn't] give up and soon we should be jointly producing the Worldbits Screen Saver with a major translation company."

What is a compatible, customized product that Meadows could create to diversify his product offering?

Throughout this book we talk about putting the customer at the center of the business. Nowhere is this more important than when the product or service is first created. The principles that have guided production-oriented corporations for 100 years are dissolving in favor of a new approach that puts the customer at the center of the design and production process. It's called **mass customization**, and evidence of its existence is everywhere, from the myriad telephone options available to customize a customer's calling habits (call waiting, call forward, conference calling, etc.) to copy centers offering professors the means to create custom books for their students using a variety of sources. David Meadows' company, ScreenShop Software (see Young Entrepreneurs—Minicase), develops customized screensavers for companies to use in such things as incentive programs. Even the commodity-based insurance industry is no longer mass producing insurance. In today's highly fragmented markets, insurance companies are finding they must tailor products to customer needs. The new paradigm requires new strategies on the part of entrepreneurial companies that want to achieve and maintain a competitive advantage in a dynamic, global environment.

The United States became the world's most powerful economy due in large part to the concept of mass production as conceived by Henry Ford and Frederick Taylor. The essence of mass production was to create demand to meet the needs of mass production—in other words, mold the customer into a common package that was good for everyone. One best way—one best car, in black—resulted in a rigid management structure with workers trained to become automatons, specialists in one small aspect of production that they repeated over and over. At the peak of the mass production paradigm, the major corporations became the dictators of the economy, concentrating more on their own needs than those of the customer. "The task became one of shaping demand to meet the needs of mass production rather than sculpting production to satisfy customer needs and tastes."[1] As a consequence, production became standardized with a focus on reducing costs and prices, and quality was not part of the equation. In 1913, when the assembly line was introduced to produce the Model T, the amount of time it took to build a car dropped from 12 hours, 8 minutes, to 2 hours, 35 minutes. Soon Ford was able to produce 1,000 cars a day.[2] Assembly-line mass production brought prices down, so more people could afford these goods; this, in turn, meant increased demand for products. And so a cycle of greed was born. One unfortunate consequence of this system was the prevailing theory of customer service: *caveat emptor,* or "let the buyer beware." Although contrary to current philosophy, this approach to business actually spawned extraordinary results at the time, producing the wealthiest economy in history.

Shifting Away from Mass Production

During the 1980s, several factors precipitated the shift away from the mass marketing paradigm.[3] For the most part, it was the Japanese who triggered the shift as they mounted an effort to gain market share from U.S. manufacturers. The results were remarkable and unprecedented:

▶ The concept of lean manufacturing, pioneered at Toyota, resulted in automated, computer-controlled production machinery.

▶ The manufacturing refinements of just-in-time, statistical process control, empowered work teams, flexible manufacturing, total quality management, and continuous improvement (all are discussed in Chapter 14) made the Japanese the most efficient mass manufacturers in the world.

▶ The ability to join mass production unit costs to the new refinements to provide a wider range of innovative products in a shorter amount of time was unchallenged.

▶ The ability to improve the quality and variety of mass-produced products at no additional cost also went unchallenged for a time.

▶ The control of economies of scope, which allowed the Japanese to implant new technologies in existing products to enhance them and to develop totally new products (the transistor, for example), was a significant competitive advantage.

Of course, none of these advancements would have been possible without the availability of low-cost computer technology, which enhanced the ability to track customer tastes and preferences, allowing for customization

AnyTime Access Inc. of Sacramento, CA has found a way to help lenders serve their customers. AnyTime provides 24-hour consumer-loan services to loan providers via phone and the Internet. Helping the customer by providing a specialized service on demand is a lucrative strategy. Thomas Bollum's business has gone from 15 employees in 1996 to 200 in 1998. (Linda Sue Scott)

of products and services to meet specific customers' needs. This chapter explores product development for entrepreneurs using a customer-centered paradigm.

Product Development for Entrepreneurs

The whole arena of product development has undergone profound change over the past decade, and the customer has been at the root of the change. As stated earlier, the time from concept to product launch has decreased dramatically (see Figures 13.1 and 13.2). As a result, companies such as Intel work on multiple generations of a product simultaneously. Intel will volume produce one generation of processor chips while beta testing another and designing yet a third chip. In fact, over the past 13 years, Intel has produced eight generations of microprocessor chips. Nevertheless, while production times have decreased, the demand for quality, reliability, and variety has increased. What used to be considered inconceivable levels of quality are now looked on as standards and expected, no matter what the cost of the product. Customers are also demanding customized lot sizes rather than merely accepting

Entrepreneurship in Action

A Product Development Strategy Even a Pig Can Like

Some entrepreneurial companies make creativity and innovation the center of everything they do, and in that environment employees and customers thrive. New Pig Corporation, a Pennsylvania-based company, is a manufacturer and direct marketer of industrial cleaning products. The company was founded in 1985 with only one product: the Pig, an absorbent sock that soaked up industrial leaks and spills. It has since seen annual sales increase an average of 40 percent annually, and in 1994 revenues exceeded $50 million. It employs more than 190 people.

While exemplary, these statistics aren't the most interesting thing about New Pig. What is really dramatic is the fact that 46 percent of those 1994 sales were generated by new products introduced within the previous three years. In 1995 alone, New Pig introduced 392 new products, 40 percent of which were developed internally. How can this incredible rate of new-product development be explained? There are four reasons New Pig excels in the area of new products and innovation:

1. *Focus on innovation.* New Pig's philosophy requires that everyone, from top management down to the janitors, focus on a constant stream of innovation; in other words, new-product ideas come from everyone in the company. New Pig has made product innovation so important that assignment to a new-product team is considered a privilege, something to work for, and anyone assigned to a new-product team has cradle-to-grave responsibility for the product.

2. *Create an environment for new ideas.* To encourage and keep track of new ideas from employees, vendors, and customers, New Pig uses a database called the PIT. As ideas are gathered, they are fed into the PIT, which currently contains more than 4,000 new-product ideas. Most of these ideas relate to customers' workplace problems. When a customer calls in to New Pig with a problem, the customer service representative dials a voice mailbox into which he or she relates the content of the conversation with the customer. That content is then coded and keyed into the PIT, which is a ready source of product ideas to test. New Pig also uses its four-color catalogs, called Pigalogs, to solicit new ideas. A postcard in the catalog asks customers to name the problems they are having and three ideas for solving them. In appreciation for their effort, customers receive a promotional reward such as a pig T-shirt or a baseball hat with the hindquarters of a pig protruding from the bill. The return rate on the cards is more than 10 percent.

3. *Humor helps.* New Pig has found that humor makes a potentially dull, industrial business lively and more interesting. Customers know that when they call with their very unusual problems and suggestions, no one is going to laugh at them because the company is already laughing at itself.

4. *Product development tool kit.* New Pig believes in using a full complement of the latest product development tools: quality function deployment (QFD), concurrent engineering, design for manufacturing (DFM), aggregate project plans, early system prototyping, and project audits. It actually prototypes the entire range of product activities, including the product, manufacturing, marketing, sales, and service, in addition to early testing of its products with the customers who suggested them. Its development efforts have been divided into several major product platforms: absorbents, workplace safety, chemical storage and handling, and spill response. The company puts its resources toward each platform in proportion to the amount of activity it is expected to generate.

New Pig Corporation is an excellent example of a scrappy entrepreneurial firm that has defined a niche in the market, exploited it, and owned it through new-product development.

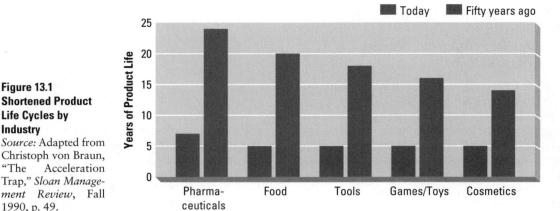

**Figure 13.1
Shortened Product
Life Cycles by
Industry**
Source: Adapted from
Christoph von Braun,
"The Acceleration
Trap," *Sloan Management
Review*, Fall
1990, p. 49.

what the manufacturer claims it customarily does. Manufacturers are no longer in a strong position to dictate anything to the customer. Quite the contrary, they are under pressure to make the customer part of the team from the very conception of the product.

Customers have also brought about the convergence of products and services into products that have services bundled with them and services that offer products as spinoffs. The video game market is a good example. Nintendo has regularly sold its game machines at cost, considering them merely a vehicle to enhance the sale of video games, its real profit center. The same can be said of Microsoft's Windows 95, which was sold very cheaply to encourage consumers to adopt it and programmers to write software to take advantage of its capabilities.

Not only young companies are affected by this new paradigm. Mature industries that have traditionally enjoyed long product life cycles and relative stability have seen their predictable environment all but disappear in the face

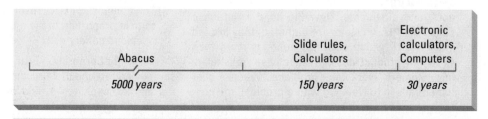

**Figure 13.2
The Shortening of the
Product Development
Timeline**

Source: Charles K. Kao, *A Choice Fulfilled: The Business of High Technology* (New York: St. Martin's Press, 1991), p. 56.

of changing customer expectations. The auto industry is a prime example. The number of world-class competitors in the auto industry has grown from 5 in the 1960s to 20 today, and each brings with it a diverse environment with distinct strategies and different technological know-how. Today an automobile manufacturer has to undertake four times as many projects as it did in the past just to maintain its market share.[4]

Why Chaotic Environments Are Good for Small Business

For entrepreneurial companies all these changes are seen as positive, because with change comes opportunity. Innovative new products and services do not generally emerge from stable environments where the comfort level is high; rather, it is at the edge of chaos, in dynamic environments, where they find a home. In fact, **breakthrough products**, those that do not derive from existing products (the fax machine is one), emerge in environments where there is high uncertainty, risk, and ambiguity. In his book *Mass Customization,* Joseph Pine says that turbulent environments consist of

- Little stability of demand
- Changing needs of customers
- Changing demographics
- Product saturation in a market
- Economic cycles, shocks, and uncertainties
- Technological shocks that cause changes in the dominant design.[5]

 The Real World of Entrepreneurship

Issues Raised by the New-Product Development Paradigm

The new-product development environment demands new approaches that will make a company more competitive and more responsive to changing customer needs. Following are five points of view entrepreneurial companies need to adopt to create value under the new paradigm:

1. Customer knowledge must be at the core of everything the company does. It is important not only to get feedback from customers during the design and prototyping process but to anticipate new uses for the product by observing how customers adapt it to their specific requirements.

2. Early prototyping will improve the ability to test the product and make adjustments and changes before more expensive product quality prototypes are built.

3. Fast failures help give a design team a "let's do it"

attitude about product development that will keep the company on the cutting edge. The time from identifying an idea for a product, to putting together the team, to the first very primitive prototype should be a matter of days.

4. **Platform products**, families of products built on the company's brand name, facilitate new-product customer awareness and simplify the choices they have to make.

5. Creating solutions to problems, not simply products, by continually working with those early customers will make it easier to take new products from the early adopter stage to the mainstream market.

SOURCE: Peter H. Farquhar, "Big Ideas for Developing Great Products and Services," Peter F. Drucker Management Center lecture, April 25, 1996.

Pine further asserts that these turbulence factors are of two types: demand and structural. **Demand factors** determine "the degree to which a firm can control, stabilize, and reduce uncertainty within its markets"; **structural factors** describe "the basic nature of the industry and are therefore less subject to manipulation by individual firms."[6]

Consequently, exciting new products and services that have the greatest impact on society tend to be born in dynamic, even volatile industries such as the computer industry. In these creative environments, successful streams of new products create enthusiasm in the firm producing them and in the marketplace as well, causing a momentum of their own. Everyone in the distribution channel, small companies and large, benefits. In fact, small companies often benefit more because their high degree of flexibility lets them respond quickly. Because of the turbulence of the environment for new products, the ability to design and produce products quickly has become a paramount issue for entrepreneurs.

Critical Issues in Product Development Today

The dynamic environment in which new products come to life has forced a new-product development paradigm with two fundamental characteristics of which all entrepreneurs should be aware: (1) the importance of effective product design and (2) the importance of reducing time to market. The importance of these characteristics will be discussed here, and strategies and tactics to facilitate their achievement will be treated later in the chapter.

The Importance of Effective Product Design

The effective design of new products takes on significantly more importance in dynamic environments for several reasons:

- Product design accounts for only about 8 percent of the product budget but determines fully *80 percent* of the cost of the product.

- Product design determines the marketability of the product by establishing the feature set and how it will work.

- Product design determines quality, reliability, and serviceability.

- Product design determines the length of time to launch and the cost to produce.

- Good product design can reduce the need for global manufacturing through significant cost savings.

- Good design gives the company the potential to set industry standards, which can be effective barriers to entry for competitors or even open up a new market, as the Sony Walkman did.

In today's environment, products will not get to market quickly enough to be competitive unless they are designed effectively from the start.

Time to Market

Time to market is a critical component of effective product development. In a volatile marketplace, if a new product is not introduced quickly, the market may change just enough to force redesign, which lengthens the development process significantly and starts a pattern of lost opportunities and higher costs. Nevertheless, it's important to underscore the reality that *the only real measure of time to market is the time to trouble-free production, which depends on getting the design right the first time.* An example of failure to properly design is the classic case of the aerospace firm whose manufacturing division designed and built a new plant that could not encompass the wing span of the new aircraft it was about to produce. All the effort to fast-cycle the product development was lost because of the need to redesign the production facility.

The biggest gains in shortening the time to market come from (1) reducing wait time between development and production tasks, (2) shortening the time to complete activities, (3) overlapping tasks where possible, and (4) most important, designing right the first time to avoid costly redesign at the end. In other words, the biggest gains in reducing costs to produce come from careful design.

Achieving effective, **fast-cycle product development** will result in momentous gains for the company (see Table 13.1). The closer the design of the product is to market introduction, the more likely it will meet customers' needs at that moment. Moreover, bringing out the next generation of product ahead of industry standard practice can mean substantial gains at the bottom line. It is estimated that a six-month jump on competitors in a market accustomed to 18- to 24-month design lives can translate into as much as

 Entrepreneurship in Action

BrainWorks Fast-Cycles

Howard Lind and Avi Telyas were looking for a way to get new products to market more quickly so that their young company, BrainWorks, Inc., could become a market leader. They found the solution in rapid prototyping.

Founded in 1993, BrainWorks, Inc., a $4 million company based in Port Washington, New York, manufactures computer accessories for kids, everything from colorful keyboards to mice, monitors, and masks. Using licenses obtained from entertainment companies with trademarked characters, it was able to design such creative devices as a mouse in the shape of a Star Trek Phaser.

Its rapid prototyping consists of initially designing three-dimensional models on a computer, then sending those designs to an engineering firm in Massachusetts that can produce plastic models, using a process called *stereolithography*, within 8 to 10 hours. Each model can cost up to $10,000, but the savings in time more than makes up for the cost. When the model has been approved, the computer models are sent via the Internet to a toolmaker in Taiwan. By using this approach, BrainWorks has managed to stay ahead of potential competition with fast-cycle new products coming out at a pace that will be difficult for competitors to duplicate.

SOURCE: Joshua Macht, "Plastics Make Perfect," *Inc. Technology* no. 4 (1995), p. 106.

Table 13.1   The Benefits of Fast-Cycle Product Development

The benefits of fast-cycle product development can be organized into four broad categories: marketing, technology, costs, and management.

Marketing	Technology	Costs	Management
▸ Better able to exploit windows of opportunity	▸ New technology is applied more quickly, which translates into recovering R&D costs sooner	▸ New generations with reduced costs can replace older, more costly generations more quickly	▸ Development team experiences shorter time to see the results of its work
▸ Design a niche and enter as the perceived and/or actual market leader	▸ Easier to take advantage of previous R&D, better resource utilization	▸ Reduced interest expense	▸ Enhances the spirit of creativity and innovation in the organization
▸ Potential for publicity		▸ Better utilization of plant and equipment	▸ Attracts the best people to work in the company
▸ Set standards for the industry		▸ Potential for premium prices or superior value	
▸ Potential for longer product life since the company is in the market first		▸ Revenue returns earlier to recoup R&D expenses	
▸ Can delay product development to further refine customer needs and come out at the same time as competitor with a better product			
▸ Better able to develop derivative products			
▸ Can start product development at same time as competitor and bring the product out sooner			

three times the profit over the market life of the design.[7] By contrast, slow-cycle product developers typically introduce a new product every two years. Better design and performance also permits the company to charge premium prices or keep prices stable and thereby create superior value for its customers. Moreover, effective, fast-cycle product development creates a sense of excitement about the company and within the company, which attracts favorable publicity and the best people to work there.

Cautions for Fast-Cycle Product Development

Fast-cycle development is not without problems. For example, when there are inaccurate assumptions about the target market or the distribution channel, a mismatch among product, process, and technology can occur. This was the case with the TI Professional home computer and the Kodak disk camera in the 1980s; both ultimately failed because the companies misread the way technology was heading. Another problem occurs when there is a mismatch between the firm and the environment: designing a product that manufacturing can't produce, for example. Or manufacturing and marketing may make different assumptions about the mix of products to be offered. Other difficulties that may be experienced during fast-cycle product development include lack of innovation in the product, technical problems that weren't anticipated, no cushion in resources for the unexpected, and lack of advance planning.

Traditionally, companies have traded off performance, cost, reliability, and time to market because they believed it was not possible to achieve them all; however, it is possible to achieve gains in all these areas without sacrificing anything.

Good design results in lower costs, and cost savings go directly to the bottom line. Consider the following simple example:

Revenue	–	Cost	=	Gross Profit
$5,000	–	$4,500	=	$500

Suppose your company desires to double its profits. You have two choices: you can double sales or lower costs:

Double sales $10,000 – $9,000 = $1,000 (doubled GP)

Lower costs 10% $ 5,000 – $4,000 = $1,000 (doubled GP)

Simply lowering costs 10 percent can produce the same effect on gross profit as doubling sales, which will require additional marketing expenses in the overhead budget and ultimately the lower net profit. Caution should be exercised when determining ways to lower costs, however, because some tactics will affect quality and may even have the reverse effect of raising costs. The following tactics should *not* be used to lower costs:

- Increase volume (this is the mass production approach)

- Omit product features, especially when you know the customer values them

- Use cheaper components and parts or a low bidder

- Redesign to lower costs (redesign always adds to the cost)

- Reduce expenditures on product development because this may ultimately affect product quality

The issue of costs related to production is discussed further in Chapter 14.

The Product Development Cycle

The product development cycle is typically portrayed as a linear process with the steps depicted in Figure 13.3. In reality, however, the product development cycle is far from linear. Instead it tends to have starts and stops, and movement forward and backward, until the production quality prototype is completed (the prototype that is equivalent to the final commercial product).

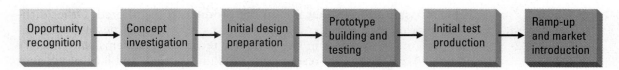

Figure 13.3
The Traditional Product Development Process

The linear depiction also suggests that the process moves through independent functions; for example, the opportunity may have been recognized by a marketer who, along with someone with financial expertise, did a feasibility analysis. It then moved to engineering design and finally to manufacturing. In fact, this is the traditional way product development has occurred in large companies. But this antiquated approach is not competitive in a dynamic marketplace; it's too slow, it's not integrated, it doesn't include the customer, and it lends itself to too much redesign, which is neither cost efficient nor timely.

Effective, fast-cycle product development for the twenty-first century integrates the functions of the entire company, whether they are within the company (in a larger company) or outsourced (as in the case of most entrepreneurial companies) to produce superior company performance. An integrated approach has engineering, manufacturing, marketing, finance, *and* the customer designing products and processes that reflect the needs of the customer. In this way, engineering doesn't create a product that is too costly to manufacture or lacks a market of sufficient size to warrant the effort. Purchasing will also work with the team by establishing reliable relationships with vendors, shortening raw materials acquisition time, fostering part standardization, and seeing that vendors deliver on time with optimal quality. Personnel will work with the team to hire the most qualified people and minimize turnover.

Outstanding development projects will

▶ Have clear objectives

▶ Focus on time to market

▶ Use a fully integrated team both within the organization and with outside resources

▶ Develop high-quality prototypes early in the process

▶ Have strong leadership from management

▶ Focus on core strengths in technology, talent, process, and so on

▶ Plan in terms of families of products (i.e., platform products)

▶ Get the customer involved early in the process to receive constant feedback throughout the process

The Product Development Strategy

It's important that a company develop a product development strategy that will give focus, direction, and integration to the various tactics it will employ. The strategy should arise from several critical questions:

1. What are the number, breadth, and depth of the products to be offered: platform (core products), derivative (enhanced products), number of different products?

2. Who will be the customers for these products?

3. How will customers purchase the products?

4. Why will customers choose these products over those of the competition?

5. How often will the company introduce new products?

6. How will these products fit into the overall strategy for the company?

In addition to answering these questions, the product development strategy must address the allocation of resources, so you need to consider the types of projects you may undertake. This process is called **aggregate project planning** and consists of identifying the various types of products the company may produce: research, breakthrough, platform, derivative, and partnered, as pictured in Figure 13.4.

Basic research consists of the technology your company may develop that will then be used on all its projects. Breakthrough products often result from basic research. These are products for which there is no precedent; in other words, the product or technology does not derive from an existing product or technology. The fax machine is one example of a breakthrough product. **Platform products** are those from which a family of products can be created,

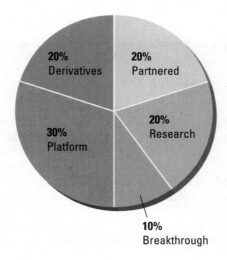

**Figure 13.4
Typical Product
Development
Projects**

and **derivatives** are products that arise from enhancements in existing products. Some companies will choose to offer platform products very infrequently but introduce a variety of derivative products on a more frequent basis, since they are easier to design and produce quickly. **Partnered projects** are those done jointly with other companies or with government research agencies.

Every company, whether or not it actually develops technology, needs a strategy for technology, that is, a way to determine which technologies are necessary to ensure the competitive success of the company and whether they will be developed, partnered, or acquired through licensing. In the case of technology the company is developing, a strategy should separate the technology, the process, and the service from the product itself so that technology is not tied solely to this product but can be used to develop additional products using the same technology and process or offered as a service to other firms in a joint venture, in a licensing agreement, or as a subcontractor.

The Unique Issues of Product Development in Small Companies

Small businesses face an entirely different set of constraints than do large mega-corporations with R&D departments and ample budgets. They work with very limited resources and typically rely on outsourcing certain functions or partnering with a more established company to achieve their objectives. But the lack of resources and established in-house departments has not hindered entrepreneurial companies' ability to compete effectively in terms of product development. Instead, it is precisely the need to bootstrap and use resources wisely that has compelled them to seek not only innovative product solutions but process solutions as well. Still, any entrepreneur undertaking product development through outsourcing should understand that initially it will take longer and cost more than it will when the growing busi-

The Real World of Entrepreneurship

One Way to Get New Product Recognition Quickly

One of the biggest problems with introducing new products is gaining recognition of the product name in the marketplace. **Licensing** an established product name is a way to achieve instant product recognition in a highly competitive market, and it's a growing trend. For example, Cohen/Gebler Associates, a corporate communications company in Boston, acquired the rights to Dilbert, the popular comic strip character, to use in its training videos. Other entrepreneurs have licensed Disney characters and other, similar name brands.

In general, licensing is much like renting, with the distinction being that in licensing the entrepreneur pays between 5 percent and 12 percent of wholesale revenues over the life of the agreement. Typically companies frequently must also pay upfront costs for product design, merchandising, and promotion, and, of course, the licenser will probably want final approval of the product. It's important for a licensee to negotiate as long an agreement as possible to have sufficient time to develop and establish the product in the marketplace.

Some of the best product ideas come directly out of a need and don't require a huge R&D investment. Mike Taggett was a rafting guide on the Colorado River where people were always losing their glasses in the rapids. Starting with a crude prototype he sewed himself, Taggett created the multimillion dollar Chums LTD, which produces adjustable eyewear retainers and a line of clothing called HelloWear. (Courtesy of Chums, Ltd.)

ness has more resources. This is because he or she will be relying on several other companies for various aspects of product development. These other companies—job shops, manufacturers, design engineers, and so forth—have other customers, so the entrepreneur's needs are one of many. Consequently, the entrepreneur may not be able to get a particular task accomplished as quickly as desired.

Entrepreneurial product development also tends to cost more because the company is asking the independent contractors to whom it is outsourcing to do one or two prototype units, and they are used to doing larger quantities. It costs more to do one of something than to do many.

Entrepreneurial companies that rely on new-product development as part of their competitive advantage often try to bring that function in-house as quickly as possible to speed up the process and decrease product development costs. Several solutions are available to overcome resource problems and should be considered by any entrepreneurial company undertaking product design and development:

▶ Prioritize development projects, focusing on those that have the highest return on investment.

▶ Focus on core competencies and design rather than parts other companies are already producing.

▶ Purchase off-the-shelf parts and components whenever possible.

▶ Consider outsourcing component design, materials specifications, machinery to produce, ergonomic design, packaging design, assembly drawings, and specifications to firms for which these tasks are core competencies.

▶ Get to a physical prototype earlier to more quickly converge on the optimal design and prevent later redesign.

▶ Check out job shops to which you will outsource to make certain they can work as quickly as you need and that they are used to working with entrepreneurs.

An Integrated Approach to Product Development

Entrepreneurial companies are driven to operate under an integrated, cross-functional, product development design, principally because they have to outsource so many of the tasks. The core functions—engineering, marketing, and manufacturing—as well as the customer are immersed in the product development process from the initial conception stage through prototype testing and market launch. The framework in Table 13.2 is a guide to an integrated approach to product development. It is based on the work of Steven Wheelwright and Kim Clark, but the financial function has been added to the framework because this key function must also play a valuable role in a fully integrated framework. In this framework, process design takes place concurrently with product design and with cross-functional input. Similarly, marketing and finance, which have input into product/process design as well, work in tandem to define prices and marketing budgets for the product launch.

Soliciting Feedback During Product Development

During the prototype phases (II through IV), it's important to test and use the product in the same manner customers will and also to compare it against competitors' products. At Deere & Company, a construction and agricultural equipment manufacturer, engineers spend considerable time in the field observing customers using the prototypes and soliciting immediate feedback. This is particularly important when designing and refining the ergonomics of the product. In the case of Deere & Company, customer feedback resulted in a redesign of the placement of controls on its equipment to make its continued use more comfortable. Deere even tests its owner's manual to ensure that the customer understands correct usage and maintenance. Once the product is launched, it is vital to receive continual feedback from everyone involved in its production, distribution, and use. This would include feedback from the following:

▶ *Manufacturing.* What would enhance the product and facilitate its manufacture?

▶ *Vendors.* How is the product being received? What can be done to improve the product, its components, and the way it's built?

Table 13.2   Framework for Integrated Approach to Product Development

Phase	I	II	III		IV	V
Functions	**Concept Development and Investigation**	**Product Planning**	**Design and Development** Stage 1	Stage 2	**Commercial Preparation**	**Market Introduction**
Engineering	Recognize opportunity; develop new technologies; build models; develop new-product ideas	Early prototypes; build supplier list; chose off-the-shelf components	Detailed design; integrate with process; build full-scale prototype and test	Refine prototype and designs based on tests	Evaluate and test pilot units Solve problems and adjust units accordingly	Evaluate product launch in the field
Marketing (customer)	With input from customer, recognize opportunities; conduct feasibility study	Define target market; estimate sales and margins; preliminary focus groups	Using prototypes, conduct customer tests	Retest refined prototypes with customers; plan market launch; plan distribution	Train sales force, field service people Prepare order/entry process system	Fill distribution channels; sell, promote, build customer relationships Get feedback on launch
Manu-facturing	Propose and test feasibility on new processes	Develop cost estimates; develop and simulate process Validate suppliers	Detailed design of process; design and develop tooling and equipment Help build full-scale prototype	Test tooling and equipment; build refined prototype; install equipment	Build pilot units in commercial process; refine process based on results Train personnel Confirm supply channel	Ramp up manufacturing to volume targets; meet targets for quality, volume, cost, and timeliness of order delivery
Finance	Work on priorities for development projects Establish budgets	Work with engineering and manufacturing on cost estimates, marketing on sales estimates	Refine estimated costs based on first prototype Estimate price Begin to establish marketing budget	Refine estimated costs based on second prototype Set preliminary price Refine marketing budget	Refine estimated costs for production and marketing based on final figures	Check actual sales and costs against projections; adjust budgets

Source: Adapted with the permission of The Free Press, a Division of Simon & Schuster from Steven C. Wheelwright and Kim B. Clark, *Revolutionizing Product Development: Quantam Leaps in Speed, Efficiency, and Quality* (New York: The Free Press, 1992). Finance phase added by author. Copyright © 1992 by Steven C. Wheelwright and Kim B. Clark.

▶ *Service personnel.* What is the reliability of the product? Are any components less reliable than others? Are customers satisfied? Is the product easy to maintain?

▶ *Customers.* Are they satisfied with the product? Is there anything they wish were different about the product? Are they pleased with their ability to get the product when they need it?

▶ *Customer service.* What is the complaint rate, and how are complaints handled? What specific aspects of the product receive the most complaints?

▶ *The media.* Is the company receiving positive publicity about the product? Has the product been reviewed in trade journals? If so, what was the result?

Doing Product Development in a Virtual Mode

Most growing, entrepreneurial companies don't have the resources to do serious new-product development on a continual basis or to enter an established market with a new product with any clout. As product development times and product life cycles shorten, it's impossible for one company in a vacuum to do it all. Moreover, in a global economy, it's very difficult for a company to maintain superior capabilities throughout the entire distribution channel from producer to end-user. Consequently, many new companies have turned to the concept of virtual or cooperative forms of organization to allow them to be competitive through new-product development. With a virtual company, new-product development capabilities can be coalesced instantaneously through the use of strategic alliances. This is a major improvement over merely outsourcing, because you are better able to control time and costs when dealing with strategic partners who have a vested interest in what you are doing.

The virtual company has been described as an alliance of core competencies distributed among several distinct entities.[8] (See Chapter 6 for a more complete discussion of the nature of virtual companies.) Each entity in the virtual organization is a peer company, so in essence the virtual company is not really owned by anyone, although typically one of the entities takes a lead role in terms of name recognition in the marketplace, much as an entrepreneurial team has a lead entrepreneur. To the customer, however, the structure of the virtual organization is not visible. This is a positive, for over the life of the virtual company, entities will come and go as competency needs change, making it a constantly evolving organization. The basis of every virtual organization is a fundamental belief in cooperation and trust. Sharing core competencies often requires sharing intellectual property, and without a sense of trust and cooperation, this will not be possible.

There are several reasons for young companies to consider the virtual route to solve product development and operations issues:

▶ A virtual network of strategic alliances allows the new venture to share other companies' resources and spread the risk at a time when its own resources are limited.

▶ Linking the core competencies of several companies enhances the ability to innovate.

▶ The integration of knowledge and skills among the entities reduces the time to market.

▶ A virtual network allows for easier access to new markets.

▶ It makes it easier to sell solutions instead of products.

◗ The ability to create open systems with plug-in components is the mainstay of a virtual organization and enhances its ability to create broader markets.

Though the virtual route has many advantages, you should remember that strategic alliances are like partnerships, with all the attendant risks and problems. The bottom line is to choose your partners very carefully.

The Importance of Technology to Virtual Product Development

It is important that entrepreneurs realize that when product development is outsourced, it often takes considerably longer. This is because you have to rely on job shops that will take on small jobs. Of course, yours will not be the only company for which they do work. So when you call on them to do some aspect of your product, they are unlikely to drop what they are doing to devote full time to your product. With the inherent time lag in outsourcing product development, it becomes doubly important to make sure the design is right the first time.

Virtual organizations are made possible because of information technology, which gives companies the ability to network electronically wherever they are located to send and receive purchase orders, monitor inventories and manufacturing processes, handle shipping and invoicing, and interact with customers. In reality, those young companies that deal with major manufacturers, distributors, or retailers probably will be required by their larger partners to establish **electronic data interchange** (EDI) systems, which link computers via telephone lines. With EDI these companies can save significant amounts of money by processing orders faster and more accurately. Moreover, by sharing point-of-sale, inventory, and forecasted sales information

Technology Tip

EDI Help

Growing companies are not left to their own devices when it comes to setting up an EDI system.

There are many publications that teach readers about EDI:

◗ *EDI Forum: The Journal of Electronic Commerce* (708-848-0135)

◗ *EDI News* (301-424-3338)

◗ *EDI Window* (514-288-3555)

◗ *EDI Bookstore* (www.pwr.com/ediworld)

You can also go online with the federal government to learn about EDI:

◗ Federal Electronic Commerce Acquisition Program Management Office (phone: 703-681-0364/9; fax: 703-681-0362/3)

◗ Department of Defense Electronic Commerce Information Center (phone: 800-EDI-3414; fax: 703-681-1225; www.acq.osd.mil/ec)

◗ Small Business Administration (phone: 1-800-827-5722; fax: 202-205-7064; http://www.sbaonline.sba.gov)

with their suppliers, they are able to maintain smaller and more precise inventories. Although EDI is an expensive and time-consuming process to implement, for growing companies it has benefits as well. EDI will help them cut costs, accelerate turnaround time on orders, augment cash flow, enhance sell-through, and build strong relationships.

First Years Inc., a $50 million distributor of infant accessories, found EDI enhanced its operations. Its products are manufactured by a plastic molding company in Massachusetts, G&F Industries Inc., which logs onto First Year's network each week to download the inventory demands for three months. With this information, G&F orders the components it needs to manufacture and ship First Year's products to a warehouse. G&F can also access the sales information to look for any changes in demand. With this approach, First Year can fill its orders on as little as a three-day turnaround for Wal-Mart without carrying excess inventory.

Designing Right the First Time

The principal benefit of designing a product right the first time is the savings in time and cost. Redesign—which involves reengineering, new drawings, and a reworking of the prototype—is more costly than the original design. Redesign may also cost the company the window of opportunity if the product is a fast-cycle product in a dynamic market.

Product Definition

Good product definition with significant input from the customer is the first requirement for "design right the first time." In entrepreneurial firms, cross-functional communication in the early stages of design comes more naturally than it does in large, traditionally organized corporations where departments are accustomed to a more linear, functional approach to product development. But even in small businesses, structured methods for problem solving help ensure that the design is right the first time. Two of those methods, quality function deployment and design for manufacturability, should be understood and employed to the fullest extent possible.

Quality Function Deployment (QFD)

Quality function deployment (QFD) is a structured method for letting the customer design the product by identifying critical customer preferences and requirements and incorporating these into the design engineering. In this way, the design focuses on those things that have perceived value to the customer and the market. QFD was developed in 1972 at Mitsubishi's Kobe shipyards and was later adopted by Toyota because it was thought to reduce design costs by 60 percent and design time by 40 percent. QFD was introduced in the United States in 1986 at Ford and Xerox.

The purpose of QFD is to insert customer input throughout the design, manufacturing, and service delivery phases of product development. The

Technology Tip

Use Software to Achieve Customer Satisfaction

Achieving customer satisfaction means designing and producing products, processes, and services that address the wants and needs of your customers. Using QFD to discover those wants and needs may seem like a very complicated way to do it. In reality, it's not, especially when you use software such as QFD/Guide™ and QFD/Capture™ from International TechneGroup Incorporated. It helps you understand and quickly get into the process.

In fact, it's so easy that you don't even need to know that you're doing QFD. The software asks you questions about your customers such as who they are, what they want, and how you can measure their satisfaction. It then lets you prioritize customer needs and displays results as either a QFD matrix or a text document. Using software to manage customer information and make decisions about products and services is something every small business can do.

market research that is done for QFD addresses strategic decisions, such as performance versus comfort, and functional or ergonomic decisions, such as where to place a handle. It does this through a principle known as "Voice of the Customer," a hierarchical set of "customer needs" that is prioritized.

Customer Needs and Requirements

The graphic in Figure 13.5 depicts a completed "house of quality." In the first step, engineers and marketing personnel establish how the customer could use the product. This is accomplished through focus groups with potential customers, interviews, questionnaires, or observation of the customer. How the customer might use the product is then translated into attributes that are important relative to this product. For example, in the case of a new portable computer, the customer may say, "It must be easily carried in a briefcase." A list of several hundred needs such as this may be developed, but they generally fall into three categories: (1) basic needs or assumptions about the product (e.g., that it must be small), (2) desired functions (e.g., what the customer wants it to do), and (3) unusual or unexpected desires (e.g., needs that may surprise or excite the customer). If, for example, the attributes for a new pen thought most desirable by the customers were (1) comfortable to hold, (2) does not smear, (3) ink lasts, and (4) consistency of ink, these attributes would be prioritized and assigned weights to represent their relative importance (see the green shading for the list of customer needs).

Hierarchy of Needs

In the second step, customer needs are structured into three categories: primary, secondary, and tertiary (see the blue area of Figure 13.5). Primary needs are strategic and consist of the top 5 to 10 customer needs. Using the pen as an example, these primary needs will direct the engineers to determine whether the size, ergonomics, or functions of the pen should be the focus of their efforts, and these then become the design parameters. Each primary

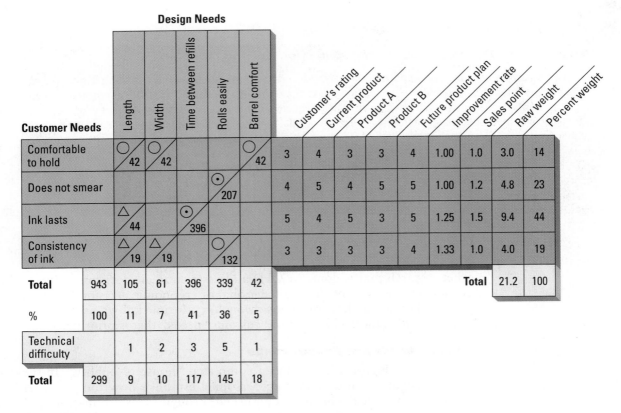

Figure 13.5
QFD Example

need is expanded into 3 to 10 secondary or tactical needs, in other words, what the product development team must do to satisfy that primary need.

For example, how is the desired length and width achieved, or what is the optimal shape? Tertiary or operational needs provide the engineers and R&D personnel with details needed to develop the solutions to the tactical requirements. For example, how do we know when the desired size is achieved?

The Relationship Matrix

In the third step, the central matrix is filled in (see the red area of Figure 13.5). Each cell links a design parameter with a customer attribute and also indicates the strength and direction (positive, negative) of that relationship. Symbols such as pluses and minuses may be used to indicate the strength and direction of the relationship.

Customer Perceptions of Performance

The fourth step, customer perceptions, is a measure of how customers perceive other competitive products in the market that are currently satisfying the need they have identified (see the purple area of Figure 13.5). Where no such products exist, it measures the way customers attempt to satisfy the need with alternative products. For the company, the results of this analysis can indicate potential problem areas as well as areas of opportunity.

The Roof of the House

The final step in QFD is building the roof of the house, which entails entering the interactions among the design parameters. The symbols in the cells indicate the strength and direction of the relationships and the trade-offs that exist in the selection of specific design parameters.

When the house of quality analysis is complete, the design team will have identified the customer's critical attributes, the design parameters related to those attributes, the interactions among the design parameters, and the potential to enhance the competitive position of the product. They will now have a framework against which to make choices about attributes versus design parameters versus costs.

The value of QFD is that it gives design teams a common language and a systematic approach to identifying key elements in the design. QFD represents a philosophy of product development that brings in all members of the team at the beginning of the design phase, including the most important member: the customer. Many entrepreneurs have used this team approach successfully without implementing the complete QFD process, which is a fairly complex method that usually requires the assistance of an outside consultant with experience in QFD. A modified version of QFD can also be used to assist service companies in designing the process for delivering their services.

Design for Manufacturability (DFM)

In the same way designing the *product* right the first time can reduce costs, designing the *process* right the first time, **design for manufacturability (DFM)**, can significantly reduce manufacturing costs and increase productivity. The key is to design the process for producing the product concurrently with the design of the product so the transition into production will be smoother and without the costly delays of engineering change orders because the process doesn't match the product. The QFD method can also be used to integrate the process for producing the product into the "house of quality" to reflect the engineer's manufacturing requirements.

DFM can be implemented in two ways: through **design rules** and through **design for producibility**. Many of the "rules of thumb" or design rules for DFM are calculated to reduce costs in labor and manufacturing and to refine quality. They define the parameters within which manufacturing can operate considering factors such as production volumes, material types, machine tolerances, and so forth based on the company's manufacturing capability. Some examples of design rules are the following:

▶ Minimize the number of parts.

▶ Simplify components; use common or standard parts.

▶ Design parts with symmetry.

▶ Minimize electrical cables.

▶ Make parts independently replaceable.

▶ Eliminate adjustments: reduce assembly errors, allow automation.

▶ Eliminate fasteners: simplify assembly, reduce direct labor.

▶ Eliminate jigs and fixtures:[9] reduce changeover costs, lower capital investment.

Design for Producibility

By contrast, design for producibility calls for a broader DFM principle that considers manufacturing to be a system so that when a decision is made in one area, the impact on other components of the system is also addressed. For example, the "minimize the number of parts" rule can result in combining many simple parts into one complex part. For this new part, assembly time, inventory carrying costs, and simplification of assembly do result in a lower cost for the product but may require a more complex, and hence more costly, mold for production. Thus, design for producibility looks at impacts of alternative designs on the entire manufacturing system and on lead time to market launch.

Designing for Quality and Reliability

If a company waits until the manufacturing process to evaluate quality and then does it through a series of inspections by various workers along the way, it can raise production costs as much as 50 percent. On the other hand, inspecting a product before it is made, during the design stage, allows the design team to engineer a manufacturing process that is stable and reliable. In other words, quality is designed into both the product and the process, and the goal is zero defects and zero engineering changes. This preventative approach is far more efficient and less costly than resorting to design reviews, numerous versions of prototypes, and beta tests to find problems. Even after the product is launched, the product team should be in a continual improvement mode, constantly seeking ways to incrementally improve and enhance the product.

The importance of quality when designing products with many parts cannot be overstated. An example will make this clear. If the quality level is a function of the probability that any part is defect free, then

$$Q^p = (Q_a)^n$$

where Q^p is the quality of the product, $(Q_a)^n$ is the average quality level of the parts in the product, and n is the number of parts. Suppose a product has 30 distinct parts and all are 98 percent defect free. Then

$$Q^p = (Q_a)^n = (.98)^{30} = .54 \text{ defect free}$$

This means that only 54 percent of the products will be defect free, assuming manufacturing quality is defect free. Choosing parts with a higher reliability rating can significantly improve the overall defect rate for the product. Suppose that parts with a 99.5 percent reliability rate are substituted. Then

$$Q^p = (Q_a)^n = (.995)^{30} = .86 \text{ defect free}$$

The bottom line is: designing for quality in both the product and the process will substantially reduce costs and increase the odds that the final product is defect free.

Achieving Mass Customization

There are many ways for any business to achieve mass customization, and they vary in the degree of implementation difficulty. The easiest way to begin the process is by *customizing services that have standardized products or services at their core*. For example, Marriott International has taken a standard offering—a hotel room—and customized how it delivers that room by creating different hotel chains to serve distinct classes of customers. Marriott Hotels, for example, fills the needs of business and leisure customers who are looking for an upscale environment. In contrast, Courtyard by Marriott is for travelers and businesspeople on a budget, whereas Residence Inn is geared toward business travelers needing extended-stay amenities. Marriott also uses a Guest Recognition System that permits it to recall a guest's preferences as to type of room for further customization possibilities. This is a fairly obvious, simple approach to customization that takes advantage of the power of electronic databases to better understand the customer and integrate a package of products and services that meet that customer's needs.

A second approach to mass customization is to *create customizable products and services* that are made to order for the customer or are virtual products, such as the digital camera, where the customer has control over the end result. Small companies in the computer hardware industry compete today based on their ability to provide the customer with a computer that contains a configuration of components that is customized to the customer's needs. No longer is a buyer limited to a standard configuration; today customers specify the quantity and type of ram, hard drive storage capacity, video ram, and CPU speed, along with type of sound card, modem, and so forth. They

If you go to Custom Foot in Westport, Connecticut you won't find just the standard shoe sizes and designs. Instead you can virtually design your own shoe to fit your foot and your taste exactly. Custom Foot's strategy is called mass customization, giving the customer exactly what they want. An electronic scanner takes precise measurments, and then customers can mix and match design style, color, and leather type. (Jonathan Saunders)

can literally build the computer from scratch with the exact components they want and upgrade it easily as new technology becomes available.

Customization of products or services sets up strong barriers to entry for competitors, but only for a period of time until others succeed in providing similar products or services. Therefore, it is critical to continually study the customer in an effort to seek new opportunities for product customization. Customization of services often involves letting customers do it themselves; this is the case with ATM machines or Internet service providers, where customers choose which services they want at the time they want them.

Perhaps the only way to really know what customers actually want is to *customize at the point of sale or point of delivery of the product or service to the customer*. Gathering information when the customer purchases a product or service gives the company important data on the who, what, where, when, and why of the purchase that can be electronically transferred to the manufacturer or producer. Point-of-delivery customization occurs when the product or service is customized at the point of purchase. For example, eyeglasses are custom fit to the customer after the purchase but before final delivery. Companies that bring services to the customer's office or home are also customizing at the point of delivery.

Yet another method of achieving mass customization is through *creating products and services with modular components* that can be configured in a variety of ways to meet customer needs. Black & Decker has been very successful in taking a small set of standardized components and, through variation, creating an entire line of tools. New companies such as Gentech Corporation, a California-based manufacturer of industrial power source machines, have made the use of modular components a competitive advantage that allows them to instantly create a machine to the specifications of the customer.

The important point to remember about mass customization is that customers do not purchase technology; they purchase perceived value. Mass customization for mass customization's sake has no value. Only when the customer perceives a benefit, a value to what the company is offering, will the company gain a loyal customer. Mass customization is a vehicle by which the company can develop a closer relationship with the customer and offer value that will set it apart from the rest of the competition in the marketplace.

Cases Relevant to This Chapter

French Rags
Pelco

Issues for Review and Discussion

1. What are the effects of the new mass customization paradigm on product development?
2. Discuss three benefits of fast-cycle product development.
3. How is product development different for small businesses?
4. How is quality function deployment used to listen to the voice of the customer in product design?
5. How can the virtual organization solve product development and operations issues for a young, growing company?

Experiencing Entrepreneurship

1. Visit a product development and manufacturing company. Look for ways it may incorporate the customer into product design. Does it employ fast-cycle product development? What specific things is it doing to improve its product development process?
2. Create an idea for a new product and make a list of where you would go to get such tasks as design, prototyping, and manufacturing accomplished.

Resources

Cohen, L. (1995). *Quality Function Deployment: How to Make QFD Work for You.*

Davidow, William H., and Michael S. Malone. (1992). *The Virtual Corporation.* New York: HarperBusiness.

Kao, Charles K. (1991). *A Choice Fulfilled: The Business of High Technology.* New York: St. Martin's Press, p. 56.

Pine II, Joseph (1993). *Mass Customization.* Boston: Harvard Business School Press.

Wheelwright, Steven C., and Kim B. Clark (1992). *Revolutionizing Product Development.* New York: The Free Press.

Internet Resources

ANSI Online

http://www.ansi.org/

This is the American National Standards Institute site, which also provides links to many other sites.

The National Technology Transfer Center

http://www.nttc.edu/

This organization helps companies work with federal laboratories to turn their work into technology that businesses can use and sell.

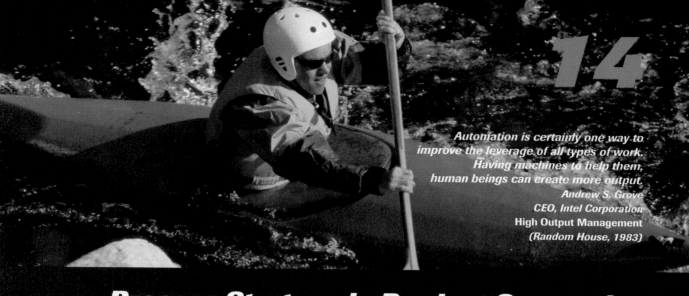

Automation is certainly one way to improve the leverage of all types of work. Having machines to help them, human beings can create more output.

Andrew S. Grove
CEO, Intel Corporation
High Output Management
(Random House, 1983)

Process Strategy in Product Companies

Preview

Understanding this chapter will give you the ability to

▶ Describe the nature of world-class manufacturing.

▶ Discuss the effect of technology on manufacturing and assembly processes.

▶ Explain the importance of agile manufacturing.

▶ Discuss the significance of TQM.

▶ List strategies for purchasing and inventory control.

▶ Describe two measures of quality.

▶ Explain how distribution is a competitive strategy for manufacturers.

▶ Identify the factors that affect site selection for manufacturers.

Terms to Know

Young Entrepreneurs—Minicase

Tyler Conrad
Colorblock Corporation

When you're born into an entrepreneurial family, no one is surprised that you too become an entrepreneur. But, almost from the beginning, Tyler Conrad had plans to grow a company much larger than any of the three owned by his entrepreneurial parents.

In 1993, at age 21, Tyler J. Conrad of Minneapolis, Minnesota, founded his first company, Colorblock Corporation (dba Minnesota Mitt & Sota) as a subchapter S-corporation in the basement of his mother's

new gift shop. While an entrepreneur major at the University of St. Thomas, Conrad has seen his mother sell 200 pairs of polar fleece mittens in a period of two months. This intrigued Conrad and, after some checking, he discovered that her contemporary women's clothing store in White Bear Lake was the only place that sold the mittens. They had been created as a hobby by a couple who had no desire to go into business. So Conrad set out to learn how to manufacture and distribute the product. In the spring of that year, he took his color-blocked, oversize fleece fashion mittens to a women's apparel trade show in New York and came back with 50 retail accounts. Meanwhile, his mother had decided to open a gift and home furnishings shop, which was to become the home of Colorblock Corporation. Later she added a coffee shop to the family's stable of business ventures. Conrad's father owns a successful real estate development company.

Minnesota Mitt has discovered a niche in the fashion accessory market. Conrad has found only one other competitor selling Polartec mittens, but he believes his product is of better quality and is more fashionable. To share the risk in this new venture, maintain low overhead, and keep costs down, Minnesota Mitt outsources patternmaking, cutting, and sewing. Conrad controls the design and quality, but does not manufacture in-house. Conrad also helps his customers, the retail outlets, promote the product by providing them with product knowledge, display suggestions, and promotional ideas.

The first season, Conrad ran the business part time and generated $46,000 in revenues. At the end of 1995, his second year, revenues totaled $732,000, and sales for 1996 were nearly $1.8 million. Growth is challenging for any entrepreneur, but when it happens almost immediately and you are growing at a rate of more than 250 percent per year, the challenge becomes immense. To raise working capital, Conrad accepted cash infusions from family, as well as three SBA-guaranteed loans over time. The company's product cycle consists of a heavy buying season in October, November, and December. By January the company is cash rich, and it uses these funds as working capital to promote sales. When Conrad first went to Norwest Bank for working capital, he had two strikes against him: his company was a start-up, and sales were very seasonal. The people at Norwest asked a lot of questions and ultimately decided to work with Conrad. They did not make a mistake. He quickly repaid the first two of his SBA-backed loans from profits; the third was structured to be paid back over a longer period of time. Conrad is very conscious of his company's financials and keeps a close eye on margins. His rule of thumb is that he will not produce a product if it can't make a gross margin of 50 percent.

Minnesota Mitt's product line has expanded to include hats, headbands, scarves, and gloves—all in fleece. In 1994, Conrad opened a seasonal kiosk at the Rosedale Shopping Center with a plan to unload some inventory, but the concept was so successful that over the next two years he opened 43 more in shopping malls located throughout Minnesota, Wisconsin, and Illinois. He did this through a type of franchising agreement whereby the owner purchased the name and the right to sell the Minnesota Mitt line of accessories. Such explosive growth concerned Conrad, however, so in 1997 he scaled back to 25 kiosks to better control growth.

In 1995 Conrad added a partner, Tom Mason, whom he had met in the entrepreneur program at the University of St. Thomas, and he also added the Sota line of fleece clothing with jackets, vests, shirts, and pants. These products retail at Nordstrom, Dayton, and Ships Ltd. of NY, as well as in Canada and Japan. In 1996, the company moved to new facilities and also rented warehouse space. Conrad and Mason use two national sales reps in addition to themselves to sell the product. They rely on temporary and contract labor to run the kiosks, which are both franchised and corporate. Conrad advises aspiring entrepreneurs to hire the necessary professionals to help manage growth. He now has a staff of 14 to better prepare the company for continued growth.

As if all this success weren't enough, Conrad was named U.S. Small Business Administration's National Young Entrepreneur of the Year for 1997. He is a prime example of an entrepreneur from an entrepreneurial family who always knew he would strike out on his own. It's a way of life for him, and Conrad can't imagine any other way to live.

What are the advantages and disadvantages of the process strategy Tyler Conrad has chosen for Colorblock?

More than 200 years ago, manufacturing was a process customized to meet the needs of the customer—a craft industry—but as customers began to value standardized goods, mass production became the new paradigm. Manufacturing was suddenly a separate function that received information through the filters of marketing, management, and finance. It was not until the Japanese assault in the 1950s and 1960s with total quality control (TQC), just-in-time (JIT), and quality function deployment (QFD) that manufacturing became part of a continual process of upstream and downstream activities and was recognized as a significant contributor to the overall performance of the firm.

Productivity in U.S. manufacturing has risen dramatically over the past decade, and the ability of small business to enter the manufacturing arena has increased tremendously. The gains can be attributed to three factors: (1) the downsizing and outsourcing of anything that is not a core competency for the company; (2) the commitment to total quality product/process management; and, most recently, (3) the trend toward *agile manufacturing* (also called *virtual manufacturing* or *networked manufacturing*). Aware of these forces, companies such as Emerson Electric and Mars, Incorporated, have merged these philosophies into their manufacturing strategies and realized substantial gains in effectiveness and profitability. New companies, however, have often fallen into the trap of focusing solely on the product in the start-up stage and then on marketing as the company grows without ever recognizing that superior process management is also a significant contributor to competitive advantage and certainly essential to cultivating an expanding bottom line. Integrating process design into all the activities of your business will save you time and money, and put your company miles ahead of product-focused companies.

Tyler Conrad (see Young Entrepreneurs—Minicase) knew he couldn't survive with high overhead costs in the early years of his business, so he decided to outsource the patternmaking, cutting, and sewing of his mittens while retaining control over the design and quality. He manages inventory and purchases carefully while being always on the lookout for new distribution channels for his products (e.g., kiosks).

This chapter looks at the processes involved in running a company that produces products as the primary source of its revenues. Those processes include manufacturing and assembly, purchasing and inventory, quality control, distribution, and site selection.

World-Class Manufacturing

World-class manufacturing process strategy consists of four primary components: the customer, state-of-the-art technology, superior resources and processes, and continuous improvement. The absence of any one of them will reduce the company's overall productivity and effectiveness. Figure 14.1 displays these components. The customer is the primary force driving world-

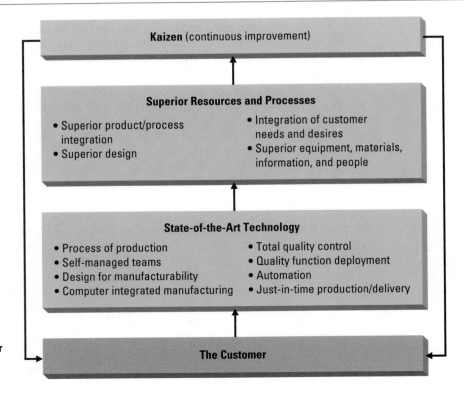

**Figure 14.1
Process Strategy for
World-Class Manu-
facturing**

class manufacturing. The customer is the foundation on which all the other functions are based, and superior performance is only achieved when the customer is involved in the manufacturing process. The following sections discuss each component in the figure in detail.

The Effect of Technology on Manufacturing and Assembly Processes

Today customers expect, and even demand, superior levels of quality, service, and response time. Therefore, manufacturers can no longer be rigidly structured, cumbersome in size, and bureaucratic in their decision making. They must instead be small, flexible, fast, organizationally flat, and simple in design. This is good news for entrepreneurs who want to start or own businesses involving the creation of products, because effective entrepreneurial businesses are inherently small, flexible, and simple in design. Flexibility on the manufacturing side means entrepreneurs need to reduce set-up times and manufacture without lots. The result is that with virtually no set-up time for production, each product produced can be different. However, to accomplish this, it is imperative that manufacturers employ the latest technology.

Probably nothing has had a greater impact on manufacturing processes than technology. Appropriate technology gives a company a strong competitive advantage and the ability to improve products and services, thereby broadening the customer base. New core technology in an industry acts as an incubator for new product/service concepts and new supply-based companies that can serve as the manufacturing core competency for another company in one or all aspects of a product. For example, large, multinational companies such as General Electric are increasingly transferring design and manufacturing to smaller vendors, and these small, entrepreneurial businesses are finding that their competitive strength in the industry lies in focusing on their core competencies and exploiting them to the benefit of much larger companies.

In fact, in some industries vendors are elaborately linked to provide a "one-stop shopping" experience for the larger company. For small-business

The Real World of Entrepreneurship

The Advantage of Smallness

If you and I are competing and I can read the market quicker, manufacture many different products on the same line, switch from one to another instantly and at low cost, make as much profit on short runs as on long ones, and bring out new offerings faster than you—or do most of these things—then I win. I can parry your every thrust, attack niches in your market that you're too bulky to squeeze into, improve faster, and maintain or even fatten profits while forcing you to follow my lead on prices.

Source: *Fortune*, September 21, 1992.

owners, this means they not only need to focus on efficiency and superior performance but must also seek to create and maintain those goals in the other companies with which they interact in their industries. When Chrysler found it had an engine part with a high failure rate, it began to examine its supply chain for weak links. All of its suppliers except one adhered strictly to world-class standards of quality and performance. The one exception was a small clay vendor that supplied a casting company, which then sold raw metal to the downstream manufacturers. The clay vendor, which was not up to the standards in the industry, finally went bankrupt, leaving the industry with no adequate supplier in that area. In effect, this small company threatened the entire supply chain and certainly the reputation of Chrysler.[1] This is just one example of the changing nature of manufacturing in a period that some call the **post–mass production paradigm**.[2]

The Importance of Agility

In their book *Agile Competitors and Virtual Organizations,* Steven Goldman, Roger Nagel, and Kenneth Preiss see **agile manufacturing** as a response to a rapidly changing environment. At a company level, agile manufacturing means operating profitably while dealing with constantly changing customer expectations and opportunities. At an individual level within an organization, it is the ability to contribute to the bottom line in a dynamic environment.[3] The ability to instantly synthesize new-product capability necessitates forming networks and strategic alliances to exploit core competencies. With agile manufacturing, choice is driven by the customer. Information technology makes its possible to treat that customer as an individual, produce to customer order in arbitrary quantities, and shrink production times.

 Entrepreneurship in Action

Using Agile Manufacturing as a Competitive Advantage

Cook Specialty of Pennsylvania has adopted the new agile manufacturing strategy. As a result, this custom manufacturer was able to help Welch Allyn, a medical instrument and diagnostic-products manufacturer, develop an enhanced line of laryngoscopes (a device for examining the larynx). The final product design is entered into the computer-aided manufacturing (CAM) program, which then generates the instructions needed by the machines that make the product. These are sent electronically to computerized machines that make the components of the final product.

Cook also maintains flexibility by incorporating manufacturing cells, which are simply integrated teams of people and equipment that can be instantly reconfigured to do a required job. Because the entire company is linked via a UNIX-based system, everyone has access to the information needed to complete a task and bring the "voice of the customer (QFD)" to the factory floor. At Cook Specialty, technology serves those who use it, not the other way around.

Source: Brian McWilliams, "Reengineering the Small Factory," *Inc. Technology* 1 (1996).

Flexibility means being able to reconfigure your manufacturing processes nearly instantaneously to meet the requirements of a customer's order. Compaq, the computer maker, uses manufacturing cells as a way to achieve flexibility. With this system each cell, or workstation, can be configured to produce a different computer model each day and is equipped to accomplish all of the manufacturing tasks from building and testing to shipping the product. (Chris Usher)

Agility is also critical to the shift from "manufacturing to knowledge-based information and service applications of manufactured products."[4] Today the success of a product is a direct function of the customer's perceived value of the knowledge, information, and services inherent in the product. Furthermore, **knowledge-based products** provide opportunities for continuing relationships with customers, a critical path to remaining competitive in the twenty-first century. Customers hold in high regard a company's ability to create value and continue to add value to what it has created over the life of the relationship.

Optimal agility (or flexibility) depends on several things:

▶ Teamwork among workers, organizations, suppliers, and customers so that all know how they fit into the big picture.

▶ Similarity of technology lines within product groupings. Using core technology to produce a variety of products is more efficient than "reinventing the wheel" over and over again.

▶ Commonality of parts, components, and product features. The ability to use common parts on different products saves design time and lets you purchase in volume more easily.

▶ Using off-the-shelf parts wherever possible. Why design a part that already exists?

▶ Letting suppliers design parts. Getting suppliers involved in the development of your product gives them a "vested interest." They are more likely to work with you and give you terms that don't constrict your ability to grow.

Essentially, agility is the ability to change quickly in response to changing demands, not as a reaction to them but in proactive anticipation of patterns of change in the industry and the market.

Total Quality Management (TQM) for Manufacturer/Entrepreneurs

Total quality management, as discussed in Chapter 7, refers to a framework or system for integrating *superior quality in all the elements of the business.* The traditional Japanese models of TQM incorporated five themes: (1) management commitment, (2) leadership, (3) customer focus, (4) total participation, and (5) process analysis and improvement.[5]* Within these themes are other principles important to process design: continuous improvement, total quality control, self-directed teams, automation, computer-integrated manufacturing, and just-in-time production and inventory. We will discuss each in more depth.

Kaizen: Continuous Improvement

If TQM is the vehicle to achieve world-class manufacturing processes, *kaizen* is the engine that drives it. *Kaizen,* which in Japanese means "gradual, unending improvement," is a principle that focuses on improving every aspect of the business. Under this philosophy, everything a company does (and this includes service companies) is a process and every element of that process is held under a microscope to see if it can be improved on. So although this chapter focuses on manufacturing, in reality the *kaizen* philosophy can be applied equally to service, marketing, finance, and so forth. There are several versions of *kaizen,* but the one we will discuss here is the USA-PDCA method, which is used by many companies worldwide. **PDCA** stands for *plan, do, check, act,* and is an acronym that embodies the essence of *kaizen.* Assuming employees are organized into self-directed teams for better productivity, the first step in PDCA is to understand the nature of the customer, the relevant needs and issues, and how your company may be failing to meet them. Once the nature of the customer is understood, the team can focus on the issue that needs improving and begin to analyze the process involved. For example, the issue may be that you don't know enough about what the customer needs to be satisfied. Focusing on the process for gathering customer information leads you to discover that the method by which you gather information from the customer may not be working effectively. The team that will deal with this issue will now need to gather information on the nature of the current process. This homework must be done before PDCA can be accomplished. PDCA then proceeds as follows:

▶ *Plan.* With the process identified and analyzed, the team now plans for the change that will take place to improve the process.

---

*Recall from Chapter 7 that Creech's five pillars of TQM are commitment, product, process, leadership, and organization.

▶ *Do*. The team implements the plan, assuming it has been determined that doing so will not pose unnecessary risk to other parts of the system.

▶ *Check*. The team proceeds to analyze the results of the change to verify that it actually improved the process. If not, the team will reexamine the plan to locate any errors in its reasoning.

▶ *Act*. Once the change has been verified, accepted, and documented, the team puts in place the changes, equipment, or whatever is required to make the change in the process routine and move on to define and research the next issue.

In this way, you will establish a process by which you can ensure that continual improvement will take place.

Total Quality Control

The term **total quality control (TQC)** derives from the work of W. Edwards Deming, J. M. Juran, and Armand V. Feigenbaum following World War II. It was the Japanese, however, who were quick to adopt this principle to overcome the perception that their products were cheap and wouldn't last. The successful implementation of TQC principles allowed Japan to substantially improve its export market and make enormous inroads into the U.S. marketplace, particularly in automobiles and electronics. Unfortunately, TQC has been practiced in the United States only for the past decade, so U.S. firms have been playing catch-up to the experienced Japanese companies. In fact, TQM is really a spin-off of the TQC philosophy.

In the past, quality was the sole province of pre-production design and testing and post-production inspection. Juran, however, suggested that quality encompasses product performance and satisfaction, and freedom from deficiencies and dissatisfaction as well.[6] The goal with TQC is to eliminate all defects at all stages of the process—in other words, to achieve perfection.

The Principles of TQC

The basic principles of TQC are as follows:

1. **Customer satisfaction**. The fundamental goal of any organization should be customer satisfaction, for without satisfied customers, there is no business. To achieve customer satisfaction requires going beyond customer expectations and providing products that never disappoint the customer. Continuous improvement—*kaizen*—is one route to the achievement of this goal. Customer input at every stage of product development is another.

2. **Quality circles**. Quality circles (QC) have been poorly received in the United States because they are believed to be better suited to the Japanese culture. The process of QC involves bringing employees together at the start of every day (or every shift) to discuss issues and daily plans. Many U.S. firms find this approach rigid in a culture that seems to thrive on sound bites and flexibility. Nevertheless, the underlying notion of

keeping everyone informed and on track, no matter how it's done, has merit and is essential to achieving total quality. Every business owner will need to develop a form of QC that is appropriate to his or her type of business if total quality is to be achieved.

3. *Hoshin.* In Japanese, *hoshin* means "policy deployment," in essence a planning and review tool that consists of annual objectives and strategies. It's very similar to the U.S. "management by objectives" (MBO) popular in the 1980s. It is a formalized process that requires a statement of objectives, how those objectives will be achieved, and how the company will know when it has achieved them. *Hoshin* is very compatible with PDCA and is an excellent tool for company annual reviews.

 The Real World of Entrepreneurship

Warranties

The company that subscribes to total quality management will likely wish to provide **warranties** with products to protect against potential liability and demonstrate that it stands behind the product. Today product warranties have also become a marketing tool to sell the product.

Some of the decisions to be made regarding warranties include the following:

▶ *Length of warranty.* This will depend on industry standards.

▶ *Covered components.* Some components may come from other manufacturers that have their own warranties. In this case, it's important to have the company's use of that component on the product certified by the OEM (original equipment manufacturer) so that the warranty is not invalidated in the new use. Then, if a warranted component from the OEM manufacturer becomes defective, it can be sent back to that manufacturer. However, it's still probably good business practice to have customers return the product to your company or to your distributors rather than to the OEM for service, repair, or exchange under the warranty that covers the whole product.

▶ *Product scope.* Will the warranty cover one or all products in a line, or will each have a separate warranty?

▶ *Market scope.* Will the same warranty apply in all markets? This will be a function of state and foreign laws.

▶ *Conditions of the warranty that the customer must fulfill.* Is there anything the customer must do to keep the warranty in force, such as servicing or replacing disposable parts? These conditions should not include registering the product via a postcard. Today a product is covered by warranty from the moment it's purchased, whether or not the purchaser returns a postcard stating when and where it was purchased or answers a short, informational questionnaire. As an incentive to get the postcard information, many companies offer update notification and potential discounts on future products.

▶ *Execution of the warranty.* The company must decide who will handle warranty claims (manufacturer, dealer, distributor), recognizing that customers do not like to mail products back to the manufacturer.

▶ *Policies for refunds/returns and shipping/handling costs.* This is a function of the company's philosophy about doing business. A customer-oriented company would probably offer a generous return policy and pay for the cost of returns.

Providing a warranty involves a cost to the manufacturer; however, that cost must be weighed against the potential loss of business if no warranty is provided. In the case of a new business with a new product, it's difficult to anticipate the number of problems that might occur as the product gets into the marketplace. Careful and adequate field testing of the product prior to market entry will go a long way toward eliminating many potential problems and the possibility of a recall, which is very costly for any firm, let alone a new, growing business.

4. *Poka yoke.* This is a Japanese term that means solutions to problems should be foolproof; that is, any process to correct a problem should be so foolproof that the problem will not occur again. Again, a sound PDCA plan will help ensure that improvements in quality remain in place.

The principles of TQC, if implemented conscientiously, ensure that everyone is focused on quality. They also enhance the probability of a defect-free process environment, a worthy goal in a highly competitive marketplace.

Self-Managed Teams

A derivative of quality circles, **self-managed teams (SMT)** have the goal of giving employees more input into what they do for the company. When employees have more control over what they do and how they do it, they are more content and have higher levels of productivity and quality.[7] SMTs also result in improved flexibility and responsiveness to changing market conditions, as decisions are made more quickly and changes are implemented with fewer problems. For SMTs to be successful, however, management must give them the power to make decisions, remove obstacles, and determine their performance rewards in alignment with the company's objectives.

Technology has made SMTs possible through electronic databases and networks so that teams have access to the customer, vendor, and production data they need to produce defect-free products on time.

Automation

One of the most far-reaching effects of technology is automation in the various forms of robotics, machinery, computers, and so forth. More often than not, automation is used not just for cost reduction but for gains in productivity, flexibility, and quality when used with simple, repetitive tasks and minimal set-ups. There are many examples of automation, and for every industry the type used will differ. These automation techniques include bar coding, computer-integrated manufacturing, and electronic data interchange.

1. *Bar coding.* This procedure was first used in the retail industry to track inventories of products, but it's also an excellent tracking device for manufacturers. Each part or product is inscribed with a bar code that contains all the relevant information about the part and avoids the need to enter this information into a computer, where the chance for entry error is high.

2. *Computer-generated manufacturing: instruction, fabrication, and assembly.* The most technologically advanced manufacturers have put computer screens on the factory floor at work areas so that workers can easily access designs, do instantaneous modification, and program parts for fabrication and/or assembly. They can all access important information on purchase orders, such as new orders, the status of orders in process, and the final disposition of an order.

3. *Electronic data interchange.* **Electronic data interchange (EDI)** allows companies to transfer designs and other graphical data between remote sites virtually in real time. It also enables retailers and wholesalers to be online with their manufacturers so that reorders are triggered electronically. This is important for companies that want to maintain minimal inventories and to ensure that high-demand items are rapidly replaced on store shelves (See "Mass Customizing for the Customer").

Computer-Integrated Manufacturing

Computer-integrated manufacturing (CIM) is simply the framework for coordinating computers, information, networks, people, and processes in a factory environment so that the manufacturing process can be more effectively controlled and information is readily available to those who need it when they need it. The importance of CIM lies in its ability to improve the accuracy of manufacturing processes, enhance the quality of design, positively affect productivity, and facilitate quicker set-ups.

CIM needs to exist in concert with **flexible manufacturing systems (FMSs)**, which seek to optimize the match between labor and automation. FMS is a "computer controlled manufacturing system using semi-independent numerically controlled (NC) machines linked together by means of a material handling network."[8] CIM and FMS have enabled many companies, large and small, to become and remain flexible and competitive over the long term.[8]

Just-in-Time Production and Inventory

One tool that is finally being recognized for its ability to improve the materials management aspect of manufacturing is **JIT** or **just-in-time production**. JIT helps companies improve cycle and delivery times, use material only when it's needed, reduce inventory and its attendant space requirements, and

 Entrepreneurship in Action

Mass Customizing for the Customer

On any given day, apparel retailers around the country are out of stock on about 30 percent of their basic items, which means the potential loss of a frustrated customer. But Pennsylvania-based VF Corporation seems to have solved that problem with a high-tech market response system that has cut restocking time from weeks to days. In stores that carry VF products such as Wrangler jeans, customers can be 90 percent certain they'll find what they are looking for.

Through a computer-driven tracking system, VF knows when a teenager buys a pair of 30/32 Wranglers in black denim at Wal-Mart in Madera, California, and can send the retailer a replacement pair within 24 hours. At the same time, VF can record which raw materials went into the making of the jeans and alert its suppliers. Both VF and VF's retailers benefit from this EDI system. Today all of Wal-Mart's more than 2,215 stores take advantage of VF's system.

What is interesting about this high-tech solution is that VF prides itself in staying one step behind in fashion.

SOURCE: Liz Seymour, "Customer Tailored for Service: VF Corporation," *Hemispheres,* March 1996, p. 25.

improve quality. Developed in the United States by Toyota, JIT has two fundamental approaches: the continuous-flow system and the *kanban* system. In manufacturing situations where a single product is being produced in high volume, the continuous-flow system is appropriate. Under this system, the correct amount of materials inventory is placed at the start of the production line and then moved from one station to the next, with the speed determined by the slowest link in the process.

Kanban, the second approach, is a system used when production is more flexible and contains more variety. *Kanban* was developed by Taiichi Ohno, the creator of the Toyota production system. The idea was based on the U.S. supermarket:

> A supermarket is where a customer can get (1) what is needed, (2) at the time needed, (3) in the amount needed. . . . From the supermarket we got the idea of viewing the earlier processes in the production line as a kind of store. The later process (customer) goes to the earlier process (supermarket) to acquire the required parts (commodities) at the time and in the quantity needed. The earlier process immediately produces the quantity just taken (restocking the shelves).[9]

Work at a station starts when a *kanban* signal card (*kanban* in Japanese actually means "visible record") is received from a previous station. Alternatively, assembly starts with bins full of parts. When the part bin nearest the work is empty, it moves to the source of supply and the next full bin moves forward. This reduces cycle time, the time to take a part through the process from start to finish, because inventory queues are eliminated.

A singular advantage of the JIT system is that defects are not passed along but discovered and corrected where they occur. In terms of productivity, the benefits include less scrap and rework, less inventory, fewer work orders, less capital investment, fewer materials handling costs, and less space.

For JIT to be successfully implemented, three major components must be in place: customer, production, and suppliers. All must subscribe to and be a part of the JIT system. The process begins with the customer, whose requirements will establish the time to delivery and the type of manufacturing process required. Production is then set up so that at each point on the production line a task is completed, with each task designed to take about the same length of time as the previous or succeeding task so there is no wait time. Under the continuous process, raw materials inventory arrives before the previous inventory is consumed, whereas in the *kanban* process, a card goes to the supply station to secure more materials when the *kanban* queue declines to a designated level. The role of the supplier becomes critical to the whole process, for if the supplier can be an integral part of the *kanban* chain through electronic data transfer or even fax transfer, the process is made more efficient. In this way, the manufacturer does not need to store supplies. This is a critical feature for small-business owners with limited resources. The ability to keep the inventory of raw materials to a minimum is important for managing cash flow and limited resources.

It is beyond the scope of this book to discuss the JIT system in depth. The goal is merely to introduce you to the concept and suggest that it be considered for the improvement of the manufacturing process.

Table 14.1 summarizes and integrates the world-class manufacturing principles and indicates how they apply across the people, materials, and equipment requirements in the manufacturing process.

Purchasing: Materials Requirements and Inventory

Any business that purchases raw materials or parts for production of goods for resale must carefully consider the quality, quantity, and timing of those purchases. Quality goods are those that meet specific needs, whereas the quantity purchased is a function of demand, manufacturing capability, and storage capability. Planning purchases so that capital and warehouse space are tied up no longer than necessary is the result of good timing. As materials account for approximately 50 percent of total manufacturing cost, it is important to balance these three factors carefully.

Locating vendors to supply raw materials or goods for resale is not difficult, but finding the best vendors for the company's purposes is another matter entirely. The first decision to make is whether to buy from one vendor or more than one vendor. Obviously, if a single vendor cannot supply all the company's needs, the latter decision is made. There are two major advantages to using a single vendor where possible. First, a single vendor will generally provide more individual attention and better service. Second, it will consolidate the company's orders, which may result in a discount based on quantity purchased.

On the other hand, the principal disadvantage of using only one vendor is that if the vendor suffers a catastrophe (e.g., its facility burns to the ground, as did that of the Japanese company that was the prime supplier of RAM chips several years ago), it may be difficult or impossible to find an alternative source in a short period of time. To insure against this type of disaster, you may want to follow the general rule of using one supplier for about 70 to 80 percent of your needs and one or more additional vendors to supply the rest. Many manufacturers are now reducing the number of suppliers they deal with to enhance relationships and quality. For example, Sun Microsystems reduced its supplier list from 450 to 150 and gave 80 percent of its business to 20 of those small firms.[10]

When considering a specific vendor as your primary or secondary source, you should ask several questions:

1. Can the vendor deliver enough of what is needed when it's needed?

2. What is the cost of transportation with this vendor? If the vendor is located at a great distance from the company, costs will be higher and it may be more difficult to get the needed service.

Table 14.1   World-Class Manufacturing

Component	Management Style	Total Quality Control	Self-Managed Teams	Quality Function Deployment	Design for Manufacturing	Automation	Computer-Integrated Manufacturing	Just-in-Time
People	Team culture focused on customer satisfaction	Quality circles to improve processes	Teams make decisions about products and processes	Cross-functional teams design products and processes according to needs of customer	Cross-functional teams design products concurrent with processes for high quality, low cost	Teams use automated machinery to improve speed and quality	People use integrated data transfer, storage, and retrieval systems to improve processes	People work where and when needed
Materials	Build JIT relationships with suppliers	Materials received from suppliers are defect free	SMTs work with suppliers and one another to improve quality and cost of supplies	Materials used meet quality requirements of customers and cost requirements of company	Number of parts and suppliers is minimized	Automated machinery minimizes the handling of materials	Electronic databases accessible throughout the plant store materials specifications, inventory, and costs	A *kanban* system provides that materials are pulled for use in the quantities needed when needed
Equipment	Equipment required to meet goals is purchased and maintained	Equipment performance is monitored and maintained	SMTs analyze equipment performance and make improvements	Equipment used meets quality requirements of customers and reduces costs	Products designed for assembly using highest-quality, lowest-cost equipment	Automated machinery, robotics, etc. are used to improve quality, cost, and flexibility	Work instructions are stored in electronic databases accessible throughout the plant	Equipment is flexible, allowing for minimal queuing or stops for quality problems

Source: Adapted from A. Richard Shores, *Reengineering the Factory* (Milwaukee: ASQC Quality Press, 1994).

3. What services does the vendor offer? For example, how often will sales representatives call on the company?

4. Is the vendor knowledgeable about the product line?

5. What are its maintenance and return policies?

It's also important to shop vendors to compare prices and check for trade discounts and quantity discounts that may make a particular vendor's deal more enticing.

Computer technology has made materials planning more of a science than ever before. Information systems can now provide purchasing managers with detailed feedback on supplier performance, delivery reliability, and quality control results. Comparing results across suppliers gives the purchasing manager more leverage when it's time to renegotiate the annual contracts with suppliers.

Inventory Requirements

Today businesses that hold inventories of raw materials for production or goods for resale have found they must reduce these inventories significantly if they are to remain competitive. Instead of purchasing large quantities and receiving them on a monthly basis, companies are purchasing daily or weekly to avoid costly inventories. Of course, some inventory of finished goods must be maintained to meet delivery deadlines; therefore, a delicate balance needs to be achieved among goods coming into the company, work in progress, and goods leaving the company to be sold.

Many extraneous costs are associated with inventories that can add as much as 25 percent to the base cost of the inventory. They include

▶ *Financing costs*—the interest paid on the money borrowed to purchase the inventory

Technology Tip

Try Purchasing from Vendors Online

Today purchasing your supplies and inventories on-line is safer, easier, and faster than ever. The Yankee Group, an industry research firm, estimates that by the year 2000, businesses will buy and sell $134 billion worth of products over the Internet. Online vendor relationships are efficient and therefore improve the bottom line.

Entrepreneurs in the apparel industry, for example, can access everything they need at Apparel.net, and businesses looking for the best long-distance rates can access Telegroup.com, which will compare rates for them. If you're a pilot or a business owner looking to buy a plane, you can find the best deal at Aircraft Shopper Online at www.aso.solid.com.

It's a good idea to check out who's online before you make that purchase offline. You may save yourself time, money, and frustration.

▶ *Opportunity cost*—the loss of use of the money that is tied up in inventory

▶ *Storage costs*—the amount spent on warehouse space to store the inventory

▶ *Insurance costs*—The cost of insuring the inventory

▶ *Shrinkage costs*—The money lost from inventory that is broken, stolen, or damaged

▶ *Obsolescence*—The cost associated with inventory that has become obsolete

Reducing inventory therefore will reduce or eliminate most of these costs.

In a start-up venture, keeping track of inventory may simply be a matter of visually inspecting and counting, since the business is growing in a fairly controlled manner in the beginning. However, once the business is growing rapidly, these simple techniques will no longer suffice, and it is best to be prepared for this eventuality early on with a system for keeping track of inventory. Three systems to consider are perpetual inventory systems, physical count systems, and combination systems.

Perpetual Inventory Systems

Perpetual inventory systems keep a running count of items in inventory. As items are sold, they are subtracted; as they are purchased, they are added. An electronic point-of-sale system (such as those now used in most grocery and retail stores) allows a business instant access to the status of its inventory. Bar coding inventory makes it easier to achieve error-free tracking. Manufacturers today are bar coding inventories of raw materials and components to facilitate tracking and reorders.

Physical Count System

Most businesses do physical counts, even if they have an electronic system, to detect errors in the system and account for items that may have been stolen or lost and would not show up as a sale. To make the counting process more efficient, it would be important to get the inventories down as low as possible before the count takes place.

Combined Inventory System

Some businesses use both perpetual and physical count systems simultaneously, perpetual for the items that make up the bulk of its sales and physical counts for less commonly sold items that are carried in smaller quantities.

Measuring Quality

The combination of an increasing desire for continual improvement and a global economy that is rapidly bringing together diverse standards of quality has resulted in the need for a common standard to ensure that minimum standards for products and services have been met. Two such measures have been used for some time now: ISO 9000 and the Malcolm Baldrige award.

Table 14.2   ISO 9000 Standards for Quality Assurance

ISO 9001	A model for quality assurance in design, development, production, installation, and servicing.
ISO 9002	Quality system requirements for assuring the quality of products designed as off-the-shelf commercial products for a general market
ISO 9003	Sets the standard for quality assurance in final assembly and testing
ISO 9004	Provides the guidelines for implementing a complete quality management system

ISO 9000

The International Organization for Standardization (ISO) developed the standards that many countries and hundreds of companies and government agencies have adopted. In fact, many companies are requiring that their suppliers also subscribe to the standards if they want to continue doing business. In general, the basic principles of **ISO 9000** are as follows:

1. Organizations should achieve and maintain the quality of a product or service in a way that meets the customer's needs.

2. The management of the organization should convey to its employees the intended level of quality and support for achieving it.

3. The organization should convey confidence in its intended quality to the customer. This may include agreed-on demonstrable requirements.

Table 14.2 gives the broad areas of quality covered by ISO 9000. Going through the ISO process is costly for a small, growing firm and includes the writing of a quality control manual. Additional costs are associated with obtaining certification, which is then subject to audit semiannually and must be renewed annually. These costs must be weighed against the advantages. With certification, the companies with which the entrepreneur does business don't have to inspect to determine the company's standards for quality. Moreover, it makes it much easier to enter the export market. At the very least, a small, growing company should attempt to meet the standards of ISO 9000 even if it's not able to go through the certification process.

The Malcolm Baldrige National Quality Award

The Malcolm Baldrige award is the United States' highest honor for quality. The competition for it is tough and the selection process daunting, but it creates a standard against which growing companies can compare themselves. The award was established by President Ronald Reagan in 1987 and named in honor of the then secretary of commerce. The significance of the honor has become so great that even in 1988, Motorola, a winner, required that its suppliers apply for the Baldrige award within five years. This is certainly a difficult accomplishment and, if achieved, means the winner must literally open its quality practices to the public, which is costly in terms of people to provide tours, training manuals, and road shows. And there is no guarantee that, once achieved, the company's performance will be enhanced or maintained. A case in point is the 1990 winner, Wallace Company. The first small company ever to win a Baldrige award, it filed for Chapter 11 bankruptcy protection two years later.[11] Nevertheless, the Baldrige award is a significant motivator for U.S. businesses to achieve the highest standards of quality. A GAO study commissioned by U.S. Representative Donald Ritter found that 20 companies that had adopted TQM as embodied in the Baldrige award and subsequently scored well on 1988 and 1989 applications had significant improvements in employee relations, quality, cost, customer satisfaction, and profitability.[12] The study has some limitations, however, so conclusive evidence of a cause-and-effect relationship is not possible to state.

Following is a list of the Baldrige criteria:

1. *Leadership.* Demonstrate evidence that senior management promotes quality values and that those values influence day-to-day management.

2. *Information and analysis.* How effectively is the company using competitive comparisons, and does it support quality objectives through data analysis?

3. *Strategic quality planning.* Does the business plan incorporate quality requirements?

4. *Human resource development and management.* What systems and practices involve employees in education, training, assessment, and recognition?

5. *Management of process quality.* Check for quality in product and service design, process control, quality assessment and documentation, and assurance of the quality of supplies.

6. *Quality and operational results.* Examine trends in and levels of improvement of products and services, business services, and suppliers' quality.

7. *Customer focus and satisfaction.* Evaluate customer service standards, customer satisfaction ratings, and the use of customer complaints and suggestions.[13]

Distribution: A Competitive Strategy for Manufacturing

In Chapter 12, we discussed distribution as a marketing strategy to reach customers (pages 353–360); refer to that discussion to review distribution channels and intermediaries. But distribution is also a physical element in the process strategy of a product company. The infrastructures of traditional distribution systems were designed with the expressed purpose of expediting mass marketing strategies that served mass markets of customers that all looked alike. Today distribution has become a significant competitive strategy in two major arenas. First, the new paradigm of mass customization calls

Sometimes the best distribution strategy is to put your business on wheels and take it to the customer. Rudy and Sharon Shepard do just that with Soft•Stitch, their alterations and embroidery shop headquartered in Greensboro, North Carolina. Loading their two stitching machines onto a trailer, they travel to flea markets, motorcycle rallies, and boat and horse shows to provide their service. (Jim Stratford)

for a different distribution strategy, one that allows a company to successfully compete in a dynamic marketplace. Some early examples of this type of strategy are direct marketing, cable TV shopping, and computer network shopping. Second, low-cost distribution is a powerful tool for value creation in a market with sophisticated customers and products and services that are less differentiated. In such a situation, price becomes the defining factor. Wal-Mart is probably the best example of successful low-cost distribution strategies that can force manufacturers to lower prices or modify their operations to deliver on price and a minimum level of quality. In commodity-type industries, such as food, manufacturers are often obligated to become their own low-cost distributors to survive. Even service industries are affected by these **category killers**. For example, information is rapidly becoming a commodity, with hundreds of companies positioning themselves as the low-cost provider of Internet services.

In his book *Value Migration,* Adrian J. Slywotzky identifies four new distribution patterns of which entrepreneurs should be aware:[14]

1. *The collapse of the middle.* In many industries, a shift from routine product sales to a customized bundling of price, distribution, support, and information has occurred. Thus, many products and services are being converted to value-added business solutions. For example, in the forms industry, for every dollar spent on forms, customers spend $20 on the system for using them: labor, routing, storage, revisions, and so forth. Consequently, the physical product itself is not what contains the value

but the system for using it. Companies that create value by improving systems or outsourcing the process will have greater success.

2. *Emergence of new customer sets.* As important as it is to identify current customers, it is equally important to recognize emerging customers. For example, in the airline industry, deregulation resulted in a whole new class of leisure travelers who were price conscious.

3. *Migration within the value chain.* The most successful companies are aware of the differential importance of individual steps in the **value chain** and concentrate on specific activities that allow them to capture maximum value at a particular step. On the computer value chain, suppliers Microsoft and Intel took over key upstream activities on the value chain—operating systems and processors—and companies such as EDS and Hewlett-Packard took over downstream activities in the delivery of computing solutions to end-users. IBM, unfortunately, recognized this value too late.

4. *Redefinition of the product/service offering.* Value migration has occurred in many products and services. Starbucks, for example, changed the way customers think about coffee. They transformed the product from a daily grind to an affordable luxury, from a beverage to an experience.

Distributors, retailers, and other outlets are one way businesses communicate to the customer, so they are very much partners in the organization, particularly in a virtual company. Their goal is to gather information from the customer so that the manufacturer can revise and improve its offerings.

The Real World of Entrepreneurship

Digital Distribution

In the software and CD-ROM industry, it's the publisher (manufacturer) that assumes all the risk for the product. This is because retailers have the right to return anything that doesn't sell within a specified period of time to the distributor, which in turn returns it to the publisher. The role of distributors in this industry is multifunctional. They order, warehouse, and ship into retail locations while also serving as the banker or escrow officer between the retailer and the publisher, collecting receivables from the myriad outlets carrying the products. Consequently, distributors bear the risk of bad debt as well as the credit burden. Generally, they have to pay the publishers within 60 days of receipt of goods and then take 90 to 120 days to collect from retailers. Because of the enormous risk the distributors bear, they are very careful about the publishers with which they choose to do business. If a publisher fails, the distributor will be left with unsold inventory that can't be returned. For multimedia publishers, this means they must demonstrate

▶ A strong balance sheet that suggests they will be in business a long time.

▶ An excellent, innovative product line.

▶ A marketing plan and sufficient capital budgeted to launch the product. This could be as much as $100,000.

▶ A plan to increase the product line to the distributor.

Source: Joanna Tamer, "New Strategies for Distribution," *Digital Media: A Seybold Report,* Vol. 4(1), June 8, 1994.

They are so important to the virtual company—they can make or break it—that finding good, loyal partners is competitively difficult. In fact, distribution, once a mundane, routine occupation, has become the glamor stock of the business world with "channel surfer" entrepreneurs who constantly seek the most productive channel.[15]

Following are just a few examples from *Inc.* of how some entrepreneurs are successfully making distribution strategy their competitive advantage:

▶ *Millstone Coffee:* Sells coffee beans to supermarket shoppers. The normal channel is food brokers; they go direct to the supermarket.

▶ *Design Basics:* A catalog of residential building plans geared toward professional residential builders and developers. The usual channel is classified ads in builders' magazines; they use direct mail.

▶ *Counterpoint Publishing:* Produces customized collections of state and federal rules and regulations for corporate-regulatory-compliance officers. The normal route is direct mail; it operates through the Internet.

Choosing the Manufacturing Site

For the manufacturer, the choice of where to locate is restricted by community zoning laws that limit manufacturing companies to certain designated areas away from residential, retail, and office commercial sites to reduce the chance of noise, odor, and pollutants affecting the citizens. Often these areas are known as *industrial parks,* and they usually are equipped with electrical power and sewage plants appropriate to manufacturing. By locating in one of these parks, a company may also benefit from the synergy of other manufacturing nearby. Opportunities for networking and sharing resources and costs are enhanced.

Another common location for manufacturing is **enterprise zones**, public-private partnerships designed to bring jobs to inner cities, downtown areas, and rural areas suffering from the shift of jobs and population to the suburbs. Thirty-five states (plus the District of Columbia) have authorized enterprise zones. The draw for businesses is tax incentives, regulatory relief, and employee training programs.

Wherever a company looks for a manufacturing site, it is concerned with four key factors: access to suppliers, cost of labor, access to transportation, and cost of utilities. These factors may not be equally weighted. Depending on the type of manufacturer, one or more factors may have greater importance in evaluating a site.

Access to Suppliers

Manufacturers and processors usually try to locate within a reasonable distance from their major suppliers to cut shipping time and save transportation costs. Certainly a food processor attempts to set up business near the growing fields so that the food is as fresh as possible when it arrives at the processing plant. Similarly, a manufacturer that uses steel as one of its main raw materials might want to locate in the same region of the country as the steel mills to save the high costs of trucking heavy steel great distances.

Cost of Labor

Today many manufacturers choose a location based on the cost of labor rather than proximity to suppliers, since labor is generally the single highest cost in the production of goods. Wages and laws relating to workers, such as workers' compensation, vary from state to state and sometimes from city to city. For example, California's laws and cost of living tend to make it a more expensive place to hire employees than those same employees might cost in Missouri. Some labor-intensive businesses have found that the only way they can compete is by having plants in Mexico or China, where labor costs are a fraction of those in the United States and laborers are protected by fewer laws. Mattel Inc., for example, has a plant in China to produce the hundreds of different toys it markets every year. The bottom line is that the entrepreneur must weigh the costs in terms of access to labor carefully when considering a particular location for a manufacturing plant.

Access to Transportation

Most manufacturers prefer to locate near major transportation networks: railways, major highways, airports, and ports of call. The reasoning is obvious: the greater the distance between the plant and a major transportation network, the higher the cost to the company and ultimately the customer. Also, the more transportation people who handle the product, the greater the cost. Thus, in terms of simple economics, to remain competitive, manufacturers must also consider the costs and benefits of locating away from a major transportation network. The higher transportation costs will result in a smaller profit margin for the company or higher costs for the customers.

Cost of Utilities

Utility rates vary from state to state and usually from city to city within a given state. If the company is heavily dependent on electricity, gas, or coal, this factor could be a significant variable in the cost of producing a product and therefore should be examined carefully.

Entrepreneurial companies that seek competitive advantages in the manufacturing arena will need to integrate into their TQM system the customer, state-of-the-art technology, superior resources and processes, and continuous improvement. Everything the company does involves a process that must be refined, improved, and updated on a continuous basis. Whether a small, growing company handles all of its production in-house or out-sources and focuses on its core competencies, it must see to it that everyone who contributes to the process and the ultimate product also integrates these four components. Today process strategy is a core competency that can mean the difference between success and failure, superior performance and mediocre effort, and a company that endures over time and one that is discontinued or fails.

Cases Relevant to This Chapter

French Rags
Pelco
SB Networks

Issues for Review and Discussion

1. Discuss the importance of agile manufacturing as a response to a rapidly changing environment.
2. What is the role of *kaizen* in achieving total quality management?
3. With what three aspects of the organization must the core principles for world-class manufacturing be integrated?
4. How can distribution be a competitive strategy for a growing company? What are three trends occurring in distribution?
5. Which factors must be considered when choosing a manufacturing site?

Experiencing Entrepreneurship

1. Find three companies that are successfully making distribution strategy their competitive advantage, and compare and contrast them.
2. Interview an entrepreneur who is using world-class manufacturing techniques to achieve TQM. How does this company compare with others in the industry?

Resources

Agility Forum. Bethlehem, PA (1-800-9BE-AGILE; http://absu.amef.lehigh.edu). Consulting, training, and education services from manufacturing experts.

Juran, J. M. (1988). *Juran on Planning for Quality.* New York: The Free Press, pp. 4–5.

Maleki, Reza A. (1991). *Flexible Manufacturing Systems.* Englewood Cliffs, NJ: Prentice-Hall, p. 8.

Manufacturing Assistance Program. Oak Ridge, TN (1-800-356-4USA). Technical assistance from U.S. Department of Energy scientists and engineers.

Manufacturing Extension Partnership. Gaithersburg, MD (1-800-MEP-4MFG). A nonprofit network of 200 field offices in 42 states providing federal, state, and local services.

Mizuno, S. (1988). *Management for Quality Improvement: The 7 New QC Tools.* Cambridge, MA: Productivity Press.

Shores, Richard (1994). *Reengineering the Factory: A Primer for World-Class Manufacturing.* Milwaukee: ASQC Quality Press.

Slywotzky, Adrian J. (1996). *Value Migration.* Cambridge, MA: Harvard Business School Press.

Internet Resources
ISO Online
http://www.iso.ch/
The International Organization for Standardization's site, which explains its work and the standards for quality management and assurance.

Technology Transfer Information Center
http://www.nal.usda.gov/ttic/
A good site to help turn federally funded research into profits.

Never reorganize except for a good business reason.
But if you haven't reorganized in a while, that's a good business reason.

John Akers
CEO, IBM
Waterman, The Renewal Factor
Bantam, 1987

Process Strategy in Retail/Wholesale and Service Businesses

Preview

Understanding this chapter will give you the ability to

▶ **Describe the nature of retail/wholesale businesses and compare it to that of service businesses.**

▶ **Discuss how to identify and analyze a trade area.**

▶ **Identify alternatives to conventional business sites.**

▶ **Explain the factors involved in facility decisions.**

▶ **Discuss the business process for retail/wholesale/service businesses.**

▶ **Plan for the management of purchasing and inventory.**

▶ **Describe ways to avoid shrinkage.**

Terms to Know

Young Entrepreneurs—Minicase

Frank Alameda
East Side Sports

Frank Alameda learned early on the value of having a vision and sticking to it. His original career plan was to be a physical education teacher, but at 18 he took an entrepreneurship class through the National Foundation for Teaching Entrepreneurship (NFTE) and caught the entrepreneurial bug. He was 21 years old, a student at Brooklyn College majoring in physical education and working part time at the Boys Club, when he started his business, East Side Sports, on Manhattan's Lower East Side. Alameda and his mother were walking down a street one day in 1993 when they spotted a run-down sporting goods store whose owner, a man in his eighties, wanted to sell. At first they thought this was the opportunity Alameda had been looking for, but it turned out the store was in a shambles. The owner had not kept good records, so the paperwork to complete the deal would be more complex than he wanted. They passed up the opportunity. Later Alameda's mother found a vacant storefront on a busy street not far from the Boys Club. The rent was $850 a month. Alameda quickly added utilities to that and figured he would have to make $60 a day to cover rent and utilities. That seemed doable. With $1,500 from his godfather and another $1,500 from his mother, Alameda was able to lease the storefront. Then the mother of a local Little League coach decided to close her business, and she gave all her displays and equipment to Alameda. It now seemed he was really going to have his business.

Because he had no money for renovations and had to do all the work himself, Alameda slept four hours a night for about six months while remodeling the store. That was a particularly rough time for Alameda because in addition to starting his business, he was still going to school and working at the Boys Club. Then his mother entered the hospital with terminal cancer. He would work all day, then visit her in the evening. In spite of what she was going through, she would always remind him, "Remember to pay the rent, Frank." Alameda attributes the success of his business to his mother's inspiration, which kept him going even during the most discouraging times.

Initially he stocked the store with T-shirts and hats that he acquired when he went to New York City to visit wholesalers and began opening up COD accounts. His plan was to stick with seasonal items, but soon people started coming in asking about team uniforms and Boys Club shirts. Alameda suddenly became an intermediary, supplying local teams and customers with whatever they needed. Within a year and a half he had the opportunity to move to a larger location in the same area, and soon the business began looking like a sporting goods store. He kept the old location and turned it into a factory to produce custom items.

Alameda was certain his business would be a success because it's located on a busy street in a neighborhood filled with teenagers and children. Consequently, Alameda has found that the best promotion for his store is community service. He works closely with neighborhood sports teams and gives them good discounts. In 1993, the New York City Housing Authority was sponsoring basketball teams for kids in the neighborhood. They came to Alameda for help, and he donated shirts for 47 kids to the leagues. The next year, he self-sponsored more than 60 kids to pay for shirts, awards, and referees. In

1995, he attracted business sponsors because the participant numbers had risen to 80 kids. The sponsoring merchants provided the teams with a budget that could be used toward supplies. In 1996, however, Alameda found he was overextending himself and, without enough staff to cover the store, he wasn't able to spend time searching for sponsors. Still, 117 kids showed up for basketball at the start of the season, so he solved the problem by asking for a nominal $10 from each child and his company covered the rest. Alameda didn't like having to charge the kids, but he quickly realized that if he didn't cover his business, he wouldn't be able to do anything for them.

Because the sporting goods he purchases from wholesalers are marked up 80 to 100 percent, he has room to give special discounts to the kids who participate in the league and to his best customers, such as the Boys Club and the YMCA.

In 1996, his revenues exceeded $150,000. In 1997, he was expecting to get his first line of credit for the business. This will be an important step forward because it will make it easier for him to handle bigger orders. He has four employees during the year and six in the summer. Alameda plans to take his business as far as he can. He's already looking ahead to a new store that will house both the retail outlet and the factory so he can do more custom work on site. His biggest challenge is building credibility for the company, but he is patient and willing to work hard. He advises young entrepreneurs to "stay strong because at the beginning it's always the hardest." And "stick to your vision," he cautions. At 21 so many other interests are competing for your focus. "You have to have some willpower."

Because he has created such a successful neighborhood business, friends and relatives now want to own their own businesses. But Alameda wisely cautions, "Don't expect anything for the first couple years." He is proud of the fact that all his equipment is paid for, something his mother ingrained in him. Frank Alameda is holding to his vision for East Side Sports, and he sees it as nothing short of a great company.

How can Alameda gain the credibility he needs to grow the business?

Every business is a process-driven system in need of continual improvement. There has been a strong tendency on the part of entrepreneur and small-business management texts to ignore the manufacturing process issues and principles discussed in Chapters 13 and 14. Perhaps readers of this book have chosen to skip those chapters as well because "no one does manufacturing anymore—we live in a service economy." Though the service sector may be the largest, the retail/wholesale and direct service businesses discussed in this chapter have a lot to learn from the TQM process strategies presented in Chapters 13 and 14. Certainly Frank Alameda (see Young Entrepreneurs—Minicase) learned very early the importance of infusing quality into all aspects of his business. And he also quickly realized that he isn't just in the retail business; he's in the solutions business.

Every business produces some type of product, and every business has a service component. The service business's product may be a solution to a customer's problem that involves consulting, training, a manual, or new equipment—in short, a process! The "product" business works with the customer to provide solutions in the form of new products and then bundles services with those products to provide a complete package. Recall Jennifer Ianollo (see Young Entrepreneurs—Minicase in Chapter 8), who through her event-planning company, Bravissimo, offers a service to customers as well as a product, the food she produces.

The principles and strategies that have produced world-class manufacturers can be applied with equal effectiveness to the processes in other types of businesses. Because of this, it is highly recommended that you read Chapters 13 and 14 prior to this chapter.

The Nature of Retail/Wholesale Businesses

In terms of risk, cost, and time commitment, retail businesses require the most of each. Because they are at the front line with the customer, they cost more in terms of storefront appearance and location, inventory, advertising and promotion, labor, and insurance. The significant initial capital outlay in facility and inventory means more risk for the company. And no one would deny that retail outlets demand enormous time commitments from their owners and employees.

Wholesale-type businesses are usually one step removed from the end-user, with the retailer in between, but today more and more wholesalers, such as PriceCostco, are selling direct "to the public" as well as in what are known as discount warehouses. Besides selling products in bulk for less, these wholesale businesses don't have the expensive storefront demands of a typical retail outlet. Customers have been "trained" to expect an out-of-the-way location, a huge warehouse, no frills, and no service, in terms of salespeople on the floor, in exchange for lower prices.

The Nature of Service Businesses

The boundary between service and product businesses is quickly dissolving as all businesses recognize they must provide service above and beyond what is typically expected. Even service businesses are packaging products for their customers. So today a service business is one that does not manufacture, inventory, or distribute products for sale. Instead, it markets an intangible

 Entrepreneurship in Action

Using Direct Marketing to Provide a Service

Andrew Morrison knows how to get to his customers, African American consumers in New York City. His company, Nia Direct, doesn't use the traditional channels—retail, wholesales, mail order—to reach his customers. Rather, he prefers to provide incentives to his customers to get them to change their behavior and come to him. Nia Direct takes advantage of Morrison's natural ability to sell by providing direct-mail coupons to African American consumers for products and services they need.

His successful business, which reached more than 5 million households by 1996, has attracted major advertisers such as AT&T, Kraft General Foods, and *Vibe Magazine*. He also supplies college and university fraternities and sororities. Morrison is a good example of an entrepreneur who understands his customers and knows how to provide a service they can use.

SOURCE: *Entrepreneur,* November 1995, p. 113.

product: the ability to do something for someone else, the ability to provide solutions to problems.

In terms of the issues discussed in this chapter, service businesses have much in common with retail businesses, particularly if the service requires that the customer come to the site. Therefore, they will be treated together and notations will be made where differences might occur.

The Trade Area

A retail or a service business deals directly with the customer, so naturally one of the first considerations is: where are these customers located? Since these companies live or die based on the number of customers who have access to the business, it's important to locate the business where there are suitable concentrations of customers.

The **trade area** is the area or region from which the company expects to draw customers. The type of business will determine, to a large extent, the size of the trade area. For example, if a company sells general merchandise that can be found almost anywhere, the trade area will be much smaller as customers will not want to travel great distances to purchase common goods. On the other hand, a specialty outlet, such as a boutique clothing store with unusual apparel or a well-known graphics designer, may draw people from other communities as well.

Once the location within the community is identified, the trade area can be calculated. Using a map of the community, the site for the business is designated; then, placing a compass on the epicenter of the proposed site, a circle that represents the distance (the radius) people are expected to drive to reach the site can be drawn. Within the circle is the trade area, which can now be studied in more detail. Employing demographics and a census tract map, census tracts within the trade area can be identified. Census data for

 Entrepreneurship in Action

Service with a Cultural Difference

The largest Vietnamese media outlet outside of Vietnam is located in Orange County, California. Little Saigon TV and Radio was started by Trang Nguyen in 1990 with the goal of learning more about her culture and trying to reconcile the differences with American culture. An immigrant at age 13, Nguyen has often found it difficult to overcome the traditional submissive role of women in her native culture and is frequently considered too assertive by people from her culture. Still, her acceptance in the business world is reflected in her audience: 100,000 radio listeners and 200,000 TV watchers.

She serves her TV audience with local news and talk shows that help Vietnamese immigrants adapt to their new culture without forsaking the traditions of the old. Her younger listeners particularly appreciate her radio broadcasts because her format replicates that of U.S. radio stations, but the songs are in Vietnamese. Some older, more traditional listeners don't like the format, but Nguyen has learned that in business, as in everything else, you can't please everyone equally.

those tracts will help to determine how many people reside within the boundaries of the trade area as well as their education level, income level, average number of children, and so forth. Alternatively, you can look by zip code. See Figure 15.1 for examples of census tract and zip code areas as well as sample data.

Competition within the trade area can also be identified. This is often accomplished by driving around the area and noting competing businesses. Some things to look for when studying the competition are their size and number as well as how busy they are at various times of the day. If competitors are located in shopping malls or strip centers, it will be important to seek out clusters of similar stores that appear to be successful and have low vacancy rates, as this would indicate a strong attraction for the site. In addition, locating near a competitor is often a wise choice because it encourages comparison shopping.

It's important to identify the routes customers might take to reach the proposed site: highways, streets, and public transportation routes. If the site is difficult to locate and hard to access, it's logical to conclude that potential customers will not exert the effort to find it. Availability of parking is also critical; consequently, most communities require a sufficient amount of parking space for new construction, through either lots or garages. In some older areas, however, street parking is the only available option, which may cause customers to seek an alternative.

A foot and car **traffic count** for the proposed site should be conducted to determine how busy the area is, because retail businesses and some service businesses rely heavily on traffic for customers. Whether or not a high volume of foot traffic is required is a function of the type of business. A coffeehouse such as Starbucks, for example, benefits immensely from a high volume of foot traffic, whereas a hardware store such as Home Depot does not depend on foot traffic for its existence. A traffic count is easily accomplished by positioning someone near the targeted site and tallying the customers going by and into the business. City planning departments and transportation departments maintain auto traffic counts for major arterials in the city.

Alternatives to Conventional Sites

Any company seeking a site for either start-up or expansion should also consider alternatives to more conventional-type locations.

Incubators

A number of communities have business **incubators** where a young company can locate and receive support services such as receptionist, copy service, or conference room; discounted fees with professional advisers such as attorneys and accountants; the ability to network with other companies in the incubator; and possibly financial aid. Generally, the company remains in the incubator for two to three years before moving to more traditional facilities.

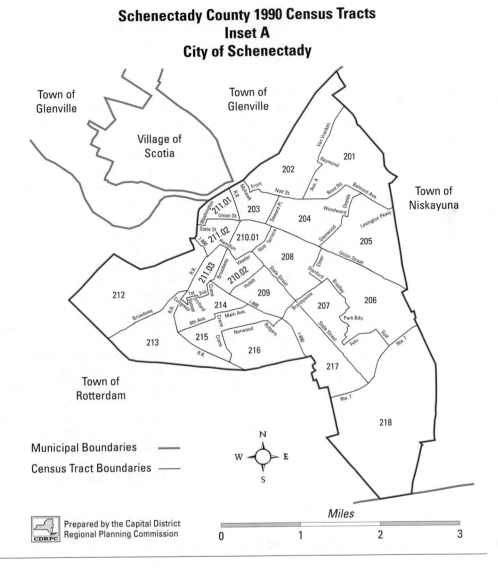

Schenectady County 1990 Census Tracts
Inset A
City of Schenectady

Figure 15.1A
Census Tract Map,
Schenectady,
New York
Reprinted with
permission.

Prepared by the Capital District
Regional Planning Commission

Sharing Space

Another choice is to locate the company within the facilities of a larger company. As the largest of the chain stores continue to downsize, opportunities to take excess space arise. This was the case for Toys 'R' Us, which rents space in 10 Montgomery Ward stores. A variation on this theme is to lease a location that has enough space to sublease to a complementary business. For example, a copy service might lease excess space to a computer graphics company.

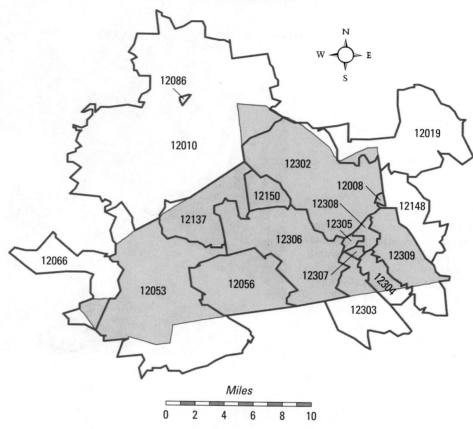

**Figure 15.1B
Schenectady,
New York**
Reprinted with
permission.

Prepared by the Capital District Regional Planning Commission

Mobile Locations

One of the more interesting ways to introduce new businesses and new prod-
ucts/services to the marketplace is through the use of **pushcarts and kiosks.**
This was the strategy of Bill Sanderson, president of CalCorn, Inc., which
owns Popcorn Palace, a chain of boutique, gourmet popcorn stores. Its typical location is a high-traffic site in an upscale regional mall. This space is one
of the more expensive in the mall; therefore, to test the potential viability of
a new site, Sanderson often starts with a pushcart location on that site before

For some business owners, operating their business from a mobile cart on the street can become a "permanent" location, at least in concept. Chuck Beek's Monorail Espresso has survived on the streets of Seattle for 18 years, fueling a coffee revolution that has spread across the country. (France Ruffenach)

committing to a long-term lease. Pushcarts and their more fixed alternative, the kiosk—a small booth—also allow a company to expand to many new locations without the high overhead of a conventional retail storefront.

Relying on experts to select a site is probably the best way to ensure a good decision. Consultants specializing in all types of business site locations are available. The advantage of using consultants is that they have a duty of confidentiality, are generally unbiased and take an objective view, and take a broader view of the needs of the business than, say, a real estate broker who is representing specific properties might.

Facility Decisions

Once a site is located, the existing building must be evaluated for a lease/buy decision. If the site is bare land, building a facility is the only choice. As a significant portion of assets can be tied up in a facility, each of these scenarios should be looked at in greater detail.

The Existing Building

Any existing building on a potential site must be examined carefully with the following questions considered:

▶ Is the building of sufficient size to meet current and reasonable future needs?

▶ Do the building and site allow for future expansion?

▶ Is there sufficient parking?

▶ Is there space for customers, storage, inventory, office space, and rest rooms?

Certainly, allowing for future growth is essential. The initial higher cost of a larger building is often offset by avoiding the extraordinarily high costs of moving and the potential for lost sales and time away from the fundamental work of the business while the business is in transition.

An examination of an existing building should begin with the exterior and answer the following questions:

1. Does the building have curbside appeal, assuming customers will come to the site?

2. Is the building compatible with its surroundings?

The Real World of Entrepreneurship

The Value of Being a Temporary Tenant

Some landlords have found that rather than sit on an empty space until the new tenant moves in, they can rent the space on a temporary basis. Such was the case with the managers of White Marsh Mall, a suburban shopping center outside Baltimore, who approached the owners of a successful seasonal goods shop, the MacCools, to take a vacant storefront until they could find a permanent tenant. There was benefit on both sides of the deal, as it gave the MacCools an opportunity to test their concept in a mall location without committing to a long-term lease.

The concept of the temporary tenant has grown so rapidly that there are now agents who specialize in that area. The most successful of these temporary tenants have the following characteristics:

▶ Personalized merchandise

▶ Opportunities to sample the product

▶ Products that can be demonstrated

▶ Products that can be used to entertain the customers

For the temporary concept to work, significant foot traffic and high customer turnover are required.

Following is a comparison of the three types of retail site based on Mall of America in Minnesota:

	Pushcart	Temporary Storefront	Permanent Storefront
	$2,000 per month to rent cart from mall.	$3,500 per month	$4,000 per month
	15% of sales above $13,333 per month	15% of sales over $23,000 per month	8% of annual sales in excess of $320,000

Source: Randy Myers, "Temporary Tenant," *Nation's Business,* August 1995, p. 39.

3. Does it have enough windows of sufficient size?

4. Is the entrance inviting?

5. Is the signage attractive, and does it satisfy the local regulations?

6. Is the parking adequate to meet customer and employee demand and satisfy local building codes?

7. Does the interior of the building meet the company's needs in terms of walls, floors, and ceilings?

8. Are there sufficient lighting fixtures, outlets, and enough power to run equipment?

These are just a few questions to be asked before finalizing a decision on a building. Most companies can answer these questions to their satisfaction, but to be certain the building is not hiding anything that could be costly for the business, it's wise to hire a licensed contractor or inspector to examine it for structural soundness.

Leasing a Building

The speed of change, innovation, and technological advancement has shortened and will continue to shorten product and service life cycles, and this has an impact on the facilities in which businesses operate. Buildings have long physical lives and typically are very expensive to refurbish and remodel. This fact is evident in the many community factories and retail outlets lying vacant for long periods of time, even years. Ultimately they are sold or leased, but at an amount far below what it cost to build the building.

One suggested solution to the problem is for companies to hold short leases of five years or less. In this way, the company does not tie up precious capital that it may not be able to recover, and it is able to move on when a product or service is deemed technologically antiquated and no longer in de-

 Entrepreneurship in Action

Try Serving a Particular Industry

In an industry filled with competing companies, entrepreneur Kerwin Neufeld has found a niche. His company, Easy PCs, located in Fresno, California, provides corporate networking and personal computer solutions to the real estate industry.

Neufeld's company is defined as a **value-added provider (VAP)**. He provides value-added service solutions to his customers for products, such as software and hardware, that are often seen as commodities. He is also a reseller of products in the computer industry.

VAPs often have difficulty distinguishing themselves from other VAPs, so many, like Neufeld, have chosen a **line-of-business approach** and focused either on certain types of products, such as databases or accounting packages, or on particular industries, such as the real estate or medical industry. This way they become the recognized "experts" in the field, providing customized solutions to specific problems.

mand. There are, however, some serious disadvantages to short-term leasing,[1] described in the following paragraphs.

1. Rents are escalated more frequently due to short-term renewal. Many a company has found itself in this awkward position. Demand for the product or service has been successful beyond initial predictions, so the company needs to remain in its current location beyond the term of the lease. When the entrepreneur renegotiates the lease terms, he or she inevitably finds that the landlord intends to raise the rent for a new lease. This is usually justified by increasing market rents; however, at the same time, the landlord is aware that it would be costly for the tenant to relocate. Moreover, the business would have little time to do so and still maintain its current production rate. Furthermore, the potential to have to replace employees and create new logistics for suppliers and buyers is daunting. All of these factors put the entrepreneur in a very weak position to negotiate a new lease.

> *Tip:* When the lease is first negotiated, a clause should be included that permits the option to renew at a specified rate, and an **escape clause** in case the business must be closed. These two clauses may, however, cost a bit more initially.

2. It will be more difficult to remodel midterm. If the company has a short-term lease, the landlord will be less likely to approve any substantial tenant improvements if they do not increase the value of the building to future tenants.

> *Tip:* When the lease is first negotiated, the entrepreneur should come prepared with a five-year plan for the facility and be able to demonstrate the benefits to the landlord of allowing the remodeling of the building.

3. The company will not be able to show a substantial asset on the balance sheet. Therefore, it will not be a good vehicle for raising capital.

> *Tip:* If the company owns the building, it can sell it later to raise needed capital and lease it back, thereby avoiding moving costs and providing the new landlord with an instant tenant, a factor that increases the value of the building to the new owner.

If you are sure you want a short-term lease, you should, at the very least, negotiate for a renewal clause in the contract that will allow you to extend the lease for an agreed-on period of time.

The cost of leasing a building is a function of the demand in the marketplace for rentals as well as a number of other factors:

- Buildings that are newer, suitable for a variety of uses, and well located generally enjoy higher lease rates, as do buildings that are in short supply.

- Since rent is normally paid based on square footage of space, the larger the space, the more costly the lease.

▶ Retail and service business sites are generally more expensive than industrial sites.

▶ A retail site in a regional mall will likely be the most expensive.

Be aware, however, that although manufacturing sites enjoy lower rental rates than commercial sites, they usually pay higher amounts for water, power, and sewage. That's why it's important to consider all the costs related to leasing a facility. Failure to include the cost of expensive utilities or a common-use area fee could spell disaster to the company's cash flow. A good lease agreement should also designate who is responsible for repairs to the structure and infrastructure of the building.

Businesses consider three basic types of leases:

▶ **Gross lease.** This lease allows the company to pay a fixed rate per month, with the landlord covering the cost (and getting the benefit) of insurance, taxes, and building operating expenses such as outdoor lighting, security, and so forth.

▶ **Net lease** (also known as *triple net*). With this lease, the company pays a fixed monthly rate plus taxes, operating expenses, and essentially everything but the mortgage and the building insurance, which the landlord pays. In essence, the company rents a shell with stipulated improvements.

▶ **Percentage lease.** This is the most complicated of all the lease types because it has several variations. It can be written as a percentage of the tenant's net income or as a flat rate plus a percentage of the gross revenues. The latter is very common in retail operations.

Fortunately for businesses seeking lease facilities, it's a renters' market and probably will remain so for the foreseeable future as demand lags the oversupply created in the 1980s. Moreover, savvy customers in the 1990s and beyond expect businesses to reflect the trend toward "less is more" by controlling costs and simplifying operations. In a renter's market, entrepreneurs can expect to negotiate leases that provide a certain period of free rent, free parking, allowances for tenant improvements, and greater flexibility to extend or shorten the lease. For example, one Chicago-based company renegotiated its high-rent lease, reducing its obligation from $36 per square foot to $22. In addition, the landlord agreed to cover the $1 million tenant improvements, which would be recovered over the term of the new 10-year lease.

Even more savings in a lease can be achieved by reading it carefully:

▶ Look for a provision for examining the landlord's books to view the costs related to the building. In this way, **pass-throughs** may be discovered. These are costs in the form of capital improvements that should not be passed on to the tenants, such as the cost of a new security system. Charges to the tenants for expenses that are rightfully the owner's, such as personal services to the owner who is also a tenant of the building, may also be found.

- Check the lease carefully for clerical mistakes, particularly the easily over-looked simple items such as addresses, suite numbers, square footage, and rental amounts.

- Talk to other tenants of the building to find out common needs that a unified effort may achieve.

- Ask for a breakdown of taxes and operating expenses for the previous three years and projections for the next five years.

- Secure a work letter that explains all improvements the landlord will make for the tenant as well as work the tenant must complete. All costs associated with the completion of these improvements should be requested.

- Make certain the building meets requirements and safety levels prescribed by the Environmental Protection Agency.

First and foremost, leases are written from the landlord's point of view and therefore are negotiable. The fact that something appears in printed form does not mean that it's true or that it has to be agreed to. A lease represents a significant portion of a company's overhead, so it's important that it provide what the company needs to do its business. The best advice is to seek the assistance of an attorney who can represent the company's interests.

Buying a Building

If a company has the resources, buying a building has some advantages. A valuable asset is immediately created on the balance sheet, which can be leveraged later on when growth capital is needed. For example, the building could be sold and leased back (called a **sale-leaseback**), withdrawing equity for other uses and negotiating favorable long-term lease terms. Sale-leasebacks are attractive options for investors, so these buildings generally sell quickly. Of course, when the building is sold, the entrepreneur effectively

Technology Tip

Go Online to Find a Business Location

As you consider where to locate your new business or where to expand it, start by going online to get information about regions of the country that are favorable to your type of business. Most larger communities now have web sites that tout the benefits of moving there. In addition, magazines such as *Inc.* and *Success* conduct annual reviews of the best places to start and grow a business (http://www.inc.com; http://www.success.com.).

You may also find an actual site online by using the *International Real Estate Directory* at http://www.ired.com. It has been called the "motherload" of real estates sites, with links to 13,000 sites in 85 countries. Here you can search by region. Many real estate brokers, such as Coldwell Banker, also have web sites that will get you started on your search for the best site for your business.

loses control of it. Therefore, it is vital to negotiate terms that allow the tenant to remodel and extend the lease should that be desired.

One advantage of owning a building is that it can be traded in a **tax-deferred exchange** for other property the company may need. For example, if the company owned an office building but needed a distribution warehouse to support a new direction it was taking, it might take advantage of a tax-deferred exchange by trading the office building for the warehouse. The exchange would defer capital gains tax on the sale of the office, and the company would have the warehouse it needed.

One other option to consider is a joint venture between the company and a real estate developer on a building in which the company will be one of the tenants and co-owner. A **joint venture** is simply a partnership created to undertake a specific project. If the company is able to occupy a substantial portion of the building, it will be easier for the developer to acquire a mortgage and additional tenants. Of course, this type of arrangement has the inherent problems of any partnership and should be considered carefully with the advice of an attorney before any agreement is executed.

Buying a building requires the signing of a contract, much as a lease agreement does. The contract will spell out the terms of the purchase and the items included in and excluded from the purchase agreement. As always, it should be read carefully to make sure that what was agreed to verbally has been translated correctly on paper. It would be wise to hire a due diligence team (inspector, contractor, CPA, attorney) to inspect the building and the agreement to protect the company's interests.

Building the Facility

When a suitable facility in the desired location can't be found, building the facility from the ground up becomes the only option. This will entail an architect, permits, possibly zoning variances, a construction bidding process, **off-site improvements** (curbs, gutters, water and power lines, roads), and a lengthy building and inspection process. This option should not be undertaken without the aid of a reputable, licensed general contractor. This is important because if the contractor has a dispute with any of the subcontractors hired for the various aspects of the job, the subcontractors have a right to lien the property, which the company owns. The company will then have to sue the contractor to resolve the issue and remove the lien (a certificate of occupancy will not be issued if any liens are present), a time-consuming and costly process.

Also, since the company is most probably responsible to the lender for the construction loan moneys, it can ensure that any subcontractors are paid by (1) using a **voucher system**, a cumbersome method whereby the subcontractor receives a voucher for work completed and must take it to the lending bank for payment and release of liens, or (2) paying the subcontractors directly and receiving lien releases. The latter method is known in the industry as "jointing a check." It prevents the general contractor from using the funds for other purposes and potentially not having the money to pay the subcontractor.

Some entrepreneurs go out of their way to provide employees a quality working environment. PRT, a software engineering company, did just that when it located its new facility on the Caribbean island of Barbados. To compete in a highly competitive market for programmers, PRT offers a turnkey existence in an information-age town that makes employees feel like they're on vacation every day. (Kathy Tarantola)

Constructing a building is no doubt the most complex option; however, the result will be a building that completely meets the company's needs. This option is most suitable when the needs for the building and/or the location are unique, when the company has time to wait, and when it intends to remain in the facility for the long term.

The Interior of the Facility

As important as the location and type of facility are, the layout of the interior of the facility can mean the difference between an operation that moves efficiently and effectively and one that is slowed and interrupted by an ineffective physical flow. A good interior design is the province of professionals who are available to you, as a small-business owner, to guide you in coming up with the best design for your particular type of business. Here we will briefly consider some of the key elements of business design.

Retail Layout and Design

Retail layouts must take into consideration the buying habits of customers. It is generally agreed that impulse items should be placed near the entrance, in the center aisle in a large store, or by the cashier. By contrast, necessities, staples, and major-expense items are normally located at the back of the store.

It's a good idea to use an expert when designing the layout, as the most efficient and effective design can mean the difference between lackluster sales and superior sales. Following are some items you should consider when designing the layout:

▶ Identify the size, quantity, and quality of all product lines.

▶ Understand the buying habits of the customer.

▶ Coordinate graphics and signage with appropriate colors and wording.

▶ Create a window display that projects the store's image.

▶ Use security systems to protect inventory.

▶ Ensure that no areas of the selling floor are invisible to the sales staff.

▶ Allow enough space for receiving and storage.[2]

See Figure 15.2 for two different layout examples, two very different approaches to arranging merchandise. The camping store on the left follows a grid plan; the shoe store on the right, an open arrangement.

Office Layout

Most businesses have office space. In fact, some service businesses are entirely office space. The layout of this space will largely determine how efficiently and effectively work flows through the organization. The goal of any layout plan should be to minimize movement and noise and maximize communication. Therefore, people who regularly work together should be located physically near one another. Computer workstations should generally be away from distractions such as conversations, and common-use items such as copy machines and water coolers should be easily accessible. A design consultant can help a company determine the optimal office layout.

Wholesale/Warehouse Layout

The goal of a wholesaler differs from that of a retailer. In a retail business, items are located to make them easier for the customer to find. In a warehouse business, by contrast, it's important to create a layout that lets employees fill orders quickly. Thus, goods that sell more rapidly are placed in one area of the warehouse, and slower-selling items are placed in another. The receiving dock is located closest to the most frequently sold items. Automated warehouse operations often use a series of conveyer belts to select items from various parts of the warehouse and send them to the receiving dock. The diversity of goods being warehoused will probably determine the methods by which items are pulled from the shelves.

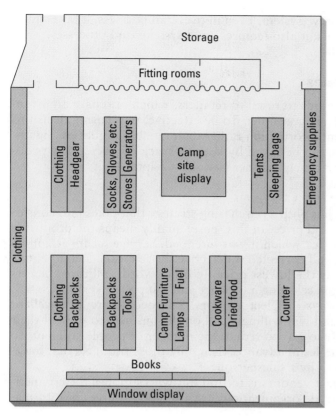

A. Grid Layout

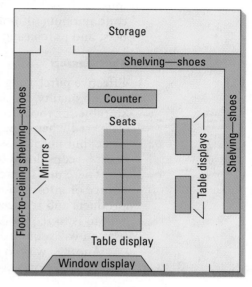

B. Open Layout

Figure 15.2
Two Retail Layout Examples
Source: Earl C. Meyer and Kathleen R. Allen, *Entrepreneurship and Small Business Management*
(New York: Glencoe/McGraw-Hill, 1994), p. 185. © 1995 by Glencoe/McGraw-Hill. Reprinted by permission.

The Business Process

Like manufacturing companies, retail/wholesale and service businesses are process oriented. Though they do not necessarily produce a product using that process, they move products and provide a service to customers. The process begins each morning before the business opens and ends each day after it closes. To properly analyze the process, a flowchart of all the activities undertaken during a typical business day in the order in which they are performed should be created. This will differ somewhat for each business. In analyzing the process, it is important to look for areas of duplication as well as activities that may require controls to avoid shrinkage through either employee or customer theft. The goal is continual improvement of the process to achieve the most effective system. Even in the retail business, it takes more than sales to create profits; it also requires good systems and processes.

Purchasing and Inventory Issues

Wholesalers purchase goods to resell to retailers, which purchase an inventory of goods to sell to the consumer. To be effective, purchasing decisions must be based on current information rather than intelligent guesses. Significant amounts of money can be saved by keeping track of prices, new products, and purchasing in a timely manner (see also Chapter 14).

Purchasing

Effective purchasing begins with a purchasing strategy that takes into consideration quality, service, and price. In this sense, quality means the product is suitable for the purpose for which it was intended. Service means it will be delivered when needed and corrected if defective. Price means a competitive price, but not necessarily the lowest price. In other words, all three factors must be considered before selecting a product and a supplier (vendor).

There are several ways to select vendors. Salespeople are an excellent source of information and will willingly call on the business to present their products and services. One way to reduce the number of people you have to talk to is to request samples in advance; then only those products that interest you will require a visit by a salesperson.

Another way to select vendors is to find out who supplies the competitors. Trade shows and trade organizations are also good sources of information on suppliers.

Once a list of vendors is compiled, it is time to evaluate them. Following are some of the issues you should address:

▶ The vendor's reputation for quality and service

▶ The vendor's credit rating (this can be checked through Dun & Bradstreet)

▶ The vendor's history

▶ The vendor's ability to provide technical assistance

Chapter 14 presented additional criteria for selecting vendors. Once selected, vendors should be evaluated on an annual basis to make sure they are still meeting the company's needs.

A good purchasing policy will also establish a clear line of authority for purchasing decisions and controls over ordering decisions. This will mean using requisitions and placing someone in charge of them.

Inventory

Inventory is basically assets purchased and held for sale. With the possible exception of some service companies, all businesses have some type of inventory. As Chapter 14 explained, inventories carry inherent costs—insurance, storage, shrinkage, and so forth—so it's vital that a growing company have a system in place to manage its inventory. To reduce some of the costs of inventory, many firms are moving toward a just-in-time system that links them electronically with their suppliers, who then know when the company reaches a trigger point at which it must replenish its inventory of a particular product.

There are three basic types of inventory: finished goods, raw materials, and work in process. The last two relate to manufacturing operations, which were discussed in Chapter 14. **Finished goods inventory** is items ready for sale, and this is the type of inventory retailers hold to ensure that they have enough on hand to meet their customers' needs. Certainly customer demand fluctuates, so retailers must have a keen sense of when to carry above-average levels of inventory. Too much inventory means high carrying costs; too little inventory results in lost sales.

Informal Inventory Tracking Methods

When a company is small and its suppliers are close, it can reorder inventory on an *as-needed basis*. One method smaller companies use is to divide the inventory into expensive and inexpensive items and then track more frequently the status of the expensive items, since they account for a larger portion of the inventory as a whole. Larger retailers, in contrast, typically use a bar code system to track inventory and establish trigger points with their suppliers to find out when to reorder. With this system, when a sale occurs, it is recorded electronically and the inventory is updated simultaneously.

Hardware stores and wholesale businesses typically use a version of *kanban* to track inventory. It is essentially a **two-bin system** suitable for small items whereby two containers of the item are carried at all times. The open container/display is placed on top of the closed container. When the open container is empty, it's time to reorder and open the bottom container. Bookstores that shelve books cover forward use a variation of this method by placing a reorder card in the last book at the back of the stack.

Yet another method involves dividing inventory into *three groups* based on price. Each group is then analyzed to determine the best tracking method for that group. Usually one group will require more frequent reordering than another.

Formal Inventory Tracking Systems

The following systems are more elaborate and sophisticated than those previously discussed, and they require computers and specialty software.

Point-of-Purchase Systems   Point-of-purchase (POP) systems exist for virtually every type of retail or wholesale business and ensure more accurate tracking of inventory in "real time." When an item is purchased, its code is entered into the terminal and the inventory is immediately reduced by that item. This makes it very easy to know when to reorder.

Bar Coding   Bar coding actually facilitates POP systems by relieving the salesperson from having to enter code. Consequently, one potential point of data entry error is eliminated, which can be a significant savings to the company. The bar code is a label containing black-and-white parallel bars encoded with information. To use a bar code system requires a computer, a laser scanner, a decoder, and the bar code symbols.

Electronic Data Interchange   Electronic data interchange (EDI) takes electronic data entry one step further by linking the retailer with the supplier so that reordering essentially becomes automatic. By linking directly or through a third party such as AOL or another Internet service provider, inventory is shipped when needed, resulting in higher inventory turnover and the elimination of the need for demand forecasting or other traditional inventory tracking devices.

Inventory Turnover

Inventory turnover is an important indicator of the effectiveness with which the company is managing its inventory. Inventory turnover is the average number of times an inventory is sold out during the year for a particular product line. The rate of turnover differs for each industry (e.g., men's clothing is 3; restaurants, 22; and some chemical manufacturers, 100), but knowing the average rate for the industry in which the company competes is an important benchmark against which to measure the company's effectiveness. For example, if it is known that a particular industry has an inventory turnover rate of 5, the following formula represents how much inventory must be kept on hand:

$$\frac{12 \text{ months}}{5 \text{ turnover rate}} = 2.4 \text{ months' supply}$$

On average, then, a 2.4-month supply of inventory will need to be on hand. Once the quantity required to be on hand is known, the cost of the inventory can be calculated by using the company's forecasted sales for the upcoming year and the cost of goods sold (COGS) (inventory) percentage. For example, if the company is forecasting $200,000 in sales and the COGS is 50% of sales, then

$$\frac{\$200,000 \times .50}{5 \text{ turnover rate}} = \$20,000$$

It will cost $20,000 to maintain a 2.4 months' supply in inventory, not including carrying costs. Naturally, if the company deals in several product lines, calculations for each line will need to be done as they may have varying turnover rates.

Using a variation of the previous formula, a company can calculate its inventory turnover rate to compare itself against the industry average. This is done by dividing the cost of sales by the average inventory:

$$\$100,000/\$20,000 = 5$$

This means the company turned over its inventory an average of five times during the year, or every 73 days (365/5).

It's important to look not only at total inventory turnover but also at turnover of individual items to find the slow-moving ones. A simple analysis of the number of any item on hand against the number sold in, say, the past 60 days will point up which products need to have their inventory on hand decreased and which need their inventory to be increased.

Shrinkage

Shrinkage is loss by theft and shoplifting from both customers and employees. It is by all accounts a significant problem in the retail industry because so many people pass through its doors. To illustrate the impact of theft on a company's profitability, consider a case where a software retailer loses a software program valued at $39.95 every day for a year. If the store operates at a 10 percent profit margin, it will have to sell an additional $145,817.50 of merchandise to compensate for the loss.

Shoplifting, the most common crime in the retail business, accounts for about 3 percent of the selling price of an item. Though it may seem that expensive items are shoplifted more often, most stolen items range from $1 to $5. Only a small percentage of shoplifters are professionals; the vast majority are juveniles (50 percent) and drug or alcohol abusers. To combat shoplifting requires that sales personnel be aware of the habits of shoplifters. They tend to act nervous and spend a considerable amount of time just looking around. They may carry large bags or wear bulky clothing. The more successful thieves arrive when the store is understaffed and travel in groups so that one or two can cause a distraction while the others steal the merchandise. Some tactics to help deter shoplifting include

▶ Keeping the store well lit and display cases low to maintain a clear view

▶ Using two-way mirrors or closed-circuit TV

▶ Using electronic, tamper-proof tags on articles of clothing

▶ Hiring a uniformed security guard

The Real World of Entrepreneurship

Warning Signs of Inventory Problems

Recognizing inventory problems well before they can damage the business is vital to a company's health. Following are some danger signals:

1. Inventories rising faster than sales
2. A significant shift in the inventory mix

3. An increase in back orders and lead times
4. Too many write-offs for obsolete inventory
5. Frequent customer complaints about back orders and missed deliveries[3]

To ensure a clear-cut case against a shoplifter, the salesperson must see the person take the merchandise, be able to prove the merchandise belongs to the store, prove it was taken with intent to steal, and prove it was not paid for. In addition, it is important to apprehend the shoplifter outside the store to strengthen the intent argument.

Though shoplifting is a frustrating problem for retailers, about 75 to 80 percent of all retail crime is actually committed by employees, who add 15 percent to the cost of consumer goods. Employees have an advantage over shoplifters; they normally have access to the business in a way no shoplifter does. A company can do several things to minimize the opportunity for employee theft:

1. Keep all non-entry or exit doors locked when not in use.

2. Control who has access to keys to the business, and change the locks if theft is suspected.

3. Periodically check the trash bins, as they are a typical hiding place for stolen items.

4. Watch for a large number of voided or no-sale transactions.

5. Don't let one person control a transaction from beginning to end.

6. Be careful about hiring, and check references.

A few precautions taken consistently will go a long way toward protecting the business and its customers.

Retail/wholesale/service businesses, like manufacturing businesses, are becoming solutions oriented. An effective, total quality process strategy should include the customer, state-of-the-art technology, superior resources and processes, and continuous improvement. Entrepreneurial companies that integrate these components into their process strategies will gain a significant competitive advantage in a dynamic marketplace.

Cases Relevant to This Chapter

French Rags
Zanart Entertainment

Issues for Review and Discussion

1. Discuss three alternatives to conventional business sites.
2. Compare the advantages and disadvantages of building, buying, and leasing a building.
3. What are four factors to consider to save money on a lease?
4. How can business owners select qualified vendors to supply them with goods that reflect quality, service, and a fair price?

Experiencing Entrepreneurship

1. Find a retail/service business in your community. Using a census tract map, draw a trade area for the company based on the type of business it is. Then do a competitive analysis of the trade area and a demographic analysis of the market. Is this business suitably located?

2. Interview the owner of a retail store to find out which specific tactics she or he uses to avoid shrinkage.

Resources

Anderson, Robert L., and John S. Dunkelberg (1987). *Managing Growing Firms.* Englewood Cliffs, NJ: Prentice-Hall.

Bar, Vilma, and Charles E. Broudy (1986). *Designing to Sell.* New York: McGraw-Hill.

Internet Resources
Barcode Server
http://www.milk.com/barcode/
Find out how bar codes work and generate your own.

U.S. Bureau of the Census
http://www.census.gov
Demographic information useful for identifying and analyzing the trade area.
Liszt

http://www.liszt.com/
Searchable directory of mailing list topics.
U.S. Bureau of the Census Tiger Map Service

http://tiger.census.gov
Source of census tract maps.

Managing Finances for Growth

VI

*The wise man understands equity;
the small man understands only profits.*
Confucius, c. 551–c. 479 B.C.

Financial Analysis for Growth

Preview

Understanding this chapter will give you the ability to

▶ Describe the accounting and recordkeeping options available to your business.

▶ Explain how to forecast sales and capital expenditures using triangulation.

▶ List and explain the purpose of the three main financial statements.

▶ Discuss the purpose of financial ratios and how they can be used to describe the health of the business.

▶ Describe how to use cost-volume-profit analysis to answer questions about your business.

Terms to Know

Young Entrepreneurs—Minicase

John Shegerian
Bulldog Root Beer™/Bulldog Brewing Company™

A concept for a new business can come from anywhere, even from classes you take at a university. In 1996, Professor Timothy Stearns of California State University at Fresno met John Shegerian, and an idea was born. Shegerian was a 1986 graduate of New York University who had worked in his family's printing business as well as starting his own insurance company before moving to California in 1988. There he hoped to find new opportunities in the real estate market. He took a position as senior vice president at a real estate development company in Los Angeles, directing 85 people. While still in this position, he also developed Homeboy Industries, which produced fresh tortillas, baked products, and other merchandise at the Grand Central Market in Los Angeles. The employees consisted of "gang-impacted youths," and profits from the business went to the Jobs for the Future Program, which helped these youths find jobs.

Shegerian's wife was from a small town outside Fresno, so when they grew tired of big-city life, they decided to relocate to Fresno. Shegerian first conceived the idea for a brewpub in the summer of 1995. For seven months, he mulled the idea around in his mind and began to do market research to learn more about the microbrewery industry. Among the many things he found out was that two of the "hottest" concepts for the next decade are microbrewed beer and "eatertainment-themed" restaurants. Beer is the second most popular drink in the world after water, and brewpubs have an 86 percent success rate, which is substantially higher than the 30 percent success rate for restaurants.

Encouraged by his findings, Shegerian met with Professor Stearns. The meeting was to become a turning point for his business concept. Their discussions led to the unique idea of linking a brewpub to the university's mascot, the bulldog. Fresno is very much a college town, and its athletic teams have a devoted following in the community. Shegerian envisioned a place where the community could gather to celebrate the Bulldogs. Stearns, who in the fall of 1996 planned to offer a course in new-venture creation that focused on product development, saw an opportunity to link the two concepts. He believed, however, that root beer was a more appropriate product for his students to work on. At first Shegerian was unsure whether it was wise to market the root beer product before the brewpub had launched, but Stearns wanted to see what the students could do with the concept. They came to agreement and decided that Shegerian would become involved in the class and act as an adviser, consultant, and motivator for the students.

In the fall of 1996, the goal of the class was to create and introduce a new brand of root beer—Bulldog Root Beer—named after the school's mascot. Stearns had a friend in Milwaukee who was a brewmaster and had developed a very successful recipe for root beer. This recipe became the basis for the development of Bulldog Root Beer™. An entrepreneur club was formed around the class, and it was to receive the profits of any sales. The students outsourced the production of the root beer and managed the marketing of the product line. In the spring of 1997, Bulldog Root Beer™ was test launched during Vintage Days, a university event that draws thousands of people from the community, and the students immediately sold out of 33 kegs of root beer. They knew they had a hit.

By then Shegerian was even more convinced that his brewpub concept would be a winner, and he began forming alliances with the key people he needed to make the business happen. As Shegerian sees it, the biggest challenge in this type of business is finding the right partners: "A great concept must be executed properly." Among the most important alliances he made was with one of the most successful beverage distributors in the United States. He also brought on board high-profile coaches for publicity purposes and a team of microbrewery experts. Bulldog Brewing Company™ is planned as a vertically integrated business with four profit centers: the eatertainment-themed brewpub; off-site wholesale and retail distribution of Bulldog® Beer; off-site wholesale and retail distribution of Bulldog™ Root Beer; and retail, direct-mail, and web site sales of a full line of Bulldog™ merchandise. Shegerian did not want to rely solely on one source of income for the business because he believed that would be too risky in a tough industry like food services.

Shegerian advises young entrepreneurs, "If you think you have a good idea that fills a void in the marketplace, then never give up. There are a million potholes in the road that become great excuses why you'll go back to work nine to five." In the summer of 1998, Shegerian was deep in the process of gathering the resources he needed to launch the venture in September 1998. He has no intention of ever going back to work for someone else.

How would you recommend that Shegerian forecast sales for his financial strategy, given that he seems to be involved in four different businesses under one roof: food services, food production, distribution, and merchandising of trademarked products?

Financial analysis is one of the tools business owners use to predict the future, study the past, and benchmark for continual improvement. No aspect of your business is left untouched by the company's financial strategy. At the same time, what every other part of the company is doing affects the overall financial strategy. To help successfully plan for the future, financial analysis must occur simultaneously with all other planning, from product design to production to marketing and customer service. Recall from the Young Entrepreneurs Minicase on Bulldog Brewing Company™ that John Shegerian's financial strategy specified that his new venture had several sources of income. This strategy has a significant impact on how he structures the business, markets his products and services, and grows the business. Even though the microbrewery industry is doing well, he wisely didn't rely on restaurant/pub-type services alone.

This chapter looks at two aspects of the financial strategy: (1) accounting systems and recordkeeping, which are the basis for all financial planning, and (2) the creation and analysis of financial statements. Chapter 17 examines cash flow planning and working capital management, which, for any business owner at any stage of the business life cycle, is critical to the health and vitality of the company.

Accounting and Recordkeeping Systems

Entrepreneurs are not expected to be accountants; in fact, most would probably abhor the tedious nature of accounting and recordkeeping. Still, entrepreneurs need to understand the accounting system and how it integrates

Accounting software is not just for accounting anymore. Companies like Somerset Farms, a Pennsylvania-based supplier of food products for prisons, have found that it also helps them manage their business better. Jay Shrager, president of the food distributor, claims that it keeps him in touch with the entire financial picture of the business at any moment and ties all of the functions of the business together. (Sal Dimarco/Black Star)

with everything else the company does. Furthermore, to be able to produce the financial statements so essential to raising capital, leasing major equipment, or securing a line of credit, effective accounting and recordkeeping systems must be established from start-up. Any accounting system must accomplish several things:

1. It should produce an accurate picture of the company's financial health.

2. It should allow for comparisons of current financials with previous periods.

3. It should yield accepted financial statements consistent with **Generally Accepted Accounting Principles (GAAP).**

4. It should facilitate the filing of financial and tax reports.

5. It should expose fraud, theft, waste, and errors.

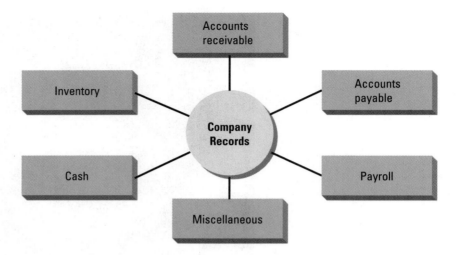

Figure 16.1
Types of Company Records

Recordkeeping

A company must keep a variety of records. These records are depicted in Figure 16.1 and include all the functional areas of the business, from purchasing to employees to inventory.

In recordkeeping, it is vital that there be checks and balances against fraud and theft in the system. For example, the person doing purchasing should not be managing the purchases journal; likewise, the bookkeeper should not be authorizing purchases. It is also important that you, as the business owner, stay in touch with the financial aspects of your business. A simple cash flow report from your bookkeeper on a weekly or even daily basis will help you stay on top of what's going on with the business.

Records should be kept for the legal period required, which is dependent on the type of record. Tax records, for example, must be kept for three years. Today, with virtually all growing companies using computers for accounting and recordkeeping, the storage problem is minimized; older files can be copied to archival disks or tape and stored easily in that form.

Journals and Ledgers

Whether the traditional paper and binder-type journals or electronic journals, journals are for recording transactions of a similar nature temporarily. For example, cash receipts are recorded in the cash receipts journal and purchases in the purchases journal. No matter how many journals a company has, all entries must ultimately be posted to the **general ledger** either as individual items or in summary form. **Subsidiary ledgers** are those kept on individual customers or accounts. Transactions that take place during the business day are recorded in the journals as **debits**, which increase asset and expense accounts and decrease liability, capital, and revenue accounts; and **credits,** which decrease asset and expense accounts and increase liability, capital, and revenue accounts (see Figure 16.2). In income accounts, a debit represents a reduction and a credit is an increase in income. In expense accounts, a debit is an increase (increased liability) and a credit is a decrease. Debits and credits must balance or you will need to look for an error.

Accounting Options

A variety of accounting systems are available to the business owner to manage recordkeeping. These systems will help you make the decisions you'll need to make about recordkeeping on a daily basis. This section briefly considers three systems: cash versus accrual accounting, single-entry versus double-entry systems, and FIFO versus LIFO inventory valuation methods.

Cash Versus Accrual Accounting

The difference between the cash and accrual accounting methods lies in the way revenue and expenses are recognized. Under the **cash method,** the easier of the two, revenue and expenses are recognized and recorded when they are realized—in other words, when the revenue has been received and the expenses have been paid.

In contrast, under the **accrual method,** used most often by growing companies, revenue is recognized and reported when, for example, a sale has taken place (the cash has not necessarily been received), and expenses are reported when they are incurred (not necessarily paid). This system is the better one for accounting purposes because it matches revenues with expenses in the same time period.

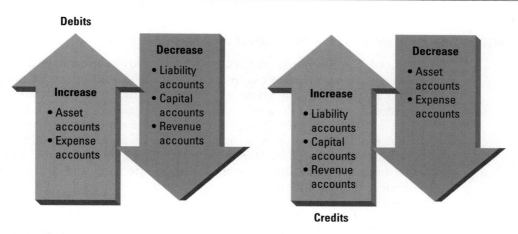

Figure 16.2
Recording Transactions: Debits Versus Credits

Single- Versus Double-Entry Systems

Many very small businesses and home-based businesses use a **single-entry system,** which is basically a checkbook system in which income and expenses are recorded in one record. A **double-entry system** uses journals and ledgers, thereby requiring that each entry be posted twice, once in the journal and once in the general ledger. The result is a built-in balancing system to check for errors and a natural basis for the financial statements. For this reason, it is highly recommended that all businesses use this system from the very beginning.

FIFO Versus LIFO Inventory Valuation

FIFO (first in, first out) and **LIFO** (last in, first out) are methods for recording the cost of a product sold—that is, inventory—when it comes in and when it goes out. Choosing one over the other is a function of your overall tax strategy. FIFO seems the more logical because the assumption is that inventory is sold in the order it is received. Needless to say, in a company dealing with perishable goods, this approach makes eminent sense. However, in reality, a perfect FIFO system never exists except in accounting records where the oldest costs are the first costs to be applied to the income statement as cost of goods sold and the most recent costs to the balance sheet as inventory assets. In practice, companies calculate the value of ending inventory, so both issues are taken care of simultaneously.

LIFO assumes the most recent inventory acquired will be the first sold. The value of this approach is in accounting for inflation, which predicts that replacement inventory will cost more than inventory sold. If costs are rising, LIFO will yield a lower profit than FIFO and thus save on taxes. LIFO will show a lower inventory asset value on the balance sheet, however, which will affect the valuation of the business at that point in time. A good accountant can help a business owner make decisions about valuation methods that are both correct and beneficial to the company's growth strategy.

Financial Statement Creation and Analysis

This book has promoted creativity and innovation in every aspect of the organization, with this one exception: creativity should normally not be reflected in the financial statements. Instead, they must follow Generally Accepted Accounting Principles (GAAP) so the reader, whether a banker, investor, or other interested party, recognizes standard terms and sees items in their normal order of presentation. This section looks at the income statement, operating cash flow statement, and balance sheet. Chapter 17 focuses on perhaps the most important tool for entrepreneurs: the cash flow statement or cash flow budget.

Pro forma financial statements are merely forecasts of the company's operations and financial position at some point in the future. Start-up ventures create pro forma statements because they have no history on which to create anything else. Growing companies create pro formas to project their position into the future based on estimated growth. If circumstances change, those projections and pro formas will change as well, but decisions about cash flow management can be made based on them. For example, if projections based on current data show that your company will become very liquid in the coming year, you might decide to begin paying your credit line down in larger payments than you have been accustomed to making.

In form, pro forma statements look like any other financial statements. Again, they are a tool entrepreneurs can use to help make the future a little less unpredictable. We will now consider how financial statements are created by first looking at a method to forecast two critical items: sales and capital expenditures.

Forecasting Sales and Capital Expenditures

Before going to the financial statements, it's important to look at how some of the items on the statements are estimated. The information needed to complete the financial statements includes demand, cost, and operating figures. To present a picture of the company at a particular point in time, current figures are used, whereas for pro forma statements, figures will have to be estimated. The goal is to either present the company's current status or forecast the company's financial condition for the next three to five years based on the information collected. The pro forma statements will reflect the best estimate of how the company will perform and what the associated expenses will be. Pro forma estimates are subject to change based on the more accurate information gained over a period of time. This is why start-up entrepreneurs typically reevaluate the financial statements on a monthly basis or at least quarterly for the first year of operations.

Sales should be calculated first because sales affect the other expenditures of the business. The method for forecasting sales for pro forma statements will vary depending on the general product or service category. For example,

 Entrepreneurship in Action

Maybe the Most Important Number in Your Business Isn't Profit or Cash

If you ask business owners to tell you what the most vital aspect of their business is, most will probably claim profit or cash. But Jack Stack, president and CEO of Springfield Remanufacturing Corporation of Missouri, asserts that the most savvy business owners will give you a different answer. He cites a hotel chain in Indiana that was losing money even though its manager focused on controlling expenses to increase profit levels. When asked how his hotels make money, the manager responded that filling rooms was how he made money, and to break even he needed to have 71 percent of his rooms occupied; he was currently running at 67 percent. So the "critical factor" for this hotel chain was not profit but occupancy rate. Knowing this changed his business strategy entirely as he now focused on ways to provide bonuses to employees as the occupancy rate increased. Ultimately, his hotel became one of the very best in the chain.

SOURCE: Jack Stack, "The Logic of Profit," *Inc.*, March 1996, p. 17.

with a new product that is a line extension or the next generation of an established product, the business owner will be able to rely on historical data that will help ensure a more accurate estimate. With a brand-new or breakthrough product, however, he or she is left to rely on market data, comparison of similar products, and the opinions of market experts. Therefore, to improve the estimate, it is useful to calculate best-case, worst-case, and most-likely-case scenarios that will cover about 90 percent of all the possible sales results.

Three sources of information will help you arrive at a good estimate of sales:

1. Industry sources such as distributors, vendors, and industry experts

2. Customers

3. Like or substitute products

By using at least three sources in a process known as **triangulation,** you can feel more confident that the estimate you arrive at will be as accurate as possible. Remember, though, these are estimates only. Any change in circumstances down the road will affect your estimates positively or negatively. Furthermore, because forecasted sales are estimates only, it is vital that they be based on a thorough understanding of your industry and market.

Forecasting Sales with Consumer Products and Services

If the product or service being offered does not exist in the market in the form in which it will be introduced, a competing product or service that is similar or is a substitute product must be found to study. The information needed includes the volume of **sell-in** to the retailer and the volume of **sell-through** to the customer, that is, the amount of product that is sold by the manufacturer or distributor to the retailer and the amount of that product that is ultimately sold to the customer. Naturally, a service business will concern itself only with the sell-through volume, as service businesses generally operate with direct channels of distribution. In addition, determining if any seasonal factors in the market could affect the volume of sales during any particular period of time is important. The mistake made by many companies that sell to distributors or retailers is focusing only on how much product they are selling to their customers and structuring their production and/or inventory accordingly without carefully monitoring retail sales to the end-user. Consequently, when consumer buying slows and the retailer cannot move sufficient product, the manufacturer or producer is left with excess inventory. The entrepreneur with a new product or service, therefore, should monitor retail sales of competing products to consumers in the same category to arrive at an estimate of sales demand as one component of the triangulation process. Best-case and worst-case scenarios should also be calculated.

One word of caution is in order when choosing competing companies for comparison purposes. If the rival company is a publicly held or a well-established company, a young, growing small business will most probably not be able to achieve the competitor's level of sales for some time. Therefore, the sales figures gathered will serve as an upper-limit benchmark; how much below that figure the sales level will actually lie will need to be determined. The percentage increase in sales over a three-to-five-year period will depend on

▶ Growth rates in the market segment in which the product or service is positioned

▶ The innovations offered that will make the product or service more attractive to the customer or consumer, even at a higher price

▶ The technological innovations employed that permit the company to produce the product or service at a lower cost than its competitors, thus making it more accessible and enticing to the customer/consumer

▶ The effectiveness of the market penetration strategies employed

Forecasting Sales with Industrial Products

With industrial products, which are generally sold business to business, it is important to understand the needs of the customer and the buying cycles of the industry. Talking to experts (e.g., distributors) in the field, getting sales figures from noncompeting product manufacturers in the same industry, and generally determining the size of the market niches the company intends to enter will all help in arriving at an estimate of sales demand. As in the consumer market, in the industrial market it is vital to bracket the estimate with best-case/worst-case, benchmark figures to cover the most likely contingencies. The rate at which sales increase will be a function of the same three factors listed under consumer products.

Forecasting Expenditures

In wholesale businesses, once the sales forecast has been determined, the figures for inventory purchases can be applied as a percentage of sales and forecast from that. So if inventory cost is 25 percent of sales, that percentage can be applied to sales across the period because inventory generally increases linearly in response to an increase in sales. Some businesses will require the forecasting of cost of goods sold, discussed next.

Forecasting Cost of Goods Sold

In manufacturing businesses, forecasting is a bit more complex because the **cost of goods sold (COGS)** must be derived first. This figure usually consists of direct labor, cost of materials, and factory overhead. Looking at the sales forecast in terms of units produced to arrive at a dollar figure for COGS and then applying cost of goods sold as a percentage of sales will probably suffice for purposes of pro forma statements when the business is starting. Month-by-month analysis of outcomes and use of a cost accounting model that considers raw materials inventory, work-in-process inventory, finished goods inventory, total inventory, factory overhead, work-in-process flow in units, and weighted-average cost per unit will give a more accurate estimate as the business grows.

In service businesses, the COGS is equivalent to the time expended for the service. The rate at which the company bills the service—say, $100 an hour—is composed of the actual expenses incurred in providing the service, a contribution to overhead, and a reasonable profit. The actual expenses incurred are the cost of goods sold equivalent.

Forecasting General and Administrative Expenses

General and administrative expenses (G&A), the expenses of running the business, are considered fixed but must be forecast separately in a detailed breakout statement. This is because some of these items may vary over a 12-month period, whereas others remain stable. Therefore, it is not recommended to do percentage of sales figures for G&A expenses. Only the totals of G&A expenses for each month are normally used in the financial statements, with a footnote directing the reader to the G&A breakout statement. Selling expenses, which include advertising, travel, sales salaries, commissions, and promotional supplies, should be handled in the same manner, with a breakout statement, and totals only in the financial statements. Table 16.1 presents some of the categories of items that may appear on the breakout statements.

Forecasting Taxes

The last item to forecast under expenditures is taxes. Although many businesses may be able to take advantage of a tax loss carry-forward for losses during R&D, ultimately the company will have to account for state, federal, and possibly local taxes that are paid at varying times of the year. Check with federal, state, and local agencies to get current rates. Apply these rates to net profit, which will be derived in the income statement; this will give a reasonable estimate of tax liability.

Income Statement

The income statement, often called the **profit and loss statement,** gives information regarding the profit or loss status of the company for a specified period of time, which could be a month, a quarter, or a year. It is normally calculated first—that is, before the cash flow statement and balance sheet—so that tax liability can be determined and reported in the cash flow statement when the taxes are paid. Figure 16.3 displays two end-of-year income statements for a corporation. Since it is a simple statement, it does not contain breakout statements. Note that if the business were structured as a sole proprietorship or partnership, the reference to taxes would be omitted, because in these two forms taxes are passed through to the owners and paid by them at their personal tax rates.

Like all financial statements, the income statement should contain footnotes referencing a page of **assumptions** or "notes to financial statements," which give supporting evidence and explain calculations that may not be obvious. The example in Figure 16.3 shows assumptions for the first three line items.

Revenue is the inflow of value from the sale of products or services. Value should not be equated with cash, as sales may have occurred using

Table 16.1   Categories for Breakout Statements

Sample Manufacturing or Construction Expenses List	
Manager's Salary Paid	Employees' Salaries
Payroll Taxes	Vehicle Lease and Maintenance
Related Travel	Packaging Costs
Supplies	Depreciation on Owned Equipment

Sample Distribution and Warehouse Expenses List	
Manager's Salary	Employees' Salaries
Drivers' Salaries	Payroll Taxes
Vehicle Lease and Maintenance	Warehouse Loading Vehicles Lease/Maintenance
Freight Expenses	Supplies
Depreciation on Owned Equipment	

Sample List of Selling Expenses	
Sales Manager's Salary	Inside Sales Salaries
Inside Sales Commissions	Telephone Sales Salaries
Telephone Sales Commissions	Field Sales Salaries
Field Sales Commissions	Payroll Taxes for Sales Employees
Sales Vehicles Lease and Maintenance	Sales-Related Travel
Advertising and Promotion	Depreciation on Owned Equipment

Sample List of General and Administrative Expenses	
Advertising	Rent
Salaries and Wages	Utilities
Office Supplies	Insurance
Office Equipment	Business Taxes
Payroll Taxes	

credit and the value received is a claim on the customer for the amount of the sale, which is known as an *account receivable*. Accountants see revenues and expenses on income statements as inflows and outflows of value, which may or may not equate to the revenues and expenses reflected on the cash flow statement. This is because the income statement uses the accrual method of accounting, whereas the cash flow statement uses the cash method. This is an important distinction because in the preceding example, the company will pay taxes for 1997 based on profit accrued in 1997 even if no cash was received. Therefore, the income statement shows that BRE Products is profitable, but we don't know if it's healthy in terms of working capital and cash flow. We will learn this when we examine the cash flow from operations statement. Indicating the difference between the two years gives you a way to more easily spot problems. For example, BRE saw sales increase by $95,000 from 1996 to 1997; yet advertising decreased by $1,485. Why did this happen? Is it the result of being farther along on the learning curve so that its advertising expenses are more targeted and effective? This would be something to examine more carefully.

BRE Products Income Statement For Year Ended December 31, 1997			
	1996	**1997**	**Difference**
Net Sales[1]	485,000	580,000	95,000
Cost of Sales[2]	244,200	320,925	76,725
Gross Profit	240,800	259,075	18,275
Operating Expenses:			
Wages and Salaries[3]	53,625	57,255	3,630
Rent and Lease Payments	8,910	5,940	(2,970)
Utilities	8,415	8,403	(12)
Insurance	20,955	20,955	0
Advertising	9,900	8,415	(1,485)
Vehicle Operation/Maintenance	33,712	32,861	(851)
Accounting and Legal	3,960	3,960	0
Payroll Taxes	7,507	14,615	7,108
Depreciation	2,970	3,300	330
Total Operating Expenses	149,954	155,704	5,750
Net Operating Income	90,846	103,371	12,525
Less: Interest Expense	(4,620)	(5,445)	(825)
Net Taxable Income	86,226	97,926	11,700
Less: Income Taxes	(31,925)	(34,209)	(2,284)
Net Income	**54,301**	**63,717**	**9,416**

1. Based on a 19% increase over the previous year, a pattern established in this industry.
2. Cost of sales was 50% in 1996; 55% in 1997 due to increasing prices from vendors.
3. Based on two employees: one full time at $40,000; one part time at $13,625.

**Figure 16.3
Sample Income
Statement**

Balance Sheet

The **balance sheet** provides information about the value of the business at a specific point in time however the end of the period is defined. It does this by looking at the company's assets (such as equipment, inventory, cash, and facilities), liabilities (e.g., notes payable and installment loans) and owners' equity (such as stock and retained earnings) in the case of a corporation. Figure 16.4 shows an example of a balance sheet.

The first section of the balance sheet is the assets, which are valued in terms of actual cost for the item. Current assets are assumed to be in a cash state and are those items that will be consumed in the operation of the business during the year, whereas fixed assets are essentially resources with long

BRE Products Balance Sheet For Years Ending December 31, 1996 and 1997	1996	1997
Assets		
Current Assets:		
Cash	21,450	4,950
Accounts Receivable	42,533	90,090
Inventory	39,875	92,606
Prepaid Expenses	0	8,250
Total Current Assets	103,858	195,896
Fixed Assets:		
Land	49,500	49,500
Building	247,500	247,500
Vehicles	52,800	57,750
Equipment	33,000	37,950
Less: Accumulated Depreciation	(34,650)	(37,950)
Total Net Fixed Assets	348,150	354,750
Total Assets	**452,008**	**550,646**
Liabilities and Owners' Equity		
Current Liabilities		
Notes Payable	34,831	62,700
Accounts Payable	20,130	27,904
Accruals Payable	3,762	6,088
Total Current Liabilities	58,723	96,692
Long-Term Liabilities		
Installment Loan Payable	0	42,354
Mortgage Payable	181,500	174,900
Total Long-Term Liabilities	181,500	217,254
Total Liabilities	**240,223**	**313,946**
Owners' Equity:		
Capital Stock	49,500	49,500
Retained Earnings	162,285	187,200
Total Owners' Equity	**211,785**	**236,700**
Total Liabilities and Owners' Equity	**452,008**	**550,646**

**Figure 16.4
Sample Balance
Sheet**

lives. They may be tangible assets that will be used over the long term or **intangible assets**, items such as patents and license agreements. Accounts receivable must be forecast, and how this is accomplished is based on the seasonality the business experiences. If the business experiences no pronounced seasonality, it may be assumed that a certain percentage of sales will not be paid in cash each month based on industry averages or on the accounts receivable turnover rate. Once the business is established, however, it will develop its own pattern of receivables, and a more accurate turnover rate can be calculated. To account for the fact that some accounts receivable will not be collected, some entrepreneurs choose to subtract from receivables an allowance for bad debt, a small percentage (2 to 5 percent) based on typical bad-debt figures for the industry. Again, the business will develop its own unique pattern over time, and it will be easier to predict more accurately what the bad-debt rate will be.

Notice that depreciation is accounted for on the balance sheet and reflects asset values. Fixed assets are presented less depreciation to show their book value, with the exception of land, which cannot be depreciated and is shown at its original cost. Thus, it is clear that the worth of the business as reflected on the balance sheet may not be (and most probably is not) the actual value of the business in the marketplace. In fact, stockholders' (or owners') equity is merely a statement of the claims of the owners on the business after all other claims have been paid.

A balance sheet does, however, generally reflect the financial state of the business based on decisions made by the entrepreneur. For example, the decision to retain earnings in the company to invest in future growth will increase the equity side of the balance sheet. A predicted increase in sales will increase

 The Real World of Entrepreneurship

Costs and Inflation

To keep track of whether a particular business expenditure has been increasing by more or less than the cumulative rate of inflation, use the following table. Multiply the expenditure in any year by the factor to the right of that year. Then compare the result with the 1995 expenditure to see if the cost has increased or decreased. For example, ABC company spent $50,000 for marketing in 1985. In 1995, it spent $175,000. Recognizing that part of that increase is due to growth of the company and new marketing vehicles, if we multiply $50,000 by the factor for 1985, 1.42, we get $71,000. This means the equivalent marketing effort the company got for $50,000 in 1985 cost $71,000 in 1995; therefore, ABC's marketing expense is substantially above the cumulative rate of inflation.

Inflation Rate Comparison Table

Year	Rate	Year	Rate	Year	Rate	Year	Rate
1970	3.93	1977	2.52	1983	1.53	1990	1.17
1971	3.76	1978	2.34	1984	1.47	1991	1.12
1972	3.65	1979	2.1	1985	1.42	1992	1.09
1973	3.43	1980	1.85	1986	1.39	1993	1.05
1974	3.09	1981	1.68	1987	1.34	1994	1.03
1975	2.83	1982	1.58	1988	1.29	1995	1.00
1976	2.68			1989	1.23		

SOURCE: U.S. Bureau of Labor Statistics. Table calculations from *Nation's Business,* February 1996.

the asset side of the balance sheet to account for an increase in inventory or equipment to meet the rise in demand.

For each year, the sum of the assets equals the combined value of the owners' equity and total liabilities, so the balance sheet must balance.

Comparing balance sheets from different periods can answer a lot of questions about the business:

1. Did the amounts of accounts receivable and inventory increase or decrease relative to sales in the same period?

2. Did the amount of debt financing increase or decrease during the period?

3. Are accounts payable at a healthy level relative to sales?

4. Have sales increased to a level that warrants further investment in capital equipment?

5. Are the operations of the business producing sufficient cash flow?

Statement of Cash Flow from Operations

The statement of cash flow from operations reports on changes in the company's cash account through inflows and outflows of cash and cash equivalents. These activities are associated with the normal operations of the company, such as purchasing, that are required to produce or sell its products and services. Thus, cash inflows include cash sales and collected accounts receivable, and cash outflows involve payment for inventory, payment of accounts payable, and payments associated with such activities as payroll taxes, rent, utilities, and so forth. **Nonoperating cash inflows** can come from loans, additional investment by the owner, or the sale of fixed assets, whereas outflows can come from the payment of principal or interest on debt, dividend distribution, the purchase of fixed assets, or the payment of legal claims.

In a financially healthy company, the principal source of cash inflows comes from operating sources and is sufficient to pay general expenses, replace and update assets, and return a reasonable rate on invested capital. This is why creditors look so carefully at a company's cash flow, because that is the source of their repayment.

Recall that profit, as reflected in the income statement, and cash flow, as reflected on the operating cash flow statement, are not the same thing. One difference is due to timing. Cash statements reflect inflows and outflows (revenues and expenses) when they occur, not when they are incurred, so it is possible that the income statement will reflect more revenues than are stated on the cash flow statement. The same is true of expenses, which may appear higher on the income statement for the same period but lower on the cash flow statement because payment has not yet been made on those items. Another difference is due to the fact that depreciation of equipment and inventory affects the income statement and balance sheet, but since it's not a cash item, it is not deducted from the cash statement.

BRE Products
Cash Flow from Operations
For the Period 1996–97

Net Sales	580,000	
Less Increase in Accounts Receivable	(47,557)	
Net Sales Adjusted to a Cash Basis		532,443
Cost of Sales	320,925	
Plus: Increase in Inventory	52,731	
Less: Increase in Accounts Payable	(7,774)	
Cost of Sales Adjusted to a Cash Basis		(365,881)
Operating Expenses	155,704	
Less: Depreciation Expense	(3,300)	
Less: Increase in Accruals	(2,326)	
Plus: Increase in Prepaids	8,250	
Less: Operating Expenses Adjusted to a Cash Basis		158,328
Taxes Paid		(34,209)
Cash Flow (Cash Drain) from Operations		(25,975)

Figure 16.5
Sample Statement of Cash Flows from Operations

Preparing a cash flow from operations statement requires that you link the income statement items with changes in the balance sheet items that arise from normal operations from one period to the next: sales, cost of sales, and operating expenses. Figure 16.5 presents a cash flow from operations statement.

A series of steps will explain how the cash flow statement was derived:

1. Adjust sales to a cash basis. Sales for 1997 were $580,000, but these were not all cash sales; some were credit. On the balance sheet, accounts receivable increased from $42,533 in 1996 to $90,090 in 1997, or $47,557. This means BRE extended more credit in 1997, resulting in a cash drain for revenues not collected. So, although sales increased, cash flow from sales did not. To recognize this on the cash flow statement requires adjusting sales down by the amount of increase in receivables:

$$\$580,000 - \$47,557 = \$532,443$$

2. Adjust cost of sales. Cost of sales is cost of goods actually sold in the accounting period. It is affected by changes in the level of inventory (current assets on the balance sheet) and changes in accounts payable (current liability on the balance sheet). In 1997, BRE had a cost of sales of $320,925. If no changes in inventory or accounts payable had occurred, this figure would have represented both the expense and the cash outflow, but as it was, inventory increased by $52,731 and accounts payable by $7,774. Each has a different effect on cash flow. The increase in inventory is an outflow of cash that is not shown on the income statement, so it needs to be added to the cost of sales. On the other hand, the increase in accounts payable means BRE was taking advantage of supplier credit and retaining more cash in the company, so the increase is deducted from the cost of sales.

3. Adjusting the operating expenses. Depreciation is a noncash expense on the income statement and reduces revenue; thus, in terms of cash flow, the operating expenses are not as large as they appear on the income statement. Accruals are unpaid obligations and as such are a current liability on the balance sheet. They represent cash retained within the company, and therefore the increase is deducted from the operating expenses. Prepaid expenses, by contrast, represent cash outflows and increase operating expenses. Therefore, the increase in prepaids should be added to the operating expense figure. With regard to taxes, they must be paid in cash; therefore, the amount representing the tax liability for 1997 ($34,209) must be deducted in full.

The resulting figure for cash flow from operations shows that BRE was not in a healthy cash position. Quite the opposite: for the period 1996 to 1997, it experienced a cash drain of $25,975. Studying the cash flow from operations statement yields some important answers to the question of how a company can be profitable and have no cash:

▶ The large growth in sales caused a cash drain in the form of working capital to support the growth.

▶ Accounts receivable increased, reducing the actual revenue from sales.

The Real World of Entrepreneurship

How Bankers Look at a Company's Financials

Bankers look at a company's financials from a totally different point of view than do investors or management. Here are some of the things they look for:

1. The primary source of repayment of a loan, the net flow of funds (net income plus depreciation, amortization, and extraordinary items). If the company is just breaking even each month, no cash is available for repayment of the loan. In general, on term loans, the lender wants to see a net funds flow/debt ratio of 1.25, which means that for every $1 of debt, there is $1.25 of funds flow.

2. The secondary source of repayment—that is, if the company defaults, what can the bank take to sell and get its money back? The lender finds this information in the balance sheet in the assets column. Accounts receivable are probably worth 60 percent of their balance sheet value if liquidated. Inventory is worth even less, anywhere from zero to about 50 percent of its value.

3. The character of the parties involved.

4. Profitability ratios, which lenders compare with those of other companies in the same industry.

5. Operating margin (revenues less cost of goods, less selling, general, and administrative expenses), which signals the health of the basic operation.

▶ Both inventory and accounts receivable grew at a much faster rate than did sales, which may suggest a management problem that should be examined further.

In summary, the logic of these adjustments is fairly simple and important to understand to interpret the information in the statement correctly; that is, an increase or a decrease in a particular account is a positive or a negative for the company. For example, an increase in accounts receivable reduces cash flow from sales because it means more customers paying on credit. Likewise, the reverse is true: a decrease in accounts receivable increases cash flow from sales.

An increase in inventory is a use of cash, whereas a decrease in inventory results in a decrease in the cost of sales. Similarly, an increase in accounts payable decreases the cost of sales because money that should be going out to pay bills is being retained in the company. A decrease in payables reflects payment of obligations and increases cost of sales.

Note that when constructing pro forma cash flow statements for a new venture, a form such as the cash flow budget is more often used. This will be discussed in Chapter 17.*

Ratios

Many tools are needed to completely analyze a company's financial picture. No one tool or technique can provide all the answers to a very complex situation. **Ratios** are a particularly good way to begin to interpret the information contained in the financial statements from a lender's or an investor's perspective. Ratios make comparisons of items in the financial statements and put them in relative terms so they can be compared to ratios in other periods to look for important changes in the company's position. It is possible to compute ratios for virtually all the items on the financial statements, but this would be a daunting and ineffective approach. A better approach is to select financial relationships that yield useful information about important aspects of the company. The three most common groups of ratios are liquidity and activity ratios, debt and financial risk ratios, and profitability ratios. In discussing ratio analysis, we will use the sample statements from BRE Products and consider the most important ratios in each category.

Liquidity and Activity Ratios

Liquidity and activity ratios provide information on the company's ability to meet short-term obligations over time as well as to maintain normal operations. The more liquid the current assets, the more easily they are converted to cash to pay off short-term obligations and maintain operations; thus, the lower the risk for creditors.

---

*For a thorough discussion of how to calculate start-up capital requirements for a new business, see Kathleen Allen, *Launching New Ventures*, 2nd ed. (Boston: Houghton Mifflin, 1998).

Current Ratio

Current ratio = Total current assets/Total current liabilities

BRE's current ratio is $195,896/$96,692 = 2.02. This means BRE has $2 in current assets for every $1 in liabilities. The higher the number, the more liquid the firm. Over time it would be important to look for increasing numbers, signaling a trend toward greater liquidity, or decreasing numbers, portending declining liquidity.

Cash Flow as a Percentage of Net Sales

Cash flow as a percentage of net sales = Cash flow/Net sales

This measure gives the amount of cash flow generated by operations per dollar of sales. If cash flow to net sales is $.20, this means that for every dollar generated by sales during the period under question, 20 cents went to cash flow. The higher this number, the more liquid the company is. Obviously, this ratio could not be calculated for BRE because the company had a negative cash flow.

Cash as a Percentage of Net Sales

Cash as a percentage of total current assets =
Cash figure from balance sheet/Total balance sheet current assets

This is another measure of the liquidity level of the company; the larger the percentage, the more liquid the company is. Note that if the company is holding excessive amounts of cash in a nonearning capacity, this cash is a negative and may actually reduce profitability. For BRE this ratio is $4,950/$195,896 = .025, which suggests very little liquidity.

Technology Tip

Automate Your Accounting

Accounting for the finances of your business can be a tedious process that many entrepreneurs avoid until tax time. By then, unfortunately, the task has become so daunting that they end up spending a lot of money unnecessarily to have a bookkeeper and an accountant figure it all out. One way to avoid the "end-of-the-year-recordkeeping blues" is to automate your recordkeeping and stay on top of it every day.

Today user-friendly software allows you to enter information one time and have it available for any type of financial report you wish to generate. Many small-business owners start with a simple package such as Intuit's Quicken® or QuickBooks®, which walks them through the process of maintaining records with virtually no need for a strong understanding of accounting principles.

As the business grows, it's easy to move on to a more elaborate system such as Peachtree®, which will do payroll, inventory, job cost, and order entry. This type of system benefits from a user who understands the basic accounting principles, something that is vitally important for every business owner.

Acid Test

Acid test = (Current assets − Inventory)/Current liabilities

This is yet another way to measure a company's ability to meet its current liabilities with its current assets. But the acid test is tougher because it removes inventory, which may be difficult to convert to cash because it's obsolete or, in the case of fraudulent practices, doesn't exist. This forces the current assets to stand on their own, which is usually more difficult. For BRE this ratio is ($195,896 − $92,606)/$96,692 = 1.07 times, or 1.07:1. Traditionally, the rule of thumb is a minimum of 1:1, so this result appears to be in line.

All of the liquidity ratios help the company find problems early so they can be more easily corrected.

Profitability Ratios

The most commonly used *profitability ratios* are the profit margin, return on assets, and return on equity.

Profit Margin

Profit margin (PM) = Net income/Net sales

This ratio uses net income from the income statement and net sales from the income statement to portray the amount of each dollar of sales remaining after all costs of normal operations are accounted for. The inverse of this percentage (100% − PM) equals the expense ratio or the portion of each sales dollar that is accounted for by expenses from normal operations. It is an important way to monitor costs. BRE's profit margin is $63,717/$580,000 = .10.

Return on Assets/Return on Investment

Return on assets (ROA) or Return on investment (ROI)
= Net income/Total assets

This measure uses net income from the income statement and total assets from the balance sheet. It gives the percentage that represents the number of dollars of income earned per dollar of invested capital. The higher the number, the greater the return. For BRE, this ratio is $63,717/$550,646 = .11. Eleven percent was earned on every dollar of invested capital.

Return on Equity

Return on equity = Net income/Owners' equity

Net income from the income statement and owners' equity from the balance sheet give a measure of the amount of net income earned per dollar of paid-in capital plus retained earnings. It is a way to look at the efficiency and effectiveness of the use of investor capital. For BRE this ratio is

$63,717/$236,700 = .26, so $.26 is earned per dollar of paid-in capital plus retained earnings.

Leverage Ratios

Leverage ratios measure the degree to which the company relies on debt. In most cases, a higher number signals a riskier company because although the firm's earnings will change, debt payments remain fixed.

Times Interest Earned

Times interest earned = (Earnings before interest and taxes)/Interest expense

This ratio measures earnings from operating income generated to meet interest charges that must be paid, so the greater the earnings relative to the interest expense, the safer the firm is. For BRE the ratio is $103,371/$5,445 = 18.9, which means earnings are 19 times interest expense. BRE's rate of 18.9 is not negative in and of itself; however, it is a decrease from the previous year's 19.7, which may signal future problems.

Debt to Asset

Debt to asset = Total debt/Total assets

This is a balance sheet ratio that measures the percentage of the firm's assets that are covered by creditors versus the percentage that is covered by the owners. It is estimated that most manufacturing firms have debt to asset ratios between .30 and .70.[1] BRE's ratio is $313,944/$550,646 = 57%, which is about average for manufacturing firms.

Ratios are important tools only as they are related to comparison periods of time or when used to compare one company with another. When looking at ratios calculated by others, it is always important to verify how the ratio was calculated—what was included—and to watch for ways in which some companies improve their appearance of liquidity by, for example, taking out a long-term loan just before the end of the fiscal year and repaying it at the start of the new year. The cash from the loan will strengthen the current ratio, but it doesn't reflect the true liquidity of the company.[2]

Cost-Volume-Profit Analysis

Analysis of financial statements gives one picture of the company: the strength of its financial position. But all the activities of the business are part of an integrated system, so it's also important to look at how changing sales levels affect operational costs, operating profits, and cash flows. This is known as **cost-volume-profit analysis** or **CVP analysis,** and it's not only valuable for determining the viability of a new company but serves as another tool to guide planning in a growing company. So numbers can be based on forecasts, in the case of new ventures, or historical data, in the case of established companies. This section looks at several ways to use CVP analysis.

Determining the Selling Price

Suppose a company has arrived at operating costs for its product; fixed costs (costs that don't change in relation to sales) are $218,750, and the variable costs per unit (those costs tied directly to sales) are $156. The company believes it can sell 5,000 units if it can come up with a market-accepted price. Furthermore, the company knows that the general price level set by competitors is $315. If the company wants to achieve a $250,000 profit level, at what price will it need to sell its product?

If total units (TU) equals fixed costs (FC) + profit (P) divided by the contribution margin (CM), which is composed of selling price (SP) minus variable costs (VC), then

$$TU = \frac{(FC + P)}{(SP - VC)}$$

Using the preceding example, the calculations would produce

$$5,000 = \frac{(\$218,750 + \$250,000)}{(SP - \$156)} = \$249.75$$

This figure of $249.75 indicates that the company has a fairly broad range of prices in which it could work and still stay at or below the competition's $315.

Maintaining the Same Profit Level with Increased Costs

Suppose a company is growing and thus expects its fixed and variable costs to increase in the coming year. This will necessitate a price increase if the company wants to retain its current profit margin. Given the following information, what price increase would be required to do this?

Fixed costs	$281,250
Variable costs per unit	$268
Selling price per unit	$415
Sales volume	3,000

The company expects fixed costs to rise by $6,875 and variable costs by $6.25 per unit. To arrive at the increased price requires calculating the **contribution margin** per unit, the total contribution margin, and the established profit, as well as new fixed and variable costs, as follows:

Contribution margin per unit:	$415 – $268 = $147
Total contribution margin:	3,000($147) = $441,000
Profit:	$441,000 – $281,250 = $159,750
New fixed costs:	$441,000 + $6,875 = $447,875
New variable costs:	$268 + $6.25 = $274.25

Using the same formula as in the previous example,

$$TU = \frac{(FC + P)}{(SP - VC)}$$

we get

$$3,000 = \frac{(\$447,875 + \$159,750)}{(SP - \$274.25)} = \$476.79$$

which is the price increase that would have to occur for the company to retain its current profit level.

Sales Required to Achieve a Specific Profit

In the final scenario, suppose a company has experienced a contribution margin of 40 percent over several years. Assuming its fixed costs are $406,250 and it wants to make a profit based on 12 percent of its sales, how much in dollars will it have to sell? In this case, total sales (TS) equal fixed costs plus profit (P) divided by the contribution margin ratio (CMR), as follows:

$$TS = \frac{(FC + P)}{CMR}$$

$$TS = \frac{\$406,250 + .12TS}{.40} = \$1,450,892 \text{ total sales}$$

We see that $1.4 million in total sales is required to achieve the desired profit. This is an important measure for entrepreneurs. The goal is to achieve a contribution margin that grows slowly over time, but monitoring the CMR regularly can forecast potential problems in the variable costs that must be addressed.

The key weakness of CVP analysis is its assumption that variable costs vary in a linear fashion with sales. It is therefore important to calculate several scenarios to prepare for any unforeseen variances in projected numbers. Large changes in an answer to an equation when only a small change is made in one of the variables signals that the model is very sensitive to that item. By testing the model using several variations on the figures, those items that affect the results the most will be found. The best solution is to arrive at a range of values into which the company's numbers will most probably fall rather than considering a result to be the exact and correct answer.

Break-Even Analysis

Break-even analysis (BE) is really another tool in the CVP package. It is essentially the fixed cost divided by the contribution margin ratio and is used to determine at what point, in terms of units produced or units sold, the company will begin to cover its fixed costs and return a profit. At break-even sales volume, total fixed costs are covered; every sale thereafter only results in variable costs of producing the product, and the remainder goes to operating profit. Using our continuing example,

$$BE = \frac{\text{Fixed costs}}{\text{Contribution margin ratio}}$$

$$BE = \frac{\$218,750}{.40} = \$546,875$$

This means sales revenues produce $218,750 of variable costs and a $328,125 contribution to margin at a break-even sales volume of $546,875.

CVP and break-even analysis can help evaluate ideas in marketing, production, services, budgeting, and pricing, and also evaluate performance. It is an important tool that entrepreneurs should use.

The next chapter looks at working capital management and the cash budget.

Cases Relevant to This Chapter

Koidra-Tek Business Plan

Issues for Review and Discussion

1. What information do the three key financial statements (income, balance sheet, cash flow) provide the entrepreneur?
2. How is it possible that a business can show a profit and not have enough cash to pay its obligations?
3. What is the advantage of the accrual system of accounting over the cash system?
4. Assume that sales for September are $575,000. Of these, 25 percent are for cash and 15 percent are collected the next month, 20 percent in the next month, 20 percent the following month, 10 percent the following month, and 10 percent the next month. Calculate the firm's cash inflow from sales for each of the six months.
5. A certain company has fixed costs of $278,740, variable costs per unit of $30, and a selling price of $50 per unit. What is the break-even quantity and what does that figure mean?

Experiencing Entrepreneurship

1. Talk to several business owners about their accounting systems and how they manage cash flow. Which system seems to work best? Why?
2. Interview a banker about ratios used to evaluate a business. Which ratios are most important to lenders, and what do they look to discover about a business by using them?

Resources

DeThomas, Art (1991). *Financial Management Techniques for Small Business.* Grants Pass, OR: The Oasis Press.

Financial Record Keeping for Small Stores. SBA Small Business Management Series, Stock No. 045-000-00142-3.

Kolb, Robert W., and Ricardo J. Rodriguez (1996). *Financial Management,* 2nd ed. Cambridge, MA: Blackwell Publishers.

Stickney, C. P. (1990). *Financial Statement Analysis: A Strategic Perspective.* New York: Harcourt Brace Jovanovich, pp. 275–290.

Internet Resources

AccountingNet

http://www.accountingnet.com

A general source of accounting information for business owners.

Internal Revenue Service—The Digital Daily

http://www.irs.ustreas.gov/prod/

This site is full of free information about the IRS and tax-related issues.

The World Bank

http://www.worldbank.org/

Offers the latest news from the World Bank, including research studies and publications.

Money is of no value; it cannot spend itself.
All depends on the skill of the spender.
Ralph Waldo Emerson, 1803–1882
American essayist and poet
The Young American

Cash Planning and Working Capital Management

Preview

Understanding this chapter will give you the ability to

▶ **Explain the cash budget, its value, and how it is calculated.**

▶ **Discuss accounts receivable financing and management methods.**

▶ **Explain the types of short-term financing available to manage cash cycles in the business.**

Terms to Know

Young Entrepreneurs—Minicase

Tracy Christian
Your Search Has Ended

At one point in Tracy Christian's young adult life, she began to wonder if she would ever stop hitting brick walls. There was no reason for this to be happening because she knew what she was capable of. Her life had been good. In 1979, Christian's father, a fashion photographer, moved the family to Los Angeles. At that time modeling schools were a fad, and Christian quickly became a child model. When it came time to go to college, Christian chose Mills College in San Francisco and then switched to California State University, Los Angeles.

Two-and-a-half years into college, Christian found herself in debt and unable to continue. She quit school to take a clerical job in advertising, but two years later was laid off. It appeared that Christian was short not only on cash but on luck. She then took a job in the fashion industry in a family-owned business, working 55 hours a week for $10 an hour. As an administrative assistant to the president, her duties included generating press releases and publicity for the company. When the president couldn't attend an event, Christian took it on herself to represent him because she saw it as a chance to network and keep the company in the public eye. She was always asking her boss for more responsibility and additional

ways to make more money. Apparently her initiative was not appreciated, for two years later she was fired because of personality conflicts. The president told her in no uncertain terms, "You're not worth more than $10 an hour, and there isn't anything you can do for this company to make more money." At that moment, Christian, now $24,000 in debt, knew she had to make it on her own. The only thing she hadn't tried yet was starting her own business.

Taking advantage of nearly 10 years of experience in the fashion, advertising, and modeling industries, she decided to start a modeling and talent search agency in Hollywood. She found an inexpensive one-room apartment near the Chinese Mann Theatre, an area of Hollywood known for its eclectic mix of people, many of whom are "starving actors." The apartment was so small that she had to jump over the bed to get to the phone.

She obtained her first clients by calling on old clients from previous positions. These were people she could rely on, and she naively figured she could ask them for favors. She soon learned that although they were willing to try out her company, Christian would have to perform or they would take their business elsewhere. Business is business—an important lesson learned.

As the business grew, she focused on providing talent for corporate events—celebrity look-alikes, trade show models, and commercial models. She also began offering seminars on different aspects of modeling, from makeup secrets to developing a portfolio and getting into television commercials. Five years into the business, she was able to buy an apartment building in the more fashionable Los Feliz area and turn the bottom floor into her office.

Today Your Search Has Ended handles talent for more than 250 events a year for such companies as Planet Hollywood and Paramount Studios. In the past, Christian always worried about selling to get more clients. Now she has to decide if it's actually worth her time to do business with certain customers. She relies on word of mouth and direct mail to reach her customers. Recently Christian has found the Internet to be an excellent source of customers, and marketing on the Internet has given her the opportunity to work with such companies as Walt Disney Studios.

Christian believes the company is now poised to really grow and compete with the very best Hollywood agencies, but for that to happen she needs to get her infrastructure in place. She would like her company to be able to compete for film roles and voiceovers, but the industry unions are very strict about agencies they will accept. She must have the right management personnel in place to be able to grow and compete, and that takes money.

The fact that she didn't finish college or take business courses has been an impediment to growth. Christian has made a lot of mistakes along the way, and she now believes finishing school would have been less costly in the long run than starting up the business without the education. To make up for it, she is taking courses whenever she can to improve her business skills.

The biggest challenge she faces is really a personal one: learning to give up control. "I'm a Type A personality. I like not taking vacations, and when I do, I love going to Vail with my cell phone on the slopes. But the reality is you can't live that way. I've lost five or six assistants because I've refused to give up control."

The other challenge is the one she has faced all her adult life: managing cash flow. Only now, it's not just her personal cash flow but her business's as well. Christian advises young entrepreneurs to spend the time learning the basics and be willing to outsource to others what you don't know how to do well.

"Believe in yourself, and never, ever, ever give up. Your business is not you. Smile every day, and don't sweat the little stuff." Christian now knows she can achieve anything she sets her mind to.

How can Christian get the infrastructure she needs on a small budget?

What would you recommend that Christian do to better manage her cash flow?

Although the focus always seems to be on profit, the reality is that for growing entrepreneurial companies, cash flow is the best indicator of financial health. Therefore, cash planning is a vital part of your company's integrated financial strategy. Tracy Christian (see Young Entrepreneurs—Minicase) learned quickly that a rapidly growing business eats up more cash than it brings in as it tries to meet demand for the product and take on more staff to manage the growth. Failure to manage cash at that point can bring about a disaster from which the company may never recover.

A good plan will include estimates for periods in which the business may experience a cash problem and periods in which it may benefit from a cash surplus. The plan will also signal when the company may need financing and how much financing it will require. In addition, making optimistic, pessimistic, and conservative calculations will give the company a range of options and scenarios to which it can prepare to respond.

Unfortunately, many companies don't do regular cash planning. Instead, they take a reactive approach that leaves them very few options during a cash crunch. For example, companies often stop or slow the payment of bills during a cash crunch. This can hurt the company significantly, particularly if suppliers delay shipments or put the company on a cash-only basis. All the effort to build up credit with suppliers will be lost, and customers will be unable to get the product. Another often-used approach is to seek emergency funding, but this sends a strong message to lenders that the company hasn't done any cash planning. Any loan secured under these conditions will not be beneficial in the long term.

The bottom line is that a company must undertake cash planning or risk running out of cash just when it needs it most. This chapter looks at cash planning techniques as well as working capital management.

The Cash Budget

Cash planning begins with a cash budget, a detailed plan for inflows and outflows to the company during a specific period of time. Typically it is an annual budget with overlays of quarterly or monthly budgets. The budget includes both operating and nonoperating cash flows divided into the two categories of inflows and outflows. To avoid confusing items that appear on the income statement and do not appear on the cash flow statement or in the cash budget, consult the following guidelines for preparing a cash budget:

▶ Do not include depreciation in the cash budget. This is a noncash expense that appears on the income statement.

▶ Cash purchases appear in the budget; credit purchases do not. Credit purchases become a cash outflow when they are paid.

▶ Cash sales are found in the cash budget. Credit sales are not. Again, the credit sales will appear as inflows to the cash budget when they are actually received.

▶ The total of principal and interest from loan payments appears in the cash budget when it is paid.

▶ Cash expenditures related to operations, such as payroll, appear in the cash budget when they are paid. They do not accrue as they do on the income statement.

Choosing a planning horizon for the cash budget will be a function of the purpose of the budget and what the company is attempting to achieve. In general, start-up and growing companies may use monthly budgets that tie into the annual budget. This is valuable for a new company that doesn't yet have a grasp on the market and how the business will respond under varying conditions. Start-up companies have no historical precedent for the numbers they project in their pro forma financial statements; thus, the budget becomes an important tool for checking the accuracy of the forecasts. Generally, a company will want to check its actual numbers at the end of each month

 The Real World of Entrepreneurship

Achieving Critical Mass

A growing business never reaches a point where the owners can sit back, relax, and just enjoy the fruits of their labor. Norm Brodsky, entrepreneur many times over, claims that a business is like a living organism: it is constantly changing. But at some point, a business moves out of the start-up stage and achieves what Brodsky terms "critical mass." **Critical mass** occurs when the business has achieved a certain level of customers or a certain level of sales—actually, any number of goals—but, most important, when the business breaks even on its cash flow. That is, the business generates enough cash from its operations to sustain itself and grow without having to go to outside sources of capital.

So, by looking at cash flow, sales, gross margins, and expenses, any company can calculate what it will take to reach critical mass, whether it be 10 strong customers or 1,000 units a month sold. Once critical mass is achieved, a whole new set of challenges confront the entrepreneur, including: Do we want the company to grow? How fast? Should we broaden our product base? The company is now producing cash flow that can make all that happen if the entrepreneur doesn't become careless in the newfound excitement of positive cash flow.

SOURCE: Bo Burlingham, "How to Succeed in Business in 4 Easy Steps," *Inc.*, July 1995, p. 30.

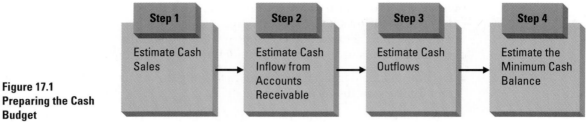

Figure 17.1 Preparing the Cash Budget

against the budget forecast to see where differences occur. Those differences signal changes the company must make in its projections; it was either too optimistic or too conservative in predicting the numbers.

Figure 17.1 outlines the steps in preparing a cash budget.

Step 1: Estimate Cash Sales

The first step in preparing the cash budget is to estimate sales volume for the period. In a new company, this is extraordinarily difficult and requires that the owners have a firm understanding of the industry and the company's competitors so their estimates are at least within a reasonable range. In a growing company, the job gets a little easier as the company develops a track record on which to base its projections.

Sales growth is rarely linear as so often depicted in budgets and financial statements. Most businesses experience some **seasonality** or variation throughout the fiscal year. For example, a retailer of outdoor barbecue equipment will probably experience a decline in sales volume in the fall and winter months. In addition, the sales forecast should reflect any specific plans the company has for growth into new markets and the addition of products or services to its product line. Refer to Chapter 16 for suggestions on forecasting sales.

The sales forecast must then be adjusted to account for the percentage of sales that are cash sales. This is accomplished by looking at patterns established since the company has been in business (a new company will probably need to use industry averages). For example, if the company has been doing business for three years, it will look at three years of sales, separate them by season, and again by whether they were cash or credit purchases. For each year and for each season, the company will figure the percentage of total sales that were cash sales (cash sales/total sales) and then average those percentages to arrive at an average percentage of cash sales for each season.

Step 2: Estimate Cash Inflow from Accounts Receivable

The cash inflow arising from the collection of accounts receivable must also be calculated. Similarly to adjusting sales in step 1, percentages are applied to dollars of accounts receivable collected during a particular season of the year over however many years the company has been in business. This analy-

Doing a cash budget can help you look at all your expenses so that you can explore ways to save money. For Larry Powell, saving money was critical to the success of his advertising and graphics design firm. Bartering for office space, sharing space, and later subleasing his excess office space are creative strategies he used to make his cash position positive. With the resulting increased cash flow, Powell has been able to purchase new office equipment. (Jesse Hornbuckle)

sis will produce results such as: 25 percent of sales are collected in the month they occurred, 50 percent in the next month, and 25 percent in the second month following the sale. Analyzing payment patterns of customers is very important and can often reveal future problems that could severely affect the company. For example, the analysis may show that one large customer is responsible for the greatest percentage of accounts receivable every month and the time to payment for that customer has been steadily increasing. This type of pattern can have a significant impact on the company's cash flow and ability to pay its vendors. See "The Way Down Goes Much Faster" for the problems one company faced when its principal customer stopped paying.

Step 3: Estimate Cash Outflows

The estimation of cash outflows is easier because most cash outflows, such as loan payments, leases, insurance, and salaries, are relatively fixed in nature for the short term. Those cash outflows that vary with the level of activity, such as wages and advertising, usually are easily predicted in the short term; and those outflows that are not easily predicted, such as utilities and phone, can be estimated from historical data. The estimation will also include looking at the company's payment pattern so that reasonable predictions can be made as to when expenses will actually be paid.

Step 4: Estimate the Minimum Cash Balance

It is critical to the success of cash budgeting to estimate the minimum cash balance that must be available for contingencies or unforeseen events as well as errors in estimation. The world of growing entrepreneurial companies is volatile, and this volatility extends to all aspects of the business, including budgeting. Deciding on the appropriate size of the **contingency balance** is really a balancing act in which estimating too low can mean being unable to meet the financial demands of an unforeseen event and estimating too high will result in wasting resources in nonearning capacities. The size of the contingency balance is a function of the volatility of the industry and the business itself, as well as the stability of cash flows. Some businesses, such as restaurants, have regular inflows of cash, whereas others, such as real estate development and manufacturing, do not. For each business, the answer to how much to keep as a contingency balance will differ, and the company will become more adept at forecasting the amount as it grows and its operations begin to develop patterns. Figure 17.2 presents a sample cash budget for six months.

Examining the sample cash budget in Figure 17.2 yields information about the three most important variables: net cash flow, required financing,

 Entrepreneurship in Action

The Way Down Goes Much Faster

PTP Industries Inc.'s ride to fame and fortune was a spectacular one. The Baltimore-based packaging company (PTP stands for Precision Thermoforming & Packaging) grew at a mind-boggling rate due to increased demand from such big-name customers as Eveready, Procter & Gamble, Revlon, and Seagram. In fact, so valuable was PTP's business in Baltimore that when it was planning to move to a larger facility in Norfolk, Virginia, Maryland's economic development officials invested $5 million in an abandoned Montgomery Ward building to retain the 150 jobs PTP was supporting. The city and state also provided $5 million in loan guarantees for renovations. Then the federal government kicked in additional incentives.

Meanwhile PTP was hiring new employees at an increasingly rapid rate to keep up with the demand of one of its biggest clients, America Online, which represented 60 percent of PTP's sales. It hired more than 300 new employees in a relatively short time and saw sales skyrocket from $24 million in 1993 to $38 million in 1996. But in early 1997, AOL owed PTP $2.2 million and wasn't paying. PTP could not operate under those conditions and very quickly went out of business.

Then PTP's lender filed a lawsuit against AOL after PTP defaulted on the loan, and PTP followed with a breach-of-contract lawsuit of its own seeking $80 million from AOL. In June 1997 PTP, which never filed for bankruptcy, was able to raise $3 million in an auction of its equipment to partially pay off creditors.

SOURCE: Kevin L. McQuaid, "Obits: Packaging Company Diss-ked by AOL," *Inc.*, September 1997, p. 31.

	Month 1	Month 2	Month 3	Month 4	Month 5	Month 6
BRE Products						
Sample Cash Budget						
Six Months						
Cash Inflows						
Total Inflows	69,315	45,000	22,000	25,000	34,020	42,720
Cash Outflows:						
Purchases	39,805	29,350	9,460	10,750	14,629	18,370
Wages and Salaries	4,399	4,399	4,399	4,399	4,399	4,399
Lease	1,000	1,000	1,000	1,000	1,000	1,000
Utilities	649	649	649	649	649	649
Insurance	1,587	1,587	1,587	1,587	1,587	1,587
Advertising	850	850	850	850	850	850
Vehicle	1,500	1,500	1,500	1,500	1,500	1,500
Accounting and Legal	300	300	300	300	300	300
Payroll Taxes	659	659	659	659	659	659
Income Taxes	0	0	6,000	0	0	9,000
Capital Expenditures	15,000	10,000	10,000	0	0	0
Total Outflows	65,749	50,294	36,404	21,694	25,573	38,314
Net Cash Flow	3,566	−5,294	(14,404)	3,306	8,447	4,406
Beginning Balance	17,000	20,566	15,272	868	4,174	12,621
Total Cash (Ending Balance)	20,566	15,272	868	4,174	12,621	17,028
Minus Minimum Balance	12,000	12,000	12,000	12,000	12,000	12,000
Required Financing	**0**	**0**	**(11,132)**	**(7,826)**	**0**	**0**
Surplus Cash	**8,566**	**3,272**	**0**	**0**	**621**	**5,028**

**Figure 17.2
Sample Cash Budget
for a Six-Month
Period**

and excess cash. The cash budget has two primary sections: the determination of net cash flow based on projected operational and nonoperational cash flows on a monthly basis and the financing section, which includes the contingency balance and any other forms of financing the company might require.

Net cash flow in the budget is the same as net cash flow on the cash flow statement: total cash inflows minus total cash outflows. Positive numbers reflect surplus cash from operations, and negative numbers represent a cash drain caused by any of a number of things, for example, seasonality or too

Even a business that on the surface appears simple can hide some very complex start-up costs. Ken Woods, co-owner of Gotta Java drive-thru coffee outlet in Pasadena, California conducted three years of research before he opened for business. Accurately figuring the costs for everything from coffee beans to a logo for the business was essential to arriving at a realistic start-up figure. (Ulf Wallin)

many receivables. The minimum amount of cash required to be on hand, if subtracted from total cash available, gives an estimation of any financing required during troughs in the sales cycle.

From the sample we can see that BRE will experience a surplus in four of the six months, due principally to increased sales. A cash deficit will occur in March and April due to decreased sales, accompanied by a capital expenditure in March and taxes paid. Consequently, BRE will require financing to make it through the period.

When Just One Budget Isn't Enough

Particularly when the company is young and patterns are not well established, it's a good idea to create different budgets for different scenarios—that is, a most-likely, most-pessimistic, and most-optimistic budget. By doing this, you will know what to expect if the worst happens and, conversely, what is the best that can be expected. You can then prepare in advance for each possible outcome. Also, if early in the year of the annual budget you suspect sales will be less than expected, you can shift operations to the most-pessimistic budget to conserve capital.

Accounts Receivable Planning

The existence of accounts receivable in the company's financial statements means the company has chosen to extend credit to its customers, which will affect its cash position. Of all the noncash assets the company has, accounts receivable are the closest to being cash because on average accounts receivable are paid within 30 to 60 days. Still, lack of good credit management practices can adversely affect cash flow by lengthening accounts receivable turnover time and increasing bad-debt write-offs. To avoid this outcome, the company should take several steps:

1. The time between shipping, invoicing, and sending billing notices should be minimized.

2. Continual review of clients' credit history should reveal potential problems early enough to solve them before they hurt the company's cash flow position. Of course, it's important to ask new clients to complete a credit application with references.

3. The company should provide incentives to customers to pay early. Two examples are discounts for early payment and an interest charge on delinquent accounts.

Technology Tip

Keeping Track of Customer Payment Patterns

One important way to keep track of how the company's customers are paying their obligations is to set up an aging report. This will quickly give a picture of how much of a company's receivables are due to one particular customer and will also highlight those customers that are costing the company money by delayed payments. The table below is an example of an aging report.

In this example, it's apparent that customer D presents a significant cash flow problem for the company.

The chart also indicates that customer B may create problems in the future.

Many accounting and financial software packages will allow you to print such a report from the account entries in your journals. Otherwise, try hiring a college student who specializes in computer applications for business to design a way to go from your customer database to a spreadsheet or other type of report so that you have to enter information only once.

Aging Report Sample

Customer	Total Sale	Current	30 Days Past	60 Days Past	90 Days Past	Over 90 Days
Customer A	$1,000	$1,000				
Customer B	$500			$500		
Customer C	$250		$250			
Customer D	$1,500	_____	$250	$100	$100	$50
Totals	**$3,250**	**$1,000**	**$500**	**$600**	**$100**	**$50**
Percent	**100%**	**31%**	**15%**	**18%**	**3%**	**2%**

4. Accounts receivable should be **aged** on a monthly (or sometimes weekly) basis to identify early any delinquent accounts (see Technology Tip on page 479).

5. The company should develop a set of effective methods for collecting overdue accounts receivable.[1] (See "Collection Policy" on page 483.)

Accounts Receivable Financing

When a company makes a credit sale, it does not generate the cash to (1) replace its inventory associated with that sale, (2) make payroll, or (3) pay creditors. Still, while the receivable is outstanding, the company must continue to meet its ongoing obligations until the receivable is paid and cash is released for use. The **cash cycle** of a business runs from the date of purchase or production of inventory to the date the inventory paid for by credit is covered by payment of the receivable. This is a long time for a business to have its precious capital tied up. For this reason, many companies speed up the cash flow from their receivables by borrowing against them. In this way, they have the use of their money 30 to 60 days sooner than they would otherwise. The two primary sources of this type of financing are commercial banks and finance companies, and they offer two types of financing: **collateral** and **factoring**. In the first case, the company's accounts receivable are pledged as collateral against a loan from the bank. Customers' payments are forwarded to the bank to repay the loan. In the second case, the company sells its accounts receivable at a discount to a finance company known as a *factor*. The factor then assumes the bad-debt risk of the receivables and collects on them.

To estimate the length of the cash cycle of the business and the required financing to support that cash cycle, the following formulas can be used. They are followed by an example.

1. *Cash cycle* = (Inventory turnover in days + Average collection period) − Average payment period for accounts payable.

2. *Average expenditures per day* = Cash operating expenses (Cost of sales + Expenses − Depreciation)/360

3. *Required financing* = Cash cycle in days × Average expenditures per day

Suppose New Venture Inc. has a cash cycle of 35 days, cost of sales of $250,000, operating expenses of $143,780, and depreciation expense of $2,862. Then the calculation of the required financing to cover its cash cycle would look like this:

Average expenditures per day = ($250,000 + $143,780 − $2,862)/360
= $1,085 (rounded) average expenditures per day

Required financing = 35 days (cash cycle) × $1,085
= $37,975 total financing required to cover cash cycle

Though the availability of immediate cash is enticing to a business, it's a very costly form of financing, with interest rates running several points above prime in addition to a fee charged by the factor for services rendered. This cost of credit must be factored into the cash budget. Furthermore, with this valuable asset removed from the balance sheet, a company may find it difficult to borrow money in general.

Credit also affects the gross margin. Suppose the company's gross profit margin is 40 percent on a product whose revenues are $40 a unit. If a sale is made for credit, an additional cost of financing is incurred, which, for discussion purposes, is $0.15 for every dollar borrowed for a year. Using the preceding example with a cash cycle to be financed of 35 days, we would find the following:

$$\text{Revenue} - \text{Cost of goods sold} - \text{Financing cost} = \text{Gross profit margin}$$

$$\$40 - \$24 - \$0.15/\$40 = 39.6\%$$

If that credit is extended to 60 days, the finance charge increases and the gross margin decreases again:

$$\text{Gross profit margin} = (\$40 - \$24 - \$0.29)/\$40 = 39.2\%$$

The unmistakable message is that using credit costs money. Unfortunately, the decision to extend or not extend credit is often out of the hands of the business owner if it is industry custom. To be competitive, the company has to offer its customers credit terms, but credit doesn't need to be handed out indiscriminately. A company can put in place policies that will minimize losses and costs to the company, such as arranging for a finance company to handle customers' credit. The following section discusses credit and collection.

Credit and Collection Policies

As you learned in the previous section, extending credit to customers entails a cost to the business; this cost consists of the costs of credit checking, keeping records (accounts receivable), bad-debt write-offs, interest cost of financing accounts receivable, and the cost of collecting on delinquent accounts.

 Entrepreneurship in Action

The Importance of Numbers

Failing to stay on top of your company's financials can cost you the company. This was the case with a Maryland electrical contractor who had an opportunity to expand his business by going into the apparently lucrative mechanical contracting field—plumbing, ductwork, and so on.

Unfortunately, the company did no research on its costs prior to winning several bids for work. Too late it discovered that those costs were higher than projected.

While its revenues were increasing, its profit margins were declining. The electrical side of the business was doing well, but the mechanical side was losing money. Had the owner kept a more watchful eye on the numbers, he may have been able to save the business. But, the discovery was too little, too late, and the company folded.

Source: Linda Elkins, "Real Numbers Don't Deceive," *Nation's Business,* March 1997, p. 51.

Therefore, it is important that the company develop a **credit policy** that (1) governs how and when credit will be extended, (2) sets credit standards or conditions customers must meet before being extended credit, (3) sets a credit period during which the company will grant credit (e.g., 30, 60, or 90 days), and (4) establishes a collection policy for those instances where customers fail to comply with the credit policy.

Credit Standards

The company can require credit applicants to fill out a standard form providing it with enough information and permission to run a credit check with a local credit bureau, in the case of a sole proprietorship or partnership, or a **Dun & Bradstreet (D&B) report,** in the case of a corporation. Credit applications usually ask for references, which can also be checked. It is important to verify the information provided and apply it against the company's credit standards. Examples of standards a company may use to judge credit applicants include the following:

▶ No delinquencies on current debt

▶ Consumer has a full-time job

▶ Income greater than a required amount

▶ Consumer has a valid credit card

▶ For a company, a D&B rating of A or better

▶ Net assets of some minimum amount

▶ A credit bureau report showing no delinquencies

 The Real World of Entrepreneurship

Handling Collections

One of the most important rules to learn about collecting unpaid accounts is that the longer a debt is outstanding, the harder it will be to collect. So the goal should be to take care of the problem as quickly as possible. During the process of trying to collect, it's effective to cancel credit, withhold products and services, and assess late charges. There are, however, several things a company cannot do under the Fair Debt Collection Practices Act:

▶ Threaten the customer in any manner that suggests force, arrest, or criminal prosecution

▶ Use abusive language

▶ Contact the customer's employer or family

▶ Falsely state or imply that a lawsuit has been filed

▶ Discuss the case with other people

▶ Send notices that misrepresent the contents (for example, sending a notice in an envelope labeled "tax information")

If all attempts to collect the debt through normal procedures fail, the company can employ a collection agency, which will charge from 15 to 25 percent of the amount collected. It will also take time, because collection agencies have procedures they must follow as well.

Whichever standards the company sets, they should be applied equally to all customers without discriminating. If credit is granted, the company should notify the customer of the dollar amount and terms of the credit.

Collection Policy

Any business that extends credit will undoubtedly face the issue of collecting from a customer who has not complied with the credit policy. It's important that the company establish a policy and standard procedure for dealing with this situation. Following is an example of a series of actions that go from mild to severe:[2]

1. Mail a past-due statement when the account is 10 days overdue.

2. Mail another past-due statement when the account is 30 days overdue.

3. Call the customer at 45 days past due.

4. Notify the customer in writing at 60 days past due that the account will be turned over to a collection agency if payment is not received within 15 days.

5. Turn the account over to a collection agency or an attorney as the case may warrant.

Of course, these suggestions are only recommendations, and every company should set up a procedure that best fits its cash flow situation and the industry in which it operates.

Short-Term Financing of Working Capital

Companies use short-term financing, often called **bridge financing,** to overcome seasonal fluctuations in their cash flow. For example, if the company is anticipating a strong selling season, it may wish to build up its inventories above the normal level, thus incurring a higher than normal level of accounts receivable. These accounts receivable must be financed until the cash comes in to pay them. Retailers often use short-term financing to build up inventories for the Christmas season, which accounts for about 25 percent of their total revenues.

Every company, in the normal course of operations, holds a certain amount of cash, accounts receivable, and inventory. Additional working capital to manage seasonal fluctuations is usually obtained through short-term financing. In addition, a firm will need to finance assets such as plant and equipment. This is usually done through long-term rather than short-term financing. However, when interest rates are high, companies don't like to commit to long-term financing that will cost them much more over the life of the asset, so bridge financing may also be used to "bridge" the period of high interest rates. When those rates come down, the company may refinance the equipment for a longer term.

There are several types of bridge financing mechanisms, including unsecured bank loans, lines of credit, revolving credit lines, secured short-term financing, and commercial paper (see Figure 17.3)

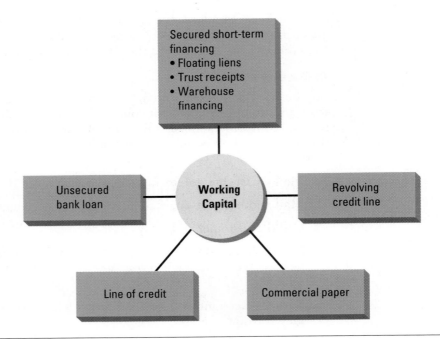

**Figure 17.3
Sources of Short-
Term Working
Capital**

Unsecured Bank Loan

Unsecured loans are based on the excellent credit of the borrower and require no collateral as in the case of secured loans where the lender can seize
company assets in the event of default. Usually the bank and the borrower—
the entrepreneur or the company—will execute a promissory note, which
specifies all the terms of the loan.

Line of Credit

Establishing a **line of credit** with a bank can mean the difference between
having to take out an expensive, short-term loan and not having to do so.
With a line of credit, the bank commits to making available to the company
a certain amount of funds on demand. The firm can then borrow the amount
when needed. Typically, a commitment fee of 0.5 to 0.1 percent of the total
committed amount is required whether or not the company actually uses the
money.

Revolving Credit Lines

In a **revolving line of credit,** the bank agrees to supply funds to the company
up to a specified amount. For example, if the credit line is for $500,000 and

the company uses $200,000 of that amount, it still has another $300,000 available. Furthermore, if the company pays down the credit line to zero, it will once again have $500,000 available. The system works much as credit cards do for consumers.

Secured Short-Term Financing

The section on accounts receivable management discussed pledging and factoring accounts receivable to enhance cash flow. These are just two types of secured short-term financing. Companies can also use inventory as collateral for a loan. The value of that inventory to the lender is determined by how quickly it can be converted to cash in the event of default by the borrowing company. There are several types of inventory loans:

▶ *Floating liens.* With a **floating lien,** the company gives the lender a blanket claim against the inventory. This type of claim is used when inventory items are of little value and difficult to distinguish (e.g., parts). In the case of larger inventory items that carry serial numbers, the lien will specify which items fall under the claim. For the lender, this is not the strongest type of claim.

The Real World of Entrepreneurship

The Value of Credit Lines

Todd Heim, owner of Future Cure Inc., an Ohio company that manufactures paint-spray booths for automotive body shops, has found a line of credit to be indispensable to successful cash flow management. When the business started, Heim used the credit line to purchase equipment and later to finance inventory and accounts receivable and even to cover payroll and other expenses. He has plans to use it again when the company moves to cover costly moving expenses.

Credit lines generally fall into two categories: lines to finance seasonal needs and lines to finance long-term growth. For seasonal lines, banks normally allow the borrower to borrow at will as long as the line is paid to zero for 30 days each year. This is known as a *30-day cleanup covenant*. Lines of credit are also used to finance rapid growth—a long-term cyclical line. Although no 30-day cleanup period is required, the line is usually renewed on an annual basis. Most banks require the line to be tied to the value of the assets being financed (e.g., 40 to 70 percent on inventory and 50 to 80 percent

on accounts receivable). The bank monitors the company through a loan base report to determine if the line balance is below the asset margins.

Entrepreneurs considering a credit line should prepare the following:

▶ The amount being requested and the justification
▶ A history of the company and description of products and services
▶ Résumés on key management
▶ Personal financial statements on the owners
▶ Business and personal credit references
▶ A detailed accounting of assets and their values
▶ Pro forma financial statements
▶ A business plan (for start-ups)

SOURCE: J. Tol Broome, Jr., "Credit on Call," *Nation's Business,* September 1995, p. 42.

- *Trust receipts*. For items that have serial numbers, **trust receipts** can be used. In this case, any proceeds from the sale are immediately forwarded to the lender.

- *Warehouse financing*. The highest form of collateral for the lender is with **warehouse financing**. If the firm has negotiated a field warehousing agreement, it can keep the claimed goods in its own warehouse but segregated from other goods. The lender then hires a warehouse company to check the goods and issue a receipt stating that in fact they are segregated in the warehouse. If the firm is under the control of a terminal warehousing agreement, the lender actually puts the inventory in a warehouse managed by the warehouse company it has hired. The borrowing company can't have access to the goods without the expressed permission of the lender. Because this method provides the most security for the lender, the lender will generally lend a higher percentage of the value of the inventory.

Commercial Paper

Commercial paper is short-term debt issued by corporations in the financial marketplace.[4] This commercial paper is backed by other firms based on the borrowing company's promise to pay. Therefore, it doesn't have to be registered with the Securities and Exchange Commission, and it can't have a maturity date longer than 270 days. Under the terms, the borrower agrees to pay the holder a fixed amount at some specified future date, and the commercial paper sells at a discount from that amount. Only larger companies with excellent credit have been able to benefit from this form of borrowing.

The Real World of Entrepreneurship

The SBA's CAPLine Credit Program

It is now possible for small businesses to finance their accounts receivable and inventory through the **CAPLine** revolving line of credit program offered by the U.S. Small Business Administration. This program is designed for manufacturers and wholesalers that need longer-term, asset-based financing. The entrepreneur works with a local bank, while the SBA shares in the approval process and guarantees repayment to the bank up to 75 percent of the credit line amount should the borrower default. In any case, the guarantee cannot exceed $750,000 and can be written for up to five years. This is a flexible line that, rather than requiring a fixed monthly payment, fluctuates with the level of the borrower's accounts receivable and inventory.

The SBA does charge a 2 percent guarantee fee, and 0.25 percent if the line is written for less than one year. The local bank also charges servicing fees. Still, a CAPLine normally is less costly than factoring and other types of loans. The company will be required to submit monthly reports and quarterly financial statements. Where loans exceed $200,000, the bank conducts semi-annual field examinations and an account must be set up at the bank to collect all accounts receivable. Advances are usually based on 50 percent of eligible inventory and 75 percent of accounts receivable.[3] For information, contact the SBA's Answer Desk at 1-800-8-ASK-SBA.

Accounts Payable Management

Cash flow management and accounts payable management are inextricably tied together, and both are affected by timing and, in some cases, negotiation. Many times a growing company will find itself in an "emergency" situation that requires it to request an extension on an obligation to a vendor or a lender. If the extension is granted, the payable remains an obligation of the company on the books but releases cash from obligation temporarily. This is an example of the effects of negotiation on cash flow. In other situations, entrepreneurs will typically attempt to use "other people's money" or borrow as much as possible to keep as much of their limited cash as possible for emergencies. This means that **trade credit**, credit extended by vendors, is a very valuable commodity to an entrepreneur. Unfortunately, most vendors offer discounts based on being paid by the 10th of the month after purchase. If the company's inflow of cash is rather irregular throughout the month, it may not generate enough cash by the 10th of the month to pay all its obligations. In the best of situations, the company should have enough liquidity to cover the obligations until cash comes in, but, unfortunately, most start-up and growing companies are short on cash and long on obligations. So leveraging their cash position by paying vendors at varying times is often the only solution.

In general, trade credit involves terms that have a cash discount; "3/10, net 30" is one example. In this case, the vendor is offering a 3 percent discount on the purchase if paid within 10 days; otherwise, the full amount is due in 30 days. Suppose a company purchased something for $50,000. Under this offering, the company has a choice of paying $48,500 on any of days 1 through 10 or $50,000 on any of days 11 through 30. The decision becomes

1. Can the company afford to take advantage of the discount? If it can, it should pay on the 10th day as there is no advantage to paying before that time and the company has the use of its money for nine days.

2. If the company can't pay the bill until after the 10th day, it may as well wait until the 30th day so that it gains 20 additional days in which to use its money.

The business incurs a definite cost by not taking advantage of discounts where offered; the interest rate based on forgoing the discount can be very high. For example, using the previous situation, the annualized interest rate amounts to

$$\text{Annualized rate} = \frac{\text{Days in the year}}{\text{Net period} - \text{Cash discount period}} \times \frac{\text{Cash discount \%}}{100\% - \text{Cash discount}}$$

$$= \frac{365}{30 - 10} \times \frac{.03}{1.00 - .03}$$

$$= 18.25 \times .030928$$

$$= 56.4\% \text{ annualized interest}$$

In this case, the company will be paying the exorbitant annual rate of 56.4 percent to use the supplier's money. Of course, this may be a relatively small amount when compared to the greater problem of writing checks that may fail to clear the bank.

There are many reasons to keep your company sufficiently liquid:

1. It allows the company to meet its operating obligations in a timely manner and maintain good vendor relationships.

2. It helps the company achieve and maintain a good credit rating.

3. It provides the company with a hedge against unforeseen expenses.

4. It helps the company reduce financing costs by allowing it to take advantage of vendor discounts.

5. It helps build a strong and trusting relationship with the company's bank.

The Real World of Entrepreneurship

Red Flags of an Unhealthy Business

Small businesses in particular need to be mindful of the warning signs that signal to a potential lender or creditor that the business is not in a healthy condition. Following are the most important red flags:

1. A highly leveraged, thinly capitalized situation, which makes the business particularly vulnerable to changing economic conditions.

2. Management by one person, which means the business relies on one individual to remain viable.

3. Poor communications, which indicates the owner is not keeping professional advisers abreast of what is happening with the business.

4. Few management reports, which suggests that the company is not analyzing key issues such as sales and orders, financial statements, and marketing strategy. Systems and controls seem outdated and ineffective.

5. Lack of financial controls and late financial statements.

6. Sales growth but no increase in profit, which signals that the emphasis is in the wrong place, suggesting lack of efficiency.

7. Lack of inventory records. The company doesn't have perpetual inventory records and relies on end-of-the-year physical counts. This may reflect inadequate cost systems.

8. Undervalued inventory, which is a hidden asset.

9. Inventory outpaces sales, which may signal that management is unwilling to mark down stock.

10. Outdated inventory.

Notice that red flags 1 through 6 are the result of management problems, while 7 through 10 are inventory problems.

Source: Coopers & Lybrand.

Small-business owners often forget that vendors also have bills to pay as they try to manage their cash flow. Several strategies will help a company take advantage of trade credit to the benefit of both the entrepreneur and the vendor:

1. Take advantage of cash discounts whenever possible. In fact, you should consider negotiating for an additional discount if you are able to take the goods COD.

2. Pay all bills on time, but not so early that you to lose the advantage of trade credit.

3. When considering vendors, attempt to find the longest terms possible as long as the vendor meets the company's quality standards.

4. Contact suppliers immediately if you cannot pay on time, and request an extension. Never ignore the vendors.

5. Stay on top of cash flow management, daily if necessary, to ensure that your company can meet its obligations.

One More Time: The Importance of Cash Flow Management

The importance of managing the cash flow of the business cannot be stressed enough. Too often small-business owners think they know how much money the business has because they know what is in the checking account. But that's only part of the story. Timing of accounts receivable, timing of accounts payable, and credit collection add three more dimensions to the picture and can make the difference between having enough cash on hand to operate and being cash poor. The next chapter looks at how to support your internal cash flows with the additional resources required to grow your company.

The Real World of Entrepreneurship

When the Company Has Too Much Debt

Rapid growth often brings unwanted debt that can strangle a company at a time when its attention is rightfully on building the company so that it can sustain itself. When a company faces too much debt, it has several options:

- It can approach the creditor to ask for lower interest rates or an extended term. Creditors may see this as a more favorable alternative to forcing the ailing company into bankruptcy.

- It can look for another lender with more favorable terms, but it shouldn't confront the current lender until another is on board.

- It can offer its creditors equity in the form of stocks or warrants in exchange for the debt.

- It can sell off assets and use the resulting cash to pay obligations.

Cases Relevant to This Chapter

SB Networks
Pelco

Issues for Review and Discussion

1. Which items found on the income statement are not present in the cash budget?
2. How can a company manage accounts receivable so as not to affect cash flow adversely?
3. Which specific actions on the part of a company would an effective credit and collection policy include?
4. List three types of bridge financing and describe how they might be used to manage business cycles.
5. What is meant by "the real cost of credit" when considering effective accounts payable management?

Experiencing Entrepreneurship

1. A certain business has a cash cycle of 32 days, cost of sales of $200,000, operating expenses of $120,000, and depreciation expense of $2,000. What is the required financing to cover its cash cycle?
2. Interview a commercial banker to determine what its lending policy is for small businesses and which types of financing it offers.

Resources

Bangs, David H., Jr. (1992). *Financial Troubleshooting*. Chicago: Upstart Publishing.

Harrison, John (1994). *Collection Techniques for a Small Business*. Grants Pass, OR: Oasis Press (1-800-228-2275).

National Association of Credit Management. Publishes *Credit Manual of Commercial Laws* (410-740-5560).

Scolo, James. *Credit and Collection Business Kit*. International Wealth Success (1-800-323-0548).

Shaw, Eric. *The Game of Credit*. New York Credit (310-827-0076).

Skiar, Leonard. *The Check Is Not in the Mail*. Baroque (1-800-348-1355).

Internet Resources

How to Make Better Credit Decisions
http://www.dbisna.com/credit/hcredit.htm
This is a Dun & Bradstreet article that offers practical guidance on assessing customers as credit risks.

Preparing a Cash Flow Forecast
http://www.sb.gov.bc.ca/smallbus/workshop/market
This article walks you through the process of preparing a cash flow forecast.

If it's not growing, it's going to die.
Michael Eisner
CEO, Walt Disney Productions
"60 Minutes" TV program, November 22, 1987

Financing Growth

Preview

Understanding this chapter will give you the ability to

▶ **Explain how growth financing differs from start-up financing.**

▶ **Discuss issues related to raising growth capital.**

▶ **Explain the venture capital market and process.**

▶ **Contrast private placement and public offerings.**

▶ **Discuss how strategic alliances can be used to fund growth.**

▶ **Explain ways to value your business for sale or investment.**

▶ **Describe how to harvest the wealth in your business.**

Terms to Know

Young Entrepreneurs—Minicase

Marc Andreesen
Netscape Communications Corporation

No collection of stories of young entrepreneurs would be complete without including perhaps the most famous member of Generation X, Marc Andreesen. Andreesen is the co-founder of Netscape Communications Corporation of Mountain View, California, and the primary thrust behind the most dynamic shift in computer technology since the arrival of the PC.

Although he has often been compared to the likes of Bill Gates of Microsoft and Steven Jobs of Apple, his background differs dramatically. He was born and raised in a small town in Wisconsin whose only real activity was junior high and high school sports. His father is a retired seed salesman; his mother works for Land's End, the catalog company. Because Andreesen had no interest in sports, he turned to something he did find fascinating—computers—and taught himself BASIC, a programming language used at the time. The first time he actually used a computer was in the sixth grade in the school library, where he developed a program to do his math homework. In the seventh grade his parents gave him a Commodore 64, and he was off and running.

Andreesen is a paradox, a person who loves junk food but also loves classical music, history, and philosophy. While attending the University of Illinois at Urbana–Champaign, he discovered the Internet, which at the time was a very unwieldy technology used principally by academics and scientists. But he quickly realized it was a way to reach out to the world and tap into global sources of information. In 1992 he approached Eric Bina, who had a master's degree in computer science and was working at the National Center for Supercomputing Applications at the university. He proposed that they write a program that would hide all the various arcane functions of the Internet behind a user-friendly graphical interface. On weekends and whenever they had a moment, the two collaborated on what was to become NCSA Mosaic.

It was a very simple code, but it made the Internet accessible to anyone. At that time, neither had any idea of the long-term impact of their creation.

By the time Andreesen graduated with a BS in computer science, millions of copies of Mosaic had been downloaded over the Net by users worldwide. The success of Mosaic gave Andreesen the opportunity he needed to leave the Midwest and head for the Silicon Valley. There he took a position with a small software company called Enterprise Integration Technologies, which was developing security software for the Internet. It was then that fate stepped in, in the form of Jim Clark, one of the co-founders of Silicon Graphics, who had just left his own company because of a dispute over the direction the company was taking. Clark contacted Andreesen to talk, and the meeting resulted in a decision to start a company together that would focus on Internet browsers and servers. Clark had the capital, and Andreesen had the creativity.

Netscape Communications was founded in April 1994 and, before it even began to make a profit, enjoyed one of the most successful IPOs in history in 1995. In the last quarter of 1996, the company made $7.7 million on sales of $100 million. Netscape is projecting revenues of $5 billion by the year 2000, which it plans to achieve by focusing on intranets, the software that runs corporate networks.

Andreesen never took any business courses in college, but business strategy fascinates him, so he reads everything he can get his hands on. "There's a triangulation between what's possible with the technology, what business needs people have, and what's actually practical. You triangulate on that, and that's where the sweet spot is for making a successful business and driving it further. That's the most interesting part."[1]

One challenge Netscape faces is the perception that it gives away its software for free. Andreesen claims the company has encouraged that perception, but "it's had a positive and negative effect on our business. I don't think it's a bad thing that our competitors are confused about what our business model has been. But now we need to be a little clearer because customers may get confused."[2] Another challenge is the ever-present threat of his giant competitors, Microsoft and Oracle. But Andreesen is focusing on what his company does best: the Internet and, more important, the intranet, where he feels its strength lies.

In 1996, Netscape acquired Collabra and Netcode, companies with technology that Netscape needed and would have taken it a long time to develop. This is a common strategy in an industry where focusing on core competencies is essential to staying ahead of the competition.

Andreesen advises that there is still a lot of opportunity in the software industry. Whenever it appears that one company, such as Microsoft, is creating what he calls a "bottleneck," it's time to start a company to "get [the] value out of smart people."[3] He predicts that in the future, there will be a lot of small start-ups that will be acquired very quickly.

What does a young entrepreneur who presides over a $400 million company worry about? " . . . [W]hat I worry about is that we'll not develop new products quickly enough, that we will target the wrong customers with the wrong feature sets, that other start-up companies will upstage us. There's no shortage of things to worry about; it keeps us motivated, and it keeps us working hard."[4]

What funding strategy did Andreesen use to grow Netscape Communications, and how did that contribute to his potential harvest strategy?

---

[1]Rick Tetzeli, "What It's Really Like to be Marc Andreesen," *Fortune,* December 9, 1996, pp. 137–156.

[2]Chrisopher J. Alden, "Bill Gates with a College Degree," *The Red Herring,* January 1996, issue 27 (http://www.herring.com/mag/issue27/degree.html).

[3]Ibid., p. 11.

[4]"15 Minutes with: Marc Andreesen" (http://www.christine.com/15mins/archives/marcand.htm).

The growth phase of a business is an exciting adventure that results from a successful start-up or acquisition. But it also places a tremendous strain on the resources of the business at a time when it most needs them. Successful growth takes capital, and often the financial resources that saw the business through start-up and early growth are not sufficient to supply the demands of rapid growth. Marc Andreesen was fortunate to have started his business with a strong financial backer (see Young Entrepreneurs—Minicase). Going public early in this high-tech industry gave him the additional capital he needed to rapidly grow the company. This strategy is not uncommon in technology industries, but is probably not viable for non-technology businesses. There are, however, other ways to finance growth.

This chapter expands on the resources discussed in Chapter 4 and gives you more options for funding the growth of your business as well as harvesting the wealth your business will create. In Chapter 4, you learned about private investors; in this chapter, you will learn about professional venture capital and methods for doing a private placement or going public.

Growth Financing

Growth capital consists of those funds needed to take the company out of the start-up phase and move it toward becoming a significant contender in the marketplace. To the extent that the entrepreneur has met the sales and earnings targets estimated in the start-up business plan and the company has reached critical mass, the financing choices available to the business will increase substantially when it seeks growth financing. This increase in choices is important because the amount of money needed to grow the business is normally significantly larger than that required to start it. One exception, however, is high-tech or biomedical companies, which generally incur considerable R&D costs prior to start-up. These types of companies may spend millions of dollars and accrue several years of negative income before their first sale.

Today most venture capital still goes to biotechnology, software, and computer ventures, but in general the best companies in any industry will have the easiest time finding capital from all sources. To become one of the "best" companies requires an excellent track record (however short it may be), a sound management team, potential for high growth, and an appropriate and effective exit strategy so that investors and the founders can reap the benefits of their investment. It has been said that the bottom-line criterion for securing a bank loan is to be a company that doesn't really need the money. The same can be said for suppliers of growth capital. Typically they will not go into a situation where their "new money" is paying off "old debt" or where a company has poor cash flow. They want to know that the infrastructure is in place, sales are increasing, and the growing venture needs capital only to take that next step toward becoming a market leader.

Raising Growth Capital

Raising growth capital is a time-consuming and costly process. For this reason, many entrepreneurs opt to grow slowly, depending exclusively on internal cash flow to fund growth. They may have a basic fear of debt and giving up any control of the company to investors. This attitude is sound if it works, but new ventures that begin with obvious high-growth potential will find themselves hamstrung by a level of growth that prohibits them from meeting demand. Consequently, it's important to plan for growth from the very beginning so that the entrepreneurial team will be prepared for the expense and the demands on their time when rapid growth comes.

Seeking Investors

The first thing to understand about raising growth capital (or any capital, for that matter) is that it will invariably take at least twice as long as projected to actually have the money in the company's bank account. If you are attempting to raise a substantial amount of money, you should expect to need several months to find the financing, several more months for the potential investor or lender to do due diligence and say yes, and up to six months more to receive the money. In other words, no growing company should wait to look for funding until it needs it; then it will be too late, which could spell disaster for the business if no backup source is available. Moreover, since this search for capital can take you away from the business at the time it needs you most, it's helpful to use financial advisers who have experience in raising money and to have a seasoned management team in place so that the business is in good hands while the search is going on.

Second, the investors identified as a financial source may not work out in the end as you learn more about them. For this reason it's important to continue to look for additional investors, if only as backups, while you are investigating a potential financial source.

Third, second-round financiers often request a buyout of the first-round funding sources if they believe those sources have nothing more to contribute to the business and no longer want to deal with them. This can be a very awkward situation, especially if the first-round financing came from friends and family. The second-round funder has nothing to lose by demanding the buyout. He or she can certainly walk away from the deal; there are thousands more out there.

The Cost of Raising Capital

In figuring out how much capital the venture needs to grow, many entrepreneurs concentrate on the cost of the capital in terms of interest rate or return on investment and fail to include the cost of seeking the capital, which can be substantial. The costs incurred before the money is received must be paid up front by the entrepreneur, whereas the costs of maintaining the capital can often be paid from the proceeds of the loan or, in the case of investment capital, from the proceeds of a sale or internally generated cash flow.

The costs of seeking funding for your business can be significant (see Figure 18.1). Maintaining current financial statements is essential as you prepare to talk to a funding source. If the capital sought is in the millions of dollars, growth capital funding sources prefer that financials have the imprimatur of a financial consultant or an investment banker, someone who regularly works with investors. This person is expert in preparing loan and investment packages that are attractive to potential funding sources. The

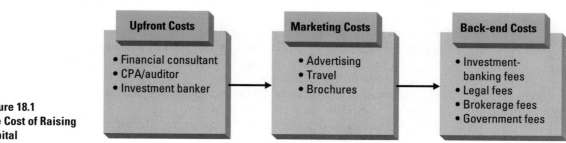

**Figure 18.1
The Cost of Raising
Capital**

Table 18.1   The Costs of Going Public

Following are average costs for the various items you'll need to complete the initial public offering process:

Legal fees	$75,000
Filing fees with the SEC and the state in which the company is doing business	$50,000–$100,000
Audited financial statements, pro forma statements	$20,000–$150,000
Financial printing fees for the prospectus, SEC registration statement, and official notices	$40,000–$100,000

company's CPA will prepare the business's financial statements and work closely with the financial consultant. All of these activities will result in costs to the entrepreneur. In addition, if the company is seeking equity capital, it will need a prospectus or an offering document, which will require legal expertise and often has significant printing costs. Then there are the costs of marketing the offering, such as advertising, travel, and brochures. Finally, there is the cost in terms of time away from the business while the entrepreneur is out seeking capital. All of these costs can amount to thousands of dollars (see Table 18.1).

In addition to the up-front costs of seeking growth capital are "back-end" costs in situations where the entrepreneur seeks capital by selling securities (shares of stock in the corporation). These can include investment banking fees, legal fees, marketing costs, brokerage fees, and various other fees charged by state and federal authorities. The total cost of raising equity capital can go as high as 25 percent of the total amount of money sought. Add that to the interest or return on investment paid to the funding source(s) and it is easy to see why it unquestionably costs money to raise money.

Mezzanine Financing

To put themselves in a better position to negotiate a deal, some entrepreneurs use *mezzanine financing*, a layer of subordinated debt between senior term debt and equity. It is used to raise capital to do an IPO, a leveraged buyout, or an expansion. Mezzanine lenders are typically financial institutions, commercial finance companies, pension funds, and private investment funds. These types of loans are usually unsecured and are used by companies with revenues in the $2 million to $5 million range. A mezzanine lender wants a company in a strong market niche with attractive growth prospects, a good financial history, a strong management team, a solid business plan, and a definite exit plan for the investor.[1]

Mezzanine debt often is structured to include warrants or options and repayment of interest only in the first two to three years. The combination of debt and equity is designed to give the lender a return of 20 to 30 percent.

The primary disadvantage of mezzanine financing is that it is a claim against your cash because you must repay the principal and interest. If your expected growth and profitability do not materialize, you could find yourself in a very difficult situation.

The Venture Capital Market

Private venture capital companies have been the bedrock of many high-growth ventures, particularly in the computer, software, biotechnology, and telecommunications industries. Since venture capitalists rarely invest in start-up ventures outside the high-tech arena, the growth stage of a new venture is where most entrepreneurs consider approaching them. Waiting until this stage is advantageous, because using venture capital in the start-up phase can mean giving up significant control of the new venture.

Professional venture capital is, quite simply, a pool of money that is managed by professionals. These professionals usually assume the role of general partner and are paid a management fee plus a percentage of the gain from the investment by their investors. The venture capital firm takes an equity position through the ownership of stock in the company in which it is investing. It also normally requires a seat on the board of directors and brings its professional management skills to the new venture in an advisory capacity.

In the 1980s, the number of private venture capital firms grew by 199 percent, and the average amount of money under professional management grew from $2.9 billion in 1979 to more than $49.5 billion in 1989. It was an easy time for entrepreneurs seeking this type of capital. However, the growth in venture capital firm formation peaked in 1987 and has been declining ever since.[2]

A survey of 600 venture capital firms (VCs) by Coopers & Lybrand in 1995 found that VCs invested more than $6.6 billion in U.S. companies.[3] Still, a couple of events have changed the nature of the venture capital market. The Small Business Job Protection Act of 1996 encouraged investment in small businesses that have chosen an S-corporation form by pension plans, trust, and other tax-exempt entities, which were previously ineligible to invest.[4] In addition, the tables have turned on venture capital firms. With so many new ventures experiencing windfalls of capital resources from IPOs, VCs now must accept a smaller equity stake and less risk. So although they are investing in new companies, they are doing so much more conservatively.

The Price Waterhouse Venture Capital Survey for the second quarter of 1997 reported that 697 companies received $3.8 billion in venture capital funds. Total investments exceeded $3.18 billion, which was a 13 percent increase over the figures reported in the second quarter of 1996. As usual, the Silicon Valley of California was the clear leader in number of companies receiving investment capital, followed by New England and the Southeast. As expected, 70 percent of all dollars invested were placed in biotechnology, communications, computers and peripherals, electronics, environmental products, medical instruments, semiconductors, and software.[5]

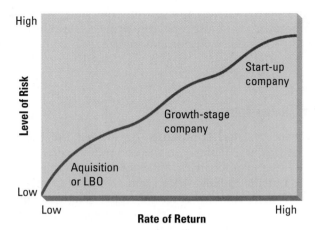

**Figure 18.2
Risk Versus Rate of
Return**

The Venture Capital Process

To determine if venture capital is the right type of funding for the growing venture, it is critical to understand the goals and motivations of venture capitalists, for they dictate the potential success or failure of the attempt. The venture capital company invests in a growing business through the use of debt and equity instruments to gain long-term appreciation on the investment within a specified period of time, typically five years. By definition, this goal often differs from that of the entrepreneur, who usually looks at the business from a much longer time frame. The venture capitalist also seeks varying rates of return depending on the risk involved. An early-stage investment, for example, will typically command a higher rate of return, as much as 50 percent or more, whereas a later-stage investment will demand a lower rate of return, perhaps 30 percent. Very simply, as the level of risk increases, so does the demand for a higher rate of return, as depicted in Figure 18.2. This relationship is certainly not surprising. Older, more established companies have a longer track record on which to make predictions about the future, so normal business cycles and sales patterns have been identified, and the company is usually in a better position to respond through experience to a dynamic environment. Consequently, investing in a mature firm through an acquisition or a **leveraged buyout (LBO)**, in which debt is used to purchase the controlling interest in the company, does not command the high rate of return realized by investing in a high-growth start-up, which may have little or no track record and no established sales patterns.

What Do Venture Capitalists Look for?

Usually (but not always) the first thing venture capitalists look at when scrutinizing a potential investment candidate is the management team to see if experienced people with a good track record are in place and able to take the company to the next level of growth. In addition to experience, they look for commitment to the company and to growth because they recognize that growing a company requires an enormous amount of time and effort on the part of the management team. Once they have determined that the management team is solid, they will look at the product and the market to see if the opportunity is substantial and if the product holds a unique or innovative position in the marketplace. Product uniqueness, especially if protected through intellectual property rights, helps to erect entry barriers in the market, commands higher prices, and adds value to the business.

The other major factor examined is the potential for significant growth and the amount of growth possible, because it is from growth and the consequent appreciation in the value of the business that the venture capitalist will derive the required return on investment. The venture capitalist will weigh that potential for growth against the risk of failure and the cost to achieve the growth projected. Therefore, when negotiating with venture capitalists, the entrepreneur should have a good sense of the value of the business, a topic discussed later in this chapter.

Dealing with Venture Capitalists

Armed with an understanding of what venture capitalists look for, you will be prepared to begin the search for the VC that will meet your needs. As the venture capital community is fairly close-knit, at least within regions of the country, it is wise not to "shop" the business around looking for the best deal. Investigating the venture capital firms in the state where your company does business will help you locate VCs who specialize in the industry or type of business you are in. Attorneys and accountants who regularly deal with business investments are excellent sources of information on VCs. In fact, the best way to approach a venture capitalist is through a referral from someone who knows the VC. Once you have chosen a venture capital company, it is preferable to stay with that company until you are certain the deal will not work. Under no circumstances should you talk to two companies at once.

The venture capital company will no doubt ask for a copy of the business plan with an executive summary. The **executive summary** is a screening device for the venture capitalist. If the VC cannot immediately determine that the entrepreneurial team's qualifications are outstanding, the product concept innovative, and the projections for growth and return on investment realistic, they will not bother to read the entire business plan. On the other hand, if, after studying the plan, the VC like what they see, they will probably call for a meeting to determine if the entrepreneurial team can deliver what it projects. This may or may not call for a formal presentation of the business plan by the entrepreneur. During this meeting, the initial terms of an agreement may also be discussed; however, you should not seem too eager to discuss issues such as owner compensation until the venture capitalist indicates that a deal is imminent. It is also very important that you not hype the business concept or make claims that you cannot substantiate. Venture capitalists have literally seen it all and will readily recognize when an entrepreneur is puffing. It's wise, however, to disclose any potential negative aspects of the business and ways to deal with them.

If the meeting goes well, the next step is for the venture capital firm to do its due diligence; that is, it will have its own team of experts check out the entrepreneurial team and the business thoroughly. If it is still sold on the business after due diligence, it will draw up legal documents detailing the nature and terms of the investment. These may appear in the form of a term sheet, which is usually written to the benefit of the venture capitalist over the entrepreneur. The term sheet will contain the terms and conditions for the investment. Typically the VC will want some form of convertible preferred stock, with common shares for the entrepreneur. This is because the VC's stock value is determined by the amount of money they contributed. If the entrepreneur received the same value for no money, there would be immediate tax implications; the entrepreneur would have to pay taxes on the gain and may not have the cash to do it. But if the stock is of a different class and the VC's stock has the benefits of preferred stock, the entrepreneur's common stock can be valued at a fraction of the VC's.

Once the VC has declared that "the check's in the mail," you should be aware that receiving that check may take some time. This is because some venture capitalists wait until they know they have a satisfactory investment before putting together a partnership to actually fund the investment. Others just have a lengthy process for releasing money from the firm.

It is not uncommon for the money to be released in stages based on meeting agreed-on goals. Moreover, the venture capital firm will continue to monitor the progress of the new venture and probably will want a seat on the board of directors so it will have a say in the direction the new venture takes.

Capital Structure

At this point, it may seem as if the entrepreneur is totally at the mercy of the venture capitalist. That, unfortunately, is true if the entrepreneur enters the negotiation from a weak position, desperately needing the money to keep the business alive. A better approach is to go into the negotiation from a position of strength. True, venture capitalists are presented with hundreds of

Technology Tip

Try Finding Capital Online

More and more businesses using a Regulation A offering (see page 505) or direct public offering (DPO) are looking for investors on the Internet to help keep their offering costs down. One such business, Interactive Holdings of New York City, put its offering circular, legal contracts, sales material, registration forms, and company bylaws online. It also posted advertising icons on other compatible sites.

Interactive Holdings received thousands of leads and many calls from its $5,000 worth of effort. Still, it took a human being to actually close a stock deal and ultimately raise the necessary capital the company was seeking.

Source: Stephanie Gruner, "When Mom & Pop Go Public," *Inc.*, December 1996, p. 66.

deals on a regular basis, but most of those deals are not big hits; in other words, the return on the investment is not worth their effort. They are always looking for that one business that will achieve high growth and return them enough gain on their investment to make up for all the average- or mediocre-performing investments in their portfolios. If you enter the negotiation with a business that has a solid record of growth and performance, you are in a good position to call many of the shots.

Any investment deal will have four components:

▶ The amount of money to be invested

▶ The timing and use of the investment moneys

▶ The return on investment to investors

▶ The level of risk involved

How these components are defined will affect the venture for a long time, not only in constructing its growth strategy but in formulating an exit strategy.

What Venture Capitalists Want

Venture capitalists often want both equity and debt—equity because it gives them an ownership interest in the business and debt because they will be paid back more quickly. Consequently, they tend to want redeemable **preferred stock** or **debentures** so that if the company does well, they can convert to common stock, and if the company does poorly or fails, they will be the first to be repaid their investment because they have preferred stock. If you have entered the negotiation from a position of strength, you will be more likely to convince them to take common stock, which makes things much easier. In another scenario, the venture capitalists may want a combination of debentures (debt) and warrants, which allows them to purchase common stock at a nominal rate later on. If this strategy is carried out correctly, they can conceivably get their entire investment back when the debt portion is repaid and still enjoy the appreciation in the value of the business as a stockholder.

Venture capitalists often ask for several other provisions to protect their investment. One is an **antidilution provision**, which ensures that the selling of stock at a later date will not decrease the economic value of their investment. In other words, the price of stock sold at a later date will be equal to or greater than the price at which the venture capitalists could buy the common stock on a conversion. One way to ensure that dilution does not occur is to have a **full ratchet clause** that lets the venture capitalist buy common stock at the lowest rate at which it has been sold. For example, if the lowest price at which the stock has been sold to this point is $1, that is the conversion rate for the VC. However, if subsequently the stock is sold at $.50, all of the VC's convertible shares can be purchased at the new lowest rate. Where the VC's $1 million investment would have bought 1 million shares at $1 per share, it now can buy 2 million shares at $.50 a share, effectively reducing the equity holding of the founders. A better method from the entrepreneur's point of view is to use a *weighted ratchet approach,* which uses the weighted price per share of all the stock issued after the founders' stock and before the lowest stock price that will cause dilution. This is certainly fairer to the founders and will prevent them from losing control of the company if the value of the stock decreases substantially.

In addition, the VC may request a **forfeiture provision,** which means that if the company does not achieve its projected performance goals, the founders may be required to give up some of their stock as a penalty to the VC to guard against the VC having paid too much for their interest in the company. This forfeited stock increases the VC's equity in the company and may even be given to new management that the VC brings on board to steer the company in a new direction. One way to mitigate this situation is for the entrepreneur to request stock bonuses as a reward for meeting or exceeding performance projections.

Using venture capital is certainly an important source for the entrepreneur with a high-growth venture. It is, however, only one source, and, with the advice of experts, the entrepreneur should consider all possible avenues. The best choice is one that will give the new venture the chance to reach its potential and the investors or financial backers an excellent return on investment.

Private Placement

Private placement is a way of raising capital from private investors by selling securities in a private corporation or partnership. Recall that these private investors are called "angels" (see Chapter 4). Securities are common and preferred stock, notes, bonds, debentures, voting-trust certificates, certificates of deposit, warrants, options, subscription rights, limited partnership shares, and undivided oil or gas interests. Private placement is a formal vehicle for seeking funding from private investors who are "sophisticated" in terms of the rules of private placement, which are stated in Regulation D of the Securities Act. **Regulation D** was designed to simplify the private offering process and allow the entrepreneur to seek funding from private investors as long as they met the requirements. Doing a private placement memorandum involves the completion of a business plan and a prospectus detailing the risks of the investment.

Private placement is a less costly, less time-consuming process than a public offering, and many states now offer standardized, easy-to-fill-out disclosure statements and offering documents. The advantages of a private offering are many. The growing venture does not have to have a lot of assets or credit references as it would need for bank financing, nor does it need a lengthy track record. It also does not have to file with the Securities and Exchange Commission. It must, however, qualify under the rules of federal Regulation D. Be aware that not all states recognize the exemptions under Reg D in their **"blue sky" laws,** the securities laws designed to protect investors against fraud, so the issuer of a private placement memorandum may have to register with the state as well.

The burden is on the issuer to document that the exemption from registration requirements have been met. Therefore, the "sophistication" of all offerees should be examined closely and the reasons they qualify carefully documented. The issuer should also number each private placement memorandum and keep a record of who has looked at the memorandum or discussed the offering with the issuer. The memorandum should include a qualifying statement that the contents must not be copied or disclosed to anyone other than the offeree. If an offeree becomes an investor, the issuer should document when and where the offeree examined the company's books and records. When the offering is complete, the issuer should place a memo in the offering log stating that only those persons listed in the log have been approached regarding the offering. It is important to note that even if the offering qualifies as exempt from registration, it is still subject to the antifraud and civil liability provisions of federal securities laws and state "blue sky" securities laws.

Small Corporate Offering: SCOR U-7

Many states have adopted the Small Corporate Offering Registration Form, also called **SCOR U-7**, which makes the registration process much simpler by providing 50 fill-in-the-blank questions that ask for the company's basic

Rinaldo Brutoco, president of Red Rose Collection mail-order company, learned that SCOR financing is a relatively simple way to do a small public offering to raise up to $1 million. And it has a side benefit as well. It's also a way to get your loyal customers and suppliers to invest in the business. (Linda Sue Scott)

financial, management, and marketing information. SCOR U-7 lets a company raise up to $1 million by selling common stock directly to the public for at least $5 per share. One key benefit of SCOR is that unless the state securities commission expressly imposes investor suitability requirements, the offering can be sold to virtually anyone in amounts as small as $1,000, and there are no restrictions on resale of shares. In fact, some states will allow SCOR companies to trade their common stock on NASDAQ's electronic OTC bulletin board. A lawyer should be consulted, as some of the adopting states restrict who can use Form U-7. See the box below for an example of a company that used SCOR.

Types of Stock Used with SCOR U-7

Within the structure of the corporate private placement, the entrepreneur can sell preferred and common stock, convertible debentures, and debt securities with warrants. Recall that preferred stock has dividend and liquidation preference over common stock in addition to antidilution protection and other rights as specified in a stockholder agreement. **Common stock,** on the other hand, carries voting rights and preserves the right of the corporation to elect Subchapter S status. **Convertible debentures** are secured or unsecured debt instruments that can be converted to equity at a later date as specified in the agreement. In its debenture form, however, it provides for a fixed rate of return (interest), which can be deducted by the corporation. Debt securities with warrants give the holder the right to purchase stock at a fixed price for a specified term, which can be very attractive for an investor who wants to share in

 Entrepreneurship in Action

The Private Placement Process*

As an example of what the private placement process is like, consider the following company that wanted to raise $1 million to grow. These are the steps it took:

1. Using a SCOR software program provided by the state securities agency, the entrepreneur, Tom Lauder, wrote a prospectus detailing the terms, conditions, risks, and rewards of the offering.

2. Lauder refined the document with the aid of his attorney. The 60-page document took about three weeks to complete at a total cost of about $50,000.

3. He hired a nationally known accounting firm to audit the corporation's most recent financial statements. This cost was approximately $15,000.

4. By comparing his company with others in the industry, he was able to arrive at a value for the company of three times present earnings, or $15 million.

5. He registered the corporation in 10 states that permitted the SCOR filing, with filing fees ranging from $50 to over $2,000.

6. He then had to decide to whom he should present the offering. A logical choice was his major customers and suppliers. To these people he sent an announcement of the offering. From the announcement he received requests from 3,000 people for a prospectus, and from that group he received enough commitments to ultimately be fully subscribed within the year.

* This example is based on a real company. The names have been changed to protect the company's anonymity.

the upside potential of the growing company by purchasing stock at rates that are usually below market value. Purchasing common stock under this instrument does not invalidate the preferred position of the debtholder as creditor, and if the warrants are issued as net-issuance warrants, the investor will not have to meet the SEC requirement of a two-year holding period before selling. This is because when the investor exercises the net-issuance warrant, no cash passes between the company and the investor. Instead, the company subtracts the cost of the conversion (the rate the investor pays) from the value of the stock being purchased and gives the investor the difference. This means that this type of warrant is more liquid.

As with any complex legal document, it is crucial that you consult with an attorney well versed in private placements in the preparation of the private placement memorandum and disclosure of information about the company and its principals. Problems usually don't arise if the business is successful; however, if the venture fails and the investors uncover a security violation, the entrepreneur and other principal equityholders may lose their protection under the corporate shield and become personally liable in the event of a lawsuit. The courts have dealt severely with security violations, and there is no statute of limitations on the filing of such a suit.

Direct Public Offering (DPO): Regulation A

Another type of small corporate offering is the **direct public offering** or **DPO** under Regulation A of the Securities and Exchange Commission. In contrast to SCOR, it permits a maximum offering of up to $5 million over a period of 12 months. Here are some things you should consider before doing a DPO:

▶ Can you show several years of profit under your management?

▶ Can you show three years of audited financial statements?

 Entrepreneurship in Action

Know When to Fold 'Em

Kwik Goal is a sports equipment manufacturer based in Quakerstown, Pennsylvania. The tremendous growth of soccer in the United States was beginning to strain the company's resources as it struggled to grow yet maintain a positive cash flow.

In 1993, annual sales at Kwik Goal, a family-owned business, were approaching $4 million. Its founder, Vincent Caruso, wanted to grow the company past the $5 million level in the coming year and needed approximately $500,000 to do it. He decided to do an IPO for $6 million to move his company beyond its increasing debt and give it a chance to grow unfettered.

On the day before the IPO, the underwriter reported to Caruso that the offering would bring only $3 per share instead of the expected $6. Caruso refused to give up 55 percent of his company for only $3 million, so, to everyone's surprise, he abandoned the IPO, which had cost him $200,000 to that point.

In 1996, Kwik Goal, still a private company, reached $9 million in sales, and Caruso believes he made the right decision. Because it is a private company, he has control over how and when it grows.

Source: David R. Evanson, "Tales of Caution in Going Public," *Nation's Business,* June 1996, p. 57.

▶ Can your business be explained quickly, in a couple of sentences? That's really all the time you have to interest a potential investor so you can then tell him or her more.

▶ Is your business exciting in any way? Again, this is about attracting interest from investors.

▶ Do you have strong, loyal customers who might invest?

▶ Do you have someone you can assign to manage the DPO, which will take a considerable amount of time (six months to a year)?

Remember, doing a DPO, SCOR, or private offering is not a quick way to raise cash. It is a serious strategic decision whose pros and cons should be carefully weighed. Companies considering doing small offerings should make the decision very carefully, since the costs of doing the offering, coupled with the costs of compliance with reporting requirements, are substantial when compared to the amount of the offering. See "Know When to Fold 'Em" (page 505) for an example of a company that decided against a public offering.

The Initial Public Offering (IPO)

There is no doubt that the **initial public offering (IPO)** or "going public" has an aura of prestige and, if chosen as the method to raise growth capital, represents an exciting time in the life of a rapidly growing business. However, the decision whether or not to do a public offering is difficult at best because once the decision to go ahead with the offering has been made, a series of events is set in motion that will change the business and the entrepreneur's relationship to it forever. Moreover, returning to private status once the company has been a public company is an almost insurmountable task.

An initial public offering is simply a more complex version of a private offering in which the founders and equity shareholders of the company agree to sell a portion of the company (via previously unissued stocks and bonds) to the public by filing with the Securities and Exchange Commission (SEC) and listing their stock on one of the stock exchanges. All the proceeds of the IPO go to the company in a primary offering. If the owners of the company subsequently sell their shares of stock, the proceeds go to the owners in what is termed a *secondary distribution*. Often a combination of the two events occurs; however, an offering may be far less attractive when a large percentage of the proceeds is destined for the owners, since it clearly signals a lack of commitment on the owners' part to the future success of the business.

More and more smaller corporations are using the IPO vehicle to raise growth capital; in fact, well more than half of all IPOs are companies with an asset value under $500,000. This trend has been helped by SEC Form S-18, which applies to offerings of less than $7.5 million and simplifies and reduces the disclosure and reporting requirements.

When to "Go Public"

There is no "rule of thumb" for when to go public, but in general many companies consider it an option when their need for growth capital has exceeded their debt capacity. On average, a potential IPO company should have an attractive rate of annual growth, at least $10 million in annual sales, $1 million in earnings, and a history of audited returns. Recently there have been notable exceptions to this rule, namely Netscape Communications Corporation, a Silicon Valley company that on August 9, 1995, went public at $28 a share and saw a 108 percent gain on the first day of trading. The unique aspect of this IPO was that at the time, Netscape was an unprofitable company that was giving away its Internet browser software, Navigator. By December of that same year, it had become a $4 billion company and its stock was selling at $150 a share. This is not an example of a typical IPO by any means. It is an example of the rush by investors to climb on board the Internet bandwagon, which is seen as the future of computer technology.

Advantages and Disadvantages of Going Public

The principal advantage of a public offering is that it provides the offering company with a tremendous source of interest-free capital for growth and expansion, paying off debt, or product development. With the IPO comes the future option of additional offerings once the company is well known and has a positive track record.

A public company has more prestige and clout in the marketplace, so it becomes easier to form alliances and negotiate deals with suppliers, customers, and creditors. It is also easier for the founders to harvest the rewards of their efforts by selling off a portion of their stock or borrowing against it as needed. In addition, public stock and stock options can be used to attract new employees and reward existing employees.

However, the public offering has some serious disadvantages:

▶ Of the 3,186 firms that went public in the 1980s, only 58 percent are still listed on one of the three major exchanges. Moreover, the stock of only one-third of these firms was selling above its issue price.[6]

▶ It is a very expensive process. Whereas a private offering can cost about $100,000, a public offering can run well over $300,000, and that figure does not include a 7 to 10 percent commission to the underwriter, which compensates the investment bank that sells the securities. One way to prevent a financial disaster should the offering fail is to ask for stop-loss statements from lawyers, accountants, consultants, and investment bankers. The stop-loss statement is essentially a promise by the investment banker not to charge the full fee if the offering fails.

▶ Going public is an enormously time-consuming process. Entrepreneurs report that they spend the better part of every week on issues related to the offering over a four-to-six-month period. Part of this time is devoted to educating the entrepreneur about the process, which is far beyond the scope of this chapter. One way many entrepreneurs deal with the knowledge gap is to spend the year prior to the offering preparing for it by talking to others who have gone through the process, reading, and putting together the team that will see the company through the offering. The IPO process can be speeded up by running the private corporation like a public corporation from the beginning, that is, doing audited financial statements and keeping good records.

▶ A public offering means that everything the company does or has becomes public information subject to the scrutiny of anyone interested in the company.

▶ The CEO of a public company is now responsible to the shareholders above all and only secondarily to anyone else.

▶ The entrepreneur, who before the offering probably owned the majority of the stock, may no longer have the controlling stock (only if the entrepreneur agreed to an offering that resulted in the loss of control), and the stock he or she does own can lose value if the company's value on the stock exchange drops, which can occur through no fault of the company's performance. World events and domestic economic policy can adversely (or positively) affect a company's stock irrespective of what the company does.

▶ A public company faces intense pressure to perform in the short term. Whereas an entrepreneur in a wholly owned corporation can afford the luxury of long-term goals and controlled growth, the CEO of a public company is pressured by stockholders to show almost immediate gains in revenues and earnings, which will translate into higher stock prices and dividends to the stockholders.

▶ Last but not least, the SEC reporting requirements for public companies are very strict, time consuming, and therefore costly.

The Public Offering Process

The first step in the public offering process is to choose an **underwriter,** or **investment banker.** This is the firm that will sell the securities and guide the corporation through the IPO process. Some of the most prestigious investment banking firms will handle only well-established companies because they believe smaller companies will not attract sufficient attention among major institutional investors. Consequently, you should contact anyone you know who has either gone public or has a connection with an investment bank to gain an entrée. The importance of investigating the reputation and track record of any underwriter cannot be stressed enough, as investment banking has become a very competitive industry, and the lure of large fees from IPOs is attracting some firms of questionable character. You should also examine the investment mix of the bank. Some underwriters focus solely on institutional investors, others on retail customers or private investors. It is often useful to have a mix of shareholders, since private investors tend to be less fickle and more stable than institutional investors. The investment bank should also be able to provide the IPO with support after the offering by way of financial advice, buying and selling stock, and helping to create and maintain interest in the stock over the long term.

Once chosen, the underwriter will draw up a letter of intent, which will outline the terms and conditions of the agreement between the underwriter

 Entrepreneurship in Action

How One IPO Happened

In 1986, Huib Geerlings and Phillip Wade founded G&W, a wine-by-mail concept that took advantage of two significant trends: mail order and the increase in consumption of premium wines. Their target market was customers who wanted to be educated on wines and how to appreciate them. In 1993, a window of opportunity opened for them to go public on sales of more than $6.4 million. Here is how it happened:

▶ Understanding completely that most investment banking firms would rather do a $100 million deal for the same effort as a $10 million deal, Geerlings and Wade began their search for an underwriter.

▶ After turn-downs by the major investment banking houses, they received a call from Needham & Company, a small New York house specializing in high-tech offerings that wanted to diversify into retail and particularly wine. They became G&W's investment banker in the spring of 1994.

▶ Needham & Company then sought a co-manager to arrange the road show, help create a market, and provide research. Fechtor & Detwiler, the firm that agreed to co-manage, also brought along 40 brokers who ultimately sold-one third of the offering. This represented significant retail interest that would boost the IPO's price and increase activity in the aftermarket.

▶ The registration statement, which documents the terms of the IPO in addition to the company's management, history, and financial condition, was drafted over a period of two months and 16-hour days in 1994. When it was ready, the company still hadn't received approval from NASDAQ for a stock listing. Ultimately NASDAQ declined, saying that G&W's financials didn't meet its requirements. This was a crucial point be-

cause G&W would now be relegated to NASDAQ's small cap market, which would definitely not attract substantial investors.

▶ Finally, on May 5, 1994, NASDAQ acquiesced and allowed G&W to file with the SEC.

▶ The SEC then spent 45 days critiquing the document while G&W distributed its "red herring," or preliminary prospectus, subject to completion. (When the SEC is satisfied with the disclosures, it declares the offering to be "effective" and the IPO can be sold to the public.)

▶ Immediately after filing, Wade, Geerlings, and their investment banker embarked on a three-week road show to present their company to institutional investors and fund managers.

▶ On June 16, 1994, based on the bids of fund managers contacted during the road show, the shares were priced at $8, less than the $9 to $11 projected. But this pricing reflected the current slump in the IPO market, and Wade and Geerlings had to decide whether or not to take it. They took it.

▶ In December, G&W stock reached $16 and landed at number 70 on the 1995 Inc. 100 fastest-growing companies list.

▶ On the day of the IPO, the founders, Geerlings and Wade, held $8.4 million and $6.7 million, respectively—which included $744,000 in cash—and the company received $8.5 million in new funds. At the same time, the founders' share of ownership went from 80 percent to less than 48 percent.

SOURCE: Robert A. Mamis, "The Making of a Millionaire," *Inc.,* May 1995, p. 86.

and the entrepreneur/selling stockholder. It will normally specify a price range for the stock, which is a tricky issue at best. Typically, underwriters estimate the price at which the stock will be sold by using a price/earnings multiple common for companies within the same industry as the IPO. That multiple is then applied to the IPO's earnings per share. This is only a rough estimate. The actual going-out price will not be determined until the night before the offering. If the entrepreneur is unhappy with the final price, the only choice is to cancel the offering, a highly unpalatable option after months of work and expense.

A registration statement must be filed with the SEC. This document is known as a **red herring**, or prospectus, because it discusses all the potential risks of investing in the IPO. This prospectus will also be given to anyone interested in investing in the IPO. Following the registration statement, an advertisement in the financial press, called a **tombstone**, announces the offering. The prospectus is valid for a period of nine months; after that time, the information becomes outdated and cannot be used except by officially amending the registration statement.

Another major decision that must be made is on which exchange to list the offering. In the past, smaller IPOs automatically listed on the AMEX (American Stock Exchange) or NASDAQ (National Association of Securities Dealers Automated Quotation) only because they couldn't meet the qualifications of the NYSE (New York Stock Exchange). Today, however, NASDAQ, which lists companies such as Microsoft and Intel Corporation, is the fastest-growing exchange in the nation. There is a difference between the way NASDAQ and the other exchanges operate. The NYSE and AMEX are auction markets with securities traded on the floor of the exchange, enabling investors to trade directly with one another. The NASDAQ, on the other hand, is a floorless exchange that trades on the National Market System through a system of broker-dealers from respected securities firms who compete for orders. In addition to these three are regional exchanges, such as the Pacific and Boston stock exchanges, that are less costly alternatives for a small, growing company.

The high point of the IPO process is the road show, a two-week, whirlwind tour of all the major institutional investors by the entrepreneur and the IPO team to market the offering. This is done so that once the registration statement has met all of the SEC requirements and the stock is priced, the offering can virtually be sold in a day. The coming-out price will determine the amount of proceeds to the IPO company, but those holding stock prior to the IPO will often see the value of their stock increase substantially immediately after the IPO. See Figure 18.3 for a summary of the IPO process.

Strategic Alliances

Earlier chapters discussed how to use strategic alliances to create the virtual company or grow the business. Strategic alliances with larger companies are also an excellent source of growth capital for young companies. Sometimes the partnership results in major financial and equity investments in the grow-

Choose an underwriter

Underwriter draws up
letter of intent

Registration statement
filed with SEC

Tombstone placed in
financial press

Choose stock exchange

Road show

Public offering

**Figure 18.3
The IPO Process**

ing venture. Such was the case of United Parcel Service of America, which acquired a 9.5 percent ownership interest in Mail Boxes Etc. for $11.3 million. This gave Mail Boxes Etc. capital to grow and UPS additional pickup and drop-off outlets. Growing companies that link with established companies can usually get a better deal than they would have gotten from a venture capitalist. In addition, they derive some associated benefits that give them more credibility in the marketplace. The large, investing partner is, at a minimum, looking for a return of the cost of capital, but in general a return of at least 10 percent on the investment.

Strategic alliances are every bit as tricky as partnerships, so it's important that the entrepreneur evaluate the potential partner carefully in addition to doing "due diligence" on the company. It is also crucial not to focus on one partner but consider several before making a final decision. For the partnership to really work, the benefits should flow in both directions; that is, both partners should derive cost savings and/or revenue enhancement from the relationship. It is probably best not to form a partnership that requires one of the partners (usually the smaller company) to be too heavily dependent on the other for a substantial portion of its revenue-generating capability. That is a dangerous position to be in should the partnership dissolve for any reason.

Valuing the Business

A key component of any growth strategy is determining the value of the company, since a realistic value figure will be needed no matter which financial strategy is undertaken to raise growth capital. However, it should be understood at the outset that *value* is a subjective term with myriad meanings. In fact, at least six different definitions of value are in common usage (see Figure 18.4):

▶ **Fair market value.** This is the price at which a willing seller would sell and a willing buyer would buy in an arm's-length transaction. By this definition, every sale would ultimately constitute a fair market value sale.

▶ **Intrinsic value.** This is perceived value arrived at by interpreting balance sheet and income statements through the use of ratios, discounting cash flow projections, and calculating liquidated asset value.

▶ **Investment value.** This is the worth of the business to an investor and is based on the individual requirements of the investor as to risk, return, tax benefits, and so forth.

The Real World of Entrepreneurship

Getting the Deal to Close

Some entrepreneurs choose to become business owners by buying an existing business. The concern becomes how to get the money to do the deal without sacrificing too much of your future equity.

Bill Black, owner of Dorchester Publishing Company, started his quest for the company by using the experiences of his consulting clients as a guide to what to do and not to do. His first contact was a venture capitalist who would do the deal only if he took the company public, something Black was not interested in. Finally, he found an investor who specialized in his industry. With a combination of investor money and bank debt, Black was able to structure a deal that suited everyone's needs.

M. John Storey, author of *Taking Money Out of Your Corporation,* believes you can find your best deal by

1. Focusing on offers that meet your criteria rather than taking a shotgun approach.

2. Talking to the specialists in your industry. They are the ones who ultimately control whether or not you can make the deal.

3. Not being discouraged if you fail several times before you get what you want.

4. Focusing on finding equity and debt partners who have the same goals you do and building long-term relationships with them.

SOURCE: M. John Storey, "Clinch the Big Deal," *Success,* September 1995, p. 29.

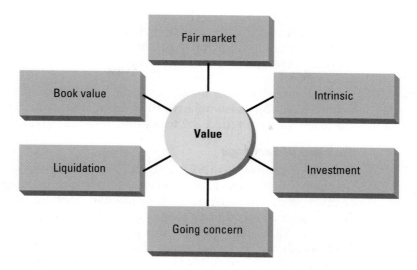

Figure 18.4
Definitions of Value

▶ **Going-concern value.** This is the current status of the business as measured by financial statements, debt load, and economic environmental factors, such as government regulation, that may affect the long-term continuation of the business.

▶ **Liquidation value.** This value assumes the selling off of all assets and calculating the amount that could be recovered from doing so.

▶ **Book value.** This is an accounting measure of value and refers to the difference between total assets and total liability. It is essentially equivalent to shareholders' or owners' equity.

See page 514 for an example of how one company valued its business.

Methods for Valuing a Business

There are numerous ways to value a business. Here we will focus on three methods that are in common use: adjusted book value, multiple of earnings, and discounted cash flow.

Adjusted Book Value

The **book value** of a going concern is simply the owner's equity, that is, the value of the assets less the outstanding debts. Adjusted book value is based on balance sheet items. The difficulty with this method lies in how assets are valued—as realizable value or as liquidation value.[7] Cash and near-cash items are easily valued, but in the case of accounts receivable, not all are readily collectible. You will need to know what your bad-debt rate is so that you can deduct it and provide a better estimate. But there will also be costs associated with collecting that have to be taken into account. Land and facilities have real estate market value that an appraiser would have to estimate. In short, both inflation and depreciation affect the value of all assets to some degree. Therefore, balance sheet items are adjusted upward or downward to reflect their fair market value.

Be aware that since many entrepreneurial companies in the early stages tend to have few assets relative to firms at later stages of development, this approach may not reflect the true value of the company.

Multiple of Earnings

Using a price/earnings (P/E) ratio to value a business is a common method among publicly owned companies because it's simple and direct. It consists of dividing the market price of the common stock by the earnings per share. For example, if a company has 200,000 shares of common stock and its net income is $250,000, the earnings per share will be 200,000/$250,000, or $.80 per share. If the price per share rose to $3, the price/earnings ratio would be $3/$.80, or 3.75. The business would then be valued at $750,000 (200,000 shares × 3.75).

Another method that typically results in a higher valuation is using a year's worth of after-tax earnings and multiplying it by the industry average multiple based on the P/E ratios of public companies in the industry. This method must be considered with care. To say that a young, private company with earnings of $250,000 in an industry where the average P/E is 12 should be valued at $3 million probably is overstating the case. It has been suggested that public firms have a premium value of about 25 percent to 35 percent over a closely held company, and so any P/E multiple used should be discounted to reflect that premium.[8] That would mean that our private com-

Entrepreneurship in Action

How One Company Valued Its Business

Physician Dispensing Systems, Inc., is a Philadelphia-based medical information company that needed to raise $1 million to launch the business. Its founder, Frank Martin, did not want to give up control of the company in the process. The first step was to value the price of the stock shares to determine the value of the company as a whole. The most common method of doing this is the price/earnings multiple or ratio, which says that a company will trade at a multiple of earnings. For example, Standard and Poor's *Analysts' Handbook* indicates that miscellaneous health care companies traded at 20.4 times earnings in the fourth quarter of 1994.

Martin estimated that by the end of 1996, the company was earning $1 million net after tax. Using the mul-

tiple of 20, the total value for the company would be $20 million. Applying a 50 percent discount rate—the rate typically used by investment bankers—and discounting the $20 million in 1996 back to 1994, the present value was calculated as $10 million. The $1 million of financing he was seeking represented 10 percent of the total value and also the percentage of ownership Martin would have had to give up in exchange.

The important lesson to learn from Martin's experience is to justify the highest multiple possible for the company because investors will discount it. This is usually accomplished by showing better margins than comparable companies or the potential for higher growth.

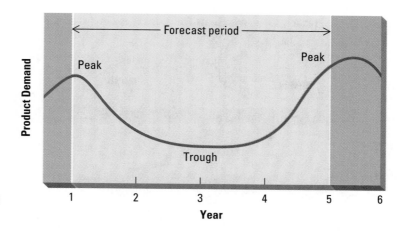

Figure 18.5
Business Cycles and
the Forecast Period

pany now has a value of $2,250,000 ($250,000 × 9). Even with discounting, the variation in the ways a company can calculate earnings and the difficulty in finding a public company that is comparable often make this a dubious measure at best for purposes of valuation.

Discounting Cash Flows

If valuing the business by its potential earning power is the goal, the most common measure and the one that gives more accurate results is future cash flows, because only cash or cash equivalents are used in the calculations. The method is called **discounted cash flow analysis** or *capitalization of future cash flows to the present value.* This simply means calculating how much an investor would pay today to have a cash flow stream of X dollars for X number of years into the future.

For this analysis, the entrepreneur uses pro forma cash flow statements for the business and determines a forecast period. (Refer to Chapters 15 and 16 for discussions of pro forma cash flows and methods for forecasting sales and expenses.) The length and nature of business cycles in the industry must also be understood so that a forecast period that goes either from trough to trough or peak to peak in a cycle is chosen. In other words, there needs to be at least one complete business cycle within the forecast period to give a fair representation of the effect on cash flow (see Figure 18.5).

Once the forecast period has been defined and the cash flow projections prepared, a discount rate must be chosen. This is not a purely arbitrary exercise. The buyer or investor's point of view must be considered, and that viewpoint will often involve the opportunity cost to the investor/buyer of investing in or buying the business. It has been suggested that the decision should be based on three factors:

1. The rate achievable in a risk-free investment such as U.S. Treasury notes over a comparable time period. For example, for a five-year forecast, the current rate on a five-year note is appropriate.

Table 18.2 One Method for Discounting Cash Flows

Assume: 6% risk-free rate
           + 14% risk factor (category 2 business)
           20% discount rate

Discount the cash flow:

End of Year	Cash Flow ($000)	Factor (20%)	Present Value ($000)
1	$200	.8333	$166.7
2	250	.6944	173.6
3	300	.5787	173.6
4	375	.4823	180.9
5	450	.4019	180.9
Totals	**$1,575**		**$874.7**

2. A risk factor based on the type of business and the industry should be added to the interest rate in item 1. Several precedents for determining what these factors are have been established over years of study. One accepted standard is that offered by James Schilt[9] in the form of five categories of business. Note that even within each category there is room for degrees of risk.

   a. Category 1: Established businesses with good market share, excellent management, and a stable history of earnings: *6–10%*

   b. Category 2: Established businesses in more competitive industries, still with good market share, excellent management, and a stable earnings history: *11–15%*

   c. Category 3: Growing businesses in very competitive industries, little capital investment, an average management team, and a stable earnings history: *16–20%*

   d. Category 4: Small businesses dependent on the entrepreneur or larger businesses in very volatile industries, and the lack of a predictable earnings picture: *21–25%*

   e. Category 5: Small service businesses operating as sole proprietorships: *26–30%*

3. The life expectancy of the business, because typically discounting is based on this factor.

The example in Table 18.2 illustrates this valuation method. Assuming the current rate on a 10-year Treasury note is 6 percent and the business is a category 2 business at a 14 percent risk factor, the adjusted discount rate becomes 20 percent. Using a calculator or a present value table, the present value of the five-year cash flow stream can be calculated. This example shows that this hypothetical business will throw off $1,575,000 of positive cash flow over five years. Hence, a buyer would be willing to pay $875,000 today for that business, given the discount rate.

If three scenarios have been created—best-, worst-, and most-likely cases or success, survival, and liquidation—there will be three values for the business. The entrepreneur then assigns a probability of occurrence to each scenario and multiplies the discounted cash flow by that probability to arrive at an adjusted present value.

A variation of this method is the *excess earnings method*, which combines the estimate of future earnings with the value of the business's existing assets minus liabilities. The advantage of this approach is that it accounts for *goodwill*, which is an intangible asset that represents the difference between an unproven business and an established, successful one. In brief, this method has the following steps:

1. Compute the adjusted tangible net worth of the business. Tangible assets are adjusted up or down for market value; then liabilities are subtracted.

2. Compute the opportunity cost of this investment. How much would the investor/buyer earn by investing the same amount in another, comparable investment?

3. Forecast net earnings. Earnings from previous income statements can provide a basis for the forecast, which is made before subtracting the owner's salary.

4. Calculate the extra earning power, which is the difference between forecasted earnings and opportunity costs.

5. Estimate the value of intangible assets or goodwill. If your business has extra earning power (some small businesses and family businesses do not), you can multiply that figure by what is known as a *years-of-profit (YOP)* figure. An average business will have a YOP of 3 to 4; a high risk business may have a YOP of 1; and an established business may have a YOP of 7.[10]

6. Calculate the value of the business by adding the figures up.

Once a mathematical estimate of value has been achieved, other factors will come into play that are difficult to put into the equation and are more rightly points of negotiation. All the projections used in the valuation of the business are based on assumptions, and the buyer/investor will likely question them and perhaps discount the value of the business even further. Another factor affecting the final valuation is the degree of legitimate control the owner has in the business. This is typically measured by the amount of stock the owner holds. Buying out an owner who holds the majority of the stock is more valuable than buying out one who does not. Finally, intangibles such as a loyal-customer list, intellectual property, and the like will also create additional value for the business. The "real" value or market value of the business will be ultimately determined through negotiation with investors, lenders, or underwriters. However, doing the calculations just discussed provides an excellent jumping-off point for the negotiations.

As careful as these procedures are, they still have a significant "crystal ball" aspect because at several critical points in the process, the entrepreneur makes subjective decisions. There is really no way to avoid this dilemma. It has been estimated that new ventures encounter more than 300 significant unexpected events that will substantially affect the business in the first three years of its life alone, and there is no way to factor all those variables into the equation.[11] Nevertheless, business owners, recognizing that everyone interprets value differently, should be prepared to discuss and defend the assumptions used to estimate value.

The bottom line is that there is no best way to value a business, particularly since each situation is different. The most prudent approach is probably to use several techniques and, through negotiation with the investor/buyer, determine the one that makes the most sense for the situation and is a win-win solution for both parties.

Return to the Investor

While the entrepreneur is attempting to place a value on the business as a whole, the potential investor/owner is looking at the business in terms of what it will *return to the investor/owner.* This is a very specific type of return and includes three categories of items: cash flow returns, appreciation, and tax benefits.

▶ *Cash flow returns.* The investor/owner can receive the benefits of cash flow through "perks" such as expense accounts and company cars, the repayment of debt (which is a tax-free transaction), interest, salary, and dividends. Each of these has personal advantages and disadvantages for the investor/owner.

▶ *Appreciation.* The investor/owner can sell off a portion of his or her interest in the company and enjoy a tax-free event up to the amount of his or her cost basis.

▶ *Tax benefits.* The investor/owner may be able to receive pass-through losses, which generally occur in the early years of a venture, if the business has elected a Subchapter S corporation status.

This chapter has focused on methods for valuing and funding young, growing businesses. Valuation is by its very nature an incremental process that involves bringing together key pieces of information that will (hopefully) give some insight into the health and future of the business. In all discussions of value, you should be clear on whose definition of value is being used and justify your own definition. The type of growth funding you will need will be a function of your growth strategy, the potential value of your business in the marketplace, the track record of the management team, and your ability to excite potential investors/lenders/buyers about the future of your business. If you have kept complete business records since you started or acquired your business, if you have had a successful start-up, and if you have developed a sound growth strategy, you will likely find it easier to locate growth funding than you did finding start-up funding.

Harvesting the Wealth

Entrepreneurship—owning a successful growing company—has always been one of the great sources of wealth creation in the world. A well-conceived business has value apart from its founders. In other words, it continues creating value and wealth even when the original founders leave.

Why would an entrepreneur ever leave a business that took so much effort and heart and soul to create? The fact is that although many entrepreneurs remain with their businesses throughout their lives, the majority decide to reap the rewards of their hard work by passing the business to a family member, selling it, or taking it public, and moving on to something else. In fact, to some entrepreneurs, starting a business is exciting and challenging, but managing a business is frustrating and mundane, so they move from venture to venture at the optimal time.

Whether you decide to stay with your business or leave, you will probably want to enjoy some of the wealth your business has created. There are several ways to accomplish this depending on whether or not you want to remain a part of the business in some manner: going public, selling the business, taking your cash out but remaining a part of the business, merging with another company, selling to your employees, and liquidating the business.

Knowing how you might want to harvest your wealth at some point in the future will help you make decisions along the way from the start of the business that will ensure you are headed in the right direction. To help you think about a harvest or exit plan, here are three steps you should take as early as possible in the life of your business:

1. Create a small, informal advisory board to guide you in your personal wealth planning. You might include an accountant, a tax attorney, and an estate planning expert. These people could actually be a subset of your more formal advisory board or board of directors.

2. Find a mentor who is leading the type of life you would enjoy and whom you would like to emulate. In general, successful entrepreneurs enjoy helping new entrepreneurs build their success.

3. Begin to focus on the aspects of your company that create value. Following are just a few:

   ▶ Do you have any intellectual property? If not, can you acquire any?

   ▶ Do you have a loyal customer base?

   ▶ Do you have or can you acquire assets that hold their value?

   ▶ Do you have a successful network of vendors, suppliers, distributors, salespeople, manufacturers, and professional advisers?

   ▶ Does your company have a system of incentives and a company culture that encourages employees to remain loyal?

Going Public

Earlier in this chapter, you learned about going public as a growth financing mechanism. Going public is also a way to harvest some of the wealth your company has created as well as recapture your initial investment. You may be able to structure an IPO deal that will pay you a portion of the funds you receive when the offering is sold.[12] A note of caution here: it's not a good idea to remove all of your investment in the business, because this sends a negative signal to stockholders who have just committed to its growth.

Selling the Business

If you would like to leave the business behind with no strings attached, the best solution may be to sell it outright. However, it's important to realize that for most entrepreneurs, selling a business you created from scratch is much more than a financial event; it's a very emotional event. And unless it's done very carefully with this in mind, you may regret the action later on. To ease the situation, you will want to find a buyer who understands the culture and values of the business you created because, certainly long before you ever thought of selling the business, your employees had already bought into that culture. Bringing aboard a new owner who has entirely different values would definitely create a culture shock. You want to be certain that the new owner will also carry on the traditions and reputation you have built up because, like it or not, you and your name will be associated with that business long after it has been sold.

The advantage of selling the business is that unless you agree to carry back debt for the new owner, you will receive your investment and capital gains in the sale. You will also be free to move on to other ventures without being tied in any way to the old one, should that be your choice.

Cashing Out but Staying In

There are several ways to remove your investment in whole or in part from the business while remaining involved in some way. You could *sell your stock* to other stockholders in the company at current market rates, assuming your shareholders' agreement allows you to do this.

If you would like to take money out of the company and put control in the hands of your children, you might consider *splitting the company in two.* You would retain control of the company that holds all the assets, such as plant and equipment, while your children would own and manage the operations of the business and lease the assets from you. In this way, you will derive an income stream off the leases.

You can also do what is known as a *phased sale,* in which you choose to sell in stages. For example, you might sell in two stages. In the first, you sell off a portion of the business but retain control of operations until the company has reached an agreed-on point. You then sell the remaining portion to the buyer.

Nautica's founder, David Chu, was looking for a way to sell his business but stay involved in it, because his real passion is design. In 1984, he sold his apparel company to State-O-Maine, Inc. (which took the Nautica name in 1993) and stayed on as executive vice president and head of design. In that position he saw the company revenues grow from $121 million in 1992 to $387 million in 1997. (Susan Salinger)

Merging

Doing a **merger** of your company with another is a cross between a sale and a partnership. Depending on how you structure the deal, you may be able to cash out some of your holdings and stay on in a paid management capacity. Or you may negotiate to sit on the board of directors of the other company. When considering the merger route, it's important to look very carefully at the other company. Make sure the two companies have similar goals, operations, and culture. Trying to merge two completely different companies is a strategy bound for failure. It's also important that the companies be located fairly close to each other to permit effective management and that the purchasing company be part of a growth industry.

Selling to Employees

If you own a company with more than 25 employees, have an annual payroll of at least $500,000, and have revenues of at least $5 million, you may be a candidate for an **employee stock ownership plan** or **ESOP**. This approach lets you cash out of the company but remain in control. Many entrepreneurs who believe employees should become owners in the company have chosen this route. In essence, ESOPs are tax-qualified pension plans governed by the Employee Retirement Income Security Act (ERISA) and IRS regulations. Basically it works as follows:

1. An ESOP trust fund is established, and new or existing shares of stock are placed in it. You can also elect to take out a bank loan to buy stock and a minority interest in the company of at least 30 percent so that any cash the owners receive from the ESOP is not taxed if they reinvest it in U.S. stocks or bonds.[13]

2. Your company then makes tax-deductible contributions to the trust of up to 25 percent of the payroll to repay any bank debt.

This process can take several years, or at least as long as it takes to repay the bank loan if one was used.

ESOPs have many advantages, but they are expensive to set up and maintain. If yours is a private company, you will have to repurchase the stock of any employees who leave the company. The biggest implication of an ESOP is that you must now share much more information with your employees than you may have previously. If you are not a believer in open-book management, you may not be happy with an ESOP strategy.

Liquidation

Liquidation is certainly not the exit strategy entrepreneurs would plan for or purposely choose if they could avoid it. There are two forms of liquidation: (1) when there is little marketable value in the business and (2) when the business can no longer survive.

Liquidating When the Business Has No Marketable Value

Many businesses, particularly sole proprietorships such as services and small retail operations, cannot effectively exist without the owner. The products and services provided derive directly from the expertise of the owner and are not easily passed on to others. Generally, in these types of businesses, a buyer will purchase only inventory and assets such as equipment and supplies or perhaps a customer list. Under this scenario, the owner is lucky to break even or make a small amount of gain.

One way to attempt to achieve a higher valuation for your small business is to do a reverse merger. Your company will become part of a large public shell, a corporation that is registered with the SEC but does no actual business. So, in effect, you merge with several small companies whose common goal is to increase the valuation of the individual business. When the shell has acquired enough small companies, it does a public offering and the small-company owners receive proceeds from the sale of their stock. This is a highly complex transaction that requires the services of a good attorney.

Liquidating When the Business Can't Survive

When the business is upside down and can no longer generate enough cash flow to meet its obligations, the only solution may be to liquidate the assets and discharge the debts through a **Chapter 7 bankruptcy** proceeding. The goal of this type of liquidation is to reduce the assets of the business to cash and distribute that cash to the creditors. Any surplus funds remaining after claimants have been paid will go to the business owner. Bankruptcy should always be considered a last resort. If your business is showing signs of trouble that could lead to failure, consult a specialist in turnarounds in your industry. Also, have your accountant audit your books to see if you might qualify for **Chapter 11 reorganization**, which would allow you to continue in business while you work out a plan to repay creditors. The ramifications of bankruptcy remain on your personal credit history for a long time in the case of sole proprietorships, partnerships, or instances where the owner has used personal guarantees, so don't make the decision without careful consideration of all alternative courses.

Here are some tips that will help you avoid a situation that could result in bankruptcy:[14]

1. Don't ever rely on only one customer for the majority of your revenues.

2. Always keep overhead expenses to a minimum. Remember, these expenses have to be paid even when no revenues are coming into the business.

3. Remain as liquid as possible; for example, keep several months of overhead expense in your account to meet unexpected situations.

4. Always keep your financial advisers apprised of the current condition of your company so there are no surprises and so they can offer advice before it's too late.

Succession Planning

Planning to have someone take over for you in the business is as important as any other component of your business planning. Succession planning is usually thought of in reference to family businesses where it's assumed that the next generation will take over the business. This is because more than 80 percent of all businesses in the United States are family owned. But succession planning is equally important for non-family-owned businesses. Over time you will have developed a cadre of loyal employees who have worked their way up in terms of responsibility and authority. They are the equivalent of the next generation in a family business.

Because family members and loyal employees often assume they will be considered to replace the owner when he or she leaves the business, it's important to put a succession strategy in place as early as possible in the life of the business. It doesn't have to be detailed, but it should lead to some broad policies to guide the decision-making process when the time comes. These broad policies may include

▶ An equitable way to determine whether or not outside talent must be brought in to compensate for a lack of appropriate skills on the part of insiders

▶ A probationary period for insiders to give them a chance to prove they are capable of doing the job

▶ A set of criteria that applies to both insiders and outsiders

▶ A plan for compensation at fair market value

In the unique case of a family member, it's important to understand that the succession process often begins when the family member is still a child becoming aware of the business and his or her potential role in it. Later, as the child becomes a teenager, he or she can work part time in the business to get a better grasp of how it works from the inside. When education is completed, the child may work for the company full time in a nonmanagerial role leading to management experience as she or he demonstrates readiness for it. When the time comes for the son or daughter to transition to the presidency of the company, the transition should take place over a period of about two years so that he or she can serve an apprenticeship in the role before assuming complete control. The same is true for an employee who may be assuming the role of president. It would be important for that employee to go through a period of apprenticeship before taking on the position fully.

Turning your business over to someone who knows it inside and out and understands and believes in the company's vision will facilitate the transition. For this reason, many of the most successful companies promote from within. If you do decide to turn the position of president over to an insider, make sure that you constantly look for fresh points of view in other important positions in the company. This will prevent the company from becoming so entrenched in tradition that it will be unable to change quickly to meet the demands of the marketplace.

Harvesting the wealth of a successful business venture is one of the great rewards of entrepreneurship. But it is the journey to the harvest that will determine how successful the harvest is. Planning early in the life of your business for growth and an eventual harvest will go a long way toward ensuring that you reach your goals.

Cases Relevant to This Chapter

Zanart Entertainment
Pelco
SB Networks
Marcus Food Co. and Buckhead Beef

Issues for Review and Discussion

1. Discuss three ways companies can finance their start-up and growth with debt.
2. What is meant by the "cost of raising capital"?
3. Explain the four components of any investment deal.
4. Discuss the differences among the six definitions of value as they pertain to a growing business.
5. Explain the differences among an IPO, a DPO, and a SCOR offering.
6. Describe two ways you can harvest the wealth your business has created.

Experiencing Entrepreneurship

1. Secure a copy of the SCOR U-7 from your state's security agency and make a list of the information required to process a registration for a small corporate offering. How is this different from the requirements for an IPO?
2. Interview a business owner with a growing company about his or her financial strategy for growth.

Resources

Bokser, Denise (1998). *Pratt's Guide to Venture Capital Sources: 1998* (22nd ed.). Newark, NJ: Venture Economics (1-800-455-5844).

Bygrave, W. D, and J. A. Timmons (1992). *Venture Capital at the Crossroads*. Cambridge, MA: Harvard Business School Press.

Canadian Reciprocal Trade Association, Box 82008, Burnaby, BC V5C 5P2 (604-521-7911; fax: 604-521-7944).

Diener, Royce (1995). *How to Finance a Growing Business: An Insider's Guide to Negotiating the Capital Markets*. Berkeley, CA: Nolo Press (1-800-638-7597).

Editors of *Inc.* (1998). *The Best of Inc. Guide to Finding Capital*. Englewood Cliffs, NJ: Prentice Hall-Press.

Garner, D. (1991). *The Ernst & Young Guide to Raising Capital*. New York: John Wiley & Sons.

Gladstone, D. (1988). *Venture Capital Handbook*. Englewood Cliffs, NJ: Prentice-Hall.

Hicks, T. G. (1990). *Business Capital Sources*. Rockville Centre, NY: International Wealth Success, Inc.

International Reciprocal Trade Association, 6305 Hawaii Court, Alexandria, VA 22312 (703-237-1829).

Tuller, L. W. (1994). *Small Business Valuation Book*. Holbrook, MA: Bob Adams, Inc.

Venture Capital Journal. Newark, NJ: Venture Economics (1-800-455-5844).

Internet Resources
FinanceHub: Venture Capital on the Web
http://www.financehub.com/
This site contains a database of 11,000 investors and links to many venture firms.

Foundation Center
http://fdncenter.org/
A nonprofit organization designed to help individuals and organizations find funding from foundations and philanthropists.

Price Waterhouse LLP National Venture Capital Survey
http://www.pw.com/vc/
This site contains a quarterly survey of venture capital trends and results from around the nation.

A Venture Capital Analysis
http://www.kcilink.com/brc/financing/vent-capt.html
This site will help you determine whether or not venture capital is right for your business.

VII

Building a Business with Character

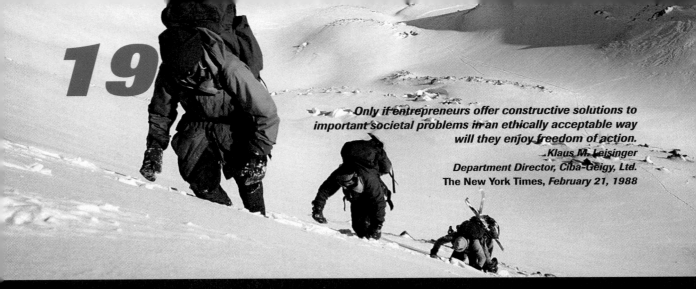

Only if entrepreneurs offer constructive solutions to important societal problems in an ethically acceptable way will they enjoy freedom of action.

Klaus M. Leisinger
Department Director, Ciba-Geigy, Ltd.
The New York Times, February 21, 1988

Ethics and Social Responsibility

Preview

Understanding this chapter will give you the ability to

▶ **Discuss the source of ethics.**

▶ **Explain some ways to develop a code of ethics for your company.**

▶ **Explain what social responsibility is and how your company can achieve it.**

Terms to Know

Psychological egoism, 533
Ethical egoism, 533
Ethical relativism, 533
Ethical subjectivism, 533
Utilitarian theories, 533
Theories of justice, 534
Theories of virtue, 534
Integrity-based programs, 534
Spamming, 539

Young Entrepreneurs—Minicase

Justin Butchert
Kings River Expeditions

Knowledge is power, and nowhere is that more apparent than when your business is with Mother Nature. Justin Butchert learned that lesson at eighteen when he took a job as a rookie guide with a river rafting company on the Kings River in Central California.

Fearless, like most young men his age, Butchert never thought anything could go wrong. But in his 18th year the snowpack in the Sierra Nevada was substantial. One spring Saturday the temperature rose way above normal. The runoff caused the rivers to rise dramatically. Butchert recalls that "it was a completely different river." Upon completing the first set of rapids, his boat with its load of customers hit what is known as a reversal hole. Butchert was thrown from the raft and found himself stuck in a hole from which he had to fight his way out. Unable to find his own rafting party, he swam about a mile until he found another boat that took him to camp. He recalls spending the next couple of days on his bike riding alongside the river studying its patterns. The experience taught him that he must always have respect for the river.

For a year after graduating from high school, Butchert traveled the country in his truck with a camper attached. While skiing in a blizzard in Yosemite he came to a major turning point in his life. There he met the cousin of the owner of Kings River Expeditions (KRE), a white-water rafting company in the central Sierra Nevada mountains, who convinced him to apply for a job as a river guide. Butchert did so and in 1978 began what was to become his life on the river.

In Butchert's fourth year at KRE, the owner decided to sell the business. At the time, Butchert owned a small cabinet shop and was expecting to spend his life in the construction business. But the opportunity to own KRE and to spend his time on the river he loved was just too great to pass up. At twenty-two, he faced the enormous challenge of needing to raise $250,000 to buy the business. Just like that fateful day on the river four years earlier when he had fallen out of the boat, luck was with him and he managed to meet two men 30 years older than he who believed in what he wanted to do. The other men came in as partners, offering Butchert all the money he needed to purchase the business. In 1981 the three formed a corporation and proceeded to buy all new equipment in order to build a first-class operation.

What the men bought was essentially goodwill, so they were virtually starting from scratch. The goodwill consisted of the customer base and the permit to operate on the river granted by the U.S. Forest Service. The Forest Service grants a maximum of three companies the right to operate on the Kings River, and since there were already three companies running, the only way Butchert could have done it was by purchasing an existing company. The partners broke even in the first year of operations after starting with 7–9 full-time seasonal employees and 600–800 customers. Today the company has 45 full-time employees and averages 9,000 customers a season.

The possibility for growth on the rafting side of the business is limited by the Forest Service. Still, Butchert has managed to grow his operations by offering "eco-tours," international adventure tours to such places as Costa Rica, where customers can raft, snorkel, kayak and rock climb along with a variety of other outdoor activities.

Butchert, who spent more than seven years as a guide on the rafting expeditions, now spends his days in a kayak alongside the rafts filming the many exciting (and often hilarious) events that occur. Using professional video editing equipment at the base camp, he's able to quickly prepare a video of the day's events that is shown at the evening meal.

Butchert learned the value of ethics early in his business career. In the industry it is common practice to employ illegal aliens from Costa Rica and New Zealand who come to the States to work while their own countries are in the off season. These people are paid cash and never count as employees, thereby avoiding payroll taxes. As a very young man, Butchert faced the temptation of becoming impressed by the success of people in the industry even though he knew that they were not leading exemplary lives. When Butchert finally met the partners who joined him in buying KRE, he learned a whole new lesson about ethics and trust. These partners did business on a handshake; their word was their bond. And it has been that way for the seventeen years they've been in business together. From them Butchert quickly learned that "if you treat people fairly, that comes back to you." The reverse is true as well: if you're not fair with people, it will eventually catch up with you.

Butchert will never let either money or business sway him from his ethics. During the spring of 1998, when weather patterns were severely affected by the *El Nino* effect, the King River sped up, moving thousands of cubic feet per second faster than normal. Butchert actually cancelled trips that included children under the age of thirteen because he believed it was too dangerous.

Today Justin "Jeb" Butchert leads the life he has always wanted. He spends a minimum of 200 days a year outdoors. He has also taken his love for outdoor sports into the classroom. California State University at Fresno asked him to teach several courses in the recreation department. There he inspires college students to challenge themselves in all sorts of outdoor activities. Along with his business partners and the U.S. Forest Service, he has sponsored the San Joaquin Valley Young Leaders Organization (YLO), a unique program that gives rural youngsters from diverse socioeconomic backgrounds the opportunity to participate in a three-year program that develops leadership skills through a variety of participatory and travel experiences.

Author's Note: At the time this interview took place, Justin told me in no uncertain terms that I needed to "experience" his business to be able to write about it. Three days later, he had me up at the base camp on the Kings River ready to begin a day-long adventure on the river. The "put-in" for the river trip is ten miles upstream. You reach it via an old white school bus on a single lane dirt road, one side of which is a sheer cliff to the river below. It is rumored that if you survive the bus trip, the river seems easy. The staff who drive the bus do it day in and day out. So driving backwards across a narrow bridge and backing downhill on the one-lane road to let another vehicle pass are just part of the day's work. Needless to say, it gives the passengers some breathtaking moments.

At the start of the journey, the quaint old bus is packed shoulder to shoulder with rafters who are feeling quite warm in their skin-tight wetsuits. That problem is soon solved, however. As the bus takes off, windows down, one of the staff turns a hose on the startled rafters in the bus. This helps cool us down for a while as the bus jolts its way up the mountain.

At the launch site, with safety checks over and boats and guides assigned, we're finally on the river. The summer of 1998 has seen some of the highest river volumes in many years. Rapids are plentiful and waves are huge. Within less than a minute of being on the river, we hit the first rapids and desperately try to remember everything we were told so that we don't fall out of the boat and become what the guides facetiously refer to as "swimmers." For two hours we make our way down the river, tackling each new challenge with growing confidence and more frequent high fives with the paddles to celebrate our victories. Justin can often be seen zipping around in his one-man kayak, filming everyone at each turn of events. We make it the entire length of the journey without losing a single person from the raft. Back at camp, 60 tired but happy rafters celebrate well into the evening with tall tales and fond remembrances.

Justin was right. His business is one that has to be experienced. For someone who spends a great deal of time in front of a computer screen, I found that this physically challenging trip on the Kings River rapids to be the perfect complement to the mental exhaustion of the daily work in my business. To be successful as an entrepreneur requires balance. And sometimes that sense of balance comes from doing things that are as far removed from what you normally do as possible.

Justin Butchert has found a unique sense of balance in his life. He has balanced making money and being socially responsible with having fun and doing what he loves.

What are some other ways Justin Butchert can demonstrate his company's social responsibility?

At no other time in history has it been more important and more challenging for a business owner to maintain his or her integrity. Yet, in a complex global marketplace, businesses that hold to their convictions often come up short. The global economy has juxtaposed U.S. businesses with cultures that define morality in very different contexts with different codes of values and ethics. The Internet and the information age have brought that global economy even closer, posing new ethical questions and challenges in an environment that didn't exist even 10 years ago.

Many writers and researchers in the field of ethics have asserted that no economic system will survive over the long term without a moral component.[1,2] Before the Industrial Revolution, economic activity was part of the larger social fabric so that business activities were governed by the same social and cultural restraints and dictates that pervaded other activities. Consequently, there was moral unity.[3] But as we moved into the Industrial Revolution, it became possible to separate a person's role in the economy from his or her role in other areas of society. As the church's hold on moral doctrines declined in the face of a more complex society, the "amoral paradigm of business" began to surface. Many writers have claimed that the misinterpretations of Adam Smith's *The Wealth of Nations* and the selective use of his ideas to support interests for personal gain contributed to the movement away from ethics in business.[4,5,6]

Because religion experienced a declining influence on economic matters in U.S. history, a distinct chasm erupted between the ideology of free enterprise, which is based on self-interest, and the altruism of religion.[7] The challenge business owners face today is to overcome the amoral theory and understand that "self-interest and concern for others are not mutually exclusive alternatives."[8] "Ethics have everything to do with management. Rarely do the character flaws of a lone actor fully explain corporate misconduct."[9] In other words, if you as a business owner choose to ignore ethics and fail to design systems that promote ethical conduct and hold your company to high standards, you will face a higher risk for corporate liability. Justin Butchert holds his company to a higher standard than other businesses in the industry. That is one of the reasons KRE is so successful.

Complementary to the issue of ethics is that of social responsibility. What responsibilities do businesses have toward the communities in which they do business and to society as a whole? This chapter explores the nature of ethics and social responsibility as they relate to all types of businesses, large and small.

The Source of Ethics

Ethics, or the moral code by which we live and conduct business, come from the cultural, social, political, and ethnic norms with which we were raised as children. Most of us don't actually sit down to think about what our value system is; we merely act instinctively based on it. Only when we face a situation that others might point out to us as immoral or unethical (the terms are used interchangeably) might we consciously ask ourselves, "What do I really

**Figure 19.1
Barriers to the De-
velopment of a Moral
Code**

believe is the correct thing to do in this situation?" In Chapter 7, we discussed creating a vision for your company that is based on your values and
beliefs. Once again, it's important to consider exactly what those values are.
The benefits of knowing your values are many:

▶ You will have an easier time making decisions because you will eliminate
from consideration alternatives that go against your value system.

▶ You will have an easier time persuading people to agree with you because
you will express a level of confidence you wouldn't have without a value
system. You are also less likely to let someone else influence you to do
something you should not do.

▶ If you always make decisions based on your value system, you will probably not regret your decisions over the long term.

▶ You will have the best chance of knowing what real success is because it
will be defined in terms of what is important to you.

In addition to understanding your value system, it is helpful to understand the additional influences on your code of ethics.

Barriers to the Acceptance of a Moral Code Based on Reason

Three barriers to moral reasoning prevent many business owners from looking at situations in an impartial and reasonable manner: psychological egoism, ethical egoism, and ethical relativism (see Figure 19.1). If you are not
aware of these barriers in your own thinking, you will not be able to accept a

rational approach to ethics and will tend to dichotomize ethics, viewing it either selfishly or altruistically.

Psychological Egoism

The theory of **psychological egoism** says that we are essentially programmed to pursue only our own selfish interests. If at times we seem to be acknowledging the needs of others, it's only because we expect to gain something by doing so.[10] This barrier would prevent a person from looking rationally or objectively at a business situation and probably is responsible for much of what is termed the "dark side" of entrepreneurship, the notion that entrepreneurs are out solely for personal gain.

Ethical Egoism

If psychological egoism means we are biologically incapable of doing anything that does not contribute to self-interest, **ethical egoism** means that although people are capable of acting unselfishly, they should instead always do what will result in a gain for them. Therefore, this is a normative theory that asks us to use reason and impartiality to make a decision about whose interests will be satisfied when we face a moral dilemma.[11]

Ethical Relativism

Ethical relativism is based on the theory that there is no universality of moral truth. Instead, morality is defined by the culture in which it occurs ("When in Rome . . ."). A business owner should make ethical decisions based on the environment in which he or she is operating at the time.[12] This theory is also applied at the individual level and is called **ethical subjectivism**. In other words, ethics is an individual thing based on one's personal feelings.

Now that we have looked at the barriers that inhibit the development of a moral code, let's consider three basic ethical theories in current use.

Basic Ethical Theories

Three fundamental ethical theories are in operation today: utilitarian theories, theories of justice, and theories of virtue. How people transact business or react in business situations derives from their expectations, which are based on their own ethical framework or theory.

Utilitarian Theories

Classical **utilitarian theory** asserts that you must consider equally the happiness of all people involved in a moral decision; that is, whether or not you do something is based on the consequences of the action. It is essentially the use of reason and impartiality in making ethical decisions.[13] So in making an ethical decision under this theory, you would look at the impact your decision might have on others around you.

Suppose one of the core values of your business is that you do not believe in giving or taking bribes. Under the utilitarian theory, you may decide that foregoing this value in countries where bribery is the norm is acceptable.

Theories of Justice

Theories of justice are based on absolute rules a person must follow no matter what the situation. In other words, people who believe in theories of justice believe in the universality of certain moral laws that everyone should follow under all conditions. In this way, decisions are made rationally.[14] Under this theory, your business would not participate in bribery under any circumstances.

Theories of Virtue

Theories of virtue are differentiated from the previous two types of theories in that the focus is not on actions but on the character traits of individuals. This theory claims that a good person will do good deeds, that the person's inherent wisdom will guide him or her to make a right and moral decision. This theory assumes that if a businessperson is a good person, he or she will do the right thing no matter what the situation. Here your business would allow its employees to make ethical decisions based on their own moral beliefs and conscience.

Let's now look at how a code of ethics can be developed from these three theories.

Developing a Code of Ethics

In developing a code of ethics for a business, Cavanaugh, Moberg, and Valasquez proposed that business owners ask three questions based on the three theories of ethics:[15]

1. Will the actions taken result in the "greatest good for all parties involved"?

2. Will the actions respect the rights of all parties?

3. Are the actions just?

These questions get at the core of a person's value system and his or her respect for others. Notice that the questions do not represent rules of conduct—what to do or not do in a particular situation. In 1994, Price Waterhouse prepared its first comprehensive report on corporate compliance programs, those that deal with compliance with company policies and laws and regulations.[16] It found that programs based on rules of conduct were less effective than those based on a "commitment to ethical values," also called **integrity-based programs**. This is because rule-based programs don't get at the cause of the problem, so often people don't understand the "why" of the rule. The codes of conduct of the companies studied had three key characteristics that are important for small-business owners who want to develop their own codes of ethics:

Whether or not an entrepreneurial business has a formal code of ethics, it is important for the entrepreneur to consider the company's core values. In an industry not often known for its ethical practices, Peter Fink's auto transmission business in Omaha, Nebraska stands out as a business customers can trust. He refuses to give estimates over the phone without seeing the car first so that his estimates will be as accurate as possible. And he always gives the worst case scenario to the customer first, so the customer knows the most the repair might cost. Then the customer usually ends up paying less. He also refuses to pay his diagnostics on a commission basis so that they can't be influenced to prescribe more repairs than are really necessary. (Randy Hampton/Black Star)

1. The code and its attendant policies were clear and easy to understand. It included such areas as conflict of interest, ethics, and foreign government payments.

2. Specifics regarding special situations that need further explanation were included (e.g., political factors in certain countries).

3. Where employee judgment was required, descriptions and examples were given to make it easier for the employee to make the decision.

Note that an effective code of ethics allows the employee to make the decision in any given situation. This means that when you establish the fundamental value system for your company, you will need to hire people who share that value system. Only when you hire people with different codes of ethics will you be forced to use rules of conduct, which, as mentioned earlier, are far less effective.

In large companies, compliance programs are managed by a committee of directors and the code of conduct is reviewed at least semiannually to determine if any changes are needed. In a small, growing company, that responsibility may fall to the board of directors or board of advisers.

Some suggestions for small companies desiring to develop a code of conduct for their business have come out of the Price Waterhouse study:

1. Make sure all employees are aware of and understand the code of conduct—the values and culture of the company.

2. Make sure your compliance committee is cross-functional, that is, represents all aspects of the company.

3. Require any employee who works in a foreign country to learn about the company's values and culture and understand how those values may conflict with norms in another country.

4. Rotate employees who work in countries where corruption risks are considered high.

5. Conduct internal audits on compliance.

6. Make sure employees know and understand the disciplinary actions that will be taken should the code be violated.

Common Ethical Problems for Entrepreneurs

Some ethical problems entrepreneurs commonly face occur in four broad categories: conflicts of interest, desperate measures, associate pressure, and legal games.[17]

 Entrepreneurship in Action

What Happens When the SEC Doesn't Like Your Values?

Apparently the government thinks that having fun is risky business, at least when it comes to an investment prospectus. AES Corporation was in the process of going public in the summer of 1991 when it submitted its proposed prospectus to the U.S. Securities and Exchange Commission according to the rules. In the company description section of the prospectus, the firm referred to its core values of fun, fairness, integrity, and social responsibility.

The SEC promptly responded that these "values" were misplaced. They belonged in the section "Risk Factors." AES executives never missed a beat. On their subsequent road show, they touted the fact that even the government believes that values are important enough to be considered risk factors. Even though AES made it a point to declare that its values were more important than "maximizing shareholder wealth," its offering was oversubscribed five-and-a-half to one.

Source: George Gendron, "Sign of the Times," *Inc.,* February 1992, p. 11.

Conflicts of Interest

Conflicts of interest are a serious problem in business dealings, principally because people have rightful interests in their careers, the success of their businesses, and the welfare of their families and communities. Because the entrepreneur's activities cross into all these areas, it's not surprising when conflicts of interest occur. Take an entrepreneur who also teaches a course in small-business management at a local university. Suppose he encounters a student in his class who would be perfect for a position in his company, or suppose that student is starting a business in which the entrepreneur would like to invest. You can readily see the conflict of interest. As a teacher, he must grade his students fairly, without bias. As an entrepreneur, he must find the best people to ensure the success of his business.

What about the student who goes to work for a company to learn on someone else's time so she can go out and start her own business? Is this ethical? Is there a conflict of interest here? Clearly there is. What about the employee who needs to balance work and family obligations, which will cause no end of conflicts? One workable solution is to develop a flexible work schedule to minimize conflicts. Entrepreneurs need to recognize that businesses are fertile grounds for conflict of interest and that not all conflict can be resolved satisfactorily. In the situations described here, you need to go back to the three basic questions: (1) Will the actions taken result in the greatest good for all parties involved? (2) Will the actions respect the rights of all parties? (3) Are the actions just?

Desperate Measures

It is often stated that you don't really know what your ethics are until they have been tested. Entrepreneurs have certainly done many things they would have preferred not to do in the name of saving the business or making that extra dollar. "Desperate times call for desperate measures" is the motto of some. But your code of ethics, just like the core values you established for your company, must be unwavering over time no matter what the situation.

 The Real World of Entrepreneurship

Simple Code of Conduct: The Jet Propulsion Laboratory

▶ I will conduct all business dealings with fairness, honesty, and integrity.

▶ I will protect all information and resources available to me from loss, theft, and misuse.

▶ I will avoid even the appearance of conflict of interest or any other impropriety.

▶ I will treat my fellow employees fairly and with dignity and respect.

▶ I will help create and sustain an atmosphere conducive to the spirit of this code.

Source: http://www.jpl.nasa.gov/JPL/ethics/ethictxt.htm. Developed by Don Cheney and Susan Birgel of the Information Technology Engineering Systems Group, JPL Section 392

It won't always be easy to live by your code of ethics, but if you don't live by it in desperate times, no one will expect that you will live by it in good times. You and your business have only one reputation to lose.

Associate Pressure

Throughout your business life, you will be pressured by the people around you to make decisions that are in their best interests. Suppose you are debating whether or not to enter the global market. Your financial adviser encourages you to do so because you will make more money. Your attorney is concerned about the legal ramifications of dealing in diverse markets. Your family doesn't want you to be traveling around the world. At every level, there will be pressure to do or not do something, and you will be torn as to which way to go because you know you can't please everyone. This is when it's important to have values firmly in place because they should be the principal guide to your decision making.

Legal Games

The law is not as clear and defined as you might like it to be. Certainly there are many gray areas where entrepreneurs can walk a fine line and probably get away with it. In fact, new businesses have been created just to help business owners work within the law in its loosest interpretation. Some entrepreneurs consider it a sport to play as close to the edge as possible when it comes to the rules and regulations of doing business. Most business owners, however, prefer to play safely within the law because they know the consequences of not doing so can be costly and time consuming, if not criminal. The legal roulette some business owners play usually comes back to haunt the business in a big way. One California real estate developer paid bribes to city officials to get his zoning requests approved. Local developers who were putting in legal requests and often getting them denied were frustrated by the lack of the justice in the system. In 1997, that developer and those city officials were indicted for bribery, and the developer is now serving time in prison. He has lost his business, his family, and his reputation. It's a big price to pay for failing to do business by the letter of the law.

Again, it all comes back to your code of ethics. If you have a serious, well-defined code of ethics based on your value system, the tough decisions of your business life will be much easier to make.

Ethics in Technology

With more information more readily available to everyone via computer technology, the way organizations operate has changed significantly. Not only have the core activities of the business changed, but the way we interact within these new environments has changed as well.[18] Consequently, new ethical challenges have arisen. The "new technology can level the playing field, but in many instances creates a whole new playing field. . . . Thus, not only do the rules change, but there may be, in fact, no rules at all."[19]

The implemention of computers in decision making presents both problems and opportunities. The degree to which a system is effective within your business is a function of whether or not you take ethical principles into consideration. When the Internet was first contrived, it was built on the honor system. The "Internet Community"—scientists, government, and academicians—was one of shared values. An unwritten code of ethics prevailed. But when the Internet attracted the attention of the general public, that environment changed. Today Internet users are "attacked" by unsolicited advertising via e-mail directly to their personal computers in a practice known as **spamming**. Most Internet service providers specifically prohibit spamming in their user agreements, and since the amount of unsolicited advertising that goes on is still relatively small, it's possible to control it to a certain extent. See the Technology Tip below for a process for tracking down an e-mail spammer.

Another significant ethical problem in cyberspace is computer hackers who break into company computer systems, sometimes just to prove they can do it and other times for criminal purposes. When you set up a web site, an

Technology Tip

Tracking Down an E-mail Spammer

Here is a brief process you can use to track down an e-mail spammer. For a more detailed example, check out a guide by Andrew C. Bulhak at http://www-ccrma.stanford.edu/~daj/spam.htm/.

Look at the sender header, for example, mail@cheapshot.com (all headers used here are fictitious). Even if the sender used a fictitious name, the source may be revealed in another header not readily visible. Some software allows you to look at the document source so that you can see the trail the mail went through from the sender to you. This will appear in the form of a *Received* line:

Received: from www.cheapshot.com (w3.cheapshot.com [555.555.555.555] by bill.xx.west.net (5.5)

Received: from spammer.xxx.com (dialup-555.provider.net [555.555.555.5]) by www.cheapshot.com (5.5.5/5.5.5)

The first line tells you that you (bill.xx.west.net) received mail from www.cheapshot.com. The second line indicates that www.cheapshot.com received a message from spammer.xxx.com, who is really dialup-555.provider.net. This type of name may mean this is a private machine run by the spammer, which is temporarily connected to a service provider by modem. The provider is provider.net. So your complaint should go to the postmaster@provider.net. Other headers to check are *Message-Id:* and *Comments*.

Here are three other tips to help you deal with this problem:

1. Spammers typically buy e-mail address lists from a variety of sources. Often the addresses are old. If you are being spammed on an old address and reply to the spammer, you may inadvertently give him or her your new address, and you will get unsolicited mail once again. Take care of it immediately and notify the postmaster.

2. If your unsolicited advertiser provides an 800 number, call and make a complaint; you will probably get quicker results.

3. If you receive verbal abuse from an advertiser, be sure to send a copy to the advertiser's postmaster. Action will be taken quickly.

intranet (a network within your company), or an extranet (a network that goes beyond your company), you should also set up a system of passwords, a firewall, to keep unwanted visitors out. A good computer consultant can help you find the best system for your company's needs.

Applying a Code of Conduct in Cyberspace

There is help for you in cyberspace in the form of the CyberAngels Organization, comprised of more than 4,000 volunteer Internet users from around the world who are attempting to defend "freedom of expression, tolerance, self-regulation, and responsibility in cyberspace." Their members, or "Netizens," have decided to take personal and proactive responsibility for ethics in the online world.

CyberAngels deals with activities and materials related to harm, fear, distress, inconvenience, offense, and concern. The organization operates under a strict code of ethics and will defend only those who act in accordance with it. You can check out its web site at http://www.cyberangels.org.

Social Responsibility

Today it's not enough to have a successful business and make a profit. Today society expects companies to hold themselves to a much higher standard of social responsibility by giving something back to the communities in which they do business and to society as a whole. This means following the laws, respecting the environment, and thinking of the impact the business has on the community, the industry, the stakeholders, and people in general. In other words, you can't operate your business in a vacuum. Social responsibility concerns all the obligations and duties that business has to society as a whole.

We have all read stories about businesses that failed to take social responsibility seriously—clear-cutting forests, fighting for the right to sell handguns while lobbying in Congress for tougher youth crime bills, claiming products that are natural and fat free while loading them with sugar and chemicals. According to Joline Godfrey of An Income of Her Own, an organization that teaches young women how to take charge of their lives, the notion of doing good [historically was not] "an act of charity or . . . something you did *after* you had figured out your yearly profit, but . . . an ever-present responsibility of life. . . ."[20] The problem today, she asserts, is that "some companies identify themselves as 'socially responsible' by pointing to the percentage of profits they give to the community, not to the decisions made to attain those profits."[21]

So for many businesses, just as "the customer is king" becomes a mantra with no deep sense of conviction behind it, social responsibility becomes just another task of the business so it will "look good" for the public. Social responsibility in its purest forms comes from the value system of the entrepreneur and the culture that is created in the company. Your value system as a business owner must contain an understanding of your business's role within the community and society at large.

Lynn Carr's Twainland Cheesecake Co. is more than just a product business. Carr is dedicated to helping the impoverished women of Hannibal, Missouri finish high school, hold down good jobs, and gain financial independence. Coming out of homelessness herself, she is dedicated to employing destitute women and providing them with benefits such as day-care and assistance in obtaining their GEDs. (Twainland Cheesecake Co. from Hannibal, MO)

A Framework for Looking at Social Responsibility

A simple framework for understanding levels of social responsibility has been suggested by the work of Sethi.[22] The framework consists of three stages companies may go through on the way to becoming socially responsible companies:

1. *Social obligation*: At this stage, the company contributes to society when there is a direct benefit to it (psychological egoism). At a minimum, the company obeys the laws and shares little information about its efforts.

2. *Social responsibility:* The company will attempt to meet social norms and contribute to noncontroversial, established causes. The company is more open to evaluation of its efforts and more willing to share information.

3. *Social responsiveness:* The company is willing to be publicly evaluated on its social activities and to contribute to more controversial causes. The

**Figure 19.2
How to Become
Socially Responsible**

company is proactive in its efforts to be socially responsible and willingly shares information.

Some businesses have chosen the route of defining themselves publicly as "socially responsible businesses." Body Shop International's original goal was to end Third World poverty. While certainly a lofty goal, it's highly unlikely that one corporation can do what entire nations have been unable to accomplish. So, in essence, Body Shop was setting itself up for failure. Moreover, since companies such as this put their social goals into all their publicity and advertising, they are held to impossibly high standards by the public and the media, who are ready and willing to remind them of their failure to achieve their goals. In the case of Body Shop International, it was accused of misleading customers in its claims, so it hired an ethicist from Stanford University, Kirk Hanson, to conduct an independent investigation into the claims. The findings scored the company low in 22 of 38 areas studied, and it also received the lowest marks for its reaction to criticism.[23]

But stories such as this should never discourage a small-business owner from finding ways to become more socially responsible. Amy Miller of Amy's Ice Cream of Austin, says, "I think about social responsibility when I worry about whether asking employees to dress in a certain way violates their rights to free expression (Nose rings and tattoos are OK; lip rings are not.)"[24] It's fine to think about saving the rain forest, but when you are growing a young company, you have to weigh everything against its survival. Unless the business of business is conducted well, there will be no business from which to achieve the goal of social responsibility.[25]

Small companies can make a difference when it comes to social responsibility. Following are some approaches you might consider for your company (see Figure 19.2).

Donating Your Product or Service

Donating your product or service is a good way to start the process of achieving social responsibility as a company. James Blackman, executive producer of the Civic Light Opera of South Bay Cities, a very successful non-profit theatre company in Southern California, donates evenings of theatre to physically challenged children and children from the inner city so they can enjoy something they have never experienced before. Saint Louis Bread Company gives bread, muffins, and so forth to homeless people to the annual tune of $700,000 retail.[26]

Get Employees Involved

Money and products are a static resource, but human beings are a dynamic resource.[27] One way to be socially responsible is to teach your employees to be philanthropic. Rhino Records of Santa Monica, California, gives employees who contribute 16 hours of personal time per year to community service a week off at Christmas with pay.[28]

Get Other Companies Involved in Social Responsibility

Organize a group of small businesses to work together on a community project. Just Desserts, a San Francisco bakery, put a group of 35 businesses together to "adopt" an elementary school. They got volunteers to plant trees

 Entrepreneurship in Action

What Would You Do?

Someone must have been whispering in the ears of the delegation from Gessto Company to get them to present such outrageous demands. At least that's what David Winston thought as he listened to them drone on. He was in France to phase out a relationship with this distributor, but the Gessto people were doing their best to make it appear that Sterling Machine—the company whose products they represented—owed them a severance package that would make most stickup artists blush. Little did he and his colleague, Joan Geske, know the surprise awaiting them as they challenged Gessto's demands. Nor were they prepared to be fingered as criminals at large.

David was an attorney for Sterling. . . . Joan's youthful appearance as an assistant vice president for distribution often lulled others into underestimating the sharpness of her mind and the magnitude of her experience. They were both part of Sterling's team, which re-cently concluded it was time to change its French distributors. They were prepared to buy back Gessto's inventory. Sterling was also ready to offer additional concessions, including what they felt was a generous offer to provide a six-month financial transition cushion. But Gessto wanted more, much more, claiming "We have evidence that Sterling violated U.S. laws prohibiting sales to Libya, Iraq, and Iran. Unless you agree to our proposal you will run into serious problems with your own government and risk public exposure of illegal sales." David was concerned that although he had always been ethical, he didn't know what some overseas sales office might have done.

What would you do in this situation?

SOURCE: Doug Wallace, "What Would You Do? Threatened by Extortion," *Business Ethics Magazine,* July/August 1996.

on the school grounds, paint the school, and refurbish the classrooms. Now the school's students have a good environment for learning.

More Ways to Be Socially Responsible

Your growing business can become socially responsible by lending its expertise in a pro bono way to nonprofit organizations and the community. You can also strive to use suppliers and seek customers who subscribe to the notion of social responsibility. Amana-Key, a Brazilian company, offers free seminars to teenagers on skills they will need in the future, and it has adopted a school. Account Executive is a Philadelphia company that bridges the gap between training programs and employees for low-income women. Its founder, Abby Siegel, co-founded a nonprofit organization that provides interview clothing to help the women "dress for success."

Companies that have worked at social responsibility report that they have an easier time retaining employees and customers, are more respected in the community, and enjoy more business success in general.

It certainly is apparent that a new breed of entrepreneur is in the making. These new entrepreneurs have been variously called *social entrepreneurs* or *philanthropic entrepreneurs*, and they are making an important impact on how we all do business. Social entrepreneurs are finding innovative ways to share the wealth they create with their communities and society at large.

Cases Relevant to This Chapter

Pelco

Marcus Food Co. and Buckhead Beef

SB Networks

Issues for Review and Discussion

1. What issues might prevent business owners from adhering to a moral code?
2. Contrast the classical three theories of ethics.
3. What can you do if you are spammed by unsolicited advertising?
4. List three ways to make your company more socially responsible.
5. Why did the Body Shop International set itself up for failure as a "socially responsible" company?

Experiencing Entrepreneurship

1. Interview an entrepreneur about how she or he is striving to make the company more socially responsible.
2. During your efforts to track down software problems in your business, you are forced to check the contents of some users' files. You find a file that proves the user is embezzling from your company. What would you do?

Resources

Rushworth M. Kidder (1995). *How Good People Make Tough Choices.* New York: William Morrow.

"Thoughts on the Business of Life," *Forbes,* September 25, 1995, p. 248.

Internet Resources

Business Ethics Magazine
http://condor.depaul.edu/ethics/biz

Corporate Conduct Quarterly
http://camden-www.rutgers.edu/~ccq/pell53.html

On the Horizon: The Environmental Scanning Publication
http://sunsite.unc.edu/horizon/pastissues/

The Online Journal of Ethics
http://www.depaul.edu/ethics/

Epilogue: The Customer-Centered Entrepreneurial Business

By now it should be clear that achieving total quality in a growing entrepreneurial company requires an integrated approach with the customer at the center of everything the company does. No company better exemplifies this philosophy than Pelco, the closed-circuit TV and surveillance equipment manufacturer featured in the case study at the end of this book. Everyone in the company, from the president down to the newest employee, understands with startling clarity that it is really the customer who writes their checks. Without the customer, they have nothing. This customer-centered philosophy took Pelco to the number one position in an industry where competition is fierce and most of the products are "me-too's." Pelco's biggest competitive advantage, and the reason for its success, is the way it treats customers; it will do literally anything to keep them happy.

Another company that certainly ranks as one of the best in terms of treating customers and employees and stands as a role model for growing entrepreneurial companies is Southwest Airlines, winner of the prestigious U.S. Department of Transportation's Triple Crown award for customer satisfaction. Its competitor, Northwest Airlines—which was very indignant over the choice—ignored the results and continued to call itself number one in customer satisfaction, to which Southwest replied quite humorously in a nationwide ad:

> After lengthy deliberation at the highest executive levels and extensive consultation with our legal department, we have arrived at an official corporate response to Northwest Airlines' claim to be number one in customer satisfaction. Liar, liar. Pants on fire.[*]

Southwest believes that humor, aimed mostly at itself, creates an organizational culture that balances the natural stress of the industry and makes it possible to be more customer centered. It must be right, because while its competition has been losing large amounts of money, Southwest has been consistently profitable with sales of more than $1 billion.

---

[*] Kathy Thacker, "Top Guns Wrestling over Ad Slogan Rights," *Adweek*, February 17, 1992.

There is, however, a great danger that this idea of "customer-centered" companies and "customer-centered" growth will become a cliche as have so many of the other management philosophies proposed in the past. In many companies that will certainly be the case, because they haven't taken the time and made the effort to infuse the customer into all the activities of the organization. They have paid lip service to the strategy with customer service departments, surveys, and promotions. What they have not done is give the customer a real voice in what the company does, from product design to distribution to billing. That takes some real effort and coordination. Most companies believe they can do just enough to keep the customer happy, but the most successful companies do more than just enough. They subscribe to a philosophy of continuous improvement, and they are constantly on the lookout for new ways to serve the customer.

Today only the most agile, customer-oriented companies will succeed in the long term. In their excellent book *Customer-Centered Growth*, Richard Whiteley and Diane Hessan assert that the entrepreneur who wants a customer-centered organization needs to ask several critical questions:[*]

1. Will you be able to fire a high-performing employee if he or she is not living the values of the company?

2. Are you prepared to work very hard for a minimum of three years to establish a customer-centered organization?

3. Are you as the entrepreneur willing to spend an extraordinary amount of time with customers?

4. Are you willing to discuss customers and employees first at every operating meeting?

5. Are you willing to forgo short-term gains to put the customer first?

6. Will you promote the customer-centered employee over the noncommitted employee?

7. Will your financials include customer satisfaction numbers as well?

The entrepreneur who truly wants this type of organization must be fully committed to the principle and carry his or her vision to everyone else within the organization as well as to all those who come in contact with it.

The viewpoint in this book has been entrepreneurial because we believe the entrepreneurial mindset is the key to successful business ventures in the next decade. Entrepreneurial companies have the greatest impact on society and on the way we do business. And they aren't found just in the high-tech arena. On the contrary, there is virtually no industry in which an astute and creative entrepreneur has not been able to carve out a unique niche in the market and grow rapidly. The key is to know the customers and give them what they want.

---

[*] Richard Whiteley and Diane Hessan, *Customer-Centered Growth: Five Proven Strategies for Building Competitive Advantage* (Reading, MA: Addison-Wesley, 1992), p. 226.

Rapidly growing, young companies have special needs and unique issues, which this book has addressed. But young, entrepreneurial companies also have a distinct advantage over large organizations when it comes to integrating the customer and total quality into the organization. It is far easier to build a company from the ground up using the bricks and mortar of total quality to establish a customer-centered culture than it is to tear down the bottom line, mass marketing, sales mentality that has been firmly implanted in some large companies for decades.

The concepts presented in this book are simple. Anyone who wants to can implement them, but it's not an easy thing to do. It requires dedication, a single-minded focus, and an intense desire to build a world-class, customer-centered company. In companies such as Southwest Airlines and Pelco where "customer-centered" is the culture, that culture survives changes in personnel and changes in the environment. "The culture is stronger than any individual," says Herb Kelleher, chair and CEO of Southwest Airlines. It is the driving force that binds everyone together to achieve the company's goals and satisfy its customers. If there is a secret to successful growth and an enduring company, it is this: *our customers are the most important people in our company.*

Koidra-Tek™
Asia Business Suite
Business Plan

Koidra-Tek *Asia Business Suite* Business Plan

KOIDRA-TEK™
ASIA BUSINESS SUITE
BUSINESS PLAN*

EXECUTIVE SUMMARY

Do you know how to present and accept a business card when in Asia? Well, if you are not aware that cultural differences do exist, you are not alone. There are hundreds of thousands of business owners who do not know the customs and etiquette needed to be successful in Asia.

Koidra-Tek incorporates education and training with technology to assist companies in expanding their global presence. Koidra-Tek's target market is companies located within the United States that are currently or plan to begin conducting business in Asia. *Asia Business Suite* will educate companies on issues relating to practicing business in Asia. The CD-ROM will be promoted through the use of direct marketing strategies and will be marketed to companies in certain retail outlets, specifically bookstores and airport shops.

The company has the necessary management team in place. Founders Esther Nguyen and Brian Wong will soon be graduating from the University of Southern California's Entrepreneur Program. Ms. Nguyen has shown tremendous executive ability as an ARCO franchisee. Mr. Wong has gained management and leadership skills through his work as part-time manager of Wilshire Serrano Motel. An advisory board has been formed consisting of Dr. C. H. Quan and Angi Ma Wong. Dr. Quan is an economist with more than 40 years of consulting experience both domestically and on an international basis. Angi Ma Wong is an award-winning author, intercultural consultant, and corporate trainer.

Three hundred surveys were distributed in the Los Angeles area to ascertain interest in *Asia Business Suite* as well as to determine the pricing strategy Koidra-Tek will ultimately implement. In addition, focus groups and interviews were conducted with the USC International Business Education and

---

* This sample business plan is used by permission from Esther Nguyen and Brian Wong. Lloyd Greif Center for Entrepreneurial Studies, University of Southern California, 1998.

Research (IBEAR) MBA program to ensure that the content and features customers desire are included in the CD-ROM.

Although competition does exist, Koidra-Tek is confident that *Asia Business Suite* will bypass its competitors through the market niche it has created. The company has identified three major competitors but feels its product is superior in quality, ease of use, and content.

Initial market penetration tactics include direct mail, personal selling, Internet shareware, cooperative advertising, and public relations efforts. Koidra-Tek's customers will see the company as being service oriented with cutting-edge technology to fulfill customers' needs. Twenty percent of gross sales will be allocated toward the planning and implementation of marketing strategies.

Start-up funding for Koidra-Tek will be received from each of the founders' parents as a graduation gift. The company forecasts profits within eight months of operations.

Koidra-Tek's chances of success are rather high considering these key factors:

- A 309 percent ROI in year one
- Unique and innovative product
- Intense guerrilla marketing effort
- Passion of the founding team
- Experienced and knowledgeable advisory board

These factors collectively are the building blocks for Koidra-Tek's success.

BUSINESS CONCEPT

Koidra-Tek's Purpose

Koidra-Tek incorporates education and training with technology to help companies succeed in achieving a global presence. Initially, the company will introduce a CD-ROM, *Asia Business Suite,* which will focus on different issues necessary to prepare companies to conduct business in Asia. The CD-ROM will be sold using direct marketing to companies located within the United States that are currently or plan to begin conducting business in Asia. In addition, *Asia Business Suite* will be available through certain retail outlets, specifically bookstores and airport shops.

Core Values

- We believe in developing quality products that will enrich and educate our customers.
- We believe in creating an enjoyable working environment and empowering our employees to build strong relationships throughout our organization.
- We believe in conducting business in an ethical and honest fashion.
- We believe in overall growth of our organization, but not without the growth of our customers and employees.

Description and Uses of *Asia Business Suite*

Asia Business Suite is a prepackaged CD-ROM that educates businesspeople on the common sayings, ethics, customs, etiquette, laws and regulations, as well as precautionary issues specifically relating to conducting business in Asia. Other features include a detailed directory of phone numbers and addresses essential for business travel throughout Asia. These directories will include information ranging from hotels, restaurants, and U.S. government agencies to emergency resources, as well as a minibusiness directory. Interactive learning of common sayings will also be included with phrases such as "How are you?" and "Hello." The other sections focusing on ethics, customs, etiquette, and laws and regulations will include such topics as bribery, greeting individuals, and dining decorum. *Asia Business Suite*'s segment addressing precautions and tips serves as a useful guide while traveling. The software will be highly graphical, user-friendly, and include true-to-life photographs and video clips. It will be compatible with existing Windows NT, 3.1, 95, 98, and Macintosh operating systems.

The Primary Customer

Koidra-Tek's main purchaser will be companies ranging from small entrepreneurial start-ups to Fortune 500 companies located throughout the United States. These companies have access to either a PC-compatible or Macintosh computer with CD-ROM capability. They may currently be conducting or plan to begin conducting business in Asia.

Distribution to the End-User

Koidra-Tek will distribute *Asia Business Suite* to the end-users via direct marketing sales, mail order, airport shops, bookstores, computer/software retail outlets, trade centers, and the Internet. In addition, *Asia Business Suite* will be available for purchase through similar retail outlets as its competitors, such as the *Culture Shock* series and De Mente's *Chinese Customs & Etiquette*.

Proprietary Rights

Koidra-Tek is in the process of filing the company with the Secretary of State of California to form a limited liability company (LLC; see Exhibits A and B). On completion, Koidra-Tek and *Asia Business Suite* will be trademarked and the CD-ROM copyrighted.

Spin-offs

Once Koidra-Tek has established itself as a small-size software publisher, it will begin to explore the industry for niche opportunities. The company will spin-off from *Asia Business Suite* by expanding this line to other regions of the world. Another possible area of exploration will be that of international education through CD-ROM and via the Internet.

Environmental Impact

Koidra-Tek will use 100 percent recycled paperboard as well as recycled plastic wrap packaging for *Asia Business Suite*.

MANAGEMENT TEAM

The founders will jointly lead and motivate Koidra-Tek to success. Together they have defined and set the company's vision, purpose, core values, and mission. Resumes are found in Exhibit C of the appendix.

Chief Executive Officer

The chief executive officer coordinates and oversees all the company's activities. In order for Koidra-Tek to remain competitive in the constantly changing industry of prepackaged software, the CEO must regularly analyze the market and industry trends. She communicates and obtains input from all levels of management and employees but plays a dominant role in the strategic planning process. The CEO's principal duty is defined as giving long-term direction to the firm and ensuring the company meets its goals.

Esther Nguyen, CEO

- Negotiated transactions and contracts as director of special projects for Compliance Monitoring Service Company
- Served as director and financial analyst for international development programs
- Received extensive training and certification by am/pm Franchise Training Program of ARCO
- Became manager with ownership interest of ARCO Monterey Mini Mart in San José, California, selling more than six million gallons of gasoline a year
- Held numerous leadership positions for the Vietnamese Student Association, including president and special event coordinator

Chief Financial Officer and Chief Operations Officer

The chief financial officer is responsible for ensuring that Koidra-Tek maintains a profitable financial position. The CFO maintains all budgets and essential statements necessary for accounting and tax purposes. Financial decisions will be made and evaluated by the CFO to help the company with daily financial operations.

The COO negotiates all transactions and maintains communications with the manufacturer, suppliers, and buyers. The COO oversees all distribution channels and control systems. He ensures the company is producing quality products that best suit the customer. The COO ensures the company's goals are satisfied and forecasted sales are met.

Brian Wong, CFO and COO

- Became assistant manager with ownership interest in the Wilshire Serrano Motel
- Involved in daily operations including customer service, property maintenance, and inventory management
- Assisted in the implementation of an internal control system to deter theft and increase profit and accountability
- Worked as administrative assistant to Sunshine Realty
- Acquired various management skills and expanded knowledge of real estate laws and practices

- Currently completing a B.S. in Business Administration with a concurrent emphasis in Finance and Entrepreneurship

Management Team: Board of Advisers

The board of advisers is responsible for formulating the policy decisions affecting management, supervision, and control of the operation of Koidra-Tek. The board will update the company's mission statement as needed. Members will establish the compensation levels of top officers, including their salaries and bonuses. A broad set of company policies on such matters as labor-management relations, product lines, and employee benefits packages will be set forth by the board. Lastly, the board shall mandate company compliance with legal and ethical dictates. The advisory board meets quarterly or on a special needs basis. See Table 1 for a breakdown of board members' positions and contributions.

C. H. Quan, Ph.D.

C. H. Quan, Ph.D., has served as an information assistant to the Acting Chief of Mission of the U.S. Special Technical and Economic Mission of Indonesia. He studied at the University of Colorado in Boulder under a Ford Foundation Fellowship and graduated with an M.S. in Journalism and Economics and a Ph.D. in Economics.

Dr. Quan has negotiated foreign joint ventures with major corporations abroad and has set up additional manufacturing facilities in Central America. He has consulted with foreign companies in negotiations to acquire licenses for overseas production and marketing of American music and movies.

Table 1 Board of Advisers

Name	Title	Contribution
Esther Nguyen	CEO/Founder	Executive decisions
Brian Wong	CFO/COO/Founder	Financial and organization adviser
Dr. C. H. Quan	Member	Economic analyst
Angi Ma Wong	Member	Intercultural consultant

Angi Ma Wong

Angi Ma Wong is an award-winning author, intercultural consultant, and corporate trainer. She has founded her own consulting service and Pacific Heritage Books to help bridge together cultures mainly for business purposes. Mrs. Wong was awarded the "Outstanding LA Businesswoman of the Year" by the National Association of Women Business Owners (NAWBO). She has dedicated much of her time mentoring and training the American Economic Development Council, NAWBO, and the Academy of Business Leadership at USC.

Mrs. Wong has written *TARGET: The U.S. Asian Market, A Practical Guide to Doing Business,* which addresses issues such as designing, marketing, and selling to Asians both in the United States and the Far East. In addition, she has written *Night of the Red Moon, The Wind-Water Wheel: A Feng Shui Tool for Transforming Your Life, The Practical Feng Shui Chart Kit,* and *Been There, Done That: 16 Secrets of Success for Entrepreneurs.*

Koidra-Tek will retain the companies shown in Table 2 for service that would benefit the company and *Asia Business Suite.*

Table 2 Outside Services

Service	Name/Address	Compensation
Attorney	Law Offices of Herman Thordsen Herman Thordsen, Esq. 6 Hutton Centre Drive, Ste. 1040 Santa Ana, CA 92707	Free consultation $125.00 per hour
Manufacturer	CD-MAN Disc Inc. Craig Arnatt 7791 Montcalm St. Vancouver, BC V6P4P1	Cost
Programmer/ Graphic Designer	Mills Group Multimedia John Mills 10677 Thomas St. Cypress, CA 90630	Project basis
Insurance	Allstate Insurance Company David Spence 11544 W. Pico Blvd. Santa Monica, CA 90024	Cost

MARKET ANALYSIS

Global Analysis

In recent years, an increasing number of companies have begun conducting business in Asia. Due to growing competition in some industries, many companies are entering the global markets.[1] For example, the U.S. computer industry is nearing saturation compared with international markets, and because of this, dramatic growth is expected internationally.[2]

According to *MegaTrends Asia* author John Naisbitt, Asian countries have rejected the Western social and political formulations that run counter to its heritage and traditions. Asia is modernizing in the "Asian way" and will not adapt to the procedures of Westerners.

Industry Analysis

Industry Profile

The prepackaged software industry is currently in the growth-stage of the product life cycle (see Figure 1). Demand for software is increasing throughout

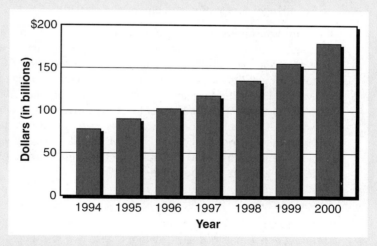

Figure 1 Software Sales
Source: International Data Corp.

9

the world with the greatest consumption in industrial areas. There are a few interesting points to consider concerning the prepackaged software industry:

- According to Anthony Picardi of International Data Corp., sales of prepackaged software worldwide rose 12 percent in 1997 and 12.8 percent in 1998 to $133 billion[3]
- By 2002, the U.S. prepackaged software market is forecast to reach approximately $87 million, increasing by 70 percent from 1997 sales[4]

Geographic Location

In terms of geographic location, the software industry is worldwide, spanning every continent. On a national level, software products may be found in computer retail outlets such as CompUSA and Egghead Software, Inc., in nearly every city throughout the United States.

Industry Trends

Multimedia technology and products are being developed at an enormous rate and are providing various opportunities to consumer electronics and communications technologies. This market will invite greater competition and challenges for existing and emerging companies.

Recently, consumers and software companies have become aware of the development of the Digital Versatile Disc (DVD), which has been coined the next generation of CD-ROM. Commercially pressed DVD-ROM will be capable of storing 4.7 gigabytes, compared with a mere 700 megabytes for CD-ROM. The DVD-ROM file and volume structure for data will be the same as that for CD-ROM. This means that file access programs, indexing schemes and routines, as well as compression processes currently in use on CD-ROM will be available for use with DVD-ROM.[5] DVD-ROM software sales are capable of generating annual revenues of $100 million by 1999 and were predicted to reach $35 million in 1997.[6]

Barriers to Entry

Entry into the software segment requires strong financial resources and manufacturing economies of scales. Without these two resources, achieving market share may be difficult. Koidra-Tek plans to overcome these barriers by its unique distribution and marketing strategies.

Profit Potential

In the prepackaged software industry, the profit potential is enormous. Average profit margins in 1997 were approximately 46 percent, a decrease of 2 percent from 1996.[7] This decrease may be associated with two key factors:

- Price wars among competitors
- Promotional campaigns undertaken by competition

Sales Patterns and Gross Margins

Sales patterns do not appear to follow any type of cyclical pattern. Software sales tend to be higher during the Christmas season as individuals buy software as gifts. Typically, software sales increase with the introduction of a new application or operating system software.

With respect to gross margins, profits on average have been determined to range from 5 to 25 percent of cost of goods sold.[8] This suggests that companies desiring greater margins must be able to obtain manufacturing economies of scale.

Target Market

Primary Target Markets

Koidra-Tek's primary target market consists of companies ranging from small entrepreneurial start-ups to Fortune 500 companies located in the United States. These companies have access to either a PC-compatible or Macintosh computer with CD-ROM capability. These companies may already be involved in the Asian market or plan to send representatives soon. The business travelers mentioned earlier are college graduates over the age of 21 who are proficient in the use of PC-compatible or Macintosh computers. These individuals also have an annual income level in excess of $25,000 and are part of the working to upper class.

Secondary Target Markets

Koidra-Tek will target certain retail outlets, specifically bookstores and airport shops. The bookstores are large in size and located nationwide. Annual sales of targeted bookstores are $200 million and up. In addition, the company will target airport shops found in international terminals of major airports. These airports will be located throughout the United States where airlines charter transPacific routes.

11

Results of Primary Research

Koidra-Tek contacted Nancy Yang, program coordinator of the 1997–1998 USC IBEAR MBA program, to distribute its surveys (see Exhibit D). Participants of the group have conducted business throughout Asia for their respective corporations or have expressed the desire to do so in the future. The USC IBEAR students come from 49 major corporations, including American Express International, Whirlpool Greater China, and Bear Stearns, representing 16 different countries.

Surveys were also distributed at the Los Angeles International Airport within the international terminals of out-bounding flights to Asia. Table 3 depicts some of the results obtained from Koidra-Tek's surveys.

Analysis of Survey Results

The distributed surveys provided Koidra-Tek with valuable information pertaining to its potential customer base. More specifically, it has determined:

- Strong interest in *Asia Business Suite*
- Consumers are willing to pay about $39.99–$49.99 for the product

Focus Group

Koidra-Tek formed a focus group with students from the USC IBEAR MBA program. The topic of the focus group was what content and features they would like to see in a product relating to conducting business in Asia. In addition, the group informed Koidra-Tek of personal mishaps that occurred overseas that could have been prevented had they been better prepared.

Table 3 Survey Results

Age Range	No. of Individuals Surveyed	No. of Computer Owners with CD-ROM Drives	No. of Individuals Planning to Conduct Business in Asia	No. of Individuals Who Would Find Business CD-ROM on Asia Helpful
18–29	117	96	31	94
30–39	60	46	27	53
40–49	68	57	19	60
50+	51	38	21	45

Interviews

Along with the surveys distributed to the USC IBEAR MBA program, Koidra-Tek also conducted numerous interviews with representatives from companies that have or are planning to send employees to Asia. One interviewee, Teresa Elaine Brown, is a representative of Chevron Corporation. She has done extensive work in the Far East and plans to return to Asia following graduation. She expressed her belief that there is a demand for preparation tools for business travelers who have not been in foreign countries before. An interview was also conducted with Veronique Le Gall, a representative of Freshfields, an English international law firm located in France. At this point, Ms. Le Gall has not conducted business in Asia, but she expressed an interest to move globally in her career path. She also voiced similar views as to the importance of a product such as *Asia Business Suite.*

An interview was also conducted with Angi Ma Wong, a renowned author and intercultural consultant for companies. Mrs. Wong stressed that business travelers are unaware of the necessary etiquette and cultural factors that may affect proper business relations.

Koidra-Tek has identified certain customer needs through its focus group and interviews. It performed additional research that led the company to define what product benefits to stress and distribution methods to employ, as shown in Table 4.

Distribution Channels

Koidra-Tek will use rather unique distribution methods compared with other software companies. The company plans to distribute its product via direct marketing to human resource departments of larger organizations as well as to owners of small and mid-size companies. In order to reach its primary target market, the company will rely on direct mailings, personal selling, advertisements in trade journals, and press releases to create awareness of *Asia Business Suite.*

The company has also decided to use the Internet as a medium to promote awareness and penetrate the market through use of shareware organizations. Through shareware organizations, start-up companies such as Koidra-Tek are able to distribute their products to a vast number of consumer groups at a relatively low cost. Shareware organizations such as Shareware Developers, located on the Internet at *www.sharewaredevelopers.com,* do not charge membership fees for their services.

13

Table 4 Product Benefits and Distribution Methods

	Companies	Retail Outlets
Customers	Small start-ups or Fortune 500 companies • Located in the United States • Intend to participate in global market *or* • Intend to send employee reps to conduct business	Bookstores • Large in size • Annual sales of $200 million + • Located nationwide	Airport Shops • Located in international terminals of major airports • Shops throughout United States
Product Benefits	• Relatively inexpensive training • Supplemental training tool • Compact and transportable • Convenient and user-friendly • Educates on various cultural issues • Reduces need for cross-referencing other sources	• High profit potential • Allows store or shop to move into technological products • Unique product	
Distribution Methods	• Direct sales to human resource departments • Direct mail • Mail order	• Through use of sales reps who negotiate with wholesale agents and distributors	• Personal selling to managers who determine if product will yield profits
Marketing Strategies	• Personal selling • Database marketing • Direct marketing • Telemarketing • 800 number • Ads in trade journals and publications • Trade shows	• Push strategy • Personal selling • Trade promotions • 800 number	

14

Distribution to retail outlets will be via distributors and wholesale agents. Koidra-Tek's founders along with sales representatives will arrange meetings with these agents in order to secure its products into retail outlets.

Entry Strategy—Initial Market Penetration

On entering the prepackaged software industry, Koidra-Tek will rely on direct mailings, personal selling, and the use of shareware. Trade shows and advertisements will be avoided initially due to the high costs associated with them. The company will also attempt to convince columnists in various newspapers, magazines, and trade journals and publications to review the product.

Emerging Products

According to extensive research conducted by Koidra-Tek, emerging products are not being produced at this time. Products with similar content do exist in the medium of books, magazines, and periodicals but are not currently being manufactured as CD-ROMs.

Substitute Products

Currently, there are numerous substitute products that may hinder the success of *Asia Business Suite,* specifically those mentioned previously (see Table 5). Koidra-Tek realizes that competitors do exist, but the company is confident that *Asia Business Suite* will be seen as a unique product with numerous benefits and features not available in conventional books.

Other potential threats include consulting groups or consulting companies. Koidra-Tek believes that many companies are seeking to globalize their operations but will not be willing or able to pay the high costs associated with such firms.

Product Service Differentiation and Competitive Advantage

Unique Features

Asia Business Suite offers many features and benefits to the end-user:

- Addresses various cultural issues pertaining to conducting business in Asia
- Covers growing Asian economies including Taiwan, Vietnam, China, Japan, Korea, Indonesia, India, and Malaysia
- Uses interactive language learning

Table 5 Competitive Grid

	Ranking by Size	Product	Unique Features/Benefits	Price	Place	Promotion	Weaknesses/Threats
Koidra-Tek	4th	*Asia Business Suite*™ • CD-ROM package covers 10 growing Asian countries • Directory of resources • Interactive language learning • Addresses travel options (hotels, restaurants, etc.)	• Reduces the need for cross-referencing • User-friendly • Compact • Transportable • Inexpensive	Direct: $39.99 Retail: $49.99	• Airport shops • Bookstores • Catalogs • Travel agencies • Direct sales • Internet • Computer retail outlets	• Direct mail • Press releases • Internet • Personal selling • Brochures • Guerrilla marketing • Trade shows • Ads in trade journals and publications	• Lack of brand recognition • Individuals may not have a laptop with CD-ROM • Potential "copycat" products • Possible buyout of company • Technological changes
Boye Lafayette De Mente (Author)	3rd	• 3-country book series • Deals with etiquette and ethics	• In-depth analysis of customs and etiquette relating to business	$51.00 (total for 3 books)	• Retail bookstores • Internet	• Internet	• Covers Japan, China, and Korea only • Numerous competitors
Culture Shock Series	2nd	• 12-country book series • Focuses on customs, culture, and etiquette	• Covers almost every Asian country • Analyzes each culture thoroughly	$156.00 (total for 12 books)	• Retail bookstores • Internet	• Internet	• Does not focus on doing business in Asia • Numerous competitors
Price Waterhouse LLP	1st	• Consulting service	• Personal consultation	Varies with size of firm	• Personnel • Direct marketing channel	• Business-to-business advertising • Referrals • Press releases	• Expensive • Technology-based consulting programs

- Provides travel directories for hotels, restaurants, and emergency resources
- Includes a plethora of photographs and video clips—highly graphical
- PC- or Macintosh-compatible

Benefits

- Time efficient—reduces the need for cross-referencing other sources
- User-friendly—incorporates icons and a search engine for ease of use
- Compact and transportable—lightweight compared with the number of books needed to cover the vast Asian market
- Increases chances for success in Asia—by knowing what to do and what not to do
- Inexpensive compared with other references—numerous books must be purchased to be equivalently informed

Potential for Innovation

At the point at which proliferation of DVD-ROM has increased, Koidra-Tek may use DVD technology in order to enhance its product. With DVD-ROM, more information can be input and excess space would be available for an increased graphical interface.

Proprietary Protection

The company has obtained FORM TX from the U.S. Copyright Office, Library of Congress in order to copyright both the content and source code for *Asia Business Suite* (see Exhibit E). The copyright endures for a term "consisting of the life of the author and fifty years after the author's death."[9] In addition to copyright protection, Koidra-Tek has filed trademark applications for *Asia Business Suite* and the company name.

Other Competitive Advantages

The main competitive advantage of Koidra-Tek's *Asia Business Suite* is that it is the first mover for this type of product combining cultural education with CD-ROM technology. After the introduction of *Asia Business Suite,* many competitors may follow in the company's footsteps, but Koidra-Tek is confident that it will be able to create brand recognition and awareness for the product.

17

Pricing

Asia Business Suite will be priced competitively using a demand-based pricing strategy. Through the company's surveys, it has determined that potential users are willing to pay $39.99–$49.99 for *Asia Business Suite.* The company feels that by pricing at this level, the product will be perceived as being of higher quality yet inexpensive. *Asia Business Suite* has also used psychological pricing, using an odd number to suggest a bargain.

Value Chain

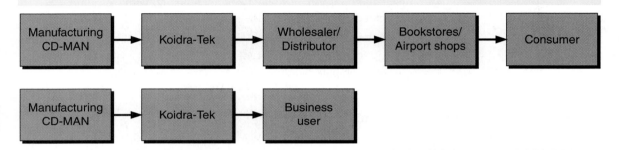

Figure 2

Table 6

	Tasks Performed	Markup
Manufacturing: CD-MAN	Duplication process, multicolor CD label screen printing, CD booklet insert printing, packaging, assembly, quality assurance	$10
Koidra-Tek	Sales and marketing, market research, R&D, process design, technical assistance	Direct: $30 Retail: $10
Wholesaler/ Distributor	Purchases and holds goods, resells to retail outlets	$5
Bookstores/ Airport shops	Provide shelf space for product	$25
Business user/ Consumer	Buys final product	Direct: $40 Retail: $50

PROCESS ANALYSIS

Technical Description of Product

Asia Business Suite will have the following recommended system requirements:

- Microsoft Windows NT, 3.1, 95, 98, or Macintosh operating system
- Personal computer using a 100 MHz processor or better
- 8 MB RAM
- Double speed CD-ROM drive or better
- Color monitor and videocard supporting 256 colors at 640 × 480
- Stereo headphones or speakers
- 8-bit sound card
- 10 MB free hard disk space for installation

Issues of Obsolescence

Due to the development of DVD-ROM, CD-ROMs may become obsolete, however DVD drives will be capable of reading CD-ROMs. The company will respond to customer preferences and industry trends as new technologies are developed.

Status of Development

The current status of development as depicted in Figure 3 is the ongoing process of research and development pertaining to *Asia Business Suite*'s content. Concurrently, market research is conducted to ensure that the final product will adhere to customers' needs and preferences.

Tasks, Time, and Cost to Complete

Tasks still to be completed include the program design and coding, alpha and beta testing, and the implementation of the company's marketing strategy. Program design and coding has been estimated at $25,000. However, the founders are currently negotiating with the USC Computer Science department in an effort to establish an internship program in which students design and code the CD-ROM. Alpha and beta testing will occur through promotional distribution of the CD-ROM to potential customers. The costs associated with testing have been allocated within the company's marketing budget. Please see the Financial Summary section for costs associated with the implementation of the company's marketing plan.

Potential Difficulties and Resolution

Difficulties may arise following the program design and coding. This will be resolved through the use of alpha and beta testing to detect glitches, bugs, or viruses within the product.

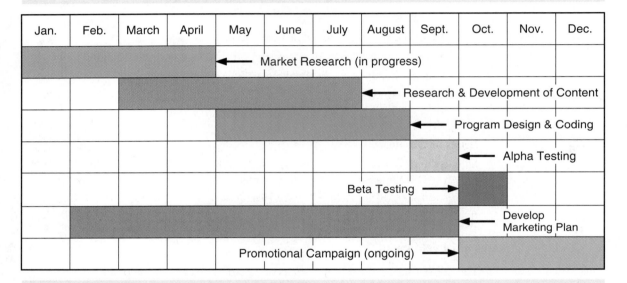

Jan.	Feb.	March	April	May	June	July	August	Sept.	Oct.	Nov.	Dec.

Market Research (in progress)

Research & Development of Content

Program Design & Coding

Alpha Testing

Beta Testing

Develop Marketing Plan

Promotional Campaign (ongoing)

Figure 3 Development Schedule

Distribution Channels and Physical Distribution Plan

Koidra-Tek will have two independent distribution channels for the accessibility of *Asia Business Suite:* direct marketing sales and retail sales. (See Figure 4.) Figure 5 displays the various processes that take place to create the product and deliver it to the customer.

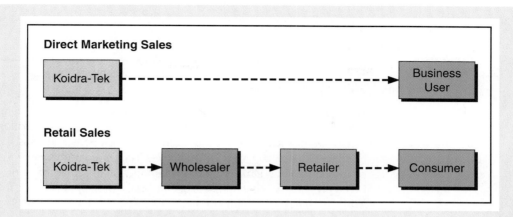

Figure 4 Distribution Channels

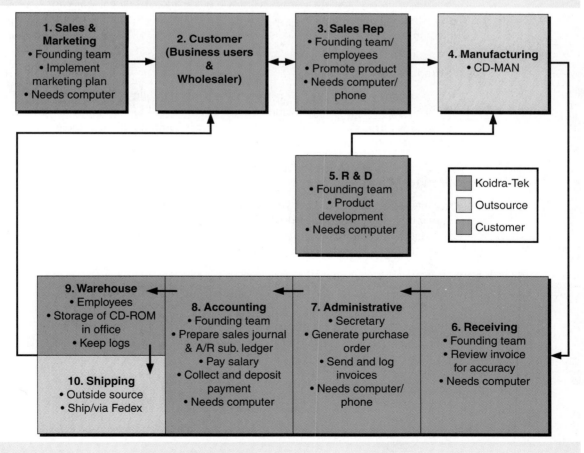

Figure 5 Process Graph

ORGANIZATIONAL PLAN

Management Philosophy and Company Culture

Koidra-Tek is committed to creating an organization that respects and listens to its employees and customers, empowers and encourages full participation of its employees, and allows everyone to share in the company's success. The company will instill a management by objectives (MBO) program similar to that first proposed by Peter Drucker to motivate individuals rather than control them. The program will encompass specific goals, participatively set, for a predetermined time period, with continual feedback on progress.

The company will create a culture that embraces an entrepreneurial-oriented haven for risk takers and innovators to build strategies around distinct competitive attitudes. Creating a strong team will guide and shape behavior consistencies and decision patterns according to the company's core values and mission.

Legal Structure

The company will initially be organized as a limited liability company (LLC) and will file articles of organization with the State of California's Secretary of State. This form was chosen due to the fact that it combines the favorable attributes of both corporations and partnerships.

Organizational Chart

Koidra-Tek's structure is a network of organizations (see Figure 6), which primarily relies on participative decision making. The company has been established as a decentralized, strategic business structure that is flat and uses cross-hierarchical and cross-functional teams.

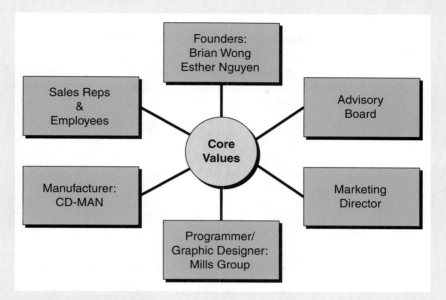

Figure 6 Organizational Network

Compensation Programs and Incentives

The two founding team members have 50 percent ownership interest each in the company but will take minimal compensation of $2,000 a month until the company reaches $100,000 in sales. When the company reaches that goal, the founding team will then increase their compensation to $6,000 a month each and will further increase compensation as the company's profits grow.

Employee Development

In order for Koidra-Tek to be competitively active, the company will incorporate an employee development program to foster the acquisition of skills, rules, concepts, and attitudes. The cost of training will benefit both the company and the employees in the long run.

23

Key Policies

Koidra-Tek's founding team and sales representatives will generate all purchase orders with customers. Internal management will assess the bookkeeping but will hire an outside accounting firm to audit and finalize all financials. The company will internally process paychecks, purchase orders, and accounts payable.

Key Benefits

Koidra-Tek will provide full-time employees with a choice of health care insurance, dental insurance, sick leave, life insurance, or paid time away from work. In order to receive additional benefits, full-time employees must be employed with Koidra-Tek for a minimum of two years.

MARKETING PLAN

The purpose of Koidra-Tek's marketing plan is to create awareness of *Asia Business Suite* and the benefits it offers companies and certain retail outlets, specifically bookstores and airport shops. For companies, product benefits include ease of use, convenience by reducing the need for cross-referencing, and relatively low cost compared with alternative sources. Retail outlets will benefit by advancing into retailing technological products and from the profit potential associated with *Asia Business Suite.* The company will enter into the niche of incorporating education and training with technology to help companies increase their chances of success in their quest for global presence. Initial marketing tactics include direct marketing strategies to companies and retail outlets, direct mail, and public relations efforts. Koidra-Tek's customers will see the company as service oriented with cutting-edge technology that fulfills customers' needs. Twenty percent of gross sales will be allocated to the planning and implementation of marketing strategies.

Purpose of the Marketing Plan

The purpose of Koidra-Tek's marketing plan is to create awareness of *Asia Business Suite* and the benefits it offers to its customers. The company will position itself as a leader in providing information through the use of technology.

Target Market

The company will target companies of all sizes located throughout the United States that have the necessary computer hardware and knowledge. These companies will either currently be or plan to begin conducting business in Asia. In addition, certain retail outlets have been targeted, specifically airport shops and bookstores. Airport shops will be located in international terminals of major airports within the United States. Bookstores will typically be large in size and located in urban areas of the United States.

Unique Market Niche

The unique market niche that Koidra-Tek has attempted to penetrate is that of serving companies that are seeking to increase their chances of success when conducting business in Asia. *Asia Business Suite* allows users to target specific areas of interest relating to business. The user can access any subject within the product with the click of a button or through the product's search engine.

Business Identity

Koidra-Tek is an innovative, quality-driven, service-oriented company that strives to provide and fulfill its customers' needs. The company is determined to increase the probability of success for its customers.

Plans to Reach First Customer

Initially, the company will rely on personal selling, shareware, and public relations efforts to create awareness of *Asia Business Suite*. Public relations efforts will be geared toward critics and columnists to review *Asia Business Suite*. Trade shows and exhibits as well as heavy advertising will be avoided initially due to the high costs associated with these marketing tools.

Marketing Tools

Koidra-Tek has determined that in order to reach its target market, it must use marketing tools geared toward other businesses. The company will use advertising, publicity, personal selling, and is planning to use trade shows and exhibits to reach customers when the marketing budget allows for these more expensive marketing tools.

Media Plan

Advertising

Koidra-Tek will rely on print media for advertising purposes (see Exhibit F). The company has determined that the costs associated with the use of broadcast media are much too great in its start-up stage. In terms of advertising, the company will use various direct marketing tools, specifically direct mail and mail order. Direct mailing lists will be obtained through various sources. See Exhibit G for mailing list companies that will be used in the company's operations.

Personal Selling

Koidra-Tek believes that the selling process consists of several steps which its sales and marketing team must perform (see Figure 7).

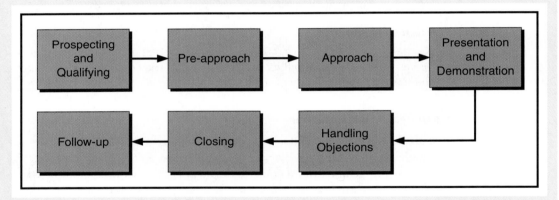

Figure 7 Personal Selling Process

Cooperative Advertising

Koidra-Tek plans to participate in a cooperative advertising program with Berlitz Language books. A majority of Berlitz's end-users travel to Asia to conduct business, making *Asia Business Suite* a complementary product to its language tutorials. The company will sell the idea of this type of coop by discussing the benefits that will be offered to Berlitz.

Publicity

Koidra-Tek's sales force and founders will be responsible for public relations efforts. The company will attempt to create awareness through the use of contacts to allow for feature articles and reviews in various business and computer-related periodicals, magazines, and trade journals.

Trade Shows and Conferences

The founders of Koidra-Tek have researched many trade shows but will currently focus on other forms of creating awareness. See Exhibit G for a list of trade shows and conferences that have been considered.

Marketing Budget

Koidra-Tek will allocate 20 percent of gross sales toward the planning and implementation of its marketing plan. The company understands the enormous costs associated with promotion within the software realm, but it is confident that through its use of public relations, cooperative advertising, and shareware distribution, awareness of *Asia Business Suite* will be created (see Table 7).

Table 7 Marketing Budget

Marketing Tool	Percentage of Marketing Budget
Publicity	0
Cooperative advertising	0
Shareware	0
Direct mailing lists	25
Personal selling (presentation materials, brochures, etc.)	75

FINANCIAL SUMMARY

Summary of Key Points and Capital Requirements

Koidra-Tek's return on investment in its first year of operation is 309 percent with a payback period of eight months. The company will begin operating following graduation of its two founders. Start-up capital in the amount of $50,000 will be supplied through family funds on graduation.

By 2002, the U.S. prepackaged software market is forecast to reach approximately $87 million, increasing by 70 percent from 1997 sales.[10] With this in mind, the company has forecasted sales to grow at 9 percent per month for direct marketing sales and 7 percent for retail sales. After year one, Koidra-Tek believes sales of _Asia Business Suite_ will level off, at which point a new product will be introduced. Sales patterns of the company's second product is expected to follow a similar growth pattern as _Asia Business Suite._ By the end of year two, sales of each product are expected to have leveled off.

Keeping in mind the highly innovative and competitive prepackaged software industry in which Koidra-Tek operates, 20 percent of gross sales will be allocated toward the marketing budget. Refer to the Marketing Plan section for an in-depth analysis of the company's strategic marketing plan.

It is clear that this venture is a profitable one. The high return on investment, the quick payback period, and its growth potential are all factors that illustrate Koidra-Tek's potential for success. The necessary management and advisory boards are in place and will begin operating in the months to come.

Financial Assumptions and Premises

Sales Forecast

Koidra-Tek has based its sales forecast on its primary research conducted throughout the Southern California area as well as its secondary research. According to Anthony Picardi of International Data Corp., sales of prepackaged software rose 12 percent in 1997 and 12.8 percent in 1998 on average.[11] The company believes it will be able to sustain 9 percent growth each month for direct marketing sales and 7 percent growth for retail sales due to the uniqueness of the product and the niche market it is entering. For the first month of business, Koidra-Tek will target a sales goal of 300 units using direct marketing methods. Retail sales are targeted at 300 units beginning in month two.

Direct marketing sales will account for 65 percent of sales revenues, whereas retail sales will account for 35 percent. These percentages have been derived from Koidra-Tek's focus on intense direct marketing strategies nationwide, using personal selling, direct mailings, and Internet shareware to create awareness for _Asia Business Suite._ Retail sales will be substantially less than direct marketing sales due to the nature of computer retail outlets, which are hesitant to carry "new" unestablished products.

In year two, the company believes sales of *Asia Business Suite* will level off and product growth will cease. Koidra-Tek will introduce a second product (name undetermined as of yet) using its established channels of distribution and brand recognition. Koidra-Tek firmly believes that the growth and success of this product will be similar to that of *Asia Business Suite.*

Cash Receipts

On graduation, the founders' parents have agreed to fund Koidra-Tek with $25,000 each as a graduation gift. This amount does not need to be reimbursed to either of the founders' parents.

On one hand, direct marketing sales will be collected on a net 30 basis due to the belief that most orders will be purchased via a credit card or check. This belief is based on surveys conducted by Koidra-Tek, which suggest that customers would prefer to pay either by credit card or check. On the other hand, retail sales will be collected on a net 60 basis, which is the average industry standard. Collection of Koidra-Tek's second product line will follow similar patterns to that of *Asia Business Suite.*

Upfront Cash

Research Materials   Various research materials were purchased by Koidra-Tek in order to develop the content of *Asia Business Suite.* These costs include purchases of books, and magazines, as well as trade journals.

Utilities and Prepaid Insurance   Utilities expense has been derived from Koidra-Tek's web site design and telephone set-up fees. The company has endorsed VS Connect to create and maintain its web site at *www.koidratek.com.* A $150 fee for the design and set-up of a web page includes InterNIC fees for the virtual domain name. Pacific Bell will service the company's telephone needs with an initial set-up cost of $160. General product liability insurance has been arranged through Allstate Insurance Company at an annual cost of $500. A $90 insurance premium has been assessed by Allstate.

SPA Membership   Koidra-Tek has decided to become a member of the Software Publishers Association (SPA) because of the many benefits the organization offers. Membership dues for start-up companies are $495 and this fee increases in correlation with company sales (see Exhibit H).

29

Legal Koidra-Tek is in the process of filing its Limited Liability Company Articles of Organization with the State of California. Trademarks for Koidra-Tek and *Asia Business Suite* will be filed with the U.S. Patent and Trademark Office. *Asia Business Suite* will be copyrighted with the U.S. Copyright Office, Library of Congress. The Law Offices of Herman Thordsen will perform all legal aspects pertaining to the formation of the company and filing of necessary documents. All future legal activities will be performed by Mr. Thordsen.

Operating Reserve An account has been established by Koidra-Tek for operating reserves to ensure that in the event that sales forecasts are not met, adequate funds are available to cover fixed expenses. This account will allow the company to operate for a period of two months in order to adjust for such events.

CD-ROM Programming John Mills, M.F.A., of Mills Group Multimedia, will program *Asia Business Suite*. The project will be completed in four to six weeks for a total cost of $25,000.

In year two, Koidra-Tek will employ Mills Group Multimedia to program the company's second product. Costs are estimated at $25,000 based on prior dealings with Mr. Mills and his company.

Variable Costs

Shipping and Handling Koidra-Tek's shipping and handling of *Asia Business Suite* and its future products will be carried out by FedEx. Shipping and handling costs have been determined to be $0.09 per unit.

Manufacturing, Printing, and Packaging Koidra-Tek will outsource all manufacturing, printing, and packaging to CD-MAN to produce *Asia Business Suite*. CD-MAN is responsible for performing the following tasks with respective costs per unit. The costs listed in Table 8 are for volumes under 3,000 units.

Sales Commission Initially, Koidra-Tek will perform all tasks associated with selling. On reaching $30,000 in sales, the company will employ one sales representative who will receive commissions of 3 percent of gross sales.*

* Throughout this discussion, note that gross sales are based on an accrual basis for tax purposes.

Table 8 Manufacturing, Printing, and Packaging Costs

Task to Be Completed	Cost/Unit (volumes under 3,000)
Duplication process	$0.89
Multicolor CD label screen printing	$0.15
CD booklet insert printing	$0.59
Packaging (including cost of jewel box, shrink wrap, and assembly)	$0.17

In year two, an additional sales representative will be employed with an equivalent compensation package. The two sales representatives will continue to be employed by Koidra-Tek throughout year three.

Research and Development   Koidra-Tek understands that in order to be successful in the increasingly competitive technology industry it must continually analyze potential products and the industry. The company will take 5 percent of gross sales after reaching $30,000 sales revenue. The research and development will be used for the growth of the company and for new product development.

Marketing   Koidra-Tek will allocate 20 percent of gross sales toward its marketing budget. The company may increase this amount if it believes it is not receiving the exposure it desires. This includes the costs associated with promotions, advertisements, and direct mailings.

Contingency Fund   The company will create a contingency fund in addition to its operating reserve to accommodate unforeseen events, such as a decline in sales, loss of key employees, changes in the U.S. economy, product liability, taxes and regulations, and other events that may occur. The fund will be derived as 3.5 percent of gross sales.

Fixed Expenses

Founding Team Salary   During the first year of operation, Koidra-Tek's founders will draw $2,000 each, per month, which the company feels is reasonable in relation to projected sales. On gross sales in excess of $55,000, each founder will receive $4,000 per month, and at $85,000 sales they will receive $5,000 each.

Employees   Koidra-Tek will employ a part-time secretary and a part-time marketing director. Initially, salary for the secretary and marketing director will be $24,000 combined. This amount will increase to $48,000 in year two and $60,000 in the company's third year of operation.

Overhead   The company's overhead will be distributed among its costs of office supplies, product liability and health insurance, telephone expense, maintenance, and travel expenses. Any unforeseen expenses in excess of the allotted amount will be drawn from the company's contingency fund.

Office—Bartering Agreement   Koidra-Tek has arranged for office space with Bridge America in an effort to reduce overhead costs. In exchange for the office space, the company will assist in the development of international projects within the company's scope of operations. Koidra-Tek will supply its own telephone lines and computers. This agreement will be valid for a period no less than one year.

In years two and three, the founders have elected to lease an office in the Irvine area. Furnishings will be brought in by each of the founders in an effort to reduce costs. The cost of the office is estimated at $1,000 per month according to the management of Koidra-Tek's current locality.

Koidra-Tek	Premise	Month 0	Month 1 Jan	Month 2 Feb	Month 3 Mar	Month 4 Apr	Month 5 May	Month 6 Jun	Month 7 Jul	Month 8 Aug	Month 9 Sep	Month 10 Oct	Month 11 Nov	Month 12 Dec	Total
Cash Needs Assessment															
Units Sold per Month															
Direct Sales	9% growth per mo		300	327	356	389	423	462	503	548	598	652	710	774	6,042
Retail Sales	7% growth per mo		–	300	321	343	368	393	421	450	482	515	552	590	4,735
Total Units			300	627	677	732	791	855	924	999	1,080	1,167	1,262	1,364	10,777
Sales Revenue															
Direct Sales	$39.99 per unit		12,000	13,080	14,257	15,540	16,939	18,463	20,125	21,936	23,911	26,063	28,408	30,957	241,681
Retail Sales	$19.99 per unit		–	6,000	6,420	6,869	7,350	7,865	8,415	9,004	9,635	10,309	11,031	11,803	94,702
Total Sales Revenue			12,000	19,080	20,677	22,410	24,289	26,328	28,541	30,941	33,545	36,372	39,439	42,760	336,382
Cash Receipts															
Direct Sales	Collection in 30 days			12,000	13,080	14,257	15,540	16,939	18,463	20,125	21,936	23,911	26,063	28,408	210,724
Retail Sales	Collection in 60 days				6,000	6,000	6,420	6,869	7,350	7,865	8,415	9,004	9,635	10,309	71,868
Total Cash Receipts			–	12,000	13,080	20,257	21,960	23,808	25,814	27,990	30,352	32,915	35,697	38,717	282,591
Upfront Cost															
Research Materials		300													
Utilities/Prepaid Insurance		400													
SPA Membership Application		495													
Legal		1,595													
Operating Reserve		11,200													
CD-ROM Programming		25,000													
Total Upfront Cash		38,990	–	–	–	–	–	–	–	–	–	–	–	–	38,990
Variable Cost															
Shipping & Handling	$0.09 per unit		27	56	61	66	71	77	83	90	97	105	114	123	970
Manufacturing Costs	$0.89 per unit		267	558	603	651	704	761	822	889	961	1,039	1,123	1,214	9,592
Printing & Packaging Costs	$0.93 per unit		279	583	630	681	736	795	859	929	1,004	1,085	1,173	1,269	10,023
Research & Development	5% of gross sales @ $30,000		–	–	–	–	–	–	–	1,547	1,677	1,819	1,972	2,138	9,153
Sales Representative	3% of gross sales @ $30,000		–	–	–	–	–	–	–	928	1,006	1,091	1,183	1,283	5,492
Marketing	20% of gross sales		2,400	3,816	4,135	4,482	4,858	5,266	5,708	6,188	6,709	7,274	7,888	8,552	67,276
Contingency Fund	3.5% of gross sales		420	668	724	784	850	921	999	1,083	1,174	1,273	1,380	1,497	11,773
Total Variable Cost			3,393	5,681	6,153	6,664	7,219	7,820	8,472	11,654	12,629	13,686	14,833	16,075	114,279
Fixed Expenses															
Founding Team															
Salary (2)	$1,500 per mo each		3,000	3,000	3,000	3,000	3,000	3,000	3,000	3,000	3,000	3,000	3,000	3,000	36,000
Employees	$2,000 per mo		2,000	2,000	2,000	2,000	2,000	2,000	2,000	2,000	2,000	2,000	2,000	2,000	24,000
Overhead	$600 per mo		600	600	600	600	600	600	600	600	600	600	600	600	7,200
Total Fixed Expenses			5,600	5,600	5,600	5,600	5,600	5,600	5,600	5,600	5,600	5,600	5,600	5,600	67,200
Total Cash Expenditures		(38,990)	8,993	11,281	11,753	12,264	12,819	13,420	14,072	17,254	18,229	19,286	20,433	21,675	220,469
Net Cash Flow for Month		–	(8,993)	719	1,327	7,993	9,142	10,389	11,742	10,736	12,123	13,629	15,264	17,042	62,122
Cash Balance: Beg. of Mo		–	(38,990)	(47,983)	(47,264)	(45,937)	(37,945)	(28,803)	(18,414)	(6,672)	4,064	16,187	29,816	45,080	62,122
Cash Balance: End of Mo		(38,990)	(47,983)	(47,264)	(45,937)	(37,945)	(28,803)	(18,414)	(6,672)	4,064	16,187	29,816	45,080	62,122	

Figure 8 Cash Needs Assessment

33

Balance Sheet		Year 1	Year 2	Year 3
As of December 31, 1999-2001				
Assets		**Year 1**	**Year 2**	**Year 3**
Current Assets				
	Cash	112,122	366,766	769,515
	Accounts Receivables	53,791	109,783	110,555
	Prepaid Assets	38,990	67,755	72,750
	Total Current Assets	204,903	544,304	952,820
Total Assets		**204,903**	**544,304**	**952,820**
Liabilities				
	Total Liabilities	—	—	—
Equity				
	Capital Stock	50,000	50,000	50,000
	Retained Earnings: Beg.	—	154,903	494,304
	Distribution of Profits	154,903	339,401	408,516
	Total Equity	154,903	494,304	902,820
Total Liabilities & Equity		**204,903**	**544,304**	**952,820**

Figure 9 Balance Sheet

Sources & Uses		Year 1	Year 2	Year 3
Sources		36,495	36,861	37,226
	Personal Funds	50,000	154,903	339,401
	Net Income	154,903	339,401	408,516
Total of Funding Sources		204,903	494,304	747,916
Applications of Funds				
	Distribution of Profits	154,903	339,401	408,516
Total Funds Applied		154,903	339,401	408,516
Net Increase in Working Capital		50,000	154,903	339,401
		204,903	494,304	747,916

Figure 10 Sources & Uses

34

Where the funds went:				
Upfront cash			38,990	
Accounts Receivables			12,000	
Start-up Profit			(3,007)	
		Total	47,983	
Capital Requirements		47,983		
Break-Even Analysis for Year 1				
Fixed Cost	67,200			
Variable Cost	11			
Selling Price				
Direct Marketing Sales	40			
Retail Sales	20			
Break-Even Point		Fixed Cost		
	Selling Price/Unit-Variable Cost/Unit			
Direct Marketing Break Even		2,287	units	
Retail Break Even		7,159	units	
Payback Period	7 months			

Figure 11 Cash Needs Assessment

Koidra-Tek Cash Flow Year 1	Premise	Start-up	Month 1 Jan	Month 2 Feb	Month 3 Mar	Month 4 Apr	Month 5 May	Month 6 Jun	Month 7 Jul	Month 8 Aug	Month 9 Sep	Month 10 Oct	Month 11 Nov	Month 12 Dec	Total
Units Sold per Month															
Direct Sales	9% growth per mo		300	327	356	389	423	462	503	548	598	652	710	774	6,042
Retail Sales	7% growth per mo		–	300	321	343	368	393	421	450	482	515	552	590	4,735
Total Units			300	627	677	732	791	855	924	999	1,080	1,167	1,262	1,364	10,777
Sales Revenue															
Direct Sales	$39.99 per unit		12,000	13,080	14,257	15,540	16,939	18,463	20,125	21,936	23,911	26,063	28,408	30,957	241,681
Retail Sales	$19.99 per unit		–	6,000	6,420	6,869	7,350	7,865	8,415	9,004	9,635	10,309	11,031	11,803	94,702
Total Sales Revenue			12,000	19,080	20,677	22,410	24,289	26,328	28,541	30,941	33,545	36,372	39,439	42,760	336,382
Cash Receipts															
Direct Sales	Collection in 30 days		–	12,000	13,080	14,257	15,540	16,939	18,463	20,125	21,936	23,911	26,063	28,408	210,724
Retail Sales	Collection in 60 days		–	–	–	6,000	6,420	6,869	7,350	7,865	8,415	9,004	9,635	10,309	71,868
Gift Funds	$50,000 Cash	50,000													50,000
Total Cash Receipts		50,000	–	12,000	13,080	20,257	21,960	23,808	25,814	27,990	30,352	32,915	35,697	38,717	332,591
Upfront Cost															
Research Materials		300													
Utilities/Prepaid Insurance		400													
SPA Membership Dues		495													
Legal		1,595													
Operating Reserve		11,200													
CD-ROM Programming		25,000													
Total Upfront Cash		38,990													38,990
Variable Cost															
Shipping & Handling	$0.09 per unit		27	56	61	66	71	77	83	90	97	105	114	123	970
Manufacturing Costs	$0.89 per unit		267	558	603	651	704	761	822	889	961	1,039	1,123	1,214	9,592
Printing & Packaging	$0.93 per unit		279	583	630	681	736	795	859	929	1,004	1,085	1,173	1,269	10,023
Research & Development	5% of gross sales @ $30,000		–	–	–	–	–	–	–	1,547	1,677	1,819	1,972	2,138	9,153
Sales Representative	3% of gross sales @ $30,000		–	–	–	–	–	–	–	928	1,006	1,091	1,183	1,283	5,492
Marketing	20% of gross sales		2,400	3,816	4,135	4,482	4,858	5,266	5,708	6,188	6,709	7,274	7,888	8,552	67,276
Contingency fund	3.5% of gross sales		420	668	724	784	850	921	999	1,083	1,174	1,273	1,380	1,497	11,773
Total Variable Cost			3,393	5,681	6,153	6,664	7,219	7,820	8,472	11,654	12,629	13,686	14,833	16,075	114,279
Fixed Expenses															
Founders Team Salary (2)	$1,500 per mo each		3,000	3,000	3,000	3,000	3,000	3,000	3,000	3,000	3,000	3,000	3,000	3,000	36,000
Employees	$2,000 per mo		2,000	2,000	2,000	2,000	2,000	2,000	2,000	2,000	2,000	2,000	2,000	2,000	24,000
Overhead	$600 per mo		600	600	600	600	600	600	600	600	600	600	600	600	7,200
Total Fixed Expenses			5,600	5,600	5,600	5,600	5,600	5,600	5,600	5,600	5,600	5,600	5,600	5,600	67,200
Total Cash Expenditures	38,990	38,990	8,993	11,281	11,753	12,264	12,819	13,420	14,072	17,254	18,229	19,286	20,433	21,675	220,469
Net Cash Flow for Month	–	11,010	(8,993)	719	1,327	7,993	9,142	10,389	11,742	10,736	12,123	13,629	15,264	17,042	112,122
Cash Balance: Beg. of Mo		–	11,010	2,017	2,736	4,063	12,055	21,197	31,586	43,328	54,064	66,187	79,816	95,080	
Cash Balance: In/Out per Mo		11,010	(8,993)	719	1,327	7,993	9,142	10,389	11,742	10,736	12,123	13,629	15,264	17,042	
Cash Balance	11,010	11,010	2,017	2,736	4,063	12,055	21,197	31,586	43,328	54,064	66,187	79,816	95,080	112,122	112,122

Figure 12 Cash Flow, Year One

36

Koidra-Tek						
Cash Flow—Year 2						
Units Sold Quarterly	**Premise**	**Qtr 1**	**Qtr 2**	**Qtr 3**	**Qtr 4**	**Total**
Direct Sales	Sustain growth of product A plus 9% growth per mo for product B	3,383	3,674	4,049	4,536	15,642
Retail Sales	Sustain growth of product A plus 7% growth per mo for product B	2,421	2,904	3,153	3,457	11,935
Total Units		5,804	6,578	7,202	7,993	27,577
Sales Revenue						
Direct Sales	$39.99 per unit	135,303	146,906	161,932	181,391	625,532
Retail Sales	$19.99 per unit	48,420	58,084	63,054	69,143	238,702
Total Sales Revenue		183,723	204,991	224,986	250,534	864,234
Cash Receipts						
Direct Sales	Collection in 30 days	120,015	142,701	156,486	174,338	593,540
Retail Sales	Collection in 60 days	34,834	55,289	59,630	64,948	214,702
Total Cash Receipts		154,849	197,990	216,116	239,286	808,242
Upfront Cost						
SPA Membership Dues						
Legal						
CD-ROM Programming						
Total Upfront Cash		28,765	–	–	–	28,765
Variable Cost						
Shipping & Handling	$0.09 per unit	522	592	648	719	2,482
Manufacturing Costs	$0.89 per unit	5,166	5,854	6,410	7,114	24,544
Printing & Packaging Costs	$0.93 per unit	5,398	6,117	6,698	7,434	25,647
Research & Development	5% of gross sales	9,186	10,250	11,249	12,527	43,212
Sales Representative (2)	3% of gross sales each	11,023	12,299	13,499	15,032	51,854
Marketing	20% of gross sales	36,745	40,998	44,997	50,107	172,847
Contingency Fund	3.5% of gross sales	6,430	7,175	7,875	8,769	30,248
Total Variable Cost		74,471	83,285	91,376	101,701	350,833
Fixed Expenses						
Founding Team Salary (2)	$4,000 per mo each	24,000	24,000	24,000	24,000	96,000
Employees	$4,000 per mo	12,000	12,000	12,000	12,000	48,000
Office	$1,000 per mo	3,000	3,000	3,000	3,000	12,000
Overhead	$1,500 per mo	4,500	4,500	4,500	4,500	18,000
Total Fixed Expenses		43,500	43,500	43,500	43,500	174,000
Total Cash Expenditures		146,736	126,785	134,876	145,201	553,598
Net Cash Flow for Month		8,113	71,205	81,240	94,086	254,644
Cash Balance: Beg. of Mo		103,944	166,709	244,326	333,773	
Cash Balance: In/Out per Mo		16,291	24,731	28,354	32,993	
Cash Balance		120,235	191,440	272,680	366,766	

Figure 13 Cash Flow, Year Two

37

Koidra-Tek						
Cash Flow—Year 3						
Units Sold Quarterly	**Premise**	**Qtr 1**	**Qtr 2**	**Qtr 3**	**Qtr 4**	**Total**
Direct Sales	Stabilize Growth	4,722	4,722	4,722	4,722	18,890
Retail Sales	Stabilize Growth	3,570	3,570	3,570	3,570	14,282
Total Units		8,293	8,293	8,293	8,293	33,171
Sales Revenue						
Direct Sales	$39.99 per unit	188,848	188,848	188,848	188,848	755,393
Retail Sales	$19.99 per unit	71,409	71,409	71,409	71,409	285,635
Total Sales Revenue		260,257	260,257	260,257	260,257	1,041,027
Cash Receipts						
Direct Sales	Collection in 30 days	188,848	188,848	188,848	188,848	755,393
Retail Sales	Collection in 60 days	70,637	71,409	71,409	71,409	284,863
Total Cash Receipts		259,485	260,257	260,257	260,257	1,040,255
Upfront Cost						
SPA Membership Dues						
Total Upfront Cash		4,995	–	–	–	4,995
Variable Cost						
Shipping & Handling	$0.09 per unit	746	746	746	746	2,985
Manufacturing Costs	$0.89 per unit	7,381	7,381	7,381	7,381	29,522
Printing & Packaging Costs	$0.93 per unit	7,712	7,712	7,712	7,712	30,849
Research & Development	5% of gross sales	13,013	13,013	13,013	13,013	52,051
Sales Representative (2)	3% of gross sales each	15,615	15,615	15,615	15,615	62,462
Marketing	20% of gross sales	52,051	52,051	52,051	52,051	208,205
Contingency Fund	3.5% of gross sales	9,109	9,109	9,109	9,109	36,436
Total Variable Cost		105,628	105,628	105,628	105,628	422,512
Fixed Expenses						
Founding Team Salary (2)	$5,000 per mo each	30,000	30,000	30,000	30,000	120,000
Employees	$5,000 per mo	15,000	15,000	15,000	15,000	60,000
Office	$1,000 per mo	3,000	3,000	3,000	3,000	12,000
Overhead	$1,500 per mo	4,500	4,500	4,500	4,500	18,000
Total Fixed Expenses		52,500	52,500	52,500	52,500	210,000
Total Cash Expenditures		163,123	158,128	158,128	158,128	637,507
Net Cash Flow for Month		96,362	102,129	102,129	102,129	402,749
Cash Balance: Beg. of Mo		429,085	531,214	633,343	735,472	
Cash Balance: In/Out per Mo		34,043	34,043	34,043	34,043	
Cash Balance		463,128	565,257	667,386	769,514	

Figure 14 Cash Flow, Year Three

Koidra-Tek							
Profit & Loss—Years 1–3	**Year 1**					**Year 2**	**Year 3**
Units Sold per Month	Qtr 1	Qtr 2	Qtr 3	Qtr 4	Total	Total	Total
Direct Sales	983	1,274	1,649	2,136	6,042	15,642	18,890
Retail Sales	621	1,104	1,353	1,657	4,735	11,935	14,282
Total Units	1,604	2,378	3,002	3,793	10,777	27,577	33,171
Sales Revenue							
Direct Sales	39,337	50,943	65,972	85,428	241,681	625,532	755,393
Retail Sales	12,420	22,084	27,054	33,143	94,702	238,702	285,635
Total Sales Revenue	51,757	73,027	93,027	118,571	336,382	864,234	1,041,027
Variable Cost							
Shipping & Handling	144	214	270	341	970	2,482	2,985
Manufacturing Costs	1,428	2,116	2,672	3,376	9,592	24,544	29,522
Printing & Packaging Costs	1,492	2,211	2,792	3,528	10,023	25,647	30,849
Research & Development	–	–	3,224	5,929	9,153	43,212	52,051
Sales Representative	–	–	1,935	3,557	5,492	51,854	62,462
Marketing	10,351	14,605	18,605	23,714	67,276	172,847	208,205
Contingency Fund	1,812	2,556	3,256	4,150	11,773	30,248	36,436
Total Variable Cost	15,227	21,703	32,754	44,595	114,279	350,833	422,512
Fixed Expenses							
Founding Team Salary (2)	9,000	9,000	9,000	9,000	36,000	96,000	120,000
Employees	6,000	6,000	6,000	6,000	24,000	48,000	60,000
Office	–	–	–	–	–	12,000	12,000
Overhead	1,800	1,800	1,800	1,800	7,200	18,000	18,000
Total Fixed Expenses	16,800	16,800	16,800	16,800	67,200	174,000	210,000
Total Cost	32,027	38,503	49,554	61,395	181,479	524,833	632,512
Net Profit (Loss)	19,730	34,524	43,473	57,177	154,903	339,401	408,516
Cummulative Profit (Loss)	19,730	54,254	97,727	154,903		494,304	902,820

Figure 15 Profit and Loss, Years 1–3

GROWTH PLAN

Strategy for Growth

Koidra-Tek will introduce a second product similar to that of its initial product, *Asia Business Suite*. This line extension will discuss similar issues of business-related conduct, but it will focus on different geographic regions of the world.

As stated previously, the company is aware of the development of DVD and will look to that form in response to customer preferences as well as storage demands.

Resources for Growth

Funding for growth will be supplied from the company's previous earnings. In addition, an account for research and development has been established to ensure that competitive advantages with respect to products and innovation are maintained.

Infrastructure Changes

Through growth, Koidra-Tek's founders will delegate responsibilities and ensure that the team buys into the growth vision. Koidra-Tek will attempt to achieve a customer-centered growth strategy. This will be accomplished by learning what customers value most and focusing on what they feel are the company's core competencies.

APPENDIX: EXIT STRATEGY

If at some point the founders of Koidra-Tek believe the company has reached a level at which professional management is needed to carry on with the day-to-day activities, it will seek the option of cashing out but will continue to participate in management. This option will be executed by selling stock in the company to an outside investor without relinquishing all participatory powers.

Koidra-Tek will employ a business broker to assist in the sale of the company. A third-party appraiser will also be employed on agreement of both Koidra-

Tek and the potential purchaser. Prior to agreeing to sell the company, the following two key aspects must be understood by the purchaser:

- Each of the founders will share equally in the selling price of the company as stated in the partnership agreement
- Each of the founders will serve as members of the board of directors for a period of no less than four years

REFERENCES

[1] Kathleen Allen, *Launching New Ventures: An Entrepreneurial Approach* (Chicago, IL: Upstart Publishing Co., 1995), p. 359.

[2] John A. Pearce and Richard B. Robinson, *An Industry Approach to Cases in Strategic Management* (Chicago, IL: Irwin Book Team, 1996), p. 244.

[3] "Software," *Business Week,* 12 January 1998, p. 86.

[4] One Source Information Systems, Inc., July 1997.

[5] Dr. Roger Hutchinson, "DVD: The Next Generation of CD-ROM," *PC Computing,* 25 January 1997, p. 38.

[6] Simba Information Inc., "Multimedia Title Publishing 1996–97: Review, Trends & Forecast," 17 February 1998.

[7] Standard & Poor, "Standard & Poor's Industry Surveys, Computers: Software," 19 June 1997, p. 16.

[8] Steven C. Hudgik, *Make Money Selling Your Shareware* (New York: Windcrest/McGraw-Hill, 1996), p. 31.

[9] K. Allen, *Launching New Ventures,* Upstart, 1995.

[10] One Source Information Systems, Inc., July 1997.

[11] "Software," *Business Week,* 12 January 1998, p. 86.

State of California
Bill Jones
Secretary of State

LLC-1

LIMITED LIABILITY COMPANY
ARTICLES OF ORGANIZATION

IMPORTANT - Read the instructions before completing the form.
This document is presented for filing pursuant to Section 17050 of the California Corporations Code.

1. Limited liability company name:
   (End the name with LLC, L.L.C., Limited Liability Company or Ltd. Liability Co.)

2. Latest date (month/day/year) on which the limited liability company is to dissolve.

3. The purpose of the limited liability company is to engage in any lawful act or activity for which a limited liability company may be organized under the Beverly-Killea Limited Liability Company Act.

4. Enter the name and address of initial agent for service of process and check the appropriate provision below:

   _____, which is

   [   ] an individual residing in California.

   [   ] a corporation which has filed a certificate pursuant to Section 1505 of the California Corporations Code. Skip Item 5 and proceed to Item 6.

5. If the initial agent for service of process is an individual, enter a business or residential street address in California:

   Street address:

   City: State: California   Zip Code:

6. The limited liability company will be managed by: **(check one)**

   [   ] one manager   [   ] more than one manager   [   ] limited liability company members

7. Describe type of business of the Limited Liability Company.

8. If other matters are to be included in the Articles of Organization attach one or more separate pages. Number of pages attached, if any: ⬜

9. It is hereby declared that I am the person who executed this instrument, which execution is my act and deed.

For Secretary of State Use

File No. _____

_____
Signature of organizer

_____
Type or print name of organizer

Date: _____ , 19 _____

SEC/STATE (REV. 8/97)   FORM LLC-1 -- FILING FEE: $70
                               Approved By Secretary Of State

Exhibit A   Articles of Organization for a Limited Liability Company

Mailing Address:

Name:

Address

City

FILING FEE: $10.00 for 1 FBN and 2 registrants plus
$2.00 for each additional FBN/registrant

FICTITIOUS BUSINESS NAME STATEMENT

THE FOLLOWING PERSON(S) IS (ARE) DOING BUSINESS AS: (Attach additional pages if required)

1 — Fictitious Business Name(s)
1

2

3.
*See "Note" Below
Articles of incorporation Number (if applicable)
AL #

2 — Street Address & City of Principal Place of Business in California (P.O. Box alone not acceptable) | Zip Code

3 — Full name of Registrant | (if corporation - incorporated in what state)

Residence Street Address | City | State | Zip Code

3A — Full name of Registrant | (if corporation - incorporated in what state)

Residence Street Address | City | State | Zip Code

3B — Full name of Registrant | (if corporation - incorporated in what state)

Residence Street Address | City | State | Zip Code

*See "Note" Below

4 — This Business is conducted by: (check one only)
( ) an individual   ( ) a general partnership   ( ) joint venture   ( ) a business trust
( ) co-partners   ( ) husband and wife   ( ) a corporation   ( ) a limited partnership
( ) an unincorporated association other than a partnership   ( ) other - please specify___

5 — ( ) The registrant commenced to transact business under the fictitious business name or names listed on (date):___
( ) Registrant has not yet begun to transact business under the fictitious business name or names listed herein.

6 — If registrant is not a corporation sign below:

SIGNATURE _____ TYPE OR PRINT NAME _____

SIGNATURE _____ TYPE OR PRINT NAME _____

SIGNATURE _____ TYPE OR PRINT NAME _____

6A — If registrant is a corporation sign below:

CORPORATION NAME

SIGNATURE & TITLE

TYPE OR PRINT OFFICERS NAME AND TITLE

This statement was filed with the County Clerk of _____ **LOS ANGELES** _____ County on date indicated by file stamp above.

NOTICE - THIS FICTITIOUS NAME STATEMENT EXPIRES FIVE YEARS FROM DATE IT WAS FILED IN THE OFFICE OF THE COUNTY CLERK. A NEW FICTITIOUS BUSINESS NAME STATEMENT MUST BE FILED PRIOR TO THAT DATE. The filing of this statement does not of itself authorize the use in this state of a fictitious business name in violation of the rights of another under federal, state, or common law (See Section 14400 et seq., Business and Professional Code).

REGISTRAR - RECORDER/COUNTY CLERK
BUSINESS FILING AND REGISTRATION
P.O. BOX 592, LOS ANGELES, CA 90053-0592
PH (310) 462-2060

THIS FORM SHOULD BE TYPED
OR PRINTED "LEGIBLY" IN BLACK INK

Exhibit B   Fictitious Business Name Statement

ESTHER NGUYEN
55 Paquita Espana Ct.
Morgan Hill, CA 95037
(408) 555-8307
estherng@scf.usc.edu

EDUCATION

UNIVERSITY OF SOUTHERN CALIFORNIA
Bachelor of Science, Entrepreneur Program, May 1998

WORK EXPERIENCE

Franchisee, ARCO Monterey Mini Mart (August 1997–Present)
• Extensive training and certification by the am/pm Franchise Training Program
• Proficient in Financial Accounting System and Point of Sale
• Established management training that is applicable in each am/pm facility

Clerk, Marc B. Hankin, Law Offices of (January 1996–May 1997)
• Updated and maintained law files and documents for court
• Researched and organized reports
• Revised drafts and memorandums

Computer Operator, University Computer Center (January 1995– January 1996)
• Processed reports and data through the Internet
• Operated programs such as UNIX with various types of PCs, Apples, and Sun Systems
• Typed, cleaned, and distributed printouts

Manager, ARCO Monterey Mini Mart (January 1991–August 1994)
• Interacted diplomatically with employees regarding wages, benefits, and work schedules
• Generated correspondence with representatives from various corporations
• Compiled and updated reports on purchases, inventory, and bookkeeping

SKILLS

IBM, Mac, and SUNS experience
Proficient in Word, Excel, PowerPoint, WorkPerfect, ECCO, Timeslips, and Internet
Fluent in Vietnamese

VOLUNTEERING & ACTIVITIES

President & Special Event Coordinator, Vietnamese Student Association (1995–1998)
• Initiated and directed events for the service/culture–oriented club
• Functioned as a liaison between various VSA organization and student programming entities
• Committee member for the Garden Grove Vietnamese New Year's festivals
• Coordinated and supervised the largest Vietnamese Café Cultural Night

Pledge, Phi Alpha Delta (1994)
• Academic national organization functioned to promote the law field
• Organized events for the service organization
• Scheduled speakers for open forum

INTERESTS

Ice Skating competitor and coach, snow skiing, snowboarding, basketball, and community work

Exhibit C-A   Founders' Resumes

BRIAN WONG
brianwon@scf.usc.edu

527 21st Street   (310) 555-7200
Santa Monica, CA 90402   (310) 555-3045

EDUCATION

University of Southern California, Marshall School of Business
B.S., Business Administration—Entrepreneurship and Finance, Dec. 1988

University of California at Los Angeles
Fulfilled general education requirements, Sept. 1994–June 1996

National Taiwan Normal University
Developed basic reading, writing, and conversational Mandarin, Summer 1996

EXPERIENCE

Assistant Manager, Wilshire Serrano Motel, July 1996–June 1997
- Involved in daily operations, including customer service and inventory management
- Assisted in the implementation of an internal control system to deter theft and increase accountability and profits

Administrative Assistant, Sunshine Realty, June 1994–June 1996
- Acquired various management skills and expanded knowledge of real estate laws and practices
- Responsible for filing, data entry, bookkeeping, and miscellaneous errands

ACTIVITIES

Member, Chinese-American Basketball League, June 1992–Present

Volunteer, Project Hunger, August 1994–Jan. 1995
- Provided food for homeless individuals
- Participated in support groups for members of the shelter

SKILLS

- Working knowledge of Microsoft Word, Excel, PowerPoint, Publisher, Windows 3.0 and 95, WordPerfect, and the Internet
- Proficient in Chinese—Mandarin

INTERESTS

Basketball, snow skiing, snowboarding, musicals, and searching the Internet

Exhibit C-B   Founders' Resumes

45

Koidra-Tek Survey

Are you a: ❏ Freshman ❏ Sophomore ❏ Jr. ❏ Sr. ❏ Graduate School
❏ Employed ❏ Other

Age: ❏ 18–21 ❏ 22–29 ❏ 30–39 ❏ 40–49 ❏ 50+

Do you own a computer?	Yes	No	
If YES, is your computer?	Desktop	Laptop	
If NO, how do you access a computer?	Home	Work	Other
Does the computer you use have a CD-ROM drive?	Yes	No	
Do you have Internet access?	Yes	No	
Do you own any CD-ROMS?	Yes	No	

If YES, what type is it? Educational Business Entertainment Other

Have you conducted business in Asia before? Yes No

Do you think you will conduct business in Asia
anytime during your career? Yes No

If you were to do business in Asia, would you find a
CD-ROM which focuses on doing business in Asia
(customs, etiquette, hotels, tourist sites, etc.) helpful? Yes No

How much would you expect to pay for such a product?
$20–$30 $31–$40 $41–$50 $51–$60 $61–$70 $71+

How much would you personally pay for such a product?
$20–$30 $31–$40 $41–$50 $51–$60 $61–$70

Koidra-Tek thanks you for taking the time to fill out this survey.

Exhibit D   Koidra-Tek Survey

SHORT FORM TX

For a Nondramatic Literary Work
UNITED STATES COPYRIGHT OFFICE

Registration Number

TX   TXU

Effective Date of Registration

Application Received

Examined By

Deposit Received
One   Two

Correspondence ☐

Fee Received

TYPE OR PRINT IN BLACK INK. DO NOT WRITE ABOVE THIS LINE.

1   **Title of This Work:**

Alternative title or title of larger work in which this work was published:

2   **Name and Address of Author and Owner of the Copyright:**

Nationality or domicile:
Phone, fax, and email:

Phone (   )   Fax (   )

Email

3   **Year of Creation:**

4   **If work has been published, Date and Nation of Publication:**

a. Date _____ _____ _____   *(Month, day, and year all required)*
     Month   Day   Year

b. Nation

5   **Type of Authorship in This Work:**

Check all that this author created.

☐ Text (includes fiction, nonfiction, poetry, computer programs, etc.)
☐ Illustrations
☐ Photographs
☐ Compilation of terms or data

6   **Signature:**

Registration cannot be completed without a signature.

I certify that the statements made by me in this application are correct to the best of my knowledge. * Check one:

☐ Author   ☐ Authorized agent

X _

7   **Name and Address of Person to Contact for Rights and Permissions:**

Phone, fax, and email:

☐ Check here if same as #2 above.

Phone (   )   Fax (   )

Email

8   Certificate will be mailed in window envelope to this address:

Name ▼

Number/Street/Apt ▼

City/State/ZIP ▼

Complete this space only if you currently hold a Deposit Account in the Copyright Office.

9   Deposit Account # _____

Name _____

DO NOT WRITE HERE   Page 1 of ____ pages

Exhibit E   Copyright Short Form TX

Koidra-Tek™
2801 Ellendale Pl., Suite A
Los Angeles, CA 90007
1-800-Koidra1
www.koidra-tek.com
koidra_tek@yahoo.com

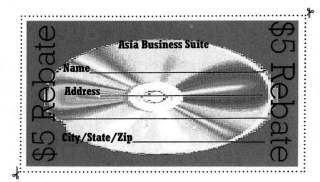

$5 Rebate

$5 Rebate

Asia Business Suite

Name _____

Address _____

City/State/Zip _____

Considering doing business in Asia?

Asia Business Suite™ is a pre-packaged CD-ROM, which educates individuals on the common sayings, ethics, customs, etiquette, precautions and laws and regulations of Asian countries, specifically relating to business.

Asia Business Suite™

- addresses various cultural issues
- reduces the need for cross-referencing to other sources
- presents highly-graphical photographs & video-clips
- provides instructions on key phrases and sayings
- incorporates icons for ease of use

Many individuals and companies find themselves unsuccessful due to a lack of knowledge necessary to conduct business in Asia.

Koidra-Tek™ will quickly and easily prepare you for success in Asia with Asia Business Suite™.

Koidra-Tek™ incorporates technology into its educational products with the purpose of serving today's expanding global market.

Exhibit F-A   Koidra-Tek Brochure (front)

48

DID YOU KNOW THAT IT IS INSULTING TO...

Southeast Asia

Asia Business Suite

Developed by Koidra-Tek

Koidra-Tek
Brian Wong & Esther Nguyen
2801 Ellendale Pl., Suite A
Los Angeles, CA 90007

Dr. Kathleen Allen
USC Marshall School of Business
The Entrepreneur Program

DID YOU KNOW THAT IT IS ILLEGAL TO...

DID YOU KNOW THAT WHEN ACCEPTING A BUSINESS CARD YOU SHOULD...

DID YOU KNOW THAT IT IS ACCEPTABLE TO...

Asia Business Suite ™

"Get it and you'll know!"

Exhibit F-B Koidra-Tek Brochure (back)

Direct Mailing List Companies

Research Projects Corp.
Pomperaug Ave.
Woodbury, CT 06798
800-243-4360

Sunshine Software Services
4255 S. Channel 10 Dr., #38
Las Vegas, NV 89119

Apogee Software
4206 Mayflower St.
Garland, TX 75043

Trade Shows and Conferences

PC Expo
P.O. Box 1026
Englewood Cliffs, NJ 07632

CD-ROM Expo
P.O. Box 4010
Dedham, MA 01776

Multimedia International Conference
945 Front St., Suite 945
San Francisco, CA 94111

MacWorld Exposition
P.O. Box 9107
Framingham, MA 01701-9107

Multimedia Expo
600 Community Dr.
New York, NY 10012

Exhibit G   Future Marketing Avenues

SPA Membership Application

COMPANY INFORMATION

Company Name _____

Street Address _____

City _____ State _____ ZIP + 4 _____ Country _____

Telephone _____ Fax _____ Web Site URL _____

Company Description (up to 50 words). This description will appear in the next membership directory. _____

_____

_____

_____

_____

CONTACT INFORMATION

Please designate a contact person who will serve as your company's primary membership representative for SPA. All member correspondence will be mailed to this individual. SPA will also send mailings to other contacts noted.

Membership Contact _____ Title _____

Direct Phone _____ Fax _____ E-mail _____

FREE MEMBERSHIP IN THE INTERNET, CONSUMER MARKET AND EDUCATION MARKET SECTIONS

As a membership benefit, SPA offers three sections that develop special publications and projects to support members involved in specific markets. Please designate a representative for each section you wish to join. That person may participate in section activities and will receive section mailings.

☐ Internet Section _____
                                (Name/Title/Phone/E-mail)

☐ Consumer Market Section _____
                                (Name/Title/Phone/E-mail)

☐ Education Market Section _____
                                (Name/Title/Phone/E-mail)

SPECIAL INTEREST GROUP (SIG) MEMBERSHIPS

Enroll in the SIGs of your choice by listing the individual SIG member. The cost is $100 per SIG for each individual in addition to company dues. Free SIG publications will be included in your Welcome Kit.

☐ Multimedia SIG _____
                                (Name/Title/Phone/E-mail)

☐ Marketing SIG _____
                                (Name/Title/Phone/E-mail)

☐ Public Relations SIG _____
                                (Name/Title/Phone/E-mail)

☐ Software Packaging SIG _____
                                (Name/Title/Phone/E-mail)

ANTI-PIRACY AUTHORIZATION – FULL MEMBERS ONLY

One of your most valuable membership privileges is the opportunity to participate in and benefit from the SPA's anti-piracy program. In the corporate environment, SPA primarily conducts audits of the allegedly infringing organization, which then must destroy any unauthorized software, purchase replacement software and pay a fine. The fines are used exclusively to fund additional anti-piracy education and enforcement programs. In cases of channel piracy and other counterfeit software, SPA employs private investigators and works with law enforcement to prepare civil or criminal actions if necessary. SPA also works with governments to deter pirate software manufacturing through title verification programs. To be included in these efforts, you must check-off the appropriate boxes and sign the following authorization:

☐ **Software audits:** SPA is hereby authorized to conduct software audits on our behalf, both domestically and internationally, and to settle and give full release from any and all claims for alleged infringement of computer software copyrights and/or trademarks held by us that arise from such audits;

☐ **Pre-litigation investigations:** SPA is hereby authorized to conduct pre-litigation investigations on our behalf, both domestically and internationally, and to settle and give full release from any and all claims for alleged infringement of computer software copyrights and/or trademarks held by us that arise from such investigations;

☐ **Title verification:** SPA is hereby authorized to act as the title verification organization for us in countries throughout the world (e.g., People's Republic of China, Bulgaria) in which verification of licenses, copyrights,etc. are required for third parties to manufacture or distribute software.

If litigation is required to pursue claims of alleged infringement of computer software copyrights and/or trademarks held by us, it is understood that a separate written authorization will be obtained before we are named as a plaintiff in a lawsuit. This authorization will continue until revoked with 30 days' written notice to SPA.

Name _____ Signature _____ Title _____ Date _____

Please return to: SPA Membership Department, Software Publishers Association, 1730 M St. NW, Washington, DC 20036-4510. Any questions? Call (202) 452-1600, ext. 399 or fax to (202) 785-3197.

Exhibit H   SPA Membership Application (front)

FULL MEMBERSHIP

The following dues schedule represents annual SPA membership fees for all companies based in North America. **SPA offers a 35% discount to those full-member companies with no presence in North America. Due to increased overhead in servicing overseas members, companies outside North America are subject to a minimum dues rate of $770.**

Companies eligible for full membership in SPA are publishers and developers of software applications, components, tools operating systems, on-line digital content and Web sites. Dues are based on gross worldwide revenue generated during the last four fiscal quarters from code or content running on desktop computers, client-server networks or the Internet. These revenues may be generated through product sales, advertising or any method where digital content value provides a basis for income. Computer hardware companies also join SPA as full members. Companies with software or digital content products whose primary interest and benefit in joining SPA is as a service provider to the industry should join as associate members.

SOFTWARE PUBLISHERS AND DEVELOPERS

Contributing Revenue	Membership Dues
$0-100,000	$770
100-250,000	850
250-500,000	1,275
500,000-1 million	1,695
1-2 million	2,495
2-3 million	3,395
3-5 million	4,250
5-7 million	4,995
7-10 million	6,795
10-15 million	10,200
15-20 million	13,600
20-30 million	17,900
30-50 million	21,000
50-100 million	26,000
100-150 million	35,000
150-200 million	42,000
200-300 million	52,000
300-500 million	59,000
500-750 million	68,000
750 million-1 billion	76,000
1 billion-2 billion	96,000
2-5 billion	112,000
5 billion-over	125,000

SPECIAL FIRST-YEAR DUES FOR START-UP COMPANIES

Contributing Revenue	Membership Dues
$0-100,000	$495

Applies to companies with five or fewer employees, first-year dues only. Not applicable to companies based outside North America.

COMPUTER HARDWARE SYSTEMS MANUFACTURERS

Aggregate Gross Revenue	Membership Dues
$0-1 billion	$14,000
1 billion-2 billion	28,000
2 billion-4 billion	42,000
4 billion-over	70,000

ASSOCIATE MEMBERSHIP

Companies eligible for associate membership in SPA support the growth of the software industry and may provide a service to the industry. Companies with more than 50 percent of revenues generated by publishing software or digital content must join as full members. Associate members' dues are based on total organizational revenues, computer-related or otherwise, for the last four fiscal quarters. Nonprofit organizations should call for information about associate membership. There is no Associate Member discount for companies based outside North America.

Aggregate Gross Revenue	Membership Dues
$0-1 million	$1,150
1-10 million	2,550
10-100 million	4,950
100 million-1 billion	6,450
1 billion and over	7,450

ALL MEMBERS

Dues payment must be included with this form. You may send a check payable to SPA or include your credit card information.

Membership Classification　☐ Full　☐ Associate　(check one)

Check all that apply　☐ Dues based on computer hardware revenues　☐ Nonprofit organization
　　　　　　　　　　　☐ Start-up company; no software sales revenue yet

Amount of Dues	$ _____	Charge My　☐ Visa　☐ MasterCard　☐ American Express
Special Interest Groups @ $100 each	$ _____	Card# _____
TOTAL	$ _____	Expiration Date _____
		Name as it appears on card _____
		Card Billing Address _____

I certify that our company is eligible for the designated membership classification as defined above, that our dues contribution is based upon the four fiscal quaters ending _____ (mm/yy) and that we agree to abide by SPA bylaws.

Name (please print) _____

Signature _____　Date _____

Immediately upon receipt of your completed application, SPA will send you an order form for free SPA publications.

Exhibit H　SPA Membership Application (back)

Case Studies

SB Networks*

As Nigel Allyn, director of strategic technology, sat at his desk in a business park outside London, he considered the situation facing SB Networks (SBN). Since joining SBN in early 1991, he had watched the firm grow from a 70-person start-up company to a 2,100+ employee global corporation. In that time he also saw the company enter a market monopolized by IBM and, over a period of six years, establish itself as the acknowledged technology leader in the world of Token Ring networks.

When he came to SBN, Allyn was to be the liaison between management and the engineering side of the company. Later he became a salesman responsible for selling "everything that was not on the price sheet." In 1996, he was responsible for 5 percent of SBN's revenue. While SBN typically took in between $2 and $3 million a year from leasing out its intellectual property, it spent less than a quarter of a million dollars paying for the intellectual property it brought in.

SBN's policy was to patent its intellectual property, about five patents per year, but SBN seldom found it cost effective to prosecute cases of infringement. This is because companies small enough to successfully prosecute tend to not have enough money to make the effort worthwhile, whereas companies large enough to be worth suing have enough money to make the prosecution effort very time consuming and costly. In instances of particularly valuable patents, industry practice is to give one's patent to a law firm with the stipulations that

---

*Graduate student Jim Mimlitsch prepared this case under the supervision of Professor Kathleen Allen, Ph.D., as the basis for class discussion rather than to illustrate either effective or ineffective handling of an administrative situation. The company name and names of all parties in this case have been changed. Copyright © 1997 by James Russell Mimlitsch, Jr.

the firm pay for all patent defense itself, pay the company a fixed amount per year, and split any profits over and above those costs with the company.

History

In 1986, Simon Brooks founded SB Networks with the goal of designing, building, and marketing Token Ring network products. At the time, IBM, who invented the technology, almost single handedly controlled the Token Ring market. Difficulty raising start-up capital for a company that wanted to challenge the biggest name in the computer industry finally led Brooks to mortgage his family's pastureland in southern England. Having literally "bet the farm" on his success, Brooks recruited several technically brilliant engineers from across the United Kingdom and began to design and build Token Ring products.

In 1987, SBN introduced its first Token Ring adapter products for personal computers and its first hub products for connectivity. Additional products quickly followed up these offerings. This second wave of products and several others that followed established SBN's name and reputation for well-designed and well-built technology. So well respected were SBN's products and reputation for technical excellence that SBN quickly took industry leadership for Token Ring away from inventor IBM and began to set the standards for the technology.

"Smart" Products

Token Ring networks allow computers, which may be of different types (like mainframes and PCs), to exchange data. This is done by installing Token Ring adapter cards in each of the computers and then connecting all the computers with cables. The adapters, which contain a protocol based on the IEEE (Institute of Electrical and Electronics Engineers) standard 802.5, create a logical ring in which each computer can send data to its neighbor. The protocol dictates that only one computer has the right to send data at a time. This "right" is signified by a piece of code called a token. When one computer on the ring wants to send data to another computer, it waits until it receives the token and then addresses the data to its destination and passes it to its neighbor. The neighbor then reads the data and checks the address to see if the data is meant for itself. If it is, it keeps the data and gives the token to the next computer in the ring; otherwise it retransmits the data along to the next computer.

This was the technology as IBM invented it and the IEEE codified it. SBN improved this technology by introducing active management that provided fault-tolerance. A ring built with all computers connected to a MultiNet hub would continue to operate even if the cable between a computer and the hub were severed, or, more important, if one computer in the ring began misbehaving, for instance sending data without having the token or not passing data on to its neighbor. SBN also introduced technology that improved the throughput of Token Ring adapters by reducing latency. A Token Ring adapter that contained the new chipset could read the destination address of the data it was being sent without having to read the data itself as other adapters did. This improved the rate at which these adapters could handle data.

In 1995, SBN acquired LANNET Data Communications, an Israeli company known for Ethernet networks. This was a major shift in focus for SBN, which had previously only manufactured and sold Token Ring network products. In 1996, SBN acquired Teleos Communications Inc., a player in the Internet market segment. This gave SBN instant access to yet more new technology, this time public-switched digital services such as T-1 and ISDN (Integrated Services Digital Network). These acquisitions allowed SBN to offer a broad range of products at a time when a new competitive environment was beginning to emerge in the network industry.

Competitive Environment

Early product successes laid the foundation for SBN's reputation in the industry, and it followed this up with a string of superior products. (Exhibit 1 provides a partial list of awards that SBN products boast.) However, SBN had come to be known as an adapter company, and adapters were generally perceived as commodity items. SBN's marketing strategy was to charge pre-

Exhibit 1   SBN Product Awards

▶ Smart Ringswitch, Tester's Choice Award, *Data Communications,* June 1996
▶ First National Bank of South Africa (SBN customer), Computerworld Smithsonian Award, *Computerworld Smithsonian,* June 1996
▶ LANswitch, Tester's Choice Award, *Data Communications,* May 1996
▶ LANswitch, Tester's Choice Award, *Data Communications,* February 1996
▶ Video Router Express, New Product Achievement Award, *ComNet,* February 1996
▶ Smart Ringswitch, Hot Product 1996, *Data Communications,* January 1996
▶ LANswitch, Best Overall Award, *BYTE* Magazine, July 1995
▶ SBN Networks, ISO 9002 Quality Certification, *International Standards Organization,* May 1995
▶ Smart 16/4 EISA Ringnode, Best Token Ring NIC, *Network Computing,* April 1995
▶ LANswitch, Best of Times, *LAN Times,* February 1995
▶ Smart 100 EISA Ringnode, Tester's Choice, *Data Communications,* July 1994
▶ Smart 100 EISA Ringnode, Product of the Year, *LAN Magazine,* February 1994
▶ Smart 16/4 EISA Ringnode, Best of Times, *LAN Times,* December 1993
▶ Smart 16/4 EISA Ringnode, Editor's Choice, *PC Magazine,* October 1992

mium prices and to offer high levels of service in support of its products, but it became harder and harder to sell SBN 16Mbit Token Ring adapters for $400 when customers could purchase 10Mbit Ethernet adapters that started at $40. Even the Ethernet manufacturers would acknowledge the superiority of SBN's adapters' performance, but the difference in price/performance ratios could no longer always support the decision to buy from SBN.

In 1993, when SBN made its IPO, the hot segment of the network industry was routers. Routers, which pass data between local network segments like Token Rings, and other "closet" products (devices which support the network infrastructure as opposed to individual computers and are kept in wiring closets) were the darlings of the industry media and of Wall Street. Router manufacturers like Wellfleet (which later merged with SynOptics to form Bay Networks) and Cisco grew at a dizzying pace and came to dominate the network industry and for some to symbolize it. These companies offered a full range of "closet" products as well as hubs and adapters. There were many Fortune 500 companies that preferred to purchase all of their network equipment from one vendor like these, believing that this would ensure interoperability and dedicated service.

The Industry

In 1996, the companies that offered a full line of products dominated the market. (Exhibit 2 shows a ranked list of industry players and their February 1997 market values.) The number of firms in the industry had decreased dramatically because of the high-profile merger of Wellfleet and SynOptics and the less well known acquisition of dozens of smaller firms. (Exhibit 3 presents a partial list of mergers and acquisitions in the network industry in 1995 and 1996.) The rush to acquire niche players was driven by a desire to offer a full range of products. The scope of the industry had expanded and now included voice and video in addition to data transmission over private and public analog and digital services. Major industry players all wanted to

Exhibit 2   Ranked List of Industry Players and Their February 1997 Market Values

1.	Cisco Systems Inc.	$41,148 (millions)
2.	3Com Corp.	12,084
3.	Cabletron Systems Inc.	5,519
4.	Newbridge Networks Corp.*	5,156
5.	Bay Networks Inc.	4,052
6.	Fore Systems Inc.*	3,061
7.	SBN NV	431

*Newbridge and Fore both derive significant portions of their income from the telecommunications industry, whereas the other companies listed do not.

Exhibit 3 Partial List of Network Industry Mergers and Acquisitions, 1995 and 1996

- SBN NV acquired LANNET Data Communications Inc., September 1995
- 3Com Corp. merged with Chipcom Corp., October 1995
- SBN NV acquired Teleos Communications Inc., January 1996
- Bay Networks Inc. acquired Performance Technology Corp., March 1996
- 3Com Corp. acquired Axon Networks Inc., March 1996
- Bay Networks Inc. acquired Armon Networking Ltd., April 1996
- Cabletron Systems Inc. acquired ZeitNet Inc., July 1996
- Bay Networks Inc. acquired Penril Datacomm Networks Inc., November 1996
- 3Com Corp. merged with OnStream Networks Inc., November 1996
- Cabletron Systems Inc. acquired Netlink Corp., December 1996

establish a presence in all of these markets in order to be well positioned when ATM (asynchronous transfer mode) networks began to replace traditional network technologies as most industry experts predicted it would.

ATM

ATM technology promised to unify the wide assortment of products and services that existed in the world of information transmission. Previously, technology needed to be matched with the type of application in order to achieve acceptable results. Data communications, for example, are optimized by sending large amounts of data only when there is data to be sent. This is termed connectionless communication and conforms to available bandwidth. Voice and especially video applications, however, require established connections and predictable service levels, also known as fixed bandwidth. ATM, which is connectionless, works by sending extremely small amounts of data extremely quickly and offers methods of ensuring service levels and emulating connections. It is widely held that ATM will replace most other methods of communication at some point in the future. ATM holds the promise of opening the telecommunications market to the network industry and the threat of opening the network market to telecommunications players. Despite this blurring of lines, consolidation has mainly stayed within traditional industries.

SBN and ATM

In 1994, SBN unveiled its strategy for integrating Token Ring with ATM and became a founding member of the Desktop ATM 25 Alliance, an industry group that promoted the 25Mbit ATM standard developed by IBM. Since that time, SBN has introduced several ATM products and taken a leadership position in the area of LAN emulation, a technology that will allow customers to extend their investment in existing technologies such as Token Ring and Ethernet. Despite this, however, SBN has not been able to offer the "one stop shop" approach to ATM that many customers desire.

Licensing in the Network Industry

Licensing intellectual property in the network industry is extremely common. More than 50 percent of all networking products contain some amount of third-party intellectual property. For example, the vast majority of ISDN solutions employ signaling code for call set-up that is licensed from another company. Companies license the intellectual property of others in order to achieve any or all of the following objectives:

1. To reduce the time it takes to bring a product to market. Products in the network industry have an average life span in the field of less than five years but can expect to be replaced by newer products in less than six months. In this environment, any means of reducing time to market is likely to be adopted.

2. To maintain compatibility with existing systems. Standards in the network industry are often incomplete and open to interpretation by various manufacturers. In order to ensure interoperability, licensed technology is often used.

3. To ease the burden of testing. Product testing is a very time-consuming process in such a fast moving industry, and employing licensed technology reduces the amount of testing that is required to bring a product to market.

4. To keep from reinventing the wheel. Most companies or at least divisions have clear focuses and are able to innovate in these areas. Outside of these areas, intellectual property is often employed to keep developers focused on their own areas of expertise.

In addition to licensing the intellectual property of others, most companies license out their own intellectual property as well. Firms do this for any or all of the following reasons:

1. As an easy means of generating revenue. Companies can inexpensively add more to their bottom lines by getting others to license their intellectual property.

2. To create an industry standard. One needs to look no further than the example of Microsoft to see that the companies who set the standards are the most successful in the long run. The lesson applies equally well to the network industry.

3. To develop a reputation in the industry. The network industry is rather small and a reputation for good products or good code benefits companies because of the halo effect.

SBN and Licensing

SBN has a long history of licensing its products within the industry. Instances of SBN licensing technology to and from others include the following:

▶ In 1988, SBN licensed the code to its Token Ring protocol stack software to Microsoft. This allowed SBN to quickly become a standard for Token Ring networking with users of the Windows operating system.

▶ In 1996, SBN again developed a licensing agreement with Microsoft, this time to have SBN's Token Ring driver code incorporated into the Windows NT operating system. As with the previous example, this allowed SBN to become a standard for Token Ring networking with users of the Windows NT operating system.

▶ In 1990, SBN licensed its Fastmac technology to Cisco for use in Cisco's routers. At the time, Cisco was better positioned to use the technology for "closet" products than SBN was, and the license agreement also helped to establish the young firm as a respected name in the network industry.

▶ In 1995, Cisco licensed SBN's RingRunner switching silicon (the software, or "microcode," that makes up the logic of an IC or chip) for use in Cisco's line of switch products. This was an expansion of SBN's earlier license with Cisco. With this license agreement SBN attempted to establish RingRunner as the standard in switching silicon.

▶ Also in 1995, SBN licensed its RingRunner silicon to Newbridge Networks. SBN and Newbridge agreed to jointly develop a line of products to be marketed and sold by Newbridge. This was a good source of income for SBN, which could not otherwise afford to develop or market to Newbridge's customers.

▶ In 1996, Cisco licensed the high-density ISDN switching technology that SBN acquired with Teleos in order to integrate it into a high-capacity universal access server. This was primarily done for the revenue. Although SBN would later develop a competing product, at the time SBN had just completed its acquisition of Teleos and needed the cash infusion.

▶ From Cisco, SBN licensed the Cisco IOS (Internetwork Operating System) for use in a WAN (wide area network) AccessSwitch. Cisco's IOS was generally considered an industry standard, and SBN could not afford to reinvent the wheel.

▶ From Novell Corp., SBN licensed NetWare Hub Services for use with its Smart 16/4 MC Hubcard. By licensing NetWare Hub Services, SBN could quickly gain access to the huge installed base that Novell had developed.

Problem

Although SBN engages in both licensing to and from other companies, the balance of licensing weighs in the favor of outgoing intellectual property. When it was a small company and focused on a single niche, SBN's licensing of its technology brought in revenue, prestige, and mindshare. However, as SBN continued to grow, it began to develop products that were in competition with those of its former partners. Can SBN continue its practice of licensing out its intellectual property and remain a competitive force in the networking industry? Does licensing out intellectual property stand in conflict with the notion of sustainable competitive advantage? Is licensing intellectual property (in or out) a short-term or a long-term strategy?

Aftermath

In July 1997, SBN announced a corporate restructuring and an accompanying layoff. The restructuring trimmed the ATM and consulting business units from the company and the layoff led to the termination of 700 employees worldwide (about one-third of the total work force). The restructuring came after several quarters of declining revenue and net losses. The financial ill health was the result of slower than expected acceptance of ATM by network industry customers.

Sources

Phone interview with SBN Public Relations, 30 January 1997.
Personal interview with SBN District Sales Manager, 31 January 1997.
Phone interview with Nigel Allyn, SBN NV, Dir. of Strategic Tech., 4 February 1997.
SBN's web site, *http://www.sbn.com/*.
Upside Magazine, various articles and advertisements, February 1997.

2

French Rags*

Finding a New Distribution Channel in the Apparel Industry

Introduction

In the business life cycle, a company may reach a point where it stagnates and dies, or the market changes such that what the company does, what it produces, or how it reaches its customers no longer works. This was the situation facing apparel company French Rags in 1989 when it began to see its carefully crafted world and $10 million niche market sales begin to fall apart.

French Rags was not alone in its plight. Other apparel manufacturers were also feeling the effects of a slump in department store sales, which meant slower payments and more returns. The solution to French Rags' turnaround was twofold: a move to computer-integrated manufacturing that permitted more customization and unique designs and a new distribution channel to get the clothes to the customer.

The History of French Rags

French Rags began as a scarf-making company founded by British-born Brenda French in a spare bedroom in 1978. French had learned to knit in grade school in Manchester, England, an area widely known for knitting; and she began making scarves from wool she purchased at Woolworth. The many retail contacts she had made during 16 years of working for manufacturers in a variety of roles told French that people not only wanted her scarves, they

*French Rags (1997) was prepared by Kathleen R. Allen, Ph.D., Lloyd Greif Center for Entrepreneurial Studies, Marshall School of Business, University of Southern California. This case is meant to serve as a basis for classroom discussion rather than to illustrate effective or ineffective handling of a management situation.

asked for sweaters as well. So French began dyeing yarn in her kitchen sink and making sweaters. From scarves and sweaters she moved into custom knitwear, moved out of her home to a factory, and hired several knitters to help with the increasing volume.

At one point, French was introduced to a special type of rayon yarn that doesn't cling, which she began to incorporate into her garments. Sales took off. She had to move to a larger factory and hire more knitters. Now her clothes were featured in leading department stores such as Neiman Marcus, Bonwit Teller, and Bloomingdale's. Her clients were upscale and soon became intensely loyal to her unique designs.

But by 1989, with sales approaching $10 million, her carefully crafted apparel world began to fall apart. Several factors contributed to the problems French began to face at that point. Department stores were no longer the cherished source for retail customers. Because they were experiencing a slump, they made life difficult for vendors like French Rags by paying late and returning merchandise sometimes for no good reason at all.

Another reason for French's problems was that retailers absolutely refused to display her garments in the best way possible. Knitwear should not be hung on hangers because "it grows if it's hung and not folded." An additional problem was that buyers would carry only a few of her styles, sizes, and colors, so sales for most of her line were slow. Moreover, retail markups made a coat, for example, which could sell profitably at $400, languish on a hanger for $1,000.

To further exasperate the struggling French, union organizers began targeting the 200+ handknitters she employed and successfully forced a National Labor Relations Board election that cost her company more than $250,000 in legal and other fees. Fortunately, she won the election by 20 votes. Had she not, she probably would have lost the company.

But French's battles were not yet over, for within a few months of winning the election, her factor dumped her. In the apparel industry, losing a factor is a blow to the heart of the business, because factors make it possible for a business to survive the slow payment of retail outlets by paying the accounts receivables and then taking a percentage of them in return. As her sales dipped below $1 million, she found she had to draw on her personal savings to make payroll. She also had to close showrooms in New York, San Francisco, and Chicago. Her only revenues came from retailers able to pay COD.

The Turning Point

The value of loyal customers was quickly made apparent to French when they called the company wondering why her clothes were no longer available in their favorite stores. One desperate New York customer offered to show French's designs in her elegant home, claiming French would make sales of $10,000. Taking a chance on this unusual scheme, French took her entire collection to New York and ended up selling $80,000 worth of clothes. That trip signaled a complete change in her marketing and distribution strategy as she switched from selling in retail outlets to using sales consultants and a retail shop at her Los Angeles factory.

About this time, French decided it was time to look for a knitting machine. She was introduced through a mutual friend to Mile Rasic, who at the time was working as a supervisor in a contract knitting company. Rasic had just purchased a Stoll knitting machine; as he talked with French, he immediately understood that her designs would be perfect for this new machine. French decided she had to have the machine. To come up with the money, she sold her house and convinced Rasic to come on board for three months as a consultant. He ultimately became her partner and has remained with the company.

The Apparel Industry

In 1996, with retail sales up 1.3 percent, the U.S. apparel industry had sales at the wholesale level of $78.4 billion and retail sales (domestic wholesale and retail markups of apparel) at approximately $211 billion, which was about 4.3 percent of disposable income.[1] Women's apparel accounted for 50 percent of all retail sales and was expected to grow because of the trend of more women in the work force. In 1996, approximately 57 percent of the work force consisted of women.[2]

National brands account for about 30 percent of all U.S. wholesale sales of apparel. The U.S. Bureau of the Census reports that 23,048 businesses are engaged in manufacture of apparel for small and private labels like French Rags, which account for the remaining 70 percent of wholesale sales. Apparel is sold principally in four major categories of outlets:

Department stores	23%
Discounters	20%
Specialty stores	18%
Major chains	15%
Other	24%

The apparel industry is characterized by simple technology and relatively low entry barriers, because typically capital requirements are minimal compared with other industries. Nevertheless, there are hurdles to overcome, such as existing brand name recognition, established distribution channels, and economies of scale that established manufacturers enjoy. Consequently, the mortality rate for companies is fairly high.[3] Because of intense competition there has been a slower rate of increase in price compared with overall inflation, and profit margins are low.[4]

Several continuing trends have been apparent in the apparel industry.

1. Customers have a markdown mentality. Customers are looking for value and are willing to wait until an item is marked down before buying.

2. Customers are buying less. Customers seem to be buying less, but they are spending more on an individual item in an effort to get quality.

3. Number of retailers is shrinking. While the total number of retailers is decreasing, the average size of retail outlets is getting larger.

4. Retailers are attempting to differentiate. Retailers are seeking expanded product offerings in an effort to stand out from the crowd.

The Product Line

Since 1990, the French Rags collection has grown from one basic collection with 14 separates in 12 solid colors to three separate collections that reflect French's view that "seasonal dressing no longer works within the rigors of modern-day life and busy travel schedules." People need clothing they can wear year round anytime day or night. Her unique knit fabrics permit layering so they can travel from winter to summer in a matter of seconds.

The garments also provide for individual sizings and a wide variety of colors and patterns. Because so many of the designs are interchangeable, they allow the customer to create a personalized wardrobe, making the designs virtually customized.

Her patterns are influenced by a variety of different sources: painters like Monet and Matisse, English tapestry weaves and paisley, as well as strong graphic designs. With 32 colors in each style, a customer can create a total of 45,000 different looks.

Operations

French Rags' operations are a combination of handknitting and electronic knitting. The reason she went to computerized knitting machines was not to increase the speed of production, although it does, but to enhance her ability to create more artistic designs.

French Rags is now housed in a 36,500-square-foot factory and showroom in West Los Angeles. French calls this location her "craftory." All aspects of production are handled in-house; the only outsourced function is the creation of the yarn itself. Close strategic alliances with spinners and dyers gives French the ability to more accurately meet her customers' needs. For example, French uses fine gauge rayon, which is less fragile and less expensive than silk and finer and more flexible than wool. Still, rayon has a tendency to snag, so French worked with spinners to develop a twist that would not snag. The result was an innovation in the knitting industry that has made her garments flexible enough to be worn in any climate. It has also given French Rags a competitive advantage in that the new rayon would be difficult to copy by overseas companies.

French's partner, Rasic, used his computer skills to design a software program that supplements those that come with the Stoll knitting machines. This new program produces portable templates that contain instructions as to which color yarns are to be loaded on which spools on top of each of the 11 Stoll knitting machines. Rasic's office is the control room where he can monitor on computer screens what is being produced on each machine. On a 500

MB Silicon Graphics workstation, Rasic can create full-color graphic images of French's sketches for new designs. On another screen, he can see video feed from eight cameras scattered around the factory as well as the camera in their one showroom at the Eldorado Hotel in Santa Fe, New Mexico.

Distribution

Essentially, Brenda French has eliminated the middleman in her industry by going directly to the customer without the overhead of a retail outlet. Her innovative strategy involved developing a sales force from her loyal, affluent customers who would sell the clothing from trunk shows in their own homes. The more than 60 agents receive a straight 14 percent commission on sales. They have virtually no start-up costs as French supplies invitations, order forms, sample garments, and fabric swatches of the 30 color choices. The agents conduct weeklong, by-appointment-only trunk shows. After a customer decides what she wants, measurements are taken, a 50 percent down payment is collected, and the order is faxed to the French Rags factory. There each item is custom made and shipped directly to the customer within four to six weeks. In this way French Rags has very little inventory.

The Future

French, who turned her company around with technology, sees technology and the Internet in the future of the business. She looks forward to the day when her agents and customers will do everything online, from designing and selecting their clothes to placing orders and paying. French believes that if agents could place orders by clicking on order numbers, sizes, and so forth, fewer errors would be made. It would also be easier to maintain customer information and get input more quickly.

Stoll America Knitting Machinery, Inc., of New York claims that French Rags is one of the fastest growing mills on the West Coast. With a new Stoll CMS 433.6 full jacquard, electronic computerized machine, French Rags now has the capability of creating anything from full-fashion designs to intarsia and three-dimensional knitting.

French Rags now stocks well over 30,000 pounds of yarn. It has 10 computerized knitting machines, 20 hand machines, and employs more than 80 people. It produces more than 600 units per week.

The challenge is to keep breaking the rules in the apparel industry while listening to customers and continually meeting their changing needs. Brenda French is always looking for new ways to stay ahead of the game.

References

[1] Standard & Poor, "Standard & Poor's Industry Surveys," June 1996, pp. 64–79.

[2] Standard & Poor, "Standard & Poor's Industry Surveys," June 1996, pp. 80–97.

[3] Standard & Poor, "Standard & Poor's Industry Surveys," September 1995, p. 76.

[4] Department of Commerce, *Textiles, Apparel & Home Furnishings* (Washington, D.C., 1997).

Sources

Nancy Rivera Brooks, "Word-of-Mouth Power," *Los Angeles Times,* 12 September 1994.

Roberta Maynard, "Managing Your Small Business," *Nation's Business,* April 1996.

Hal Plotkin, "Riches from Rags," *Inc. Technology* (summer 1995), pp. 62–67.

Several interviews by author with Brenda French in February and March 1997.

Kathlyn Swantko, "West Coast: French Rags to L.A. Riches," *Knitting Times,* special printing.

3

Marcus Food Co. and Buckhead Beef*

A Case Study of Corporate Ethics and Entrepreneurial Growth

On December 12, 1988, Jerry Marcus, president of Marcus Food Co. in Wichita, Kansas, telephoned his brother Howard, founder, chief executive officer, and chairman of the board.

"Howard, something is wrong here. You had better meet me in Texas." Together, the two eventually discovered an employee collusion and embezzlement scheme leading to a $5 million net loss for Marcus Food and to the demise of Landrum Distribution, a Texas-based affiliate. One of the two perpetrators was convicted and subsequently incarcerated at a federal penitentiary for five years.

"The woman went to jail," explains Howard. "We couldn't convict her partner, a guy I hired because she took all of the rap in criminal court. We went after him civilly and got a $21 million judgment against him. He's a very clever guy, though, and showed no assets in his name, so we still couldn't touch him despite the judgment."

About the time that the embezzlement had been discovered, the Marcus family, long active philanthropists in the Wichita community, had made a $350 thousand donation to Wichita State University to fund improvements for a Center for Continuing Education which today bears the family name. Howard notes in retrospect, "I trusted him too much. The biggest mistake I made was leaving the books in his lap, letting him run the bank checkbook. I let my two accountants do a review rather than a full audit. When Jerry came into the business, I had him oversee their books. That's when we discovered

---

*Management cooperated in the field research for this case, which was written solely for the purpose of stimulating student discussion. All events and individuals are real. Written by Sandra Honig-Haftel, Wichita State University.

the trouble. They had a check kiting scheme and kept two sets of books. They showed inventory that didn't exist, at falsified addresses."

"If I had joined Howard in 1980," Jerry claims, "it never would have happened. I'm a finance guy. Howard's the marketeer. I'm also executive vice president of Buckhead Beef, an Atlanta-based company that Howard owns with Howard Halpern, the president."

Industry Environment

The meatpacking industry consists of several different groups of companies performing specialized functions and serving different customers. The beef industry is different from the pork and poultry industry.

In the beef industry, producers concentrate on calf production. They may be a small farm with a few cows and a bull, or a large ranch with a highly sophisticated cow-calf operation. Feeders buy the calves and place them on grass and then place them into feedlots to fatten for slaughter. Within the feeding industry, there are industry players who own their own supply and control their feeding in their own feedlots, or rent space in other's feedlots. There are also sizable groups of speculative investors who know little or nothing about feeding per se; however, they enjoy the return on their investment when feeding is profitable.

At the slaughter level, there are three major packers, IBP, Excel, and Monfort, who perform more than 80 percent of the slaughter of cattle in the United States. There are many additional small- to medium-size packers who exist in regional markets providing specialized services to the industry. Some restrict their operations to killing cows, dairy breeds, or selected heavy-weight cattle and are able to compete with the majors.

At the processing level, there are many facilities that have expanded beyond the major slaughter operations. Some of these facilities are enormous and provide tremendous economies of scale. Some packers process their product only to provide raw material to the wholesale trade in the form of cryovac subprimals. Some have gone a step further, attempting to create consumer packages and cooked, ready-to-eat products. There are also freestanding processors which produce specialized products for the food service, retail, or institutional market. The poultry industry has made this transition more rapidly than the beef industry.

At the wholesale level, there are several different kinds of companies competing with each other. A full-line hotel/restaurant institutional supply company such as Sysco supplies thousands of items to the food service industry, of which meat may be only a fraction. They may be very competitive in their pricing of meat as most of their profit comes from paper goods and many other items. Competing with them are the small independents who offer a high level of service and high-quality specialty products. Also at this level of the industry are the specialized purveyors of meat items to the center-of-the-plate, white tablecloth customers. These companies are generally small- to medium-size regional wholesalers. This is a very competitive area of the industry with a few large, efficient operations and many small, somewhat noncompetitive followers who are having a difficult time surviving.

At the marketing level, most packers handle their own product; however, there has always been room for traders and brokers. The traders survive within the industry as specialists in buying products that the packer has not been able to readily move. Some traders provide a marketing service for the small packer. Meat is a perishable product and must be moved in an orderly manner as it is produced. For a packer, speculating on its own production by freezing and holding is a risk it is generally unwilling to accept. Traders also exist within the industry because they may sell their product to customers that the packer may consider an unreasonable credit risk.

Financial Characteristics

In the meat industry, the volumes handled by firms competing with each other are generally large, whereas the margins are notably thin. Large, concentrated accounts receivables represent huge potential losses to most companies within the industry if their customers go out of business. Coupled with high volume, the earnings of the major packers are respectable with other industries, as can be observed from average returns on investment. Capital requirements differ for each segment of the industry. Feeding is generally funded through chattel mortgages, limited only by the willingness of the banks. Slaughter and processing facilities are expensive, costing upward of $100 million for a new complete plant. Entry into this end of the business is limited. Specialized processors require moderate capitalization and working capital to be efficient. Entry here is not difficult; however, survival is, as available market share is limited. The characteristics of the successful leaders in the industry are high volume at low relative operating cost. Traders are limited by the credit and working capital lines established.

Industry Competitors

The major packers compete internationally through economies of scale associated with production efficiencies and have had the capital to do most of the innovative R&D for new product development. The smaller packers compete on a regional basis through customized service and specialization of producers. The more vertically integrated firms spread the risk because all segments are not necessarily profitable at any one time.

Marcus Food Co. and Buckhead Beef: History and Overview

Marcus Food, a food trading and marketing company, was founded in 1980 by Howard Marcus. Marcus was the son of Samuel H. Marcus, founder of the Excel Packing Company in Chicago. This firm became Kansas Beef Industries (KBI), which was formed with the merger of Excel Packing and a group of affiliated and independent companies (see Exhibit 1). KBI became a

Exhibit 1   Chronology of Events for Founding of Marcus Food Co. and Buckhead Beef

1936   Samuel H. Marcus founds Excel Packing Co. in Chicago.

1941   Marcus moves Excel to Wichita, Kans.

1962   Circle E Ranch founded as part of Excel, Potwin, Kans.

1964   Missouri Beef Packers (MBP) founded in Rock Port, Mo., later to be merged with Excel. Jerry Marcus joins MBP after obtaining B.A. from Wharton School of Business at the University of Pennsylvania.

1966   MBP opens plant in Rock Port, Mo.

1968   MBP opens plant in Friona, Tex.

1969   Kansas Beef Industries (KBI), Wichita, Kans., formed by merging Excel Packing, Kansas Packing, Dunn Packing, Circle E Ranch in Potwin, Kans., and Philadelphia, Pa.; Excel Packing is one of the divisions.

1970   KBI becomes a public company. Samuel Marcus is president and director, succeeding to chairman of the board in 1971; Jerry Marcus serves as vice president and director and general manager of Excel Division. Howard Marcus is vice president and director and general manager of KBI's Kansas Packing Division. MBP establishes corporate office in Amarillo, Tex.

1971   MBP opens plant in Plainview, Tex.

1973   MBP opens plant in Boise, Id.

1974   KBI merges with MBP, creating MBPXL. KBI had been wholesaling beef under the XL brand name.

1977   Samuel Marcus retires.

1979   Cargill buys MBPXL after ConAgra sues Cargill, claiming it had a previous acquisition agreement. ConAgra loses suit. MBPXL opens slaughter plant in Dodge City, Kans.

1980   Howard Marcus founds Marcus Food Co., Wichita, Kans.

1983   Howard Marcus purchases Buckhead Beef, Atlanta, Ga. Excel opens boxed-beef fabrication unit in Dodge City, Kans., buys plants in Cozab, Neb.

1985   Howard Marcus acquires Landrum Distribution Co., Arlington, Tex.

1987   Jerry Marcus joins Marcus Food, overseeing accounting and financial operations.

1988   Embezzlement due to employee collusion occurs at Landrum Distribution Co., costing Marcus Food Co. $5 million.

1989   Excel closes Wichita, Kans., plant, blaming high cattle prices, high sewer costs, and tight supplies.

1992   Excel buys Emge Packing Co., a pork processing firm with plants in Fort Branch and Anderson, Ind.

1995   Excel opens new plant in Nebraska City, Neb., to produce fully cooked products such as prime rib and barbecued beef and pork. Excel employment worldwide exceeds 14,000.

public company in 1970, with Samuel H. Marcus succeeding to chairman of the board in 1971. Howard Marcus, his oldest son, was vice president and general manager of KBI's Kansas Packing Division. Jerry Marcus was vice president and director and general manager of Excel Division of KBI.

In 1974, KBI merged with Missouri Beef Packers (MBP), creating MBPXL. In 1979, Cargill bought MBPXL after the firm waged a successful battle against ConAgra, which had sued Cargill, claiming that it had a previous acquisition agreement with MBPXL. With proceeds from the sale of his holdings in MBPXL, Howard Marcus founded Marcus Food Co. in 1980. "I left MBPXL with my marketing experience and with my knowledge of the customer," says Howard.

His brother, Jerry, went his own way, experimenting with several entrepreneurial ventures until he joined Marcus Food in 1987, overseeing accounting and financial operations.

In 1983, Howard had purchased Buckhead Beef in Atlanta, Georgia, with Howard Halpern, who became president. "I took over Buckhead Beef, supplying its working capital needs," Howard Marcus explains. Jerry Marcus eventually assumed the role of executive vice president of Buckhead Beef, frequently traveling between Wichita and Atlanta to track financial operations. Landrum Distribution in Arlington, Texas, was founded in 1985.

Both brothers had been formally trained in business, Howard in marketing at the University of Colorado and Jerry in finance at the Wharton Business School of the University of Pennsylvania. It was Jerry who first discovered the extent of the missing funds at Landrum, although it could have happened much sooner.

Jerry remarks: "I joined Howard's company in May of 1987. Instead of letting me focus on the financial side of the business, Howard had me sitting at a desk near him trying to sell. Marketing is not my strength. We relied on two rather immature accountants—CPAs—to review financial operations at Landrum. Then, about a year and a half after I joined the company, I suggested to Howard that we go to Atlanta to make sure that all was operating correctly at Buckhead."

"If I had just said, 'Let's go to Texas first,' rather than to Atlanta, we could have stopped the criminal fund drainage perhaps a year or so earlier," bemoans Howard.

"I asked the accountants to do an inventory reconciliation with confirmations. Well, they got one back with an address that didn't exist and they never said anything. It took us six months before we found it—just four days before we made a major contribution to Wichita State University," recalls Howard.

"At the time, we didn't know the extent of the embezzlement. Nobody knew the magnitude. We thought that it might be a million dollars, then three million. We had no idea until mid-January how much it really was. Imagine what I could have done with that money for the community and for myself. What if we can't help Wichita? I hope that somebody is using that money somewhere for some good," Howard Marcus states.

Present Structure, Mission, and Objectives

The surviving Marcus Food and Buckhead Beef companies boosted their collective sales from $150 million in 1995 to $225 million for 1996. This was largely due to the acquisition of several major sales contracts.

Buckhead Beef provided meat for the Olympic athletes during the 1996 Olympic games in Atlanta, Georgia. They would also supply one of the fastest-growing public restaurant firms (Lone Star Steakhouse) with its "center-of-the-plate" menu items, including beef, shrimp, and pork.

"We are structured as two separate corporations. I owned 100 percent of the stock of Buckhead Beef until several years ago, when I gave my partner 49 percent of the stock. Now I am a 51 percent stockholder," says Howard Marcus. He goes on to explain, "I have the controlling interest as chief executive officer and majority shareholder, so I can set policy—to a point. Howard Halpern is the president—the operating officer. We have some conflict there due to the long distance relationship, but it is a highly successful company."

The two separate firms together employed more than 200 people in 1995. Buckhead Beef has captured most of the U.S. Southeast market for its products plus the Caribbean, while Marcus Food Co. has expanded considerably into international markets in the Pacific Rim countries, Mexico, Canada, Russia, and elsewhere. Credit, payroll, accounts receivable and payable, and order processing are tracked and monitored in Wichita under the direction of Jerry Marcus (see Exhibit 2).

Today, Buckhead Beef ranks about third in the United States in its class in sales and volume as a hotel/restaurant supply company. It has one of the lowest operating costs of any company in its competitive group. That's phenomenal growth in a 10–12 year period. "In the past three years alone, we have grown from 20–40 percent per year," says Jerry. "Today we are continually sharpening our accounting controls. We monitor all aspects of the accounting functions, including cash."

"Each company has its own accounting center in Atlanta and in Wichita. We have several controllers in Atlanta. One of the things that was really mysterious and somewhat caused us to miss what was going on in Landrum was that Buckhead and Marcus Food were both making profits similar to Landrum relevant to the size and scope of the operation," Howard notes. "For the volume that they were showing, it looked totally reasonable. If you looked at some of the margins of the transactions, you would have known that they weren't real."

Marcus Food Co.

"Today our goal at Marcus Food is to remain a significant factor in marketing and to make decent returns on investment," says Howard.

Jerry adds, "When we started the trading business, Marcus Food was in a narrow channel of the beef industry. We diversified, developing expertise in

Exhibit 2   Organizational Chart

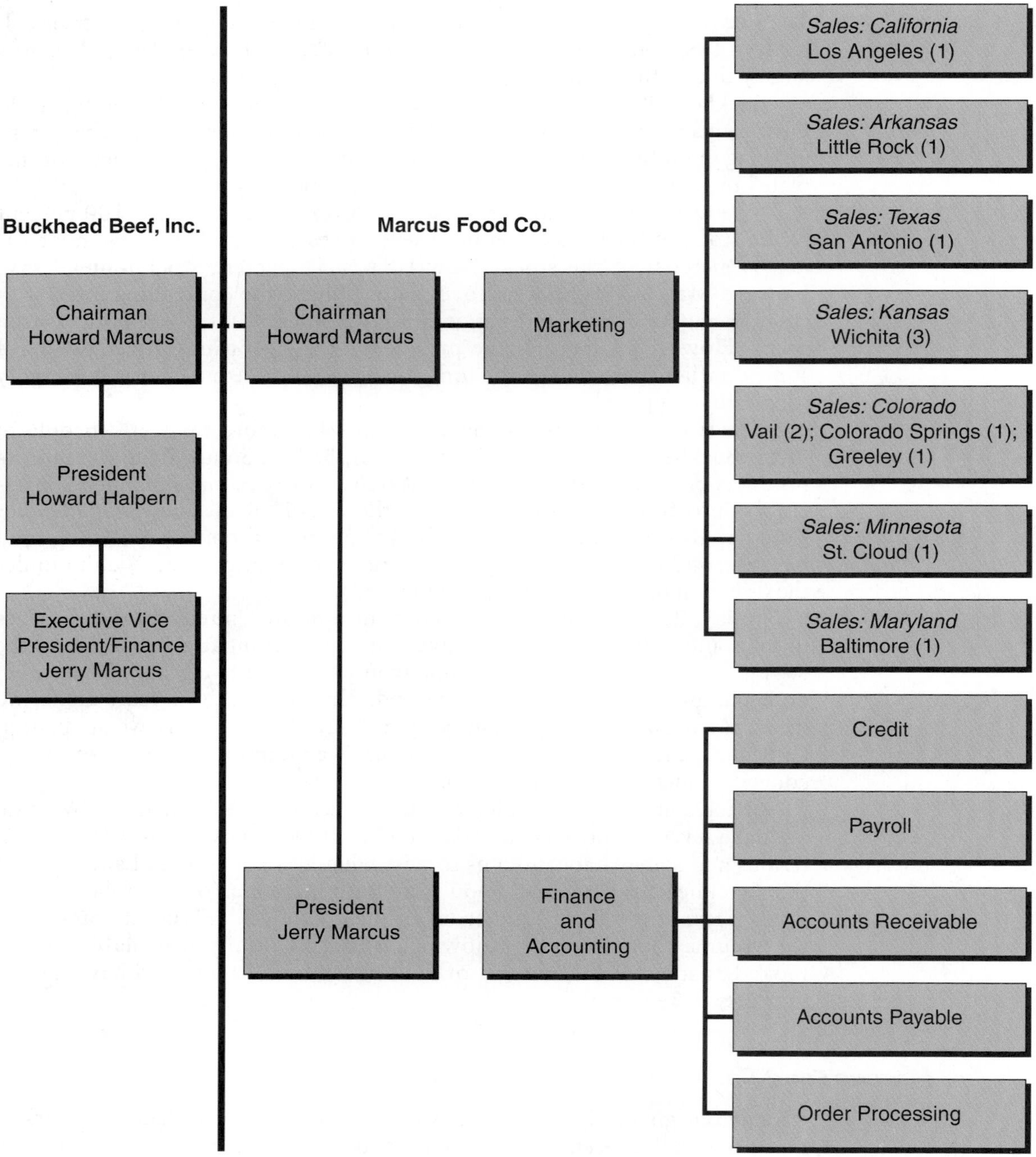

Buckhead Beef, Inc.

Chairman
Howard Marcus

President
Howard Halpern

Executive Vice
President/Finance
Jerry Marcus

Marcus Food Co.

Chairman
Howard Marcus

Marketing

Sales: *California*
Los Angeles (1)

Sales: *Arkansas*
Little Rock (1)

Sales: *Texas*
San Antonio (1)

Sales: *Kansas*
Wichita (3)

Sales: *Colorado*
Vail (2); Colorado Springs (1);
Greeley (1)

Sales: *Minnesota*
St. Cloud (1)

Sales: *Maryland*
Baltimore (1)

President
Jerry Marcus

Finance
and
Accounting

Credit

Payroll

Accounts Receivable

Accounts Payable

Order Processing

other areas—pork, poultry, and fish and processed foods—to expand our marketing base and knowledge of the products that we could sell, buy, and trade."

"The reward system at Marcus Food drives sales with a generous incentive program which attracts excellent and experienced people away from the industry giants," according to Howard. "I typically give our people 40 percent of the bottom line of every transaction, keeping 60 percent for Marcus Food. The cost of operations is about 20 percent of the profit. This gives our salespeople the same return as Marcus Food." Howard continues to explain, "Our salespeople also assume the risk. If there is bad debt, they assume risk for 40 percent of that risk. Our salespeople are true entrepreneurs, leaving secure, salaried jobs for high-risk opportunities."

The firm functions as a trading company, taking title to product that major meatpackers cannot (or do not wish to) sell. It also functions as the marketing arm for many of the minor meatpackers.

"We take bigger risks than the majors," Jerry Marcus says. "We take on the marginal credit risk customers that for one reason or another the major packer does not choose to accept. They don't want the risk."

The firm has a diversified product line, offering squid and sardines under its own brand name as one of its specialty products and selling it to the Philippines and China. "In 1995, we bought a $1 million boat, a 70-foot, 110-ton boat, to catch 90 tons of squid a night that we will pack and send to China and the Philippines," Jerry remarks.

"The trading company is capital intensive, and sales growth goals are only limited by access to capital. We are only constrained by working capital, and the banks keep giving us more money," says Jerry. "Many people go into business without proper capitalization or lines of credit. Most people don't know how much money a business takes."

"We're lucky," says Howard. "Our bank extended our line of credit and saw us through the major embezzlement problem so our credit rating wouldn't be hurt. It took us five years to get back the equity position that we had in 1988."

"Today, we're an international company. We go to Canada, the Caribbean, Greece, Holland, the Philippines, Taiwan, China, Australia. Exporting is a major factor," Howard boasts. "We're driven by profit, and I want an efficient return on working capital, diversification, and the right kind of salespeople. The way we handle ourselves in terms of ethics is very important. We sell the product for what it is. We are not going to misrepresent the product. It is my reputation that is at stake. If a product has a quality problem, we don't misrepresent it to the customer. That's my ethics and morality . . . these are the things that my father taught me about good business. My dad was as honest as they come. He would never cheat anybody out of one pound of anything or misrepresent the product," says Howard.

"We may have a large amount of inventory in the freezer that we bought from somebody. We froze it on speculation, and then the market may go against us. We may have no recourse but to sell it for a loss. That is part of the game. We are taking the risk, and that is part of the risk that we take. We sometimes have losses, but we're probably wrong only 10–15 percent of the time," Howard explains.

"We can store it in the freezer for as long as a year, maybe for two years, depending on how it is wrapped. Sometimes we throw out some products. That's also part of the game. I have a philosophy," says Howard. "We have had growth, and we have diversified into a multifaceted company. We are not a beef marketing company. We are a 'center-of-the-plate' marketing company. We are selling every red and white meat item. We cannot be solely dependent on the major producers. I would rather diversify with 150 suppliers. The customer can go direct to suppliers and cut us out if they want to. Once they have the working capital and the connections and they know where the product is, there is nothing to prevent anyone from being dishonest with me," notes Howard. "We're in the finance business for the customer, and we're service oriented and have the benefit of market knowledge from every supplier in the country for any particular commodity that a customer may be looking for."

"Remember," says Jerry, "the broker only makes the connection between the buyer and the seller and takes a brokerage fee. A trader takes possession. We buy the product and we own it and sell it. The margins are much greater, but we have greater risk."

Buckhead Beef

Buckhead Beef continues to exceed its growth goal of 20 percent according to Howard Halpern, the president in Atlanta. "Growth is my choice. All entrepreneurs are driven and I am a classic entrepreneur in many ways. By continuing to grow at a rate of 20 percent, it is my belief that I will be able to continue to enhance the quality of the organization and the operation. Prior to 1990, I was the general manager, the operations manager, and the production manager. I made all the buying decisions, and I ran the company."

Howard Halpern has considerable experience in the wholesale food business and in the hotel and restaurant business. He had identified a market niche in 1983 with Howard Marcus, focusing on the beef industry and on "center-of-the-plate" specialty products.

"All my salespeople have culinary training. In fact, one of my salespeople was a certified executive chef. He was past president of the Chef's Association and captain of my Culinary Olympic Team. I was chairman of the Culinary Olympic Team for the Chaîne des Rôtisserers (a culinary society) for the United States. We competed in France in 1988 and 1992, and we also brought a team from Johnson & Wales University and placed third in the world competition. My salespeople are very professional. They know the business and understand what the customers want. We have no middle management here, no vice presidents of anything, no sales managers, and no regional managers. The salespeople report directly to me and we work directly with the customers," explains Halpern.

"Continued growth has allowed us to bring in quality, talented people. My chief financial officer is in charge of our computer system. In today's world of technology, our company requires this expertise. Talented and experienced people with designated areas of responsibility have formed our steering committee. I have all these young lions and lionesses running around here with an average age of 35 or so. They want to be part of a growth-oriented company," Halpern remarks.

Today, Buckhead exceeds standard key industry operating ratios on all measures. Cash flow is managed on a percent of current accounts receivables or 50 percent of inventory, depending on the ratio of inventory to accounts receivables.

"Maintaining inventory and receivable turns are vital in our industry. We use a 16-day inventory turn," says Halpern.

"I consider Howard Marcus our capital partner, but not our venture capitalist. Venture capitalists always have exit plans. We don't at this time. We might want to sell in the future, but not now," says Halpern. "I really depend on Howard Marcus' experience in the business, on his love for the business, his entrepreneurship, and on his will to win and to succeed. He and Jerry have commitment to this business. Howard was raised in this business, so he's not just a venture capitalist partner. Howard and Jerry have always been on the meatpacking side and I have always been on the food service purveying end of it. Yet we both love the business . . . love the idea of growing the cattle, getting it fabricated, getting them slaughtered, getting them to market efficiently and getting product to customers at prices they can afford."

Howard Halpern, once only the "sweat equity" partner of Buckhead Beef, envisioned himself as a capital equity partner with Howard Marcus. "In order for Howard Marcus to be comfortable with the continued growth, I have taken a substantial position in subordinating debt and retaining earnings that equal his. In 1991, we renegotiated my contract and based earnings on earnings of the company. I don't get paid a large salary. Unless we sell the product and the company collects it and makes money, I don't get paid. We set up an incentive bonus program. This is a classic entrepreneurial opportunity designed to pay me what the chief operating officer of a company would make. It was good for Howard Marcus because it did not guarantee me income if the company did not make money. We can continue to fund growth as we accelerate retained earnings," Halpern explains.

"Here at Buckhead, we put in the controls. The bank insisted that we have certified audits," says Halpern. "At our board meetings we do a review of accounts receivable collections by salespeople, by days outstanding. We do a very detailed look at gross profits and sales by customers, by salesperson, and by specific items. When I go to a board meeting, I bring this material and Howard Marcus and I sit down and review it. Jerry grasps the numbers, and he is good at listening."

Halpern says, "A major challenge for the future is succession. I have within this company now the people who will be running it 20 years from now. My son, Kirk Halpern, was in the top half of his class at Duke University and passed the bar with flying colors. He is an amazing individual and has the respect of all his peers. He took a big cut in salary when he joined us after being in legal practice for a few years. Yet he came here with $1,500 a week of business the first week that he started. My wife, Lynne, has the lowest bad debt ratios in the industry. She just smells them out, because she considers it our money. I also have five married couples who work here. We are a family kind of business and I like it that way."

"Jerry Marcus is the best thing that happened to Howard Marcus and Marcus Food. He's done a good job of brainstorming with us and in coming up with control mechanisms for our business," says Halpern. "As for Howard Marcus, I appreciate his great sense of family and commitment to family and community."

Buckhead has informal, but comprehensive board meetings once a year. "Howard Marcus and I have a great relationship. He comes and sees me once a year and I go and see him once a year," Halpern notes.

Epilogue

In 1996, Buckhead Beef Co. established a five-person, formal board of directors, with Howard Marcus as chairman of the board, Howard Halpern, and with three outside directors. "We have accounting controls and structure, and we're thinking about the future," says Howard Marcus.

4

Pelco*

Maintaining a Successful Customer–Centered Culture and an Entrepreneurial Spirit in the Face of Rapid Growth

Introduction

From 1987 to 1996, Pelco, Inc., a California-based manufacturer of video surveillance equipment, grew more than 700 percent—from 90 employees and under $10 million in revenues in 1987 to more than 600 employees and just under $100 million in revenues in 1996. David McDonald, the president, and his management team who acquired the small company in 1987, established a corporate culture and competitive strategy based on Tom Peters' *In Search of Excellence* philosophy that put the customer at the center of everything they did. It was their intent that employees in every area of the organization know specifically what they do to satisfy the customer, and they are rewarded for their efforts with a myriad of incentives and rewards. As a result, everyone in company talks about the customer because they all believe that it is the customer who pays them, not management.

Pelco is now poised to grow to more than 1,000 employees with half a billion dollars in revenues, but McDonald believes the challenge it faces with that kind of growth is "to maintain our entrepreneurial style, our culture, and our values in a larger environment where the chain of command is more complicated, where new people don't just walk in the door and automatically take on those values. . . . The opportunity for non-Pelco type values is

*This case study was prepared by Kathleen R. Allen, Ph.D., Lloyd Greif Center for Entrepreneurial Studies, University of Southern California, October 1996.

very high." Another challenge is to focus more of its resources on new product development, which has not been a strength of the management team to this point.

The Vision

Pelco's Commitment to Excellence

At Pelco, we firmly believe in providing our customers with innovative, superior quality products that are competitively priced and nearly always available off-the-shelf. We offer by far the most aggressive, complete array of customer services ever made available to the closed-circuit video market. Furthermore, we GUARANTEE 100% CUSTOMER SATISFACTION. Simply stated, this means we will always do whatever it takes to fully satisfy every customer, every time. You should accept absolutely nothing less from PELCO, because we accept nothing less from ourselves.

Being FANATICALLY CUSTOMER DRIVEN is an integral part of every PELCO job description. All of our people who deal with potential customer problems are authorized, and required, to make on-the-spot decisions as necessary in order to completely satisfy our customers every time, without needing approval from anyone. No PELCO employee will ever be criticized for going too far in trying to help a customer.

I personally stand behind PELCO'S COMMITMENT TO EXCELLENCE. If our organization ever fails to provide you with this level of support, then please contact me. I personally handle every customer issue brought to my attention. As I'm sure you can tell, we appreciate your business.

David L. McDonald
President

Pelco's History

Pelco was founded as Pelco T.V. in Hawthorne, California, in 1954 by E. L. Heinrich, known to all as "Erv." Pelco T.V. was really just a sideline of the more established Pelco Aviation machine shop. Its first manufactured products were simple pan and tilts and joysticks, which were used to remotely position T.V. cameras. As time went on, demand suggested a need for more elaborate controls such as variable speed and scan as well as heavier-duty pan and tilts.

The operation was soon moved from Hawthorne to the rear of the Pelco Aviation building in Gardena, California. The tiny four-employee company became six, then ten as its specialty item list grew to include weather-resistant housings and explosion-proof pan and tilts. The name of the company also changed to Pelco Sales, Inc. As production demand overcame Pelco's outside vendors' ability to handle, Pelco Sales added more new buildings, increased electronics production, and added a painting department. Heinrich ultimately purchased some adjacent land and erected a building to house a sheet metal fabricating department as well as a larger finished goods warehouse. Yet another building was purchased and remodeled next to the sheet metal department to house the ever-expanding sales and accounting departments.

About this time, Erv decided to turn the business over to his son, Rod Heinrich, who saw the need for a single new building that would put all of Pelco's departments under one roof. After considering the cost of doing this in Los Angeles, the younger Heinrich decided to move the company to Fresno, California, where there was a more available work force and more economical real estate costs. Within three years, however, the company had used up every square foot of floor space in the Fresno facility. With demand requiring new production lines, Heinrich made plans to build an 80,000-square-foot facility in Clovis, a community adjacent to Fresno.

Meanwhile, across town at Vendo, a NYSE company that manufactures vending machines, David McDonald, senior vice president of operations, was beginning to have the desire to run his own company. With several other executives at Vendo, he came up with a plan to find a project that had good growth potential and was a good candidate for the implementation of the Tom Peters' *In Search of Excellence* philosophy. McDonald firmly believed that a "philosophy built around excellence in the management of people and excellence in customer service and customer relations was a surefire formula for success, and actually few companies had made a serious attempt to adopt it." McDonald and his partners were also looking for something close to their own experience and joint knowledge, and they found the opportunity in the security industry with Heinrich's company. The team conducted a market study to determine how Pelco was positioned, what its strengths and weaknesses were, and what some of the "hot buttons" were with customers that were not being fulfilled. This gave them a better understanding of what was driving the market.

At that time, 1987, the Closed Circuit TV (CCTV) segment of the security industry was low on the maturation curve, so supply of product was the primary driver. Simply getting product to customers when they needed it would produce sales. Because it was a growth market, the "search for excellence" was not there; instead, the attitude was, "if you make it, they will come." Demand was always greater than supply. "When it's too easy," McDonald comments, "it's very tempting for manufacturers to be very insensitive to customer needs. Why try to make it perfect?" But McDonald and his team believed that the industry would mature, that supply would eventually meet and even exceed demand, and that therefore the market would ultimately be driven by completely different things.

McDonald's group, Freedom Acquisitions, Inc., and a silent partner, Lyles Diversified, Inc., of Fresno approached Heinrich to buy Pelco Sales, Inc., and in June 1987, they completed the purchase. Pelco Sales, Inc., became Pelco, Inc., owned equally by Freedom Acquisition, Inc. (which is entirely owned by Pelco management) and Lyles Diversified, Inc. At the time of purchase, Pelco Sales was doing under $10 million in revenues and had 90 employees. It was tied for second place in the market with seven other companies that were doing the same volume in different niches. A year and a half later, Pelco was already outselling its largest competitor. Today, the company is the industry leader in its niche, doing over $100 million in revenues with more than 600 employees in three buildings totaling over 260,000 square feet. A fourth building is on the drawing boards. *Industry Week* magazine named Pelco one of the top 25 plants in the United States.

The Industry

What began as simply a new medium—CCTV—is now considered essential to solving security problems in all types of venues. CCTV technology for general security applications has grown significantly over the past ten years, and this growth is expected to continue. The Freedonia Group projects a 16 percent growth rate per year through the year 2000. Similarly, a study by market observer Frost & Sullivan finds that because of technological advances, U.S. sales of commercial and industrial security equipment will grow 14 percent annually from $1.65 billion to $4.08 billion by the year 2001. Interior security devices will rise in total market revenue from 41 percent in 1994 to 46 percent in 2001, while the electronic access control segment will dip from 58 percent to 54 percent in the same period. This result is attributed to rising commercial and industrial crime and the increasing availability of multiple cost-effective security products.[1] CCTV is the largest component of the interior security product market with projected annual compound growth of 16 percent. Dropping prices of color cameras and end-user affinity for visual techniques are cited as the precipitators of this growth.

The number of CCTV applications has increased directly with technological advancements that have enhanced not only CCTV cameras but VCRs, monitors, video transmission systems, and many other areas within video systems.

In the early years of this young industry, the demand for new CCTV products was so great that all manufacturers had to worry about was meeting that demand. Consequently, they did not consider devising sound policies that would serve the entire industry. As a result, many companies that should have prospered as the industry grew were stagnating. According to Donald N. Horn, in the *American Society for Industrial Security Management* journal, there are two reasons for this.[2]

First, according to Horn, while every company desires favorable publicity about its products, many of the articles and books in the industry are self-serving and often tout products and services that in the end don't work or that inflate product capabilities to create unrealistic expectations on the part of buyers. This hurts the industry as a whole.

Second, the industry has been inhibited from becoming mature by confusing marketing policies which have created ambiguous relationships among distributors, dealers/installers, and end-users, often resulting in one dealer initiating a sale and another completing the sale.

Competitors

Three of Pelco's significant industry competitors are briefly discussed in this section. Note that all of these companies are public companies.

Sensormatic–Florida

Sensormatic manufactures high-tech security devices, which include closed-circuit television cameras, access control systems, photo-imaging equipment, as well as other security products. With more than 60 percent of the anti-theft technology market, it is the leading provider. It is best known for the white plastic "alligator" tags used by retailers to prevent shoplifting.

Incorporated in 1968, Sensormatic experienced steady growth until the early 1980s when sales slowed reflecting the maturing of the security tag segment of the industry. In 1986, after cutting costs, Sensormatic began a diversification program and in 1992 acquired its chief rival, ALPS (Automated Loss Prevention Systems), the European market leader. In 1994, it acquired Advanced Entry Systems, a systems integrator with CCTV expertise, and in 1995, systems integrator Glen Industrial Communications. These last two acquisitions put it directly in competition with Pelco.

Vicon Industries, Inc.

A New York–based company, Vicon makes CCTV components and systems for security surveillance, safety, and other applications. Its products range from $10 mounting brackets to $100,000 digital control and video switching systems.

The company was founded in 1967 to supply components to the CCTV industry. In 1981, it established a U.K. subsidiary, and, like Sensormatic, by the mid 1980s, it experienced slow sales, so the company moved into designing and manufacturing a broader array of products and systems.

In 1987, it successfully fought off a hostile takeover bid by rival Sensormatic. In that same year it signed an agreement with Chun Shin to manufacture its products in South Korea.

Since 1988, however, the company has turned only one small profit. Its strategy has been to cut low-margin products to concentrate on state-of-the-art surveillance systems and to expand in the Pacific Rim and Latin America. In 1995, the company introduced several new products including the Nova series of digital matrix switchers and controllers and DigiTek, a sophisticated intrusion detector. It also unveiled ProTech, a Windows-based command and control software package, which allows users to graphically program and operate the company's digital control and video processing systems from a PC.

Checkpoint Systems, Inc.

Checkpoint produces and markets electronic article surveillance (EAS) and closed-circuit television systems in stores and libraries. It holds a 15 percent share of the EAS market behind Sensormatic's 68 percent share.

Checkpoint was founded in 1969. In 1977, with $3 million in sales, Checkpoint was spun off to the shareholders of its former parent, Logistics

Industries. In 1986, the company acquired Sielox Systems, a designer, manufacturer, and marketer of electronic access-control systems. Desiring to target the retail and library markets internationally, Checkpoint acquired a Canadian distributor in 1992 and an Argentine distributor in 1993. It also set up subsidiaries in Mexico and Australia. Its 1993 acquisition of ID Systems International B.V. and ID Systems Europe B.V. gave the company direct access to six countries in Western Europe.

In 1995, Checkpoint acquired Alarmex, a leading supplier of CCTV, POS monitoring systems, and alarms.

Products and Customers

Pelco produces 2,500 different finished products for the CCTV/video surveillance segment of the security industry and is the leader in that segment worldwide. Pelco's equipment and systems can be found throughout the world. At one end of the market, they are found in large department stores, casinos such as the Mirage, as well as small corner drug stores. At the other end of the market, Pelco equipment is used in airports, in and around government agencies, on warships, and at Cape Canaveral to monitor rocket launches. In the television and film industries, Pelco equipment is used to move cameras or dish antennas and featured in many movies like *The Bodyguard*. Most U.S. embassies and many U.S. and foreign military installations have Pelco equipment. Pelco's television surveillance products also exist in high-profile sites such as the Olympics, Buckingham Palace, China's Tiananmen Square, and Denver's new airport, as well as in cities like Santiago, Chile, where crime is controlled through "video patrol." The installation of 22 closed-circuit security cameras at strategic street locations in downtown Santiago has reduced crime and disorder dramatically.

Pelco gives its customers complete surveillance systems, from CCTV video cameras designed to blend with their surroundings to complete systems control panels that allow a technician to monitor several sites at once. The only aspect of the product that Pelco outsources is the actual cameras and control monitors (CRTs), because this specialized technology does not fall within their core competencies. Pelco's products are sold through a network of 3,000 authorized dealers, and Pelco enjoys a 45 percent share of the market, which has approximately 20 competitors.

In the summer of 1995, Pelco announced that the company had reached an agreement with the Sony Corporation that would make Pelco Sony's exclusive customer for the Japanese market. This historic agreement provided that Sony will not sell products that compete with Pelco products in that market. The products are marketed under the Sony name and include all standard Pelco products modified only to accommodate electrical differences and labeling. This arrangement is more than a typical customer/supplier situation. Rather, it's a partnership where both companies have agreed to combine product lines—and technologies—resulting in complete systems for Sony's Japanese customers.

Competitive Strategy

There is little doubt about the fact that in a "me-too" industry, Pelco's competitive advantage lies in its relationship with its customers. Pelco became a pioneer in addressing customer service in the CCTV industry at a time when it didn't have to. Industry customers were feeling that they weren't being treated well, but they accepted it as the norm for the industry. Pelco decided to change all that. David McDonald, president, recalls: "One of the first things we did to make a statement in this direction was a policy on products that came in to be serviced from the field." The typical turnaround for the industry was six weeks, and Pelco's research had found that this was a "hot button" for customers. They put in place a policy that products that came in for service would be turned around in one day. If the factory received it on Tuesday, it would go back out to the customer on Wednesday. The safety net on that policy was that if they couldn't fix it in a day, they would give the customer a new or like new product within 24 hours. "This was a profound statement to the marketplace." Internally they had to put systems and procedures in place to make it happen.

> Part of the theory behind that was . . . a customer who had bought and paid for a product and then had a problem somewhere along the line, either a routine problem or a problem that was our fault because there was something wrong with the design and it broke in two weeks or two months, [it] had to have priority over anything else we did; [it] had to have priority over new products or new customers . . . that's the distinction that a lot of companies have trouble making—protect and serve the customers you already have. Blow their socks off every time and be absolutely fanatical about how you make that happen. A one-week turnaround would have been astounding to the marketplace. But our whole philosophy here is to be almost as good as you theoretically can be so nobody can ever come along and say "I do it better." A week would have been OK, but a day made one hell of a statement about our culture and philosophy. It works to a degree of perfection that academically couldn't be supported.

Statistically, there should always be a mean failure rate; but Pelco refused to look at it that way. There was no minuscule failure rate that was OK. McDonald and his employees believed there was always a way to achieve the goal.

One question that McDonald is continually faced with is, "What is the financial impact of the customer service you provide?" He loves that question:

> One of the greatest myths of extreme levels of customer service is, can you afford to do that? And here's the truth of the matter. When you look at extreme customer service, things we do around here, if you completely ignore and discount the positive business we get . . . and

strictly look at the short term financial impact. If we had the possibility of gaining new business and higher levels of customer loyalty, or any other ancillary or longer term benefit, it saves us probably in the order of magnitude of a couple million dollars a year by doing these things as opposed to not doing them—*saves us that money.*

For example, in the service department when the 24-hour turnaround was put in place, the psychology of putting people who had never been seen in the spotlight as a huge marketing tool resulted in a work pace and intensity that increased so much that they had to reduce the staffing in that department by two people because they soon had excess capacity. That in a company that was now ten times larger than it was at that time.

Line Functions

Pelco has a very flat structure that goes from the president to the vice presidents in charge of each functional area and then to line managers and teams who carry out all the activities related to the production of its products, from R&D to manufacturing, assembly, and distribution.

Research and Development

In the spring of 1996, Pelco made an important strategic move to focus more of its energies and resources on new product development with the hiring of Glenn Waehner, a highly respected technical person in the CCTV industry, as senior vice president, product development. Waehner's job is to drive Pelco to become the "clear technological leader in the CCTV industry."

When McDonald and his group purchased Pelco in 1987, they purchased it from founder Erv Heinrich, an inventor with a focus on the product side of the business. McDonald candidly admits he "lacked the industry knowledge and product knowhow" of the Heinrichs, and so he and his partners focused on creating "high people values, extreme levels of customer performance, vertical integration, business integrity, and a professional organization." That approach grew the company to ten times its original size. Still, McDonald is concerned:

> I've always been concerned that, while we do most things very well, we've never been seen as the industry's technical leader. At times I've felt very disadvantaged in trying to direct our company's R&D activities. It's not my background. It's my primary weakness as Pelco's CEO.

McDonald knew that he had to attract someone of the stature of Glenn Waehner, CEO of American Dynamics and later corporate vice president at Sensormatic, Pelco's principal competitor. It took several years and "relentless pursuit," but McDonald achieved what he calls "the most strategically important event in Pelco's history."

Manufacturing

Tim Glines is the vice president of manufacturing and also an owner of the company. He believes that every job in the company, including those of the vice presidents, is multifaceted. "We haven't developed at Pelco . . . a lot of king-ships." For everyone, the normal job is customer service. The chain of command in manufacturing goes from the president to the vice president to the line foreman, who sets up team leaders who are in charge of functional cells that do such things as lathe work, assembly, and punching. The machine operators within the cells are in charge of an 8×8 foot area. It is Glines' job to make sure that everyone is properly trained and given the appropriate equipment and to see that the team successfully completes the schedule on time.

Pelco produces 2,500 finished goods products. The average product has six manufactured parts and multiple purchased parts. Every nut, bolt, screw, and casting is controlled by the team leader whose team uses those materials. With steel, for example, workers are responsible for inventory in stock, ordering all material, cutting it to first operation size, and quality. Anyone can stop the manufacturing process for quality issues. Asserts Glines, "We don't care about productivity. Within manufacturing we expense all labor, and I don't even track the hours it takes to do a job. I don't care. All I care about is 100 percent quality."

They used to do traditional time-and-motion studies but found that if employees are motivated to produce quality products, productivity will be a natural by-product.

The customer is involved in issues of manufacturing and product design from the first day. Prototype designs come to the manufacturing floor and are built on real equipment, put in the work-in-process storage area, and pulled as a regular job in the assembly area. The assembly team puts it together on the line, and if at any point a worker does not like the way the prototype is going together, he or she stops the product and it goes back to engineering for redesign.

Many times new products will originate in manufacturing rather than in engineering or R&D. For example, in one case a dealer asked for a certain product with enhanced features that he couldn't get from anyone else. With the help of marketing, it was designed in manufacturing in one afternoon, programmed the next week, and the prototype was tested in the field. It came back to manufacturing with some changes; the changes were made, and three weeks later it was a completed part that engineering never touched.

When Pelco was acquired, there were holes in the product line, so it had to design "me-toos," or products everyone else was doing, just to have a complete selection. Once that was accomplished, however, the next challenge was to take the production line from what was traditionally an electromechanical line to a microprocessor-based line using the best equipment to accomplish the job. Initially, Pelco outsourced its turning and milling, and the machine shop started out with duplicators for punching and standard mills. All of the sophisticated equipment came in the period from 1987 to 1996. Glines recalls that when they first added new technology to the machine shop, "my guys bet me they could outrun that machine on a regular mill—and were sure of it, by the way—until about two hours into the run. . . . I actually ran [the new machine] myself. I figured if a VP could run it and beat 'em, they'd love the machine—I was probably 70 percent ahead of them in two hours." Glines believes that buying that machine was really a training device to prove to the workers that you could go from standard equipment to technology-based equipment and it would contribute to quality and productivity. This prepared them for the more advanced equipment later on. Over a period of two years, all manufacturing was brought in-house.

Glines doesn't feel that, with the exception of start-ups, any company can be successful in a highly competitive marketplace while outsourcing. This is because in an industry the upper value is set, even if you add more features. So the only place to manipulate the numbers is in the raw materials, which are cheaper if Pelco does it in-house. With manufacturing in-house, Pelco is 100 percent in control of quality and engineering changes. "If I had to call Taiwan [for an engineering change] it might take months." However, every one of Pelco's major competitors has actually quit manufacturing in-house.

Glines meets with all manufacturing employees once a week to show them what contributed or detracted from their profit sharing in terms of performance. He notes that when incentives become standardized over time, it becomes a challenge to continue to teach the basics. A new goal for quality must always be set, and employees are the ones who set the goals. They're harder on themselves than management ever would be. When a new employee comes onto a team, for example, and produces good output during the 90-day probationary period, the team will request that the person be hired permanently. The team also determines when not to hire someone, and its decisions are respected. Pelco promotes from within. According to Glines, "they can have my job tomorrow; there's always things to do."

Procedures in manufacturing run half a page. If they run longer, they don't use them. Employees are responsible for quality, and they take that responsibility very seriously. In 1995, the quality index for manufacturing was 99.87. Glines missed his goal by one tenth of one percent. "People will rise to the level you let them rise to. Most of this stuff is so common sense, it's ridiculous . . . but common sense is not common."

Production

The vice president of production (assembly) is Steve Jensen, who is also one of the owners of the company. His role is to ensure the correct distribution of personnel for a production schedule that varies monthly. He is in charge of 260 employees who are divided into 20 teams with team leaders and assistants. He also has three managers. Each team is responsible for a family of similar products, and within each team those who want to can learn several positions and cross-train. There are also opportunities for advancement to a leader or manager position.

The stockroom pulls parts fabricated in the manufacturing plant into a kit for production using an internal just-in-time system. Those raw materials that are purchased, such as sheet metal and castings, come from suppliers who have agreements with Pelco to supply what it needs in a very short period of time, usually about once a week. This allows Pelco to keep inventory to a minimum.

Production builds a large variety of product to stock so that it always has a 60-day inventory of finished goods. The exact number of finished goods that it needs to keep on hand is determined by a customized computer schedule that publishes graphs to show weekly usage as well as to project sales and trigger the replenishing of items. Its goal is to maintain 95 percent off the shelf for the top 100 requested items and 90 percent for the remaining several thousand products.

The in-house computer system allows anybody in the company to call up a product to check on the status—how many in stock, how many allocated to sales orders, and what the production schedule is. People on the production floor use terminals to do sales order reservations showing the product is complete and ready to ship. Virtually 99 percent of shipments are made on autopilot, that is, the order is scheduled by computer and the delivery date determined. On average, 75 different products are packed in a single day.

In the fall of 1996, Pelco shifted to a new printed circuit board process called surface mount where all the components and circuitry are placed on the surface of the PC board rather than drilling holes in the board to secure the wires. This method avoids the step of soldering the back side of the board and allows for more functions in less space. This is the technology that made things like beepers and cell phones possible, but it hadn't yet been used in this industry. As the industry attempts to cram more capabilities in the same amount of space, however, surface mount technology becomes a big issue. Pelco has products under development that will specifically use this technology.

Quality assurance is dealt with in every aspect of manufacturing and production; it is not really a separate department. Team members are charged with the challenge of finding things wrong in the task completed before the product gets to them on the assembly line. The quality audit (in the traditional sense) is accomplished by random inspection of roughly one out of every hundred items they build. Based on those findings, there's a quality index number that's generated every day for every team and that score is used as the basis for a multitude of recognition and reward systems. A team leader, for example, whose team runs a 100 percent quality index can just about double his or her income. The assistant leader will receive half of that, and all of the team members will have a variety of incentives available to them. If the quality index is 100 percent for three months, the whole team goes to lunch, and each team member receives one of the more expensive gift items that Pelco offers. According to President David McDonald,

> All of these incentives are driven by only one measure . . . quality. It's a singular focus . . . because what the customer expects of that person sitting down on the line—they don't care how productive they are or how efficient they are, or even if they made their scheduled amount of production for the day. What they care about is that what they made is right, and when they open up the box and plug it in, it

works. That's how we make the lowest-level person on that line customer focused. We translate customer focus in that case to what they do that makes a difference for the customer—quality—therefore, we have the highest quality in the industry with a QA department one tenth the size of what you'd normally expect in a company this size.

The costs associated with incentive programs amount to about 20 percent of the cost of maintaining a traditional QA department. While competitors typically try to inspect the quality in the finished product, the people on the line at Pelco know that they're the last people to see the product before the customer gets it, so they're the ones responsible for quality.

Marketing and Distribution

Pelco has three types of customers: end-users, dealers, and manufacturer's reps. There are several ways that these customers are involved in Pelco's business. Twice a year the top dealers come to Pelco for a President's Council Meeting to voice their opinions on how Pelco is doing and where it needs to go. Also, end-users often call in and enquire about Pelco's willingness to do a new product. The Blue Ribbon Dealer program encourages dealers to develop new ways to expand territories and types of outlets, such as retail. In addition, Pelco does several trade shows, which are used for relationship building. In fact, 90 percent of the people at these trade shows have been doing business with Pelco for years.

Pelco uses a network of dealers and manufacturer's reps. The reps are managed by three regional managers, and their job is to make contacts and establish a dealer base. Even major clients like the Mirage casino go through dealers, in this case, one that specializes in the needs of casinos. Pelco's sales representatives have the ability to instantly check the status of customer orders from anywhere in North America through the use of a phone line, a computer, and a modem. Through this Intranet system they can access information regarding product pricing and availability, inventory levels, purchase order status, credit information, and shipping dates. They can also check for special pricing availability or substitute products for items not in stock.

Customer Support

Customer support manager Joe Schanda started with Pelco as a technical writer and worked his way up through marketing. His background before coming to Pelco was as a customer field service repair technician for the Southern California division of a New York–based company and as a regional manager for another company. Schanda is in charge of technical support, both pre-sale and post. His duties vary from scheduling technicians for on-site visits to customers, to supporting salespeople, expediting products with time-sensitive deadlines, handling calls from customers, and technical training for customers, dealers, and reps. Schanda also attends the various trade shows in which Pelco is involved and then travels to meet with dealers and reps to see how Pelco can support their needs.

All technical support comes from the factory via phone. On-site support comes first from the dealer, then the rep, and finally, if necessary, the factory will send a factory technician to the site, which is something most competitors don't do. According to Schanda, "Everyone understands what their job function is—to support the customer." Technicians will not get in trouble for decisions they make in the field to please the customer, even if that means installing a new system to repair a defect within the 24-hour guaranteed repair time frame. For example, a technician was in San Bernadino in Southern California where he discovered a problem that was occurring in four locations. He brought the part back to the factory, worked on a solution, and drove back to San Bernadino the next day, a five-hour drive, to install it. If customers need technical help, they can go to anyone in the factory who is on the personal contact list, so that no customer ever sits on hold or doesn't speak to a human being. One-day training seminars are held on a case-by-case basis as requested by the customer and Pelco does not charge for this. In the spring of 1996, Pelco began comprehensive CCTV instruction at its training facility. Besides the technical seminars, President David McDonald speaks on topics such as "How to Build a Highly Prosperous Small Business" and "Using Fanatical Customer Service as a Business Strategy."

Staff Functions

Management and Organization

Vicki Garcia really knows Pelco from many perspectives. In the seven years she has been employed there, she has held seven different jobs. Starting as a stock clerk, she moved to receiving and shipping, where she turned her data entry job into a coordinator position. Soon she began hearing rumors that a job was in the works to supervise and maintain the Early Warning System, so she went to her boss and said, "that job's mine; I can do it better than anyone—I know I can." The EWS was put in place when Pelco began to experience extraordinary growth and was concerned about getting products shipped on time. Not only did their 24-hour turnaround promise require that someone make sure "must ship tomorrow" products made their deadlines, but any product had to meet the delivery date given to the customer or Pelco would pick up the cost to overnight the shipment. Garcia's job is to work with every department to facilitate the achievement of that promise. As of August 1996, she had experienced only three "misses" which necessitated contacting the customer. This is a remarkable achievement considering Pelco ships about 3,500 to 4,000 line items a day. If a product ships late, the customer is contacted by Garcia, the president—David McDonald—and Garcia's boss, a vice president. They also receive a faxed letter of apology as well as a FedEx delivered letter. And, of course, their order is shipped overnight at Pelco's expense.

According to Garcia, everyone at Pelco is in the customer service business. Anyone who has a telephone will help a customer. "It's very satisfying to be able to solve [customers'] problems and give them information and help them to get through their day." But this means that she is on the factory floor, in fact, all over the plant, daily. She needs to understand the workings of every department and how it may affect her ability to get a product out on time. If she asks an employee to do something, he knows there's a customer at the other end of the request, so he never gives her a problem. Garcia believes her professional reputation is always on the line, so she has to be very creative in her problem solving, and she always has a backup plan even where there's no problem.

Human Resources

Gloria Miller is the human resources director, and, in her words, she does "everything but make the product." This includes overseeing the Blue Pride Café (the employees' restaurant), choosing vendors, fitness programs, training, the video library, hiring, termination, safety, and incentive programs. Prior to joining Pelco, Miller spent nine years in city government, and when McDonald interviewed her for the position of human resources director at Pelco, he told her that his only concern was that she might not spend money; he wanted her to be free to do things for people. Miller found this very refreshing. She is a frugal person by nature, but McDonald's philosophy toward spending money on incentive programs gave her the freedom of thought to implement new programs to motivate and reward the efforts of Pelco's employees—things like the wellness program where employees listen to experts talk about health issues during lunch. When an employee attends one of these wellness lunches, she or he gets healthy points that can be redeemed for gifts.

Once a month the company provides lunch for all its employees, along with an annual company picnic and a dinner/dance during the holidays. Every Friday there are free donuts. Remarkably, Miller has no budget for her department. When she wants to implement a program, she estimates the cost and submits a requisition. She has never been turned down.

"They're all my kids out there," Miller jokes, "and they all know that when I yell at them . . . when I say, 'get your safety glasses on,' I still love 'em." She knows everyone's name and what's going on in their lives. She is an attorney, psychiatrist, social worker, and psychologist. Not only employees come to her, but their supervisors and managers as well. Before any action can be taken against an employee, supervisors must go through Miller. Because of this procedure, Pelco has a remarkable record of no lawsuits. And where former employees have filed inappropriately for unemployment benefits, Miller has never lost an appeal. This comes from the fact that "if someone's fired, they fire themselves." They know the reason because the issues have been discussed many times with them. Every employee has a probationary period of 90 days during which everything they do, both positive and negative, is documented. Usually, the problem is absenteeism; in only a few instances is the problem that they can't do the work. She calls it a "gentle termination." "I give them a hug and I wish them good luck . . . they walk out feeling . . . they know they've lost their job, but they don't go out angry, ever."

Finance

Carrie Migliori is a senior vice president and the chief financial officer. She has been with the company since 1988, and since that time she has used her strong analytical skills to do much more than be the CFO. Three years ago, she redesigned the MRP process; for a time she filled in for the vice president of sales; in the summer of 1996, she was heading the engineering department until the new VP came on board.

Migliori defends the requisition system used in most departments in the company, saying that "if you have a budget, you're going to spend that budget so that it's not reduced the next year. Since it's developed ahead of time, it doesn't easily allow for current, up-to-date decisions based on the market." Each individual requisition stands on its own. If human resources develops a program that benefits employees, then it's justified. By contrast, if HR were on a budget, some of these programs would never be implemented because going over budget could never be justified in and of itself.

At the end of each month, some departments look at expenses compared with a trend. If the department is growing and wants to justify a new machine, for example, it would do a feasibility analysis to look at the benefit and the payback period. The one exception is the marketing department, which does have a budget because, as Migliori puts it, that's one area where "everything sounds good to do."

The accounting department, like production, manufacturing, and marketing, has incentive systems. For example, employees in reception and data entry are rewarded based on lack of errors; in accounts receivable rewards are based on collection of past due accounts. In short, rewards are always based on good performance that translates to quality for the customer.

Once a year, Migliori as CFO does a forecast of growth, new equipment, facility requirements, and cash flow—in other words, how much bank money will be needed to make it through the year. Its positive relationship with its bankers allows Pelco to remain flexible in meeting the needs of its customers throughout the year.

Executive compensation is different for every vice president and is geared to the individual position, experience, and contribution to the company. Where bonuses are given, they are based on bottom line profit. In this way, all VPs are aware of everything in the company that improves the bottom line even if it's not within their designated purview. Regional sales managers receive bonuses based on sales in their territory as well as incentives for product promotions, while managers at the production level have bonus plans based on production and quality.

Pelco does not believe in open-book management, the philosophy that all employees know and understand the company financials. However, Pelco does provide employees with a profit-sharing scoreboard. At the end of the month, Migliori does a schedule showing areas that have helped profit sharing for employees (i.e., the shipping department met its goals) and also inefficiencies or things that worked against profit sharing (i.e., scrapping metal for a machine that didn't work properly). These are areas where employees can make a difference. Employees who make suggestions for cost savings that are implemented get 10 percent of the savings.

Conclusion

Since Pelco was acquired from its original founder in 1987, it has become a solid industry leader in its niche. Capitalizing on the strengths of its management team, Pelco has parlayed a strategy of high people values, extreme levels of customer performance, vertical integration, and business integrity into a superior performing company in an industry where growth and product demand are no longer givens.

Now Pelco is looking to grow to the next level without sacrificing the customer-centered culture it has so carefully created. How can Pelco grow and still ensure that the quality and service it is known for will be important to everyone who works there? How can it maintain a sense of "family" when employee numbers go over 1,000, and they're working in four different buildings? How does it maintain an entrepreneurial spirit in such a large company?

Pelco also has to look seriously at a product development focus if it is to maintain its leadership position. In an industry affected by rapidly changing technology, Pelco must develop a product development strategy that will give it yet another competitive advantage in a very dynamic market. What is the appropriate strategy, and how should it be implemented are just two of the questions facing the company.

References

[1] "Keeping It Under Lock and Key," *Electronic Design,* 18 March 1996.

[2] Horn, Donald N. (1990). "Are We Being Misled? Closed-Circuit Television in Security," *American Society for Industrial Security Management* 34, no. 8, p. 150. Note that Horn is the chair of Vicon Industries, one of Pelco's competitors and a company that has experienced stagnating growth.

One of Tom Zotos' daily rituals was to have breakfast at one of LA's local delis. On a muggy morning during the summer of 1990, Tom entered the eatery, and, as he was approaching the counter, he heard his friend from many years call him over to his booth.

Tom, you look like hell. What's going on?

His friend Bob Stein was genuinely concerned about Tom's apparent distress. Tom sat down and just shook his head.

Bob, the Disney people have decided not to renew their license. The company I work for is completely dependent upon that license, after ten years of hard work, I am back at the beginning. The new owner is 60 and he doesn't have the energy to do it again. I still see a big market for our product. I just don't know what to do.

Tom Zotos

Tom was born in Southbridge, Massachusetts, the middle of three sons of parents who had emigrated from Albania. His father worked in Southbridge's optical glass mill before WWII, then learned barbering in the army. After the war, he went into business for himself as a one-chair barbershop in

---

*This case was researched and written by Professors William H. Crookston and Thomas J. O'Malia. This case is intended to be an introduction into the people side of entrepreneurship. Some details have been changed in order to protect the confidences of actual individuals. Copyright © 1995.

this same town. Tom's mother was a homemaker, and the home was filled with exuberance, music, and love in an old-fashioned Eastern European traditional way.

Tom remembers that his first entrepreneurial experience was to make $5 shoveling snow for a neighbor. He grew in pride and stature when he gave the money to his mom. He fondly remembers the feeling of satisfaction he got from doing something on his own. Several years later, Tom loaned his dad money to open a successful custom glass scientific apparatus business in the garage. Tom, the teenager, financed his dad's dream. He felt he was being trained to be an entrepreneur from early childhood.

Tom's parents exposed their young boys to culture—primarily art and music. Tom's art was music: he played guitar, formed a band, and did gigs for high school dances featuring many of the songs he had written himself. He got pretty good at this music-making business and on some weekends netted $400. He finished high school and went on to Quinsigamond Community College to study business. From this base, Tom made as much as $1,000 per week on the college concert circuit.

Tom's life was music, but after 250 music gigs his interest was waning. His first exposure to printed art was when, as a teenager, he was given a book of illustrated art by Allen Aldridge. This book and its contents made quite an impression on Tom. As Tom's interest in art grew, he moved his young family, now a wife and eight-year-old daughter, to Los Angeles, a better scene for art than New England. By chance, he met his teenage idol and began an association with Aldridge that would help form his future.

Aldridge's work had featured a number of superstar musicians including the Beatles, Elton John, and others. Their meeting and friendship began shortly after the unfortunate death of John Lennon. A musician at heart, Tom did an art piece on Lennon and decided to sell it commercially as a memorial. With Aldridge as lead blocker, Tom was able to meet Yoko Ono and convince her to let him go forward with the project. The piece was successful and got the recognition Tom needed to begin his new career.

These serendipitous events—the gift of the book, meeting Aldridge, his Lennon poster—combined with Tom's networking and the mentoring of his new friend, led to his first formal job. Tom had never worked for a company before; he always had worked for himself. This first LA job at OSP (One Stop Posters) was really an informal loose partnership where Tom ran the art arm of the company. This firm designed, printed, and distributed posters, buttons, and high-end gallery art.

In 1986, Tom tried to get the Disney organization in Burbank interested in upscale art designed for adults. Trying a direct approach, Tom had been pestering the licensing agents at Disney to take a chance on stocking art posters and showed his designs based on pictures of Walt Disney. The agents would have none of this departure from the low-end art items which they sold to tourists. Tom felt that the market was ripe for a more classy image in poster art and who better to buy a picture of Walt than Disneyland visitors?

The licensing people could not figure into which category of merchandise this type of art might fall. After several attempts to get rid of him, the licensing managers told Tom to meet the head legal person at Disney. Tom asked if this person would negotiate a license with him. No, they said, he just likes art, and maybe he will understand you; we can't.

> They simply didn't know what to do with me because they didn't know what I was talking about. They always had two dollar posters in their stores. I told them I wanted something I could hang in my office. They asked, "Why?"

Tom describes the meeting with the head legal person as a "godsend." He walked into an office where a Dali and a Picasso hung on the wall along with other art prints. He asked the attorney if a Disney shouldn't be on the wall as well. Sure, he was told, but what kind of Disney? Tom explained his idea for a four-part series. The man said go ahead and show him some rough paste-ups. They were done without all the formalities of a contract, but with a handshake from the head lawyer and a big dose of hope from Tom.

Tom developed the pieces that featured a young Walt Disney standing in a doorway with a cartoon shadow of Mickey Mouse cast on the open door. The head of legal loved the artwork, gave Tom a license, and OSP had its first significant success. The Walt/Mickey poster remains a classic.

The success with the Lennon and Disney posters gave Tom the nucleus of his new career. He was secure at his position with OSP. Then changes occurred. In 1989, the company went through a transition that forced a buyout from an individual within the firm. The buyer and new owner regarded Tom as just an employee. His boss was approaching 60, and Tom was approaching 40. "My career could have been funded by this person in the company, but we were on different wavelengths. I have a family and monthly expenses, and I was at an age and time when I had to be careful with my decisions."

Bob Stein

Bob was born and raised on Long Island, another middle of three sons. His father, who emigrated from Austria, worked for a stock brokerage firm in New York City as a market maker for several stocks. Family conversations allowed Bob to share in the basics of his father's career. His parents were very supportive of any of his endeavors. Through high school, Bob wrote music and played tournament tennis.

He attended two years (1974–1976) at the University of Rhode Island on a tennis scholarship but left school because he felt he was not getting enough out of it. "Business School let me down, I didn't respect my professors." After a short break, Bob came back for one year of liberal arts study—philosophy, art, and history—which was much more to his liking; but he never finished college.

The music bug eventually drew him to New York City where he was determined to become a songwriter. He admits he never read a note of music in his life; he just heard it in his head. Using his tennis background, at age 20, he started working at the Gramercy Racquet Club where his responsibility was to open the club at 7:00 a.m. each morning. One day, one of the tennis pros was sick, and Bob took over one of his lessons. In the waiting area, Walter Cronkite watched Bob give this lesson and was impressed with his patience and teaching style. He asked Bob to give him a lesson, so Bob, the new employee, told the head pro, "Mr. Cronkite would like a lesson with me." The pro was a bit intimidated, Cronkite intervened, and Bob was promoted to instructor on the spot.

Bob continued to work on his music while paying his way with the tennis lessons. His music writing was doing well, but his efforts to market his music ran into conflicts with the record companies.

On his twenty-first birthday, Bob flew to Los Angeles.

> It seems that lawyers controlled how music was made and if I wanted to be involved in promoting my music, then I had to think like they did.

As a result of his earlier networking and apparent good tennis teaching, Cronkite wrote a recommendation letter for Bob to Southwestern School of Law. This letter, Bob's glibness, and his high LSAT score persuaded admissions, and he was accepted, without a Bachelor's degree, to law school.

Bob had an internship experience at ABC Records during his final year in law school. The job was to prepare "fair use" letters, which let licensees use bits of songs for other uses. In effect, the letter grants a specific license. This became boring work. ABC had lost $40 million that year and was being acquired by MCA. With lawyers leaving ABC, Bob got the opportunity to handle option contracts.

Bob got his J.D. degree in 1980. In 1985, he wrote and produced a record with Rudy Vallee, the old-time crooner. It was Bob's type of music. His passion for it was without measure. He loved his product, but the record companies did not share his passion. Music would have to take a back seat.

> You can only be different and successful if you can find a market that is totally discontent. You will be totally successful or completely rejected. It's all or nothing if you are different. I don't want to be like anyone else.

Within the next year, Bob took a job with a small legal firm and studied for the bar, which he passed in Hawaii in 1987.

His law career continued through 1990. Most of the work dealt with taking firms public. He attributed his skill in part to his exposure to Wall Street through his dad. What he liked most was the chance to see many firms try to develop new ideas. He loved the creative part of expanding the scope of the client's offerings and accepted the legal mechanics as a necessary evil. He knew that his creative talents were being underutilized, and he was growing restless.

One of his friends throughout this time was Tom Zotos. Tom's brother was part of the band that Bob had formed in the mid-eighties and was part of the Rudy Vallee record deal. Bob and Tom often met and talked for hours on end about music, art, and their futures. The meeting at the deli this morning was typical of their frequent sessions:

At the deli, Bob was concerned as he looked at his friend:

Stein: Tom, what are your choices? What can this company do over the next decade?

Zotos: Bob, you know what I believe. The world is changing. The time for merchandising is coming. The product that sells the movies and records and the movies and records that sell the products are integrating. You can't separate the two any more.

Stein: If you stay at the company, what are you going to work on next?

Zotos: I hear that Warner Brothers is finally ready to talk about licensing Looney Tunes and Batman. That's going to be a big part of the next years for someone. I just don't know.

Stein: Do you believe in this?

Zotos: Of course I do. I've got eleven years in this industry. It will happen!

Stein: How much will it take?

Zotos: Probably a hundred grand. A little more, a little less.

Stein: I think it's possible.

Zotos: It doesn't matter if you don't have any money. All I've got is $20,000 in an account for my daughter's college and that's just not negotiable. And I need funds to live. But, yes, I believe having the rights to Bugs Bunny on an art poster is the most exciting thing that could happen to us. I just don't know if this is the time to go after it.

Stein: If you wait for a hundred percent thing, it will never happen.

The two exchanged pros and cons for the next hour. What's next? What makes sense? Bob and Tom were exhausted. The conversation ended with the two friends leaving and promising to meet in two days.

Tom's and Bob's story continues in Case 6.

6

A cartoon revolution is about to happen. Bob and I expect a major change—from a market with no merchandise being available to Baby Boomers who want to buy something from their time period—to a market waiting for this demand to be filled. This expected phenomenon created a constant urgency and self-imposed pressure for us to drive this potential market. I know we are on the right track. But I have no control over the company I work for.

Zanart Entertainment*

Tom Zotos summarized the conversation with Bob Stein in the deli that summer morning. Tom felt a great deal of pressure on himself at OSP over the Walt/Mickey proposal. Without the Disney deal, OSP would be hurting for sales volume; but even with this deal, his position was not secure and there was no upside for him.

Tom needed time to reflect. He went home to Massachusetts for a week and talked with his father. The two philosophized; the senior Zotos advised his son. Dad shared that he might not have made the right moves in his life because of personal and family security reasons. Costa at age 80 was reflecting on his own earlier indecision and suggested that Tom go for it, because Tom had a clear vision on how to go forward.

Tom had $20,000 saved for his daughter's college fund, which he did not want to touch. He knew he could fall back on his credit cards. He avoided sharing the impending storm at OSP with his wife. He had to isolate her from stress as she was expecting their second child and was also ill at the time. It became a silent time. Tom knew that if he started a new company and it failed, he would be buried financially, but he only focused on success. He felt the weight on his shoulders.

Bob was single; his pressure was not similar to Tom's. He would gladly give up his legal position. His dad agreed to make a loan of $15,000 to help his son over the same time period. Bob never had any self-doubts.

---

*This case was researched and written by Professors William H. Crookston and Thomas J. O'Malia. This case is intended to be an introduction to the enterprise formation process. Some details have been changed in order to protect the confidences of actual individuals and companies involved. Copyright © 1995.

Zany Art Was Born

So Zanart Entertainment (ZE) was launched. Tom Zotos and Bob Stein decided that they should pursue their common dreams together—publishing zany art. Why is the word "entertainment" in their name? It indicates what the two felt they were always involved in: entertainment. ZE believes it produced entertainment that you hang on a wall: visual entertainment.

Bob had worked on "blind pools" that had been raising money with an eye toward investing in various companies. The pool was called Xuma and controlled about $50,000. Zanart ultimately merged with this pool and now had access to limited funds as a public company.

A friend of Bob's, Steven B. Adelman, the son of a Polish emigrant father, became the third original shareholder. His investment in ZE was to do legal work and share, for two and one-half years, his penthouse offices and office equipment in the Unisys building in Westwood Village.

The company initially consisted of four equal owners: the shell provided $50,000 in cash for 25 percent; Adelman got 25 percent for providing free rent, advice, and use of equipment; and Zotos and Stein would get 25 percent each for the sweat equity to come.

Even though the offices made them look good, the active partners were so cash poor they had to park on residential streets in Westwood to avoid building parking fees. When and if any money came into the company—there was not a lot of it at the beginning—Bob felt he had a moral obligation to let Tom have the majority of money. Bob knew that for ZE's survival, the first funds had to go to Tom to support his family. But Tom took no funds and lived on his credit cards.

The first effort the fledgling company undertook would take all of their available cash. They wanted to buy the Looney Tunes® and Batman® licenses from Warner Brothers for wall decoration art. Tom felt that Warner Brothers characters had not been exploited to the extent that the Disney characters had been, and thus was an opportunity for Zanart.

> Does anybody remember Mickey Mouse cartoons? No, except for ten seconds of the historical "Steamboat Willie." But people certainly remember almost every chase scene of Bugs, Elmer Fudd, and Roadrunner.

There was no marketing research. All of the players just "felt" that spending all of the company's money on the two licenses was right. They were trying something new. Older people feel adult art—cartoons on a wall—is a waste of money. Baby Boomers yearned for nostalgia.

> We felt like the one Warner brother who held out for sound added to movies. We felt like the people who introduced the paper towel: everybody used rags for chores, but Scott Paper pushed disposable towels on rolls. We felt like Las Vegas in the Nevada desert: "you're going to gamble where?" We were pioneers!

The two principals sat on their rent-free chairs at their rent-free desks in their rent-free office and contemplated how quickly they had changed their entire lives while waiting for the rent-free fax machine to run. The calendar read February 1990.

Reality

ZE had spent the majority of its initial funds for the two licenses. The owners had not yet agreed on where or how to sell the products. The license was for high-end art and artistic print derivatives of that art. The license covered one industry category: "wall decoration." Tom and Bob asked themselves, now that we have the two licenses, where can we sell our product—Warner Brothers characters—as wall decoration?

The sales plan was that the balance of the funds be spent on two trade shows, the first, Art Expo in LA, and the second, a major show in New York. An elaborate last minute, "smoke-and-mirror" booth was constructed. In addition to their Looney Tunes® and Batman® art, they negotiated a consignment license arrangement. This deal provided no upfront payment, but it paid a higher percentage for products sold from a portfolio of Marilyn Monroe photographs and the work of a little-known art deco artist, Tamara DeLempicka. With these two additions, ZE's product retail price line at the show would range from under ten to over a thousand dollars.

Interest and sales at both shows did not materialize. The gallery buyers would look at Marilyn and Bugs prints placed next to each other in the booth and come away quite confused. The pricing and positioning left some buyers puzzled. The costs of the shows were not even covered by their few sales. Everything was wrong. The good news was the Batman creator came by the booth and remarked at how fine the art was. Tom was devastated! Bob was more philosophical:

> I'm in tune with rejection from my music experience, being turned down wasn't really new to me. What would keep us going was basically a lot of things: owning popular art was a smart thing, but there was not yet a natural sales channel for enough sales to sustain our business.

ZE explored other distribution channels. It thought that its line might be a new visionary product, an "executive gift." Would sales go through Sharper Image, Hammacher Schlemmer, or American Express?

ZE felt that it could do better than Scoreboard. It was producing a high quality collectible that was different from the products people had already seen. It was not like a thousand baseballs stamped with a signature. The issue became, can ZE go out and sell a higher-end collectible?

This experience really tested Tom and Bob. Bob trusted Tom's instincts. Tom instinctively knew that the market for popular art was coming. The two returned to LA with no cash but with more determination. The calendar read April 1990.

Credibility

The first significant order came across the rent-free fax machine when an art print company distributor bought six $12.00 prints. "What is it? It's a PO!" They didn't know what to do with it, but it sure felt good. During the next several months, more and more small orders dribbled in from the shows. The two spent all their time in sales. Bob was on the phone with every show attendee and a long list of art distributors. Tom spent his time constantly visiting the studios. Anything was important as long as it rang the cash register.

> We can't refuse any business. Even if it's only ten percent over our cost, we have to take the order. We need to build credibility. We need to let buyers know we are out there and can do a great job.

Tom received a call from the Spielberg organization. A major party was to be held the following weekend to introduce *Tiny Toons*, a new generation of baby Looney Tunes® characters. Spielberg wanted to give each guest a memento about the film. ZE was contacted about making 2,000 souvenir art prints. Tom quickly designed them and called back with a price of $10 each. "Too high," said the buyer, and Tom went back to the drawing board. He came up with a new printing technique which allowed an inexpensive print to be done on glossy stock. It took on the look of an expensive cel. "Pseudo-Cel" was the newly coined product name, and this new concept would later provide the major breakthrough for Zanart. ZE got the order and the bragging rights that came from making an innovative product for Spielberg's company. Tom and Bob used the proceeds to buy the license rights to classic properties such as *Superman*. These new products showed the world that the young company might have a good idea. Tom summarized their thinking:

> We were skirting around limited edition art, just to show the world something. We looked like an art company and we looked like a merchandise company. We were trying every avenue until we could find a breakthrough. I knew three properties were enough. Bob and Steve felt limited. We looked better than we were, top quality on all. Bob thinks we have changed the company. I think that the credo was the same.

The Warner Brothers Era

Zanart's positive reputation traveled around and opened doors in this select industry. Tom and Bob received a call from an account executive at Warner Brothers. WB had recently decided to begin marketing its library of characters in direct competition with Disney and others. Prior contacts, mutual friends, and knowledge of the industry created a situation where the account executive at WB was supportive and wanted to work with ZE. WB wanted to use ZE because it was capable of delivering. There were no surprises: WB liked the products that Tom had done for Disney in the past. The real value recognized by WB was the creativity seen in Tom's Disney experience and the fine art work ZE published with Tamara DeLempicka.

> It was a combination of all the things that gave us credibility. They knew we were in a penthouse, though they never visited us there. WB had seen the 70-color piece we had done with Tamara and they loved our creativity in the Disney and Lennon posters. They wanted to do business with Zanart Entertainment!

Bob and Tom knew WB needed help in finding a direction for its lines. They worked long hours at no charge—free consulting. The first Warner Brothers offering would be a catalog of its line. Steve Adelman had a contact at the new division and opened the door wider. The question was what pieces would be included? Certainly the existing licensed products. But WB wanted something special. So did ZE!

When Mel Blanc passed away in 1989, *Variety* ran a commemorative tribute page that showed a spotlight on a lone microphone with the WB cartoon characters standing silently by with their heads bowed. Tom and Bob wanted to work with this piece and make it ZE's flagship. He experimented at length with the printing process he used on the Tiny Toons® Pseudo-Cel. Trying different combinations of glossy papers, filtered inks, and application techniques, he created a product that was even richer and still could be produced at affordable costs. It looked like a real cel even though it was much larger. When matted and framed, the image jumped off the wall. It was the right look and gave the impression of being a *one-of-a-kind custom work of art*—truly a collector's item.

"Speechless" was the first item produced by ZE for the WB catalog. It carried a $150 retail price. It was new and daring. Most of the catalog items were lower priced. Items in the catalog began to sell. "Speechless" began to sell. ZE felt it had turned the corner.

WB and ZE debated about "Speechless" as a retail item. WB felt that it would be construed as an old product. Bob sang "Unforgettable" to the retail group of WB executives to demonstrate that "Speechless" would not go away in a few months. It was a standard—timeless. The "Speechless" original was scheduled to be a limited edition, but ZE persisted and WB made it an open edition. It would have been limited to 1,000 pieces; but sold many, many more. ZE knew that the piece had a great deal of emotional grabbing power. WB and ZE had synchronicity about this Mel Blanc concept. But ZE was still just a vendor—each day it had to prove itself all over again.

Bob and Tom were willing to put in the time and be persistent enough to wait and earn the right to meet very busy people. ZE provided an idea source. This was key to getting into WB, the biggest entertainment company in the world.

> We knew that getting further involved with Warner Brothers was very important. We had no idea what would keep selling our products. We knew what was right, but we didn't know how big. This

was a point where we began to generate money. The niceness of "Speechless" impressed other buyers and what we could do for them. It was an exciting time!

The first Warner Brothers Studio Store was close to opening. Warner Brothers wanted to make a big splash. *Casablanca* was a WB film, and Tom knew the Hollywood Wax Museum manager. He was able to "borrow" the Bogart wax figure for the store opening. Warner people thought the ZE people were real team players. They did more than just favors; they made the buyers look good.

Outside retailers saw the success of ZE at WB. The WB store carried litho prints and lobby card portfolios made by ZE. Suncoast/Musicland saw these and contracted ZE to make similar items for its stores. Sales materialized and ZE used the funds and added more licenses.

> We were like Cannon Films who would sign hot stars to their studio without money, but gave the talent a bigger piece of the deal. We may not have been that smart to think of this so we copied their idea and began to give higher royalty percentages than what others would offer for licenses, but we paid less up front.

In the early years of movies, 11 × 14-inch promotional placards were displayed in theater lobbies. This was the only way movies were promoted from the early 1900s through the 1960s. The placards became a new collectible. "Do you have a program?" buyers would ask (which meant a line of products). "We don't sell programs, we sell lobby cards." Bob thought the buyer meant the type of program ushers handed out in theaters.

As ZE continued to get closer to WB, it began to get better market feedback and the learning curve got shorter. The "sell through" issue is very important to retail, especially with impulse items. ZE got close enough to WB stores that it tracked what shipped last Friday from when it went on the shelves, giving it quick measurement of sales—or not. This channel flow of products was in real time so ZE and WB could react quickly; they could add more similar products if they moved, or change lines if they did not.

When did Tom and Bob think "it" would really happen? Tom remembered exactly, he knew it was September 4, 1991, a Saturday afternoon at the Beverly Center when 5,000 people were fighting to get into the WB store. Tom sat and watched from the floor above the Warner store:

> All my life I had waited for this moment. This was the fulfillment of my vision. The revolution was happening and I was not only watching—I was a part of it.

Bob reflected:

> We got a first down and stayed in the game. We went into this black tunnel, an unknown area, without any money flowing through. We were taking out small draws now. We tried to start repaying my dad, but he kept sending the checks back to us. Unless you have a backer

(or are independently wealthy) you will have to use the money from your family and friends in order to take it to the next level. And you do not have to be ashamed of this.

The Investor

ZE had grown to the point where it had employed a part-time accountant to do its books. The management realized the company needed financing to grow. Growth could not be financed in a trickle-down manner any more. There was a payroll to be met. Bob's family was aware of a gentleman who had just successfully sold a large company and who liked to do private investments. A meeting was arranged with the investor. He was the chair and majority shareholder of a major public company. Previously, he had successfully built another company and sold it for stock.

> I recall going down there with a copy of every art piece we had ever done and laying them out in the conference room. We wanted to dazzle him. It was an impressive array of products.

The investor enjoyed the principals of Zanart and the chemistry was good. He was more impressed with the perseverance and conviction of Tom and Bob than he was with the product. He was amazed that they had gone almost two years without a salary and that every dollar had gone into buying more licenses. Tom was certain that something would come of the meeting, and when the investor asked why they didn't put characters on other products, like paper plates, the duo explained the intricacies of the licensing business and the capital required to expand to other product categories.

The investor was so taken by the focus, conviction, and the strong reaction of the team that he agreed to make a $500,000 bridge loan on the spot. The investor concluded:

> If you two guys could do this much without any money, imagine what you could do with money.

With funds now in place, the tempo of the game increased. Bob and Tom were able to enjoy their first real payday. Additional personnel were hired and additional licenses purchased. During this time, Zanart hosted a USC Management internship program project. Based on the MBAs recommendations, prices were raised, with a positive result and very little impact on customers. Dr. Ben Enis of the marketing department was the professor. Both Zanart principals felt that the experience was very enjoyable and profitable.

With time, money, and people now working for them, the ZE principals made plans for the next stage of growth. They produced a catalog of their new offerings, organized their sales efforts, and built a distribution system.

The two and a half years of free rent was coming to an end and new offices were needed. But the most important thing that the bridge funding did was to give Tom and Bob the time to build their company.

The next 18 months saw growth in revenues with sales in the $2 million range. The company's reputation and product line grew. Companies now came to Zanart Entertainment looking for it to do things for them. As Tom's efforts moved more and more into product development, Bob took on the additional challenge of exploring the feasibility of doing a secondary offering.

When asked when he first thought about doing a secondary offering, Bob replied without hesitation:

> Day One. We knew we were not properly capitalized. We never questioned that we couldn't go public. But we knew we needed enough substance to get there. We had to!

Using his legal contacts, Bob quickly found the difference between someone saying he was interested and someone actually willing to seriously take on the challenge of taking a marginally profitable company, with untested management, public. He felt the challenges would never end. A new challenge seemed to arrive just as the last one was answered.

Investor to Public Market for Secondary Offering

The investor gave Zanart a $500,000 bridge loan in February 1994 at 10 percent per year. The principal would be paid at the closure of a public offering or on any other permanent financing arrangement. In addition to the interest payments, the loan granted 250,000 shares of stock in the public company and a warrant to purchase another 250,000 shares at $4.00 per share.

The investor's funds were to be used mainly for working capital (specifically to finance additional inventory and accounts receivable), to acquire new licenses, and to add key management personnel, including a CFO and a national sales manager.

When the offering was delayed and certain capital requirements were needed to be met pursuant to the letter of intent from the investment bankers, the investor agreed to convert $100,000 of this loan to equity at $4.00 per share. This left the note at $400,000 and gave the investor 33,333 additional shares of stock. By the fall of 1995, the investor owned 283,333 shares of ZE, approximately 10 percent of the total number of shares then outstanding (2,902,983).

Public Offering Timetable

During March 1994, Arthur Andersen LLP was engaged to do the required audits and accounting work preparatory to the secondary offering. These were the first full audits that ZE had undergone, and they entailed a great drain on management time and money over 12 months.

The company talked with several underwriters. The investor was able to introduce ZE to a senior executive at First Equity Corporation, investment bankers of Miami. They were excited about doing a deal with ZE and the investor.

In October 1994, Todd Slayton was hired as chief financial officer. Todd is a CPA, received his MBA in Corporate Finance and Financial Accounting from USC in May 1991, and was a senior consultant/accountant with the middle market practice of Deloitte & Touche in Los Angeles.

The grueling and frustrating process of writing a prospectus and preparing the SEC registration ran from November 1994 through March 1995. This process involved the coordination of no less than six parties: the company, the company's counsel, the underwriters, the underwriters' counsel, the auditors, and the SEC.

There were constant hurdles to overcome in order to make the deal happen. There were several SEC filings with continuous changes based on its comments, upgrading the financials (certain financials grew "stale" over time), amendments, and endless tinkering with the language and presentation. Todd commented in hindsight:

> This road was fraught with surprises at every turn, and several potential events that could have been "deal killers" were skillfully avoided.

The offering called for ZE to sell 800,000 units at $6.00 (the original plan called for 1 million units). Each unit consisted of one share of common stock and one warrant allowing the redeemer to purchase a share of stock at $6.00 within five years. First Equity had the option to sell an overallotment of shares of 120,000 units (the "Green Shoe").

The "red herrings" (prospectus) were printed in early April and Tom, Bob, and Todd hit the road. The roadshow involved a multimedia presentation to brokerages and private offering meetings with potential investors. The three reflect:

> The process was incredibly stressful.

The slide presentation which posed the question, "Why Invest in Zanart?" had five main points:

▶ Product innovation and market niche

▶ Emerging channels of distribution

▶ Stable of blue-chip properties

▶ Strong relationships with licensers

▶ Dedicated management surrounded by successful businesspersons

ZANART
ENTERTAINMENT

800,000 Units
Each Unit Comprised of One Share of Common Stock
and One Series A Warrant

Zanart Entertainment Incorporated (the "Company") hereby offers units ("Units"), each Unit consisting of one share of Common Stock par value $.0001 per share (the "Common Stock") and one Series A Warrant (the "Series A Warrant") exercisable for one share of Common Stock at a price of $6.00, subject to certain anti-dilutive adjustments, at any time during the 60 months following the date of this Prospectus. The Company has the right to accelerate the expiration date of the Series A Warrants under certain circumstances. The Common Stock and the Series A Warrants will be detachable and separately transferable 90 days after the date of this Prospectus or on such earlier date as may be determined by First Equity Corporation of Florida (the "Representative"), as the representative of the several underwriters named herein (the "Underwriters"). See "Description of Securities." The Company has listed its Units, Common Stock and Series A Warrants for quotation on the NASDAQ Small-Cap Market.

The initial public offering price of the Units offered hereby has been arbitrarily determined by negotiation between the Company and the Representative and does not bear any relationship to such established valuation criteria such as assets, book value or prospective earnings. It is currently contemplated that certain shareholders of the Company intend to purchase Units in this offering. Any such purchases will be on the same terms and conditions as those offered unaffiliated investors. See "Underwriting" for a discussion of factors considered in determining the initial public offering price.

THIS OFFERING INVOLVES A HIGH DEGREE OF RISK AND IMMEDIATE SUBSTANTIAL DILUTION AND SHOULD BE CONSIDERED ONLY BY INVESTORS WHO CAN AFFORD THE LOSS OF THEIR ENTIRE INVESTMENT. SEE "RISK FACTORS" AND "DILUTION."

THESE SECURITIES HAVE NOT BEEN APPROVED OR DISAPPROVED BY THE SECURITIES AND EXCHANGE COMMISSION NOR HAS THE COMMISSION PASSED UPON THE ACCURACY OR ADEQUACY OF THIS PROSPECTUS. ANY REPRESENTATION TO THE CONTRARY IS A CRIMINAL OFFENSE.

	Price to the Public	Underwriting Discounts and Commissions (1)	Proceeds to the Company (2) (3)
Per Unit	$6.00	$.585	$5.415
Totals.	$4,800,000	$468,000	$4,332,000

(1) Excludes additional compensation to the Representative in the form of a 3% non-accountable expense allowance. Additionally, the Company has agreed to sell to the Representative, at nominal consideration, options to purchase 80,000 Representative Units and has further agreed to certain indemnification and contribution arrangements with the Underwriters. See "Underwriting."

(2) Before deducting expenses of the offering, payable by the Company, estimated to be $422,410, or $444,010 if the over-allotment option is exercised in full, including the 3% non-accountable expense allowance payable to the Representative.

(3) The Company has granted the Representative an option to purchase up to an additional 120,000 Units, upon the same terms as set forth above, solely to cover over-allotments, if any. See "Underwriting." If that over-allotment option is fully exercised, the total Price to the Public, Underwriting Discounts and Commissions, and Proceeds to the Company will be $5,520,000, $538,200 and $4,981,800, respectively.

The Units are offered by the several Underwriters, subject to prior sale, when, as and if received and accepted by them, subject to their right to reject orders in whole or in part and to certain other conditions. It is expected that delivery of the certificates for such Units will be made against payment therefore on or about May 18, 1995.

FIRST EQUITY CORPORATION
The date of this Prospectus is May 11, 1995

Figure 6.1
Prospectus

The roadshow was a success, and the three returned home exhilarated and ready to jump through the final hoops to close the deal.

After a final night of endless phone calls, cold sweats, and nervous stomachs, the deal was declared effective by the SEC on May 11, 1995 (commencement of trading), and the final prospectus was printed. The deal closed one week later on May 18, and the company received a check for $4,188,000 on that day [$4.8 million gross proceeds less 12.75 percent ($612 thousand) in commission and fees to First Equity]. The investor was repaid immediately. On June 28, First Equity exercised the overallotment of 120,000 shares and ZE received an additional check for $628,000.

Summary of Offering

The offering is summarized as follows:

- 920,000 units sold at $6.00 for gross proceeds of $5.5 million
- Yielded approximately $4 million after commissions, expenses, fees, and repayment of debt
- Funds in U.S. Treasury Fund at brokerage earning 5.5–6.0 percent

Operations

The company's products are manufactured by a coordination of vendors mainly in Southern California. The company uses three printing vendors and various independent artists to produce the prints. Warner Brothers Stores (approximately 50 percent of revenue) buy mostly framed products that are finished by a firm with a framing facility adjacent to Zanart's offices in Van Nuys. Most licensed merchandise (both matted and matted/framed) is assembled by a vendor located in Gardena. The company uses other vendors as "overflow" producers as needed.

Zanart grew out of its small warehouse space in Van Nuys, and in August 1995, leased approximately 10,000 square feet of space adjacent to the Gardena vendor's 75,000-square-foot warehouse and set up the main distribution facility. Gardena is where most raw materials and finished goods are maintained and where most shipping of licensed merchandise takes place. The facility has an operations manager and two to three warehouse staff.

The company has 16 full-time employees including officers. Other than the three officers discussed previously (Tom, Bob, and Todd), there is another four-year veteran of the company, Vice-President Mark Politi, who coordinates the Warner Brothers "show" and is key to overall company operations.

Sales are headed up by a national sales manager who attends trade shows, makes visits to national key accounts, and manages the more than 25 outside "rep" companies, which show Zanart's lines. He is supported by a sales coordinator, a customer service manager, and order entry staff.

The company recently established an internal art department with an art director to create ads and displays, sell materials, catalogs, new product prototypes, and so on, using the latest computer equipment.

ZE also recently hired a director of special projects to coordinate the development of a Zanart web site on the Internet, oversee catalogs and ad placements, develop programs for home shopping channels, and assist in other new business development.

The company has a Novell network with ten Windows-based workstations with Windows-based accounting software designed for small to midsize companies. Accounting staff consists of a staff accountant (who also handles accounts payable) and a customer service manager (who also handles accounts receivable, credit, and collections).

References

Chapter 1

1. Peter Senge, *The Fifth Discipline: The Art and Practice of the Learning Organization* (New York: Currency/Doubleday, 1990).
2. Kathleen R. Allen, *Launching New Ventures*, 2nd ed. (Boston: Houghton Mifflin, 1999).
3. David L. Birch. Birch's firm Cognetics, Inc. tracks employment and sales records of more than 9 million firms listed with Dun & Bradstreet.
4. William J. Dennis, Jr., Bruce D. Phillips, and Edward Starr, "Small Business Job Creation: The Findings and Their Critics, "*Business Economics*, July 1994, pp. 23–30.
5. Zoltan J. Acs, "Small Is Beautiful! Big Is Best!" *Inc.*, The State of Small Business special edition, 1995.
6. Ibid., p. 8.
7. Ibid.
8. John Case, "The Age of the Gazelle," *Inc.*, The State of Small Business, special edition, May 1996.
9. *D&B Annual Survey of Small Business* (Murray Hill, NJ: Dun and Bradstreet, 1991, 1997).
10. Elyse M. Friedman, ed., "The New Economy Almanac," *Inc.*, The State of Small Business special edition, 1997, pp. 108–121.
11. Paul D. Reynolds, "Who Starts New Firms? Preliminary Explorations of Firms-in-Gestation," in Paul Reynolds and Sammis White, eds., *Small Business Economics* (*Wisconsin's Entrepreneurial Climate Study*, Final Report to the Wisconsin Housing and Economic Development Authority, (Marquette University Center for the Study of Entrepreneurship, Milwaukee, WI, 1996).
12. Briefing Report, Entrepreneurial Research Consortium, December 13, 1996, p. 13.
13. Ibid., p.117.
14. Janean Chun, Debra Phillips, et al., "Young Millionaires," *Entrepreneur,* November 1996, pp. 118–134.
15. Thomas J. Stanley and William D. Danko, *The Millionaire Next Door* (Marietta, GA: Longstreet Press, Inc. 1996).
16. Ibid., p.12.
17. R. H. Brockhaus, "Risk-Taking Propensity of Entrepreneurs." *Academy of Management Journal* 23(1980), pp. 509–520; Peter F. Drucker, *Innovation and Entrepreneurship* (New York: Harper and Row, 1985).
18. D. B. Greenberger and D. L. Sexton, "An Interactive Model of New Venture Initiation." *Journal of Small Business Management,* 26 (1988), pp. 1–7.
19. W. Gartner, "Who Is the Entrepreneur Is the Wrong Question," *American Journal of Small Business*, Spring 1988, pp. 11–31.
20. E. B. Roberts, "Influences upon Performance of New Technical Enterprises," in A. Cooper and J. Komives, eds., *Technical Entrepreneurship: A Symposium* (Milwaukee: The Center for Venture Management, 1972), pp. 126–149. Mark P. Rice, *Growing New Ventures, Creating New Jobs: Principles and Practices of Successful Business Incubation.* (Westport, CT: Quorum, 1995).
21. G. L. S. Shackle, in R. F. Hebert and A. N. Link, eds., *The Entrepreneur* (New York: Praeger Publishers, 1955).
22. William B. Gartner, "What Are We Talking About When We Talk About Entrepreneurship?" *Journal of Business Venturing* 5 (1990), pp. 15–28.
23. Stanley Kaish and Benjamin Gilad, "Characteristics of Opportunities Search of Entrepreneurs versus Executives: Sources, Interest, General Alertness," *Journal of Business Venturing* 6 (1991), 45–61.
24. I. M. Kirzner, *Competition and Entrepreneurship* (Chicago: University of Chicago Press, 1973).
25. Kaish and Gilad, p. 59.
26. Tom Richman, "Creators of the New Economy," *Inc.,* The State of Small Business special edition, 1997. p. 48.
27. Ibid., pp. 44–48.

Chapter 2

1. W. H. Starbuck, "Organizations and Their Environments," in M. D. Dunnette ed., *Handbook of Industrial and Oganization Psychology* (Chicago:

Rand McNally, (1976). These are conceptually identical to those proposed by Child, 1972 (illiberality, variability, and complexity) Pfeffer J. & Salancik, G.R. 1978; and H. Mintzberg, *The Structuring of Organizations* (Englewood Cliffs, NJ: Prentice-Hall, 1979). The External Control of Organizations. New York: Harper & Row

2. H. Aldrich and G. Wiedenmayer, *From Traits to Rates: An Ecological Perspective on Organizational Foundings* (Paper presented at the Gateway Conference on Entrepreneurship, St. Louis University, St. Louis, Missouri, 1989).

3. G. Dess and D. W. Beard, "Dimensions of Organizational Task Environments," *Administrative Science Quarterly* 28 (1984), pp. 101–128.

4. J. R. Galbraith, *Designing Complex Organizations* (Reading, MA: Addison-Wesley, 1973).

5. W. M. Evan, "The Organizational Set: Toward a Theory of Interoganizational Relationships," in J. D. Thompson, ed., *Approaches to Organizational Design* (Pittsburgh: University of Pittsburgh Press, 1966).

6. J. M. Pennings, "The Relevance of the Structural-Contingency Model for Organizational Effectiveness," *Administrative Science Quarterly* 20 (1975), pp. 393–410; J. D. Thompson, *Organizations in Action* (New York: McGraw-Hill, 1967).

7. W. W. Keep, D. L. Wardlow, and G. S. Omura, "Survivability of Entrepreneurs as a Function of Evolutionary Market Change and Task Complexity," in G. Hills, R. LaForge, and B. Parker, eds., *Research at the Marketing/Entrepreneurship Interface* (Chicago: University of Illinois at Chicago, 1988), pp. 47–61.

8. Ibid.

9. Jay B. Barney, "Looking Inside for Competitive Advantage," *The Academy of Management Executive* IX, 4 (1995), p. 49.

10. Ibid.

11. Alex Hamilton in Jerry Jasinowski and Robert Hamrin, *Making It in America: Proven Paths to Success from 50 Top Companies* (New York: Simon & Schuster, 1995).

12. Ibid.

13. Charles Taylor and Gail D. Fosler, "The Necessity of Being Global," *Across the Board,* February 1994, p. 41.

14. Bureau of Labor Statistics, *Monthly Labor Review,* October 1995.

15. Hamilton, p. 25.

16. David Freedman, "Who Wins the Looking Glass War," *Inc.,* The State of Small Business special edition, May 1996, p. 48.

17. Ibid., p. 49.

18. Bethany McLean, "Promising Industries for 1997," *Fortune,* December 23, 1996, p. 155.

19. Ibid., p. 160.

20. Ibid.

Chapter 3

1. "Liabilities, Awards, Settlements," *The Financial Times Limited, World Insurance Report,* January 14, 1994.

2. "McDonald's Faces Another Hot Coffee Suit," *The Charleston Gazette,* May 2, 1995.

3. Kathleen Allen, *Launching New Ventures,* 2nd ed. (Boston: Hougton Mifflin, 1999).

4. Ibid.

5. Tom Williams, Selected Topics on Internet Law (Unpublished paper, University of Southern California Law Center, May 1996).

6. Ibid., p.10.

7. Ibid., p. 17.

8. Raymond Nimmer, (1985). *Law of Computer Technology 55;* Edward Cavanos and Gavino Morin, *Cyberspace and the Law, 44* (1994, Boston: MIT Press).

9. Baum, Ian, *EDI and the Law,* (I. Walden, ed., 1991). Boston: Blackwell Publishers.

Chapter 4

1. David E. Terpstra and Philip D. Olson, "Entrepreneurial Start-up and Growth: A Classification of Problems," *Entrepreneurship, Theory & Practice,* Spring 1993, pp. 5–20.

2. D. F. Kuratko and R. M. Hodgetts, *Entrepreneurship: A Contemporary Approach* (Hinsdale, IL: Dryden Press, 1989).

3. Neil C. Churchill and Virginia L. Lewis, "The Five Stages of Small Business Growth," in William A. Sahlman and Howard H. Stevenson, eds., *The Entrepreneurial Venture* (Boston: Harvard Business School Publications, 1992).

4. Jeffry Timmons, *The Entrepreneurial Mind.* (Acton, MA: Brickhouse Publishing, 1989).

5. Susan Greco, "The Incredible Upbeatness of Being," Inc. 500, 1997, p. 24.

6. Martha E. Mangelsdorf, "How to Build an Inc. 500 Company," Inc. 500, 1997, p. 26.

7. Susan Greco, "The Need for Speed," Inc. 500, 1997, p. 28.
8. Susan Greco, "Employee Package Deal," Inc. 500, 1997, p. 30.
9. W. Keith Schilit, *Rising Stars and Fast Fades: Successes and Failures of Fast-Growth Companies* (New York: Lexington Books, 1994).
10. Ibid., p. 54.
11. Ibid., p. 6.
12. Ibid., p. 17.
13. Martha E. Manelsdorf, "The Class of '85," *Inc.*, 1995, p. 76.
14. A. Bhide, "Bootstrapping Finance: The Art of Start-Ups," *Harvard Business Review*, 70, no. 6 (1992), pp. 109–117.
15. "Start-ups from Scratch," *Inc.*, September 1994, p. 76.
16. Jay Finegan, "A Bootstrapper's Primer," *Inc.*, August 1995, p. 49.
17. Paul Suplizio, International Reciprocal Trade Association, in Marsha Bertrand, "Let's Make a Deal," *Nation's Business*, February 1995, p. 27.
18. Ibid.
19. John Freear and William Wetzel, Jr., "Who Bankrolls High-Tech Entrepreneurs?" *Journal of Business Venturing*, March 1990, pp. 77–89.
20. Ibid.
21. Ibid., p. 36.
22. Kathleen Allen, *Launching New Ventures* (Chicago: Upstart Publishing, 1995), p. 292.
23. Ibid., p. 293.
24. Joan C. Szabo, "Matching Investors and Entrepreneurs," *Nation's Business,* February 1995, p. 46.
25. "SBA Loans Spur Start-up Growth," *Inc.*, November 1992, p. 66.
26. Allen, p. 294.

Chapter 5

1. Arnold C. Cooper et al., *New Business in America* (Washington, DC: The NFIB Foundation, 1990).
2. Donald A. Duchesnau and William B. Gartner, "A Profile of Success and Failure in an Emerging Industry," *Journal of Business Venturing*, September 1990, p. 297.
3. Doug Hall and David Wecker, *Jumpstart Your Brain* (New York: Warner Books, 1995).
4. Ibid., p. 219.
5. Stanley R. Rich & David E. Gumpert, "How to Write a Winning Business Plan," In William A. Sahlman and Howard H. Stevenson eds., *The*

Entrepreneurial Venture (Boston: Harvard Business School Press, 1992).
6. Collins and Lazier.
7. From an unpublished business plan written by Tara Barrett, class of 1996, The Entrepreneur Program, University of Southern California.
8. Zenas Block and Ian C. Macmillan, "Milestones for Successful Venture Planning," in William A. Sahlman and Howard H. Stevenson, eds., *The Entrepreneurial Venture* (Boston: Harvard Business School Press, 1992) pp. 138–148.

Chapter 6

1. Sally Helgesen, *The Web of Inclusion* (New York: Currency/Doubleday, 1995).
2. Steven L. Goldman, Roger N. Nagel, and Kenneth Preiss, *Agile Competitors and Virtual Organizations* (New York: Van Nostrand Reinhold, 1995).
3. Ibid, p. 220.
4. Ibid, p.211.
5. Robert B. Reich, "Entrepreneurship Reconsidered: The Team as Hero," in William A. Sahlman and Howard H. Stevenson, eds., *The Entrepreneurial Venture* (Boston: Harvard Business School Publications, 1992).
6. A. H. Van de Ven, R. Hudson, and D. M. Schroeder, "Designing New Business Start-ups," *Journal of Management* 10 (1984).
7. Kathleen R. Allen, *Launching New Ventures* (Chicago: Upstart Publishing, 1995).
8. Amar Bhide and Howard H. Stevenson, "Attracting Stakeholders," in William A. Sahlman and Howard H. Stevenson, eds., *The Entrepreneurial Venture* (Boston: Harvard Business School Publications, 1992).
9. Robert A. Mamis, "Company Protection: Crash Course," *Inc.*, February 1995, p. 54.
10. Allen, *Launching New Ventures*.
11. Dale D. Buss, "How Advisers Can Help You Grow," *Nation's Business*, March 1996, p. 47.

Chapter 7

1. Michael Porter, *Competitive Strategy* (New York: The Free Press, 1980).
2. A. P. Chandler, *Strategy and Structure* (Cambridge, MA: MIT Press, 1962); J. Bain, *Industrial Organizations* (New York: John Wiley and Sons, 1959); I. Ansoff, *Corporate Strategy* (New York: McGraw-Hill, 1965).
3. K. Andrews, *The Concept of Corporate Strategy* (Homewood, IL: Irwin, 1971).

4. D. Lewin and P. D. Sherer, "Does Strategic Choice Explain Senior Executives' Preferences on Employee Voice and Representation?" in Kaufman, B. F., and Kleiner, M. M., eds., *Employee Representation.* (Madison, WI: Industrial Relations Research Association, 1993), pp. 235–263.

5. P. R. Lawrence and J. W. Lorsch, *Organization and Environment: Managing Differentiation and Integration* (Boston: Graduate School of Business Administration, Harvard University, 1967).

6. James C. Collins and William C. Lazier, *Beyond Entrepreneurship: Turning Your Business into an Enduring Great Company* (Englewood Cliffs, NJ: Prentice-Hall, 1992).

7. James C. Collins and Jerry I. Porras, *Built to Last: Successful Habits of Visionary Companies* (New York: HarperBusiness, 1994).

8. Ibid., p. 2.

9. Ibid., p. 3.

10. Ibid., p. 7.

11. Collins and Lazier, *Beyond Entrepreneurship.*

12. Collins and Porras, *Built to Last.*

13. A portion of the full credo written by R. W. Johnson, Jr., in 1943. In Francis J. Aguilar and Arvind Bhambri, "Johnson & Johnson (A)," Harvard Business School Case No. 384–053, p. 4.

14. Collins and Porras, *Built to Last.*

15. Akio Morita, *Made in Japan* (New York: Dutton, 1986), pp. 147–148.

16. L. Smircich, "Concepts of Culture and Organizational Analysis," *Administrative Science Quarterly* 28 (1983), pp. 339–358.

17. S. Davis, *Managing Corporate Culture* (Cambridge, MA: Ballinger, 1984).

18. Terrence Deal and Allan Kennedy, *Corporate Cultures: The Rites and Rituals of Corporate Life* (Reading, MA: Addison-Wesley, 1982).

19. D. Ulrich and D. Kale, *Organizational Capability: Competing from the Inside/Out* (New York: John Wiley & Sons, 1990).

20. J. Kotter and J. Heskett, *Culture and Performance* (New York: The Free Press, 1992).

21. Charles W. Hofer and Ram Charan, "The Transition to Professional Management: Mission Impossible?" *American Journal of Small Business,* Summer 1984, p. 3.

22. Howard H. Stevenson and David E. Gumpert, "The Heart of Entrepreneurship," *Harvard Business Review,* March/April 1985; p. 85.

23. Peter Senge *The Fifth Discipline: The Art and Practice of the Learning Organization* (New York: Currency/Doubleday, 1990).

24. Ibid., p. 150.

25. C. Argyris. *Reasoning, Learning and Action: Individual and Organizational* (San Francisco: Jossey-Bass, 1982).

26. Senge, *The Fifth Discipline,* p. 221.

27. Ibid., p. 61.

28. Eileen C. Shapiro, *Fad Surfing in the Boardroom* (Reading, MA: Addison-Wesley, 1995).

29. Ibid., p. 176.

30. Bill Creech, *The Five Pillars of TQM* (New York: Truman Talley Books/Plume, 1994).

31. Creech, Tom Peters, forward to book written by Tom Peters.

32. Creech, *The Five Pillars,* p. 196.

33. John Case, *Open-Book Management: The Coming Business Revolution* (New York: HarperBusiness, 1995).

34. Jack Stack, *The Great Game of Business* (New York: Doubleday/Currency, 1992).

35. James W. Walker, "The Ultimate Human Resources Planning: Integrating the Human Resources Function with the Business," in Gerald R. Ferris, Sherman D. Rosen, and Darold T. Barnum, eds., *Handbook of Human Resource Management* (Cambridge MA: Blackwell Publishers, 1995).

36. J. E. Butler, G. R. Ferris, and N. K. Napier, *Strategy and Human Resources Management* (Cincinnati: South-Western, 1991); C. A. Lengnick-Hall, and M. L. Lengnick-Hall, *Interactive Human Resource Management and Strategic Planning* (Westport, CT: Quorum, 1990).

37. Perrin Towers, "Repositioning the Human Resource Function: Transformation or Demise?" *Academy of Management Executive* 4, no. 3 (1990), pp. 49–60.

38. E. H. McWhirter, "Empowerment in Counseling," *Journal of Counseling and Development* 69 pp. 222–227.

39. D. B. Greenberger and S. Strasser, "The Role of Situational and Dispositional Factors in the Enhancement of Personal Control in Organizations, *Research in Organizational Behavior,* 13 (1991), pp. 111–145.

40. A. Bandura, "Self-efficacy Mechanism in Human Agency," *American Psychologist* 37, (1982), pp. 122–147.

41. W. A. Pasmore and M. R. Fagans, "Participation, Individual Development and Organization Change: A Review and Synthesis," *Journal of Management* 18 (1992), pp. 375–397.

42. J. R. Hackman, and G. R. Oldham, "Motivation Through the Design of Work: Test of a Theory," *Organizational Behavior and Human Performance* 16 (1976), pp. 250–279.

43. J. B. Rotter, "Generalized Expectancies for Internal Versus External Control of Reinforcement," *Psychological Monographs* 80, no. 1 (1966).

44. F. Herzberg, B. Mausner, and B. B. Snyderman, *The Motivation to Work,* 2nd ed. (New York: John Wiley & sons, 1959).

45. R. Likert, *The Human Organization* (New York: McGraw-Hill, 1967).

46. Shapiro, *Fad Surfing,* p. 93.

47. Robert C. Liden and Thomas W. Tewksbury, "Empowerment and Work Teams," in Gerald R. Ferris, Sherman D. Rosen, and Darold T. Barnum, eds., *Handbook of Human Resource Management* (Cambridge, MA: Blackwell Publishers, 1995).

Chapter 8

1. Donna Fenn, "When to Go Pro," *Inc.,* Inc. 500 1995, p. 72.

2. Ibid.

3. George F. Dreher and Daniel W. Kendall, "Organizational Staffing," in Gerald R. Ferris, Sherman D. Rosen, and Darold T. Barnum eds., *Handbook of Human Resource Management* (Cambridge, MA: Blackwell Publishers, 1995).

4. Ibid., p. 451.

5. R. A. Noe, J. R. Hollenbeck, B. Gerhart, and P. M. Wright, *Human Resource Management: Gaining a Competitive Advantage* (Burr Ridge, IL: Austin Press/Irwin, 1994).

6. L. R. Gomez-Mejia and D. B. Balkin, *Compensation, Organizational Strategy, and Firm Performance* (Cincinnati: South-Western, 1992).

7. B. R. Ellig, "Compensation Elements: Market Phase Determines the Mix," *Compensation Review,* Third Quarter 1981, pp. 30–38.

8. J. L. Kerr, "Diversification Strategies and Managerial Rewards," *Academy of Management Journal* 28 (1985), pp. 155–179.

9. E. A. Locke, D. B. Feren, V. M. McCaleb, K. N. Shaw, and A. T. Denny, "The Relative Effectiveness of Four Methods of Motivating Employee Performance," in K. D. Duncan, M. M. Gruenberg, and D. Wallis, eds., *Changes in Working Life* (New York: John Wiley & Sons, 1980), pp. 363–388.

10. M. L. Weitzman and D. L. Kruse, "Profit Sharing and Productivity," in A. S. Blinder, ed., *Paying for Productivity* (Washington, DC: Brookings Institution, 1990); D. L. Kruse, *Profit Sharing: Does It Make a Difference?* (Kalamazoo, MI: Upjohn Institute, 1993).

11. D. C. Jones and K. Takao, "The Scope, Nature, and Effects of Employee Stock Ownership Plans in Japan," *Industrial and Labor Relations Review* 46 (1993), pp. 352–367.

12. E. E. Lawler III "Pay for Performance: A Strategic Analysis," in L. R. Gomez-Mejia, ed., *Compensation and Benefits* (Washington, DC: Bureau of National Affairs, 1989).

13. Noe, Hollenbeck, Gerhart, and Wright, P. M.

14. "The State of the Art of Small Business," *Inc.,* May 21, 1996, p. 66.

15. Roger Thompson, "Benefit Costs Shift into Reverse," *Nation's Business,* February 1996, p. 50.

16. Laura M. Litvan, "Switching to Self-Insurance," *Nation's Business*, March 1996, p. 16.

17. Edward O. Welles, "What CEOs Make," *Inc.,* September 1995.

18. Ibid.

19. Ibid., p. 559.

20. Jerry McAdams, *The Reward Plan Advantage* (San Francisco: Jossey-Bass, 1996).

21. Charles Coonradt, "The Game of Work," *Inc.,* May 1997, p. 117.

22. McAdams, *The Reward Plan Advantage,* p. 117.

23. Michael H. LeRoy and James M. Schultz, "The Legal Context of Human Resource Management: Conflict, Confusion, Cost, and Role-Conversion," in Gerald R. Ferris, Sherman D. Rosen, and Darold T. Barnum, eds., *Handbook of Human Resource Management* (Cambridge, MA: Blackwell Publishers, 1995).

24. Janine S. Pouliot, "Rising Complaints of Religious Bias," *Nation's Business,* February 1996, p. 36.

25. Kathleen R. Allen, *Launching New Ventures: An Entrepreneurial Approach* (Chicago: Upstart Publishing, 1995).

26. James Walsh, *Rightful Termination* (Santa Monica, CA: Merritt Publishing, 1994).

27. G. W. Florkowski and R. Nath, "MNC Responses to the Legal Environment of International

Human Resource Management," *International Journal of Human Resource Management* 42 (1990), pp. 303–324.

28. Nancy K. Napier, Jacques Tibau, Maddy Janssens, and Ronald C. Pilenzo, "Juggling on a High Wire: The Role of the International Human Resources Manager," in Gerald R. Ferris, Sherman D. Rosen, and Darold T. Barnum, eds., *Handbook of Human Resource Management* (Cambridge, MA: Blackwell Publishers, 1995).

29. Ibid.

30. R. B. Peterson, J. Sargent, N. K. Napier, and W. S. Shim, *International Human Resource Management in the World's Largest Industrial MNCs* (Paper presented at the Academy of International Business meeting, Hawaii, 1993).

Chapter 9

1. "The 1996 Inc. 500 List," *Inc. 500 1996,* p.16.
2. Ibid. INC 500, p. 24.
3. Richard Whiteley & Diane Hessan. (1996). *Customer-Centered Growth*. Reading, MA: Addison-Wesley Publishing Co.
4. Ibid., p.26.
5. Ibid., p.99
6. Echo Montgomery Garrett, "The 21st Century Franchise," *Inc. Magazine,* January 1995, p. 83.
7. Jay Finegan, "The Smartest Franchisees in America," *Inc. Magazine,* November 1995, p. 48.
8. International Franchise Association, *Franchise Times*, Department of Commerce, U.S. Small Business Administration, *Financial World, USA Today.*
9. *Ibid.* p. 48. Results of a study by Timothy Bates, Wayne State University, Detroit.
10. Janean Huber, "Thrill Seekers," *Entrepreneur,* May 1995, p. 128.
11. Timothy Bates, "Look Before You Leap," *Inc. Magazine,* July 1995, p. 23.
12. "The Next Big Thing," *Inc. Magazine,* November 1995, p. 62.
13. Jay Finegan, "Strength in Numbers," *Inc. Magazine,* December 1995, p. 94.
14. Ibid.
15. Dale D. Buss, "Growing More By Doing Less," *Nation's Business,* December 1995, p. 18.
16. Ibid.
17. Michael F. Corbett, "Outsourcing: Redesigning the Corporation of the Future," The Outsourcing Institute, special advertising section, *Fortune,* December 12, 1994.

18. Ibid., p. 19.
19. James Worsham, "A Global Reach for Small Firms," *Nation's Business,* October 1995, p. 40.
20. Teri Lammers Prior, "The Worldly Wise Letter of Credit," *Inc. Magazine,* March 1996, p. 57.
21. Joshua D. Macht, "Growing Global," *Inc. Technology,* Summer 1995, p. 86.
22. Erika Kotite, "On a Mission," *Entrepreneur,* July 1995, p. 78.
23. Roberta Maynard, "Why Franchisers Look Abroad," *Nation's Business,* October 1995, p. 65.
24. Erika Kotite, "Danger Zones," *Entrepreneur,* July 1995, p. 84.
25. Ibid.

Chapter 10

1. A. E. Pearson and C.L. Irwin, *Coca-Cola vs. Pepsi-Cola (A),* Case No. 9–387–108 (Cambridge, MA: Harvard Business School, 1988).
2. Frederick F. Reichheld and W. Earl Sasser, Jr. "Zero Defections: Quality Comes to Services," *Harvard Business Review,* September/October 1990.
3. Regis McKenna, *Relationship Marketing* (Reading, MA: Addison-Wesley, 1991).
4. William H. Davidow and Michael S. Malone, *The Virtual Corporation* (New York: Edward Burlingame Books/HarperBusiness, 1992), p. 3.
5. B. Joseph Pine II, Don Peppers, and Martha Rogers, "Do You Want to Keep Your Customers Forever?" *Harvard Business Review,* March/April, 1995.
6. Don Peppers, "Digitizing Desire, Part Two: How Technology Has Changed Marketing," *Forbes,* (April 10, 1995), p.76, via Lexus/Nexus.
7. Don Peppers and Martha Rogers, *The One to One Future: Building Relationships One Customer at a Time* (New York: Currency/Doubleday, 1993).
8. Don Peppers and Martha Rogers (1993). The One to One Future. New York: Currency Doubleday.
9. Lawrence G. Foster, IA Company that Cares (*New Brunswick*, NJ: Johnson & Johnson, 1986), 17.
10. R.W. Johnson, Jr., *Try Reality*, a pamphlet he wrote in 1935.
11. Becki Walker. "Relationship Marketing: The Cornerstone of Distribution Planning," *CD-ROM Professional,* January 1995.
12. Peppers and Rogers, *The One to One Future,* p. 52.
13. American Management Association, New York, NY.

14. Customer Service Institute, Silver Spring, MD.
15. Technical Assistance Research Programs, Washington, DC.

Chapter 11

1. Jay Conrad Levinson, *Guerrilla Marketing* (Boston: Houghton Mifflin, 1993).
2. Wayne D. Hoyer, and Deborah J. MacInnis, *Consumer Behavior* (Boston: Houghton Mifflin, 1997).
3. *McWilliams Wines, Pty. Ltd. v. McDonald's System of Australia, Pty. Ltd.* (1980).
4. Judith Lynne Zaichowsky, *Defending Your Brand Against Imitation* (Westport, CT: Quorum Books, 1994).
5. Sarah Schafer, "When It's Time for a Makeover," *Inc.,* December 1995, p. 118.
6. James C. Collins and William C. Lazier, *Beyond Entrepreneurship: Turning Your Business into an Enduring Great Company* (Englewood Cliffs, NJ: Prentice-Hall, 1992).
7. Marilyn Yung, "Star Power," *Business96,* February/March 1996, p. 22.
8. D. Peppers and M. Rogers, *The One to One Future: Building Relationships One Customer at a Time* (New York: Currency/Doubleday, 1993).
9. Ibid., p. 184.
10. Ibid.
11. Terry G. Vavra, *Aftermarketing: How to Keep Customers for Life Through Relationship Marketing* (Homewood, IL: Business One Irwin, 1992).
12. Peppers and Rogers, *The One to One Future,* p. 36.
13. "Ask the Marketing Doctors," *Inc.,* October 1995, p. 68.
14. Donna Fenn, "Leader of the Pack," *Inc.,* February 1996.
15. Peppers and Rogers, *The One to One Future,* p. 83.
16. Vavra, *Aftermarketing,* p. 129
17. Ibid., p. 206.
18. Laura Liswood, *Serving Them Right* (New York: HarperBusiness, 1990), p. 93; Vavra, *Aftermarketing,* p. 104.
19. F. R. Reichheld and W. E. Sasser, Jr., "Zero Defections: Quality Comes to Services," *Harvard Business Review,* September/October 1990.
20. Vavra, *Aftermarkteing.*
21. Richard Whiteley and Diane Hessan, *Customer-Centered Growth* (Reading, MA: Addison-Wesley, 1996).

Chapter 12

1. Barry H. Minkin, *Future in Sight* (New York: Macmillan, 1995).
2. Ibid.
3. Marilyn Kern-Foxworth, "Colorizing Advertising," *American Advertising,* Winter 1991–92, pp. 26–28.
4. Joel Kotkin, "Still the Best Places to do Business," *Inc.,* July 1996, p. 42.
5. Charles K. Kao, *A Choice Fulfilled: The Business of High Technology* (New York: St. Martin's Press, 1991).
6. P. N. Golder and G. J. Tellis, "Pioneer Advantage: Marketing Logic or Marketing Legend?" *Journal of Marketing Research* 30 (1993), pp. 158–170.
7. A. Ali, "Pioneering Versus Incremental Innovation: Review and Research Propositions," *Journal of Product Innovation Management* 11 (1994), pp. 46–61.
8. Golder and Tellis, "Pioneer Advantages."
9. Ali, "Pioneering."
10. J. Utterback, *Mastering the Dynamics of Innovation* (Cambridge, MA: Harvard Business Press, 1994).
11. Geoffrey A. Moore, *Inside the Tornado: Marketing Strategies from Silicon Valley's Cutting Edge* (New York: HarperCollins, 1995).
12. Ibid.
13. Ibid.
14. Business wire, New York, October 30, 1995.
15. "Bulletin Boards' Global Reach," *Nation's Business,* February 1995, p. 33.
16. "What's in an Internet Name?" *Inc.,* January 1995, p.101.
17. *Expanding Your Business Globally,* Deloitte & Touche LLP (http://www.dtonline.com/expand/exglobal.htm).
18. Ibid.
19. Case, John, "Is America Really Different?" *Inc.,* The State of Small Business special edition, 1996, p. 108.
20. Ibid. Statistic from Chris Hall, University of Technology, Sydney, Australia.
21. "Global Market Opportunities," *Expanding Your Business Globally,* Deloitte & Touche LLP (http://www.dtonline.com/expand/exglobop.htm).
22. Ibid.
23. Douglas F. Lamont, *Global Marketing* (Cambridge, MA: Blackwell Publishers, 1996).
24. Ibid, p. 12.

25. Allison Lucas,"Market Researchers Study Abroad," *Sales and Marketing Management,* February 1996, p. 13.
26. Ibid., p. 71.
27. "Mexico: The Revolution Continues." *The Economist,* January 22, 1994, p. 19.
28. Anthony DePalma, "Mexico Unloads State Companies, Pocketing Billions, but Hits Snags," *The New York Times,* October 27, 1993, pp. A1, A6.
29. Geri Smith, "Free Trade Isn't Coming Cheap," *Business Week,* December 6, 1993, pp. 58–59.
30. Gianluigi Guido, "What U.S. Marketers Should Consider in Planning a Pan-European Approach," *Journal of Consumer Marketing,* Spring 1992, p. 30–131.
31. Gary Mead, "Hunting the Euro-Consumer," *Financial Times,* June 28, 1993, p. 4.
32. Sudhit H. Kale and John W. Barnes, "Understanding the Domain of Cross-National Buyer-Seller Interactions," *Journal of International Business Studies,* First Quarter 1992.
33. Lamont, *Global Marketing.*
34. Yves Marbeau, "Harmonisation of Demographics in Europe 1991: The State of the Art, Part 1: Eurodemographics? Nearly There!" *Marketing and Research Today,* March 1992, pp. 33–40; Jean Quatresooz and Dominique Vancraeynest, "Part 2: Using the ESOMAR Harmonised Demographics: External and Internal Validation of the Results of the EURO-BAROMETER Test," *Marketing and Research Today,* March 1992, pp. 41–50.
35. Greg Lipper, "Finding a Partner in Japan," text of a speech delivered to the Los Angeles Venture Association of the Pacific Rim Strategic Alliance Conference, June 16, 1995.
36. Shuppan Kagaku Kenkyujo, "The Manga Market," *Mangajin,* April 1991, pp. 14–17.
37. Karen Lowry, "You Just Can't Talk to These Kids," *Business Week,* April 19, 1993, p. 106.
38. Robert Thomson, "Japan Enters the World of Fantasy," *Financial Times,* May 6, 1993, p. 8.
39. Lowry, "You Just Can't Talk," p. 104.
40. Lamont, *Global Marketing,* p. 184.
41. Xu Bai Yi, *Marketing to China: One Billion New Customers* (Lincolnwood, IL: NTC Business Books, 1990).
42. Ibid.
43. James McGregor, "U.S. Companies in China Find Patience, Persistence and Salesmanship Pay Off," *The Wall Street Journal,* April 3, 1992, p. B1.
44. Andrew Tanzer, "Ding-Dong, Capitalism Calling," *Forbes,* October 14, 1991, p. 186.
45. McGregor, "U.S. Companies."
46. "Coke v. Pepsi (cont): Chinese Fizz," *The Economist,* January 29, 1994, pp. 67–68.
47. Susan Greco, "Selling the Superstores," *Inc.,* July 1995, pp. 55–61.
48. Joshua Hyatt, "Hot Commodity," *Inc.,* February 1996, pp. 50–61.

Chapter 13

1. William H. Davidow and Michael S. Malone, *The Virtual Corporation* (New York: Harper-Business, 1992).
2. B. Joseph Pine II, *Mass Customization* (Boston: Harvard Business School Press, 1993).
3. Steven L. Goldman, Roger N. Nagel, and Kenneth Preiss, *Agile Competitors and Virtual Organizations* (New York: Van Nostrand Reinhold, 1995).
4. Steven C. Wheelwright and Kim B. Clark, *Revolutionizing Product Development* (New York: The Free Press, 1992).
5. Pine, *Mass Customization,* p. 54.
6. Ibid.
7. Ibid., p. 21.
8. Goldman, Nagel, and Preiss, *Agile Competitors.*
9. Wheelwright and Clark, *Revolutionizing Product Development,* p. 235

Chapter 14

1. David Friedman, "The Enemy Within," *Inc.,* October 1995, p. 47.
2. Steven l. Goldman, Roger N. Nagel, and Kenneth Preiss, *Agile Competitors and Virtual Organizations* (New York:Van Nostrand Reinhold, 1995).
3. Ibid., p. 3.
4. Ibid., p. 22.
5. A. Richard Shores, *Reengineering the Factory: A Primer for World-Class Manufacturing,* Milwaukee: ASQC Quality Press, 1994.
6. J. M. Juran, *Juran on Planning for Quality* (New York: The Free Press, 1988) pp. 4–5.
7. Robert C. Liden and Thomas W. Tewksbury, "Empowerment and Work Teams," in Gerald R. Ferris et al., eds., *Handbook of Human Resource Management* (Cambridge, MA: Blackwell Publishers, 1995).
8. Reza A. Maleki, *Flexible Manufacturing Systems* (Englewood Cliffs, NJ: Prentice-Hall, 1991), p. 8.

9. Taiichi Ohno, *Toyota Production System* (Cambridge, MA: Productivity Press, 1988), pp. 25–26.
10. William H. Davidow and Michael S. Malone, *The Virtual Corporation* (New York: HarperBusiness, (1992), p. 146.
11. R. C. Hill, "When the Going Gets Rough: A Baldrige Award Winner on the Line," *Academy of Management Executive* 7, no. 3 (1993), pp. 75–79.
12. D. A. Garvin, "How the Baldrige Award Really Works," *Harvard Business Review* 6 (1991), pp. 80–93.
13. Adapted from Warren H. Schmidt and Jerome P. Finnigan, "The Race Without a Finish Line," *Small Business Reports,* February 1993.
14. Adrian J. Slywotzky, *Value Migration* (Cambridge, MA: Harvard Business School Press, 1996).
15. Teri Lammers Prior, "Channel Surfers," *Inc.,* February 1995, p. 65.

Chapter 15
1. Kathleen R. Allen, *Launching New Ventures: An Entrepreneurial Approach* (Chicago: Upstart Publishing, 1995).
2. Vilma Bar and Charles E. Broudy, *Designing to Sell* (New York: McGraw-Hill, 1986).
3. Robert L. Anderson and John S. Dunkelberg, *Managing Growing Firms* (Englewood Cliffs, NJ: Prentice-Hall, 1987), p. 223.

Chapter 16
1. Robert W. Kolb and Ricardo J. Rodriguez, *Financial Management,* 2nd ed. (Cambridge, MA: Blackwell Publications, 1996).
2. Ibid.

Chapter 17
1. Justin G. Longenecker and Carlos W. Moore, *Small Business Management: An Entrepreneurial Emphasis,* 8th ed. (Cincinnati: South-Western Publishing, 1991).
2. Robert L. Anderson and John S. Dunkelberg, *Managing Small Businesses* (Minneapolis/St. Paul: West Publishing, 1993).
3. J. Tol Broome, Jr., "SBA's CAPLine Credit Program," *Nation's Business,* October 1995, p. 77.
4. Robert W. Kolb and Ricardo J. Rodriguez, *Financial Management,* 2nd ed. (Cambridge, MA: Blackwell Publishers, 1996).

Chapter 18
1. Courtney Price and Kathleen Allen, *Tips and Traps for Entrepreneurs* (New York: McGraw-Hill, 1988).
2. W. D. Bygrave and J. A. Timmons, *Venture Capital at the Crossroads* (Boston: Harvard Business School Press, 1992).
3. Jill Andresky Fraser, "Benchmark: Where Does Venture Capital Go?" *Inc.,* June 1996, p. 120.
4. Robert A. Mamis, "New for '97," *Inc.,* January 1997, p. 54.
5. Price Waterhouse Venture Capital Survey, Results for Second Quarter 1997 (http://www.pw.com/vc/).
6. Gary D. Zeune, "Ducks in a Row: Orchestrating the Flawless Stock Offering," *Corporate Cashflow,* February 1993.
7. Donald E. Vaughn, *Financial Planning for the Entrepreneur* (Englewood Cliffs, NJ: Prentice-Hall, 1997) p. 67.
8. Ibid., p. 68.
9. James H. Schilt, "A Rational Approach to Capitalization Rates for Discounting the Future Income Stream of Closely Held Companies," *The Financial Planner,* January 1982.
10. Thomas W. Zimmerer and Norman M. Scarborough, *Essentials of Entrepreneurship and Small Business Management,* 2nd ed. (Englewood Cliffs, NJ: Prentice-Hall, 1998).
11. Tiffany Haugen, "The Vegas Element of Venture Valuation," *Orange County Business Journal,* July 15, 1991.
12. Price and Allen, *Tips and Traps.*
13. Ibid.
14. Ibid.

Chapter 19
1. R. E. Palmer, "Let's Be Bullish on Ethics," *New York Times,* June 20, 1986, p. 23.
2. L. W. Porter and L. E. McKibbin, *Management Education and Development* (New York: McGraw-Hill, 1988).
3. Jon M. Shepard, Michael G. Goldsby, and Virginia W. Gerde, "Teaching Business Ethics Through Literature," *The Online Journal of Ethics* 1, no. 1 (1997) (http://www.depaul.edu/ethics/gerde.html).
4. D. Collins, "Social Contract: The Proper Role of Individual Liberty and Government Intervention in 18th Century Society," *Business and Professional Ethics Journal* 7 (1988), pp. 119–146.

5. Ph. H. De Vries, "Adam Smith's Theory of Justice: Business Ethics Themes in *The Wealth of Nations*," *Business & Professional Ethics Journal* 8 (1989), pp. 37–55.

6. J. M. Shepard et al., "The Problem of Business Ethics: Oxymoron or Inadequate Vocabulary?" *Journal of Business and Psychology* 6 (1991), pp. 9–23.

7. T. H. Tawney, *Religion and the Rise of Capitalism* (New York: Harcourt, Brace, & Company, 1962/1926).

8. Shepard et al., "Teaching Business Ethics."

9. Lynn Sharp-Pine, "Managing for Organizational Integrity," *Harvard Business Review,* March/April 1994, pp. 106–117.

10. T. Hobbes, *Leviathan,* ed. C. B. Macpherson (New York: Penguin Books, 1968/1651).

11. A. MacIntyre, "Egoism and Altruism," in P. Edwards, ed., *The Encyclopedia of Philosophy* (New York: Macmillan and Free Press, 1967).

12. J. Ladd, ed., *Ethical Relativism* (Belmont, CA: Wadsworth, 1973).

13. J. S. Mill, *Utilitarianism* (Indianapolis: Bobbs-Merrill, 1957/1861).

14. I. Kant, *Groundwork for the Metaphysics of Morals,* trans. J. W. Ellington Indianapolis: Hackett, 1981/1785).

15. G. F. Cavanaugh, D. J. Moberg, and M. Valasquez, "The Ethics of Organizational Politics," *Academy of Management Review* 6 (1981), pp. 363–374.

16. Gary Pell, "Corporate Compliance Programs: Leading Edge Practices," *Corporate Conduct*

Quarterly 5, no.3 (http://camden-www.rutgers.edu/~ccq/pell53.html).

17. Courtney Price and Kathleen Allen, *Tips and Traps for Entrepreneurs* (New York: McGraw-Hill, 1998).

18. Kirk D. Fiedler, Louis E. Raho, L. Floyd Lewis, and James A. Belohlav, "Managing Complex Decisions" *Information Executive* 1 (1999), pp. 49–53.

19. J. Belohlav, D. Drehmer, and L. Raho, "Ethical Issues of Expert Systems," *The Online Journal of Ethics* (http://www.depaul.edu/ethics/expert.html), copyright 1997.

20. Joline Godfrey, "Seeing Is Believing," *Inc.,* September 1994, p. 27.

21. Ibid.

22. S. Prakash Sethi, "A Conceptual Framework for Environmental Analysis of Social Issues and Evaluation of Business Response Patterns," *Academy of Management Journal*, January 1979, p. 68.

23. "Front Line Articles: Be Careful What You Wish For," *Business Ethics Magazine* (http://condor.depaul.edu/ethics/biz_aug1.html), copyright 1996.

24. Amy Miller, "Sundae School," *Inc.,* December 1995, p. 29.

25. Kathleen Allen, *Launching New Ventures* (Chicago: Upstart Publishing, 1995).

26. Ellyn E. Spragins, "Making Good," *Inc.,* May 1993, p. 114.

27. Ibid.

28. Ibid.

Index